VOICES

OF A

PEOPLE

VOICES
OF A
PEOPLE

THE STORY OF YIDDISH FOLKSONG

Ruth Rubin

SECOND EDITION

McGRAW-HILL BOOK COMPANY

New York St. Louis San Francisco Düsseldorf Johannesburg

Kuala Lumpur London Mexico Montreal New Delhi

Panama Rio de Janeiro Singapore Sydney Toronto

Library of Congress Cataloging in Publication Data

Rubin, Ruth, 1906–
   Voices of a people.

   Bibliography: p. 525
   1. Folk-songs, Jewish (Yiddish)—History and criticism. 2. Folk-songs, Jewish (Yiddish) 3. Folk-songs, Jewish (Yiddish)—Translations into English.   4. English poetry—Translations from Yiddish.
I. Title.
PJ5122.R8 1973   784.7'6'924   73-6983
ISBN 0-07-054194-9

Music typography by Music Art of New York.

1234567890 KPKP   76543

DEDICATION

This work is tenderly dedicated to
my son
MICHAEL
1937–1959

Guide to Transliterated Texts

Yiddish can roughly be classified into three main pronunciations: Lithuanian, Polish, and Southern (Ukrainian, Podolian, Rumanian). The Lithuanian is used here; occasionally, Polish or Bessarabian sounds are retained for the sake of a rhyme. The Hebrew texts and words are given in the Ashkenazic or idiomatic pronunciation.

Sound	Example in Text	English Equivalent	Remarks
Vowels:			
a	harts	part	The *e* is alway short and
e	ven	hen	*always* sounded.
i	visn	pin	
i	tayer	fire	
o	hot	got	Except for the diphthongs *oy*,
u	unter	room	*ay*, and *ey*, all other vowels
oy	groys	boy	are voiced full in pronunci-
ey	freyd	way	ation.
Consonants:			
g	gib	give	Except as indicated, all con-
ch	chosn*	Loch (as in Scottish)	sonants are the same as in English.
ts	tants or tsores	huts	
tsh	mentsh	chair or munch	
dz	undzer	sounds	
zh	shpil-zhe	seizure	

Unless otherwise indicated, all translations into the English are by the author.

* Some authorities use *kh* instead of *ch* here.

7

Preface

THE JEWS HAVE ALWAYS BEEN A SINGING PEOPLE. ON THEIR WANDERINGS from one land to another, they bore with them, along with other cultural treasures, a talent for music. In every land where they settled, they left traces of their own culture, in turn absorbing and recreating portions of the cultures they came in contact with: tales and legends; dances and songs; customs, beliefs, and ways of life.

The folk-song treasure of the Jews as a whole is much richer and more varied than is generally supposed. Included are the folk songs of the Oriental Jews (Yemenite, Sephardic, Persian, Daghestanian, Babylonian, Moroccan), the Ladino songs of the Spaniolic Jews with their large collection of liturgical melodies (*piyutim*), the Yiddish folk songs and Chasidic tunes, with and without words, of the Eastern European Jews. The innumerable synagogal chants (religious folk songs) and prayers, which differ musically one from the other depending upon the community where they prevail, are to be found among Jews the world over.

Eastern European Yiddish folk song, with which this book is concerned, is the youngest offspring of Jewish *folk* music and one of the richest stores of popular music in modern times. Varied in topical content, intimate in its use of the Yiddish vernacular, it reflects vividly the life of a community of many millions over a period of many generations. In the songs, we catch the manner of speech and phrase, the wit and humor, the dreams and aspirations, the nonsense, jollity, the pathos and struggle of an entire people. These are the songs which served the needs, moods, creative impulses, and purposes of a particular environment at particular periods in the history of the largest Jewish community of modern times.

The creative, pulsating force, the wellspring that for centuries had fed and nourished all other Yiddish-speaking communities in the world, the sphere of Eastern European Jewish life is no more. The migrants during the nineteenth and early twentieth centuries transformed and

9

transmuted segments of their former Eastern European Jewish cultural heritage, as they lived in their new homelands. Although many elements of the previous mode of life were preserved, the dynamic creative process—a phenomenon of the whole people that had existed in the "old home"—was not possible in the lands of more recent settlement. In our own time and before our very eyes, the violent destruction of vast numbers of creators and carriers of Jewish knowledge and science, language and lore, literature and song in the Yiddish language brought *living* Yiddish folklore and song of the Eastern European phase to an historic close.

This work is an attempt to present some of the aspects of that Jewish, Eastern European life as it speaks to us through the thousands of folk songs and songs in folk style, at times directly, at times obliquely. These songs, which are scattered in many publications still extant and are also retained in the memory of many people still among us, represent a varied and rich repository as yet well preserved in the United States. Many Yiddish-speaking institutions operate in this country through the Yiddish press, literature, publications, schools, fraternal organizations, theater, songs both popular and art, and over the radio and in recordings. The American-Jewish community, within its Yiddish-speaking segment, thus retains both the threads that bind it to the Eastern European community, which is no more, and that tie-in with the first migratory years and later development of the American Jewish community—the largest Jewish community of modern times.

RUTH RUBIN.

Contents

VOICES
OF A
PEOPLE

Prologue

To UNDERSTAND ANY ASPECT OF THE CULTURE OF A PEOPLE, ONE SHOULD be familiar with its history. This is especially true of the Jewish people, which speaks various tongues and has a plurality of cultures and among whom the cultures of various communities are different from each other. Jewish history has shifted its center of gravity from one country to another several times over the centuries. Through the ages, the Jew has expressed himself musically in chant and cantillation, in song and recitative, in regular and irregular rhythms, in simple and ornamented melodies. While the Bible reveals hardly a trace of the actual music of the songs of the ancient Jews, it does supply numerous references which show that these songs existed and that they played an important part in religious ceremonies, as well as in the social and secular life of the people.

After the destruction of the first Temple in Palestine, the remnants of Judea were taken into captivity, sold into slavery, and dispersed throughout the Roman Empire as far as the Iberian peninsula, the Rhine, and the Danube.[1] In the centuries that followed the destruction of the second Temple, music among the Jews seemed doomed to be silenced forever. The spiritual leaders suppressed everything of a secular nature : all instrumental music for religious purposes, even at weddings, was prohibited; and the entire art of the instrumental music of the Levites fell into oblivion.

By the eighth and ninth centuries, "art music was almost non-existent and instrumental music had been forbidden since the fall of the Temple. What remained was a traditional chanting of the prayers and the cantillation of the scriptural lessons, according to certain ancient modes."[2] But the musical instincts of the Jews persisted. About the same time in the regions of North Africa and Spain a type of religious bard (*paytan*) became prominent, who created a form of Hebrew poetry that was often set to a fixed melody, composed either by the poet himself or the precentor (*chazzan*) of a synagogue. These melodies were frequently adapted

17

Feast of Ahaseurus. Anonymous German woodcut from *Der Spiegel der Menschen en Behaltnis* (The Mirror of Salvation) Speyer, 1479–1481

or even adopted from the outside world, and some of them became part of the repertoire of sacred songs in the synagogue. One source of these melodies might well have been the songs of the troubadours and minne-singers, while others were based on Oriental, Turkish, and Moorish-Spanish melodies.[3]

The practice of adapting and adopting tunes from the outside, secular world for use in prayers in the synagogue spread to other European Jewish communities. From the tenth to the fourteenth centuries in Germany, almost all the rabbis composed sacred songs instinctively in a folk manner and functioned as precentors either permanently or at least on feast and fast days. Some of their tunes gained popularity, spreading throughout the German congregations, while others fell into oblivion.[4] In time, the sacred songs became traditional, marking every important occasion in the life of the Jew in the Middle Ages.[5] A number of them became banquet or home songs (*zemiroth*), enhancing Sabbath meals, serving as the bridge between the human and the Divine as the family sat for hours around the table, singing hymns during the meals on Friday night and Sabbath noon, afternoon, and evening.[6]

A Hebrew Sabbath song which has come down to us from the Middle Ages and is still current is "Eliyohu hanovi," sung at the outgoing of the Sabbath. Already well known to all Jewish communities by the eleventh century, it tells of the prophet Elijah, legendary watcher over Israel and the future messenger of the Messianic era. Among the *zemiroth* were the cumulative songs for the Passover seder — in Aramaic — "Echod mi yodea" and "Chad gadyo," to which new tunes were set during the medieval period, as well as songs for the Chanukah and Purim festivals, for circumcisions and weddings.

The centuries before the Reformation in Germany were marked for the Jews by constant fear of extinction. No sooner did they recover from the horrible blood bath of the first Crusade (1096) than a second (1147) reduced them to utter misery. The horrors of the Black Death (1348/9), the persecutions of the Church, the expulsions and excessive taxation, the exclusion from land and handicrafts made up a long chain of injustices, repressions, and cruelty. The Jewish communities were scattered, weak, and under the constant threat of economic and physical ruin.

Yet, at the close of the eleventh century, Jews had been leading a settled community life for generations in Cologne, Mainz, the Rhineland, and a number of other German regions. Talmudic students (*bachurim*) wandered about the countryside, very much like the German *Wanderschüler* or the Italian *vagantes;* and like the Goliards some of them were accomplished musicians, acquainted with German secular and church music. Jews were diligent readers of the German poets, well acquainted with medieval poetry and, from the thirteenth to the fifteenth centuries, even shared in the creation of national epics and romances of chivalry.[7] In twelfth-century Germany there even lived the rare phenomenon of a Jewish minnesinger, Susskind of Trimberg, who sang "in beautiful strains, knew how to handle rhyme, meter, strophes in the vernacular, and was so warmly appreciated that he was received into the circle of poets."[8]

Whereas no specifically Jewish secular songs are traceable from the early medieval period, during the twelfth and thirteenth centuries French-Jewish poets translated Hebrew prayers into French, and Jewish women knew the songs of the troubadours. Susskind of Trimberg was not alone in his love of the troubadour's art, as "love songs and ballads were read in the twelfth century by Jews, though reading of the *Romance* was not recommended as a holy recreation,"[9] and the rabbis were often dismayed by the deep inroads German folkways and culture made into Jewish life.

Thus during the fourteenth and fifteenth centuries in Germany, despite the barriers and restrictions of the Church and the ruling circles, a whole secular world became known to the Jews through current German oral literature and music.[10] This is the period of the sung or intoned epic poetry in Judeo-German (Yiddish)[11] when Yiddish literature of the *older epoch* had its own troubadours and minnesingers and when, in the Jewish ghettos of Germany and Italy, there existed an original corps of literary creators of secular poetry and song — folk singers (*Spielmänner*) who followed close upon the declining period of the German *Spielmann* epoch.[12]

As the German *Spielmann* two centuries before him, so the Yiddish *Spielmann*, through his combined repertoire of Jewish and non-Jewish materials, sought to educate and entertain people through his epic poems and gnomic lyrics. Borrowing from current German literature and song, he endowed many a theme from Hebrew literature, lore, and song with German rhyme, phraseology, and idiom. Though at times he demonstrated some of the skills of the lighter genre of entertainers (clowns, acrobats, instrumentalists, jugglers, tumblers), his performance was distinct from theirs. With true romantic passion and in recitative style, he performed in the evenings at the homes of the well to do (then the patrons of contemporary secular art), where his audiences included women and at times even some scholars. The epic tales and ballads which had fired the previous generations of German Crusaders with religious fervor and were accompanied by many excesses against the Jews themselves now became in turn a popular vehicle in the Jewish ghettos of Germany, where they served as a basis for new, original works.

Along with the current religious literature in Yiddish, the Jewish minstrel of the fourteenth and fifteenth centuries dominated the creative literary-musical scene with a repertoire which included original epic adaptations from the Bible, Talmud, and Midrash and German and Italian chivalric lays, as well as his own creations set to contemporary German melodies. First in importance were the traditional songs of the Jewish holidays and festivals. "Purim, he sang Esther poems; during the Pentecost and Simchas Torah he sang Torah songs; on Passover and Pentecost he sang a poem entitled 'Medresh m'yosi,' which tells about Moses and the exodus from Egypt."[13] Other songs in his Yiddish repertoire included "Dovid's Shire" ("David's Song"), "Akeydes yitschok" ("The Sacrifice of Isaac"), and the *Shmuel Buch* (Book of Samuel), which was 1,800 stanzas long, first published in 1544 and the oldest and most important, anonymous, Yiddish epic poem of the archaic Yiddish period.

Written by an author supposedly from Southern Germany, the *Shmuel Buch* instructed its readers to sing "in the tune which is known and popular among all of Israel." However, although two manuscripts are still extant and a number of references attest to its great popularity and dissemination, the actual melody has been unfortunately lost. Not a direct translation of the Biblical tale, the *Shmuel Buch* is a secular poem based on the Bible story, employing current German epithets and phraseology, molded in the Nibelungen rhyme, and sung, it is assumed, to a contemporary German tune. Seeking to resemble the epic themes of knights, battles, and the love cult of German epic tales, the anonymous, Yiddish folk song of the *Shmuel Buch* found natural source material in the ancient story of the prophet Samuel and in the battles, love, and devotion of the Jewish warriors and kings of ancient Israel which endowed the work with lustiness, humor, and dramatic descriptions of love and battles. Current possibly prior to the Black Death, the *Shmuel Buch* continued to be popular up to the end of the seventeenth century, with many a contemporary work indicating that it was to be intoned or sung *b'nigun shmuel buch,* in the rhyme or to the tune of the Book of Samuel.

The repertoire of the Yiddish folk singer of the late Middle Ages also included translations from the German, some of the most popular of which were: "Dietrich von Bern" (to the tune of "Herzog Ernst"[14]), "Hildebrant,"[15] and "Artus Hof."[16] The last named, which is based upon the Arthurian cycle of legends about the Round Table, was so widespread that "two hundred years ago, every Jew knew its name, and when you wanted to describe a person living in style, you would say: his home reminds you of King Arthur's Court!"[17]

Some other songs and bardic epics from the German repertoire which Yiddish minstrels performed before their Jewish audiences were: "Der royzngartn," "Shmid Wieland," "Tristan und Isolde," "Florus und Blancheflur," "Paris und Viene," and the long poetic romance, the *Bovo Buch.*[18]

Some of these works were short performances; others took two to three evenings to complete. Some had a standard melody, while others were chanted. In general, lyrics in the Middle Ages were made to be sung, and the line of demarcation between *singen und sagn* was not as sharply defined then as it is today. Even the parts that were read aloud were performed in a kind of melodic recitative. Although it may be true that these professional Yiddish folk singers overshadowed the general flow of folk compositions from the *anonymous* folk, they served nevertheless as a stimulant and a channel for the lyrical and poetic creativeness of the people as a whole and provoked new categories of songs never before current in the Jewish community: dance and love songs, satirical and nonsense songs, historical and popular songs, and even a kind of secularized religious song.

During the fifteenth century, Italian Jews emigrated to Germany and the Slavic lands, and the emigration increased during the sixteenth century. Among the travelers were Jewish *klezmer* (bandsmen), who became an important factor in the social life of the new communities, exerting a strong influence on the tunes and techniques of both their musical brethren and the listening public. The highways of the Middle Ages were swarming with travelers. Together with dislocated craftsmen, small-scale tradesmen, merchants, often side by side with beggars and thieves, these bandsmen, along with clerical men, clowns, and the Yiddish minstrels, wandered from Germany to Bohemia, Lithuania, Poland, Northern Italy. During the second half of the sixteenth century and into the seventeenth, the migrants also included *magidim* (moralistic orators), *darshonim* (mentors), scribes, and booksellers.

The sixteenth century witnessed the disappearance of the Yiddish minstrel and with it, whole groups of literary and entertainment professions. Only the light performances of the clown, acrobat, dancer, and *badchen* (marriage entertainer), who sang at weddings, combining the humorous with the serious, remained. The *badchen* carried on the old tradition and some of the practices of the former Jewish minstrel.

During the sixteenth century also, the permanent settlement of large numbers of Jews displaced from the middle Rhine into Bohemia, Poland, Lithuania, and Russia takes place. Although the migration of German Jews to Poland began in the thirteenth century, the compact communities in towns and cities became important during the fifteenth and sixteenth centuries. To the Slavic lands the German Jews brought their Judeo-German (Yiddish) tongue, their intellectual baggage, and former mode of life. Separated from their "old home," they craved for the spiritual food to which they had been accustomed, yearning for the "stories with which their ancestors had whiled away their hours of leisure in the cities along the Rhine. And so it happened that when the legendary lore of the Nibelungen, of Siegfried, of Dietrich of Bern, of Wigalois, of King Arthur, had begun to fade away even from the folk books of Germany, it lived on in the Slavic countries and continued to evoke pleasure and admiration."[19]

Poland now became the main concentration of Jewish settlement and the ruling spiritual center of all other Jewish communities in Europe.[20] Although Poland had enjoyed the creations of the old Yiddish minstrels, the country is not known to have contributed a single romance, epic poem, or historical song throughout this secular literary epoch that had centered in Germany, with occasional contributions from Italy, Prague, and Amsterdam.

By the beginning of the seventeenth century, the secular *Shmuel Buch* had ceased to be published. A wave of religiosity spread over all literary endeavor, and the number of religious and pious songs greatly increased in number. The highways now drew ever-increasing numbers of Talmudic scholars and students from Amsterdam, Prague, and Germany, from Wolin, Lithuania, and the Ukraine to Poland, now recognized as the Talmudic and religious center of the Jews. After the Cossack excesses of 1648 (Chmelnitski), large numbers of Jews fled from Poland to Germany, but the German-Jewish center had already lost its leading position, and the German influence had already receded. Only the patronesses of Yiddish literature remained, and until the end of the seventeenth century, they managed to keep alive for a little longer the art of the Yiddish minstrel, who was still occasionally heard in their homes during weddings, festivals, and holidays.[21]

By the eighteenth century, the break with the old Yiddish (Judeo-German) literary, secular era was complete. And by the beginning of the nineteenth century, Yiddish folk song had disappeared from Western and Central Europe. In the Slavic lands, under the new cultural and territorial influences, German medievalism was dispelled, and the modern period began. A distinct phase was introduced which in no way resembled that of the three hundred years that preceded it — a phase developed entirely on a new basis and in no way a direct continuation of the older period.

Although it vanished from Western and Central Europe, Jewish secular folk song, recast in its modern Yiddish vernacular, burst into full bloom in the Slavic lands during the nineteenth century. Recalling the creative period of Jewish minstrelsy of the sixteenth century, many new categories of secular song now welled from the depths of the people, including cradle and love songs, ballads and dance songs, drinking and humorous songs, work and children's songs, soldier and topical songs, nonsense and satirical songs, as well as the previous categories of wedding, religious, holiday, ethical, and historical songs, and many others.

Contrary to the type of Yiddish songs of the earlier archaic epoch, these folk songs were almost completely anonymous. They reflected the light and shadow of many generations of Jewish life in the Eastern European communities, a life which included both the old and the new — the old patterns to which the people had clung for generations and even centuries and the new forms emerging under the influences and pressures of the surrounding Slavic culture and history.

Notes

PROLOGUE

1. Long before the destruction of the first Temple in Jerusalem, Jewish settlements were established throughout the ancient world. After the Babylonian captivity, there were always more Jews outside Palestine than within it. The great Jewish migrations from the Near East westward began about 900 C.E. In Germany the oldest Jewish communities, in the southwestern part, were already established at the time of Charlemagne. As for Eastern Europe, the largest center until the close of World War II, the Jewish population traces its traditions partly from Germany, partly from the Oriental communities, and, from the point of view of antiquity, may equal that of the West.

2. Werner, p. 957 (*see* Bibliography for references).

3. *See* Oesterly, p. 58. Until the period of the *paytanim,* there were only a few prayers with music. The most celebrated *paytan* was Rabbi Israel Najara, who adapted more than 650 prayers to secular music and composed several hundred original Hebrew melodies. Another was Judah Halevi, foremost Hebrew poet of the Middle Ages.

4. Idelsohn, p. 134. For centuries, Jewish life concentrated in the synagogue, and much of the ancient character of Jewish tradition was deposited in its liturgical music, which up to the seventeenth century was largely Jewish folklore in its most stylized form. Wherever Jews settled, they adapted local airs for use in their religious services. These, added to fundamental, traditional material common to Jews living in different lands, produced a great variety in synagogal music.

5. The Middle Ages, as applied to Jewish historiography, extends to the end of the eighteenth century, almost into the French Revolution.

6. Not all the songs at meals were religious in content. "Praises of wine and love, both in Hebrew and in the vernacular, found their way into Jewish circles, especially in Spain, where . . . these secular songs were even interpolated into the grace after meals and were set to Arabian tunes" (Abrahams, p. 137).

7. Karpeles, p. 87.

8. Graetz, III, pp. 419–420. Recently, some scholars have questioned the Jewish origin of Susskind of Trimberg.

9. Abrahams, p. 361.

10. "One can say with certainty, that at that time, approximately more Jews *read* the tales of King Arthur's Court and Smid Weiland than the number of Germans who had *heard* them" (Güdemann—Shtif, p. 14).

11. Originating around 1000 C.E. in the Rhine basin, *Yiddish* is a Jewish language with a structure of its own, comparable to Hebrew and Aramaic. As early as the seventeenth century, it had already developed a unique set of dialects quite different from those of German. Spoken by Jewish communities in Southern, Central, and

Northern Germany, Bohemia, Poland, Lithuania, Northern Italy, Ukraine, and Holland, it reached its widest usage in the eighteenth century. Then it declined in Italy and Germany but expanded in the Western Hemisphere, Palestine, Australia, and South Africa. Before World War II, some eleven million Jews spoke Yiddish. The largest Yiddish-speaking community in the world today is in the United States.

Most forms of folklore are represented in Yiddish : songs, tales, plays, proverbs, and the like. Yiddish literature is no younger than Russian or Polish and only a century or two behind the earliest writings in French, German, and Italian. Yiddish in America is about eighty years old and counts its authors in the hundreds and its books in the thousands.

12. Erik, p. 21. The Jewish *Spielmann* became active about the fourteenth and functioned until the first half of the sixteenth century. He sang in Judeo-German (archaic Yiddish) for Jewish audiences in the ghettos only, being prohibited by the Church to perform before Christians.

13. Erik, p. 91.

14. Toward the end of the fourteenth and through the fifteenth and sixteenth centuries, this German, twelfth-century fantasy, based on Henry the Lion's Crusade of 1172, seems to have been one of the most popular songs among the Jews in Germany, and its tune was used for a number of songs and bardic epics.

15. This is the oldest-known German folk song about that German legendary hero. Two old Yiddish versions are extant. This legend and "Dietrich von Bern" were very popular among the Jews, to which the rabbis strongly objected.

16. The Yiddish work, paraphrased in rhyme, was based on the German tale of Wigalois by Wirnt von Grafenberg. Several handwritten manuscripts and a number of printed copies are extant.

17. Weinreich, p. 64.

18. Possibly the first Yiddish book *printed,* this work in verse, by Eliyahu Bachur (Levita), is a free translation of the Italian legend of Bevis of Hampton (Buovo d'Antona). In the introduction to the 1507 publication, Levita comments on the tune to which the work is to be sung :

Ober der nign, der deroyf vird geyn,	But the tune, to which this is to be sung,
Den kon ich nit gebn tsu fershteyn,	Is not possible for me to explain,
Den eyner kent muzika oder solfa,	But if one knows music or sol-fa,
Zo volt ich im hobn geholfa.	Then, I could have helped him.
Ober ich zing es mit eynem Velshn gezang.	However, I sing it with an Italian tune.
Kon der deroyf machn eynen besern,	If one can create a better one,
Zo hob er dank. (Shiper, I, p. 41.)	He has my thanks.

The *Bovo Buch* continued to be popular until the end of the seventeenth century. Due to its title, it became, thanks to popular usage, synonymous with *bobe mayse* — a "grandmother's tale." A copy is to be found in the Jewish Theological Seminary, New York.

19. Wiener, p. 4.

20. While the Jewish colonies on the shores of the Black Sea and on the territory of modern southern Russia were the result of immigration from the lands of the Greco-Byzantine and Mohammedan East, the Jewish settlements in Poland were founded by Jews from Western Europe, from the lands of German culture and the Latin faith. During the twelfth century, German Jews occasionally traveled to the Slavic lands, and the Jews of Russia used to address inquiries to the Jewish scholars of Germany. The eighteenth century saw a reversal of this process when Poland became the center of Jewish culture and learning. This situation was maintained until World War II.

21. After the advent of the printing press, as the reading public increased during the sixteenth and seventeenth centuries, there emerged the rich, well-to-do woman, who played an important part in the economic life of the Jewish-German community of those days. She often supported the entire family, making it possible for the males to further their Talmudic learning. Around her, a whole literature in Yiddish sprang up; she became the patroness of this literature, and at weddings, celebrations, and holidays, the Jewish minstrel, clown, acrobat, and dancer performed, depending on her for support. Yiddish books in folk style were specially written for these patronesses and for women in general, not only to entertain them but also to keep them preoccupied and concentrated on piety and religious duties. It may be assumed that it was primarily the women who also assimilated the literature of the surrounding world and who must have helped introduce it into Jewish society of that day. These patronesses were still prominent during the eighteenth century, and women as promoters of contemporary secular literature and song were still an institution in Eastern Europe at the turn of the nineteenth century.

CHAPTER I

At The Cradle

THE MODERN YIDDISH LULLABIES ECHO THE DREAMS AND ASPIRATIONS of the average Jewish mother in the Czarist Pale of Settlement. Although in the nineteenth century these songs abounded in number and variety, many a scholar has sought in vain in the Bible and Talmud for traces of Jewish cradle songs. "In the Middle Ages, some religious authorities disapproved of lulling a Jewish child to sleep with non-Jewish lullabies. But this does not prove that genuinely Jewish lullabies did not exist in those times."[1] The paucity in the distant past of those humming, crooning, soothing melodies, pure improvisations of the moment, seems generally accepted as fact. There are even scholars, investigating the ancient period and observing the scantiness of such material, who maintain that antiquity lacked the cradle song entirely!

During the nineteenth century, however, there was no dearth of lullabies, both as spontaneous expressions in the simplest structure, created at the cradleside, and as poetic creations of more literary origin, current among the folk. These modern cradle songs include a variety of forms, motifs, and moods and sincerely reflect the patterns of life which were prevalent at the time.

Within the confines of the Pale, with the exception of a thin, upper layer, the majority lived in the direst poverty. The daily life was forever under the pall of insecurity, persecution, humiliation, and general cultural isolation from the outside world. Parents and children together endured its rigors. A religious way of life dominated the internal existence of the Pale. Boys were sent to Hebrew school at the tender age of four and five and sometimes even three. Little girls, not expected to master these studies, were in some cases provided with rudimentary instruction in reading and writing Yiddish and a bit of arithmetic. But more often, they remained at home to help with the household chores. Most Jewish

29

Дочь твоя — года с ребенком   А. Касьян 57-59 г.

mothers of that period supported the family so that their males could devote themselves to studying the Holy Writ.

"My mother," writes Mendele Moycher Sforim, "always lived in want and simply never had enough with which to pull through the day. She would knit socks, pluck hens, assist at childbirth, and help with the baking of the *matses* before Passover. She worked day and night, poor soul, and, out of it all, we barely had a mouthful to eat."[2]

The cradle songs thus served two purposes: on the one hand, they reflected the prevailing social and religious patterns of life; and, on the other, they served as tender, crooning songs to induce the little baby to slumber peacefully. The main motif, however, which flows through most of the older lullabies that were composed at the beginning of the nineteenth century, was the aspiration toward Torah learning and piety, bringing economic security, and prestige in the community. Within the simple structure of the cradle song, the motif that her son become a scholar develops into a deep yearning on the part of the hard-working mother. And if her infant happens to be a little girl, the mother's ambition is that she may marry a man of pious and scholarly pursuits.

"Riches, bodily advantages, and talents of every kind have indeed a certain worth . . . but . . . no merit is superior to that of a good Talmudist. He has the first claim upon all offices and positions of honor in the community. . . . The most honorable place is assigned to him."[3] The aspiration for Talmudic learning becomes bound up with the conviction that such an achievement would bring not only economic security on earth but also celestial approval in heaven. Small wonder, then, that the working mothers constantly aspired to and sacrificed themselves toward this end, which promised prestige and recognition for themselves and their children in the Jewish community, though their own economic origin might have been of the lowliest.

Unter yankele's vigele	Under Yankele's cradle
Shteyt a vaysinke tsigele.	Stands a little white kid.
Tsigele iz geforn handlen	The little kid went off to trade
Rozhinkes mit mandlen;	With raisins and almonds;
Dos iz di beste s'choyre,	These are the best of wares,
Yankele vet lernen toyre.	Yankele will study the Torah.
Toyre vet er lernen,	He will study the Torah,
Sforim vet er shraybn,	He will write learned volumes,
Un a guter un a frumer	And a good and pious man
Vet er tomid blaybn.[4]	He will always be.

In most of the lullabies of the older genre, the tender sentiments of the mother are intermingled with her personal social and religious ambitions for her child. In one, the mother imagines her son grown and a prominent Talmudic scholar in the community. In another, she sees her infant delivering a brilliant oration at his thirteenth birthday ceremonial (*bar mitzvah*). In a third, the mother marks each important stage in the life of her child, as she sings her baby to sleep.

Shlof, shlof, mayn zun,	Sleep, sleep, my son,
Ch'vel dir koyfn shtivelech;	I will buy little boots for you;
Shtivelech vel ich dir koyfn,	Little boots I'll buy for you,
In cheder vestu loyfn,	You will run to cheder,
Loyfn vestu in cheder,	To cheder you will run,
Lernen vestu k'seder. . . .	And study regularly. . . .
Gute b'sures un gute mayles,	A good reputation and fine virtues,
Tsu achtsn yor vestu paskenen shayles;	At eighteen you'll solve rabbinical problems;
Shayles vestu paskenen,	Problems you will solve,
Droshes vestu darshenen.[5]	Speeches you will make.

This particular lullaby goes on to describe the coming of the match-maker, always on the lookout for desirable young men for his wealthy "clients," the drawing up of the engagement contract, the exchange of gifts between the bride and groom, the wedding date being set and the marriage and blessing of the newlyweds. Such were the fond dreams of the mother as she crooned and rocked her baby to sleep, in health and in sickness, through the "measles and the chicken pox," soothing the fretful, whimpering child.[6]

Where the infant was a baby girl, the dreams and hopes took the following form in the cradle song:

Davnen un shraybn un taytsh leyenen,	To pray and write and read Yiddish,
Taytsh leyenen oys di bichlech,	To read Yiddish out of the books,
Neyen un heftn shtern-tichlech. . . .	To sew and embroider headbands . . .
Vayl m'iz kleyn darf men zich lernen,	One must learn when one is young,
Me zol di eltern nit dertsernen;	So as not to aggravate the parents;
Nit dertsernen, mit a freylech ponim,	Not to worry them, but be of good cheer,
Heybn zich on dreyen di shadchonim. . . .	Then the matchmakers begin to come. . . .

Sorele's chosn vet zayn a talmid-
    chochem,
A talmid-chochem mit gute mayles,
Sorele's chosn vet kenen paskenen
    shayles.[7]

Sorele's groom will be a wise scholar,
A wise scholar with fine virtues,
Sorele's groom will know how to
    solve problems.

Occasionally a domestic problem is revealed in a lullaby, as in the following, in which it becomes evident that the parents are not in agreement as to the proper upbringing of the child. The mother wants the baby to be a learned man, but apparently the father is indifferent in matters of religion and piety. The mother sees in the father's attitude a serious threat, not only to the family's position in the community, but also to the peace and acceptance she expects to find in the afterlife as the mother of a pious man. The mother's deep concern is expressed in her passionate appeal to her child, still in the cradle, to follow the accepted ways of the religious requirements, so that even the father might be spared the "tortures of hell" which were surely awaiting him in the afterlife for his transgressions on earth.

Der tate hot dem kind nit gelernt vos
    got hot gebotn,
Vet men im af yener velt brenen un
    brotn;
Un du mayn lib kind, mit dayne
    tsidkes, zolst zich mi-en,
Dayn tatn fun genem aroystsutsi-en.

    Refrain: Shlof mayn kind,
    Zolst mir ru-en un zayn gezint.

Az ich vel amol darfn af yener velt
    geyn,
Veln di tirn fun gan-eydn ofn shteyn.

Du mayn kind, zolst mir zayn a
    frumer un a guter,
Vet men zogn af yener velt : lozt
    arayn dem tsadik's muter ! [8]

Your father didn't teach you the
    Lord's ways,
And he will be burned and roasted in
    the other world;
And you, my dear child, with your
    saintly ways, you will endeavor,
To save your father from hell.

Sleep, my child,
May you rest and be healthy.

And when I shall have to go to that
    other world,
The gates of Paradise will be open
    for me.

You, my child, will be good and
    pious,
So that they may say there : open the
    gates for the mother of the saint !

Religious life penetrated into everything in the Pale. The Jewish community maintained its own network of religious schools (cheder), houses of study, Talmudic academies (yeshiva), synagogues, and was governed by its own community councils of elders (kohol). The middle of

the nineteenth century witnessed a strong swing towards the secularization of these ways of life, expressed through the Haskalah (Enlightenment) movement, which sought to introduce secular schools, modernize
the mode of dress, and stimulate the pursuit of secular knowledge. In
many a home, the father became "touched" by this movement, whereas
the mother persistently clung to the old ways. In the following fragment,
we find the mother shrewdly planning to marry the child off early, in
spite of the fact that she knows the father will scoff at her ideas:

Tsu tsvelf yor vel ich dich chasene machn,	I will marry you off at the age of twelve,
Ch'vel dir neyen kleyder un ale gute zachn.	I will sew clothes for you and other nice things.
Der tate der apikoyres lacht derfun gor,	Your father, the non-believer, scoffs at this,
Chasene, zogt er, nor tsu achtsn yor.[9]	Marriage, says he, only at the age of eighteen.

Rocking her child to sleep, the mother would reflect upon her own
hard life, hoping for something better for her baby in a world full of
temptations and hardships:

Shlof, zo lang dayn eygele iz noch nit oysgetrert,	Sleep, as long as your little eyes are not dried up with weeping,
Shlof geshmak, mayn feygele, yetst iz yedes regele	Sleep well, my birdie, now every little moment
Milionen far dir vert.	Is worth millions for you.
Shpeter vet dos shverlech zayn, yesurim fun altsding.	Later it will be hard and you will have worries about everything.
Veln vestu erlech zayn un datsu bagerlech zayn,	You will want to be honest as well as desirable,
Ay, dos iz nit gring!	Ah, that is not simple!
Lib iz dir dayn tseltunye, zo lang du bizt noch blind	Your little cradle is now dear to you, as long as you are still innocent
Un du kenst nit undzer veltunye, vu men koyft far geltunye,	And you don't know our world, where everything can be bought for money,
A man, a vayb, a kind.[10]	A husband, a wife, a child.

The injection into the lullabies of themes relating to the adult world
was a natural one. For although the adult beside the cradle hummed and
crooned soothingly, the singer was aware that the infant could not be

touched by the texts themselves. Consequently many an adult unburdened his heavy heart, pouring into the lullabies sad thoughts and troublesome problems. When the cradle rocker was a servant girl, a maiden aunt, or an older sister, the lullaby often became the receptacle of a tale of heartbreak in a love affair:

Er hot mir tsugezogt, er hot mir tsugezogt,	He promised me, he promised me,
Er hot mir tsugezogt tsu nemen.	He promised me to marry.
Er geyt avek tsu anander meydl,	He went off with another girl,
Tut mayn harts klemen.	And my heart aches.
Refrain: Shlof mayn kind, shlof,	Sleep, my child, sleep,
In dayn zisn shlof.	In your sweet slumber.
Got zol im batsoln far der falsher libe,	May the Lord punish him for his false love,
Dos zol zayn zayn shtrof.	Let that be his punishment.
Ch'ob zich oysgeneyt a zaydn kleydele,	I made myself a silk dress,
Finef arshin di breyt.	Five yards in width.
Kayn guts un kayn naches zol der mentsh nit hobn,	No good nor pleasure shall that one have,
Vos er hot undz in undzer libe tsusheydt.	Who separated us in our love.
Azoy vi s'iz nito kayn royt epele,	As there is no little red apple,
S'zol nit zayn kayn veriml derinen.	Without its little worm inside it,
Azoy iz nito der mansparshoyn,	So there is no male
Vos zol nit hobn kayn falshn zinen.[11]	Without his false intentions.

In another lullaby, the adult singer combines three elements in her song: she croons and hums sweetly as she tells the child a cumulative tale about a king and queen, a vineyard, a tree, a branch, a birdie and its wing. The singer manages at the same time to weave her own heartbreak into the refrain and the concluding stanza of the song, of which several stanzas and the refrain are given below:

Amol iz geven a mayse. . . .	Once upon a time,
Di mayse is gornit freylech—	The story is not a happy one—
Di mayse heybt zich onet	The story begins
Mit a yidishn meylech.	With a Jewish king.

Refrain: Lulinke mayn feygele	Hushaby my birdie,
Lulinke mayn kind.	Hushaby my child.
Ch'ob ongevoyrn aza libe—	I have lost my own true love—
Vey iz mir un vind.	Woe is unto me.
Der meylech iz opgeshtorbn,	The king died,
Di malke iz gevorn fardorbn,	The queen pined away,
Der tsvayg iz opgebrochn,	The branch broke off,
Dos feygele fun nest—antlofn.	And the birdie flew away.
Vu nemt men aza chochem	Where is the wise man
Der zol kenen di shtern tseyln?	Who can count the stars?
Vu nemt men aza dokter	Where is the doctor
Er zol kenen mayn harts heyln? [12]	To heal my aching heart?

With mothers working, the baby was often cradled in the arms of a grandmother or rocked by a neighbor or a neighbor's child. The following is sung by a little girl who is upset, for she would rather be outdoors skipping with her friends and eating sugar candy than rocking the neighbor's baby:

Refrain: A-lu-lu, sha, sha, sha,	Hushaby, hush, hush, hush,
Dayn mameshi'z geganen in gas ara';	Your mother's gone out;
A-lu-lu, shlof mayn kind!	Hushaby, sleep my child!
Di mameshi vet kumen gich un geshvind!	Your mommy will soon return!
Andere meydelech tantsn un shpringen,	Other little girls dance and play,
Un ich muz n'kind vign un zingen.	And I have to rock the baby and sing.
Andere meydelech tsukerlech nashn,	Other little girls eat sugar candy,
Un ich muz n'kind's vindelech vashn.[13]	And I have to wash the baby's diapers.

The tenderest lullabies were created by the mothers themselves. No matter how difficult their life, these hard-working, self-sacrificing women spun their sweetest dreams beside the cradle. Motherhood, love and concern for their baby, delight in their charm and beauty are contained in these sensitive songs.

Du host shoyn dayne eygelech tsugemacht,	You have closed your little eyes now,
Vi di sheyne zun geyt unter farnacht. . . .	Like the setting sun at the day's end. . . .

Dem keyser's oytsres iz gornisht optsutsoln,
Dos sheynkayt fun mayn kind iz gornit optsumoln! [14]

The king's treasures are beyond purchase,
My child's beauty is beyond description!

But when the infant whimpered, tossed, and was restless, the weary mother would plead with the little one to close its eyes and go to sleep. Failing there, the poor woman was sometimes compelled to conjure up the well-known "bogeyman," as in the following:

Pestest zich un veynst, un shlofn, vilstu nit,
Machst doch on dayn muter shmertsn mit dermit.
Zingen un vign iz dayn gantser grunt;
Shlof-zhe mayn kind, shlof-zhe gezunt!

You whimper and cry and won't sleep,
Causing your mother anguish thereby.
Singing and rocking is all you want;
Sleep then, my child, sleep in good health!

Zhabes mit bern ton oyf droysn zitsn,
Mit di hoyche shtekns, mit di lange shpitsn.
A meydele, vos veynt un vil nit ru-ig zayn,
Nemen zey zi tsu un varfn in torbe arayn. [15]

Toads and bears sit outdoors
With their tall, pointed sticks.

A little girl that cries and refuses to be quiet
Is taken away by them and thrown into a sack.

Since it was not expected of little girls to be learned in the Holy Writ, their main hope lay in marrying a lad who was going to be proficient therein. Through his excellence in Talmudic learning, the poorest boy could aspire to the daughter of even the richest man in town. Thus the problem of dowry literally hung menacingly over all girls, even babies in the cradle. The following example reflects the prevailing customs in approaching a marriage, the role of the matchmaker, the terms of the dowry, the role of the parents, and the whole drama and byplay of the marriage "transaction."

Vos iz di beste s'choyre?
Sorele's chosn vet lernen toyre.
Toyre, toyre in kepele,
Kashe mit milch in tepele;
Broyt mit puter 'et men shmirn,
Der tate mit der mame veln derlebn

What is the best of wares?
Sorele's groom will study the Torah.
Torah, Torah in the little head,
Gruel and milk in the little pot;
Bread with butter will be spread,
Father and mother will live to see

Sorelen tsu der chupe tsu firn.	Their Sorele led to the marriage ceremony.
Tsu der chupe tsu firn un gants sheyn zich tsirn. . . .	To the canopy dressed in finery. . . .
Foter un muter vet men fregn,	Father and mother will be consulted,
Toyznt toler 'et men legn,	A thousand thalers will be put up,
Toyznt toler 'et men tsuborgn;	Another thousand will be borrowed;
Ver s'et nemen sorelen vet nisht hobn vos tsu zorgn.[16]	Whoever marries Sorele, will have nothing to worry about.

Side by side with the above type of lullabies, there were those which treated only of one theme — to rock the baby tenderly to sleep with images and sounds of sweetness and beauty, such as the following:

Shlof, shlof, shlof,	Sleep, sleep, sleep,
Der tate vet forn in dorf,	Daddy will go to the village,
Vet er brengen an epele,	He will bring a little apple,
Vet zayn gezunt dos kepele.	To make your little head strong.
Shlof, shlof, shlof,	Sleep, sleep, sleep,
Der tate vet forn in dorf,	Daddy will go to the village,
Vet er brengen a hezele,	He will bring a little hare,
Vet zayn gezunt dos nezele, etc.[17]	To make your little nose strong.

The above proceeds with its simple rhyming device, bringing an *entele* ("a little duck") to make the baby's little hand (*hentele*) strong, a *nisele* ("a little nut") to make the baby's little foot (*fisele*) strong, etc.

In the following, the green forest and the twittering birds combine with beautiful rings, auguring marriage, to create a tender little lullaby for a baby girl:

Shlof, dvoyrele, shlof,	Sleep, little Deborah, sleep,
Di feygelech zingen in vald,	The birdies are singing in the wood,
Zey zingen un shpringen in grinem groz,	They sing and hop about in the green grass,
Zey veln dvoyrelen brengen vos.	They will bring little Deborah something.
Vos veln zey brengen?	What will they bring?
Sheyne, fayne ringen.	Lovely, fine rings.
Di ringen veln zayn mit gold bashlogn,	The rings will be wrought with gold,
Dos vet dvoyrele trogn.[18]	That's what little Deborah will wear.

During the eighties and nineties of the nineteenth century, a lullaby that reflected the political atmosphere in Czarist Russia at the time became popular. It utilized a theme, which was employed in several work songs and which contrasted the poor man and the rich man, registering the dissatisfaction and protest of the workingmen against poverty and exploitation. Following are three stanzas:

Shlof mayn kind, shlof k'seyder,	Sleep, my child, sleep,
Zingen vel ich dir a lid.	I will sing you a song.
Az du mayn kind vest elter vern,	When you, my child, will grow older,
Vestu visn an untershid.	You will understand the difference.
Az du mayn kind, vest elter vern,	When you, my child, will grow older,
Vestu vern mit laytn glaych.	Then you will be like the rest of us.
Demolst vestu gevoyre vern	Then you will find out
Vos heyst orim un vos heyst raych.	What it means to be rich or poor.
Di tayerste palatsn, di shenste hayzer,	The finest palaces, the loveliest houses,
Dos alts macht der oriman.	All of these are made by the poor man.
Nor veystu ver es tut in zay voynen?	But do you know who inhabits them?
Gor nisht er, nor der raycher man.[19]	Not he at all, but the rich man.

At that time too, the great mass migrations from Eastern Europe to America were taking place. The Jewish immigrants seeking economic security and political and social liberties in the New World were at first deeply disillusioned by the stark reality of the sweatshops. The magic of the "golden land of opportunity" was proving, for the majority who had uprooted themselves from their old home in the Slavic lands, to be merely a myth. A poem entitled "Mayn yingele" ("My Little Boy"), written by Morris Rosenfeld in 1889, was set to an anonymous tune and quickly spread among Yiddish-speaking immigrants. Current in several variants on both sides of the Atlantic, it is still alive today and reflects an economic environment that has since disappeared from our midst. In the lullaby, a father sings about the long hours and hard work in a sweatshop on New York's East Side. He expresses his anguish in not being able ever to see his baby son awake — for when he departs for work in the morning, the child is still asleep, and when he returns at dusk, the infant slumbers once again.[20]

One of the most popular lullabies at the close of the century was

Sholem Aleichem's "Shlof mayn kind" ("Sleep, My Child"), which gained wide usage in Eastern Europe. Migrating to America with tens of thousands of immigrants, it is still popular wherever Yiddish is spoken today. It mirrors the separations and suffering, the waiting and longing which immigrants and their families experienced in their search for a better life in the New World. Although both text and tune were originally derived from classical music and literature, this song has acquired many musical and textual variants, achieving a greater popularity than many an old folk song of its day. Following are several stanzas:

In Amerike iz der tate,	Your daddy's in America,
Dayner, zunenyu,	Your daddy, little son,
Du bizt noch a kind les-ate,	But you are still a child,
Shlof-zhe, lu-lu-lu.	Sleep then, hushaby.
Dortn est men in der vochn	There they eat even on the weekdays
Chale, zunenyu,	White bread, little son;
Yaychelech vel ich dir kochn,	I will cook chicken broth there for you,
Shlof-zhe, lu-lu-lu.	Sleep then, hushaby.
Er vet shikn tsvantsig doler,	He will send us twenty dollars
Zayn portret dertsu,	And his picture, too,
Un vet nemen, lebn zol er!	And will take us—long life to him!—
Undz ahintsutsu.[21]	To America.

On the whole, however, the lullabies of the nineteenth century remain for the most part preoccupied with the theme of Talmudic learning and the respected, honored place in the community that it enjoyed. In the following excerpt, the parent hopes for a better future for her child than the one she had had.

Dayne yunge yorelech bin ich dir mekane,	I envy you your little young life,
Du vest zayn a groysinker, vestu zayn a tane,	When you grow up, you'll be a scholar,
Vestu dayne eltern batsirn un bashaynen,	Honoring and enhancing your parents,
Past doch nit far dir, zolst pishtshenen un veynen.[22]	Therefore it's not nice for you to be whimpering and crying.

Talmudic learning was the magic key to the doors of success. The tired parent, bowed down by the strain of daily problems and responsi-

bilities, couldn't help but envy the little baby lying there so innocently
in the cradle, not knowing what the world might hold in store for it.

Shlof mayn feygele,	Sleep, my birdie,
Mach tsu dayn eygele, ay-lu-lu-lu.	Close your little eyes, hushaby.
Shlof geshmak mayn kind,	Sleep well, my child,
Shlof un zay gezunt, ay-lu-lu-lu.	Sleep and be well, hushaby.
Shlof un cholem zis,	Slumber and dream sweetly,
Fun der velt genis, ay-lu-lu,	Enjoy this world, hushaby,
Bizvanen du bizt yung,	As long as you are young,
Konstu shlofn gring,	You can sleep at ease,
Lachn fun altsding, ay-lu-lu.[23]	And laugh at everything, hushaby.

Occasionally we come across a tragic lullaby, sung by a widowed
mother to her orphaned child, excerpts of one of which are given below:

Ich klog vos ich hob dich geborn,	I weep that I bore you
Oyf tsores, ovf umglik, oyf shmerts.	Into trouble, sorrow, and pain.
Ven ich hob dayn foter farlorn,	When I lost your father,
Biztu geven bay mir untern herts.	You were still under my heart.
Horeven vestu dayn gantsn lebn,	You will toil your whole life long,
Mit noyt vet dir onkumen dayn broyt.	Earning your bread by the sweat of your brow.
Blut vet fun dayne oygn rinen,	Bloody tears will flow from your eyes,
Vayl dayn foter iz toyt.[24]	Because your father is dead.

Sorrowful, too, is the lullaby sung by strangers, as they lull to sleep a
baby whose mother died in giving it birth:

Ver vet dir mayn kind, gletn un kamen?	My child, who will comb and caress you?
Ver vet dir mayn kind di vigele oysramen?	My child, who will clean your cradle?
Refrain: Nito kayn mame, nito kayn nechame!	Without a mother, there is no comfort!
Ver vet dir mayn kind putsn un tsirn?	My child, who will clothe and adorn you?
Ver vet dir mayn kind in cheder firn?	My child, who will take you to cheder?
Ver vet dir mayn kind machn far a mentshn?	My child, who will make a man out of you?
Un ver vet dir mayn kind unter der chupe bentshn?[25]	My child, who will bless you under the canopy?

Bearing the characteristics of a bitter lament, perhaps even uttered by the mother lying on her deathbed, this tragic lullaby breathes with tenderness towards the innocent baby in the cradle, with a life of sorrow facing it so soon.

It may be that the chapter of anonymous Yiddish lullabies ended with the close of the nineteenth century. Yiddish cradle songs, however, continued to be written by Jewish poets and composers during the twentieth century, both in Eastern Europe and America and wherever Yiddish-speaking Jews settled. It is true that these never achieved the wide usage of the earlier ones that were born spontaneously and anonymously and were sung naturally in a centuries-old environment, which gave birth not only to cradle songs but to a host of other categories as well.

Notes

AT THE CRADLE

1. Schauss, p. 80.
2. Mendele, VI, p. 17.
3. Maimon, p. 16.
4. Cahan, 1957, No. 337.
5. D. and Y., p. 39, No. 5.
6. ". . . during those sleepless nights, she was so skillful in translating her troubles and burdens into songs, that I never knew whether she had created them herself or whether she had heard them from someone. *Oy pokelech, oy mozelech, oy-oy un oy-oy,* she would hum to herself." (*pokelech*: "little pox"; *mozelech*: "little measles"). (Teitelbaum, p. 35.)
7. Cahan, 1957, No. 340.
8. D. and Y., p. 48, No. 19.
9. *Ibid.,* p. 48, No. 20.
10. *Ibid.,* p. 53, No. 25.
11. Rubin, MSS.
12. Rubin, 1950, p. 20.
13. Cahan, 1957, No. 331.
14. *Ibid.,* No. 332.
15. B. and F., p. 310.
16. Cahan, 1957, No. 339.
17. B. and F., p. 304.
18. *Ibid.,* p. 306.
19. Rubin, 1950, pp. 22–23.
20. *See*: Chapter XIII, "To America," pp. 12–13 f., No. 22.
21. Rubin, 1950, pp. 23–24.
22. Rubin, MSS.
23. B. and F., pp. 314–315.
24. G. and M., No. 81.
25. *Ibid.,* No. 79.

CHAPTER II

The Children's World

THE LIFE OF THE CHILD IN THE JEWISH ENVIRONMENT OF THE PALE OF A century ago was circumscribed and limited, and the moments of pure joy and happy abandoned playfulness were short-lived. The responsibilities imposed by the exacting, difficult, enclosed life, coupled with the harsh rule of the Czarist regime, actually breathed down the infant's neck while it was still in the cradle. From the day it was born, the child heard songs which were intended to prepare it for the seriousness of the adult life that lay ahead.

Before the little boy could actually walk or talk, he was already being groomed for the cheder. During the long winter months, the teacher's assistant (*behelfer*) would carry the hungry, ill-clothed, half-asleep little boys from their home to school, which Mendele Moycher Sforim described as "a grave in which to bury Jewish children, to stuff up their heads and tear them away from the world."[1] But Mendele was referring to the secular world of life and nature, which the Jewish child only occasionally glimpsed during the summer months or the holidays when the cheder was closed. The rest of the year the little boys remained from early morning till dark under the teacher's (*rebe* or *melamed*) stern eye and cat-o-nine-tails, studying the Bible (Torah, Tanach) and then, in the Yeshiva, poring over the Talmud and its commentaries[2] until their wedding day and often after their marriage as well.

Jewish school life in Poland and Lithuania was for centuries a firmly established institution. Already during the first half of the seventeenth century, there was scarcely a Hebrew house in the whole kingdom of Poland where the Tanach was not studied and where either the head of the family or his son-in-law, or the Yeshiva student boarding with the family, was not an expert in Jewish learning. The class of scholars that resulted looked down upon the uneducated multitude and actually

44

became an intellectual aristocracy, wielding considerable social power in the life of Polish and Lithuanian Jewry.

Much of the emphasis on study still prevailed in the nineteenth century, and it was an accepted thing for a woman to work to maintain her males at their studies, so that they might, in achieving excellence in Torah learning, also secure for the family social privileges on earth as well as heavenly rewards in the afterlife. But no matter how hard the working mothers tried to keep their males studying the Holy Writ, economic conditions relentlessly forced most families to follow the course of sending their children to work, and the number of tailors, seamstresses, tinsmiths, cobblers, bakers, carpenters, and blacksmiths, etc., increased.

In this environment two types of children's songs sprang up : the "natural" ones, characteristic of the child's world, e.g., play songs, counting-out rhymes, taunts and teasers; and the "unnatural" songs that reflected the adult world, e.g., work songs, recruitment and soldier songs, topical songs. Both the natural and unnatural children's songs were permeated with the particular flavor of a personal life influenced by the pursuit of Torah learning on the one hand and the external pressures and persecutions of an anti-Semitic and cruel Czarist government, on the other.

From earliest infancy the Jewish child in the Pale heard singing and chanting, humming and intoning. In the home, in the back yard, in the narrow village street, in the cheder, in the synagogue, at the Sabbath table, during holidays, the children created rhymes, play songs, ditties, riddles, nonsense songs, even satirical rhymes. Despite the difficult surroundings and the multiple restrictions imposed upon the child by his adult environment, these songs are very numerous and reflect the many facets of his own brief, intense life in the children's world of fantasy and play, as well as some of the aspects of the grown-up world around him.

Children's folk song is one of the most interesting categories of folk material. The ditty, the counting-out rhyme, the chant, all play an important part in the life of the child. In these two worlds are mirrored the feelings of the child itself, its temperament, imagination, playfulness, wisdom, humor, and often satire, and the views and sentiments of its elders, as well as certain current events. Adult and child have both created for children; both have at one time or another edited and improved each other's compositions, and it is often difficult to determine where one influence ends and the other begins.

Children's songs may contain remnants of a custom that existed centuries ago, or they may possess social or poetic significance. In a rhyme, sung to jumping rope, skipping, playing hopscotch, turning in a ring, or bouncing ball, we may encounter an expression which has long since disappeared from current speech. And again, we may come across songs and chants which were written only yesterday and relate to an occurrence transpiring in our own day.

Y. L. Cahan, an outstanding collector of Yiddish folk songs, writes: "Many of our children's rhymes are remnants, bits of old, long-forgotten songs, which were once sung by adults. Some are centuries old and their origin is difficult to trace. Others seem to be not so old, and yet it is difficult to determine the time of their birth."[3] Leo Wiener, historian of Yiddish literature, writes: "The number of ditties sung by children is very great. They do not in general differ from similar popular productions of other nations, either in form or content. . . . But there are two classes of songs peculiarly Jewish: the mnemonic lines for the study of Hebrew words, and those that depict the ideal course of a boy's life."[4]

The Counting-out Rhyme

In many games the counting-out rhyme is of primary importance. Who will be it? The counting-out rhyme decides this. Sung, chanted, or merely shouted, these rhymes are usually constructed of syllables that have an intriguing sound but seldom any logical meaning, side by side with some other words that do have meaning, as in the following (only meaningful words are translated):

Eyndl-beyndl, tsuker shteyndl,	Eyndl-bone, sugar stone,
Artse-bartse, rimen shvartse,	Artse-bartse, black belt
Kale royte, sik-sak,	Red bride, sik-sak,
Oybn on, shteyt der hon,	Up on top, stands the cock,
Shlipe-shlape, aroys![5]	Shlipe-shlape, out!

Some follow logical number sequences as the rhyme proceeds to count a series of unrelated objects until the last one named is *it*:

Eyns—a nisl, tsvey—a tsviling,	One—a nut, two—a twin,
Dray—mezumen, fir—reder,	Three—cash, four—wheels,
Finf—finger, zeks—kinder,	Five—fingers, six—children,
Zibn—geklibn, acht—getracht,	Seven—chosen, eight—thought,
Nayn—grad, tsen—gezen,	Nine—even, ten—seen,

Elf—a peyger, tsvelf—a zeyger,
Draytsn—baytshn, fertsn—shertsn,
Fuftsn—groshn iz a halber guldn.[6]

Eleven—a corpse, twelve—a clock,
Thirteen—whips, fourteen—aprons,
Fifteen *groshn* equal half a *guldn.*

Occasionally a counting-out rhyme includes a fragmentary allusion to a current political situation, as in the following two which precede the game of tag:

(1)

Oy, undzere poyln zenen antkegn Yidn!
Oy, undzere felder zenen fargosn mit blut.
Heybt men on arumtsuyogn,
Heybt men on arumtsuplogn,
Dali oyf di ferd, dali tsum gever!
Eyns, tsvey, dray—machn mir pleyte aray![7]

Oh, our Poland is against the Jews!
Oh, our fields are covered with blood.
We begin to chase about,
We begin to wander about,
Forward to horse, forward to arms!
One, two, three—off we run and away!

(2)

Eyne kleyne vayse taybl,
Firte mich in engeland.
Engeland iz tsugeshlosn,
Un di shlisl iz opgebrochn.
Eyns, tsvey, dray, poyln iz farbay.
Russ iz gelofn mit ale harmatn,
Poyln iz geblibn on soldatn.[8]

One small white dove,
Lead me to England.
England is locked,
And the key is broken.
One, two, three, Poland is done for.
Russia pursued with all the guns,
Poland was left without soldiers.

Sometimes we find multilingual rhymes current among the children, utilizing Russian, Polish, Ukrainian, side by side with Yiddish and Hebrew, depending on the geographical location in the Pale, a category which was current among the adults too. The following uses Hebrew, Russian, and Yiddish:

Ani holachti baderech
Upogabi ish chozok, ushmoy kozak,

Nagayke b'yodoi
V'cherev b'tsidoi. Omar elay:
Dyengi davay!
Eyns, tsvey, dray! Du geyst fray![9]

I was walking on the road
When I met a strong man, and his name was Cossack.

He had a cat-o-nine-tails in his hand,
A sword at his side, and said to me:
Hand over your money!
One, two, three! You go free!

The following fleetingly reflects trading transactions in the market place:

Eyne yudn kumen koyfn,
Koyfn zey ayn, di-es un das.
Tseyln zey op dray-un-draysig.
Eyns, tsvey, dray, du binst fray.[10]

Jews come to buy,
They buy this and that.
They count out thirty-three.
One, two, three, you are free.

Play and Game Songs

After the rhyme, the game follows, and the children in the Pale created a host of games and play songs, played in pairs or threes, in groups or alone. There were games for boys only and others for girls only. Both the counting-out rhymes and the play and game songs were either chanted, sung, or shouted. The following, for instance, preceded the game of blindman's buff, when the blindfolded child is surrounded by the others, and all engage in this taunting question-and-answer rhyme. After the phrase of "catch a bird," they scatter, and the blindfolded one tries to catch one of them.

Oyf vos shteystu? — Oyf a fas.
Vos trinkstu? — Epl kvas.
Vos bakstu? — Beygl.
Chap a feygl![11]

Where do you stand? — On a barrel.
What do you drink? — Apple cider.
What do you bake — Bagels.
Catch a bird!

The following sardonic rhyme was used by children in the Pale in many solitary games: running along, skipping, hopping on one foot, striding along holding hands with a friend, or shooting marbles:

A zun mit a regn, di kale iz gelegn,
Vos hot zi gehat? — A yingele.
Vi azoy hot es geheysn? — Moyshele.
Vu hot men es gevigt? — In a vigele.
Vu hot men es bagrobn? — In a gribele.[12]

Sun and rain, the bride had a baby,
What did she have? — A little boy.
What did they call him? — Moyshele.
Where was it rocked? — In a cradle.
Where was it buried? — In a little hole.

The game of cat and mouse, in which two children are picked to represent the groom and bride, was played to the following songs:

Hey, hey, hemerl,
Kum tsu mir in kemerl!
Ch'vel dir epes vayzn,
Shiselech mit rayzn,
Shiselech mit loyter gold,
Chosn-kale hobn zich holt.
A por ferd yogn zich,

Hey, hey, little hammer,
Come to me in my little room!
I will show you something,
Little bowls of rice,
Little bowls of pure gold,
Groom and bride love each other.
A pair of horses are racing,

Mechutonim shlogn zich,
Redele dreyt zich,
Un chosn-kale freyt zich.
Tsimbl, bimbl, tu a klung,
Chosn-kale, tu a shprung! [13]

In-laws are fighting,
The little ring is turning,
And groom and bride are happy.
Tsimbl, bimbl, let it ring,
Groom and bride, take a jump!

Games of hopscotch, rope skipping, ball bouncing, skipping along on one foot, were accompanied by chants and ditties like these:

(1)

Kestele, kestele, gib zich a drey!
Vintele, vintele, gib zich a vey!
Hendele, hendele, gib nor a krey!
Hindele, hindele, leyg mir an ey! [14]

Little box, turn around;
Little wind, blow a bit;
Little cock, crow a little!
Little hen, lay an egg!

(2)

Got, Got, gib a regn,
Fun di kleyne kinder's vegn!
A lebele broyt optsuvegn
An oriman avektsugebn. [15]

God, God, let it rain,
For the little children's sake.
A loaf of bread to be weighed
To be given to a poor man.

A fast "swing around" of little girls was sung to the following:

Kan-vasser, veych vasser,
Dos redl dreyt zich!
Di mame kocht lokshn,
Der tate freyt zich. [16]

Can of water, soft water,
The ring goes round!
Mother's cooking noodles,
Father is happy.

Bride and Groom Songs

Since the high point in the life of every boy and girl in the Pale was the marriage day, a host of children's songs, ditties, and rhymes contain references to that important occurrence, and many bride-and-groom games were played by little girls. These games often assumed the form of a dramatic production, in which the little girls, utilizing pantomime, songs, and dance, acted out the various characters of a Jewish wedding. Many such songs are humorous caricatures, but they also reflect a number of the prevailing mores, customs, and beliefs, although these were naturally fragmentary in this framework.

Prior to the wedding ceremony, in one of these bride-and-groom games, the "bride's friends" are bidding her adieu, singing:

Tants, mirele, tants,
Es shoklt zich der krants,

Dance, Mirele, dance,
The wreath is shaking,

Es shoklt zich der morgnshtern,	The morning star is rocking,
Bald vestu a kale vern,	Soon you'll be a bride,
Tants, mirele, tants.[17]	Dance, Mirele, dance.

To this, the bride replies, half in earnest, half in jest :

Sheyn, bin ich, sheyn,	Pretty am I, so pretty,
Un sheyn iz och mayn nomen,	Pretty too, is my name,
Redt men mir shiduchim mit loyter rabonim.	Wedding matches only of rabbis come my way.
Rabonishe Toyre iz doch zeyer groys,	Torah learning is indeed very great,
Bin ich bay mayn mamen a lichtige royz.	I am my mother's bright rose.
A sheyn meydele bin ich, bin ich,	A pretty maid am I, am I,
Bloye zekelech trog ich, trog ich.	Blue socks do I wear, wear,
Gelt in di tashn, vayn in di flashn,	Money in the purses, wine in the bottles,
Med in di krigelech, kinder in di vigelech,	Mead in the little pitchers, children in the little cradles,
Shrayen vi di tsigelech: me, me, me.[18]	Cry like little kids: ma, ma, ma.

The children in the "marriage" game also impersonated the in-laws, the *marshalik* or *badchen* ("wedding entertainer"), the wedding guests, and, of course, all accompanied by the "proper" songs.

Some of these "bride-and-groom" songs speak to the "groom"; others are in dialogue or conversation form involving the bride's mother or other members of the wedding party. The ceremonies prior to the wedding, during the wedding, and also after the wedding are depicted. Naturally the largest number of this type of children's songs revolve around games which simulate the feasting, dancing, and gaiety during the seven days of feasting following the wedding. Among these is the ring game "Shpits Boydim," which was popular in many variants in different parts of the Pale. Following is a portion of the Polish variant :

Shpits boydim on der erd,	From the top of the attic to the ground
Ale shtibelech tsugekert,	All the huts have been swept clean,
Ale betelech tsugebet	All the little beds have been made,
Ale meydelech tsugeglet,	All the little girls have been prettied up,
Ale veybelech oysgestroyet,	All the little women have been decked out.

Ale ferdelech ongepoyet.	All the little horses have been watered.
Kumt arayn di mume, shtelt zi zich tantsn,	In comes the aunt, she begins to dance,
Tantsn di vantsn, shpringen di griln,	The bugs dance, the crickets jump,
Kumt arayn der zeyde, far-reychert er di lyulke,	In comes grandpa, lights up his pipe,
Kumt arayn di bobe, grizhet di dare bulke.[19]	In comes grandma, gnaws the hard bun.

As a rule, in these games, the parents of the young couple are quite satisfied with the match, and the girls express this sentiment in their songs:

Mechutenesteshi, mazl tov,	Dear in-law, good luck,
Ch'ob bakumen an even tov,	I have received a precious jewel,
Lang gehart un lang gevart,	I have been patient and waited long
A gutn eydim oysgenart,	And finally got me a good son-in-law;
Lang gehart un lang gevart,	I have been patient and waited long
A gute shnur oysgenart.[20]	And finally got me a good daughter-in-law.

In the children's ring games, the choosing of a mate is done directly and simply by the children as in the following:

Kumt der liber zumer, shpiln mir in zamd;	When the summer comes, we play in the sand;
Vu s' iz undzer voynung, dort iz undzer land.	Wherever our home is, that is our land.
Shvartse karshn raysn mir, royte lozn mir shteyn;	We pick the black cherries, and leave the red alone;
Sheyne chasanim nemen mir, mise lozn mir geyn.[21]	We take the handsome grooms and the ugly ones let go.

In actual life, however, this was decidedly out of the question. Parents and matchmakers performed these functions, and young people rarely participated in such procedures. Love was considered an emotion which one felt for parents and relatives and to a member of the opposite sex, only if they were your husband or wife, and then—after the marriage ceremony. Parents were the ones to decide when the time came for a young person to be wedded, and only with rare exceptions were the wishes or the desires of the marriageable young boy or girl inquired into.

Cheder Boys' Songs

In these, the specific flavor peculiar to the Jewish environment con-
ditioned by the network of schools dedicated to religious instruction is
evident. Secular studies were not included in the boys' schools, although
the girls were taught, in addition to the prayers, to read and write, some
arithmetic, and how to write an address in Russian. The latter was included in the event that in later years, when the girl was married to a
scholar of the Torah, she would have to supervise or attend to the livelihood of the family. Girls were also taught to knit, crochet, embroider,
darn, and how to make a patch.

The tender age at which little boys were brought to the cheder and
the surrounding of the occasion with pleasurable associations is vividly
described by a Polish novelist in the following memoir, depicting the end
of the nineteenth century :

One morning, when I had turned three, my father wrapped me up in his
prayer shawl . . . took me into his arms and carried me off to *Rebe* Meyer,
the teacher in the *cheder*. . . . The teacher . . . immediately started to teach
me the Torah, pointing . . . to the ABC's and chanting : "See now, little
fellow, the first letter is an *aleph* . . . the second, which looks like a little hut
with three walls, is a *beys*. . . . After that, is the *giml*. . . . The fourth letter,
which looks like a little ax to chop wood, is a *daled*. . . . Repeat now : *daled,*
little fellow, *daled!* . . . When we reached the tenth letter, *yud,* he told me
to close my eyes. When I opened them . . . raisins and almonds were strewn
over the ABC's. "The angel from Heaven has thrown these down to you for
studying the Torah," *Rebe* Meyer said. "Eat." [22]

When the little boys had mastered the alphabet, the *rebe* began to
teach the boys the Bible by rote, translating word for word from the
Hebrew or Aramaic text into Yiddish, and the Yiddish translation,
together with the Hebrew and Aramaic, would be studied all together,
with a traditional tune. The children were taught the traditional chanting
of the cantillations as well as Sabbath and other prayers, all of which
had their traditional tunes.

Although the main creators of the secular songs of the children's world
were the girls, many of these carried over into the boys' world as well.
Drilled in keenness towards mastering the Holy Writ at a tender age, the
cheder boys and later Talmudic students exercised this faculty in composing a certain type of song which utilized the practice of translating

Zuni Maud, 1929

from the Hebrew and Aramaic texts into the current Yiddish vernacular, setting it in a cross-rhyming form. The following is a portion of such a song :

Ov—a foter, keyder—a toter,
Toter—keyder, b'godim—kleyder,
Kleyder—b'godim, chut iz a fodim,
Fodim iz chut, lechem iz broyt,
Broyt iz lechem, tracht iz rechem,
Rechem iz tracht, shmoyne iz acht,
Acht iz shmoyne, a toyb iz yoyne,
Yoyne iz a toyb, mitsnefet iz a
     hoyb,
A hoyb iz mitsnefet, a shtal iz
     refet,
Refet iz a shtal, mara iz gal,
Gal iz mara, a ku iz pora,
Pora iz a ku, boyker iz fri,
Fri iz boyker, tayer is yoyker,

Yoyker iz tayer, eysh iz fayer,
Fayer iz eysh, bosser iz fleysh,
Fleysh iz bosser, chazer iz osser,
Osser is chazer, mayim iz vasser,
Vasser iz mayim, l'shono habo
     b'Yerusholayim ! [23]

Ov—a father, *keyder*—a Tartar,
Tartar—*keyder, b'godim*—clothes,
Clothes—*b'godim, chut* is a thread,
Thread is *chut, lechem* is bread,
Bread is *lechem,* womb is *rechem,*
Rechem is womb, *shmoyne* is eight,
Eight is *shmoyne,* a dove is *yoyne,*
Yoyne is a dove, *mitsnefet* is a
     headdress,
A headdress is *mitsnefet,* a barn is
     refet,
Refet is a barn, *mara* is gall,
Gall is *mara,* a cow is *pora,*
Pora is a cow, *boyker* is morning,
Morning is *boyker,* expensive is
     yoyker,
Yoyker is expensive, *eysh* is fire,
Fire is *eysh, bosser* is meat,
Meat is *bosser,* pork is forbidden,
Forbidden is pork, *mayim* is water,
Water is *mayim,* may we be in
     Jerusalem next year !

This type of chant at times became a means of contest among the schoolboys to achieve sharper wits and improve the memory. The longer a fellow held out in composing these translations or acrostics in rhyme, the greater recognition and respect he gained from his fellow students and, better still, the envy of his enemies. This manner of chanting sometimes resulted in a more involved type of cross rhyme, which even touched upon philosophy, as in the following, which utilizes the opening lines of the Book of Ecclesiastes in the Bible :

Un hevel iz hevolim,
Un di velt iz a cholem,
Un a cholem iz di velt,
Un alts koyft men far gelt,

Un far gelt koyft men bir,
Un vos dray iz nit fir,

Oh, vanity of vanities,
And the world is but a dream,
Oh, a dream is this world,
And all is bought for gold,

For gold one buys beer,
And what's three is not four,

Un vos fir iz nit dray,	What is four is not three,
Un vos alt iz nit nay,	What is old is not new,
Un vos nay iz nit alt,	What is new is not old.
Un vos varem iz nit kalt,	And what's warm is not cold,
Un vos kalt iz nit varem,	What is cold is not warm,
Un vos raych iz nit orem, etc.[24]	And what's rich is not poor, etc.

It did not take the girls long to imitate this pattern of cross rhyming in their own songs, like the following which is in the rhythm of jumping rope :

Hey, hey, gib mir tey,	Hey, hey, give me tea,
Tey iz bitter, gib mir tsuker,	Tea is bitter, give me sugar,
Tsuker is zis, gib mir nis,	Sugar is sweet, give me nuts,
Nis iz fet, leyg mir in bet,	Nuts are fat, put me to bed,
In bet iz nas, leyg mir in gas,	The bed is wet, put me in the street,
In gas iz kalt, leyg mir in vald,	The street is cold, put me in the woods,
In vald iz kil, leyg mir in mil,	The woods are cool, put me in the mill,
Di mil dreyt zich, di alte bobe Sosye freyt zich.[25]	The mill is turning, old granny Sosye is happy.

Imitating the *rebe* in his instruction of the ABC's the cheder boys composed many alphabet songs, which they used as counting-out rhymes and in their own games. Some of these are very picturesque, as the following, given here in part :

Aleph—a odler tut untern himl fli-en,	*Aleph*—an eagle flying under the sky,
Beys—a barnboym tut ale zumer bli-en,	*Beys*—a pear tree, blooming every summer,
Giml—a galech tut zich tsu der avoyde zore kni-en,	*Giml*—a priest, kneeling to the idols,
Daled—a dokter tut gebn oyf shvitsn,	*Daled*—a doctor prescribes something to make you perspire,
Hey—a himl tut ale zumer dunern un blitsn,	*Hey*—a sky, thundering and lightening every summer,
Vov—a vayner tut oyf di feslech vayn zitsn,	*Vov*—a wine merchant, sitting on the barrels of wine,
Zayin—a zelner tut in der milchome shisn,	*Zayin*—a soldier, shooting in war,

Ches—a chazn tut zich baym davnen   *Ches*—a cantor who weeps bitterly
    mit trern bagisn,   during his prayers,
Tes—a taych tut loyfn un flisn,   *Tes*—a river which rushes and flows,
Yud—a yatkeklots, me tut oyf ir   *Yud*—a meat block, where the meat
    fleysh hakn, etc.[26]   is chopped up.

The counting-out rhymes and games of the cheder boys often reflected the opinions on religious and current matters of their elders. Some of these contain allusions to religious customs and beliefs, others are taunts leveled against apikorsim ("non-believers") and Maskilim ("freethinkers"). Following is such an example :

Oyfn hoychn barg, oyfn grinem groz,   On the high hill, on the green grass,
Shteyen a por daytshn   Stand a pair of Germans
Mit di lange baytshn.   With their long whips,
Hoyche manen zenen zey,   Tall men are they,
Kertse kleyder trogn zey,   Short clothes do they wear.
Ovinu meylech,   Our Father, our King,
Dos harts iz mir freylech,   My heart is gay,
Freylech veln mir zayn,   Gay we will be,
Trinken veln mir vayn,   Wine we will drink,
Vayn veln mir trinken,   We will drink wine,
Kreplech veln mir esn,   Pasties we will eat,
Un in undzer libn Got keynmol nisht   And our loving God we will never
    fargesn.[27]   forget.

It may well be that the allusion to the "Germans" and their "short clothes" reveals the struggle between the religious orthodoxy and the Maskilim, followers of the Enlightenment Movement (Haskalah) and their German-Jewish founder, Moses Mendelssohn. For despite the strict adherence to non-secular studies, it did on occasions happen that some young men strayed from the Talmud to indulge secretly in the study of secular sciences or to read "forbidden" literature in Hebrew, thus falling into the "trap" of the Maskilim, who preached general as well as Jewish learning, shaved their chins, and donned short jackets in contrast to the long coats of the religious Jews.

The following counting-out rhyme, current among the cheder boys, carries a warning to the non-believers who start with "eating butter with their meat" and end up forgetting the Word of the Lord altogether.

Royte fatsheyle, grin un bloy,   Red kerchief, green and blue,
Lomir forn in podaloy,   Let us go to Podoloy,

Podaloy t' gehat a zun,	Podoloy had a son,
Hot er gegesn puter mit hun.	He ate butter with his hen.
Puter mit hun hot er gegesn,	Butter with his hen he did eat,
Davnen un bentshn hot er fargesn.[28]	To pray and bless he did forget.

The sharp struggle between the two groups — the orthodox and the Haskalah followers — expressed briefly in the examples given above, often reached the most intense levels of hatred between the partisans of each group. In the children's world, it was translated in conjuring up the wonderful rewards which awaited these who remained true to the word of God and the Jewish Law and who would live to see the glory of the coming of the Messiah.

However, the life of the cheder and Yeshiva boys also included moments of free abandon under the clear blue sky on Friday afternoons when cheder was let out for the Sabbath preparations, or during the half days off before an important festival. These times were filled with true childish delight in games of all kinds : tug of war and leapfrog, hide-and-seek and tag, all accompanied by a variety of chants, tunes, and shouts, full of imaginativeness, humor, and ingenuity.

Baraban, baraban !	Rat-a-tat, rat-a-tat,
Glokn klingen, glokn klingen !	Bells are ringing, bells are ringing,
Vemes kinder forn dos?	Whose children ride there?
Dem keyser's, dem keyser's !	The king's, the king's,
In vos geyen zey ongeton?	What are they wearing?
In gold un zilber !	Clothes of gold and silver.
Oyf vos tu-en zey raytn?	What are they riding on?
Oyf shof un rinder !	On sheep and cattle.
Oyfn oyvn zitsn zey,	On the stove do they sit,
Shvebelech raybn zey,	Little matches do they rub,
Katshkelech fartraybn zey,	Little ducks they chase away,
In chaloshes blaybn zey ! [29]	In a faint they fall away !

After a long day at the study table, the cheder and Yeshiva boys marched lustily home, swinging their lanterns which lit up the dark, unpaved, narrow roads of the small, unlit town. Glad to be breathing the fresh air of the outdoors, their Yiddish and Hebrew songs rang out into the night, as they sang one ditty after another, one song after another, the old chants side by side with the Yiddish secular songs, creating new ones spontaneously as they walked together.

The Number and Cumulative Songs

There are many children's rhymes in every language that are based on a structure of numbers. The peculiar interest of many of these lies in the fact that "they retain obvious traces of the stages by which prehistoric man first learned to count."[30] They usually ran up to five or ten, and "sometimes the scheme is . . . an attempt to fix in the memory, by means of numbers, the most solemn facts of religion."[31]

"Echod mi yodea," the Passover chant, is perhaps one of the oldest of the number songs. Sung during the Passover feast, it is found in many folk-song treasuries around the world, and its variants employ both religious symbols as well as secular objects. Certain musicologists contend that its use of religious symbols traces its origins to ancient times. However, within the Passover ceremonial, it lists the symbols of the *one* God, the *two* tables of the Covenant, the *three* patriarchs Abraham, Isaac, and Jacob, the *four* matrons Sarah, Rebecca, Leah, and Rachel, the *five* Books of Moses, the *six* Books of the Mishna, the *seven* days of the week, the *eight* days preceding circumcision, the *nine* months before childbirth, the *ten* Commandments, the *eleven* stars of Joseph's dream, the *twelve* tribes of Israel, the *thirteen* attributes of God.

Among children, the number songs were particularly popular, and their counting of a given number of things included the listing of animals, instruments, actions, objects, and the like, all of which may seem far removed from the original Passover chant. The following example, however, does employ the Hebrew beginning of the Passover song, applying it humorously to secular objects, up to the number five.

Echod mi yodea, echod ani yodea,	Who knows one? I know one.
Eyns iz a yidene,	One is a woman,
Nit zi lebt un nit zi shvebt	She neither lives nor floats,
Nit oyfn himl un nit oyf dr'erd.	Not in the sky nor on the earth.

The above proceeds in the use of other symbols as follows:

Finf finger iz a chap,	Five fingers in a catch,
Fir fislech in a bet,	Four legs on a bed,
Dray ekn in a krepl,	Three corners in a pasty,
Tsvey ekn in a shtekn,	Two ends on a stick,
Eyns iz a yidene, etc.[32]	One is a woman, etc.

Since, in their daily prayer, religious boys thanked the good Lord for "not having created me a woman," the above is obviously the satirical composition of cheder boys.

A more popular and widespread song is that of the "Chad gadyo" chant, also sung towards the end of the Passover feast. It, too, has numerous variations in practically every part of the world. The following was current among the Jewish children of the Pale:

Hot Hashem Yisborech aropgeshikt a boymele arop,	The Lord, blessed be His Name, sent a little tree down
Boymele zol barelech vaksn.	To grow little pears.
Boymele vil nit barelech vaksn,	The little tree will not grow little pears;
Barelech viln nit faln.	The little pears will not fall.

The story proceeds to tell us that the Lord then sent Yekele (Jacob) down to pick the pears, and then a dog, a stick, a fire, water, an ox, a butcher, and the Angel of Death. And although the Angel of Death threatened to kill the butcher, the butcher to slaughter the ox, the ox to drink the water, the water to quench the fire, the fire to burn the stick, the stick to beat the dog, the dog to bite Yekele, Yekele could not make the tree grow its pears nor the pears to fall. So the Lord, blessed be His Name, came down Himself. And lo and behold, everything started to move in the right direction, and the little tree finally bore its fruit, and the little pears ripened and fell.[33]

A number of children's songs follow the structural cumulative pattern of the old "Chad gadyo" chant, as for example, the following, which was obviously current in an area where German must have been spoken.

Bin ich ayne yunge,	I am a young man
Bedarf ich ayne frau habn,	And need to have a wife
Bedarf ich visn vi mayn frau vet haysn:	And must know what my wife's name will be:
Chayele-Chayo, hayst mayn libe frau.	Chayele-Chayo is my dear wife's name.

Proceeding in this manner, the young man in the song then acquires a child, a cradle, a carriage, a horse, and a coachman, each with its own inimitable name:

Ayser-shmayser hayst der shmayser,	Ayser-shmayser is the coachman's name,
Erde-merde hayst der ferde,	Erde-merde is the horse's name,

Etshe-metshe hayst di karete,	Etshe-metshe is the carriage's name,
Tsire-mire hayst di dire,	Tsire-mire is the house's name,
Igele-migele hayst dos vigele,	Igele-migele is the cradle's name,
Inde-minde hayst di kinde,	Inde-minde is the child's name,
Chayele-Chayo, hayst mayn libe frau.[34]	Chayelo-Chayo is my dear wife's name.

Cumulative songs took many forms in the children's world. One ring game utilized musical instruments and their functions; the Yiddish version of the English "Old King Cole," led the *Rebe* Elimelech through a series of festivities to a state of drunkenness; a game song listed a cock that crows, a hen that lays an egg, a wheel that turns, and a wind that blows; still another, started with the general and proceeded to the particular : with the lovely root from which the tree came and which rests in the earth since the beginning of time, to the branch, nest, bird, feather, and prosaic pillow. An interesting example of this type of cumulative song is "Hob Ich A Por Oksn," which builds its rhyme in an apparent nonsensical manner but which reveals, upon closer scrutiny, that all the characters as well as the tasks assigned to them fit properly into the Eastern European Jewish environment : with oxen chopping noodles, goats rocking babies in the cradle, cocks gathering kindling wood, bears sweeping the houses, dogs making the annual supply of ink, birdies making doughnuts, and kittens baking cookies.

Riddle Songs

A curious and delightful category is that of the riddle song, which, like the cumulative and number songs, is closely tied to universal folk song the world over. During the Middle Ages, young folks in certain lands used the riddle song as a form of test in courtship. The following children's example might well have had such an origin :

Du meydele du fayns, du meydele du sheyns,	Pretty little maiden, fine little maiden,
Ch'vel dir epes fregn a retenish a kleyns.	I will ask you a little riddle.
Vu zenen do benk on tish?	Where are there benches without tables?
Vu iz do vasser on fish?	Where is there water without fish?
Du narisher bocher, du narisher chlop,	You silly fellow, you foolish clod,

Vi hostu nit kayn seychl in daynem kop !

You haven't a brain inside your head !

In bod zenen do benk on tish,

In the bathhouse are benches and no tables,

In mikve iz do vasser on a fish.

In the ritual pool there is water and no fish.

This same song proceeds to pose a series of other riddles, to which the "bright" maiden has all the answers. Here are two of her questions :

Vu iz do a vasser on zamd?
Vu iz do a meylech on a land?
—Dos vasser fun oyg iz on zamd.

Der meylech in kortn iz on land.[35]

Where is there water without sand?
Where is there a king without a land?
—Tears from the eyes are without sand.

The king of cards has no land.

Although an adult form of sing, riddle songs were current among the children as well.

For the Very Young

Following close upon the heels of the lullabies were many songs for very young children. Written and composed in a great measure by the adults in the family, these were later "improved" upon by the children themselves. There were ditties for the children in the cradle, as they began to walk, talk, feed, and tend themselves — little rhyming songs endowed with charm and tenderness created by parents, an older sister, a grandmother, or aunt. There were "bouncing" songs, when a child was picked up out of the cradle or lifted off the floor as it was crawling underfoot and tossed up and down in the air or on one's knee, such as the following :

Tsigele, migele, vaksn in krigele,

Royte brenseliye. . . .
Az der tate shlogt di mame,
Raysn di kinderlech kri-e.

Little kid *migele,* grow in the little jug,

Red bracelets. . . .
When daddy beats mommy,
The children rend their clothes in sorrow.

Tsigele migele, vaksn in krigele,

Royte pomerantsn.
Az der tate kusht di mame,
Geyen di kinderlech tantsn.[36]

Little kid *migele,* grow in the little jug,

Red oranges.
When daddy kisses mommy,
The little children go dancing.

Usually, these little rhymes, at first obviously composed by adults, were
caught up by the other children in the house, occasionally distorted by
the baby itself as it was learning to talk, and found their way into the
village streets, where they were turned to other uses. They became skipping and game songs or even taunts and teasers in the mouths of
cheder boys.

When a baby, lying in the cradle, played with its little hands and feet,
finger songs and games were composed, such as the following:

In a shtetele pityepoy,
Shteyt a hayzele badekt mit
    shtroy,
Trift a regendl, geyt a shney,
Voynen dortn sh'cheyndelech tsvey:
Sotiki, motiki, sotse, motse, abetsotse
    ruft men zey.[37]

In a little town called Pityepoy,
Stands a little hut covered with
    straw;
A rain is sifting, a snow is falling,
Two little neighbors live inside:
Sotiki, Motiki, Sotse, Motse,
    Abetsotse they are called.

After the bath, a child would be rubbed dry and its hair combed out.
A fine comb would be used to remove any undesirables from the hair, and
a little delousing story-rhyme like the following might have accompanied
this soothing ritual:

Bubi, bubi, layzele,
In kroke shteyt a hayzele.
Ver voynt drinen? yash mit marinen.
Dray panes zitsn un shpinen.
Eyne shpint zayd,
Di tsveyte shpint zilber,
Di drite shpint gold,
Dos kindele hob ich gevolt.[38]

Bubi, bubi, little louse,
In Cracow stands a little house,
Who lives in it? Yash with Marine.
Three ladies sit spinning.
One spins silk,
The second spins silver,
The third spins gold,
I wanted my little baby.

Piggyback was played to the chant:

Hop-tshik-tshak,
Nem di bob n'shtup in zak.

Trog zi aroys oyfn mark,
N'farkoyf zi far a gutn fayg![39]

Hop-tshik-tshak,
Take granny and stuff her into a
    sack.
Carry her out to the marketplace,
And sell her for a good fig!

Teaching the child to walk went with a little dance song like this:

Mitn fisele noch a bisele, tants
    zunele, tants,

With your little foot another little
    bit, dance little son, dance,

Mitn kepele, vi an epele, tants,
    etc.
Mitn maylele, vi a g'daylele, tants,
    etc.
Mitn nezele, vi a hezele, tants,
    etc.
Mit di zaytelech, vi di laytelech,
    tants, etc.
Mitn toches tsu di mishpoches, tants,
    etc.[40]

With your little head like a little
    apple, dance, etc.
With your little mouth like a delight,
    dance, etc.
With your little nose like a little
    hare, dance, etc.
With your little sides to the nice
    people, dance, etc.
With your backside to the families,
    dance, little son, dance.

When the little one could totter a bit, the first ring games were taught the child:

A rod in a rane,
A shtroyene pane,
Zibn mol arum—
Chayke, ker zich um![41]

A ring around,
A straw lady,
Seven times round—
Chayke, turn about!

Teaching the children the names of the members of the family was done to the following, possibly chanted by an older brother:

Mich ruft men zalmen,
Der tate heyst kalmen,
Mayn bruder heyst zorech,
Der zeyde heyst borech,
Di mame heyst beyle,
Di shvester heyst keyle,
Dos ferdl heyst sirke,
Dos ketsl heyst mirke,
Di bobe heyst yoche—
Di gantse mishpoche![42]

I am called Zalmen,
Father's name is Kalmen,
My brother's name is Zorech,
Grandpa is called Borech,
Mother's name is Beyle,
Sister's name is Keyle,
The horse is called Sirke,
The kitten's name is Mirke,
Granny's called Yoche—
And that's the whole family!

Other games for the little one were designed to teach the child to count, to understand, to experience and to feel, to listen to sounds and to perceive, to sing and talk, dance and walk. One such song introduced the child to a series of instruments and the sounds they make: a whistle that makes flu-flu-flu; a trumpet that makes tru-tru-tru; a drum that makes tarabambambam; a triangle that makes tsim-tsim-tsim; and a fiddle that makes fidl-didl-didl.

Pat-a-cake was accompanied by a rhyme which slipped right into the traditional pattern of preparing the child for his future life of piety, economic well-being, and scholarship and the social demands which awaited him in the adult world :

Patshn, patshn kichelech,	Clap, clap, little cookies,
Koyfn, koyfn shichelech.	We will buy little shoes.
Shichelech koyfn,	Little shoes we will buy,
In cheder vet dos kind loyfn.	The child will run to cheder.
Loyfn vet es in cheder,	He will run to cheder
Lernen vet es gor k'seyder.	And study constantly.
Vet es oplernen etleche shures,	He will study several lines,
Vet men hern gute b'sures.	And the good news will get around.
B'sures toyves tsu hern,	May good news get around,
Abi dem oylem a eytse tsu gebn.	So long as the people get good advice.
Eyne, eyne tsu gebn mit fil mayles,	Each to be given, with many virtues,
Vet dos kind paskenen shayles.	The child will one day solve rabbinical problems.
Shayles vet er paskenen,	Rabbinical problems he will solve,
Droshes vet er darshenen.[43]	Scholarly speeches he will make.

Peekaboo was played to the following question-and-answer ditty :

Feygele, feygele, pi, pi, pi,	Birdie, birdie, tweet, tweet, tweet,
Vu'z der tate? — Nito hi.	Where's daddy? — Not here.
Ven't er kumen? — Morgn fri.	When'll he come? — Tomorrow morning.
Vos't er brengen? — A fesele bir.	What'll he bring? — A little keg of beer.
Vu't men es shteln? — Hinter tir.	Where'll we put it? — Behind the door.
Mit vos't men es tsudeken? — Mit a shtikele papir.	What'll we cover it with? — A little piece of paper.
Ver vet trinken? — Ich mit dir ! [44]	Who will drink it? — You and I !

When children quarreled, they were taught to make up quickly and not to carry around a grudge. Hooking each other's little finger of the right hand, they chanted the following as they rocked the fingers back and forth :

Rikele, rikele, roygez,	Little hook, little hook, anger,
Ze'mir gevorn broygez.	We had been "mad,"
Rikele, rikele, rik,	Little hook, little hook, back,
Ze'mir chaver tsurik.	We are friends again.
Chaver, chaver oyf di velt,	Friendship all over the world,

Got 'et gebn a zekele gelt.	The Lord will give a little sack of money.
Vos ich vel hobn vel ich dir gebn;	What I'll have, I'll give to you,
Vos du vest hobn vestu mir gebn.	What you will have, you'll give to me,
Vos vilstu : — a retech tsi a rib?	What do you want : — a radish or a turnip?
— A retech.	— A radish.
Ch'el dir gebn a lekech.	I'll give you cake.
Vos vilstu : — a retech tsi a rib?	What do you want : a radish or a turnip?
— A rib.	— A turnip.
Ch'ob dich lib.[45]	I love you!

When a child was fretful in illness or whimpered and would not go to sleep, a granny would soothe it with a little humorous, crooning rhyme like this :

Nish geshlofn, nish gevacht,	Not sleeping, not waking,
Groyse tsores tog un nacht,	Great troubles, day and night.
Veyn-zhe nish mayn rochelshe,	Don't cry then my little Rachel,
Vest noch zayn a bobeshi.[46]	You'll yet grow up to be a grandmother.

And when a child was stubborn, someone tried to threaten it thus :

Az der kleyner moyshele folgt mir nit,	And when little Moses doesn't listen to me,
Veystu vos ich tu?	Do you know what I do?
Ich shtop es arayn in a zekele	I stuff him into a little sack,
Un bind fun oybn tsu.[47]	And tie it at the top.

And if this didn't make an impression, and the little offender was old enough to know a punishment when he heard it, the following was used :

Zhabes un babes tu-en droysn zitsn,	Toads and witches sit outdoors,
Mit di hoyche hitlen un mit di lange shpitsn,	With their high hats and long points,
A yingele vos veynt un vil nit ru-ig zayn,	A little fellow who cries and refuses to be still,
Lozt men arop di heyzelech un shmayst men im arayn.[48]	They pull his little pants down and spank him well.

With the mother away at work, the old granny was usually the one to rock and soothe the little ones at home. They were the ones with the patience and the time to tell the children a story, such as the following chanted tale, also directed to a whimpering child:

Amol iz geven a bobetske	Once upon a time there was a granny,
Hot zi gehat a hindele a rabetski.	And she had a little speckled hen.
Hindele hot geleygt an eyele,	Little hen laid a little egg.
Iz gevorn tsveyele.	So there were two.
Hot genumen di bobetske	So granny took the egg
Bahaltn dos eyele untern tishele;	And hid it under the little table,
Iz gekumen doz mayzele,	Came the little mouse
Un tsubrochn dos eyele mitn fisele.	And broke it with her little foot.
Der dyed veynt, di bobetske chlipet,	Grandpa is weeping, granny is crying,
Dos toyerl skripet,	The little gate is creaking,
Un dos feygele svishtshet,	And the little bird is whistling,
Un yankele pishtshet! [49]	And little Jacob is twittering!

And when this story or other tales were done, little rhymes, such as the following, were chanted by the elders to their children, rhymes which later were taken out into the street to become skipping songs, game songs, hopping rhymes, and ditties of all kinds.

(1)

Amol iz geven a mayse;	Once upon a time there was
A tsigele a vayse,	A little white kid,
A ki-ele a royte	A little red calf,
Berele iz a shoyte.[50]	Berele is a silly boy!

(2)

A shtekele arayn, a shtekele aroys,	A stick in, a stick out,
Dos maysele iz oys.	The story is done.
A shtekele arayn,	A stick out, a stick in,
Dos maysele iz gor fayn! [51]	The story is very fine!

And so we leave the children's world, rich in rhyme and song, game and fantasy, colorful and spontaneous, tender and charming, collective product of both adult and child. This portion of the Yiddish folk-song treasure of modern times is varied and delightful, mirroring the many facets of the intense, brief life of the Jewish child in the Pale.

Notes

THE CHILDREN'S WORLD

1. Mendele, VI, p. 14.
2. *Tanach*: includes all of the books in the Bible. It was written in Hebrew, with certain portions in Genesis, Jeremiah, and some chapters in Daniel and Ezra in Aramaic. *Talmud*: is the basic study of Jewish religious life, embracing many works which deal with the laws and customs and their interpretations by many scholars through the ages. It consists of *Halacha*, the juridical exposition and interpretations of the law, and *Haggada*, the ethical and poetic interpretation of the Scripture by means of the storytelling. There are two Talmuds: the Jerusalem and the Babylonian, but the latter exerted by far the greater influence on Jewish life. The Babylonian Talmud was written in Babylonian Aramaic mixed with Hebrew and was first published in Venice in 1520/22.
3. Cahan, 1952, p. 36.
4. Wiener, p. 56.
5. Rubin, MSS.
6. *Hob Ich Mir,* p. 13.
7. Cahan, 1957, No. 360.
8. G. and M., No. 90.
9. *Ibid.,* No. 84.
10. *Ibid.,* No. 94.
11. Rubin, MSS.
12. Mendele, VII, p. 50.
13. Cahan, 1957, No. 381.
14. *Ibid.,* No. 377.
15. *Ibid.,* No. 371.
16. *Ibid.,* No. 366.
17. Shtern, p. 69.
18. *Ibid.,* pp. 69–70.
19. *Ibid.,* p. 70.
20. *Ibid.,* p. 73.
21. Cahan, 1957, No. 281.
22. Singer, pp. 24–25.
23. Rubin, MSS.
24. B. and F., p. 384.
25. Rubin, MSS.
26. Cahan, 1957, No. 447.
27. Rubin, MSS.
28. G. and M., No. 95.
29. Cahan, 1957, No. 342.
30. Bett, p. 45.
31. *Ibid.,* pp. 48–49.
32. Cahan, 1957, No. 506.

33. G. and M., No. 126.

Both the "Echod mi yodea" and "Chad gadyo" chants at the end of the Passover service were sung in Aramaic. The latter has been traced to the sixteenth century and has been accepted as the source of all similar stories and songs. "The Rabbis explained it as a parable of the persecutions of Israel: The Hebrew nation is the kid; the two *zuzim* ("pieces of money") were Moses and Aaron; the cat represented Assyria; the dog—Babylonia; the stick—Persia; the fire—Alexander the Great; the water—Rome; the ox—the Saracens; the butcher—the Crusaders; the Angel of Death—the Turks; the Holy One is the Messiah" (Bett, p. 86). ". . . there are versions of these . . . in French, German, Italian, Spanish, Danish, Norwegian, Hungarian, Serb, Romaic, Persian, Arabic, Aramaic, Siamese, Sanskrit, and in several of the Indian and African languages. . . . There is a Hottentot version . . . a Swahili version from Zanzibar . . . a delightful Kabyle version from Algeria . . . a version from the Punjab . . . a version in modern Greek . . ." (Bett, pp. 89–92).

34. Rubin, MSS.

35. Cahan, 1957, No. 499. *See*: Riddle Songs in Chapter III, "Love and Courtship."

Parallels are to be found among the riddle songs of many peoples. A passage in the Talmud runs as follows: "Iron breaks stone; fire melts iron; water extinguishes fire; the clouds consume water; the storm dispels clouds; man withstands the storm; fear conquers man; wine banishes fire; sleep overcomes wine, and death is the matter of sleep, but 'charity,' says Solomon, 'saves from death' " (Bett, pp. 106–107). The following French riddle is an interesting comparison: "What is stronger than iron? —Fire. What is stronger than fire? —Water. What is stronger than water? —The sun. What is stronger than the sun? —The clouds. What is stronger than the clouds? —The mountain. What is stronger than the mountain? —Man. What is stronger than man? —Woman" (Bett, pp. 105–106).

36. Wengeroff, I, p. 28.
37. Rubin, MSS.
38. D. and Y., p. 36, No. 36.
39. Rubin, MSS.
40. D. and Y., p. 37, No. 37.
41. *Ibid.*, p. 31, No. 20.
42. *Ibid.*, p. 30, No. 16.
43. Wengeroff, p. 26.
44. Rubin, MSS.
45. Lehman, 1923, No. 160.
46. Cahan, 1957, No. 411.
47. D. and Y., p. 34, No. 29.
48. Idelsohn, IX, No. 60.
49. D. and Y., p. 30, No. 19. Said to have been adapted by L. Kvitko from the Ukrainian.
50. Cahan, 1957, No. 394.
51. Rubin, MSS.

CHAPTER III

Love and Courtship

ONE OF THE OLDEST TYPES OF SONG IS THE LOVE SONG. THE *Song of Songs,* which became a book in the Bible, may have been originally a secular love song, yet as far back as the second century C.E., its secularity was interpreted allegorically as a dialogue between God and Israel. The sages who sought to prevent its use as a love poem tried to suppress the opinion that the *Song of Songs* was secular, and, although the authorship was accredited to King Solomon, it was specified that he wrote it under holy inspiration.

In the Middle Ages, as a general rule, "songs in praise of a woman's beauty were rejected . . . as indecorous, though the Talmud had allowed them. . . . In the Talmud and the medieval Jewish records may be found genuine cases of courtship, in the modern sense of the word."[1] The eleventh-century, Spanish-Jewish writer, Moses Ibn Izra (b. 1070), "whose liturgical pieces turn mostly on the subject of sin and reconciliation . . . was, nevertheless, the author of Hebrew love-songs worthy of the most light-hearted troubadour."[2] Judah Halevi, greatest Spanish-Jewish poet of the Middle Ages, who achieved a high degree of exaltation in his liturgical poems, also wrote love poems of great beauty. At times, his inspirational religious and national meditations and songs are expressed in such ardent terms that it is not always easy to distinguish between his sacred and secular poems. Note the following lines in one of his devotional poems:

May my sweet song be pleasing in Thy sight, and the goodness of my praise,
O Beloved, who art flown afar from me, at the evil of my deeds!
But I have held fast unto the corner of the garment of love of Him who is
       tremendous and wonderful.
Enough for me is the glory of Thy name; that is my portion alone from all
       my labour.

69

Increase the sorrow, I shall love but more, for wonderful is Thy love to me.[3]

As for the following, contained in a poem "to be sung on the Sabbath following a wedding," although during the Middle Ages love songs were forbidden between the bride and groom prior to the wedding, the passion it breathes is unmistakably secular!

> Dove beside the water brooks—
> A delight is she to the eyes.
>
> Her bosom hath taken spoil of my heart
> And wrought upon me
> Enchantments, which the magicians
> Of Egypt could not do.
>
> Cheek of lilies, and mine eyes gathering;
> Breasts of pomegranates, and mine hands harvesting;
> If thy lips be glowing coals
> Then let my jaws be tongs!
>
> Thy two locks of hair are like an ambush
> For the wolves of evening;
> The light of thy cheek mingleth with them
> Like morning light amid the shadows.[4]

The love of which the Hebrew poets of the twelfth and thirteenth centuries sang was the prerogative of the poets. So far as the ordinary Jews were concerned, courtship seemed entirely of the man's making. That the woman should display prenuptial love was repulsive to the Jewish conception of womanliness. "Says a tenth or eleventh century authority: 'It is the habit of all Jewish maidens, even if they be as much as twenty years old, to leave the arrangement of their marriage in the hands of their fathers; nor are they indelicate or impudent enough to express their own fancies, and to say—I would like to wed such and such an one.' "[5]

In Eastern Europe of the nineteenth century, of all the categories of Yiddish folk songs, love songs were the most numerous, popular, melodious, and poetic. This fact for a time challenged a number of writers on Jewish literature and folklore, who were not able to justify this rich body of song within a community which was essentially patriarchal in structure and restrictive in its religious observances. Regardless of the constant struggle against secularity by the rabbinate, love songs were current among the people and, within their genre, were excellent reflectors of prevailing customs of mating prior to marriage, of the struggle to break away from the rigid rules imposed upon the young generation by the community and parents, as well as of sentiments of great tenderness and beauty.

Although in many ring games played by children, the selection of a mate was performed in a matter-of-fact way, in the actual environment of that day, this was decidedly not carried out by the young people. Mating was seldom left to accident. The current belief that "marriages were made in heaven" did not deter parents, who, with the aid of professional matchmakers, energetically performed this task on earth and in an environment where the average boy and girl were often married at the tender age of twelve. A vivid description of such a marriage at the turn of the nineteenth century is given by the folklorist and historian Saul M. Ginzburg:

. . . The bride had just turned twelve. As was the custom in those days, her father, together with other relatives and scholars, "tested" the groom's scholarship before the engagement papers were signed. Everyone was quite satisfied. The bride, too, had to demonstrate her virtues before the groom's parents by unraveling a ball of thread which they had tangled and by picking up from the ground a number of objects which they had supposedly dropped accidentally. She also "passed the examination," demonstrating that she was a girl of patience and tact. . . . The wedding was soon arranged. . . . After the wedding, this barely thirteen-year-old "woman" could often be seen playing various games in the courtyard with other such "women" and girls.[6]

In a premarriage procedure of another family half a century later — in 1849 — the young pair were given the opportunity to get acquainted and were actually left alone for a few minutes. In those days, this was quite a step forward. New ideas were beginning to filter into even the most patriarchal homes. The bride's older sister, who had been married only several years earlier, first saw her husband-to-be just before the marriage ceremony![7]

In such an environment, the term "love" as we understand it today rarely expressed the emotion between the sexes prior to marriage. Whenever it was used, it most often described the affection for parents, family, or friends. For the boy or girl to dream of love, let alone sing about it, was considered alien and sinful. This led several prominent writers on Jewish literature and folklore to assume that, not only was the term *libe* ("love") absent from the Yiddish vernacular of that day, but that the passion itself was non-existent! Thus wrote Leo Wiener: "The word *love* does not exist in the Judeo-German (Yiddish) dictionary, and wherever that feeling, with which they have been acquainted only since the middle of this century, is to be named, the Jews have to use the German word *liebe*."[8] Similarly, in his popular history of Yiddish literature, M. Pines came to the conclusion that:

. . . at a time when children at the age of twelve or fourteen were usually married, the natural romantic emotion between the sexes could not occur. . . . Not until the middle of the nineteenth century, when changes in the life of the Jews in the Pale resulted in the abandonment of, among other things, the early marriages and when secular literature began to penetrate even into the most backward sections of the people, acquainting them for the first time with the meaning of such terms as *love, beloved,* etc., then the first Yiddish love songs were born.[9]

But secular love songs *were* current among the people during the *first* half of the nineteenth century, and the passion of true love *was* known to the Jewish community in the Pale — a fact illuminated by the eminent Yiddish folklorist, Y. L. Cahan, who wrote:

. . . Obviously a serious error has here been committed. Instead of seeking the facts among the lower strata of the people . . . they have looked for them among the higher and middle groups, that is, the economically secure, religious-patriarchal environment, which up to the period mentioned, contributed very little to our secular folk song in general.[10]

As is evident among other peoples, so too among the Jews the creative process was most intense among the lower social strata, which until the second half of the nineteenth century were the only ones to create and preserve the bulk of Yiddish folk song. Here, where economic gain from a marriage could obviously not be expected, the "luxury" of love for its own sake was possible and the "playing at love" prior to marriage, not unusual. Even Mendele had something to say on this subject:

. . . There among the workers songs are often sung — their own creation too — which then go out into the world among the people, fall into the mouths of girls, servant girls, and are called *folk songs*. . . . The themes vary. There are some about love. A servant girl far from home yearns for her beloved. She remembers tearfully the good, sweet moments when they walked together like a pair of turtledoves, sometimes in the greenwood and sometimes in the fields of wheat and corn. Another girl pours out her heart, longing for a mate, like a child with its hands outstretched towards the shining moon. . . . One can rightly say that among the working folk there glowed the poetic spark, there fluttered a fresh, young soul.[11]

However, some of the ancestors of Yiddish love song can be traced to a period several centuries earlier.

Already in the sixteenth century, the Jewish mass in Western Europe leaned strongly to the then current, paraphrased works and adaptations from the German (into Judeo-German) of such *abendtoyer Romanen und Sagn* like *Dietrich von Bern, Koenig Artus, Di Liebschaft von Florus und Blanche-flur, Tyl Eulenspiegel,* and many others. These works were at the time so beloved and popular in Jewish circles, that not rarely would Rabbis in the prefaces to their ethical-religious works complain bitterly about them.[12]

In those days too, the community dance hall which served for weddings and family festivals and also as a social hall where young Jewish men and women gathered and danced together became the milieu where some of the earliest love songs were born. A sixteenth-century publication of old Yiddish (Judeo-German) songs includes some of these old love and dance songs, of which the following is an example :

Yungfreulein, wolt ir nicht	Maiden, will you not
Mit mir ein tentslein tun	Go dancing with me?
Ich bit, ir wolt mirs nit faribl hon,	I beg of you, do not be angry with me,
Frelich muss ich sein,	I must be gay
Dervayln ich es hab und kan.	When I have the opportunity.
Ayer tsarter yunger leib,	Your soft young body
Hot mich in lieb fervundt	Has wounded me with love.
Euch ayer euglein klein,	Also your little eyes,
Dartsu ayer roter mund;	And your red mouth too;
Shlist euer arme ayn,	Link your arm,
Feinslib, vol in di mayn,	Dearest, firmly in mine,
Zo wird mein herts gezund.[13]	Thus will my heart be whole.

Another old, Yiddish love song, more than four hundred years old and considered to be one of the first love songs in archaic Yiddish, is the following, which was copied from a manuscript on parchment in the Ambrosian Library in Milan, Italy, part of a collection dating from the times of Lucrezia Borgia.

Vu zol ich hin, vu zol ich her,	Where shall I go, Whither shall I turn?
Vu zol ich michs hinkern?	Where then shall I wander?
Ich bin eyntsindt, mayn harts dos brent,	I am aflame, my heart's on fire,
Ich kons nit fray vern.	I cannot free myself from it.
Do shpeyt dos herts, aler libst mayn	I feel my heart is full of love,
Di ich hob oyf erdn.[14]	For my beloved on the earth.

An examination of nineteenth-century, Yiddish love songs will reveal many parallels with old, German love songs of several centuries ago, while others contain only fragmentary evidences of this early ancestry. The bulk of Yiddish folk songs today, however, relate mainly to nineteenth-century life of the Jews in the Czarist Pale of Settlement. Within this framework, these love songs were the forerunners which inspired the first generations of Yiddish lyric poets in modern Yiddish literature. Into their own lyrics, the simple folk poured their finest sentiments, their most tender emotions, their most intimate thoughts which could not be uttered to anyone.

Many influences tended to break down the old patriarchal pattern of marriage-matchmaker-parent which forbade free mating and condemned the "alien" pastime of "playing at love." The very term "playing at love" stamped the love emotion as a passing sentiment to be taken lightly in the serious matter of marriage. On the other hand, however, the economic circumstances compelled more and more parents to send their young boys and girls into early apprenticeship, where, deprived of close adult supervision and in the environment of workingmen and women, they were indeed free to "play at love," to sing and dance, romance and dream. Following one's emotional impulses, however, bore its own responsibilities and consequences. This new-found freedom brought down upon the romancing youth the censure of the community in general as well as the heartbreak and heartache of the casual love affair, which was often ephemeral, transient, and impermanent. But youth and love would not be denied, and on a Sabbath afternoon, when the pious men and

Перчик со своей Шейкой

А.Каплан 57-59 гг.

women went off to the synagogue to listen to a *magid* ("mentor"), the
young folks gathered in some basement or attic dwelling to dance and
sing songs. ". . . And mostly love songs . . . and love affairs went on in
secret, hidden, on the bypaths and sideroads where young lovers went
strolling together, just as it is described in the very songs they sang."[15]

Geyen mir shpatsirn in dem groysn vald;	We go strolling in the great forest.
Oy-vey dushe-lebn, s'iz mir zeyer kalt.	Oh, my darling love, I am very cold.
Er hot mich ongehoybn ayntsuviklen un ayntsuhiln,	He began to hold me and enfold me,
Oy-vey dushe-lebn, shver a libe tsu firn.[16]	Oh, my darling love, it's hard to play at love.

But it was not simple, defying the age-old traditions. Prying eyes and
vicious tongues spied and slandered the romancing couples as they sought
out the secret walks and nooks of the countryside at the edge of town.
The following suggests the break-up of a love affair by village scandal-
mongers, despite the determination of the young girl to hold on to her
lover.

Fishelech in vasser mern zich,	Fish in the water multiply,
Falshe tsinger shvern zich.	False tongues swear to truth.
Falshe tsinger — beyze layt,	False tongues — evil folk,
Zey hobn undz gebracht tsu troyerkayt.	They brought sadness to us.
Fishelech in vasser, zey lebn zich gor fayn,	Fish in the water live happily,
Un ich bin a meydele mit eygene gedanken.	And I am a maiden with independent mind.
Ich hob ongehoybn a libe shpiln,	I began to play at love,
Un kon zi nit derlangen.[17]	But cannot achieve it.

Unable to stand up against these pressures, young lovers poured their
sentiments into songs, which became the receptacles for their dreams and
desires.

Papir iz doch vays, un tint iz doch shvarts,	Paper is white and ink is black,
Tsu dir, mayn zis-lebn, tsit doch mayn harts!	My heart, sweet love, yearns for you!

Ch'volt shtendik gezesn dray tog nochanand,	I could sit for three days on end,
Tsu kushn dayn sheyn ponim un tsu haltn dayn hant.	Kissing your pretty face and holding your hand.

Nechtn banacht bin ich af a chasene geven,	Last night I went to a wedding,
Fil sheyne meydlech hob ich gezen;	I saw many pretty girls there;
File sheyne meydlech, tsu dir kumt es nit gor,	Many pretty girls, but none to compare
Tsu dayne shvartse eygelech, tsu dayn shvartse hor!	With your little black eyes and raven hair!

Dayn talye, dayn mine, dayn eydeler fason,	Your figure, your manner, your gentle ways,
In hartsn brent a fayer, me zet es nisht on!	My heart's aflame all unseen!
Nishto aza mentsh, vos zol filn, vi es brent;	There's none to feel how strongly it burns;
Der toyt un dos lebn iz ba dir in di hent.[18]	My life and death are in your hands.

The outlines of the small sleeping town almost come to life in some of the love songs, as the youthful pairs walked dreamily together.

Es dremlt a shtetele, di lodns farmacht,	The town is slumbering, the shutters are closed,
Kum tsu mir libster in finsterer nacht.	Come to me, my love, in the dark of the night.
Kum tsu mir un breng dayn gitare mit,	Come to me and bring your guitar
Un zing mir un zing mir a troyerig lid.[19]	And sing to me, sing me a sad song.

Occasionally a small-town Romeo serenaded his Juliet in the silence of the night, when prying eyes of disapproving adults were not about:

Indroysn iz finster, s'iz shpet baynacht,	It is dark and late at night,
Men hert kayn zhum, kayn shorch, kayn feygele fli-en oyf der gas.	Not a buzz, not a rustle, not a bird on the wing is heard in the street.
Avu biztu geven? ch'vil mit dir tsvey verter reydn.	Where have you been? I want to have a word with you.
Avu biztu geven? ch'vil mit dir tsuzamen geyn.[20]	Where have you been? I want to go walking with you.

Although the nature motif seems to be generally absent in the bulk of nineteenth-century folk song, it occurs frequently in the love songs as an accompaniment to the love theme itself, as the texts reveal the secret meeting, the clandestine affairs in the greenwood or fields at the edge of town during moonlit nights or nights too dark for anyone to see.

Oy, a nacht a sheyne,	Oh, what a beautiful night,
Di nacht iz geven azoy sheyn.	The night was so lovely.
Oyf a benkele zenen mir gezesn,	We sat on a bench together,
Di levone hot genumen avekgeyn.[21]	As the moon began to wane.

To avoid the open clash with strict parents, young girls waited impatiently to meet their lovers after the parents had gone to bed. Mothers lay wide-eyed worrying about their wayward daughters. *Oy vey tochter, s'iz shoyn tsen azeyger; / Gey in shtub arayn / Un zol zich dir oysvayzn / Du bizt mit im gegan* (Oh, my daughter, it's ten o'clock. Come into the house and pretend that you went with him").[22]

The children on the street taunted the maidens who flaunted their love in the face of propriety:

Her chasi! me tor nit geyn,	Listen Chasye, one must not go,
Me darf nit geyn,	One need not go,
Me tor nit geyn mit keynem.	One must not go with anyone.
Az du vest geyn, shpet baynacht,	If you will go (walking) late at night,
Vestu shpeter veynen![23]	You will weep afterwards.

Many songs reflected the conversations between mother and daughter during these difficult times, revealing the problems which distressed the heart and mind of the young girls striking out for themselves. Parents tried to arrange for marriages in haste, but no matter what desirable young man was presented to the maidens, they yearned only for their "true love," the one they had chosen for themselves.

S'iz farhanen briliantn velche zenen sheyn,	There are very lovely gems,
Az men kukt zich in zey gut ayn, zenen zey gemeyn;	But when one examines them closely, they are cheap.
Ober mayn briliant in der gantser velt, ken men nisht gefinen	But my jewel is the only one of its kind in all the world.
Vu ich gey un vu ich shtey, hob ich im in zinen![24]	Wherever I am, wherever I go, he is in my mind.

Uppermost in the eyes of the parents were the economic considerations, which were the most pressing and most threatening problems in the Pale. "Falling in love," when no proposal of marriage was forthcoming, was considered highly impractical. Young girls who were willing to "gamble away" their young life on some good-for-nothing romantic were considered foolhardy and headed straight for the pit of iniquity. The following conversation song, though primitively constructed, is a vivid example of the battle for "pure, true love" which the young daughters now demanded, even in an arranged marriage!

Tochter libe, getraye, vos hostu zich
    in bocher farlibt,
Vos host in em derzen?
Er iz naket, borvis, an oriman!
Farlib zich besser in ayn raychn.
Vos nitst dir der oriman?
Baken zich beser in dayn glaychn,

Az er zol kenen zayn dayn man.

Beloved, devoted daughter, why did
    you fall in love with that fellow?
What do you see in him?
He is naked, barefoot, a poor man!
Fall in love rather, with a rich man!
What do you want with a pauper?
Try and meet someone of your own
    kind,
So that he shall be a fit husband for
    you.

Muter libe, getraye,
Mach mir di kop nit dul.
Lesh shoyn mir opet dem fayer,
Un gib shoyn mir vemen ich vil.

Beloved, devoted mother,
Don't try to change my mind.
Quench the fire that is within me,
And let me marry the man of my
    choice.

Farlibt hob ich zich in zayn sheyn
    ponim,
Gekrogn hot er ba mir cheyn.
Di gantse velt zogt az er iz mi-es un
    orim,
Un ba mir iz er tayer un sheyn.[25]

I have fallen in love with his
    handsome face,
He has charmed me.
The whole world says he is ugly and
    poor,
But to me he is precious and lovely.

Parents of scholarly lads destined to a life of leadership and importance in the community, "moved heaven and earth" to prevent their "son and heir" from marrying for love beneath his station. When such a love occurred, it was almost always doomed from the start, despite the sincere assurances on the part of the lover to his maiden:

Veyn nish' kroyneshi, veyn nish'
    dushenyu,   ·
Ch'vel noch tsu dir tsurik-kumen.
Zolst nisht hern vos layt redn,
Bay mir hostu cheyn gefunen.

Don't cry my jewel, don't weep my
    soul,
I'll return to you.
Don't listen to the talk of the town;
In my eyes you are charming.

Mayne eltern tu-en mich betn,	My parents plead with me
Ch'zol shoyn on dir fargesn.	That I should forget you.
Nisht eyn vaserl vet farbayloyfn,	But not one little stream will flow by,
Undzer libe vet keyner nish'	And our burning love will be
farleshn.[26]	quenched by no one.

A strong pressure was brought to bear upon the Jewish community in the Pale by the Haskalah movement, which through its efforts to broaden and reconstruct the economic and cultural life of the Eastern European Jews, attracted large sections of young people. Tracing its origin to the intellectual impetus given it by Moses Mendelssohn in Germany, it sought to introduce Western European ways of life into the economically backward, socially oppressed Jewish community, often incorporating into its campaign for universal education the right of the young generation to decide its own fate in the choosing of a mate. "The patriarchal and primitive Eastern European way of life which, in marriage customs, remained prevalent among the Jews forced the Haskalah to deal with this problem. It felt that this decision must be taken out of the hands of the old-fashioned parents and placed in the hands of the parties concerned : the sons and daughters themselves."[27]

By the 1860's, the Enlightenment (Haskalah) movement had already been active for thirty years, and whole waves of new influences had flowed into Jewish life, "wrecking the old." Distressed by the upheavals of that time, an elderly memoirist speaks with bitterness of the young generation of her day, which, according to her, was growing up without any knowledge of its true cultural and traditional heritage and whose sympathies and interests were drawing it ever more rapidly towards the "outside" world.[28]

But the times were working against those who yearned for the "old patriarchal" days, and the inroads were affecting even the protected daughters of the rich, who were beginning to chafe under the weight of parental control and to sing their own songs about it.

Oy mir orime meydelech,	Oh, we unhappy maidens,
Vos toyg undzer sach nadn,	Of what use is our rich dowry,
Az men putst undz oys a ferd far a man !	When we're given a circus horse for a husband !
Undzere eltern tu-en shiduchim,	Our parents arrange the match,
Zey tu-en undz gornit fregn,	They never consult us,
Darum farbrengen mir zeyer shlecht dem lebn.[29]	And we live our life unhappily.

Whereas in the Jewish patriarchal environment, the wedding was dependent on economic and scholarship considerations, among the propertyless the privilege of a life of scholarship was almost entirely denied, and the economic element was not decisive in the consummation of a match. Thus, pure, true love, as a precursor to marriage, became possible mainly among the lower classes. Only a humble person, who did not look for economic gain from his wedding, could permit himself the "luxury" of engaging in a love affair. Consequently the truly pure tones of deep affection, passionate love, longing for the opposite sex are heard only in the love songs from the environment of the lower strata of the population. It is in these anonymous lyrics that we encounter the recklessness of youth, the self-sacrificing ardor of lovers, the firm faith that love will overcome all obstacles.

A conversation song between two lovers, which takes place as the lad is about to leave for "distant climes," for economic reasons possibly, reveals the readiness of the maiden to accompany him and share all his hardships with him. "What will you do on the long road?" he asks, and she replies: "I will wash clothes for strangers, so long as I can be with you!" "Where will you wash the clothes and where will you dry them?" he asks. "You must think I am weak," she counters, "I will wash them in the river and dry them on a rope which I shall trade in for my costume . . . so long as I can be with you!" "Where will you sleep, what will cover you at night and what will you eat?" he persists. And she replies: "I shall eat bread and salt and forget my parents; I am still young and can sleep on a straw bed; the dew from heaven will cover me and the birds at morn will wake me, so long as I can be with you, my love!" [30]

The constant shifting of the population, some to the towns and cities in quest of jobs, others into the army to serve the Czar for four or five years, created a situation of constant separation, and not every maiden was equal to the self-sacrificing role which the one in the foregoing example chose for herself. These songs of parting range from the temporary separation to the permanent break, reflecting in various degrees the suffering endured by the young lovers. The following is an example of longing during such a separation:

Mayn zis-lebn fort avek	My sweet darling's gone away
Un ich blayb aleyn,	And I am left alone,

Ven ich dermon zich on mayn zis-lebn,	When I recall my darling love,
Zits ich nor un veyn.	I sit me down and cry.
Volt ich geven a feygele,	If I were a little bird,
Volt ich tsu im gefloygn,	I would fly to him,
Nechay volt er oych gezen	So that he too may see
Mayne farveynte oygn.[31]	My weeping eyes.

Another example in this category is the following, which achieves a high poetic quality :

Afn barg shteyt a taybele,	On the hill there stands a little dove,
Zi tut mit ir por brumen,	Cooing with her mate.
Ich hob gehat a gutn fraynt,	I once had a good friend,
Un ken tsu im nit kumen.	And cannot get to him.
Taychn trern tu-en zich	Rivers of tears do flow
Fun mayne oygn rinen,	From my eyes.
Ich bin geblibn vi a shpendele	I am like a little piece of driftwood
Af dem vasser shvimen.[32]	Floating down the stream.

Many tragic parting songs were created when lovers were recruited into the army for a period of four to five years. Left behind, the girls were apprehensive lest they be jilted when their lovers returned. "I'll wait for you, even if it takes four years," one unhappy maiden assures her soldier boy, "and if you don't marry me then, my disgrace will be terrible!" Whereupon her lover assures her : "Weep not, my soul, weep not, my love; I swear to you that I truly love you, and at every station where the train will stop I'll write a letter to you."[33]

Longing, yearning, the pain of unfulfilled love, were the themes of many of the love songs. Added to these were the motifs of false love and the bitterness of the jilted woman suffering a pain often as sharp as the pain of death.

Ale vasserlech flisn avek,	All the rivulets ripple away,
Di gribelech blaybn leydig.	The little ditches are empty.
Nito aza mentsh oyf gor der velt,	There's not a soul upon this earth,
Vos zol farshteyn mayn veytig.	To understand my anguish.
Un az a meydele shpilt a libe,	And when a maiden falls in love,
Shpiln in ir ale farbn,	Her cheeks are rosy and gay,
Un az zi shpilt ir libe nit oys,	And when her love is unfulfilled,
Kon zi cholile noch shtarbn.[34]	She can almost die.

The jilted woman cursed the day that she was born, bemoaning her life of emptiness that stretched before her. These songs of false lovers were prevalent especially among the women after the 1870's, when women entered industry. Along with the motifs of bewailing the cruel fate that had doomed them to a life of long hours, tedious toil, and low pay, these girls mourned their "young years" which were "chained to the needle and the wheel," despised by the upper strata of their society, lonely, helpless, celibate often their entire life. Starved for love and affection, they easily fell prey to flirtations and conniving fellows who thought nothing of "loving and leaving" them, squandering the generosity of these naïve, self-sacrificing working girls. The following examples are excerpted from two songs dealing with such a situation.

(1)

Er kumt tsu mir tsugeyn
Mitn shtekele in hant,
Er geyt avek tsu anandere,
S'iz far mir a shand! . . .

He comes to me
With his cane in his hand,
He goes off to another,
And I am so ashamed!

Er kumt tsu mir tsugeyn,
Un zogt mir a sod oyfn oyer (eyver),
Er geyt avek tsu anandere,
Grobt er far mir a keyver.[35]

He comes to me
And whispers in my ear,
He goes off to another,
Digging a grave for me.

(2)

Ich hob mit im gefirt a libe,
Un er hot mich opgenart,
Ale meydelech vos firn libes,
Zey vern doch ayngedart.

I was in love with him,
And he was false to me,
All the maidens who fall in love,
Become shriveled up.

Mayne tsores hobn mich
    arumgeringlt,
Azoy vi a bonder a fas.
Hayntike yingelech iz azoy fil tsu
    gleybn,
Azoy vi dem hunt af der gas.[36]

My troubles have ringed me
    round,
Like the barrelmaker rings the barrel.
Today's fellows are to be
    trusted,
Like the dog on the street.

Unable to confide in anyone, the jilted maiden poured her heart into her song: "I sit and play on my guitar and sing a song about myself. Only the Lord knows my anguish, only He knows how I suffer."[37] Occasionally, a young girl involved in an illicit love affair was driven to confide in her mother:

(Daughter):

Mir veln avekforn in a fremder medine,	— We will go to a strange land,
Un dortn a chupele shteln.	And be married there properly.

(Mother):

Tsi s'vet zayn git, tsi s'vet zayn shlecht,	— For better or for worse,
Bay mir far kinder zent ir shoyn oysgemekt!	You are no longer my children!

(Daughter):

Oy mame mayne, oy mame getraye,	— Oh, mother mine, oh, devoted mother,
S'iz mir a shande far laytn.	I cannot face the town for shame.
Ch'ob doch mamenyu, mayn lebn farshpilt,	I have gambled away my life, mother dear,
Ich bin doch shoyn in di hoyche monatn.[38]	For I am about to give birth.

Where young people were unable to face the anger of their parents, they resorted to elopement. The following brief excerpt draws a picture which is familiar to our own modern period.

Klayb tsunoyf dayne zachn,	Gather your things together,
Un leyg arayn in korbn,	And put them into baskets,
Un ganve zich aroys fun a fensterl	And sneak out of the window,
Un mir veln beyde chupe hobn.[39]	And we shall be married.

Sometimes, the young lovers ran off to distant America, where, they heard, economic differences in a marriage were not so important, where social inequalities had leveled off and love was primary. The following ditty, half in jest, half in earnest, touches upon this new-found freedom in the *goldene medine* ("kingdom of gold") across the Atlantic:

In amerike forn furn,	In America, wagons go
Barg aruf, barg arop.	Uphill and downhill.
Un az der bocher libt di meydl,	And when a fellow loves his girl,
Leygt er far ir di kop!	He goes all out for her!
In amerike bakt men challes	In America, they bake the twisted loaves
Far di gantse velt.	For the whole world.
Un az der bocher libt di meydl,	And when a fellow loves his girl,
Nemt er ir on a kopke gelt!	He marries her without a penny!

In amerike bakt men beygl	In America, they bake bagels
Oyf a gantsn yor.	For the entire year.
Ich dayn chosn un du mayn kale.	I'll be your groom and you my bride,
Zenen mir beyde a glayche por ! [40]	For we are a well-matched pair !

A dramatic treatment of the struggle between parents and children is to be found in S. Anski's play, *The Dybbuk* ("The Evil Spirit"), written in 1911–1914. Anski (Shloyme Z. Rappaport, 1863–1920) makes use of the supernatural belief in the transference of spirits and invests a young girl with the voice of her poor, Talmudic student-lover, who dies when he learns that his beloved has been promised to a wealthy suitor by her parents. Although the girl is taken to a great rabbi, all efforts fail to exorcise the "demon" that has entered her body to "claim his own," and the girl dies. This play gained widespread popularity following World War I, reflecting as it did the tragedy of the mismated and the yearning of lovers to decide their own fate in their choice of a mate.

As the century progressed, the love motif gained ground, and the number of "natural" love songs—mischievous, playful, teasing, flirtatious, humorous—increased in number. Following are two such examples:

(1)

Oy vos ch'ob gevolt hob ich oysgefirt,	Oh, I got what I desired,
Zol ich azoy lebn!	You may well believe me!
Ch'ob gevolt a sheyn yingele,	I wanted a handsome lad,
Hot mir got gegebn.	And the Lord did give him to me.

Ch'ob gemeynt, az er iz shoyn mayn,	I thought, that he was all mine,
Ch'ob im shoyn bakumen;	And mine he'd always be!
Iz gekumen a shener meydele	When along came a prettier girl
Un hot im tsugenumen. [41]	And took him away from me.

(2)

Oy abram, ich ken on dir nisht zayn,	Oh, Abraham, I cannot live without you,
Ich on dir, un du on mir, kenen mir beyde nisht zayn.	We cannot live without each other.
Gedenkstu, gedenkstu ba dem toyer,	Do you remember at the gate,
Hostu mir gezogt a sod in oyer;	When you whispered in my ear:
Oy vey rivkenyu, gib-zhe mir dos piskenyu ! [42]	Oh, my little Rebecca, give me just one kiss!

The maidens, sitting with their fancywork behind "latticed windows," began to sing and on occasion compose love songs, and even young fellows, Talmudic students, sat whispering under a tree "about girls." Boasted one: "I went about all day without eating and sat for hours before her house. Neither storm, wind, rain, nor snow scared me, and Mother waited for me at home with a stick. As for father, he beat me soundly with his belt and drove me outdoors."[43]

Love songs, in all their variety of moods and colors, came into their own, with longing, passion, yearning, desire expressed in the terms of the daily, homespun vernacular:

Volkn, volkn, shling mich ayn	Cloud, cloud, swallow me up
Un tu mit mir avekshvebn;	And float away with me;
Un tu mich dortn anidershteln,	And set me down way off there
Vu mayn harts tut gleybn.	Where my heart longs to be.
Mayn harts, mayn harts tsit tsu dir,	My heart, my heart, is drawn to you,
Azoyvi magnet tsu shtol;	As a magnet is to steel;
Ich volt tsu dir amol gekumen,	I would come to you,
Iz der veg tsu shmol.[44]	But the road is too narrow.

The pain of the occasional love affair was lessened, and the playfulness of the flirtation took its normal place in the life of the young people. It even became possible to sing lightly about a broken promise:

Gey ich mir shpatsirn, tra-lalalalala	As I went awalking, tra-lalalalala,
Bagegnt mich a bocher, aha, aha.	I met a handsome fellow, aha, aha.
Er zogt er vil mich nemen, tra-lalalalala,	He says he wants to marry me, etc.
Er leygt es op oyf vinter, aha, aha.	He postpones it till the winter, etc.
Der vinter iz gekumen, tra-lalalalala,	Winter came, etc.
Er hot mich nit genumen, aha, aha.	But he did not marry me, etc.
Itst vil er mich shoyn nemen, tra-lalalalala,	Now he wants to marry me, etc.
Ober ich vil im nit kenen! aha, aha![45]	But I won't have him! aha, aha!

The above song in couplets, suggesting an old, German dance song, shares, together with several Yiddish ballads, elements which can be traced to the archaic period of Yiddish folk song mentioned earlier. The following, for example, which tells of a dramatic situation between a lord and his knight, deals with a theme which had long since disappeared from Yiddish literature and song.

S'amol geforn a har mit a knecht,	There once rode a lord and his knight,
Hot er nit gevust vu links un vu recht.	He knew not whether to turn left or right.
Iz er aleyn afn teytlboym gekrochn,	So he climbed to the top of a date tree,
Hot er zich di hent mit di fis tsebrochn.	And broke his hands and feet.

The unfortunate lord pleads with his knight not to leave him alone to be devoured by wild animals and offers the knight his valuable horse, his coach inlaid with gold and silver, even his wife and only child! But to each offer, the knight replies:

Ach mayn har, ich bin nit tsufridn, Ich for avek un dir loz ich lign.	Oh, my lord, I am not satisfied, I shall ride away and leave you lying there.

Upon which the lord cries out:

Ach mayn got, tsi i'dos azoy recht, Az fun a har zol vern a knecht? [46]	Oh, my God, is this then just, That a lord shall become a slave?

The reference to the "date tree" in the above example might even hark back to an old, German epic of a lord and his knight who had gone on a Crusade. The following, too, relates to the epoch when "knighthood was in flower" and the cult of "love and the lady fair" was carefully nurtured.

—Eyn gut morgn libster har.	—Good morning, my dear lord.
—Eyn gut yor mayn libster knecht,	—Good day, my dear knight.
—Tsi kenstu mir nit gebn Dayn shvester far a vayb?	—Will you not give me Your sister to wife?

The lord refuses the hand of his sister to his knight, since this would mean marrying beneath her social position. Whereupon the knight informs the lord that his sister had only recently given birth to his child! In a rage, the lord saddles his horses and rides off to verify the knight's claim. The sister testifies to the truth of the knight's statement, and the lord, her brother, is pacified, since he had learned about it from the lovers themselves and not from the gossip of vicious tongues.

Mazl tov dir, mazl tov dir, far dayn eygn kind.	Good luck to you upon the birth of your own child.

Volt dos mir ver es gezogt,
Volt ich yenem af tsveyen geplogt.

Volt dos mir ver es iz geredt,
Volt ich im af tsveyen di kop
    geplet.[47]

Had a stranger told me of this,
I would have split him in two.

Had anyone else apprised me of it,
I would have split his skull.

One of the oldest types in the category is a song about a night visit which is well-known all over Europe and refers to a practice relating possibly to a pre-Aryan state when husband and wife did not live together, the wife remaining with her kinsmen and admitting the husband only at certain times. Such songs were probably the precursors of the serenade, developed later by the troubadours in southern France, and begin with the lover knocking at his sweetheart's door late at night, pleading to be admitted. The maiden hesitates, giving all manner of excuses, which the lover attempts to explain away. In Yiddish folk song, there are several kinds of this particular conversation song, of which the following is an older example :

—Klip-klap in goldn-tir,
  Mayne libe, efn mir!
—Shlofn, shlof ich afile nit,
  Nor efenen vel ich avade nit.

  Vuhin-zhe zol ich raytn,
  Az me shloft ba laytn?
—Der regn get, der vint veyt,
  Ich vel farnetsn mayn zaydn kleyd.

—Nem dayn kleyd untern hant,
  Gey avek in tifn vald.
  In tifn vald inem grinem groz,

  Shlof zich oys vi a yunger hoz.

—Mit vos zol ich zich tsudekn,
  Un ver vet mich dort ufvekn?
—Der blat fun boym vet dich
    tsudekn,
  Di shayn funem tog vet dich
    ufvekn.[48]

—Knock-knock in the golden door,
  My beloved, open up for me.
—Although I am not sleeping,
  I shall certainly not open the door.

  Where then shall I ride,
  When all the folks are asleep?
—It is raining and the wind blows,
  And I shall wet my satin dress.

—Take your dress up in your hand,
  Go into the deep forest.
  Into the deep forest in the green
    grass,
  And sleep there soundly like a
    young hare.

—What will I cover myself with?
  And who will wake me there?
—The leaf of the tree will cover
    you,
  The daylight will awaken you.

A more modern version, which lists the members of the family in the house, is the following, which mockingly refers to the lover as a drunkard:

Ver-zhe klapt dort in mayn tir?
—Zhamele der shiker.
Ze nechamele efn mir,
Du bizt bay mir der iker.

Who is knocking at my door?
—Zhamele the drunkard.
Nechamele, open the door for me,
You are my only one!

Nechamele refuses to let Zhamele in: "I'm afraid of Mother," she says. "I won't be long," says he. "I'm afraid of my father," says she. "It won't hurt you," he replies. "I fear my brother," she insists. "I'll not make any noise," he pleads. With the final excuse of fearing her sister, she finally lets him in with: "You are my handsomest!"[49]

The modern Yiddish ballad, however, deals with problems and incidents of current interest, narrating experiences of a topical nature. One such ballad, of a jilted woman, begins with: *"Ach mentshn, ir mentshn / ich tu aych bashvern, / ir zolt fun mayn lebn / dos lidl oyshern"* ("People, oh people, I beg of you to listen to this song about my life") and goes on to describe the sweet childhood of this beautiful maiden. "When my beauty was realized, many matchmakers came to my door, but I begged them to leave me be. And when I was eighteen, my appearance changed, and the spark went out of me. I fell in love and a flame consumed my heart. My beauty faded and a fear lodged within me when my lover left me. . . . I cannot find my love. . . . Love cannot be bought."[50]

A number of ballads describe the tragedy of suicides, several of which tell the sad tale of lovers whose parents refused to sanction their marriage and who chose death instead. One example tells of the death of a twenty-year-old girl, describing in funereal terms the anguish which drove her to her horrible death.

Mayne eltern hob ich geton zogn,
Hobn zey gemeynt, az ich trayb mit zey katoves;
Azoy hob ich opgereshet bald,
Az di krenitse zol zayn mayn malchamoves.

I told my parents,
But they thought I was joking;

So I decided immediately,
To drown myself in the well.

Ot bald vet zayn di mite mayn bet,
Un di tachrichim veln zayn mayne kleyder,

Soon my bed will be a board,
And my clothes, the shroud,

Un der keyver vet zayn mayn kabinet,	And my grave, my bedroom,
Un di verem veln esn yedn eyver.[51]	And the worms will gnaw every limb in my body.

Another topical ballad of a double suicide tells the tale of a false lover who refuses to marry his sweetheart because "her father is a poor man," whereupon she swallows poison and is rushed to the hospital. Although she had threatened to do so if he doesn't marry her, he is shocked at the reality, as she accuses him of being responsible for her death.

Dayn mame hot dich gehodevet mit vaysn koyletsh,	Your mother fed you white bread,
Un aleyn hob ich gegesn shvarts broyt,	While I ate the black;
Gants kamenets vet geyn zogn eydes,	All of Kamenets will testify
Az du host gehat a cheylek in mayn toyt.	That you had a part in my death.

Having taken their love lightly, he is now fully aware that he truly loves her, whereupon he jumps into the river and drowns himself for sorrow.[52]

Most of these suicide and murder ballads accuse the parents in their blind rigidity and stubborn will. "People, dear people, remember this : God is not responsible for my death, but my devoted parents are!"[53] Another contains the following lines : "Gather together, you mothers, and see what can happen when lovers court such a long time and the parents refuse their permission for them to marry."[54]

Another is reminiscent of the "cruel mother" motif in which the son pleads with his hardhearted parent, who simply will not agree to her son's marrying the girl of his choice. "You are breaking my heart and I shall die young," he pleads, but the mother is adamant and says that she is taking him to Vienna to find a suitable bride. He rushes to his love, bids her adieu, comes home, and takes poison. When his beloved hears of it, she flies to him but finds him already dead, laid out, and lying "with his feet to the door." The cruel mother begs forgiveness but the bereft maiden vows to remain forever true to her dead love, accusing the mother of having perpetuated this tragedy.[55]

A curious ballad, recalling the Barbara Allen motif, is the following :

S'iz geven a bocher fun achtsn yor,	There was a lad of eighteen years,
Er libt a meydele fun zechtsn yor;	Who loved a maid of sixteen;

Er libt zi yo, er libt zi neyn —
Er libt kayn tsveyte, nor zi nisht
  meyn.

He loved her yea, he loved her nay —
He loved only her and no one else.

Dos meydl iz avek in a fremd
  land,
Es iz gekumen a briv fun meydls
  kant.
Der bocher farlozt ales glik,
Iz geforn zen vos dos meydele tut.

The maid went off into a strange
  land.
When he received a letter from the
  girl's town,
The lad, he left his happy home
And traveled to the maid alone.

—Gut morgn, meydele, vos tut ir
  azoy?
Vos ligt ir azoy af dem krankn-bet?
—A dank, a dank far ayer vizit,
S'iz shoyn nit veyt fun bet biz tsu
  grub.

—Good morning little maid, what
  are you doing there?
Why do you lie on the bed so ill?
—Thank you kindly for your visit,
But I am near unto death.

Di lipn zaynen bloy, di bakn —
  vays,
Zi iz shoyn kalt, azoy vi a shtik ayz.
Er nemt dos meser fun dem sheyd
Un shtekt arayn in zaynem layb.

Her lips were blue and her cheeks
  white;
She is as cold as a slab of ice,
He draws his sword from his sheath
And thrusts it into his body.

Af der matseyve shteyt geshribn,
Az tsvey gelibte tsuzamen lign.[56]

On the tombstone it is inscribed,
That two lovers there together lie.

Riddle Songs

Another type of love song, cast in the form of a riddle, served as a courtship procedure long ago. On occasion, riddles were also performed as part of the entertainment at weddings. One such beautiful riddle is preserved in the Bible: "What is sweeter than honey / And what is stronger than a lion?—Love" (Judges 14 : 12–17). An old, Yiddish riddle song, revealing ties with European riddle songs, is the following, in which the young man poses his difficult queries to the maiden and already anticipates his victory over her:

A' der bocher nemt di meydl
Meynt er di velt i' zayn.
Un du zolst mir vasser shepn,
Der yam zol trukn zayn.
Un du zolst mir fish chapn,
Vifil in yam i' faran.

When a fellow gets his girl,
He thinks the world is his.
And you shall draw water for me,
Until the sea goes dry.
And you shall catch fish for me,
As many as there are in the sea.

However, the maiden in this riddle song is not so easily caught off her guard! "If I must catch all the fish in the sea, then you must scrape them clean for me, and yet leave their skin to be!" she replies. Whereupon he counters with: "If I'm to scrape the fish and leave the skin entire, then you must cook the fish without any fire." The maid agrees to do so, provided he eats the fish, yet leaves it whole, to which he agrees, if she will have seven children for him, and yet remain a virgin![57]

A more recent riddle song, which makes use of problems of a universal nature, is the following:

Tsvey zadatshes vel ich dir fargebn,	Two problems I will give you,
Un di zadatshes machn zolstu mir:	And you shall solve them both for me:
Az du vest mir ibertseyln di tropn funem yam,	When you have counted the drops in the ocean,
Denstmol konstu zayn a por tsu mir.	Then you can be a mate to me.
Di tsveyte zadatshe vel ich dir fargebn,	The second problem I will give you,
Un di zadatshe machn zolstu mir:	And this one you shall solve for me:
Az du vest ibertseyln di shtern funem himl,	When you have counted the stars in the sky,
Denstmol konstu zayn a por tsu mir.[58]	Then you can be a mate to me.

Nineteenth-century riddle songs pattern their questions and answers on objects more typical of the secular environment and traditional beliefs in the Pale. Six such riddles and their answers are contained in the following:

Velches iz hecher far dem hoyz?	What is taller than the house?
Velches iz flinker far der moyz?	What is faster than the mouse?
—Der koymen iz hecher far dem hoyz,	—The chimney is taller than the house,
Di kats is flinker far der moyz.	The cat is faster than the mouse.
Vu iz farhanen a shnayder on a sher?	Where is there a tailor without shears?
Vu iz farhanen a zelner on gever?	Where is there a soldier without arms?
—A toyter shnayder hot kayn sher,	—A dead tailor has no shears,
An oysgedinter zelner hot kayn gever.	A discharged soldier has no arms.
Velches iz tifer far der kval?	What is deeper than the spring?
Velches iz bitterer far der gal?	What is more bitter than gall?

—Der yam iz tifer far der kval,
Der toyt iz bitterer far der gal.[59]

—The sea is deeper than the spring,
Death is more bitter than gall.

Another song utilizes current problems: "What miller has no mill? What spoon has no handle?—A burned-out miller has no mill, a broken spoon has no handle. . . . What parochial teacher has no children? What butcher has no beef?—A blind teacher has no children, and a poor butcher has no meat."[60] Yet another utilizes the riddle song to teach the young the meaning of the marriage institution and the roles of husband, wife, and parents in their proper order of importance.

Vos iz royter fun a flam?
Vos iz getrayer fun a man?

What is redder than the flame?
What is more devoted than a husband?

Di fon iz royter fun a flam,
Un a tate iz getrayer fun a man.

The banner is redder than a flame,
A father is more devoted than a husband.

Vos iz hecher fun dem layb
Un vos iz getrayer fun a vayb?

What is higher on the body?
And what is more devoted than a wife?

Dos harts iz hecher fun dem layb
Un a mame iz getrayer fun a vayb.[61]

The heart is higher on the body
And a mother is more devoted than a wife.

The love songs were the receptacles which held the tender, secret sentiments of generations of young people in the nineteenth century. The religious and patriarchal patterns which restricted free emotional expression between the sexes prior to marriage bottled up for a time the lyric, poetic genius of the people. Stern restrictions which cloaked all secular thought and feelings in religious symbols persisted to the threshold of our own times. I. J. Singer, in his autobiographical work mentioned earlier, recalls his two cousins who "used quietly to hum a song about a love between a king and a queen: The bird flew a day and a night, a day and a night, came to the queen, found the shutters closed tight. Oh, awake, golden face, for I've brought you a message from the king. . . ." Although women in his grandfather's house were not allowed to sing, this particular love song was tolerated because it was not about an ordinary love affair, but an allegory about God and the people of Israel: the king was the Lord, and the queen, the people of Israel; the bird was the messenger from the Lord, bringing the good tidings of liberation to the people of Israel.[62]

The freeing of the emotions of longing and yearning, love and desire for the opposite sex came as part of a general change in the ideas and practices that ran dramatically through almost every phase of nineteenth-century life in Europe. Once the sluices were opened, the dam flowed wide and free, and the number of love songs literally tumbled over each other in great numbers, touching upon every conceivable emotion growing out of the closer relationships between the sexes, "during the mating season."

The examples given here are but a few of the hundreds upon hundreds of love songs of courtship and flirtation, humor and sophistication, naïveté and experience, innocence and guilt. There were songs of true love and false love, unfulfilled and unrequited love, depression and loneliness in rejection, the anger of the jilted woman, despair of the unmarried mother, the struggle with cruel parents. There were the odd songs about suicides and murders and the curious love songs of the "gangster and his moll" of the underworld.

All of these mirrored the tilt between the old and new ways of life and served to channel the tender sentiments of love and passion, which the established society of that day did not countenance in the open. More than any other category, the love song achieved a degree of poetic quality and melodic beauty which helped to inspire the generation of Yiddish poets in Eastern Europe towards the close of the nineteenth century as well as those in the United States following World War I.

Notes

LOVE AND COURTSHIP

1. Abrahams, p. 155, p. 161.
2. *Ibid.*, p. 163.
3. Halevi, p. 117, No. 62.
4. *Ibid.*, pp. 66–67, No. 37.
5. Abrahams, p. 166.
6. Ginzburg, II, "Hundert Yor Familien Geshichte," p. 29.
7. *See*: Wengeroff, II, pp. 39–40.
8. Wiener, pp. 57–58.
9. Pines, I, p. 55.
10. Cahan, 1952, p. 71.
11. Mendele, II, pp. 87–88.
12. Cahan, 1912, I, Intro. xxvi.
13. *Ibid.*, Intro. xxix (from the Walich collection; *see* Appendix).
14. Erik, p. 173.
15. Cahan, 1912, I, Intro. xxxii.
16. Rubin, MSS.
17. D. and Y., p. 101, No. 6.
18. *Ibid.*, pp. 72–73, No. 28.
19. Rubin, MSS.
20. *Ibid.*
21. *Ibid.*
22. Kipnis, p. 23.
23. Skuditsky, 1936, p. 161, No. 17.
24. Cahan, 1957, No. 98.
25. G. and M., No. 229.
26. Bassin, p. 115.
27. Viner, I, p. 347.
28. Wengeroff, II, p. 179.
29. G. and M., No. 240.
30. D. and Y., pp. 76–78, No. 36.
31. G. and M., No. 135.
32. D. and Y., p. 86, No. 51.
33. *Ibid.*, p. 89, No. 54.
34. Rubin, MSS.
35. G. and M., No. 215.
36. D. and Y., pp. 114–115, No. 27.
37. B. and F., p. 236.
38. Rubin, MSS.
39. G. and M., No. 175.
40. *Ibid.*, No. 228. (*beygl*: a kind of doughnut.)
41. Cahan, 1957, No. 255.

42. D. and Y., p. 84, No. 46.
43. *Ibid.,* pp. 94–95, No. 62.
44. *Ibid.,* pp. 80–81, No. 40.
45. Rubin, MSS.
46. Skuditsky, 1936, pp. 280–281, No. 11.
47. G. and M., No. 359.
48. B. and F., p. 127.
49. Rubin, MSS.
50. D. and Y., pp. 149–150, No. 75.
51. *Ibid.,* pp. 180–181, No. 31.
52. Skuditsky, 1936, pp. 210–211, No. 69. Kamenets is a city in southern Ukraine.
53. D. and Y., pp. 182–183, No. 33.
54. *Ibid.,* pp. 184–185, No. 34.
55. *Ibid.,* pp. 185–187, No. 35.
56. *Ibid.,* pp. 189–190, No. 38.
57. Ansky, p. 177.
58. D. and Y. p. 75, No. 32.
59. Cahan, 1957, No. 500.
60. G. and M., No. 357.
61. *Cahan,* 1957, No. 499.
62. Singer, pp. 131–132.

CHAPTER IV

Marriage

THE THREE IMPORTANT MILESTONES IN THE LIFE OF THE JEW IN THE Pale were birth, marriage, and death. The most colorful practices attended the preparations for the wedding and the day of the marriage ceremony itself. According to the Talmud, the match was made in heaven even before the young man and woman were born. This belief was very widespread and has persisted into our own day. "I would lead thee and bring thee into my mother's house," says the girl to her beloved in the *Song of Songs*.

Fir ich dich in shtibele	I lead you to the hut
Fun mayn mamen aleyn.	Of my own mother,
Chosn-kale veln mir zayn	Groom and bride we both shall be
Un tsu der chupe geyn! [1]	And go to the wedding ceremony.

Such is the lilting form taken by a nineteenth-century, Yiddish folk song of Eastern Europe.

The marriage customs of Biblical days have undergone a number of transformations both in the Orient and in the Western European countries. Many of them still prevail in the Eastern European-Jewish community and are practiced in our very midst among Jews of Eastern European origin. Marriage was always considered a most desirable state by the leading religious scholars of long ago. "If thou hast sons . . . give them wives in their youth. . . . Get thy daughter married . . . bestow her on a sensible man."[2] The general feeling that bachelorhood or spinsterhood was to be frowned upon still prevails. "Any man who has not a wife is not a proper man. . . . Any man who has no wife lives without joy, without blessing, and without happiness."[3]

Through the centuries, the emphasis in consummating a match was laid upon culture and knowledge. Among Jews, nobility of culture and

97

aristocracy of learning took precedence over nobility of blood or wealth,[4] and the custom of dowry, coming to us from the days preceding the second destruction of Jerusalem, was a device to help maintain the scholar and his wife during his prolonged years of Talmudic studies.

During the Crusades, when whole Jewish communities were decimated and destroyed, the air was charged with constant fear and tragedy. The custom of "child marriages" suddenly came into being and with it, too, the professional matchmaker, or *shadchen,* who "enjoys a legal status at least as early as the twelfth century."[5] This custom of early marriages is defended by a twelfth-century authority: "As to our custom . . . of betrothing our daughters before they are fully twelve years old, the cause is that persecutions are more frequent every day, and if a man can afford to give his daughter a dowry, he fears that tomorrow he may not be able to do it, and then his daughter would remain forever unmarried."[6]

From here it was but a step towards marrying the young off without their consent. During the fourteenth and fifteenth centuries, among the Jews in Germany, young people had no say in the matter whatsoever; and even little children would be mated, and the marriage contract signed. Matchmaking became a religious act (*mitzvo*) and a number of prominent rabbis engaged in it. However, the *shadchen* remained the favorite means of arranging a marriage in the Middle Ages, and he often toiled in vain, earning his fee by the sweat of his brow. Harking back to those days, the following excerpt of a *current* Yiddish, Eastern European song describes half seriously and half in jest the trials and tribulations of a matchmaker before he succeeds in bringing "the two together."

A shadchen darf men kenen zayn—	A matchmaker's trade is a special one,
Es iz fun got a broche!	It is a blessing from the Lord!
Ich fardin mir mayn kerbl gring,	I earn my ruble easily,
On a shum meloche.	Without a bit of effort.
Oy, eyder ich por zey beydn tsunoyf,	But before I bring them both together,
Tserays ich tsen por shich!	I wear out ten pairs of shoes!
Dernochdem zog ich: vayivrech moyshe!	And then I say: And Moses fled!
Chapt aych beydn der ri-ech![7]	May the devil take both of you!

By the sixteenth century, when the rabbinical supremacy of Polish Jewry over the Jews of Europe was firmly established, young men flocked to the rabbinical schools. "At the end of the term, the teachers and their numerous pupils went to the Polish fairs, in summer to Zaslaw and Jaroslaw, in winter to Lemberg and Lublin. Thus several thousand students of the Talmud met. . . . The keener intellects received wealthy brides as a reward for their mental exertions. Rich parents took pride in having sons-in-law educated in Talmudic schools, and sought them at the fairs." [8] For many generations a Jew could achieve eminence by religious learning in Poland and Russia, and the following gay, little, nineteenth-century, Yiddish love song retains elements of this pattern of life of previous generations:

Di mame iz gegangen in mark arayn noch koyln,	Mother went to market to get some coal,
Hot zi mir gebracht a yingele fun poyln;	And she brought me a lad from Poland;
Oy, iz dos a yingele, a sheyns un a fayns,	Oh, what a lad, so handsome and fine,
Mit di shvartse eygelech, ketsele du mayns.[9]	With his little black eyes, kitten mine!

It was also considered a *mitzvo* to participate in the preparations and celebration of a wedding or to contribute in any way to the joy of bride and groom. Consequently, a wedding was considered a community occurrence, and the whole community was invited as a matter of course. A traditional wedding procession consisted not only of family and friends but was headed by the rabbi and leading members of the community, preceded by the bandsmen (*klezmorim, klezmer*) and followed by the townspeople. Music, singing, dancing, shouting, clapping were always part of every wedding procession through the ages, although the ceremony in the synagogue itself was performed in an atmosphere of solemn dignity. But as soon as it was over, songs were sung, merry tales and fables were told, and even ribald jokes passed at the expense of the young couple.

The music at every wedding was provided by Jewish musicians. Throughout medieval times instrumental music at religious celebrations was customary, and at weddings it was considered indispensable, since it contributed to the religious precept of gladdening the bridegroom and bride. The *klezmorim* led both the groom's and bride's procession. They were the ones who greeted the arrival of the wedding parties prior to and upon their return from the ceremony. They entertained at the wedding feast and played for the dancing guests.[10]

The central figure both in the preparations and after the ceremony was the *badchen,* that professional jester and merrymaker, who retained some of the traditions of fifteenth-century Jewish life in the Middle Ages and even earlier.[11] The *badchen,* or *marshalik,* was also a folk poet and preacher who improvised his jests and witticisms, basing his rhymes on verses of the Bible and passages from the Talmud, weaving into his songs and ditties the prevailing mores of his God-fearing people. Although there were rabbis who frowned upon the unrestrained drolleries of the *badchen,* their protestations were of no avail. By the 1890's, although the *badchen* was not as indispensable as the *klezmorim,* his role was still an important and integral part of the wedding celebration, particularly in Poland and the Ukraine. Filling his double task of evoking laughter from the guests and tears from the bride and groom, on occasion he also utilized the opportunity to point up the unpleasant conditions under which his people lived, often bitterly satirizing those who were responsible for them.

The most important part of the *badchen's* repertoire were the songs about the bride and groom. About fifteen of these have come down to us, ranging from the fifteenth to the seventeenth centuries. Some of these songs were directed to the groom only, some to the bride only; most of them, however, were usually directed to both bride and groom together.[12]

In the literature of these professional wedding entertainers, three wedding customs are singled out. The first is when the groom is escorted by a large crowd together with the *klezmer* to the courtyard of the synagogue; then the bride is similarly escorted there, the groom goes out to greet her, and wheat, corn, or sweetmeats are thrown at them to the thrice-repeated phrase: "be fruitful and multiply"; then the bride is escorted back home while the groom proceeds with the crowd to the synagogue to pray. In the lines of the following example one can almost hear the measured tread of the processional as it accompanies first the groom and then the bride to the courtyard of the town synagogue, through the narrow winding streets of the medieval Jewish community. The *badchen* admonishes the bridal pair, exhorting them to good deeds and liberal gifts to charity after their marriage.

Es izt kayn gresser freyd of erden,	There is no greater joy on earth
Als ven tsvey lib tsuzamengebn verden :	Than when two lovers are mated.
Tsu dizer freyd zol zich zayn bereyt,	For this joy, let every man prepare himself,

Knecht un mayd,
Chosn un kale tsu ern.
Hart tsu, chosn un kale, vos ich aych
    zog
Ayer zind verden aych firgebn of
    dizn tog.

Knight (man) and maid,
To honor the groom and bride.
Listen, groom and bride, to what I
    say
Your sins will be forgiven this day.

. . . Iber di armen tut aych
    derbarmen,
Entfanget zi liblich mit den armen,
Teylet gitlich und gern.[13]

Have compassion for the poor,

Embrace them kindly,
Share with them willingly.

The second ceremonial figuring largely in the song literature of the old-time marriage entertainers takes place in the home of the bride, prior to the wedding. She is seated on a chair in the middle of the room, surrounded by her friends and female relatives, while her hair is being braided, preparatory to being cut. The *badchen* sings *bazetsenish* ("to the seating") songs to her, while the ritual of the braiding of her hair proceeds.

Sheyne libe kale,
Her, ich zog dir for :
Dayn mazl zol dir shaynen
Vi di zun iz klor.[14]

Beautiful, lovely bride,
Listen, I prophecy to you :
May your fortune shine
As clearly as the sun.

The largest number of old wedding songs to survive seem to be these *bazetsenish* songs.[15] In some areas, the seating of the bride is accompanied by the music of the *klezmorim,* who play melancholy tunes which stir the hearts of the women. These are followed by the *badchen,* who in rhymes and a chanting singsong exhorts the bride, reminding her of the solemnity of this day.[16] Following is an example of a *bazetsenish* song, published in the eighteenth century but obviously current long before that :

Kale, kale, mazl tov,
Tu ich dir vintshn far ale dingen.
Dernoch vel ich dir ayn lidche
    zingen.
Dos zolstu nemen tsu hertsn,
Den an chupe tog tustu fastn,
Dos got di zind fargibt, tustu dich
    flachtin,
Hit dich vayter far bitre shmertsn.[17]

Bride, bride, good luck
I wish you in all things.
Then I will sing you a little
    song,
Which you must take to heart,
For on your wedding day you fast.
That God may forgive your sins, you
    are braiding your hair.
Guard yourself from bitter pain.

Another example goes into greater detail in describing the prevailing customs, possibly even before the seventeenth century.

Sheyn kale, loz dir zingen und zogn,	Lovely bride, let me sing and tell you
Vol fun der alte zitn,	About the old customs.
Vi du dich zolst farhaltn un fartrogn,	How you shall behave and what you shall do,
Vayl nun der shtul shteyt in dermitn,	Because this stool stands in the middle of the room,
Den shtul in di mitn :	The stool is in the center.
Biz mitvoch muztu fri oyfshteyn,	Till Wednesday you must rise early,
Zo firt man dich tsu der main,	When you will be led to the Main (river)
Varft man dich mit veyts un korn,	And wheat and corn will be thrown at you,
Dertsu kumt groys un kleyn	To which old and young will come,
Ach, di gants gemeyn (gemeynde).	Ah, the whole community.
Ach, di gants gemeyn (gemeynde).	Ah, the whole community.
Do tut man dich antshpuzn,	Here, you will be betrothed,
Mit ayn gold ringlein.	With a little gold ring.
Sheyne kale, du darfst zich farlozn,	Lovely bride, you may be sure,
Noch der chupe vert es zayn dayn,	That after the ceremony, it will become yours,
Noch der chupe vert es zayn dayn;	That after the ceremony, it will become yours;
Nun libe kale farnem mich gor ebn,	Well then, dear bride, understand me well,
Un batracht dich vol in dayn grestn freydn.	And ponder now during your greatest joy.
Un denk du verst nit eybig lebn.	Realize that you will not live forever.
Un fun der velt du must maydn.	And you must avoid the evils of the world.
Un fun der velt du must maydn.[18]	And you must avoid the evils of the world.

The *badchen* thoroughly exploited the seriousness of the moment, never forgetting that he was half showman and half instructor in his important function. Bringing the bride to tears, he reminded her of the temptations of the world and the inevitability of death. A nineteenth-century children's taunt utilizes this situation and weaves into its humorous nonsense rhymes fragments of practices prevalent before the wedding ceremony, which were current two centuries earlier. Following is the rhyme :

Kaleshi, kalèshi, veyn-zhe
Der chosn et dir shikn a lefele
    chreyn,
Vestu dich basmarken
Biz tsu di tseyn.

Bride, oh, bride, weep,
The groom will send you a spoonful
    of horseradish,
So that you will snivel
Right down to your teeth.

Di toybn, di toybn,
Shteyen oyf di lodn;
S'iz shoyn tsayt tsu gebn
A shtikele flodn.

The doves . . .
Stand on the shutters.
It's time to give everyone
A little piece of wedding cake.

Di toybn, di toybn,
Shteyen oyf di betn;
S'iz shoyn tsayt
Di kale tsu badekn.

The doves . . .
Stand on the beds.
It's time
For the bride to be veiled.

Di toybn, di toybn,
Shteyen oyf di tishn;
S'iz shoyn tsayt
Di kale zol zich bapishn.[19]

The doves . . .
Stand on the tables.
It's time
For the bride to wet her pants.

There were other kinds of songs, too, sung during the *bazetsenish* ceremonial, such as the following ballad sung by Jews in Germany, culled from a publication of the second half of the seventeenth century. In this song, a young man is wandering in the field one evening, deploring his celibacy and pleading with the Lord to send him his mate. "Our holy writ has taught us," he says, "that it is not good for a man to live alone." Thereupon a *Jungfräulein* wanders across his path, and he forthwith proposes marriage to her. She insists that she is too young to marry, but he tries ever so hard to convince her that their meeting was obviously arranged by an act of God. Following are excerpts from this interesting old Yiddish ballad, which is a good example of the influence of German folk song upon the Yiddish songs of the latter Middle Ages:

Ayn arim kreatur iz doch . . . ayn
    vayb,
Ayn ripf var zi genumen oys zaynem
    layb.
Van zi nicht zol habn ires mans
    genos,
Zo var zi aler froydn bloz. . . .

A poor creature indeed is a wife,

A rib taken from her husband's
    body.
Without the delight of her husband,

All other pleasures would be empty
    indeed.

The *badchen* then concludes his song with several stanzas of good advice :

Mit shtilshvaygn far, erfaret men fil,	Through modesty one learns much,
Sheyne kale, ich zing dir dos bayshpil,	Lovely bride, I sing you of this,
Dos man dich hot gezucht zo vayt,	That you have been sought for far and wide,
Biz man dich hot gefunden hayt.	Until you have been found today.
Zay im tray, zay im hold	Be true to him, love him
Far zilber un far roytes gold.	Better than silver and red gold,
Far im zolst du farhoyln nicht,	Do not conceal anything from him,
Desglaychn dir oych fun im geshicht.	As he should not from you.
Altsayt zols tu folgn zaynem rat,	At all times, follow his council,
Zolst im oych bayshteyn in zayner noyt, . . .[20]	Stand by him too, in his need, . . .

Songs were sung also during another ceremony called the *mazltov* dance (or *kosher* or *mitzvah* dance), during which the *badchen* called aloud the name of each woman present, who then came forward, embraced the bride and completed a circle with her. These songs were usually in the form of brief, often humorous rhymes such as the following :

Dos gelt gib mir,	Give me the money,
Di kale nem dir,	And you take the bride,
Un mach mit ir,	And take her for a
A sheynem shpatsir.[21]	Nice promenade.

A number of songs related to the ceremony when bride and groom were escorted to their sleeping quarters, and the *badchen* gave his last oration to the pair. These seem to breathe of the haste of the moment when the young couple is hurrying to get away, and the *badchen* reminds them for the last time of their religious and moral duties to God and each other.

(1)

Ich efn mayn mund mit zisem gezang,	I open my mouth with sweet song,
Dem chosn tsu er, der kale tsu dank;	To honor the groom, to thank the bride,
Ich vil es aych nit machn lang :	I will not be too long about it :
Gotes-furcht zol zayn der ershter onfang ! [22]	Your first duty shall be to serve the Lord !

(2)

Mir hobn gezungen mit freylichkayt,	We have sung with jollity,
Chosn un kale tsu er,	Honoring the groom and bride,
Ach andere gute layt kumen nun her,	And all other good people who have come here.
Es izt kumen di tsayt	The time has come
Dos der chosn mit der kale tsu bete aylt.[23]	For the groom and bride to hurry to bed.

In another song of this type, the *badchen* attempts to break down the bashfulness of the blushing bride, so that the pair may the sooner happily become fertile and multiply.

Gimgold tut zich farblaychn	Spun gold turns pale
Vol far der kale tsart.	Before the gentle bride.
Zi iz azoy tsichtiglaychn,	She is so pure,
Zi iz kosher un reyn	She is clean and chaste,
Iber ale geshteyn.	And stands over all.
Kale, vilstu mich farnemen,	Bride, listen to me,
Ich zing dir fun daynem chosn,	I sing to you of your groom.
Du derfst zich zayner nit shemen,	You must not be bashful before him,
Er izt dayn man,	He is your husband,
Vi vol er di toyre kan. . . .	How well he knows the Torah!
Nun firt zi hin in ern,	Then lead her here in honor,
Vol heym in ir gemach.	Happily to her home.
Ir zoymen zol zich mern,	May her seeds multiply,
Als got tsu avrohom shprach—	As God to Abraham said—
Alde tsu guter nacht! [24]	And a good night to you all!

During the nineteenth century the motifs and tone of the wedding and marriage songs took a sharp turn away from the religious to the secular. The older type of wedding songs of the *badchen* were still heard, but the new period, with its profound changes in the thoughts and aspirations of Eastern European Jews, is reflected both in the subject matter and in its treatment. The inner struggles among the religious groups, the penetration of new social and political ideas from the West, the ethical and cultural program of the Enlightenment movement (Haskalah) brought out into the open the struggle for a re-evaluation of the relationship between the sexes. The tenacity of the age-old customs, the rigidity of the patriarchal family structure, coupled with the widespread growing anger against this procedure, compelled the Haskalah movement of the middle 1850's to treat this problem actively. Against the economic and social considerations in the marriage match, it posed the higher values of true love and human worth.

Yiddish folk song, in general, naturally reflected all these changes and

Jewish wedding in Germany, 16th century

stirrings on the part of the young generation, seeking to break through the magic ring created by the religious leaders in the Pale. Although many still listened eagerly to the stylized songs and rhymes of the professional marriage entertainers, the *badchonim* themselves sought to extend their sphere of exhortations. Not only did they guide the newly wedded pair in the traditional customs but also dramatized the difficult life of the people as a whole, occasionally satirizing the communal leaders who were guilty of excesses against the poverty-stricken mass.

The most outstanding of these was Elyokum Zunser (1836–1913), who became famous in the sixties and seventies of the past century. Elyokum "Badchen" was in demand everywhere at Jewish weddings, which during the mid-nineteenth century still incorporated a host of rituals and observances and whose festivities lasted over seven days. But Zunser the Badchen sang songs that were not only directed towards the specific bridal pair. With a deep affection and regard for his suffering people, he sang of his times, pointed up the evils, satirized the guilty, stressed the good.

Following are several lines from his song, "Dos lid fun rubl" ("Song of the Ruble"), written in 1858, in which Zunser derides the evil of money, and which he often sang at weddings of the poor.

Fun berg, fun erd kumstu aroys,
Un vilst dem mentshn's shtoltsirer zayn;
Du machst im kleyn, du machst im groys,
Du machst im prost, du machst im fayn.

Vu men geyt, vos men redt,

Biztu rak do in der mit;
Vos men tracht, vos men zet,
Iz on dir—noch nit a trit.

Du gist im kovid fil,
Yiches bimli-e,
Men git im shoyn in shul
Di tayerste aliye.
Er iz zich mischatn
Mit rabonim shiduchim ton.
Er leyknt shoyn dem tatn,
Varum es shteyt far im nit on.[25]

From mountains and earth you come
And wish to be man's pride.

You make him small, you make him great,
You make him cheap, you make him fine.

Wherever one goes, whatever one says,
You are always in the midst of it;
What one thinks, what one sees,
Nothing moves a step forward without you.

You give one much honor
And prestige,
The finest recognition
In the synagogue.
He marries into families
Of rabbis.
He even denies his own father,
Because he is ashamed of him.

Vividly mirroring the times, Zunser reacted to the many spirited movements stirring among the Jews in the Pale. He wrote his "Der poylisher
myatezh" ("The Polish Insurrection"), which he sang at weddings and
which reflected his sympathies with Alexander II at the outbreak of the
Polish Insurrection in 1863. Some years later, in 1882, he sang his lengthy
poem, "Der sandik" ("he who presides at the ceremony of circumcision"),
in which he draws a picture of the times facing the newborn, male child.
Following is an excerpt, revealing Zunser's ideas of love and romance,
which reflect the views of the majority at that time :

Bay yidn shpilt men andersh libe,	Jews play at love differently,
Men zucht zich nor a mitsve sibe.	They seek a religious reason.
Hot ir nor fri-er kayn romansn getribn,	If you have not romanced before,
Vet ir zich shpeter beser libn.	Then you will love each other better afterwards.
Treft by yidn ven di sibe,	When it sometimes happens among Jews,
Zich tsu shisn tsulib libe,	That one shoots oneself because of love,
Oder hengen, oder trenken,	Or one hangs or drowns oneself,
Noch a meydl zich farbenken,	Or one yearns for a maiden,
Oder fraylins zich tsu nemen,	Or takes a mistress,
Vayb un kinder shtark tsu klemen,	Deeply hurting wife and children,
Zi libt dem, er libt yene—	Loving this one, loving that one,
Ach ! Es groylt mir fun der s'tsene ! [26]	Oh ! I shudder at the scene !

Zunser's songs treated the Haskalah movement and the Zionist movement, the general struggle against the religious hierarchy and the widespread economic degeneration. He was the most popular *badchen* of
modern times and also the last one of his kind, when the anonymous folk
songs springing up everywhere were making deep inroads in the old
marriage entertainer's repertoire.

The anonymous, Yiddish folk songs of marriage and weddings touch
upon rituals and customs only cursorily, treating instead the whole complexity of human and family relationships that came into play with the
consummation of a wedding match : the eligibility of the male or female,
the dowry problem, the economic responsibilities facing the future couple,
the relationship with the in-laws and the mother-in-law problem, the
tragedy of celibacy, the bitterness of the abandoned wife. Gone from the

songs was the moralizing and preaching. Gone, too, were the clownish effects and showmanship attempts. Gone were the detailed descriptions of ceremonials, which in the new situation were rapidly losing their meaning for ever larger sections of the population. Even when a primitive fertility rite is indicated, as in the example below, it appears fragmentarily, with its meaning already silted over and lost within the secular framework of the song:

Hober un korn, hober un korn,	Oats and corn, oats and corn,
Rivke hot dem fartech farlorn,	Rebecca lost her apron.
Yankl hot gefunen, yankl hot gefunen,	Jacob found it, Jacob found it,
Voltn zey zich beyde genumen.	Now they will be married.
Rifke zitst un kukt in shpigl,	Rebecca sits and looks into the mirror,
Un kamt zich fanander di herelech.	Combing out her hair.
Iz tsugegangen tsu ir yankl	Jacob came up to her,
Un hot zi bashotn mit kerelech.[27]	And scattered seeds over her.

So difficult was the economic situation, which touched the vast majority with its hardships, that it indeed became the decisive factor in a wedding match. Self-sacrificing mothers, less and less able to keep their male children in the house of study, were compelled to send them to work. This deprived the poor of the privilege to attain an honored position among the aristocracy of culture and learning, creating at the same time a new aristocracy which now included in its charmed circle, not only the religious leaders but also the small group of wealthy members in the community. The wedding and marriage songs became songs about marriage problems, which treated personally the people concerned with them; in short, the anonymous *mass* now created songs dealing with marriage and the wedding.

The economic stresses spared practically no one. Now that scholarship and piety were not the sole decisive factors in a match, as the "cobbler went barefoot," so, too, might a poor matchmaker's daughter remain a spinster:

Vos iz fun dem az ich bin sheyn?	Of what use is my fair face?
Tsu der chupe volt ich shoyn gegangen,	I would long since have been married,
Hob ich nisht kayn naye kleyder,	But I have no new clothes,
Vil mich keyner, keyner, keyner,	And no one wants me, no one, no one.

Mayn tate hot chasanim on a tsol, My father has many grooms,
Bot er shtendig fremde on. But he offers them to others.
Zey vern ale vi nay geborn, They all become newly born,
Un ich farlir mayne yorn.[28] While I fade away.

Chastity, piety, dowry, social position were not the only attributes sought in a woman by parents seeking a match for their scholarly son. Where the dowry was not too considerable, a young woman was expected to be able to read and write the Slavic vernacular and to know some arithmetic, for the pall of economic reverses hovered over all, and she might be called upon to assume the economic responsibilities, to maintain her husband at his studies. But the time for these patterns was running out, and a deep-rooted protest and anger was rising against the whole system of matchmaking and the hardheartedness of the parents who controlled the destiny of their children.

Hert ir ale, eltern beyde, Listen everybody, and both parents,
Ir nemt a kind, a kale You take a child, a bride,
Un firt ir tsu der akeyde. And lead her to the sacrificial block.
Di oygn iz farbunden, Her eyes are blindfolded,
Di harts iz ful mit vunden.[29] Her heart is full of pain.

The matchmaker, too, came in for his share of abuse, since he was regarded by the young generation as the one who shuffled young humans back and forth without sympathy for their personal feelings.

Shadchen, shadchen, a klog tsu Matchmaker, matchmaker, woe to
 dir ! you,
Vos hostu gehat tsu mir ! Oh, what did you want with me?
Tsugenumen di shadchones, You took my dowry,
Opgekoylet on rachmones— And slaughtered me without pity.
A klog tsu dir, a klog tsu dir ! [30] A curse on you ! A curse on you !

This sentiment was shared by all strata of the population, by the daughters of the rich as well as the poor :

Vos toyg undzer sach nadan? . . . What use is our big dowry? . . .
Vos toyg undzer reydn, What good is our polite conversation,
Vos toyg undzer klern, Our intelligence,
Az fun raych ken men orim vern, When the rich can become poor,
Un fun orim ken men vern raych, And the poor can become rich,
Az me krigt a man a mentshn, But if you get a "real" man,
Iz men shoyn laytn glaych ! [31] Then you can face the world !

During the seventies of the nineteenth century, when young women were entering the sewing professions in large numbers out of necessity, they were leaving the warm shelter of home and parents and entering the hard world of labor. These women were not like the working mothers who supported their males in their pursuit of learning, bearing the sacrifice with a measure of dignity, serene in the knowledge that they were assuring for their family and themselves a social position in the community and a place in heaven in the afterlife. These working women in going to work suffered loss of social prestige, while the mother, who was compelled to send her children into apprenticeship, thus denying her son a life of Torah and piety or her daughter the privilege of a match with a scholarly man, regarded such a step only as a last resort and a tragic sign of the deterioration of her family. True, these working women were now tasting for the first time a so-called freedom and equality in the world of men. They were at liberty to "play at love," to marry the man of their own choice, but their choice was now restricted to the economic insecurity and low social positions of the life of artisans and workers.

Without social standing or economic prestige, a maiden had often only her beauty and charm to commend her. The following conversation song between two young people reveals the sentiments of a maid who knows what it means to be married and raise a family in poverty and who saucily rejects the young suitor who seeks to flatter her:

She:
Un kayn chosn vil ich nit
Vayl ich darf im noch nit hobn,
Un az me hot yung chasene,
Vert men yung bagrobn.

I don't want a groom
Because I don't need him yet,
And when one gets married,
One is buried young.

He:
Vayl du bizt azoy yung un sheyn,
Vi-zhe kumstu o-dos tsu visn?

Because you are so young and pretty
How do you know all this?

She:
Vayl ich bin noch yung un sheyn
Vil ich kayn shidech nit shlisn.

Because I am still so young and pretty
I don't want to arrange a match.

Vayl ich bin noch yung un sheyn,
Vil ich mir lebn fray,
Ch'kon noch vartn a yor un tsvey,
Un efsher take dray.[32]

Because I am still so young and pretty
I want to live and be free,
I can wait a year or two,
And even all of three.

The further along in the century we go, the more saucy do the songs become. Dowry, social standing, religious prestige are all relegated to secondary positions among the lower strata of the population, and only true love is considered of primary binding importance, as in the following:

Ch'ob doch dir gezogt un gezogt un gezogt,	I've told you and told you and told you
Kayn gelt hob ich nit!	That I have no money.
Hostu mich lib, kum arayn,	If you love me, come on in,
Vilstu a rayche, halt zich ayn!	If you want a wealthy girl, stay away!
Ch'ob doch dir gezogt un gezogt un gezogt,	I've told you and told you and told you
Kayn yiches hob ich nit!	That I have no social standing.
Hostu mich lib, kum arayn,	If you love me, come on in,
Vilstu yiches, halt zich ayn! [33]	If you want a girl with a pedigree, stay away!

But such goings on were not the rule in those circles where the old requirements still predominated and marrying "below your station" was considered tragic. Reflecting this contempt for artisans, a number of conversation songs between mother and daughter sprang up, which deal with the eligibility of the young man in question. The pattern usually assumes a series of questions put to the daughter by the mother: Do you want a tailor for a husband? A cobbler? A blacksmith? A coachman? To which the daughter usually renders a categorical NO but replies YES to a suitor who will secure her position in the community as heretofore — a scribe, a cantor, a Talmudic scholar. She will almost always reject the craftsman, seeking the security of the patriarchal environment into which she had been born, refusing to marry a workman, who, in her circle, was considered socially inferior, intellectually backward, and economically always on the brink of starvation. In the following excerpted lines several crafts are listed, together with the reasons the women gave for rejecting the men who followed them:

Di shusterske vayber . . .	Cobblers' wives
darfn di dratve machn . . .	must make the thread . . .
Di shnayderske vayber . . .	Tailors' wives
darfn biz shpet zitsn . . .	must sit up late . . .
Di furmanishe vayber . . .	Coachmen's wives
darfn di aksn shmirn . . .	must tar the axles . . .

Di studentske vayber . . .	Students' wives
hobn giche kinder . . .	bear many children . . .
Di katsovishe vayber . . .	Butchers' wives
darfn di fleysh trogn . . .	must carry the meat . . .
Di vebershe vayber . . .	Weavers' wives
darfn di shpindl varfn . . .	must throw the spindle . . .
Di shlayferske vayber . . .	Filers' wives
darfn dem redl dreyen . . .	must turn the wheel . . .
Di farberske vayber . . .	Painters' wives
darfn di farb mishn . . .	must mix the paint . . .
Di stolershe vayber . . .	Carpenters' wives
darfn di breter zegn . . .[34]	must saw the boards . . .

Small wonder that many a craftsman, at the bottom of the social and economic ladder, adopted a devil-may-care attitude of "loving and leaving" the naïve young working girl, who permitted herself the rare moment of happiness experienced in the casual romance. These young vulnerables, exposed to indiscriminate romantics, were often misled and then jilted — an experience of deep tragic moment in an environment witnessing the breakdown of the old mores, when the new ones had not yet become firmly established. The jilted woman in the following song is prepared to marry anybody or none at all in her desperation :

Zol ich nemen an altn man,	If I marry an old man,
Kuk ich nit af im;	I'll not look at him;
Zol ich nemen a yungn man,	If I marry a young man,
Kukt er nit af mir.	He'll not look at me.
Zol ich nemen gornit,	If I marry no one,
Zogn layt : M'tor nit;	Folks say : it's wrong;
Zol ich nemen a shlimezalnik,	If I marry a ne'er-do-well,
Iz shoyn glaycher gornit ! [35]	I'd rather not marry at all !

The interference of parents in the mating of the young people often had cruel consequences, in which young people committed suicide or died pining for each other. Others with courage eloped to another town and there got married, without benefit of witnesses or the blessings of parents, relatives, and friends. The greatest number, for a long time, submitted sadly to their fate, as did the young bride in the following example, who is marrying a man of her parents' choice and is bidding adieu to her friends on the day of her wedding.

Zayt mir gezunt, chavertes ale,	Farewell, all my friends,
Mayn letsn ade zog ich aych.	My last farewell I say to you.
Nit zayt mich mekane mitn nomen kale,	Do not envy me that I am a bride,
Vayl nit far yedn shaynt dos glaych.	For it is not the same for all.
Tsu der chupe vert men gefirt,	One is led to the canopy,
Men vert ibergegebn tsu a tsveyter perzon,	One is given to another one.
Un damit vert men rizikirt,	And thereby is the risk,
Un dos lebn shteyt vi in kon.	And one's life hangs in the balance.
Dos shpeterdige lebn vet ersht darfn bashtimen,	Only later in life will it be proven,
Tsi iz dos a glaychn, tsi iz dos a por?	Whether the pair were properly mated.
Durchtsufirn vos men hot untergenumen,	To carry through what they assumed,
Lebn in fridn, un dos iz gor.	To live in peace, and that is all.
Oy, lebn un libn, vi es shteyt geshribn,	Oh, to live and love, as it is written,
Dos iz doch nor a mazl aza.	That is but a matter of luck.
Men darf zich stayen un ales fartsayen,	One must try to forgive everything
Un fun lebn nit nemen kayn ade.[36]	And not bid adieu to life.

Another example of this kind, in which the apprehensions entertained by the very young groom are revealed as he is led from one ceremonial to the other on his wedding day, is the following:

Ale mentshn tantsndig un shpringendig,	All the folks are dancing, jumping,
Un lachndig un zingendig,	Laughing and singing,
Un moyshele shteyt alts veynendig.	And Moyshele stands crying.
—Moyshe, moyshe, vos du veynst?	—Moyshe, Moyshe, why are you crying?
—Ich veyn, vos ich meyn:	—I know why I'm crying:
Es iz shoyn tsayt tsu der chupe tsu geyn!	It's time to go to the canopy!

The subsequent stanzas list the other reasons for Moyshele's ("little Moses,") fears: "It's time to go to the wedding supper. . . . It's time to participate in the *mitsvo* dance. . . . It's time to go to bed!"[37]

Whatever fate may have decreed for the "marriages made in heaven," the marriages made on earth by parents and matchmakers often resulted in tragedy. An interesting ballad in the form of a conversation between a mother and her son tells the sad tale of the domineering mother, who would not permit her son to marry the girl he loved. When all his pleas with his cruel mother fail, he takes poison. His brokenhearted sweetheart laments:

Ach mentshn, ir mentshn, ir ale mentshn,
Zets nor, vos a muter hot gemacht!

Oh, people, you people, all of you people,
See then what a mother has brought about!

Fil nefashes volt fun undz aroysgekumen,
Zi hot zey fun der velt gebracht.

We would have brought many souls into the world,
And she murdered them all.

Ach mentshn, ir mentshn, ir ale mentshn,
Zets nor ver do ligt toyt!
A halbe velt mentshn tu ich tsushvern,
Az ich vel blaybn a moyd.[38]

Oh people, you people, all of you people,
See then who lies dead here!
I swear to half of the people of the world
That I shall remain an old maid.

Where both young lovers had the courage, they eloped and were married in another town, as the following dancing song reveals:

Ich mit mayn chosn,
Mayn mameshi in der mit;
Ich vil tnoyim shraybn,

I and my fiancé,
My mother is between us;
I want to sign the engagement contract,

Mayn mameshi lozt mich nisht.
Ch'vel nisht kukn oyf mayn mamen,
Ch'vel machn an ek;
Ch'vel nemen mayn chosn
Un vel mit im avek.[39]

But my mother won't let me.
I won't pay attention to my mother
And make an end of it all;
I'll take my fiancé
And run away with him.

In many cases, young people ran off to America, where economic and social inequalities were secondary.

In the climate of the constant economic depression that prevailed in the Pale, the haggling over the dowry at the drawing up of the marriage contract was considered a matter of fact. For some, however, it proved a disillusioning experience, as for the naïve Talmudic student, in the following excerpted example. In this song, the prospective father-in-law had evidently agreed to support the young couple for a number of years. However, soon after the wedding, the student suddenly awoke to the stark reality of having to fend for himself, since his father-in-law had stopped giving the young couple their *kest* ("board and keep").

Ver ich mir a chosn	I became engaged
Gor in eyn minut,	In a minute,
Un es ducht zich oys,	And it seemed to me
Az s'vet mir zayn gants gut!	That I would have everything just fine.
Der shver vet gebn kest	My father-in-law would support us
Un a sach gelt	And give us a lot of money,
Un dertsu a meydl	And I would have a girl,
An oysnam fun der velt.	One of a kind.
Neyn, bruder, neyn,	No, brother, no,
Hob-zhe nit kayn to-es;	Make no mistake,
Der shver vet nit gebn kayn kest	Your father-in-law won't give you *kest*
Un nit kayn-mo-es!	Nor any money.
Na dir a vayb	Take your wife
Un halt zich mit ir,	And hang on to her,
Un tsores vestu hobn	And you'll have troubles
Gor on a shir! [40]	Without end.

The dowry problem was like a thorn in the life of the young people, who sought to become independent of their parents' domination and interference. Wherever the choice of a young person was frowned upon, parents would raise the dowry situation into prominence and rattle the spectre of impending pauperism. In the following example, a sophisticated fellow taunts a pretty maiden with her poverty. She attempts to point up to him the importance of true, enduring love over the ephemeral, transitory role of money. In the end, he leaves her to her bitter disillusionment.

He:

Sheyn binsti, binsti,	You are pretty
Vi di gantse velt,	As the whole world,
Nor eyn chesorn iz on dir,	But you have just one fault:
Vos di binst on a kopike gelt.	You haven't a single penny.

She:

Gelt iz doch kaylechdig,	Money is only round,
Gelt geyt avek,	It rolls away,
Ich hob zich in dir ayngelibt,	But I have fallen in love with you,
Vi in a sheynem portret.	As with a pretty picture.

Indroysn iz a regn,
Ale shteyner zenen nas.
Itstike bochurim iz tsu gloybn
Vi a hunt afn gas! [41]

It is raining out of doors,
All the stones are wet.
Fellows of today are to be believed
Like a dog on the street!

The custom of living with the in-laws (usually with the parents of the

Herzl T. Rome, 1950

groom) after marriage resulted in a number of songs which describe the plight of the young wife in the strange home, her loneliness for her parents, and the humiliations and cruelties she suffered at the hands of her mother-in-law. The tenor of the songs varies between anger and sorrow; on occasion a song takes on a dire tone and reveals a tragic incident of a young wife, dying in childbirth because of the neglect and indifference of her in-laws. No matter what the young daughter-in-law did, the groom's mother was dissatisfied.

Knet ich chale—	I knead the bread—
zogt zi : shiter!	she says : it lacks consistency!
Mach ich fish—	I prepare the fish—
shrayt zi : biter!	she shouts : it's bitter!
Farbet ich dos bet—	I make the bed—
zogt zi : hoych!	she says : too high!
Heyts ich in oyvn—	I heat the stove—
filt zi roych,	she smells smoke.
Gey ich pamelich—	I walk slowly—
zogt zi : ich krich!	she says : I'm crawling!
Gey ich gich—	I walk quickly—
"zi rayst di shich." [42]	"she's tearing her shoes!"

Here and there some nineteenth-century marriage and wedding songs contain fragments of old wedding and marriage customs that prevailed generations earlier. The following, for example, mentions the ceremonial of leading the bride to the ritual bath on Thursday evening, before the wedding day. First, the bride would invite her female friends and relatives, serve them tea and cake, and then she would be led by both mothers and the bathhouse attendant to the ritual pool. Several generations earlier, the *klezmorim,* too, would have joined in the procession. This particular song may well have been the creation of cheder boys, who were well versed in all of these traditional rituals and ceremonials.

Farbay mil, farbay rod	Past the mill, past the wheel,
Firt men di kale glaych in bod	They lead the bride right to the bath.
Farbay di naye brukn,	Past the new bridges,
Firt men di kale tukn.	They lead the bride to be ducked.
Firt men di kale tukn,	They lead the bride to be ducked,
Loyfn di vayber kukn :	All the women run to look.
Vi men firt nor di kale aroys,	As the bride is led out,
Geyt der chosn fun kloyz aroys.	The groom comes out of the synagogue.

Mit a glezele vayn, mit a shtikele flodn,
Me zol ir gicher opbodn.
Me zol ir nit dertrenken,
Me zol ir kosher shvenken.

Chapt men on far a hentele,
Shvenkt men op a hentele.
Chapt men on far a fisele,
Shvenkt men op a fisele, etc.

With a little glass of wine and a little piece of cake,
May they bathe her all the sooner.
But may they not drown her,
May they ritually rinse her.

They grab one little hand,
They rinse one little hand.
They grab one little foot,
They rinse one little foot, etc.

The same song recalls in merry mood the older ritual, when the bridal pair was escorted by a band of *klezmorim* from the bath to their sleeping quarters :

Leybele beder, gilderne reder,

Abele brum, zelikl shtum.
Drey zich di kale, dray mol arum.
Fidlt di moyz, tantst di loyz,
Flit di floy durchn fentster aroys.
Yunge shnayders shnaydn tsu,
Blotike n'keyves nemen tsu.
Tsugenumen, avekgeleygt,
A vare macht, der chosn geyt.
A vare macht, dem chosn gebracht,
Tsu di kale, a gantse nacht.[43]

Leybele the bath attendant, golden wheels,
Abele roars, Zelikl is dumb.
Turn bride, three times round.
The mouse fiddles, the louse dances,
The flea flies out the window.
Young tailors cut the patterns,
Muddy females take them away.
Taken away, put away,
Make way, the groom is coming !
Make way, the groom is brought
To the bride for the whole night.

At the bride's home, the *badchen*, even on the threshold of the twentieth century, was conscientiously preparing the bride for the wedding ceremony and putting her into the "proper" somber mood.

Recalling the old *bazetsenish* songs, the following reminds the bride of her religious duties and responsibilities :

Sheyne libe kale,
Her ich zog dir for :
Dayn mazl zol dir shaynen
Vi di zun iz klor !
Cheyn zolstu gefinen
Bay got un bay layt;
Licht zolstu bentshn
Tsu der rechter tsayt,
Mel zolstu koyfn,
Volvl oder tayer;

Lovely, dear bride,
I say unto you :
May your luck shine
As clear as the sun !
May God and the people
Be pleased with you;
Bless the candles
At the proper time.
Buy your flour,
Cheap or dear,

Chale zolstu nemen
Un varfn in dem fayer.
Fleysh zolstu koyfn,
Kosher zolstu machn;
Dos vert doch gerechnt
Far ale yidishe zachn.
Tvile zolstu geyn
Tsu der rechter tsayt,
Vestu hobn kinder,
Gute, frume layt.
Sheyne, libe kale,
Hit dich far a zind!
Alts vert opgerechnt,
Ven men geyt tsu kind.[44]

A piece of *chale*
Throw into the fire;
Buy your meat
And make it kosher;
For these are the ways
Of Jewish life.
Go to the ritual bath
At the proper time,
Then you will bear
Good and pious children.
Lovely dear bride,
Beware of sin!
For all is remembered,
When you are in childbirth.

A large number of the wedding songs of the modern period dealt with the gaiety and abandon following the ceremony and the atmosphere of excitement and expectation in the village on the wedding day. The bride awaited the groom with bated breath, peeking through the curtained windows from time to time:

Ver s'vet mir kumen zogn,
Az mayn chosn geyt—
A rubl far'n veg
Ligt shoyn ongegreyt!

Whoever will let me know
That my groom is coming
Will get a ruble
For his deed.

Mayn chosn iz gekumen,
Me hot im fayn tsugenumen,
Me hot getrunken med un vayn
Un dernoch gegangen in gas arayn.[45]

My groom has come
And was well received,
They drank mead and wine,
And then went into the street.

Children ran through the streets, wild with excitement. Saucy, often naughty and even ribald rhymes were created "hot off the griddle" and shouted at the wedding parties moving from one house to the other in their preparations for the ceremony.

Untern shlos perehoz
Shteyt ester di grine;
Ester shteyt, der chosn geyt,
Meynt zi—Avrom Ovinu.
Volt zi visn, ver dos iz,
Volt zi tsu im vinken;
Volt zi hobn a glezl vayn,
Volt zi tsu im trinken.
Volt zi hobn ferd-un-vogn,

Back of the castle Perehoz,
Stands Esther the green one;
Esther stands, the groom is coming,
So she thinks it's Father Abraham.
If she knew who it was,
She would wink to him.
If she had a glass of wine,
She would drink to him.
If she had a horse and wagon,

Volt zi tsu im loyfn;	She would race to him;
Volt zi hobn a zekele gelt,	If she had a little sack of money,
Volt zi im opkoyfn.[46]	She would buy him off.

No sooner was the ceremony over than the somber atmosphere was dispelled and joy reigned supreme, with dancing, singing, feasting for days. However, the family conflicts broke through, even in some of the wedding songs, during the festivities, as in the following, in which the mother of the bride is trying to soften the haughty demeanor of the groom's mother towards her daughter. The song concludes, however, with the mother's threat that: "If you prove to be a nasty mother-in-law, then my daughter too, can be a shrew!"

Mechuteneste mayne, mechuteneste getraye,	Dear relation, true relation,
Lomir zayn oyf eybig mechutonim.	Let us be relatives forever.
Ich gib aych avek mayn tochter far a shnur,	I give you my daughter for a daughter-in-law
Zi zol bay aych nit onvern dos ponim.	May she not lose face with you.
Mechuteneste mayne, mechuteneste getraye,	Dear relation, true relation,
Oyf kinder hobn tut men blut fargisn.	Blood is spilled to bear children.
Un tomir vet ir zen az der zun hot lib di shnur,	And should you see that your son loves your daughter-in-law,
Zol es aych gornit fardrisn.[47]	Do not take it so to heart.

And when the feast was laid and the wedding supper was in full swing, each course was accompanied with some singing and dancing. In some areas of the Pale, feasting lasted as much as seven and eight days. In the following interesting song, the "seven feast days" (*sheva broches*—"seven blessings") are cumulatively symbolized as follows:

Eyns iz dos chasene-hoyz,	ONE is the wedding house,
in vos me est, in vos me trinkt,	where one eats, where one drinks,
in vos me tantst, in vos me [shpringt.	where one dances, where one hops.
Tsvey zenen di chosn-kale,	TWO are the groom and bride,
vos der eybershter iz zey m'male.	whom the Lord has raised up high.
Dray zenen di mechutonim,	THREE are the in-laws,
vos zey tseyln di mezumonim.	who count out the cash.
Fir zenen di chupe-shtangen.	FOUR are the canopy posts,
Vos chosn-kale vern gefangen.	which entrap the groom and bride.

Finf zenen di klezmorim, 　　vos zenen m'sameyech raych un 　　orim.	FIVE are the bandsmen, 　　who entertain rich and poor.
Zeks zenen di licht-havdoles, 　　vos der oybershter shikt mazoles.	SIX are the lighted tapers, 　　with which the Lord sends us His 　　blessings.
Zibn zenen di sheva-broches, 　　vos der oybershter shikt 　　hatsloches.[48]	SEVEN are the seven blessings, 　　through which the Lord will send 　　us good luck.

The further along in the feasting and celebrating, the more abandoned was the singing, the louder the stamping and the stomping, the more furious the handclapping and the shouting. The rafters rang and the floorboards creaked as the guests sang and danced.

Nemt zich yidn ale gor ineynim,	Everyone, take hands together,
Nemt arum zich, shlist a groysn rod,	Put your arms around each other in 　　a big ring.
Lozt nit durch cholile v'chas keynem,	Don't leave anyone out, heaven help 　　us,
Lomir ale geyn a karahod.	Let us all dance a ring-around.
Freylech, lustig, lebedig klezmorim,	Happy, gay, jolly bandsmen,
Shpilt a tentsl munter, breyt un 　　raych,	Play a dance of joy and wealth and 　　grandeur,
Tantsn zoln ale, raych un orim,	Let all dance, rich and poor,
Oys yachsones, kovid ale glaych.[49]	No exceptions, and respect for all.

The gaiety, the drinking, loosened the tongues and relaxed the tensions which existed between the in-laws and between members of the same family occupying different social positions in the community. With restraint removed, temporarily at least, the poor could be as gay as the rich, as the following two examples illustrate.

(1)

A dank un loyb dir mayn got!	I thank and praise You, my God,
Far yeder zach bazunder.	For every little thing.
Ale choyves opgetsolt,	I've paid up all my debts,
Un chasene gemacht di kinder!	And married off my children.
Ersht mayn man, tants mit mir,	Now, my husband, dance with me,
Ze s'a eydim, ze s'a shnur,	What a fine son-in-law and what a 　　fine daughter-in-law,
Mach l'chayim, trink a glezele bir![50]	Let's drink a toast with a little glass 　　of beer!

(2)

Ot azoy, ot azoy,
Macht men chasene kinder,
Mit a sloy ayngemachts,
Zet nor got's vunder.

This is how, this is how,
We marry off our children,
With a jar of preserves,
Witness the Lord's miracles.

Es iz mir gut, es iz mir voyl,
A tentsl un a hotske,
Yidl-fidl, mechl-poyk,
Shpilt mir a kazatske!

I am happy, I feel good,
I dance and hop about,
Yidl with his fiddle, Mechl with his
Play me a kazatske!   [drum,

Avrom-ber, kum aher,
Farkatshe nor di poles,
Di mezinke gib ich oys,
Poter funem dalis! [51]

Avrom-Ber, come on here,
Lift the ends of your long frock,
I am marrying off my youngest now
And am through with poverty!

Often, under the influence of whiskey and wine, "what was buried on the lung," suddenly "came out on the tongue," in the form of a dancing rhyme:

Ot azoy, ot azoy,
Nart men op a chosn,
Men zogt im tsu a sach nadn
Men git im nit a groshn.[52]

This is how, this is how
You fool a groom,
You promise him a big dowry
And give him not a penny.

Grandmothers danced sturdily to: *Ayzik-mazik, di bobe geyt a kozik; on ayn hore, zet nor zet, vi zi tupet, vi zi tret, oy a simche, oy a freyd* ("Isaac you rascal, grandmother is stepping to a *kozik* [*kazatske*]; may no evil eye harm her, but see now how she stamps and stomps, what a joy, what a pleasure!")[53] Even bashful brides joined in the festivities as soon as the somber marriage rites were over, dancing with their girl friends as the spirits ran high and were uplifted in merriment.

A sheyn epele iz doch vaynig,
A koshere kale iz a taynig!
A vaynig epele iz zeyer zis,
A treyfe kale iz zeyer mis!

A pretty little apple is delicious,
A chaste bride is a delight!
A juicy apple is very sweet,
An unclean bride is very ugly!

Keyle, keyle, greyt tsum tish,
Veln mir esn yoych mit fish!
Veln mir trinken med un vayn,
Freylech, lustig veln mir zayn! [54]

Keyle, Keyle, set the table,
Let us eat the soup and fish!
We will drink the mead and wine,
And be jolly as can be!

At the weddings of the poor, where the dowry often consisted of but a pretty face and a good disposition, the young men and women would dance and sing to rhymes such as the following — rhymes which had probably been created during their socials and dancing sessions:

Tantst meydn, hulyet vayber,	Dance maidens, be gay, women,
Moshke's tochter nemet a shnayder,	Moshke's daughter is marrying a tailor,
On kleyder, on nadan,	Without a trousseau, without a dowry,
Abi a sheyner yungerman.[55]	So long as he's a handsome young man.

Who, at that wonderful moment, thought of the poverty of the morrow, of the hard life facing the young couple, of the pain of parenthood and bringing up a family in the economic oppressions and other stresses of the Czarist Pale? And yet, some of the songs, as in the rhyme above, do hint subtly at these sentiments, which hovered over all and which at that wonderful moment were pushed out of sight.

S'iz a chasenke, me loyft, me flit,	There's a wedding, folks rush about,
Karetn, mechutonim feln nit.	Carriages, wedding guests without number.
Shpiln muzikantn oysgeputste frantn,	Musicians play, folks are dressed up,
Un ale sheyne yunge damen tantsn zich tsuzamen.	And all the pretty young ladies dance together.
Un fun chosn's tsad mit groys freyd,	The groom's family joyfully
Di kale tut men on di chupe-kleyd.	Dress the bride in her wedding gown.
Azoy ringlt men ir arum, fraynt fun umetum;	Thus she is surrounded by friends from everywhere,
Do git men ir a blumen-krentsele,	Now they give her a little flower wreath
Un me geyt mit ir a groysartikn tentsele.	And dance a lovely little dance with her.
Es iz nochn tantsn, s'iz arop der glants,	Now the dance is over and the sheen is dulled,
S'iz geblibn di ritelech fun blumen-krants.[56]	Only the stems of the wreath remain.

Notes

MARRIAGE

1. Rubin, 1950, p. 71.
2. Schauss, p. 144.
3. *Ibid.,* p. 146.
4. "The study of the Talmud is the chief object of higher education among our people. . . . A wealthy merchant, leaseholder, or professional man with a marriageable daughter does everything in his power to acquire a good Talmudist as son-in-law. In other respects, the scholar may be deformed, diseased, and ignorant; he will still have the advantage over rivals." (Maimon, p. 16. Maimon [1754–1800] at the age of eleven, was able to pass as a full rabbi.)
5. Abrahams, p. 170.
6. *Ibid.,* p. 169.
7. Rubin, MSS.
8. Graetz, IV, p. 640.
9. D. and Y., p. 62, No. 8.
10. ". . . The tradition of Jewish fiddlers (*klezmorim*) in the Eastern European countries was still alive in the middle of the nineteenth century, whereas it was completely forgotten and obsolete in Central and Western Europe. These fiddlers functioned as dance bands and as teachers, furnishing the cultural life of East European Jewry with a strongly artistic element" (Werner, p. 979).
11. The professional *badchen* (marriage entertainer) existed "already in the first centuries of the Common Era, . . . whose task it was to cheer the sad and to make peace between enemies. . . . They sought to elevate and to instruct the masses while entertaining them . . . through witty and subtle satire. . . . Their songs, the *badchonim* invented extemporaneously according to the particular conditions at each wedding" (Idelsohn pp. 435–436). In the sixteenth century, when the *Spielmann* disappeared, the *badchen* took his place at weddings, together with the clowns. The jester's repertoire included humorous, light, often bawdy songs, as well as instrumental and acrobatic antics, dances, and even small dramatic presentations. The *badchen,* on the other hand, delivered the more serious discourses, together with the rabbi and the bridegroom. Gradually, both types of entertainment became intertwined, and, by the nineteenth century, the *badchen* was performing in a manner and with a repertoire which combined the art of both former wedding entertainers. "He improvised verses upon the various stages of the marriage ceremony, he delivered the solemn discourses to bridegroom and bride, and furnished the wit during the banquet. . . . His verses were mere rhyming lines, without form or rhythm, and his jests were often of a low order and even coarse" (Wiener, p. 91).
12. This chapter speaks of *Yiddish* wedding songs as distinct from the liturgical *Hebrew* marriage hymn, which appears during the tenth century, and the wedding odes, for example, of Judah Halevi. In the Middle Ages, "on the Sabbath following a wedding, the bridegroom attended synagogue accompanied by a concourse of friends. He ascended the reading-desk during the recitation of the weekly portion of the Pentateuch, and as he walked from his place the assembled worshippers . . . broke

forth into gleeful Hebrew songs" (Abrahams, p. 11). At the beginning of the eighteenth century, the great Jewish poet, Moses Chayim Luzzatto, "like Jehuda Halevi . . . was much in demand as a turner of marriage verses" (Abrahams, p. 190). "Songs of this type were sung in the home or in the wedding house rather than in the synagogue, though . . . the Yemen Jews appear to have chanted the wedding odes of Jehuda Halevi during public worship." (Abrahams, pp. 191–192).

13. Bassin, pp. 40–41. (Walich collection.)

14. Idelsohn, IX, No. 547.

15. "The orthodox Jews of Russia, Poland and Galicia observe very strictly the following custom: Just before her wedding, a bride has her head shaved. She is then covered with a kerchief, and is led under the canopy. During the remainder of her life she wears a wig. . . . The custom has died out in the United States, however, and one is reminded of it only on meeting old women who still wear their European wigs" (Yoffie, p. 415). Describing a nineteenth-century Jewish wedding in Eastern Europe, Schauss states: "A generation previously, the hair of the bride was shorn at the ceremony of *bazetsens,* but . . . this custom was discarded. Married women did not crop their hair but they wore wigs covering and matching the color of their own hair" (p. 190).

16. The belief that on the wedding day the bridal pair was menaced by evil powers resulted in various ruses to make the demons believe that this was an occasion of mourning. The bride wept, both wore shrouds at the wedding ceremony, the face of the bride was veiled, etc. (*See:* Schauss, pp. 212–213.)

17. Kirch-han, Song No. 12.

18. Erik, pp. 159–160. In an old custom in Frankfurt-am-Main, possibly prior to the seventeenth century, virgins were married on Wednesday; widows on Thursday. Later, all weddings took place on Friday.

19. Lehman, 1923, p. 123, No. 68. The ceremony following *bazetsens* is *badekens* (when the bride's face is covered). "A group of women of the bride's party, preceded by the *klezmorim* and the *badchen,* now pay a visit to the bridegroom, inviting him to *badekens.* . . . The bridegroom, escorted by his father and the rabbi, walks between the two rows of girls holding the lighted candles until he approaches the bride's chair. The two mothers stand in front of the chair holding a plate of raisins or hops covered with a silk kerchief. The rabbi and the bridegroom seize the kerchief by two corners, lift it hastily, and cover the bride's face. At this moment, a mass of raisins and hops is showered upon both bride and groom" (Schauss, p. 191).

20. Bassin, I, p. 50. Curiously similar to this motif is a stanza from a poem by Judah Halevi: "This lover hath no friend at his side; / Come thou, be a help for him. / For it is not good that man should be alone, / But goodly to be twain" (Salaman, p. 68).

21. Rubin, MSS.

22. Bassin, I, p. 40. (Walich collection.)

23. Erik, p. 162. (This is another stanza from the above song.)

24. *Ibid.,* pp. 158, 162. (Walich collection.)

25. Zunser, I, pp. 62–64.

26. *Ibid.,* III, pp. 122–123.

27. Fibix, p. 6.

28. Rubin, MSS.

29. D. and Y., pp. 196–197, No. 6.

30. Cahan, 1957, No. 290.

31. D. and Y., p. 196, No. 5.

32. *Ibid.,* p. 65, No. 14.

33. Rubin, MSS.

34. G. and M., No. 313.

35. D. and Y., pp. 100–101, No. 4.

36. Rubin, MSS.
37. Bassin, I, p. 117.
38. Cahan, 1957, No. 20.
39. *Ibid.,* No. 60.
40. D. and Y., p. 199, No. 10. (*kest*: room and board given the young couple by the bride's parents for a period of time.)
41. G. and M., No. 141.
42. Bassin, I, p. 120.
43. G. and M., No. 260. "A Chasidic custom of dancing on the wedding day occurred when the bride was being led to the ritual bath. Chasidim would accompany her with music and then continue to dance in front of the bathhouse. . . . There was an inspiring dance, too, when the *rebe* danced with the bride, holding one end of a kerchief while she held another end of it. A lusty Chasidic dance also took place when the groom was being led to bed. . . . The Chasidim then danced in front of the house, singing all kinds of gay tunes . . ." (Unger, 1946, p. 129).
44. Cahan, 1957, No. 301. (*chale*: the twisted white loaf; *kosher*: according to the Jewish dietary laws.)
45. *Ibid.,* No. 276.
46. D. and Y., p. 58, No. 2.
47. Rubin, 1950, pp. 112–113.
48. Cahan, 1957, No. 309.
49. Idelsohn, IX, No. 262.
50. *Ibid.,* No. 538.
51. Rubin, MSS.
52. Idelsohn, IX, No. 260.
53. Warshawsky, p. 14.
54. Cahan, 1957, No. 293.
55. Skuditsky, 1936, p. 284, No. 17.
56. D. and Y., p. 198, No. 9.

CHAPTER V

Customs and Beliefs

FOLKLORE DEALS WITH THREE CHIEF AREAS: CUSTOMS, BELIEFS, AND folk literature.[1] Coined more than a hundred years ago (1846) by the English antiquarian William John Thomas to replace the earlier expression "popular antiquities," the new term soon established itself in countries outside of England.Folklore has been defined as the unwritten law of a people and the history of its life in primitive ages. It is also the psychology and religion, social organization and ceremonial life of early man, manifested in beliefs and customs still practiced by force of habit and tradition, current among the people in folk tales, legends, sayings, proverbs, maxims, myths, and songs.[2] In the course of time, ancient customs, beliefs, observances, and practices are gradually rejected, becoming superstitions and traditions. "Folklore is the scholar's word for something that is as simple and natural as singing songs and spinning yarns among the folk who know the nature and the meaning but not the name . . . of folklore."[3]

The folklore of the Jews is distinguished from that of other nations, primitive and civilized, by its monotheistic and ethical background. "Abraham Ibn Ezra, the distinguished poet and scholar, writing eight hundred years ago, recognized the ethnological truth that every people fashions its songs to suit its spirit, and reflects in its chant its inner mood and characteristics. Thus, he says in one of his Hebrew epigrams:

> The Arabs sing of love and lust,
> The Christians of war and revenge,
> The Greeks of wisdom and cunning,
> The Hindus of proverbs and riddles,
> But Israel's song is to the Lord of Hosts."[4]

Jewish folklore also spans a long and continuous history, a wide range of productivity in many lands and a rich variety that bears the imprint of the diverse cultures assimilated by the Jews through the centuries.

Originating in Palestine when the Canaanites and Amorites dwelt in the ancient land, Jewish folklore was subsequently carried to Babylon and Persia, when Israel went into exile. Preserved there, as well as absorbing a measure of the Babylonian and Persian beliefs and customs, it was in the course of centuries swelled by other folklore streams : Indian, Greek, Roman. "During the Middle Ages . . . the Jews were responsible for the diffusion in Europe of many Oriental tales and legends and enriched the Folklore of Western nations with many substrata and motifs. . . . In addition to the old tales and legends bequeathed to them by the Talmud and the Midrashim, they invented new ones."[5] The ancient survivals from Persia and Greece, the later adoptions of Teutonic folklore, were endowed with Jewish coloration, carefully cast in the mold of its particular religion and ethical practices. "They have cherished and preserved their tradition of learning ever since . . . the 6th century B.C. In large measure this tradition was derived from the religious obligation of every Jew to study Scriptures ceaselessly. . . . In later centuries, this study also embraced the *Mishna,* the Talmud and the *Midrash,* of which folklore was an integral part. . . . This universal duty to study *as a religious act* broadened the base of Jewish culture. . . ."[6]

Another basic difference between Jewish folklore and the folklore of other peoples is that it was not founded on nature but was created on the foundations of written literature. From the very first between it and the folk stood "the Book" (Torah). In the Torah, folk creativity on the basis of nature was but faintly evident; as for the Haggada, which followed it, it was built entirely on the foundations of the Torah. Jewish folklore, thus based on Torah and Haggada and not springing spontaneously from the surrounding natural world, is almost entirely devoid of animal lore and the primitive naïveté which is natural in the folklore of other peoples.[7]

Modern Jewish folklore in its *outer* cloak is in the main identical with the folklore of other peoples. In content, however, it is permeated with the motifs and moods of the Bible and the Talmud, regardless of the fact that literally thousands of years separated the modern period from distant antiquity. This religious-ethical influence is especially strong in the mass of spiritual folklore, strongly didactic, which is represented in stories, legends, tales, superstitions, daily mores, proverbs, sayings, jokes, and anecdotes. The bulk of the songs, however, are mainly lyrical and retain only fragmentary survivals of traditional customs, rituals, beliefs, or superstitions.

Aside from the spoken word, the outstanding folk expression was the song. The combination of swaying and singsong was familiar from the cradle on, in the cheder, the Yeshiva, the synagogue, the home. The man of the *shtetl* (small town) habitually swayed and crooned when he studied or thought, even if he were pondering a business problem. "Swaying as one reads and chanting the words in a fixed melody . . . are considered necessary for successful study."[8]

In addition to the ritual music for the melodic chanting of prayers, the individual religious melodies of the Chasidic rabbis, or the home songs at the family table during the Sabbath meals and festivals and holidays,[9] there were countless secular songs current among the people. But so permeated was every phase of life of the Jew in the Pale with the religious patterns evolved through the centuries, that many cradle songs, children's songs, marriage and holiday songs, retained surviving remnants of religious rituals, customs, beliefs, superstitions. Thus, in addition to purely secular Yiddish folk songs, there were also Yiddish folk songs which dealt with religious or biblical themes, superstitions, and ceremonial practices, most of them constantly stressing the central purpose and main pursuit in the life of the Jew : to study the Torah, observe the laws within it, guard the Sabbath, and serve the one and only God.

With the invention of printing, when sung poetry began more and more to be read, some of the old historical and pious songs did not cease entirely to exist. Though current since the fourteenth and fifteenth centuries, they could still be heard during the seventeenth and even the eighteenth centuries, almost up to the threshold of our times. The *T'chines* (special prayers for women in Yiddish), for example, recall these old pious songs. Many cradle songs have as their central theme Jewish piety and scholarship — a theme which assumed a practical approach towards life, recognizing the benefits of prestige and economic security guaranteed by a position of knowledge and piety in the Jewish community, as well as the promise of spiritual asylum in paradise in the afterlife. Small wonder that the working mother was willing to sacrifice herself for her male children and her husband to enable them and herself to achieve that desired position, for once her men were successful, then she automatically became the beneficiary of their good life, also.

In addition to the dangers from divine wrath for those who strayed from the ways indicated by the Lord's teachings, there was also the constant menace from the demons, ghosts, and spirits swarming between heaven and earth. Fear and awe of the supernatural filled the life of the young child and were part of its upbringing, as this element was carried over in tales from pagan myths and biblical legends. In the following lullaby, a mother rocking her restless baby is concerned about the "evil eye," one of the most widespread fears, of which some of the symptoms were pallor, fever, emaciation, excessive yawning. The whispered charm was considered the most effective remedy for injuries caused by an evil eye and several generations ago, in every Jewish community in Eastern Europe, there was one man or woman or several who knew how to "whisper off an evil eye." [10]

Vos iz dos fara shteyger,	What kind of behavior is this,
Es iz shoyn tsvelf azeyger,	It is already midnight,
Un du shlofst noch nit ayn!	And you are not yet asleep!
Es iz kayn ander s'vore,	There can be no other reason,
Az du host an ayn-hore,	But that you have the "evil-eye,"
Shlof-zhe ayn mayn kind!	Sleep then, my child!
Ven es volt nit zayn shpet,	If it were not so late,
Volt ich arop fun bet	I would get off the bed
Un volt an ayn-orele opshprechn,	And whisper the evil eye away,
Arop fun dayn guf,	Away from your body,
Biz di vayber zaynen noch nit uf,	Until the women awake,
Vos hostu azoy dos kepele farvorfn? [11]	Why is your head so limp?

To protect her child from the evil spirits, a mother would call on the good angels to guard over her slumbering baby: *Der malech vet dich tsudekn mit zayn fligele / Biz morgn klor-vaysn tog.* ("The angel will cover you with his wing till the morrow's bright clear morning.") [12] Crooning to her infant the mother thus expressed the thoughts and beliefs of her time:

In shlofn geyt di neshome aroyf,	In sleep, our soul goes up to heaven,
Un shraybt di aveyres in bicher.	And enters our sins in books.
Un du mayn kind, host noch kayn zind,	But you, my child, have not yet sinned,
Kenst shlofn ru-ig un zicher. [13]	You can sleep peacefully and secure.

Whereas piety and Torah learning were considered the pillar of strength in the struggle with the evil spirits roaming the earth, the Torah was not merely a code of laws. It was also a code of ethics and a handbook of daily behavior.

"Every detail—social, religious, economic, moral—is examined and discussed, and a definite rule is set for it, with exceptions, limitations, and implications fully defined. . . . A large part of this monumental literature is devoted to human relations, . . . situations involving honesty, love, the ties between man and wife, parent and child, conduct at table or at public assemblies." [14] The example below again describes the advantages of spiritual nourishment as the bulwark against all temptations:

Gey mayn kind in cheder :	Go, my child, to cheder,
Lern Toyre k'seyder	Study the Torah always.
Fun ivre biz tsu g'more,	From reading to the Gemara,
Dos vet dich hitn fun beyz un tsore !	This will shield you from all evil.
Loyf mayn kind, tsum rebn,	Run, my child, to the *rebe,*
Er vet dayn neshomele shpayz gebn,	He will nourish your soul.
Loyf tsu im, un lern	Run to him, and study,
Un vi got zolstu im hern.	And listen to him as you would to God.
Gots mitsves zenen vi honig zis,	The Lord's deeds are as sweet as honey,
Zayn toyre shitst undz, vi vaser fish,	His Torah protects us, as water does the fish;
In ir rechte hant—lebn oyf der velt	In its right hand—life in the world,
In der linker—kovid un gelt.	In its left—honor and security.
Gey, mayn kind, lern,	Go, my child and study,
Lern mit groys cheyshek,	Study with great desire;
Dos iz oyf der velt	That is, in this world,
Der bester eysek.[15]	The best of professions.

Mitsves (good deeds) derived not alone from serving the Lord and fulfilling his laws. They also extended to the responsibilities of man to man and pictured the many rewards to be reaped both in this life and the life to come. A popular legend tells that when a man dies and his soul enters heaven, it is met by his good deeds and his bad deeds, and, according to the amount of each, the soul remains either in heaven or is sent to hell. An interesting folk ballad, twenty-eight stanzas long, based on this legend, carries the humanitarian message still further, decrying the evil of avariciousness and the cruelty often suffered by the poor at the hands of the rich. In the ballad, a rich brother casts off his poor brother and when death calls to them, each faces it in a different way. The poor brother weeps at having to part from his wife and child; the rich brother wails at having to leave his gold and silver behind. At the place of judgment, when asked to account for themselves, the poor brother humbly denies his good deeds on earth, while the rich brother attempts to enter the gates of paradise by concealing the evil that had filled his life. But — the good and true triumph in the end, as the excerpts below testify:

Poor Brother:

Aveyres un g'zeyles hob ich ye geton,	Sinning and thieving I did do,
Mitsves un tsidkes hob ich nit geton!	Good and holy deeds I did not do!

Angels:

Reb moyshe, reb moyshe,	Moses, Moses,
Ir zogt doch alts farkert!	You speak to us in riddles!
Aveyres un g'zeyles hot ir nit geton,	Sinning and stealing you did not do,
Mitsves un tsidkes hot ir ye geton.	Good and holy deeds you did do.

Derfar kumt aych tsu zitsn oybn on,	Therefore you shall sit on high,
In gold un in zilber ongeton;	Dressed in gold and silver,
Goldene sforim oyf dem tish	Golden books upon the table,
Un a goldenem benkele unter di fis.	And a golden footstool at your feet.

*   *   *   *   *   *

Rich Brother:

Aveyres un g'zeyles hob ich nit geton,	Sinning and thieving I did not do,
Mitsves un tsidkes hob ich ye geton.	Good and holy deeds I did do.

Angels:

Reb shloyme, reb shloyme,	Solomon, Solomon,
Du zogst doch alts farkert!	You speak to us in riddles!
Aveyres un g'zeyles hostu ye geton,	Sinning and stealing you did do,
Mitsves un tsidkes hostu nit geton!	Good and holy deeds you did not do!

Derfar kumt dir tsu zitsn untern hon,	Therefore you shall sit under the cock,
In pech un in shvebl ongeton;	Dressed in pitch and brimstone;
Fun fayerdike riter iz dayn tish,	Your table will be of fiery rods,
A fayerdikn benkl unter dayne fis.[16]	And a burning footstool at your feet!

It has been assumed that religious song flourished only during periods of great religious fervor. In the case of the Jewish people, however, religious fervor was constantly fostered and stimulated throughout the centuries by its religious leaders, scholars, mentors, prophets, not only during times of stress but also as a daily preoccupation and as a continuous source of inspiration. A religiosity surrounded the daily secular duties, and this carried over into the mores and ethical beliefs.

Though, in the main, Yiddish folk song is secular, the religious-ethical motif is to be found in many songs.

Sabbath Songs

Yiddish folk song is a song of the "week" and does not as a rule figure prominently during the holy Sabbath. Yet, there are a number of Yiddish Sabbath songs which describe the sweet spirituality of the holy day, its peacefulness, the good things to eat, the clean clothes one wears, and the beautiful songs one sings on that day. A nineteenth-century song in couplets contains the following lines:

Shabes licht un shabes lompn,	Sabbath candles and Sabbath lamps,
O, vi zis iz ayer shayn.	Oh, how sweet is your glow.
Refrain: Shabes, o shabes, o heyliger shabes!	Sabbath, O Sabbath, O holy Sabbath!
Vifil brengt ir treyst dem yidn	You bring much comfort to the Jew
In zayn elnt in zayn payn. . . .	In his loneliness and his anguish. . . .
Kumt tsu undz der shabes-koydesh,	When the holy Sabbath comes to us,
Vi es vern licht gebentsht. . . .	The candle lights are blessed. . . .
Bald antloyft di more-sh'choyre,	All the sadness soon disappears,
Un men vert a nayer mentsh. . . .[17]	And one becomes newly born. . . .

An eighteenth-century song, "to be sung Friday evening," is didactic in tone and instructs the Jews to follow a mode of behavior on the Sabbath to induce rest and peace, security and joy.

Der heylign shabes veln mir antfangen mit freydn;	We will greet the holy Sabbath with joy;
Im onton zayn g'vir veln mir nit fer-maydn.	Nor shall we fail to render it its due respect.
Gut esn, gut trinken, vos got tut beshern	Eat well, drink well, as God has decreed,
Kayn tsar, kayn roygez tsu vayzn un lozn hern,	No sorrow, no quarrel to be seen or heard,
Chuts Toyre lernen den libn got tsu ern.[18]	Except the study of the Torah, to honor our dear Lord.

An interesting, seventeenth-century Sabbath song, which the author calls "a beautiful song . . . to be sung with fresh, gay voice, to honor the holy queen, Sabbath, known to all," likens the "queen" to a bird, plagued and troubled, driven from pillar to post and exiled for six days, until she comes to rest on the seventh. The song then proceeds to instruct its readers and singers to light the Sabbath candles "not too early and not too late, but when the sun goes down," to place the twisted loaves and all good things to eat on the table, to light up the lamp brightly and sing praises to the Sabbath queen. Then, "all the demons will flee before her into the deepest pit, gnashing their teeth; for during the Sabbath, no sorrow will be found, only peace and joy will reign supreme." The song goes on to describe additional rituals: "you go to the synagogue and two angels will accompany you and guard you from all evil. And when you return, you will bless the wine and sit down to table and everyone, to right and left of you, will know the joy of peace and good food and drink." Like many a pious song of those difficult times, this song reminds the good Lord of his promise made to the Jews through their prophets, that he would hasten to bring the day closer when they will be liberated from their exile.[19]

Thus these songs combined the secular and the pious, on the one hand instructing the Jew in his behavior and rituals for the Sabbath and, on the other, urging him to enjoy to the full the peace and comfort that it afforded. In one song, visions of heaven with the angels joyously observing the Sabbath are intertwined with the warning that on the Sabbath "no money or fire" may be handled:

Boruch eloheynu, undzer guter fraynt!	Blessed be our Lord, our good friend!
Shabes-koydesh iz doch bay undz haynt.	Today is our holy Sabbath.
Shabes hot doch a ponim fun yener velt,	Sabbath looks like the other world,
Shabes tor men nit haltn fayer un gelt.	On the Sabbath, we must not hold fire or money.
Shabes in himl is fayer fil,	On the Sabbath, the heavens are full of fire,
Hobn di malochim zeyer shpil:	And the angels have their festivity:
Tantsn un shpringen un loybn got,	Dancing and jumping and praising God,

Vos er hot bashafn undzer gebot.[20]	For having created our Commandments.

The Chasidic sects sang passionately about the Sabbath. In old Safed, in Palestine, even as late as the eighteenth century they would greet the Sabbath as a queen, come to dwell in their midst, walking out into the fields amid the mountains, dressed in white, to watch the sunset over Mt. Meron and to sense in the caressing, sweet-smelling breezes the coming of the Sabbath queen. During the nineteenth century, they sang and shouted :

Oy gevald ! shabes !	Oh help ! Sabbath !
Shabes, shabes, shabes !	Sabbath, Sabbath, Sabbath !
Shabes vil mich nemen,	Sabbath wants me,
Ich vil nemen shabes !	I want Sabbath !
Volt ich gehat koyech,	If I had the strength,
Volt ich gelofn in ale gasn,	I would run through the streets,
Un geshrign : shabes !	Shouting : Sabbath !
Oy gevald ! shabes ! [21]	Oh help ! Sabbath !

The need to create a protective shell around themselves in the midst of the surrounding hostile atmosphere created by the Czarist government endowed Jewish religiosity with a quality of passion and absorption. On the Sabbath, the Jew felt himself to be the king and his "bride" — the Sabbath — the queen. In order to achieve this difference, even the lowliest was prepared to toil and borrow, so that on that one day a week, he could at least *feel* like a king. *A gantse voch, horevet men doch, oyf Shabes darf men layen* ("all week long, one toils, and for the Sabbath one must borrow"), one song tells us, and this was accepted as a normal procedure. Whether the average Jew in the Pale ate three meals a day during the week or not did not matter; on the Sabbath, it was his duty to eat thrice, so that his body as well as his soul could be nourished. And when that was achieved, he really felt like a king !

O bruder zog, vi heyst der tog	Oh, brother, tell me the name of the day
Vos mir ale zenen freylech?	When we are all happy?
Der yidele der kleyner, der kosherer, der sheyner,	The dear little, pious, decent Jew
Iz doch dan a meylech.	Is then a king.
Shabes aleyn, kumt tsugeyn,	Sabbath herself comes,
Zayt-zhe freylech ale !	Be gay, everyone !

Tanst kinder, yederer bazunder,   Dance, children, each and everyone,
L'kovid der heyliger kale! [22]   Honoring the holy bride!

A number of Yiddish Sabbath folk songs deal with the food which was so heartily consumed and so carefully prepared for the Sabbath. The following example describes different dishes eaten during the three meals on the Sabbath.

L'kovid shabes, l'kovid shabes,   In honor of the Sabbath,
Fraytig, fraytig tsunacht,   Friday evening
Esn mir ale fish!   We all eat fish!
Un a tsimesl fun pasternak,   And a parsnip stew,
Un a tsimesl fun merelech,   And a carrot compote,
Un a kishkele?   And a stuffed derma?
Un a kishkele oychet!   And a stuffed derma too!

Refrain: Kishkele heystu,   Your name is stuffed derma
           In oyvn shteystu,   You stand in the oven,
           In moyl tsegeystu,   You melt in my mouth,
           L'kovid shabes! [23]   In honor of the Sabbath!

The above song lists the other dishes eaten on the Sabbath morn: "sweet and sour stew, and a bean mush and chickpea mush, and a pudding, too!" and on Sabbath evening: "cold fish and a noodle pudding and a fruit pastry, too!" The third meal on the Sabbath was more solemn and included prayers which pleaded for a happy, secure week to come. For some Chasidim it was a time of gay singing and abandoned drinking:

L'chayim rebe, hot a gute voch,   To health, *rebe,* have a good week,
Shrayt yederer bazunder: och, och! Everyone shouts: hey, hey!
Kayn mashke nit gezhalevet, lomir   Let's not stint on whiskey, let's drink
   trinken noch!   more!
Mir hobn oysgebetn a gute voch! [24] For our prayers will assure a good
                                       week!

For others, it included the plaintive chants of the head of the house, as he anticipated the coming week and its problems with apprehension and concern. This time of the day, when the Sabbath "queen" departed, is always pictured in gentle hues of twilight, when mother or grandmother sat near the window, catching the last rays of the setting sun, softly intoning the prayers specially written for women, which called upon the angels to protect the family from sorrow and woe. Such a scene, interwoven with song, is contained in the following description:

". . . Grandmother would sit in the big kitchen which was full of the evening shadows of the departing Sabbath, intoning her *T'chines* and prayers. She would say, not only Hebrew prayers, but also Yiddish ones, putting into her 'God of Abraham' a lot of heart and feeling. I still remember her evening melody: 'God of Abraham and Isaac and Jacob, protect your people of Israel from evil' . . . Then . . . she would sing a song in rhyme about Elijah the Prophet who was to bring the news about the coming of the Messiah. I still remember some of the lines:

Oyf a barg vayt ergets, vayter,	On a hill far away and farther,
Shteyt tsvishn himl un erd a leyter,	There stands a ladder between heaven and earth,
Eliyohu der Tishbi shteyt oyf der leyter,	Elijah the Prophet stands on the ladder,
Un zogt on folk Yisroel a b'sure mit a tromeyter.	Trumpeting and calling to the people of Israel.
Eliyohu hagilodi, tromeyter noch,	Elijah the Gileadite, continue your trumpeting,
Moshiach ben dovid zol kumen di voch." [25]	So that the Messiah, Son of David, may come this week.

Current much earlier, religious songs in praise of the Lord, often containing references to sin and death, were widespread among the Jews during the seventeenth and eighteenth centuries. At that time, even on the holy Sabbath, the Jews could not easily shut out the difficult life which they were compelled to lead.

Barimhertsiger got, tu dayne shtarke hent oys-shtrekn,	Compassionate God, stretch out, your strong hands,
Tsu aynzamlen di do zaynen fershpreyt in ale ekn,	Gather together all those scattered far and wide,
Mit dayn genod undz nit shtekn,	Do not deprive us of your mercy,
Tu a z'chus oves dervekn.[26]	Rouse your sympathy for the sake of our forefathers.

So, too, during the nineteenth century, this compassionate plea to God is heard in the prayers intoned and chanted by the women of the Jewish households, many of whom were the breadwinners of their families, as they pleaded with God to make life a little easier for them. The following

Zuni Maud

Elijah the Prophet

lengthy excerpt from a prayer song, like a previous example, calls upon the gentle prophet Elijah, to bring good tidings, but this time the tidings relate to the everyday needs of the family.

Liber got, es zol undz geyn voyl,	Dear God, may it go well with us,
Mir zoln hobn undzer zalts un broyt,	That we may have our bread and salt,
Mir zoln chas v'sholem nit visn fun kayn hunger un fun kayn noyt,	That we may not, heaven forbid, know of hunger and want,
Mir zoln hobn undzer lechem l'chol un beged lilbosh,	That we may have our bread to eat and our garment to wear,
Omen, omen, v'omen.	Amen, amen, and amen.
Kumt eliyohu hanovi in undzer shtub arayn,	Elijah the prophet comes into our house,
Tut er undz onzogn ale gute b'sures un m'vaser zayn :	And tells us good news, and brings good tidings :
Ale krume zoln glaych vern,	All the lame shall walk straight again,

Ale orime zoln raych vern,	All the poor shall become rich,
Ale kranke zoln geheylt vern,	All the sick shall be healed,
Ale nakete zoln gekleydt vern,	All the naked shall be clothed,
Ale shvere un bitere hertser,	All the heavy, bitter hearts
Zoln liber got, derfreyt vern.[27]	Shall be uplifted, dear God.

Messiah Songs

Of all the prophets, Elijah seems to have been the most popular to appear in Jewish folklore. In the tales and legends, he usually takes the various forms of a merchant, peasant, coachman, wanderer, or beggar, whose holy mission is to strengthen the pious, aid the needy, give warning of some impending disaster threatening the Jewish community. On occasion, he even helps a dying Jew to outwit the Angel of Death.

In folk song, the prophet Elijah appears as an intermediary for the Jews, pleading their case with the Lord to return them once and for all to the security and sanctuary of their ancient homeland. In most of the songs, he is identified with the Messiah, Son of David, and often foretells the time of the coming of the Messiah, as in this children's song:

Shnirele, perele, gilderne fon,	Little ribbon, little pearl, golden banner,
Moshiach ben dovid zitst oybn-on,	Messiah, son of David, sits on high,
In gold un zilber ongeton.	Dressed in silver and in gold.
Halt er a becher in der rechter hant,	He holds a goblet in his right hand,
Macht er a broche iber gor dem land.	Making the blessing over all the land.
Omen v'omen, dos iz vor:	Amen and Amen, that is true:
Moshiach vet kumen hayntign yor,	The Messiah is coming this very year.
Vet er kumen tsu raytn,	Should he come on horseback,
Veln mir hobn gute tsaytn;	Then we will have good times;
Vet er kumen tsu forn,	Should he come in a coach,
Veln mir hobn gute yorn;	Then we will have good years;
Vet er kumen tsugeyn,	Should he come on foot,
Veln ale maysim oyfshteyn.[28]	Then all the dead will rise up.

Among the Chasidim, vivid descriptions of feasting and celebrating "when the Messiah will come" is described in a number of songs. One such cumulative example, in question and answer style, contains a series of queries which are all answered in the final stanza, as follows:

. . . Got aleyn mit zayn kovid vet dort zayn,	The Lord himself, in his glory, will be there,

In gan-eydn veln mir zitsn,
Arn hakohen vet undz bentshn,
Moyshe rabeynu vet undz toyre
zogn,
Miriam han'viyo vet tantsn,
Dovid hameylech vet undz shpiln,
Shloyme hameylech vet undz zingen,
Yayin hamshomer veln mir trinken,
Shor habor mitn levyosn veln mir
esn,
Oyf der sude, oy! [29]

We will sit in the Garden of Eden,
Aaron the priest will bless us,
Moses our teacher will read the
Torah for us,
Miriam the prophetess will dance,
David the king will play for us,
Solomon the king will sing for us,
We will drink the hallowed wine,
We will eat the legendary ox and the
Leviathan
At the feast, oh!

A humorous version endows the coming of the Messiah with local color, bringing the current situation into play:

Un az moshiach vet kumen,
Vet undz alemen vern besser,
Un vayn un bronfn,
Veln mir zupn fun di fesser.

And when the Messiah will come,
It will be easier for all of us,
And wine and whiskey
We will guzzle from the barrels.

Un ver vet dos alts tsuzen?
Dos heylige folk yisroel.
Un take ich oych:
Ot, ot, ot, ot, ot, ot, getsele michoel.
Un mir veln noch ale shrayen:
Riboyno shel oylom, hura! [30]

And who will witness all of this?
The holy people of Israel.
And I too:
I, I, I, I, I, I, Getsele Michoel.
And we will all shout then:
Creator of the Universe: hurrah!

Among the Yiddish Messiah songs, there are several that reflect the struggle between the Chasidim and Maskilim. Though the following employs the Chasidic style, it pokes fun at the Chasidim, who, according to the Maskilim, practiced outlandish rituals and thought only of food and drink, "when the Messiah comes."

Vos vet zayn fun dem rebn dem
frumen,
Az der melech hamoshiach vet
kumen?
Der rebe vet zayn, oy, a b'chor
Un vet geyn vi a nozir mit di lange
hor . . .

What will happen to the pious
rebe,
When the Messiah, the king, will
come?
The *rebe* will be, oh, the eldest
And wear his hair long, like a
recluse.

Oyf ale boymelech veln vaksn
chalelech mit bulkes,
Oyf ale tsvaygelech veln vaksn
tsibilikes mit lulkes,

Rolls and buns will grow on all the
trees,
Long-stemmed pipes will grow upon
all the branches,

Oyf ale bletelech veln vaksn titun,	Tobacco will grow upon all the leaves,
Un mir di ch'sidimlech veln roychern derfun. . . .	And we, Chasidim, will smoke it.
. . . Dos klayzl vet nit zayn fun leym oder tsigl,	Our prayer hut will not be of clay or brick,
Nor fun tsimes mit lokshnkugel . . .	But of stew and noodle pudding.
Fun bronfn vet zayn a kval,	There will be a whiskey fountain,
Baym rebn in mitn zal.	Right in the middle of the *rebe*'s dining room.
Un nevuchadnetser vet kumen fun bovl kayn yerusholayim,	And Nebuchadnezzar will come from Babylonia to Jerusalem,
Un vet gebn dem rebn lechayim, lechayim ! [31]	And drink with the *rebe,* to health, to health !

Songs about Death

The coming of the Messiah occupied the thinking of scholars and sages through the centuries, creating the belief that when the Messiah came, then all the dead would rise from the earth. This promise of the good life after death colored many rituals surrounding the death and burial practices and occupied a prominent place in the general folk lore of the Jews. In the songs, however, the theme of death rarely occurred as a subject of rituals but appeared rather in its human association — when tragedy orphaned children at the death of a parent, when a widow was left alone in the bloom of her life, when a jilted woman wept over the death of her illegitimate baby, or when a lover committed suicide over an unfulfilled love.

However, occasionally a song does philosophize on the transitoriness of life and its brief span, commenting on the sorrowful aspects of old age, as in the following excerpted example :

Vi der mentsh vert geboyrn,	When man is born,
Iz er zeyer kleyn,	He is very small.
Vi er kumt in di mitele yorn,	In middle age,
Iz er zeyer sheyn,	He is very handsome,
Un vi er kumt in di eltere yorn,	And when old age comes,
Ruft men im aheym.	He is called home.

Vi der mentsh vert geboyrn,	When man is born,
Iz er zeyer royt,	He is very red.
Vi er kumt in di mitele yorn,	In middle age,
Zucht er dos shtikl broyt,	He seeks his daily bread,
Un vi er kumt in di eltere yorn,	And when old age comes,
Kumt af im der toyt.[32]	Death overtakes him.

Another refers fragmentarily to the custom of hiring a band of musicians to play during the final moments of a dying man, who apparently regrets that he had foolishly wasted his years.

Klezmorimlech mayne libinke,	Dear little bandsmen,
Klezmorimlech mayne zisinke!	Sweet little bandsmen,
Shpilt mir abisinke koydem hamise!	Play for me before I die!
Oy, az ich volt afn sof getracht,	Ah, had I thought about my end,
Volt ich mayn velt azoy narish nit farbracht! [33]	I would not have spent my life so foolishly!

An unusual song is the following, which uses numbers up to twelve to list rituals attending the death, burial, and mourning of a person.

Eyns—dos iz di shverenes fun bitern toyt.	1—is the bitter pain of death.
Tsvey—klep in shul, di g'zeyre iz far ful.	2—knocks in the synagogue, the penalty is paid in full.
Dray—bitere tropn bay mentshn tsukopn.	3—bitter drops at a man's head.
Fir—vochn noch a mentshn shloyshim.	4—weeks after death, the memorial of the thirty days.
Finf—kloger, vos baklogn a mentshn.	5—weepers, weeping over a dead man.
Zeks—breter, tut'n a mentshn leygn.	6—boards, to lay the man on.
Zibn—teg shive tut'n noch a mentshn zitsn.	7—days sitting in mourning after the dead man.
Acht—erley kleyder, tut'n a mentshn onton.	8—kinds of garments to clothe the corpse.
Nayn—T'pochim tut'n a keyver grobn.	9—handbreadths deep to dig the grave.
Tsen—mentshn hobn a shure geton leynen.	10—men each read a line from the Psalms.
Elf—chadoshim tut'n kadish zogn.	11—months to say the prayer for the dead.
Tsvelf—chadoshim arum tut men yortsayt hobn.[34]	12—months later, to observe the memorial for the dead.

The above example embodies a number of rites observed upon the death of a person: the uncoffined burial in the garments in which the person died, plus the shroud; the laying out of the corpse, following the washing and purification by members of the Burial Brotherhood (*Chevre Kedishe*); the boards lining the grave; the seven days of mourning in the house of the deceased; the reading of portions of the Psalms and other passages from the Bible during the services held in the house of the deceased; the eleven months in which the prayer for the dead is chanted (*kadish*); and the memorial observed when the year is up and mourning officially ceases.

In the following excerpted lines in which a dying man reflects on his past life, certain other ceremonials are mentioned: placing the corpse with his feet towards the door, hiring bandsmen to play the dirges of the dead until "the feet have cooled," giving charity in the dead man's name, readying the burial clothes, and intoning the prayers for the dead.

. . . Haynt leygt men mich mit di fis tsum tir.	Today I am laid out with my feet to the door,
. . . Chevre kedishe, ton shpiln zolt ir mir koydem hamise.	Brothers of the Burial Society, play the dirges of the dead for me
. . . Bizvanen mayne fis veln ton opkiln.	Until my feet have cooled.
. . . Ts'doke zolt ir ton gebn. . . . Kadish zolt ir noch mir ton zogn.	You shall give charity and say the prayer of the dead for me
. . . Tachrichim zolt ir mir ton gebn.[35]	And clothe me in my burial clothes.

The Bible and Its Heroes

An interesting group of Yiddish folk songs are those which deal with Biblical themes and heroes. Endowed with delightful folk charm and simplicity, they are vivid and at times also humorous. Following is an example which describes the dramatic pilgrimage of the Lord, from one nation to another, offering his monotheistic religion to them. However, he is rejected by them all, until the prophet Elijah suggests the Jews to him and the "match" is forthwith consummated with the Jewish people's wedding to the Torah!

Ich vel aych dertseyln a mayse,	I will tell you a story,
Di mayse iz zeyer freylech.	The story is a very happy one.
Di mayse heybt zich on	The story begins
Mit a yidishn meylech.	With a Jewish king.

Der yidisher meylech hot gehat a bas
  y'chide,
Dos meynt men undzere toyre,
Kol alofim shono, ale toyznt yor,
Iz der meylech geforn mit ir a
  shidech ton.

Iz er gekumen tsu der ume goyim,
Hobn zey im ge-enfert vi di rishoyim.
Iz er geganen tsu der ume pritsim,
Hobn zey im ge-enfert falshe teritsim.

Af di falshe teritsim
Hot der boyre ongeheybn tsu
  zidn;
Iz gekumen eliyohu hanovi,
Hot di toyre narayet di idn.

Di toyre iz di idn zeyer gefeln,
In dray teg arum di chup tsu
  shteln.[36]

The Jewish king had an only
  daughter,
This is—our Torah,
And for thousands of years
The king traveled about with her to
  find her a mate.

He came to the nations of other faith,
And they replied to him like villains.
He came to the Lords of other faith,
And they gave him false reasons.

At their false reasons
The Creator began to boil with
  wrath:
When Elijah the prophet came
And recommended the Torah to the
  Jews.
The Jews liked the Torah very much,
And arranged for the wedding in
  three days.

In another song of this type, the motif is even more vividly secularized. In it, the Lord is the "father" and the people of Israel is the "daughter." The "father" suggests a number of suitors to his marriageable "daughter": Adam, the first man; Noah; the patriarchs Abraham, Isaac, and Jacob; the kings David and Solomon; Aaron and Moses, etc. The "daughter" rejects each suitor because each has sinned in one way or another: Noah bears the sin of too much wine; Abraham had one wife who was his concubine; Isaac bears the sin of Esau; Jacob, the sin of having wedded two sisters; David bears the sin of Bathsheba; Solomon, the sin of a thousand wives; Aaron sinned with the golden calf, etc. Below is the portion wherein Adam is rejected:

Tochter du mayn, libste du fayn,
Odom horishon geyt in der velt
  arayn.
Er geyt, er geyt, er geyt,

Far a libn chosn-man, gey-zhe nem
  im on!

—Neyn foter, neyn, es ken dos gornit
  zayn

My daughter, beloved and fine,
Adam the first man is coming into
  the world.
He is coming, he is coming, he is
  coming,
For a beloved husband, receive thou
  him!

—No father, no, it cannot be at all

Az odom horishon zol mayn man zayn.

That Adam the first man shall be my husband.

Tsi vet er mir kenen m'farnes zayn?
—To zog-zhe mir farvos?
Der chet fun eyts-hadas vet doch bay im zayn!
Darum vil ich zitsn bay dir afn shoys,
Vi a tochter ba ir foter, biz ich'l vern groys!

Shall he then be able to support me?
—Tell me then, why not?
Because the sin of the Tree of Wisdom will be within him!
That is why I shall sit on your lap,
Like a daughter to her father, until I am full-grown!

However, Moses is finally accepted, for he is the one who brought the Ten Commandments, the tablets down from Mt. Zion:

Ye, foter, ye, dos ken graylich zayn,
Az Moyshe rabeynu zol mayn man zayn.
Er vet zitsn fertsig teg afn himl,
Vet er mir kenen m'farnes zayn.[37]

Yes, father, yes, that can surely be,
That Moses our teacher shall my husband be.
He will sit forty days in heaven,
And he will be able to support me.

The story of Adam and Eve occurs in several old Yiddish folk songs. In the following, the scene in the Garden of Eden is idyllically presented, until Eve bites into the apple, which, in this song, is placed in her hand by Adam himself!

Got hot bashafn himl un erd,
Odem iz geven der ershter oyf der erd.

The Lord created heaven and earth,
Adam was the first upon this earth.

Odem, odem, pashet di shof,
Oy, falt im tsu a ziser shlof.

Adam, Adam, watching the sheep,
Oh, he fell into a sweet sleep.

Chapt er zich oyf un chave iz do,
Kukt er oyf ir in der gebentshter sho.

When he awoke, Eve was there,
He gazed at her in the blessed hour.

Er nemt zi on bay der rechter hant,
Un firt zi ibern gantsn land.

He took her by the right hand,
And led her all through the land.

Er firt zi arayn in vayngortn arayn,
Shprotst ir an epl in der hant.

He led her into the vineyard,
And planted an apple in her hand.

Nemt zi dem epl un git im a bis,
Kukt zi zich arum vi zindig zi iz.

She took the apple and bit into it,
And realized how sinful she was.

The song proceeds to call Adam and Eve before the highest court to account for their crime:

Ruft men chave'n in mishpet arayn, . . .	Eve is called to be judged, . . .
Oy chave, chave, vos hostu getracht,	Oh, Eve, Eve, what was in your mind,
Vos hostu a velt mit mentshn umgebracht?	Why did you destroy the world of mankind?

The song concludes with the verdict that Eve was to be banished from the Garden of Eden and would forever afterwards be condemned to a childbirth fraught with hardship and pain. As for the snake, it was convicted to "crawl on its belly, seek food in the wilderness and eat flies and worms forever." [38]

Mixed-Language Songs

A curious group are the mixed-language songs which utilize Russian, Ukrainian, and Polish dialects mixed with Yiddish and Hebrew phrases. Occasionally they deal with Bible themes, endowing the patriarchs, matriarchs, kings, and sages with secular simplicity, as they extol the monotheistic Jewish religion. In the following, the base is Russian, with an occasional Yiddish and Hebrew word:

Abramlyenko nash, abramshenko nash,	Our dear little Abraham,
Prodiadka ti nash,	Our dear little father,
Prosh ti boga sa nas,	Plead for us with the Lord,
Abi nas vekupil	So that he may
Oys dem golus viprovadzil,	Take us out of exile,
L'artsenu zaprovadzil,	And bring us to our land,
L'artsenu nash. [39]	To our own land.

Another uses the Hebrew base, with occasional Russian words, to describe the exile to Babylonia:

Al naharos Bovel,	On the rivers of Babylon,
Shom yoshavnu gam bochinu,	We sat there and wept,
B'zichroynu es tsion, da!	Remembering Zion, yes!
Mnogo iz nas pogybili,	Many of us were killed,
V'golus bovel nas! zagnyali! [40]	And driven into exile in Babylonia!

In the following example which mixes Ukrainian and a few Hebrew words, the joy of Hannah is described when she gives birth to her son Samuel, destined to become a prophet of the Lord.

Uvstavala chana rano,	Hannah awoke early,
Ey i ranenko izbudila svoyi slugi, ey i dobrenenki :	And early awakened her good little servants, saying :
"Uvstavayte, mo-i slugi dobrenenki;	"Get up, my good little servants,
Zazhigayte svetshetshonki, ey yerusalimki.	And light the fire and the candelabra,
A ya tim tshasom, chana,	While I, Hannah, in the meantime,
Pochazhu, da i sina talmid chacham a oy urozhu."	Will tend to my son, the wise scholar."
I uradilsya shmuel hanovi dobrim tshasom,	And Samuel the prophet was born at the proper hour,
Spo-ivala yevo chana sholkim pasom.	And Hannah sang a song of praise for him,
Sore, rivke, rochl, leye, babkami buvali,	Sarah, Rebecca, Rachel, Leah, were the midwives there,
Avrom, yitschok, yankev, ovinu sand'ka buvali;	Abraham, Isaac, Jacob, our patriarchs officiated at the circumcision,
Moyshe, aron, dovid i shloyme kvateri buvali.	Moses, Aaron, David, and Solomon carried the baby to the ceremonial.
Hakodesh borchu i malochim shmuel hanovi nazvali.[41]	The Lord, Blessed be He and the angels called Samuel, the Prophet.

Occasionally the sorrows and tribulations of the Jews break through in a fragmentary example of this type of song in which Hebrew, Yiddish, and Russian are intermingled and a Biblical promise made to Jacob by the Lord is recalled.

Omar adonoy l'yankev, oy tatenyu	And the Lord spoke to Jacob, oh, Father dear,
Host doch mir tsugezogt : al tiro avdi yankev,	You promised me : fear not, my servant Jacob,
Oy vey tatenyu.	Oh, woe is me, Father dear.
Farvos-zhe shlogt men undz, tatenyu?	Why then are they beating us, Father dear?
Farvos-zhe plogt men undz, tatenyu?	Why then are they torturing us, Father dear?
Ven vet zayn a sof, oy ven? [42]	When, oh when will there be an end to all this?

The stress on faith in the one God, the pursuit of knowledge of his teachings, and the observance of the many rites, ceremonials, and customs which developed through the ages, appear in a number of Yiddish folk songs. Such songs reflect the influence and vernacular of Talmudic students and adults constantly preoccupied with Talmudic learning, whose entire life centered around this way of life. The following chant describes the day-to-day rituals in the life of a religious Jew the whole year round.

Refrain: Ver mir zenen, zenen mir	Whoever we are, we are,
Ober yidn zenen mir.	But we are Jews.
Vos mir tu-en, tu-en mir,	Whatever we do, we do,
Ober davnen, davnen mir.	But we pray.
... Ober zmires zingen mir.	We sing songs.
... Ober hoyshanes zogn mir.	We say the prayers during the Feast of Tabernacles.
... Ober chanuke-licht bentshn mir.	We bless the Chanukah candles.
... Ober yom-kiper fastn mir.	We fast on the Day of Atonement.
... Ober lernen, lernen mir.	We study.
... Ober matse esn mir.	We eat matzos.
... Ober nedoves gibn mir.	We give charity.
... Ober in suke zitsn mir.	We sit in the booth during the Feast of Tabernacles.
... Ober shabes ru-en mir.[43]	We rest on the Sabbath.

Other variants of the above chant list additional customs observed by the orthodox Jews: to know the liturgy, cleanse oneself of one's sins, wear phylacteries, don the prayer shawl, kiss its fringes, bless the Sabbath wine. Some of these songs warn the careless ones of the punishment awaiting them in the afterlife: How will you face the final judgment day? What good are you in this world if you don't pray? Others describe the glorious descent of Moses from the mount, bearing the gleaming tablets with the Ten Commandments, expressing their joy in their faith. Still others descend to the secular delights of the delicious dishes which are served during the Sabbath and holidays, some of which have become an integral part of the actual religious observances themselves: milk dishes (*blintses*) during the Feast of Tabernacles, noodles and noodle pudding, chicken soup, and compote during the Sabbath, pastries (*homntashn*) during the *Purim* festival, pancakes during the Chanukah holiday, matzos and nuts during Passover, etc.

Leaning on the Lord served two ends. It was a source of hope within the difficult situation on the one hand, while, on the other, it acted as a crutch for those who sought the easiest solution to the prevailing problems. Many a Talmudic student and scholar, even after marriage and with a family, sat in the house of study, poring over the Holy Writ, demanding little from life in a materialistic way, not concerned with the requirements of his household. While his wife busied herself with providing the family with the meager sustenance of life, he was mainly concerned to gain for himself and his household the proper recognition given to a family of a Talmudic scholar in the community and a warm reception in heaven, when the time came.

Farvos zoln mir zorgn	Why should we worry
Vos vet zayn mit undz morgn?	What the morrow may bring?
Lomir besser farechtn.	Let us rather mend
Vos mir hobn gezindigt nechtn.	Our sins committed yesterday.
Nisht zorgn un nisht tun a krechts.	Let us not worry or complain.
Nor got dinen, veln mir nisht visn	But serve the Lord and then no evil
fun shlechts.[44]	will come to us.

To the desperate pleas of their poor wives, who worked their fingers to the bone to make both ends meet, these perennial Talmudic students replied calmly that the Lord would take care of everything.

Vu nemt men karge mel af tsi bakn broyt?	Where shall I get flour to bake bread?
Ver vet borgn, ver vet layen,	Who will borrow, who will loan,
Ver vet knetn, ver vet bakn?	Who will knead, who will bake?
Es iz nito kayn gelt!	There is no money!
—Ay, me vet borgn, me vet layen,	—Oh, someone will borrow, and someone will lend,
Me vet knetn, me vet bakn,	Some one will knead and someone will bake,
Es iz do a got, vos vet gebn gelt,	There is a God above, who will give money,
Un groypn oych! [45]	And flour too!

The sympathies of these heads of families were rarely with their harassed wives, who bore the daily burdens not only of the secular world during the weekdays but also had to guard the many religious duties that attended the care and education of their children, as described in the following:

Ich loyf in bes-medresh,	I run to the house of study,
Ich leyen oys di sedres.	Read my prayers.
Ich shrayb oys kameyes,	I prepare amulets,
Ich grayzl oys di peyes.	And curl the earlocks.
In mark darf men loyfn,	I must run to the marketplace,
Holts darf men koyfn,	And buy some wood,
Broyt darf ich bakn,	And bake some bread,
Holts darf ich hakn,	And chop the wood,
Di kinder darf ich nyantshen,	And nurse the children,
Eyne leygn shlofn,	I must put one to bed,
Di andere aroysfirn,	Lead another to the privy,
Di drite bashmirn,	Apply salve to a third,
Dos iz noch nit gor,	And that's not all,
A kind ale yor! [46]	I have a child every year!

There were times, however, when life for these professional students of the Torah weighed heavily on them, and the sacrifices of their womenfolk were not enough to provide them even with their minimal daily needs. The Torah may have been as sweet as honey, but the true reality was often bitter as gall.

There were some who treated the tribulations of the secular world lightly, as the young married student, turned tutor, in the following.

Bin ich mir a melamedl,	I am a little tutor,
Knel ich oyfn dorf a zman,	I teach a season in the village,
Nem ich dortn melamdis gelt,	I get paid my tutor's fee
An achtl kartofl fun dem pan.	In ("an eighth" of) potatoes from the Polish landowner.
Lern ich dortn ivri,	I teach them to read there,
Mit di poyershe kep,	Those peasant heads,
Un ich rays di meydelech	And pull the little girls'
Far di groyse tsep.	Long braids.
Kontshe ich biz peysech,	I finish in time for Passover,
Dem groysn zman,	The big season is over,
For ich tsu mayn vayb aheym	And I return home to my wife
Mit a pustn karman.	With an empty pocketbook.
Doch iz zi a malke,	Still, she is a queen,
Un ich bin a keyser,	And I am a king,
Un mir dertseyln nisim,	And we tell each other about the miracles
Vos tut got der groyser. [47]	Which our great God performs.

There were others, however, the unmarried *orim bochurim* ("poor fellows"), studying in the Talmudic academies often far from home, who had to depend upon the chance charitable handouts from the well-to-do members of the Jewish community, eating *kest,* a meal here and there, simply to survive. A song which reflects some of these hardships is the following :

Zibn-acht vochn tu ich in eyn hemd geyn,	I wear a shirt seven–eight weeks,
Bizvanen ich vash zi oys aleyn.	Until I have to wash it myself.
Chotsh di toyre iz zeyer gut,	Although the Torah is very good,
Nor zi tsapt aroys di bisele blut.	It drains you of your last drop of blood.
Taychn trern tu-en fun mir gisn,	Rivers of tears flow from me,
Bizvanen ich tu dem shiyur visn.	Until I memorize the lesson.
Leyg ich mir shlofn oyfn hoyln bank,	I lay me down to sleep on the bare bench,
Shtey ich mir oyf toyt un krank.	And get up deathly sick.
Muter un foter hobn gehodevet mich oyf puter,	My parents fed me with butter,
Un yetst darf ich zayn ayn patron a guter.	And now I must be a meek boarder.
Tsigaretkes un papiroskes zenen zeyer geshmak,	Cigarettes and smokes are very delicious,
Az der rebe derzet, git er in bak.[48]	But when the teacher catches you, he smacks you on the cheek.

The last two lines of the above reveal the first warning notes of the penetration of ideas and habits of the non-believers (Maskilim) among the orthodox Jewish youth. These followers of the Emancipation movement, carriers of Western European cultural, political, and social ideas and movements, were finding ardent adherents among Eastern European Jews and reaching into religious homes, schools, Talmudic academies, and making themselves felt in the Czarist Pale before the mid-nineteenth century. The following criticizes the "loose" behaviour of young Jewish government workers (excise-tax collectors) :

Un aktsizne yunge layt	The young excise fellows
Zenen farshayt.	Are very wild.
Goln di berdelech,	They shave their beards,

Un raytn oyf ferdelech,	And ride on horses.
Geyen in galoshn,	They wear rubbers,
Un esn ungevashn.[49]	And eat without washing.

The "creeping" influences from the West towards secularization and the violent opposition towards them from the Jewish orthodoxy was dramatically expressed in the Lilienthal incident. In 1841, the efforts of the Russian Minister of Education, Uvarov, to establish a network of secular schools in the Pale, where Jewish children would be taught the Russian language, secular sciences, Hebrew, and "religion according to the Holy Writ," met with dismal failure. Although he "imported" Dr. Max Lilienthal from Riga to help in this project, the reaction on the part of religious Jews was extremely hostile. Coming from a government which under military edict was hunting Jewish children down in the streets at that time, impressing them into the army as soldiers and deporting them to distant provinces, it was impossible for Lilienthal to enlist any mass sympathy from his project. The slander against him in the streets and the demonstrations of the cheder boys, obviously organized by their teachers (*melamdim*), who feared that the new schools would render them jobless, rang out with: *shkoles nye zhelayim!* ("we don't want schools!") The following song reflects this violent reaction to the Uvarov project, accusing all those who supported it, among whom were many leading Maskilim, as evil — men who shave their beards, women who do not wear the *sheytl,* are not strict with their dietary laws, are lax in their observation of traditional customs, and even break with fundamental Jewish beliefs. Following each of the ten lines given below, the mocking refrain of: *Shrayt men, shrayt men, liliental, / liliental iz der bester fal!* ("They shout, they shout, Lilienthal, Lilienthal is the best thing!") was chanted.

A klog tsu di yorn, az apikorsim zenen yidishe manhigim gevorn,	Woe to the years, when non-believers have become Jewish leaders,
Berdelech gegolte, tsurkes gemolte,	Shaved chins, painted faces,
Gekleydet vi goyim, machn yidishe kinder far resho-im.	Dressed like non-Jews, they turn children into wicked people.
Davnen nit a vort, in ale klubn iz zeyer ort.	They don't pray, and they hang out in every club.
Hultayes, yungatses, peysech on matses.	Do-nothings, bums, who don't eat matzos during the Passover.
Vayber mit eygene hor, oyf kurtse yor.	Women who wear their own hair, shortening their lives.

Zingen treyfe lider, es tsugeyt zey in ale glider.	They sing forbidden songs and enjoy them immensely.
Chazer un tarfes tu-en zey esn, on got hobn zey fargesn.	They eat pork and non-kosher food and have forgotten our Lord.
Trefnyakes, ochley n'veyles, machn bay yidn shkoles.	Carcass eaters, non-believers are building schools for Jews.
Leydakes, hultayes, vern di talmidim fun di shkoles.[50]	Do-nothings, bums, become students in these schools.

Already by the 1860's the impact of these ideas and practices played havoc with the medieval patterns of life which prevailed in the Jewish Pale, and contemporary writers of those days spoke of the dramatic changes that were corrupting the youth.

And indeed many young people walked the streets "brazenly" arm-in-arm with girls (an unknown and forbidden practice among the orthodox Jews), donned short jackets instead of the long *kaftans,* smoked on the Sabbath, incurring the approval of the devil himself, read secular literature in Yiddish and Hebrew and also in Russian and German, following a path that in the judgment of the religious Jews was leading straight to hell. As for the solemn thought of what such sinners might have to face in the afterlife, this did not even occupy the minds of the young offenders.

And yet, though the strange wonderful world of secular knowledge—science, literature, social ideas, habits of dress, and new ways of life—beckoned and even embraced ever larger numbers of Jewish youth in Eastern Europe, it was the rare occasion when any member of the Jewish community sought to break with his Jewish faith. When such an occurrence did take place, the wrath of the orthodox was expressed in a custom that declared the turncoat dead and proceeded with the seven days of mourning! The helplessness and anguish of the parents—village dwellers—whose daughter has embraced Christianity is expressed in the following lines of a song:

Sorele mayn vayb,	Sarah my wife,
A klog tsu undzere yorn!	Woe unto our years,
Shpan ayn dem ferd	Harness the horse
Un nomir ingichn arayn forn.	And let us ride quickly.
Feygele undzer tochter,	Feygele, dear daughter,
Kum tsu undz aheym,	Come home to us,
Mir veln dir gebn	We will give you
Vos du vilst aleyn.	Anything you desire.

Yankele der gabe	Jacob the elder
Hot ongeton dem zaydenem chalat,	Donned his silken coat,
Feygele undzer tochter	Feygele, our daughter,
Hot zich opgeshmadt.	Left our faith.
Refrain: Oy vey, a yomer,	Oh, oh, what weeping
Oy vey, a klog !	And what wailing !
Ich hob ongevorn feygelen	I've lost my Feygele
Biz hayntign tog ! [51]	Forever and forever !

During the first half of the nineteenth century, the Haskalah movement touched only members of the intelligentsia and the merchant class, while the majority of the Jews in the Pale remained solidly behind the religious leaders, who fought passionately against every encroachment upon their domain of influence. The rapid strides towards assimilation on the part of some followers of the Haskalah, however, stirred the orthodox to deep concern and even wrath, regarding as they did the slightest step "away from the fold" as leading straight to paganism and the devil. This brought a type of song into currency that taunted the "non-believers," who, the religious Jews maintained, were serving only clay idols that could not respond to anyone's prayers. The following taunt is such an example:

Zog mir, getshinke, vos-zhe machstu?	Tell me, little idol, how are you?
Zog mir, getshinke, vos-zhe trachstu?	Tell me, little idol, what are you thinking?
Az och un vey iz tsu zey !	Woe is to them !
A leymenem got hobn zey !	They have a clay god !
Du host a moyechl un kenst nit klern,	You have a little brain but cannot think,
Du host oyerlech un kenst nit hern.	You have little ears but cannot hear,
Az och un vey iz tsu zey !	Woe is to them !
A toybn got hobn zey !	They have a deaf god !
Du host eygelech un kenst nit kukn,	You have little eyes and cannot see,
Du host kni-elech un kenst zich nit bukn.	You have little knees and cannot kneel.
Az och un vey iz tsu zey !	Woe is to them !
A blindn got hobn zey. [52]	They have a blind god !

And so, despite the persistent rhythm of centuries of life, customs, rites, rituals, superstitions that had prevailed in the Eastern European

Jewish communities, the second half of the nineteenth century saw the inexorable coming of a new impulse and new currents. These did not transplant the old ways immediately but gradually infiltrated the Jewish Pale, taking their place side by side with the old and even the ancient, outmoded, and outdated ways of life.[53] The central core of Jewish faith : respect for scholarship, piety, honesty, charity (the Talmud lists seven types of charity), the ethical content of Jewish Holy Writ remained, to be poured into newer, more modern vessels, to feed and inspire anew the generations that followed. The passionate plea *Helf undz tate heyliger Oy vey tate, foter hartsiger* ("Help us holy Father, Oh, Father, dear Father"), was about to be joined with the passionate search for social justice in the world of ideas and translated into actions to improve this life on earth. "God helps those who help themselves," became the trend of men seeking in the real world around them the answers to their problems and the practical realization of their dreams.

Notes

CUSTOMS AND BELIEFS

1. The *customs* deal with the fixed dates of feasts and social institutions, birth and death, marriage and occupations, even games. The *beliefs* relate to the conceptions of a given people about the origin and structure of the world, inanimate things, the vegetable and animal kingdoms, human, half-human, superhuman beings, the corporal remains and the spiritual manifestations of the dead, etc. The *folk literature* embraces the folk tales and legends, myths and epics, riddles and proverbs, songs and ballads.

2. The consensus of opinion of the majority of students of folklore is that *folklore is the study of the mental equipment of the simple folk,* as distinguished from technical skills (popular artifacts such as buildings, furnishings, clothing and utensils, implements, ornaments, etc.), the latter of which are studied by its sister science, ethnology.

3. Botkin, Intro. xxi.

4. Idelsohn, p. 360.

5. Rappoport, p. 3.

6. Ausubel, Intro. xix. Shtif maintains that the chant to which the Scriptures were taught to cheder boys in the sixteenth century may be the same as the cantillation used today for the prayers approaching the Day of Atonement. *See* p. 80.

7. Ansky, p. 22.

8. Z. and H., p. 324, p. 92. Different parts of the tanach are set to different, fixed melodies.

9. Already in the fourteenth century, the prayers had set musical patterns. Certain main motifs served several prayers, while others were for special prayers only. (*See* Güdemann—Shtif, p. 71.)

"And when the child crossed the threshold of the cheder, it began to study . . . and always with a tune : the A B C . . . with a tune : the prayers . . . with a tune; the commentaries and reviews of the Scriptures . . . with a tune; the *akdomes* (Pentecost hymn), the Book of Ruth, the Song of Songs (*Shir hashirim*) with its magical melody; the Story of Esther, the Passover story, even the Book of Lamentations . . . with its heartrending tune! Everything—with a tune! (Gelbart, p. 117).

10. Schauss, p. 89.

11. D. and Y., p. 42, No. 9. Haskalah men of letters decried the widespread superstitions among the people. David Apotheker, 1855–1911, in a poem in his *Hanevel,* "Czernowitz," 1881, which was sung along with others he had written, contained a stanza of a lullaby which said : "Your nurse probably teaches you to be afraid of your own shadow. She tells you that there are devils in the basement and demons in the attic and scares you to death" (p. 39).

12. *Ibid.,* p. 50, No. 22.

13. Kisselgof, p 12, No. 22.

14. Z. and H., p. 112.

15. Kisselgof, p. 12, No. 21.

16. Cahan, 1957, No. 495. Note the angry tone when the angel is addressing the rich brother with the formal *ir* ("thou") and the kindly voice he assumes when addressing the poor brother with the informal *du* ("you").

17. Rubin, 1950, pp. 142–143.

18. Bassin, I, p. 66, Kirch-han, Song No. 1.

19. *Ibid.*, pp. 45–47.

20. G. and M., No. 31.

21. Cahan, 1957, No. 496.

22. Kisselgof, No. 56.

23. Cahan, 1957, No. 516.

24. Rubin, MSS.

25. Singer, pp. 130–131.

26. Kirch-han, Song No. 3.

27. Idelsohn, IX, No. 735.

28. Bassin, I, p. 101.

29. *Ibid.*, p. 103.

30. Idelsohn, IX, No. 216.

31. Idelsohn, X, Intro. xix, No. 235–I.

32. B. and F., pp. 424–425.

33. *Ibid.* pp. 436–437.

34. G. and M., No. 358.

35. *Ibid.*, No. 350.

36. *Ibid.*, No. 2.

37. *Ibid.*, No. 5.

38. Rubin, MSS.

39. Kipnis, p. 131. Living among different Slavic communities in Eastern Europe, Jews often incorporated into their speech and song Russian, Ukrainian, Polish, and terms of Slavic dialects. Some Yiddish-Hebrew folk songs, in which a Hebrew phrase or line was followed by its Yiddish equivalent, often added the Slavic equivalent. Such mixed-language songs are to be found among the children's songs, soldier songs, drinking and dance songs, humorous songs, songs of Biblical themes and Chasidic songs.

40. Idelsohn, IX, No. 508.

41. Ansky, p. 52.

42. Kaufmann, pp. 6–7.

43. Kisselgof, 9, No. 14.

44. G. and M., No. 20.

45. *Ibid.*, No. 21.

46. *Ibid.*, No. 278.

47. *Ibid.*, No. 316.

48. *Ibid.*, No. 315.

49. Wengeroff, II, p. 133.

50. *Zichron Yankev*, p. 80.

51. G. and M., No. 355.

52. Cahan, 1957, No. 528.

53. "In their many wanderings, the Jews have borrowed customs and ideas from other people, and have added them to the traditions of their race. . . . Most of the customs and rites . . . are so old that it is well-nigh impossible to trace them to their origin. . . . By far the greater mass of their traditions and ancient practices still clings to burial-ceremonies and mourning for the dead" (Yoffie, p. 413).

CHAPTER VI

Merriment

DESPITE THE BITTER LIFE IN THE PALE, A MASS OF HUMOROUS ANECDOTES, jokes, witticisms, jests, taunts, riddles, and teasers abounded, representing a rich source of oral literature in which the Jews in the Eastern European areas "laughed through their tears." Humor became the protective shield worn by the Jews, who in time of sorrow and stress, clutched at the straw of lightheartedness. In time, this portion of oral literature grew to become an important source of not only the humor but also the caustic commentaries of the folk on the prevailing practices that stemmed from the evils of bureaucratic institutions, ignorance, avarice, hypocrisy.

The capacity to laugh in moments of stress or to create imaginatively and humorously at work or in moments of relaxation is well revealed in the many humorous anecdotes of the Eastern European Jews. Yiddish folk song, however, also contains a number of songs which reflect this ability to entertain oneself merrily on the one hand and, on the other, to point a finger of mockery at those personages in the Pale who were often responsible for some of the ills and problems. Although many of the songs satirize the smug rich or the wonder-working Chasidic "saints" (*tsadikim*) and their gullible followers, the butt of most of the songs is the all-consuming poverty which hung like a pall over the vast majority of the many millions of Jews in Czarist Russia. In an attempt to "sing away one's troubles," or "whistle in the dark," many a somber text was set to a gay tune, thus endowing many of the songs with a sardonic flavor. The well-known potato song, "Bulbes," the popular rent song, "Dire-gelt," the ditties about tailors, cobblers, tinsmiths, and other personages in the Pale lilt tunefully on the brink of starvation, as they dwell humorously on the bitter aspects of the life, work, and community problems of the people who sang them. This wonderful capacity to poke fun at oneself is reflected in the following little song of an incompetent tailor.

159

Bin ich mir a shnayderl,	I am a little tailor,
A nodl ken ich nit haltn in hant.	But can't hold a needle in my hand.
Shtel ich mir aroys a viveske :	So I hang out my shingle :
Az ich pres gevant!	That I press cloth!
Fregt vos ken ich? — Tidlidldam!	If you ask what I know — tidlidldam!
Az ich pres, farbren ich! —	When I press, I burn the cloth —
Tidlidldam!	tidlidldam!
Hot nit kayn faribl, hot nit kayn	But don't you worry, don't you
faribl—	worry —
Tidlidl-idlidl-dam-pam-pam! [1]	Tidlidl-idlidl-dam-pam-pam!

At the beginning of the nineteenth century when industry was still not developed, there were only small artisan or semiartisan shops and a mass of tailors, cobblers, watchmakers, capmakers, barbers, professional match-makers, and other such craftsmen. Restricted in their choice of occupa-tions, barred from the villages and agricultural pursuits, the mass of dislocated poor, along with the many traders in all manner of wares and merchandise, were crowded into the small towns and cities, with the majority of the people living from day to day, from hand to mouth. Poverty was the "hero" of many a song and ballad, such as the following, in which the singer cumulatively satirizes his sad experiences with a long coat of "ancient stuff" which was literally falling to pieces. The singer attempts to make of the cloth, first a coat and then in turn a jacket, a vest, a pocket, a tie, and finally a button. But the old, worn-out material simply cannot survive any of these transformations, until the poor tailor is left with nothing but his song! Below are the first and last stanzas of this merry song :

Hob ich mir a mantl fun fartsaytign	I have a coat of ancient stuff,
shtof, tralalalalalala, la, la, la.	trala, etc.
Hot er nit in sich kayn eyntsign	It hasn't a whole stitch in it.
shtoch, tra, etc.	
Darum hob ich zich batracht,	Therefore, I made up my mind
Fun dem mantl a rekl gemacht,	To make a jacket out of the coat.
Tralalalalalala, tralalalalalala,	Trala, etc.
Fun dem mantl a rekl gemacht.	To make a jacket out of the coat.
Hob ich mir a gornisht fun	I have nothing left of ancient stuff,
fartsaytign shtof, trala, etc.	trala, etc.
Hot es in zich kayn eyntsign shtoch,	It hasn't a whole stitch in it,
trala, etc.	trala, etc.
Darum, hob ich zich batracht,	Therefore, I made up my mind,

Fun dem gornisht a lidele gemacht!	To make a little song out of the nothing!
Trala, etc.	
Fun dem gornisht a lidele gemacht.[2]	To make a little song out of the nothing!

A nonsense song which employs the lucky number "seven" describes the fancy loot that a thief ran off with, after having broken into the house of a poor *rebe* in the town.

Refrain: Bay mayn rebn iz gevezn,	In my *rebe*'s house there was,
Iz gevezn bay mayn rebn,	There was in my *rebe*'s house,
Bay mayn rebn iz gevezn :	In my *rebe*'s house there was :
A geneyve!	A robbery!

| Zibn hemder vi di becher, | Seven shirts like goblets, |
| Dray mit lates fir mit lecher! | Three with patches, four with holes! |

| Zibn laychter vi di shtern, | Seven candlesticks like stars, |
| Dray on fis un fir on rern! | Three without legs and four without sockets! |

| Zibn hener vi di tsigl, | Seven cocks like bricks, |
| Dray on kep un fir on fligl! | Three without heads and four without wings! |

| Zibn meydn vi di sosnes, | Seven maids like pine trees, |
| Dray on tseyn on fir on yosles.[3] | Three without teeth and four without gums! |

The deep chasm that existed between the solitary rich and the mass of the poor resulted in a host of anecdotes and tales on motifs which dealt with the life of the fortunate wealthy. Men sat round the potbellied stove in the synagogue or house of study, spinning yarns and weaving tales about that wonderful world which was so unattainable to them.

A song which naïvely attempts to fathom the very peak of affluence enjoyed by the mighty Czar describes how the Czar drinks tea, eats potatoes, and sleeps at night. In it, the poverty-stricken, imaginative singer endows these simple tasks with all the grandeur and majesty that he is able to muster. Partly recitative, following the question-and-answer pattern (with the group posing the questions to the elders and these "wisely" responding), the replies to the three queries are as follows :

Me nemt a hitele tsuker,	They take a cone of sugar,
Me macht in dem a lechele,	And make a hole in it,
Me gist arayn heys vasser,	And they pour hot water into it,

Un me misht, un me misht.	And they stir and stir.
Oy, ot azoy, ot azoy,	Oh, that is how, that is how,
Ot azoy trinkt der keyser tey. ·	That is how the Czar drinks tea.
Me shtelt avek a vant mit puter,	They put up a wall of butter,
Un a soldatl mit a harmatl	And a soldier with a gun
Shist durch di puter mit a heyser bulbe	Shoots hot potatoes through the butter
Un treft dem keyser glaych in moyl arayn.	Straight into the Czar's mouth.
Oy, ot azoy, ot azoy,	Oh, that is how, that is how,
Ot azoy est der keyser bulbes.	That is how the Czar eats potatoes.
Me shit on a fuln cheder mit federn	They fill a room full of feathers
Un me shlaydert arayn ahintsu dem keyser,	And toss the Czar into it,
Un rotes soldatn shteyen un shrayen :	And regiments of soldiers stand shouting :
Sha! sha! sha!	Hush! Hush! Hush!
Oy, ot azoy, ot azoy,	Oh, that is how, that is how,
Ot azoy shloft der keyser baynacht.[4]	That is how the Czar sleeps at night.

Utilizing a prevailing slander that cantors were a bit on the simple side and were Jacks-of-all-trades and masters of none, one song describes the meeting of a cantor with an acquaintance, who doesn't seem to recognize him. "Do you remember me?" asks the cantor. "You seem familiar, but I can't quite place you," answers the other. "You must be a honey maker, or a rope twirler, or perhaps—a thief?" The cantor is beside himself. "Good heavens!" he exclaims, "I am certainly none of these! And what's more, my father and my grandfather were none of these! I can see that you don't know who I am!" The "joker" finally stops tormenting the naïve cantor and says : *Oy, oy, oy, / Ich hob zich shoyn dermont / Ich hob aych derkont. / Ir zayt mistame a yid a chazn!* ("Oh, oh, oh, I remember now, and I know who you are. You are probably a cantor"). To which the cantor coyly replies : *A bisele yo, / un a bisele neyn. / Ich ze, az ir veyst shoyn, ver ich bin* ("A bit yes and a bit no, but I see now that you know who I am").[5]

The butt of many humorous and satirical songs were certain corrupt elders of the town council (*kahal*) and their unproductive hangers-on. The higher up their position, the sharper the barb leveled at them; the lower the job holder, the kinder the comedy. One such good-humored song pokes fun at the melamed, the poor parochial teacher entrusted with the first grades of the cheder and the youngest male children in the community. Although the melamed in this song is exposed as an ignorant man in a backward community, the basic motif is the abysmal poverty, helplessness, and pathos of the pious and the poor. The song is cast in the words of the melamed himself, as he proudly boasts of his three "prize" students: "One already knows his ABCs, . . . the other beats his mother, . . . and the third is getting married." Following are the concluding stanzas, which deal with the third student's approaching marriage and apprise us of the bride's pedigree and the terms of the marriage contract:

Un veyst ir, vemen er nemt?	And do you know whom he is marrying?
Er nemt, er nemt, er nemt.	Whom, whom he's marrying.
Un veyst ir vemen er nemt?	And do you know whom he is marrying?
Un bald vel ich aych zogn. . . .	And soon I will tell you. . . .
—Dem beder's techterl.	—The bathhouse keeper's daughter.
Un veyst ir vifil nadn er nemt?	And do you know how much dowry he's getting?
Er nemt, er nemt, er nemt.	How much, how much dowry he's getting.
Un veyst ir vifil nadn er nemt?	And do you know how much dowry he's getting?
Un bald vel ich aych zogn. . . .	And soon I will tell you. . . .
—Fuftsig kerblech, fuftsig kerblech.	—Fifty rubles, fifty rubles.
Fuftsig—zogt men, fertsig— meynt men,	Fifty—is promised, forty— is intended,
Draysig—tseylt men, tvantsig— git men,	Thirty—is counted out, twenty— is given,
Tsen kerblech iz nito!	Ten rubles there are none!
Tsen kerblech iz nito! [6]	Ten rubles there are none!

A conversation song, which treats the struggle between the young and old generations on the choice of a mate in marriage, is "Meyerke, mayn zun," ("Meyerke, My Son"), which was current in a number of variants. In each, the conversation takes place between father and son, with the son striving subtly to apprise the father that he already settled on the girl he's going to marry, without the benefit of his parent's advice. As the nineteenth century progressed, professional matches played a lesser role in the life of the young generations. In the following variant, in this case,

"Nochemke," the son has not only selected his own mate without the knowledge or blessing of his father but has gone off and gotten married secretly and is already himself the father of a son:

Refrain:

Nochemke mayn zun, Nochemke mayn zun,
Vos biztu azoy fartracht, Nochemke mayn zun?
—Ch'ob lib a sheyn meydele, tatenyu.

Un ver-zhe iz dos meydele, zunenyu?
—S'iz a fayn meydele tatenyu.

Un vifil git zi nadn, zunenyu?

—Kayn nadn git zi nit, tatenyu.

Es gefelt mir nit der shidech, zunenyu!
—Me fregt ba dir kayn deyes nit, tatenyu.

Ich vel nit kumen af dayn chasene zunenyu!
—Vest kumen tsum bris, tatenyu.

Ven-zhe iz di chasene, zunenyu?

—Ich vel shikn noch dir dos eynikl, tatenyu.[7]

Nochemke, my son, Nochemke, my son,
Why are you so thoughtful, Nochemke, my son?
—I love a pretty maiden, father dear.

And who is this maiden, dear son?
—She's a fine girl, father dear.

And how much dowry is she giving, dear son?
—None at all, father dear.

I don't like this match, dear son!
—Nobody's asking your advice, father.

I won't come to the wedding, dear son!
—You'll come to the circumcision, father dear.

When then is the wedding taking place, dear son?
—I'll send your grandson to tell you, father dear.

The humorous song treated the personal and collective burdens in the Pale with a light touch, toning down the tragic implications, pointing up instead the comic aspects. It stimulated laughter and merriment, dispelled the gloom, stirred the imagination, and lightened the heavy heart. Even in the matter of unhappy marriages, the singer of the humorous song chose to emphasize the comedy in the situation, rather than the tragedy, as in the following, which describes the marital difficulties between a couple. She is a terrible housekeeper and an awful cook; he beats her, and she runs home to father. He finally prevails upon his neighbors to bring her back; whereupon she returns, and the merry-go-round starts all over again:

Fun montig in der fri biz fraytig farnacht,	From Monday morning till Friday eve,
Mayn vayb tshipe-trayne hot dem kugl gemacht.	My wife Tshipe-trayne made the pudding.
Refrain: Hot a yid a vaybele, Hot a vayb a yidele . . .	Oh, this Jew had a little wife, This wife had a dear little Jew.
Vi es iz gekumen shabes tsum esn,	And when the Sabbath table was set,
Hot zi dem kugl in oyvn fargesn.	She forgot to take the pudding out of the oven.
Hot er genumen dem grobn shtekn	So he took his thick stick
Un hot ongehoybn dos vaybl tsu dekn.	And began to beat his wife.
Hot zi genumen di alte shkrabes	So she grabbed her old rags
Un iz antlofn tsum tatn af shabes.	And ran home to her father for the Sabbath.
Hot er genumen di sh'cheynim spekulirn,	So he urged his neighbors to do what they could,
Me zol zayn vaybl brengen tsu firn.	To bring his wife back to him again.
Hot men shoyn dos vaybl gebracht,	So they brought her back to him again,
Fun montig inderfri biz fraytig farnacht.[8]	From Monday morning to Friday eve.

A considerable number of humorous and satirical songs were leveled at the Chasidic *rebeyim* ("rabbis") and their followers. These songs scoffed at the ignorance and superstition of the *tsadikim* ("saints," *gute yidn*), who believed in miracles and feared secular knowledge, and poked fun at the happy-go-lucky Chasidim who spent so much of their time singing, dancing, journeying to and from their revered holy men, and contenting themselves with the crumbs from the festive boards of their saints. Although the following illustrates the capacity of the Chasid to sing and dance in the face of dire poverty, the tone of bitterness is unmistakable.

Avremele, a chosidl, a lustige bri-e,	Abraham, a little Chasid, a happy creature,
Un on a z'chi-e.	But without a bit of luck.
Refrain: Un fun oybn dem rimak, Veln mir tantsn hop-tshik-tshak!	And over all, the leather belt, We will dance the hop-tshik-tshak!

Hoyle lecher iz mayn kapote,	My long coat is full of holes,
Un ayngeshmirt in gole blote.	And spattered with mud from top to bottom.
Sorele mayn vayb, a broch oyf dir,	Sorele, my dear wife, woe unto you,
Ich hob a firer nisht bay mir.	I haven't four kopeks to my name.
Eyder ich fardin mir a shtikl broyt	Before I earn a crust of bread,
Kumt es mir on glaych mitn toyt.[9]	I have to work until I'm almost dead.

The large number of anti-Chasidic songs of merriment attest to the prolonged and bitter struggle which went on between the Chasidim and their opponents—the Misnagdim and the Maskilim. The following ridicules the fright of a Chasid, when, journeying to his revered *tsadik,* he sees a steam engine for the first time.

Ver hot dos gezen	Who has ever seen
Un ver hot dos gehert,	Or heard such a thing,
Az fayer mit vasser	That fire and water
Zoln firn vi a ferd?	Should pull like a horse?
Refrain: Oy hot er a fayfer,	Oh, it has a whistle
Mit an ayzernem koyech,	With the strength of iron,
Fun untn gist zich vasser,	Water pours from below
Fun oybn shpart a royech.	And smoke belches from the top.
Heyse koyln	Hot coals
Iz bay im a maychl,	Are its delight,
Kalte vasser	Cold water
Iz bay im a yaychl.	Is its broth.
G'vald reboynoy-shel-oylom,	Help, Creator of the world,
Nem bay im op di yorn,	Cut its life short,
Er zol nit kenen fayfn,	Stop its whistling
Un zol nit kenen forn.[10]	And its running.

Many songs poked fun at the *rebe*'s miracles: "He went into the water and came out—wet; he walked into the mud and soiled his coat, . . . he told a mute—not to speak; he ordered a blind man—not to look; he instructed a lame man—not to walk!"[11]

Another ditty, which reveals the *rebetsin*'s (*rebe*'s wife) uneasiness at the arrival of a rowdy bunch of Chasidim given to mischievous pranks, at the same time defends their merriment and their reputation:

Efnt rebetsin, ch'sidim geyen,

Ch'sidim geyen, viln zich freyen.

—Ch'sidim geyen in pantofl,

Zey veln doch tsuganvenen di
zilberne lefl.

—Rebetsin, rebetsin, hot kayn moyre,
Ch'sidim geyen lernen toyre.[12]

Open the door, *rebetsin,* Chasidim
are coming,
Chasidim are coming to be merry.

—Chasidim are coming in their
slippers,
They will steal my silver spoons.

Rebetsin, rebetsin, have no fear,
Chasidim are coming to study the
Torah.

Jolly songs were created in the artisan's workshop, where, as the hands
worked busily, the mind engaged in flights of fancy, and the voices rang
out in merry song. In this environment, the butt of ridicule was naturally
the master workman or his wife, who acted as overseer of the apprentices
and workhands. Set to the rhythm of the tasks performed (stitching,
hammering, pressing, the turning of a primitive machine), the songs were
robust, hearty and gay, and the laughter they induced was deep and full.
A number of these songs created in the workshop were cumulative in
structure, indicating the group effort that went into their composition.

A cumulative song popular among artisans was the one about ten
brothers who traded in different wares, and one by one each met his
end at the hands of the capricious accidental rhyme. Starting with the
number ten and working backwards, a variant of this song proceeds in
this way: "Ten brothers traded in wine, and then there were nine. Nine
handled freight, and then there were eight. Eight sold turnips, and
then there were seven. Seven dealt with baked goods, and that left six.
Six sold hosiery, and then there were five. Five traded in beer, and then
there were four. Four sold lead, leaving three; three dealt with tea, leaving
two, and two sold bones, leaving one."

Eyn guter bruder bin ich mir geven,
Hob ich mir gehandlt mit tron.
Iz fun mir gevorn—a groyser hon.
Refrain: Shmerl mit dem fidl,
    Yekl mit dem bas,
    Shpilt mir oyf a lidl
    Oyfn mitn gas.
    Oy, oy, oy. . . .[13]

One good brother was I,
I traded with blubber.
So I became—a big rooster.
    Shmerl with his fiddle,
    Yekl with his bass,
    Play that little tune for me
    Right here on the street.
    Oh, oh, oh. . . .

Popular too was a cumulative humorous song that lists a number of objects, which, according to the singer, are necessary to "land a man through his stomach." The song begins in this way:

Gevald, vu nemt men, vu nemt men, vu nemt men	Help, where shall I find, where shall I find
A lokshnbret af katshen di varnitshkes?	A pastry board to roll my *varnitshkes?*
Oy, a lokshnbret af katshen di varnitshkes?	Oh, a pastry board to roll my *varnitshkes?*
On heyvn un on shmalts, un on fefer un on zalts,	Without yeast or shortening, without pepper or salt,
Oy, a lokshnbret tsu katshen di varnitshkes?	Oh, a pastry board to roll the *varnitshkes?*

But the poor girl in this song seems to lack not only yeast, shortening, pepper and salt, but also the pastry board, the knife, the pot, as well as the man, who was to eat the triangular-shaped pasties.

Gevald, vu nemt men, vu nemt men, vu nemt men	Help, where shall I find, where shall I find
A bocher af tsu esn di varnitshkes?	A fellow to eat my *varnitshkes?*
On heyvn un on shmalts, un on fefer un on zalts,	Without yeast or shortening, without pepper or salt,
Oy, a bocher af tsu esn di varnitshkes? [14]	Oh, a fellow to eat my *varnitshkes!*

Another cumulative song playfully combines the use of the alphabet with the listing of a rich man's ten daughters, their mates, and the gifts which the young men brought the maidens they were courting. Adapted from the Ukrainian, the song speaks in the name of the professional matchmaker, who begins his tale in this way:

Amol iz geven a groyser gvir,	Once upon a time there was a very rich man,
Hot er gehat gelt on a shir.	And he had a great deal of money.
Hot er gehat tsen techter,	He had ten daughters,
Zenen zey geven af laytishn gelechter.	And they were the laughing stock of the town.
Di ershte eyde, di tsveyte beyle,	The first was called Ida; the second, Bella;
Di drite golde, di ferte dvoyre,	The third, Golde; the fourth, Deborah;

Di finfte hene, di zekste vichne,	The fifth, Hene; the sixth, Vichne;
Di zibete zelde, di achte chane,	The seventh, Zelda; the eighth, Hannah;
Di naynte toybe, di tsente yidashne.	The ninth, Toba; the tenth, Yidashne.
Hot er mich far a shadchn gemacht,	So he appointed me the matchmaker,
Hob ich im di shiduchim in shtub arayngebracht,	And I brought the prospects to his house,
Zey veln mir danken kolzman zey veln lebn	As long as they live they will be grateful to me
Far di shiduchim vos ich vel zey gebn.	For the matches that I will arrange for them.

The matchmaker then lists the prospective sons-in-law and the gifts each brought to the bride, following the same alphabetical sequence: Ida got chickpeas, Bella—beans, Golde—oats, Deborah—fish, Hene—herrings, Vichne—currants, Zelda—buns, Hannah—horseradish roots, Toba —doves, and Yidashne—broth.[15]

The Drinking Songs[16]

The songs of merriment were often the fruit of good fellowship around a bottle of wine. Consequently, a number of the songs appear to *begin* with the wine cup, while others seem to *end* around the whiskey glass. The drinking songs sung around the festive table had an air of well-being, of expansiveness. One song which describes the delicious dishes served by a charming hostess begins with: *Baleboste zisinke, zisinke, zisinke, zise baleboste* ("Sweet little hostess, sweet, sweet little hostess") and goes on to list the delicious preparations served by her: *zisinke ugerkelech, ... frishinke bulkelech, ... tsapldike fishelech, ... fetinke yaychelech, ... heysinke kartofelech* ("Sweet little cucumbers, ... fresh little rolls, ... wriggling little fishes, ... little bowls of fat soup, ... hot little potatoes).[17]

At another time perhaps, no sooner did the group sit down to the table than the call rang out for whiskey!

Mir zenen nichter, mir zenen nichter,	We are sober, we are sober,
Trukn iz bay undz in haldz!	Our throats are parched!
Git abisl mashke, git abisl mashke	Bring on the whiskey, bring on the whiskey
Veln mir zingen bald! [18]	And we'll soon begin to sing!

Drinking and singing, singing and drinking, seemed to go hand in hand. The glasses would be filled and refilled as the host and each of the guests were gaily greeted with a toast.

Lomir ale, ineynim, ineynim,
Dem rebn m'kabl ponim zayn;
Lomir ale ineynim, lomir ale
  ineynim,
Dem rebn m'sameyech zayn.
Lomir ale ineynim, lomir ale
  ineynim,
Trinken a glezele vayn.[19]

Let us all together, together,
Greet the *rebe;*
Let us all together, let us all
  together,
Bring joyousness to the *rebe.*
Let us all together, let us all
  together,
Drink a little glass of wine.

The more one drank, the more voluble one became. The gayer the mood, the freer the tongue:

Lomir ale ineynim, ineynim,
Oy, lomir zich nit shemen, nit
  shemen.
Lomir ale ineynim freylech zayn.
Lomir ale trinken vayn, gisn mashke
  in haldz arayn,
Hulyen bizn groyen tog arayn.[20]

Let us all together, together,
Oh, let us not be bashful or shy.

Let us all be gay together.
Let's all drink wine and pour the
  whiskey down our gullets,
Raise a rumpus till the break of day.

A festive gathering of the well-to-do would usually include a houseful of guests, among whom there would be present several prominent members of the community, the town council, the synagogue. The table would be loaded with bottles of wine and whiskey, platters of roast goose, and other traditional, favorite delicacies. The guests would be eating and drinking steadily, becoming inebriated gradually but surely. Their Yiddish songs would most likely be interspersed with Hebrew words and an occasional Russian or Ukrainian phrase, as in the following:

Evyoynim haholchim iber di hayzer,
V'shosim yayin iber di brayzer.
Elu voelu hatso-akim boch!
A trunk bronfn vilt zich doch!

Paupers going from house to house,
Drink wine in all the saloons.
They shout aloud to the Lord!
We want a drink of whiskey!

Balebatim hayoyshvim b'botehem,
V'shoysim yayin bichleyhem.
Elu voelu hatso-akim chay!
A trunk bronfn podavay!

Property owners sit in their houses,
Drinking wine out of their dishes.
They shout aloud: to life!
Give us a drink of whiskey!

Purimshpiler, 17th century, German

Dayonim hayoyshvim eytsel haknesl,	Judges sit near the house of worship,
Hashoysim yayin a fule fleshl,	Drinking wine out of the bottle,
Elu voelu hatso-akim boch!	They shout aloud to the Lord!
A trunk bronfn vilt zich doch!	We want a drink of whiskey!
Hendler hayoyshvim eytsel hahendl,	Merchants sit beside their business,
V'shoysim yayin a fule kendl,	Drinking wine by the ladle,
Elu voelu hatso-akim chay!	They shout aloud: to life!
A trunk bronfn podavay! [21]	Give us a drink of whiskey!

A variant of the above, obviously created by artisans, jibes at other members of the community, both respectable and otherwise: "Rabbis, who study with authority, drink whiskey with delight. . . . Doctors, who make their patients sicker, drink whiskey from the keg. . . . Teachers, who teach their students the Gemara, drink whiskey in deep sorrow. . . . Thieves, who sit in jail, drink whiskey out of a potsherd. . . . Workers from the factories and workshops drink whiskey and toast each other!" [22]

There were those who drank to be merry and those who imbibed in order to relieve their misery. Still others drank to excess out of bitterness and suffering, and a few drank because they really liked the "bitter drop." Some of the best drinking songs are credited to the Chasidim, to whom merriment and "gladdening the soul" in good fellowship were part of their religious beliefs and practices. Consequently, their opponents sought to create songs, which followed the manner and structure of the Chasidic songs but served to ridicule the Chasidic movement.

The drinking songs created by the Chasidim and their opponents were both adopted by the people as a whole. It is thus often difficult to determine the source of a song of merriment, and many a non-believer has often regaled himself and his friends with a jolly song that had been composed by his bitter opponents. Two such examples are given below:

(1)

Yoshke, yoshke, shpan dem loshik,	Yoshke, Yoshke, harness the colt,
Lomir gicher loyfn!	Let us race quickly!
Tomer vet er zich opshteln,	And if he should stop short,
Veln mir im nit koyfn.	Then we will not buy him.

Refrain: Der rebe hot geheysn	The *rebe* told us to be gay,
freylech zayn,	
Trinken bronfn un nit	To drink whiskey, not wine.
kayn vayn. [23]	

(2)

A volechl lomir zingen,	Let us sing a little *volech*,
A volechl lomir shrayen,	Let us shout a little *volech*,
A volechl lomir zingen, lomir shrayen !	Let us sing it, let us shout it !
A gantse voch, horevet men doch,	All week long, we toil and moil,
Oyf shabes darf men layen.[24]	For the Sabbath we must borrow.

The widespread poverty reduced everyone to the absolute necessities of life. Yet, no matter what one ate during the week, even if it were only a dry crust of bread, on the holy Sabbath every effort was made to spread the table with the traditional dishes of fish, meat, soup, compote, and wine. Then the poor man, too, was a king, regaling his queen — the Sabbath. But where was he to procure these unattainables? The singer of the following drinking song, who seems to value his whiskey above all Sabbath fare and is gradually reduced to a state of inebriation in which he is no longer master of the situation, nevertheless seems strangely aware of the "delights" of his erring ways.

Layen, layen, layen, layen, layen,	To borrow, borrow, borrow, borrow,
Zol men nisht badarfn,	Oh, that I should not have to do it,
Shabes on chreyn, kon men zich begeyn,	I could manage without the horseradish on the Sabbath,
Ober nisht on bronfn.	But I cannot do without my whiskey.
Bronfn, bronfn, bronfn . . .	Whiskey, whiskey, whiskey . . .
Dos iz doch mayn nechome,	That is my only comfort,
Az ich mach a kos noch a kos,	And when I drink glass after glass,
Derkvik ich mayn neshome.	My soul is refreshed.
Mayn neshome, mayn neshome, mit mayn nechome,	My soul, my soul, and my comfort,
Zenen doch ingantsn,	That is all that matters,
Az ich nem a kos noch a kos,	When I drink up again and again,
Geyen di fiselech tantsn.	My feet begin to dance.
Tantsn, tantsn, tantsn . . .	Dance, dance, dance . . .
Iz gor a hoyche mide;	This is a holy custom;
Un az ich nem noch amol a kos,	And when I drink glass after glass,
Tants ich mit a ch'side.	I dance with a *ch'side*.
Mit a ch'side, mit a ch'side . . .	With a *ch'side*, a *ch'side* . . .
Iz doch a groyse aveyre;	Why, that is a great sin;
Ober az ich nem a kos noch a kos,	But when I drink again and again,
Hob ich nisht kayn breyre.[25]	I have no other choice.

A charming song is the one that describes a happy-go-lucky little Chasid, journeying to his *rebe*. A rainstorm compels him to seek shelter at a roadside inn, where he takes a nip or two and becomes tipsy. He begins to flirt with a pretty young girl, and, although she eagerly accepts his gifts (a string of beads, a calico dress, a hat), she rejects his amorous advances. Whereupon he demands the return of his gifts, and she "laughs in his face." Like a true little Chasid, however, although he leaves shame-faced, he continues on his merry way, humming his little tune of "bim-bam, bimbam."[26]

Although the different strata of the Jewish population in the Pale each had their own brand of drinking songs, they borrowed freely one from the other. One drinking song that was popular among workmen was the following:

Eyn kol, eyn kol, eyn kol vayn,	There is no, there is no wine,
Ch'kon on dir nit zayn.	I cannot be without you.
Eyn kol, eyn kol, eyn kol bir,	There is no, there is no beer,
Ch'kon nit zayn on dir.	I cannot be without you.
Eyn kol, eyn kol, eyn kol yash,	There is no, there is no whiskey,
Ch'vil a fule flash.	I want a full bottle.
Eyn kol, eyn kol, eyn kol koniak,	There is no, there is no cognac,
Ay, iz dos geshmak.	Oh, how delicious it is.
Eyn kol, eyn kol, eyn kol kvas,	There is no, there is no cider,
Ch'vil a fule fas.[27]	I want a full barrel.

Towards the close of the nineteenth century, Michl Gordon's "Di mashke" ("The Whiskey") was set to an anonymous tune and gained wide currency in a number of variants. In this song, Gordon ridiculed the constant use of wine during the ceremonials marking the different stages in the life of a Jew: birth, circumcision, entering the cheder, beginning the study of the Torah, the *bar mitzvah* (thirteenth birthday) of a male child, the consummation of a marriage match, the engagement party, the wedding. Excerpts from one of these popular variants are given below:

Refrain: Ich vel dir mashke, erlich haltn,	Whiskey, I will treat you right
Un shteyn far dir, vi far an altn,	And respect you, like an elder,

Ich vil dir haltn erlich mashke,
Vayl ich darf doch dayn laske.

I will treat you right, whiskey,
Because I need your favors.

Ich gedenk bay mir oyfn bris,
Iz di mashke nit arop fun tish.
M'hot getrunken un gevuntshn mazl-tov,
Dos kind zol vaksn un zayn a rov.

I remember at my circumcision,
Whiskey didn't leave the table.
They drank and congratulated each other
That the child may grow up to be a rabbi.

Un fun damols on, trink ich a rov-kos,
Un dos rov, on a mos!

And from then on I drink a full glass,
And most of the time without counting!

Bay mir oyf der bar-mitsvah hob ich gezogt a droshe;
Az trinken bronfn, iz gor nishkoshe.

At my *bar mitzvah,* I made a speech
That drinking whiskey wasn't bad at all.

Un ale hobn mayn droshe oysgehert,

Un ale vayle arayngekert.

And everybody listened to my oration
And tipped their glasses all the while.

Darum brider, orim un raych,
Lomir trinken ale glaych.[28]

Therefore brothers, poor and rich,
Let us drink together equally.

In sharp contrast to Michl Gordon's caustic "Di mashke" is Mark Warshawsky's benign "Der becher" ("The Goblet"), which is sentimental and overflowing with loving kindness. Following is an excerpt:

Tayere malke—gezunt zolstu zayn!
Gis on in becher, in becher dem vayn.

Dear Malke, may you be well!
Fill the goblet, the goblet with wine.

Refrain: Bimbom, bimbom, bimbom, bimbom,

Bimbom, bimbom, bimbom, bimbom,

Fun dem dozign becher, er glantst azoy sheyn,
Hot getrunken mayn zeyde, mayn zeyde aleyn.

From this sparkling, lovely goblet,
My own grandfather once drank.

Er hot m'sameyech geven ale kinder, bakent iz dos dir,
Funem tatn iz der becher gekumen tsu mir![29]

It cheered all the children, this you know,
And from father the goblet came to me!

Some songs employ complex structures of cross rhyming, others endow their rhymes with a profound subtlety, philosophy, or downright bitterness, intermingling their Yiddish with Hebrew words.

. . . Mayim iz doch vasser, vasser iz mayim,
Trinken mir a lechayim, lechayim, lechayim.
Az ich nem, az ich nem mayn glezele in hant,
Azoy bin ich mit aych alemen bakant.
Oy brider, brider, zogt-zhe lechayim,
Dos glezele mit yash iz ful mit mayim. . . .[30]

Mayim is water, water is *mayim,*
We drink to life, a toast to life, to life.
When I take the little glass in my hand,
Then I become acquainted with you all.
Oh brothers, brothers, say then : to life,
The little glass of whiskey is full of water. . . .

The fear of the morrow, the insecurity hovering over all, is revealed in the following two song fragments, which plead for life while it is still possible to live it.

(1)

S'iz nito kayn nechtn, s'noch nito der morgn,
S'iz nor do a pitsele haynt — shtert im nit mit zorgn.
Chapt arayn a shnepsl, kolzman ir zayt baym lebn;
Mirtseshem af yener velt vet men aych nit gebn.[31]

There's no yesterday, and the morrow has not yet come,
There's only a little bit of now, so don't spoil it with sorrow.
Snatch a bit of whiskey, so long as you're alive;
With the will of God, in the afterlife you will not get any.

(2)

Az me brent, brent men bronfn,
Az me bakt, bakt men broyt,
Un az me shtarbt ligt men toyt.

When you burn, you burn whiskey,
And when you bake, you bake bread,
And when you die, you lie there dead.

Vaksene lichtlech in der zayt,
Un shtarbn muz men tsu der tsayt.

Wax tapers on the side,
And when the time comes you must die.

Gold un zilber lozt men shteyn,
Az men ruft tsum mishpet : muz men geyn![32]

Gold and silver are left behind,
When you're called to the judgment: you must go!

It was unusual for a Yiddish folk song to deal with the perennial drunkard who was cruel to his family. The following excerpt describes this rare phenomenon in Jewish life, whose wife in this case, however, was far from docile.

Ach du lotre un du pianitse,
Zolstu azoy lebn,
Tsi den az mir oyf di hoytsoe veynig,

Darfstu mir ibern pleytse gebn?

Tomer fardinstu a grivnikl,

Trogstu avek in shenk.
Du gist arayn in dayn heldzele,
Un aheym brengstu a krenk! [33]

Oh, you rogue and drunkard,
May you have a bad life for yourself,
It's not enough that you don't support me,
Must you also beat me?

Even when you earn a tiny ten-kopek piece,
You carry it off to the saloon.
You pour it down your little throat,
And bring curses home to me!

In another of this type, the singer is so much in love with the bottle that he prays that when he is dead and buried, whiskey may be poured over his grave.

Ich nem nor dem butl in hant,
Un klap di probke aroys,
Der butl blaybt ba mir in hant
Un dem bronfn trink ich oys.

Du gotenyu, du tayerer, du ziser,
Du bizt doch a voyler un a guter.
Shik mir tsu a regndl fun bronfn,
Ich zol zayn k'seyder shiker.

Mayn keyver zol zayn mit spirt
    bagosn,
Dos iz ba mir der iker,
Un afn keyver zol zayn ongeshribn,
Az do ligt yoshkele der shiker. [34]

I take the bottle in my hand,
And knock out the cork,
The bottle remains in my hand
And the whiskey I drink up.

Dear God, you dear, sweet God,
You are so good and kind.
Send me a rainfall of whiskey,
To keep me drunk forever.

May my grave be watered with
    whiskey,
That is the main thing with me,
And may it be written on my grave,
That Yoshkele the drunkard lies here.

An uproarious ballad, which constructs its humorous text on wild exaggerations and garbled accounts of the stories of the Bible, was probably the creation of gay blades who created their song under the influence of the whiskey bottle. Following are excerpts from this ballad:

Ich ken chumesh un biblie oych,

Un homen hatsadik hot gehat a
    groysn moyech,

I know the Pentateuch and the Bible
    too,

And Haman the saint had a big
    brain,

Un shloyme hamelech's tate, der
    alter terach,
Iz geven a shiker—dos shver ich.

And King Solomon's father, old
    Terah,
Was a drunkard—this I swear.

Koyrech iz oych geven a groyser
    shiker,
Vayl dos bronfn iz geven ba im der
    iker.
Un lotn hot derfar genumen di erd,
Vayl bronfn hot ba im nit gehat
    kayn vert. . . .

Korah too was an awful tippler,
Because whiskey meant everything to
    him.
And Lot was buried just because
Whiskey didn't mean a thing to
    him. . . .

Az di brider hobn farkoyft noyech'n
    kayn mitsrayim,
Hobn zey b'eys-mayse gemacht a
    lechayim.
Zey hobn fun im aropgetsit dos
    hemdl,
Un hobn farkoyft di plishtim far a
    rendl.
Un az di brider zaynen geforn koyfn
    borshtsh kayn mitsrayim,
Hot nevuchadnetser gemacht mit zey
    a lechayim.

And when the brothers sold Noah to
    the Egyptians,
They drank a toast thereby.

They pulled off his little shirt,

And sold him to the Philistines for a
    gold piece.
And when the brothers went to buy
    borscht in Egypt,
Nebuchadnezzar drank a toast to
    them.

Achashverish der kenig hot lib gehat
    di mashke,
Er flegt zi zupn glaych fun der
    fliashke.
Er hot gemacht a sude far vayber
    aleyn,
Un bilem's eyzl iz dort oych geven.
Un avrom ovinu iz geshtanen untern
    tir,
Un estern hot men ufgehangen, vey
    iz mir. . . .[35]

King Ahasuerus loved his whiskey,

He'd guzzle it right out of the bottle.

He made a banquet for women only,

And Balaam's ass was also there.
And Abraham, our Father, stood
    behind the door,
And Esther was hung, oh, woe is
    me. . . .

The gay, uninhibited mood evident in the above song was usually not tolerated by the elders and religious leaders in the Jewish community in the Pale. Excessive drinking was accepted by them only on Simchas Torah, when a Jew could even roll in the gutter, or on Purim, when he could be so drunk that he wouldn't know the difference between "boruch mordekay" ("blessed be Mordecai") and "arur homen" ("cursed be Haman"). These strict bounds, however, were obviously not always adhered to throughout the rest of the year, and this is evident by the rich store of Yiddish lore and songs of merriment.

The merry songs were comical and ironic, sardonic and scornful, good-humored and jolly, occasionally even suggestive and bawdy. With tongue-in-cheek, a twinkle in the eye, mischievously and gaily, the merry, Yiddish folk songs elicited wholesome laughter and broke through the pall of misery and hardships. They were a delightful and welcome phenomenon in an intolerable environment of oppression from within and without, where the will to live, the capacity for joyousness, the subtlety and variety of the folk imagination were over and over again reaffirmed.

Notes

MERRIMENT

1. Rubin, MSS.
2. *Ibid.*
3. Rubin, 1950, p. 131.
4. D. and Y., pp. 264–266, No. 23.
5. *Ibid.,* pp. 257–258, No. 15.
6. *Ibid.,* pp. 259–260, No. 16.
7. *Ibid.,* p. 269, No. 30.
8. *Ibid.,* pp. 266–267, No. 24.
9. Cahan, 1957, No. 508.
10. G. and M., No. 326.
11. *Nayntsig Geklibene,* pp. 22–23.
12. Kipnis, pp. 52–53.
13. *Ibid.,* No. 130.
14. D. and Y., p. 270, No. 32 (*varnitshkes*: a triangular-shaped dough pastry).
15. *Ibid.,* pp. 254–255, No. 10. The alphabetical sequence of the Yiddish song naturally does not apply to the English translation.
16. Abrahams comments on wine songs in the Jewish communities in Germany during the Middle Ages: ". . . the favourite Jewish wine songs . . . were merry but they contained not one syllable of licentiousness. Drunkenness was never a prevalent vice. The sanctified use of wine at every Jewish ceremony produced a real *instinct* for temperance without destroying an equally strong instinct for sociability" (p. 137). Although certain Jewish satirists of that period "were exhausting all their powers of drollery over the joys of drunkenness," Abrahams maintains that their works were mostly imitations of "Arabic and other originals" and not truly representative of the actual Jewish environment at that time (p. 87).
17. Kipnis, pp. 57–58. Said by Kipnis to have been authored by Sholem Aleichem.
18. Kipnis, p. 51.
19. *Ibid.,* p. 53.
20. Rubin, MSS.
21. G. and M., No. 376.
22. Kipnis, pp. 79–81.
23. Cahan, 1957, No. 559.
24. Kipnis, p. 72 (*volechl*: a Wallachian tune).
25. *Ibid.,* pp. 69–70. (*ch'side*: wife of a Chasid; however, in this song, it merely means a female.)
26. B. and F., pp. 374–375.
27. Rubin, MSS.
28. *Nayntsig Geklibene,* pp. 13–15. This song utilizes the play on the Hebrew words: *rov* (rabbi), *rov-kos* (full glass), and the Yiddish-Hebrew expression *dos rov* (usually). *See* Chapter X on "Of Literary Origin."
29. Warshawsky. pp. 19–20.
30. Rubin, MSS.

31. D. and Y., p. 272, No. 34. Written by Chaim Zhitlowsky.
32. Cahan, 1957, No. 558.
33. G. and M., No. 293.
34. D. and Y., p. 279, No. 43.
35. *Ibid.*, p. 277, No. 41.

CHAPTER VII

Dancing Songs

SOON AFTER THE BLACK DEATH (1348/9), AN EPIDEMIC OF DANCING spread throughout Germany, especially in the Rhineland, "where hundreds of men and women appear in groups, dancing to utter exhaustion."[1] Lasting until the beginning of the fifteenth century, this "epidemic" carried over also into the Jewish ghettos, where a *Tanzhaus* was to be found in many a Jewish community.[2]

The excesses of the Black Death and the excessive dancing which followed as its aftermath brought into play the bizarre phenomenon of the dance of death (*danse macabre*), a form of artistic entertainment which became a popular dramatic presentation among Jews as well as non-Jews.

Prevalent during the latter years of the Middle Ages, the *danse macabre* might have been at first a revival of an ancient custom designed to stay a plague. In its professional enactment, however, with musical and vocal accompaniments, it came to be a prominent form of entertainment during weddings and other family gatherings in many Jewish homes, even as late as the seventeenth century.[3]

In its dramatic treatment, the dance of death usually portrayed Death in his dance with the different members of society, presented by an array of characters from the highest status to the lowest, each appearing in his final struggle for ephemeral life. Perhaps one of the oldest dance songs of this kind, attributed to a Spanish Jew, is the following, in which the rabbi argues with Death:

O, Elohim, fun Avrohom der got !
Zay mir moychl di zind !
Trayb mich nisht mit dayn sharfn
   gebot !
Ich zol tantsn atsind !
Machmes vos iz keyner nisht faran
   oyf der velt

O, Lord, God of Abraham !
Forgive me my sins !
Do not turn away from me with
   your sharp command !
I must dance now !
For is there anyone in the world

182

Vos zol lebn, hagam dem toyt dos nisht gefelt?	Who lives, when Death does not wish it?
Don rabi mit der langer bord,	Don Rabbi with the long beard,
Host shtendig talmid un m' forshim geknelt,	You have always studied Talmud and the Holy Writ,
Un gemitn dem emes in der velt!	And sought the truth in the world!
To tants un zol dir nisht zayn bang!	Dance, then, and do not regret it!
To zing, zol fun dayn broche vern gezang!	Sing, then, and may your blessing be turned into song!
Un ru zich dan oys mit ashi geport![4]	And then you can rest together with Ashi.

During the Middle Ages, dancing among Jews was regarded, not so much as a personal pleasure, but as a means of rousing friendly enthusiasm at festive gatherings. At the same time, the most popular *athletic* amusement among Jews was *the dance*. Dancing between the sexes, however, was quite out of keeping with the current mores, although a husband might dance with his wife, a father with his daughter, a mother with her son, a brother with his sister. This concession, however, was apparently far from adequate for the popular needs. Despite the rabbinical prohibition of mixed dancing, young men and women, with some married couples, "not only danced together, but did so in the communal dancing-hall on the Sabbath and festivals."[5]

Chasidic Dance

The artistic *danse macabre* was quite distinct from the kind of communal dancing performed in the dancing halls. Quite distinct, too, was the kind of dancing which the Chasidic movement encouraged and made, along with its song, part of its religious observations and even of its liturgy. This was in character and in the spirit of its central credo, which bade its followers turn away from sorrow towards joy and serve the Lord with passion and enthusiasm, pleasure and joyousness. "If laments can open the gates of Heaven, then joyousness can break down walls," said the Baal-Shem-Tov (Besht), who believed too that "melody and joyousness and dance together can lift man up and lead him into the higher realms."[6]

Serving the Lord with enthusiasm and passion led the Besht to teach his pupils not to inhibit themselves during prayers but to move their body about freely, shake and rock from side to side, so that every part of the body, too, served the Lord! Chasidim came to believe that not only through their fervent prayers but also through their fervent dancing they could achieve the answers to their prayers and at times heal the sick and sometimes even soften the heart of the most cruel tyrant.

Thus, Chasidim rarely stood still during prayers, and the Chasidic *rebeyim* and their followers sought to inject bodily movements and actual dance steps whenever possible, while some of the most violent criticism leveled against them by their opponents, the Misnagdim, was the fact that they were always singing, dancing, clapping their hands, emitting wild cries during prayers, "which is entirely against Jewish tradition."[7]

But the Chasidic use of the dance and song was basic to their religious beliefs. Reb Shneyer Zalmen of Liadi was once described as "dancing with remarkable grace and lightness, . . . jumping so high as to touch the beams."[8] Chasidim danced on the Sabbath, during the holidays and especially on Simchas Torah, at weddings and even when memorializing their dead. Reb Nachman Bratslaver, who often sang his own compositions, is described by his pupils during his singing: "He would begin to dance, and he who has not seen him dance, has never seen anything worthwhile in his life! . . ."[9] For Reb Nachman Bratslaver taught his pupils the unity of song and dance in this wise: "The tune has to fit the words of the song, and the movements of the dance, too, must be fitted to the melody, because all three — the melody, words, and dance — are one. And fortunate is he who hears such a tune that binds the words and the dance, where everything is blended together. Then your soul could almost expire with delight, for there is no greater joy in this world than this joy."[10] So intent was Reb Nachman in his instructions that he maintained that "just as there are different notes to a melody, so are there different gestures in each limb of the body which are suitable to each tone in the melody. And every Chasid who wants to understand a melody must also know how to dance it, interpreting each tone with a specific movement of his body, according to the mood of the melody."[11]

Thus, *dance tunes* form a considerable part of the musical tradition of the Chasidic movement; and many Chasidic tunes that were at first not intended to be danced to, almost inevitably become woven together with dance rhythms. "For no sooner did one begin to sing, than immediately one's soul and body were literally lifted up. You couldn't sit still anymore, and you had to form a ring."[12]

A world away from this, it seems, are the dance songs of the nineteenth century, which literally sprang up as the wild flowers in the field among young men and women, in the main the working youth, of the cities and towns of the Jewish Pale. The secular atmosphere of the *Tanzhaus* was perhaps carried over, but the formality was gone and the environment was markedly changed, as were already many patterns of life and mores. Where several centuries earlier many of the Jewish communities of Western and Central Europe might have had a single dance hall to serve the whole community, in the nineteenth century in the Eastern European Jewish communities, every town or city had one or more dance halls, where young men and women gathered to dance for their enjoyment. "In Warsaw, for example, such dance halls were called *knaypi-es,* where the line between a family get-together and a public gathering was still not too sharply drawn. A *knaypi-e* could even be in the basement dwelling of a poor family, where young people could dance without interference, even during holidays and on the Sabbath. . . . Naturally, the pious regarded such goings-on with disfavor. . . . But who listened to them? Singing and dancing went right on, and some of the loveliest romantic songs and ballads originated in this environment." [13]

These Yiddish dance songs and ditties are in large measure a collective folk product, arising from the actual milieu of the group dance. They originated as a kind of spontaneous singing (humming, rhyming), resulting from the dance activity, usually unadorned and primitive. Designed at first merely to serve the needs of the moment, acting as an accompaniment to the bodily movements and the rhythm of the particular dance, the song actually performed the function of a musical accompaniment in the absence of any kind of instrumental ensemble.

Since the Jewish environment through the centuries was almost constantly under the watchful eye of its religious leaders and mentors, the formality between the sexes prior to marriage, even when the old social fabric was beginning to give way, still persisted. It is evident, even in some of the early nineteenth-century dance songs that indicate an origin dating back to the *Tanzhaus* period. Y. L. Cahan maintains that in the dance song there rested the latent seed of the Yiddish love song and, in reverse, that "perhaps even before the sixteenth century, there must have existed a rich song repertoire, original love lyrics, possibly in the form of short dance songs." [14] The close relationship between the dance songs and love songs was natural. Children's rhymes, for instance, that still retain the shards of old love songs similarly show traces of dance songs, as the following seems to indicate :

Kumt der liber zumer,	When the gentle summer comes,
Shpiln mir in zamd;	We play in the sand;
Kumt der liber vinter,	When the good winter comes,
Forn mir tsum land.	We go to the shore.
Shvartse karshn raysn mir,	We pick the black cherries,
Royte lozn mir shteyn,	And leave the red ones alone,
Sheyne bocherim nemen mir,	We take the handsome fellows,
Mi-ese lozn mir geyn.[15]	And let the ugly ones go.

In the more recent period, however, not only was the atmosphere more informal, but the dances too reflected this changed environment. Modern dances from the non-Jewish environment were eagerly absorbed, and Jewish young men and women gaily danced around in waltzes, polkas, mazurkas, quadrilles, krakoviaks, rhinelanders, kozatskas, side by side with their own traditional dances of a *sher,* a Chasidic *hopke,* a *broygez* dance, a *volech,* and others. Of course, wherever instrumental accompaniments were added, the patterns became more strictly regulated and the dance songs took on a more poetic contour. But where the dances were still in the process of being absorbed, the dance songs were primitive and formed part of the instructor's directives.

The instructor was not always a professional *Tanzmeister*. Within the confines of the small-town home or the dance hall of the Jewish quarter in the big city, a member of the young dancing group itself occasionally assumed the responsibility for teaching the dance steps to the rest of the young people. Only where the group in the small town could afford to do so, a *Tanzmeister* was "brought down" from the big city, and under his tutelage, in many cases without benefit of instrumental accompaniment, the new dances got under way. The dance ditties and rhymes thus became an appendage to his instruction and were chanted or lilted to the tune and rhythm of the dance being taught.

Where the Chasidic dancers accented their religious prayers and songs through bodily movements and gestures, these secular dance songs also used lyrics to mark the rhythm of the steps and patterns of the particular dances. Attesting to the uninhibited informality of the atmosphere of these dance get-togethers are the following dance songs:

Oy vey mameshi, ch'vel dir epes zogn :	Oh, oh, mother dear, I will tell you something :
A sheyn yingele hob ich lib, ch'shem zich oystsuzogn !	I'm in love with a handsome lad and am too shy to tell you !

Zog, zog, tochtershi, ch'vel dir
    gornisht ti-en,
Ch'vel nor nemen a tepel vasser un
    vel dich opbri-en ! [16]

Tell me, tell me, daughter dear, I'll
    not punish you for it,
I'll only take a little pot of water and
    only scald you nicely !

Hert-zhe oys mayn naye polke
Git a kuk, vi azoy ich tants.
Ich gey a kleydl mit uborkes,
Un di shichlech mit a glants.

Listen to my brand new polka,
Look at me, see how I dance.
I wear a dress with fancy trimmings,
And my shoes are brightly shined.

Ch'tu zich a drey ahin, aher,
Geyt doch tsu der kavaler,
Ch'tu zich a drey aher, ahin,
Tut mich a bis in haldz a bin. [17]

I turn myself this way and that,
And my partner approaches me,
I turn about that way and this,
When a bee bites the nape of my
    neck.

Reflecting a transition period, where the bridge between arranged marriages and free mating was being crossed, these little dance songs give us the flavor of young joyousness in the meeting of the sexes in an atmosphere free from the stern eye of the parent or chaperon. They contain an element of taunting and teasing, as well as a quality of humor and often slight satire. In the following two examples, the interplay between caller and dancers is evident :

(1)

Raytse ! Raytse !
Tsu mir mitn ponim !
Yente, Yente,
Geyen zi adurch.

Reytse ! Reytse !
Turn your face toward me.
Yente, Yente,
You can go right through.

Ich hob in geheysn tantsn,
Hobn zi kalye gemacht ingantsn;
Ch'ob in gelozt adorch,
Hobn zi mich nisht gehorcht. [18]

I told you to dance,
But you spoiled it altogether;
I did let you pass through
But you didn't listen to me.

(2)

Damen mit hern
A broch tsu aych !
Vos geyt ir nit gicher,
Vos i'do mit aych?
Hot nit kayn faribl
Vos mir geyen nit gich.
Mir geyen doch nebech
In tserisene shich. [19]

Ladies and gentlemen,
Woe to you !
Why don't you walk faster,
What's the matter with you?
Don't hold it against us
That we do not walk fast.
We are walking, alas,
In torn shoes.

Gleaning their tunes from itinerant bandsmen and wandering folk musicians, the small-town youth incorporated their melodies into songs and dances of their own creation. As for the traveling musicians, they were like the pollen-gathering bees, who on the one hand bore tunes to the small towns from the cities and, on the other, adapted tunes from the countryside for their city performances.

Dipping into his childhood memories in northern Hungary, a young man resurrects the atmosphere, the song, and the dance steps of a social where a *Zepperltants* ("Chain Dance") was being performed:

"When I was a boy, I was taken to socials . . . on the Sabbath day, when the young people got together. In summer it was outdoors. In winter it was in the house of a woman who lived alone, earning her livelihood as a baby sitter. . . . Avrom would hold one end of a kerchief, while Miriam held another . . . and they would dance on the freshly whitewashed, clay floor, singing:

Mayer hebt den rachten fuss,	Meyer raise your right foot
Un den linken schleppt er nuch,	And drag the left one along,
Hüpke ans un hüpke zwa,	Hop once and hop twice
Un dernuch hüpke dra.	And then hop a third time.
Schön mit di fisslech changieren,	Change your feet nicely
Un a bissele promenieren,	And promenade a bit.
Dradel dich im grinem kranz,	Turn about within the green ring,
Un des iz der zepperltanz.[20]"	And this is the Chain Dance.

Another memoir attests to the inroads that popular non-Jewish dances made into procedures even at weddings, where ordinarily only traditional Jewish dances were performed and where, even to the present day in orthodox circles, dancing between the sexes is forbidden.

"At my sister Pearl's wedding . . . Yontl . . . played the dance music like a true artist, with a flourish, seeing to it also that the dances—a lancier, a czardas, a contradanse, and krakoviak, are executed by the caller according to the rules. I recall how strange the calls sounded in my ears in Polish and how queer the fop who led the dances appeared to me as he called out: *Zmyana dam!* ("Change your lady-partners!"); *Panovie do shrodke!* ("Gentlemen into the center!"); *Para v'levo, Para v'pravo!* ("One pair to the left, one pair to the right!").[21]

Judging from the limited number of dance songs extant today, most of which are fragmentary, it becomes evident that the majority of them had served a local and immediate need and were then quickly forgotten or discarded. Shards though they are, they remain delightful reminders of the happy hours spent by hard-working young men and women, retaining some of the rhythms, accents, and patterns of dances, some of which have long since disappeared, while others are still danced (completely or in part) at the present day. The following two ditties accompanied the dancing of a polka:

(1)

Eyns, tsvey, dray, fir, finf, zeks, zibn,	One, two, three, four, five, six, seven,
A sheyn meydele hob ich zich oysgeklibn.	I have chosen a pretty maiden.
Tsi di vilst mich yo, tsi di vilst mich neyn,	Whether you want me, or whether you don't,
A polke megn mir beyde geyn.[22]	We can both dance the polka.

(2)

Eyns, tsvey, dray, fir, finf, zeks, zibn,	One, two, three, four, five, six, seven,
Shpilt-zhe mir di polke, vi es shteyt geshribn;	Play me the polka, as it is written.
Shift zi zich aher, shift zi zich ahin,	Rocking forward, rocking back,
Azoy vi di rozeve blumen bli-en.[23]	Just as the roses bloom so pink.

When the dance was being taught in the inital stages, the rhyme was brief, often primitive, but when the dance was mastered, then the rhyme at times achieved a degree of poetic texture and the stature of a full-fledged song. The majority, however, remained primitive, as is the following:

Iber felder, iber velder,	Over the fields, over the woods,
Hot gehopslt yente-broche mit di zelner.	Yente-Broche hopped about with the soldiers.
Gekumen der tate, di mame: a ma-aroche:	Father came, and mother in the proper order:
Kum aheym, kum aheym, yente-broche!	Come on home, come on home, Yente-Broche!
Ich vil nit geyn, geyt aleyn,	I don't want to go, go on home without me,
Ich vel do hopslen mit di zelner eyne aleyn.	I want to dance with the soldiers by myself.
Zey zaynen gegangen, zi iz geblibn,	They went away and she remained behind,

Zi hot gehopslt mit di zelner biz
azeyger zibn.[24]

Dancing, hopping, with the soldiers
till seven o'clock.

The following, which contains overtones of the Odessa underworld,
includes a refrain which occurs in a number of other songs set to a
similar lilting tune and rhythm :

Bin ich geforn kayn ades,
Oyf der moldavanke,
Hob ich getantst a polonez,
Mit a sharlatanke !

I went to Odessa city,
To the Moldavanka,
There I danced a polonaise
With a loose woman !

Refrain: Heyse tey, kalte tey,
Teyglech mit fasolyes;
Ale sheyne meydelech
Hobn miese dolyes !

Hot tea, cold tea,
Doughballs and beans
All pretty girls
Have such mean luck !

Vos hostu gekocht a gantse voch?
Teyglech mit fasolyes;
Vos hostu gekocht oyf shabes noch?

What did you cook all week?
Doughballs with beans;
What did you cook on the Sabbath
then?

Farfl mit barbolyes.[25]

Doughcrumbs and spuds.

The following two examples retain elements of children's skipping
songs. The first refers to a kozak, a Cossack dance, and the second marks
the rhythm of a Polish krakoviak :

(1)

Mame, mame, di kale geyt,
Tu dir on dos chupe-kleyd !
Tate, tate, der chosn geyt,
Tu dir on dem spodik,
Veln mir tantsn a kozak.

Mother, mother, the bride's coming,
Put on your wedding dress !
Father, father, the groom is coming,
Put on your fancy coat,
And we will dance a kozak.

Ich tsu dir, du tsu mir,
Lomir tantsn ale fir.
Ich bin grob, du bist grob,
Lomir tantsn hop, hop, hop.

I towards you, you towards me,
Let the four of us dance.
I am plump, you are plump,
Let us dance, hop, hop, hop.

Ich bin din, du bist din,
Lomir tantsn arim un arim.
Ich bin eydl, du bist eydl,
Lomir ale tantsn a reydl.[26]

I am thin, you are thin,
Let us dance round and round.
I am refined, you are refined,
Let us dance in a ring around.

(2)

Yakov, yakoviane,	Jacob, Jacob-iana,
Shtup aroys di pane !	Push the lady out !
Di pane vil nit geyn,	The lady won't go,
Zets ir oys di tseyn !	Knock her teeth out !
Di tseyn tor men nit zetsn,	One must not knock one's teeth out,
Dos ponim tor men nit netsn;	One must not wet one's face;
Azoy vi in ades,	As in Odessa,
Azoy in bukarest ! [27]	So in Bucharest.

The teasing, taunting quality of some of these dance rhymes give us a flavor of the flirtatiousness and the courtship inherent in these dance get-togethers, as well as the actual rhythms and accents of the dances. A kolomeika was danced to the following rhyme:

Fun vanen kumt ir gute brider?	Where do you come from, good brothers?
—Fun der kolomeyke !	—From the kolomeika !
Hot ir nish' gezen a meydele,	Perhaps you've seen a maiden there,
Velche heyst leyke?	Whose name is Leyke?
Yo gezen, nish' gezen,	Whether we have or whether we haven't
Viln mir aych nisht zogn;	We will not tell you.
Tut a chap a ferd un vogn,	Grab a horse and wagon,
Un tut ir noch-yogn. [28]	And chase after her.

A waltz song which sways gracefully along in three-quarter time mentions other dances popular at that time:

Vos toyg di polke-mazurke,	What use is the polka-mazurka,
Az tantsn tants ich zi nit.	When I do not know how to dance it.
Vos toyg mir di sheyne figurke,	What good is her lovely figure,
Az nemen nemt zi mich nit,	When she refuses to have me.

Refrain: Eyns-tsvey, eyns-tsvey-dray,	One-two, one-two-three,
Ay, vay iz tsu mir.	Oh, woe is me.
Vey iz tsu mayne yor.	Woe is my life.
A libe hob ich gefirt	My love affair has lasted
Felike dray-fertl yor.	A full three-quarter year.

Vos toyg mir di naye kozatske,	What use is the new kozatska,
Az tantsn tants ich zi nit.	When I do not know how to dance it.

Vos toyg mir di meydl di chvatske,	What good is the sturdy, fine girl,
Az viln, vil zi mich nit.	When she does not desire me.
Vos toyg mir di naye kadriln,	What use are all the new quadrilles,
Az tantsn tants ich zey nit.	When I do not know how to dance them.
Un dos meydele vos iz mir gefeln,	And the maiden whom I have selected,
Gefeln, gefel ich ir nit.[29]	Does not like me, oh, at all.

This element of "choosing" one's mate was self-evident in these youthful gatherings, where the dance and the dance song went hand-in-hand. Thus the dance song was also a primitive form of courtship and love song, which, on the one hand, may have been the preserver of love-song fragments from long ago, and, on the other, bore the first sprouts of love songs in the making. Most of the time, humor dominated the dance songs, as in the three courting rhymes below, which gibe mildly at girls of other towns and cities.

(1)

Bialistoker koketkes,	Bialystok coquettes,
Blondinkes un brunetkes,	Blonds and brunettes,
Zey klaybn zich oyf ineynim	Gather together
Un zuchn a bocher a sheynem.	To seek a handsome fellow.

(2)

Pinsker meydelech, varshavyankes	Pinsk maidens and Warsaw girls,
Tantsn, tantsn zey vi galagankes,	They dance, they dance like turkey cocks,
Un dos rufn zey oych a lebn.	And that's what they call living.
Kadoches hobn zey dem klezmer tsu gebn.	They haven't even a penny to give the bandsman.

(3)

Hayntige meydelech, zey hobn gor kayn seychl,	The girls of today have no brains at all,
Zey brikenen nor vi di ferd;	They kick with their feet, just like horses,
Papadyen zey a bocher fun a falsher libe,	They fall into the clutches of a false-hearted lover,
Leygt er zey yungerheyt in dr'erd.[30]	He drives them young into the ground.

The Chasidim danced their hopkes and volechlech; the young people danced their vengerkes, patispans, and kamarinskis; even the children had their social, square, and ring dances, accompanied by dance songs often borrowed from the adult world, such as the following:

Hot zich mir di zip tsezipt,	My sieve is all worn out
Hot zich mir tsebrochn.	And broken altogether.
Hot zich mir di shich tserisn,	My shoes are torn to shreds,
Tants ich in di hoyle zokn.	So I dance in my stocking feet.
Tants, tants antkegn mir,	Dance, dance opposite me,
Un ich antkegn dir,	And I will dance toward you.
Du'st nemen dem eydim,	You will take the son-in-law,
Un ich'l nemen di shnur.[31]	And I the daughter-in-law.

The dances varied: there were the ring dances, in which everyone participated together; there were the square dances, which assumed patterns of four and eight or whatever the dance called for; there was the social dancing, which was confined to couples. There was a type of ring dance which was popular among workmen. The men would form a tightly knit ring with their arms around each other's shoulders, singing and stamping their feet as they accented the rhythm. The humorous and satirical quality of the following excerpts of such a ring-dance song is heightened by the use of the nonsense term, *lyokum bembe,* and the corruption of the Hebrew words *bachtsi halaylo,* taken from the Passover Haggada, but which, in this context, sounds like a sneeze!

Vilner lasunes, lyokum bembe!	Vilna dandies with a sweet tooth, lyokum bembe!
Vishniver klotnikes, lyokum bembe!	Brawlers of Vishnive, lyokum bembe!
Zupraner tsign, lyokum bembe!	Goats of Zuprane, lyokum bembe!
Zaskvitser bek, lyokum bembe!	Rams of Zaskvits, lyokum bembe!
... Minsker chazerim, lyokum bembe!	Minsk pigs, lyokum bembe!
Smargoner bern-trayber, lyokum bembe!	Bear chasers of Smargon, lyokum bembe!
Zaynen zey gegangen, lyokum bembe!	All went, lyokum bembe!
Af a milchome, lyokum bembe!	To war, lyokum bembe!
Hobn zey geshosn, lyokum bembe!	And they shot, lyokum bembe!
Mit shroyene koyln, lyokum bembe!	With straw bullets, lyokum bembe!
Mit papirene biksn, lyokum bembe!	With paper guns, lyokum bembe!
Haptshi halaylo![32]	At midnight!

Another ring-dance song of this type is the following, which proceeds to count up to twelve bottles of beer and then counts the same number backwards. In the dance, the ring goes forward in one direction and then, on the backward count, reverses itself. The dance song follows this sequence : *Eyn butl bir, tsvey butl bir, dray butl-butl bir; fir butl bir, finf butl bir, zeks butl-butl bir,* etc." ("One bottle of beer, two bottles of beer, three bottles-bottles of beer, etc.").[33] In another ring-dance song of this type the count goes up to twenty-one and then counts backward till *one* is reached again.[34]

Because of the close relationship between certain activities and rhythmic associations, it often happened that certain children's rhymes were incorporated into dance songs, some dance songs carried over into work songs, fragments of love songs became children's songs, and love songs grew out of certain fragmentary dance songs. The texts of these various songs always served their specific function faithfully. In a ballad, the text was constructed to tell a story and create a mood; in a children's rhyme, the text served to accent the child's hopping to the bouncing of a ball or jumping rope. In the dance songs, the primary function of the text was to accent the dance patterns, steps, and rhythm and to adjust to the bodily movements which gave birth to the text in the first place.

The same process also exists in some of the work songs, where the mechanical movement of the task being performed becomes the father of the song, with text and tune as supplementary attendants to the work being done. Many folk-song collectors have been made aware of this fact, when an informant has had to simulate the movements of a work task as an aid to memory in recalling a forgotten work song.

As the "learning period" of modern dancing passed, the number of dance songs blossoming out into love songs increased. With the growing familiarity with the dances and the occasional presence of one or two musicians, the dancers were now free to exercise their poetic talents and imaginativeness in the creation of songs which may have sprung up in the atmosphere of the dance hall but now went out into the world as full-fledged love songs. The following might have passed through this transformation and taken such a course :

Shpilt-zhe mir dem nayem sher	Play for me the new sher dance,
Vos iz aroysgekumen.	Which is all the rage.
Ch'ob zich farlibt in a yingele a sheynem	I fell in love with a handsome lad
Un kon tsu im nisht kumen.	And cannot seem to reach him.
Ch'volt tsu im gekumen,	I would go to him, o yes,

Voynt er zeyer vayt.
Ch'volt doch im a kush gegebn,
Shem ich zich far layt.
Nisht azoy far layt,
Vi far got aleyn,
Ch'volt mit im farbracht di tsayt
Az keyner zol nisht zeyn.[35]

But he lives far away.
I would give him a kiss so sweet,
But what would people say?
And not so much what people said,
But how about God himself?
Oh, I would like to be with him
With nobody else around.

We may not find pearls of literary creation in these incidental, often accidental little rhymes, which at first performed a utilitarian function of rhythmically accompanying the social dancing of the young people. Upon closer scrutiny, however, it is clear that these fragments contain values pointing in two directions. One represents the preserved remains of old dance and love songs of several hundred years ago; the other, latent seeds of love songs in the making. This endows these fragments with a quality that, in its entirety, represents a wellspring of primitive folk poetry of a high order.

Notes

DANCING SONGS

1. Erik, p. 83.
2. The *Tanzhaus* was a type of hall where weddings took place and where, during the holidays, Christian bandsmen were permitted to play and the dancing of Jews to their music was tolerated. However, the rabbis in Germany were not in favor of these practices. Nevertheless, the dancing halls soon spread throughout France and Germany, until most of the Jewish communities had one.
3. ". . . When the guests of honor had eaten of the fruit and cakes and had done justice to the wine, the table was cleared and removed. Then appeared masked performers who bowed prettily and played all manner of entertaining pranks. They concluded their performance with a truly splendid 'dance of death' " (Glückel, pp. 98–99).
4. Shiper, pp. 30–31. Shiper attributes this macabre song and dance to an anonymous Spanish Jew. In this presentation, there appear, among others, the kaiser, the cardinal, the lord and the archbishop, the duke and the bishop, the doctor, the priest, the monk, the moneylender, and the *rabi barbudo* ("the rabbi and his beard"), each struggling in the dance with Death, at the most intense moment of his consciousness. *Ashi* (352–427 C.E.), born in Babylonia, headed the academy at Sura, where he began the Babylonian Talmud and was its editor. He spent thirty years on it, and the task was finally completed by his disciple Rabina, just before 500 A.D.
5. Abrahams, pp. 380–381. Abrahams describes Jewish dances of "ancient and medieval times" as consisting of "gesticulations, violent leaps and bounds, hopping in a circle, rather than graceful pose or soft rhythmic movement"; performed by men, while "the women danced in line or circle, without any prescribed steps," where the "leader would improvise a movement which the rest, striking cymbals the while, would attempt to imitate" (p. 380).
6. Unger, 1946, p. 118.
7. Dancing was part of the ritual in the Bible. Miriam, the prophetess, danced after the defeat of the Egyptians at the Red Sea. After Jephthah's victory over the Ammonites, his daughter came out towards him with drum and dances. There was dancing when David brought the holy Ark to the City of David. During the agricultural festivals, the daughters of Israel came out dancing. In the Psalms we often encounter references which say: "Let us praise the Lord with drums and dancing." The prophets, too, would occasionally dance as they prophesied. Dancing before the bride was considered a holy function and one that the Chasidim practiced. This custom is supposed to have been taken over from the Cabalists in the holy city of Safed, who, though they studied and communed in isolation, would break into ecstatic dancing when in a group. It was their custom, every Friday evening, to walk out to the outskirts of their city and there in the mountains surrounding Safed to dance and pray, as they greeted the coming of the Sabbath.
8. Unger, 1946, p. 126.
9. *Ibid.*, p. 102.
10. *Ibid.*, pp. 103–104.

11. *Ibid.*, p. 117.

12. *Ibid.*, p. 117. An elaborate ceremonial, in which dance figured prominently, that was conducted in the house of worship of the Kozhenitser Magid, when he came to pray, is described below:

"Before him and behind him walked an attendant carrying two lighted candles. Between the two, walked the Kozhenitser Magid carrying a small scroll. . . . When the *rebe* entered the house of worship, the first attendant placed the candles near the platform and the second placed his on the pulpit. The *rebe* then danced opposite the holy Ark, three dance steps forward and three backward. Then he placed the little scroll into the holy Ark and once more danced three steps forward and three backward. And *then* only did the *rebe* begin to pray. And as he prayed, he danced with such fire and inspiration that when he was almost done . . . he fell away in a faint. And then the *rebe,* who was a very frail man, was wrapped in lambskins, so that his emaciated frame would be warmed, and carried back to his private chamber, worn out and exhausted from his ecstatic dancing during his prayers. . . . And with this inspiration the Kozhenitser Magid prayed every day . . ." (Unger, 1946, pp. 98–99).

Yiddish folk song, which reflects a variety of attitudes, includes a humorous song in which a poor tailor scoffs bitterly both at his own poverty and at the Kozhenitser Magid's practicality when dealing with earthly matters.

Bin ich mir a shnayderl, a guter,　　I am a little tailor and a good one,
Ch'ney farn Kozhenitser rebn a futer;　　I am making a fur coat for the Kozhen-
Ich nem aroys di gute vate,　　I remove the good padding, [itser *rebe;*
Un leyg arayn an alte shmate, tralalala.　　And replace it with an old rag, tralalala.

Der beged shoyn gants fartik,　　The garment is now quite finished,
Trog ich im op sheyn un artik;　　I take it up there in style;
Er nemt im kern, er nemt im dreyen,　　He turns it about, this way and that,
Un heyst mir a knepl ibertsuneyen, tra-　　And bids me resew a button, tralalala.
　　lalala.

Er zogt az der beged iz nisht gut,　　He says the garment is not satisfactory,
Un tsapt fun mir oys dos blut;　　And makes me feel miserable;
Der beged iz gut, vi di velt,　　The garment is good, as good as can be,
Er vil mir nisht batsoln kayn groshn　　But he refuses to pay me a penny for it,
　　gelt, tralalala.　　　　tralalala.

(D. and Y., pp. 261–262, No. 18.)

13. Cahan, 1952, p. 94.
14. *Ibid.*, p. 88.
15. D. and Y., p. 68, No. 20.
16. Cahan, 1957, No. 51. Cahan lists this as a love song.
17. Skuditsky, 1936, p. 284, No. 16.
18. Cahan, 1951, No. 218.
19. G. and M., No. 360. "To be sung to the first figure of *Lancier.*"
20. Cahan, 1952, p. 91, p. 92.
21. Teitelbaum, p. 28.
22. Rubin, MSS.
23. Cahan, 1957, No. 221. Some time later, a similar rhyme referred to an "American" dance, which was popular in a town in the Vilna region:

Eyns, tsvey, dray, fir, finf, zeks, zibn,　　One, two, three, four, five, six, seven,
A sheynem bocherl hob ich mir oysgek-　　I have chosen a handsome lad.
Der tants iz doch sheyn, richtig, ye, [libn.　　The dance is pretty, right, yes,
Ich ken tantsn amerike!　　I can dance "America"!

(Cahan, 1957, No. 220.)

24. Rubin, MSS.

25. Cahan, 1957, No. 239. A humorous variant is the following:

Tsu libstu ye, tsu libstu neyn,
Royte pomerantsn,
Az der tate shlogt der mamen,
Geyen di kinderlech tantsn.

Whether you love me or whether you
Red, red oranges,   [don't,
When dad gives mother a beating,
The children dance about.

Refrain: Ay, tidiridi tutn tutn,
          Ay tidiridi, tutn,
          Vayl ich bin a zibele,
          Derfar bin ich gerotn.

          Ay, tidiridi tutn tutn,
          Ay tidiridi, tutn,   [months,
          Because I was born in seven
          That's why I'm so bright.

Heyse tey un kalte tey,
Bekelech mit royzn.
Der vos trogt kayn shleykes nit,
Der farlirt di hoyzn. . . .

Hot tea and cold tea,
Cheeks so rosy red.
He who wears no suspenders,
Will surely lose his pants. . . .

    (Rubin, MSS.)

    26. Cahan, 1957, No. 263.
    27. *Ibid.,* No. 227.
    28. *Ibid.,* No. 254.
    29. Rubin, MSS.
    30. Cahan, 1957, Nos. 240, 243, 244.
    31. Rubin, MSS.
    32. D. and Y., pp. 244–245, No. 13.
    33. Cahan, 1957, No. 259. Heard by Cahan's informant "during the nineties sung by tailors as they danced in a ring and at every *butl-butl-bir* they stamped their feet heavily but rhythmically." Cahan's comment on this song was: "It seems to be of German origin."
    34. A work song, which starts with the following refrain: *Uha, ich libe dir, darfstu mir merer* ("Uha, I love you, What more do you want"), proceeds to count from twenty-one forward, covering ten counts to a stanza. The singer's comment was: "I heard it in the Ukraine, during the First World War, from stocking workers at a hand-manipulated machine. They sang it to the regular rhythmic turning of the stocking-machine wheel" (Rubin, MSS).
    35. Rubin, 1950, p. 71.

CHAPTER VIII

Historical and Topical

S. Anski (1863–1920), folklorist, author, and dramatist once said that the folklore of a given people is like a geological stratum in which the historian may on occasion discover deeper traces of the life of a people in its distant past. Indeed, where other written documents are often not extant, old customs and songs, tales and proverbs at times provide clues to bygone eras. Great historical events have been treated in songs. Similarly occurrences of lesser moment have been sung about in topical ballads or fragmentary lilting ditties. From ancient times, folklore and folk song have kept in step with history, although the opinions and facts entertained by the folk have often differed from those of the official chroniclers. There are even some scholars who feel that no written history of a people should be considered reliable if it conflicts basically with the people's folklore!

In the Middle Ages, although local fasts and feasts took the place of the political elements which Jewish life lacked, these events, described occasionally in extant songs and ballads, in turn relate to local events of a political nature. The fasts were usually initiated after some tragic occurrence, and the Hebrew elegies recited in the synagogue served to inspire ordinary men and women to heroic endurance.

Yiddish folk song, too, is a reflector of a variety of attitudes toward specific social phenomena and events and serves, together with the eye-witness account and the memoir, as a valuable source for historical and sociological studies. The historical song, the topical ballad, the taunt and teaser of social significance all reveal the current opinions about particular occurrences in bygone eras as well as those in modern times.

Topical Songs of the Seventeenth and Eighteenth Centuries

An important Yiddish historical song of the seventeenth century is
"Megiles vints," which relates the hardships of the Jews of Frankfurt
during the uprising led by Vincenz Fettmilch during the years 1612–1616.
Jewish properties were burned and looted (September, 1614) and the
Jews were forced to leave the city. On February 28, 1616, however, the
Jews happily returned to Frankfurt and witnessed the execution of Fett-
milch and his aides. "Megiles vints" was set to the tune of the German
"Paavia die Schlacht" and described these occurrences in 103 stanzas,
of which the following excerpted lines are given in their English translation:

"In the year 1614, at that time; / it happened in the city of Frankfurt.
/ A great struggle began, / the like of which we had never seen on earth./
We were naturally frightened, / since we were in the very midst of it.
. . . / . . . We had no one to go to for protection, / and the rebels had
the upper hand. / They wanted to cut us down. . . . / . . . And we had to
suffer. . . . / The rabble gathered at our gates. / Our sorrows multiplied.
. . . / We shut the gates, went to the synagogue to pray. / When we were
saying the haftorah, we heard a great cry. / The enemies had battered
down the gates and were upon us! / . . . We ran out of the synagogue.
. . . / . . . Some of them stood there with large weapons, / till one of us
was shot down and several severely wounded. / . . . How great must have
been our sins! / . . . The evil men started a huge fire, burning our holy
books in it. / And over the flames . . . / they roasted the meat they had
stolen from us. / . . . Then the rebels had a big argument: / one said:
let them live; / The other: let them be driven from the city. / The Lord
must have tipped the scales, / so that our lives were spared / and we
were permitted to leave the city. . . ."[1]

A ballad related to the rebellion of the Ukrainian Cossack, Bogdan
Chmelnitski, and the horrendous massacres of Jews in the spring of 1648
in Bar (Ukraine, Podolia region) contains the following excerpted stanzas,
which describe a scene in which Jews, who had been tortured and held
prisoners, are led out to face the Cossack leaders Krivonos (Krivno) and
Lysenko:

Ver fun undz yidishe kinder	Which of us Jewish children
Veyst nisht fun di kozakn	Does not know of the Cossack
milchomes?	wars?

Ver fun undz ayeder bazunder
Veyst nisht fun di haydamakn
    nekomes?

Denstmol in der biterer tsayt,
Shteyt in Bar, Krivno der
    kozakn-held.
Nebn im, Lisenko mit di gute layt,

Un a tseylem hobn zey
    anidergeshtelt.

Farchoyshecht, mit tsubrochene
    glider,
Fun a vistn grub, a finstere nest,
Firt men tsu, undzere umglikliche
    brider,
Un Krivno hot zey mit di diburim
    getreyst:

—Ch'ob shoyn geshmust mit ayere
    roshim un g'virim,—
Ruft er zich on un tut derbay a lach,
—Atsindert zog ich aych mayne
    letste diburim
Far mayne layt un far aych:

Genug hot ir un ayer vayb un kind
Gelitn tsores, hunger, dorsht un
    kelt,
Bukt zich tsum tseylem un zayt nisht
    blind,
Vet ir lebn gliklich oyf der velt!—

—Shtum, du roshe, un red nisht mer
    a vort!"
Hobn ale yidn ge-entfert azoy:
"Toyt undz beser do oyfn ort,
Ober baytn undzer emune, loy, loy!

Undzer emune shaynt vi di zun,
S'vet dir, roshe, gornisht gerotn.
Kayn ander emune nemen mir nisht
    in zin,
Megst undz hakn un brenen un
    brotn!"

Which one of us, each and all
Does not know of the bitter
    Haydamakn cruelties?

Then, in those bitter times,
Krivno, the Cossack hero, stood
    at Bar.
Beside him, Lysenko and his "good"
    men,
Near the crucifix which they had
    set up.

Doomed, with broken limbs,

Out of a dismal pit, a dark grave,
Our unfortunate brethren are led
    out,
And Krivno comforted them with
    these words:

"I've already spoken with your
    elders and wealthy men,"
He says to them, laughing therewith,
"Now, I will give you my final
    words
Before my men and before you:

You and your wives and children
Have suffered enough hunger, thirst
    and cold,
Bow down to the cross and don't be
    stubborn,
And you can live happily in this
    world!"

"Be silent, evil man, and say not
    another word!"
All the Jews answered together.
"Put us to death rather on the spot,
But change our faith? no, no!

Our faith shines like the sun,
Nothing will avail you, wicked man.
No other faith will we entertain,

Though you cut us up, burn, and
    roast us!"

Bald hot men gezen a shreklech bild,
Oyf kidesh-hashem zenen zey ale
geshtorbn.
Dos ort iz geblibn pust un vild,
Ful mit beyner funem yidishn
korbn.[2]

Soon a dreadful scene unfolded;
They all died in the name of the
Holy One.
The area was laid waste and barren,
Covered with the bones of the Jewish
martyrs.

After a short respite, the Cossack wars broke out again in 1651 and, advancing from the south, Chmelnitski's hordes of Cossacks and Orthodox Ukrainian peasants perpetrated additional untold suffering on many Jewish cities, burning, looting, torturing, and murdering helpless men, women, and children. The following excerpts are from a lament of seventy-eight stanzas, set to the tune of "Adir ayom v'noyro," which chronicles the bloody march of Chmelnitski to the north, in 1656, through the cities of Tultshin, Uman, Mezhbezh, Bar, Ostre, Vinnitsa, Sharigrad, Krasny, Polone, Nemirov.

Ir libe fraynt, lozt undz veynen un
klogn
Oyf di gzeyres vos geshen zayn in
undzere togn!
B'shonas chavley moshiach tetn undz
kozakn yogn,
Mit groys achzoryes, iz nit miglech
tsu zogn!

Dear people, let us weep and
wail
Over the dread events occurring in
our days,
In the year of the coming of the
Messiah, the Cossacks pursued us
With a dreadful cruelty, impossible
to describe!

Gerush nemirov di kehile k'doyshe
far langen;
Veln shraybn vi es b'oynoyseynu
harabim iz dergangen:
Mit koses zenen di reshoyim gelofn
az men shnayd zangen;
Zi hetn zich libersht lozn fun tatren
fangen.

The holy old community of Nemirov
was dispersed;
About this much will yet be
written:
With scythes the evil ones ran about,
cutting us down like sheaves;
Rather had we been taken prisoner
by the Tartars.

Yogn, shlogn tetn zi ale glaych,

Es dertranken fil im tifn taych;

Di shoyn varn oysgeshvumen varn
derharget onderbarmiglaych,
Nit geshoynt yung noch alt, arim
oder raych.

They chased and killed everyone
alike,
Many were drowned in the deep
river;
Those who swam out were slain
without mercy;
No one was spared, young or old,
poor or rich.

Sifrey-toyres tsehakt, deroys gemacht posteles oyf fisn,	Holy scrolls were mutilated and made into slippers,
Heylige toyre, vi zol dich dos nit fardrisn?	Holy Torah, how can it not anger you?
Oy vey, vi hot men farumreynigt dayne red zo zisn,	Oh, woe, how they defiled your sweet words,
Derum mayn oygn mit trern az ayn bach flisn.	That is why my eyes flow in a river of tears.
Ofn lagn di meysim unter der zun;	Unburied the dead lie under the sun,
Eyn kodesh den andern bedekt, der untersht hots gevunen.	One holy martyr covers another, the one underneath is the better off.
Oy vey iber der make urplitsling un farzonen,	Oh, this unexpected terrible horror,
Finf hundert kinder tsu gefinen in brunen.	Five hundred children drowned in wells.
Noshim un b'sules m'tume gevezn un geshent,	Women and maidens defiled and raped,
Oych fil koyfer gevezn, fun y'chod vek gevent,	Many forced to turn from their faith in the one God,
Fil shuln ayngeleygt biz oyf fir vent.	Many synagogues destroyed down to the four walls.
Liber got, varum halstu dich oyf, ze unzer elnt!	Dear Lord, why do you withhold your mercy? Witness our helplessness!
Her got vi konstu dich oyfhaltn,	Lord, how can you restrain your mercy,
Az zi di trognde vayber di baych shpaltn?	Witnessing the bellies of pregnant women split open?
Nun, ven shoyn hobn gezindigt di altn,	And if the old ones have sinned
Varum zol men mit kleyne kinder azoy shaltn un valtn? [3]	Why should the little children be the terrible victims?

So hopeless was the situation and so helpless were the Jewish communities before this brutal onslaught, that among pious Cabalists a great deal of speculation was taking place to determine the exact date of arrival of the Messiah, who was to put an end to these dreadful tribulations. The year 1648 is actually referred to in the above ballad, which then concludes with a fervent appeal to the prophet Elijah, Son of David, to come and lead his suffering people back to the Holy Land and the city of Jerusalem.

For centuries, Jews had nurtured the idea of the coming of the Messiah and at this particular time, the Smyrna Jew, Sabbatai Zvi (1626–1676), claimed to be he. There had been Messianic movements among the Jews in the past, but the Sabbatai Zvi movement exceeded all others in scope and fervor. "Curious reports flew from mouth to mouth. It was said, that in the North of Scotland a ship had appeared, with silken sails and ropes, manned by sailors who spoke Hebrew. The flag bore the inscription, The Twelve Tribes or Families of Israel. . . . The little community of Avignon, which was not treated in the mildest manner by the papal officers, prepared to emigrate to the Kingdom of Judah in the Spring of 1666. . . . With few exceptions, all were convinced of Sabbatai's Messiahship, and of a speedy redemption, in two years at the latest. . . . In Hungary they began to unroof their houses. In large commercial cities . . such as Amsterdam, Leghorn and Hamburg, stagnation of trade ensued. . . ."[4]

In 1666 a Yiddish poem, written by Jacob Toisk and entitled "Eyn sheyn nay lid fun moshiach" ("A Lovely New Song About the Messiah"), was published in Amsterdam. It was probably written to be recited, and Toisk may have been one of those professional singers who entertained in wedding halls, inns, and drinking houses.[5] Obviously Toisk was a follower of the Sabbatai Zvi movement and his seventy-five stanzas are filled with fanatic fervor and descriptions of the miracle-working Smyrna Messiah, who consorted with angels, appeared in a ball of fire, and, though imprisoned, could go free if he so desired. Following are eight stanzas:

Bidenkt, ir libn brider mayn, iberal
    oyf al di zaytn,
Vi mir vern in erets yisrol kumen tsu
    forn un tsu raytn!
Hashem yisborech vil undz nit mer
    in golus lozn,

Mir veln bald hern shoyfer moshiach
    blozn.
Refrain: Omen, v'omen, omen.

Tut aych nit zoymen, brider mayn,
    kayn gelt zolt ir nit shporn;
Ven mir kumen in heylign land
    arayn, zaynen mir nay geborn;

Reflect my dear brothers, from
    everywhere,
How we will go to Israel, on wheels
    and on horseback!
The Lord, blessed be He, does not
    wish us to remain in exile
    anymore,
We will soon hear the trumpet of the
    Messiah blowing.
        Amen and amen, amen.

Don't tarry, my brothers, don't spare
    your money;
When we come to the Holy Land,
    we will become newly born;

Vayl undz vil gebn der liber got,
Vos er undz farshprochn hot.

Liber her got, loz kumen di g'ule
   bald, nit mit groysn shrekn!
Undzer goles hot nor lang gevert,
   verst undz nit lozn shtekn.
Mir hobn gelitn groys elnt—
Mach undzer goles bald ayn end.

Tsi den terkn iz undzer meylech
   kumen in der heypt-shtot fun
   terkay;
Undzer brider varn ez gevor, vi tetn
   zi zich freyen!
Tsu den meylech hoyb er shprechn
   on:
Dayn kroyn muz ich fun dir han.

Kumt her, ir libn brider mayn, ich
   vil aych eyn teyl fun di
   chidushim shraybn,
Vi zi antbitn shaynperlich, mir vern
   nit lang in goles blaybn;
Der terkish meylech hot lozn tafsen
   meylech moshiach, den frumen
   man,
Hobn zich al di tirn kegn im
   oyfgetan.

Al di terkn in irn land, di vern zeyer
   dershrekn,
Vi eliyohu hanovi vert shoyfer
   moshiach blozn,
Eliyo vert blozn mit groysn shal,
Zi oyf ir ponim fall.

Vi fartsaytn undzer eltern, tsu fir finf
   hundert yor vern mir ale lebn;

Dos land vos undz got farshprochn
   hot vert er undz vider gebn.
Dos glaychn iz nit fun undzer got,
Der himl un erd beshafn hot.

Vi vert dos ayn groyse simche zayn
   in al undzer glider!

Because the Lord wants to give us
What he has promised us.

Dear Lord, may the redemption come
   soon, and without great dread!
Our exile has lasted long, don't let us
   stay in it any longer.
We have suffered great desolation—
End our exile soon.

Our king came to the Turks in their
   capital city;

Our brothers learned of it and how
   happy they were!
To their king he began to speak
   thus:
Your crown I must have.

Come my brothers, I want to tell you
   some of the marvels

Which are now clear, that we will
   not remain long in exile;
The Turkish ruler imprisoned King
   Messiah, the pious man,

Yet all the gates opened wide for
   him.

The Turks in their land will tremble
   with fear
When Elijah the Prophet will blow
   his ram's horn.
Elijah will trumpet and blast,
And they will fall on their faces.

As our forefathers in ancient times,
   we too will live four or five
   hundred years.
The land God promised us, he will
   give us once again.
There is no one equal to our Lord,
Who created heaven and earth.

What a great joy will then be in all
   our limbs!

In erets yisrol vert eyner den andren
   derkenen, shvester un oych
   brider;
Atsindert veys eyner fun andern nit
   tsu zogn,
Biz mir vern ferzamlt in kurtsn
   togn.[6]

In Israel, each will know the other,
   sisters and brothers;

Now, no one knows of one another,

Until we all assemble, in a matter of
   days.

Accounts of conflagrations, plagues, pogroms—even the rare topical ballad of a love triangle revealed the current mores of the times—are reflected in the extant seventeenth- and eighteenth-century songs. An anonymous ballad, published in 1717, describing an attack led by Jesuit teachers and students on the Jewish quarter in Poznan in 1618, reveals the degradation and suffering of the Jews in this hotbed of anti-Jewish agitation. Following are some twoscore excerpted lines from this ballad, which describes the plotting against the Jewish population, the cryers running through the streets yelling "death to the Jews!", the peasants incited to sharpen their scythes and hatchets to vent their misery in the killing of innocent, young and old.

. . . Ober mir hobn gemeynt zey vern
   nemen undzer hob un gut,
Mir hobn ober nit getracht zey vern
   nemen undzer blut :
. . . Roshey . . . kehile hobn far di
   aniyem v'evyoynim ton zorgn,
Un . . . geton do eyn srore hot zi
   hundert shefl korn ton borgn :
Un dos folk no-ent on mokim
   gekumen,
Un hobn di miln avekgenumen.
Vi biter iz gevezn undzer lebn,
Mir hobn nit gehat ayn kind ayn
   shtikl broyt tsu gebn. . . .
Oych hobn mir nisht gehat tsu
   trinken,
Saydn vaser vos do hobn tan
   shtinken. . . .
. . . Hobn gezogt : tsum ershtn viln
   mir nemen ayer gelt;
Dernoch muzt ir kumen fun di
   velt. . . .

We thought they just wanted our
   material goods,
Never thinking that they were after
   our blood :
The community elders took care of
   the poor,
And arranged to borrow a hundred
   bushels of corn from a lord.
But the rabble came up

And took away the mills.
How bitter was our life,
We hadn't a crust of bread for our
   children.
We also had no water to drink

Except water that stank . . .

They said : first we'll take your
   money;
Then, we'll take your life.

. . . Ayn g'zeyre iz dos gevezn
Dos ayn foter hot nisht gevust fun
    zayn kind.
Un az dos kind hot gezen men vil
    zayn foter un muter hargen,

What a terrible calamity it was
When a father was estranged from
    his child.
And when the child saw that they
    were about to kill his father and
    mother,

Iz es avekgelofn geshvind,
Un hobn zich in lecher tun farshtekn,
Mit shtroy hobn zey zich ton tsudekn.
Vi hot dos kenen got tsuzen,
Zint titus roshe iz dos nit geshen.

It ran off quickly
And hid in the deepest holes,
Covering itself with straw.
How could God have witnessed this,
Which has not happened since the
    times of the wicked tyrant Titus.

Zey hobn geshprochn : vu iz ayer
    got?
Loz er zich onemen az ir kumt tsu
    shpot ! [7]

They said : Where is your God?

Let Him protect you from this
    shame !

Possibly the above lament was sung and chanted in the manner of other topical ballads of this genre and period. So, too, the following eye witness account of the big fire in Frankfurt on January 4, 1711, may have been chanted and recited before Jewish listeners of that and other cities. Three stanzas follow :

Groyse yelole iz glaych in der kehile
    gevorn,
Men hot glaych mit ayln farshlosn di
    torn.
Ober zi hetn di mi un arbet vol
    kenen shporn,
Den zi zayn doch gi-efnt un farbrent
    gevorn.

A great cry arose in the community,

The gates were immediately locked
    in haste.
But they could have spared
    themselves the effort,
For the blaze opened and burned
    them anyway.

Durch di gasn zayn di layt az di
    meshugoim ahin un her gelofn,
Un hobn ales tsu eyn beshrung ton
    hofn.
Ober dos fayer iz ales fun eyn hoyz
    tsu den andern gelofn,
Dos hot orim un raych b'oylom haze
    betrofn,

People ran like madmen through the
    streets,
Hoping desperately for some
    salvation.
But the fire spread from house to
    house
Sparing no one, neither rich nor
    poor in the world.

Kley-koydesh ukley-kesef, tsin, mesh,
    kuper iz ales in frankfurt ful
    gevezn,

Holy vessels and vessels of silver,
    zinc, copper, of which there
    was much in Frankfurt,

Als farbrent un fargeshmoltsn, un veynig der fun genezn.	Were all burned and melted and little was saved.
Zelche tsore iz in oylem noch nit gevezn,	Such a catastrophe was not known in the world;
Mir hobn lang derfun tsu shraybn un tsu lezn.[8]	We shall long read and write about it.

Another lament, which describes in a hundred stanzas the dreadful plague in Prague during the year 1713, concludes with a tabulation of the daily death of the many who perished. Following are three stanzas from this tragic song, which, like other topical songs of this period, served as a living newspaper in chant and rhyme.

Yontev un tishe-bov iz gevezn tsuglaychn,	Feast day and fast day were alike,
Men hot nit erkent orim als raychn.	There was no difference between poor and rich.
Als iz mit gebiktn kop gegangen,	Everyone went about with bowed head,
Den er hot ni gevust oyb er den morgedign tog vert erlangen.	Not knowing whether he would survive until the morrow.
Kegn hundert kind betrin zayn oyfgegangen,	A hundred women were writhing in birth pains,
Kayn heybam iz do gevezn di dos kind hot zoln empfangen,	And no midwife was there to receive the newborn babes.
Der man hot fil mol di heybam zelbstn muzn zayn,	The husband many times had to be the midwife himself
Dies hot ale beyde gebracht in der erden anayn.	And then buried mother and child together in one grave.
Nit kenen mayne oygn fun trern trukn vern,	My eyes cannot cease their weeping,
Acht ober nayn hundert meysim zoln mit eynmol lign oyf der erdn.	To see eight or nine hundred corpses on the ground unburied.
Gantse gezinder zayn varn oysgerisn,	Whole families torn asunder,
Iber dizn mayn oygn bach trern flisn.[9]	That is why my eyes weep rivers of tears!

Up to the middle of the eighteenth century, the differences between the Jews of the West and those of Eastern Europe were not too great. At the beginning of the nineteenth century, the contrast between the two could not have been greater. The center of gravity of Jewish settlement had now shifted to Russia, where the Jewish population outnumbered that of the rest of Europe and took a cultural course different from that of the West.

Under Czarist rule, compressed into the Pale of Settlement, limited in their pursuits, constantly persecuted and deprived of economic, religious, social, and cultural freedom, the Jewish population was forever at the mercy of each succeeding Czarist monarch and the mounting fury of his edicts, ukases, and decrees. Yet, the Jewish communities of Eastern Europe continued to preserve their traditional heritage for generations and achieved a higher degree of Jewish cultural development than the Jews of other countries.

No other Jewish community created a body of anonymous folk song to equal the Yiddish folk songs of the nineteenth century. Among these, a large number serve to illuminate the popular sentiments towards historical and social phenomena during that period.

Recruitment, Soldiers, and Wars

Of great historical significance are the songs which relate to the period when "Alexander Pavlovitsh" (Nicholas I) issued his infamous military edict of 1827. This decree ordered all Russian subjects to supply the Czarist army with a quota of soldiers who were to serve for twenty-five years! For the Jews, the period of this ukase is known as the dark days of the *rekruchine* ("recruitment"), the *chaperlech* ("snatchers"), and the *kantonistn* ("child recruits") and represents a bloody page of Jewish martyrology in Czarist Russia.

This was not an ordinary military edict, and every paragraph relating to the Jewish population carried punitive orders. To fill the quota, Jewish recruits could be taken at the tender age of twelve, trained, and serviced out to rich Russian peasants till the age of eighteen, when their military service officially began! The feeling of doom which characterizes the recruitment songs of this period is revealed in the following two excerpted examples:

(1)

Az aleksander pavlovitsh iz meylech gevorn,	When Nicholas I became king,
Zenen yidishe hertser freylech gevorn, oyvey, oyvey!	Jewish hearts became "gay," oh, woe!

Pogrom in Frankfurt-am-Main, August 22–23, 1614.
Copper engraving, German, 1624

Der ershter ukaz iz aropgekumen oyf yidishe zelner,	The first decree for Jewish soldiers was issued,
Zenen zich ale tselofn in di puste yelder, oyvey, oyvey ! [10]	Then all fled to the wild woods, oh, woe !

(2)

Vi es iz biter, mayn libe muter,	As it is bitter, mother dear,
A shefele afn grinen groz.	For a little lamb alone on the grass
Azoy iz biter, mayn libe muter,	So it is bitter, mother dear,
Me tut doch mir chapn vi a hoz.	To be caught like a hare.

Vi es iz biter, mayn libe muter,	As it is bitter, mother dear,
A beymele on riter.	For a little tree so bare,
Azoy iz biter, mayn libe muter,	So it is bitter, mother dear,
Me tut doch mir machn far a moskoviter.[11]	When they turn me into a Muscovite.

The Jewish community leaders (*kahal*), which were held strictly accountable for the Jewish quota of recruits, were forced to assume the role of Czarist police agents, often performing their function mercilessly, impressing into the army young men who did not meet the health requirements, kidnapping the sons of the poor who lacked the necessary funds to be released from military service. In default of a sufficient number of adults, little children were seized.[12] Bribery was rampant, and the impoverished mass was the tragic scapegoat.[13] Following are excerpted stanzas from a longer ballad, in which a young man, trying to hide from the *kahal* "snatchers," is caught by them.

Vi er hot genumen dem ershtn vort bentshn,	No sooner did he begin to pray,
Zenen arayngekumen a fule shtub mentshn.	Then a whole crowd of people came into the house.
—Yidn, ich veys ir zayt gekumen nit noch veyts un nit noch korn,	"Jews, I know you didn't come for wheat nor corn,
Ir zayt doch gekumen noch mayne yunge yorn!	But have come for my young life!
Ch'ob nit kayn gelt fun aych zich oystsukoyfn,	I have no money to bribe you with,
Di vegn t'ir mir farshtelt, ich hob nit vu tsu antloyfn.	You have barred all the roads, and I have nowhere to run."
M'hot im avekgeleygt af dr'erd, di keytn tsu shlisn,	They put him on the ground to bind him in chains,
Di letste kapotke hot men im f'breklech tsurisn.	They tore his only coat to shreds.
Di muter iz tsu di kohols-layt glaych gelofn,	His mother ran to the *kahal* elders immediately,
Hot zi far tsores di tir nit getrofn.[14]	But in her anguish, she could not find the right door.

Another anonymous song of that period, which expresses the deep hatred of the poor for the cruelties perpetrated upon them by their community elders, is the following:

Trern gisn zich in di gasn	Tears flow in the streets,
In kindershe blut ken men zich vashn.	One can bathe in the blood of children.
Gevald, vos iz dos far a klog?	Woe, what a dreadful time!
Tsi den vet keynmol nit vern tog?	Will the dawn then never come?

Kleyne oyfelech rayst men fun cheyder,
Men tut zey on y'vonishe kleyder.
Undzere parneysim, undzere rabonim,
Helfn noch optsugebn zey far y'vonim.

Es iz a mitsve optsugebn prostakes,

Shuster, shnayder, zenen doch leydakes!
Kretsige chay-itseklech fun a mishpoche a sheyner,
Tor bay undz nit avekgeyn nit eyner! [15]

Infants are dragged out of school,
They are dressed in military clothes.
Our elders, our rabbis,

Only help to send them into the military.

It is a good deed to give up the common folk,
Cobblers, tailors, are mere do-nothings!
But lousy kids from a nice family,

Not one of them must go for a soldier!

During this recruiting inquisition of Nicholas I, the Crimean War was in progress and thousands of Jewish soldiers were fighting and dying and being interred in "brotherly graves" together with the hundreds of thousands of Russian soldiers who fell beneath the walls of Sevastopol. A sarcastic ditty of that period, is the following:

Velches meydl s'nemt a zelner
Iz nit vert kayn prute.
Geyn, geyn kayn sevastopol,
Vi an oks tsu der sh'chite.

Velches meydl s'nemt a zelner,
Iz zi nit vert kayn drayer,
Geyn, geyn kayn sevastopol,
In dos ershte fayer. [16]

Any girl who marries a soldier,
Isn't worth a coin.
For he goes off to Sevastopol,
Like an ox led to the slaughter.

Any girl who marries a soldier,
Isn't worth a threepenny piece,
For he goes off to Sevastopol,
Into the firing lines.

In 1856 juvenile conscription was abolished, and in 1874 the last stringent laws of the older recruitment edicts were abandoned, and normal military service was introduced for all citizens alike. Below, three excerpted stanzas of a song are given, in which the sons of the poor express their glee with the new "equality" laws.

Negidishe kinder, hert uf tsu shtifn,
Ir shpilt shoyn nit kayn groyse role,
Ot bald vet men aych tsum zhereb rufn,
Soldatn vet ir shoyn zayn ale.

Rich men's sons, stop your frolicking,
You're not so important any more.
Soon, you will be called to the service,
And you will all have to be soldiers then.

Pervegilde kuptses, oys meyuchosim,	"First guilders" are not special now!
Dvoryanes hobn shoyn oych kayn vert;	The nobility doesn't mean a thing either.
Glaych mit dem gemeynem bidnem yosim,	Together with the common, poor orphan,
Vet ir geyn oych, oyb aych iz bashert.	You too will have to serve, if it's your fate.
Nachotnikes veln shoyn far aych nit geyn.	Substitutes won't go for you any more.
Ir vet shoyn kayn kapores nit shlogn,	Others won't be your scapegoats.
Di kapores vet ir shoyn zayn aleyn,	The victims you yourselves will be.
Ir megt avade veynen un klogn.[17]	You'd better cry, you'd better weep.

At the turn of the century, the Czarist government was training recruits for service in the Far East, and Jewish soldiers marched away, often with only a vague idea where Manchuria was, to assist Russia in making it a part of Siberia—an area in which Jews were forbidden to reside. The stanza below speaks of the distant Amur River on the Russian-Manchurian border and the Dniester River on the Podolian-Bessarabian border, from which the recruits in this particular song came.

Tsvishn tol un barg tut men undz fartraybn,	Between vale and hill we are being driven,
Men traybt undz kayn amur avek;	We are being driven to the Amur;
Vi azoy veln mir ariber dem nester?	How will we cross the Dniester?
Men traybt undz kayn amur avek![18]	We are being driven to the far-off Amur!

The following excerpt speaks of a "roundup" in 1899 and the anguish of parting lovers, as the raw recruit is being sent off to the Far East.

Inem toyznt acht hundert nayn-un-nayntsigstn yor,	In the year 1899,
Hot zich ge-efnt a nayer *nabor*,	A new roundup began,
Oy vey mamenyu, fun veynen bin ich mat,	Oh, mother dear, I am weak with weeping,
Ich hob nisht kayn *legote*, ch'bin a fartiger soldat.	I have no exemption and am a full-fledged soldier.
Ade, ade, mayn gelibte kale,	Adieu, adieu, my beloved bride,
Noch dir vel ich benken mer vi noch ale,	I will miss you more than anyone else,

Mayn gelibte kale, oy, bet far mir got,	Beloved bride, oh, pray to God for me,
Men zol mich nit *zasnatshen* in *dalni vostok*.[19]	That I'm not sent to the Far East.

Yiddish folk song of the nineteenth century does not include lyrical descriptions of battles nor epic songs glorifying war. Wherever war is mentioned, it deals with the suffering of the soldiers and the miseries that come in its wake. The earlier, nineteenth-century soldier songs were laments and cries, chanted or intoned, expressing the loneliness of the raw recruit far from home, the hardships of the pious in the hostile, anti-Semitic, Czarist army, where Jews suffered as second-class citizens at the hands of the sadistic military. The pain of parting from one's loved ones, one's home, is especially poignant, as revealed in the following lonely cry :

Nit kayn shtub, nit kayn balkn,	No house, no ceiling,
Nit kayn mamen, nit kayn tatn,	No mother, no father,
Refrain: Nemt mich on a geveyn,	My heart weeps,
In soldatn muz men geyn.	I must go for a soldier.
Nit kayn dach, nit kayn fenster,	No roof, no window,
Nit kayn bruder, nit kayn shvester. . . .	No brother, no sister. . . .
Nit kayn tir, nit kayn breter,	No door, no floorboards,
Nit kayn mumen, nit kayn feter. . . .[20]	No aunt, no uncle. . . .

In another, which employs a simple rhyming device set to the rhythm of marching feet and the cry of "one-two-three-four" following each line, the contrast is drawn between the tragedy of enforced recruitment and the warm security of one's family, the glow of the Sabbath eve, and the good traditional dishes to eat.

Fraytig-tsunachts derlangt men di chales, eyns-tsvey-dray-fir,	Sabbath eve, the twisted loaf is served, one-two-three-four,
Nemt men tsu chasanim fun kales, eyns-tsvey-dray-fir.	Grooms are taken from their brides, one-two-three-four.
Fraytig-tsunachts derlangt men di fish, etc.	Sabbath eve, the fish is served, etc.
Nemt men tsu mayn zun fun tish, . . .	My son is snatched away from the table, . . .

Fraytig-tsunachts derlangt men di lokshn, etc.	Sabbath eve, the noodles are served, etc.
Undz traybt men avek, azoy vi di oksn, . . .	We are driven off, like oxen, . . .
Fraytig-tsunachts derlangt men di fleysh, etc.	Sabbath eve, the meat is served, etc.
Undz traybt men avek in blutign shveys, . . .	We are driven off in bloody sweat, . . .
Fraytig-tsunachts derlangt men dem tsimes, etc.	Sabbath eve, the compote is served, etc.
Undz traybt men avek in vayte medines, . . .[21]	We are driven off into distant lands, . . .

A large number of love songs of the nineteenth century deal with the impact of recruitment and war, separation and the wrecked lives of lovers and young married people, parents deprived of their children, children orphaned and bereft. On the whole, no one wanted to serve in the army of the Czar, who only oppressed and persecuted the Jews in civilian life. No man wanted to sleep in the barracks on "cold bunks, . . . eat rotten cabbage, . . . go to Japan and be buried in far-off Manchuria in a common grave with dead horses. . . . To serve the Russian pig is no good—oh, he bathes in our blood."[22] In the following stanzas, a young woman cries out to heaven in anguish, upon parting from her beloved:

Kayn esn un kayn trinken mame, nemt mich nit,	I cannot eat or drink, mother,
Ich bin mit mayne heyse trern, oy-vey zat.	Only my tears now satisfy me.
Ich freg un freg, un keyner enfert nit,	I ask and ask but no one has the answer,
Farvos zol zayn mayn chosn a soldat?	Why must my darling be a soldier?
Oy, du tayerer got,	Oh, dear God,
Vi azoy vel ich es konen tsuzen!	How shall I be able to bear it!
Der keyser vet tsunemen mayn tayern briliant,	The Czar will take away my precious jewel,
Un ich vel darfn fundervaytns shteyn.[23]	And I shall have to stand by helplessly.

Miscellaneous Topical Songs

The nineteenth century was rich in social, religious, political, and cultural movements: Chasidism; Haskalah; the development of the trade unions and the struggle of the working class against tyranny; mass migrations to America; the settling in Palestine. These deep-rooted movements, punctuated by specific events, are revealed in whole groups of songs (treated elsewhere in this book) which mirror the popular sentiments of the times. There are other songs which mirror fragmentarily certain reactions to current events. Such for instance is the brief rhyme given below, which refers to a law of May 1, 1850, which imposed a tax on the traditional Jewish attire and created a calamitous situation among the Chasidic masses of Poland.

A zun mit a tatn, tut oys di chalatn,	Son and father, remove your long coats,
Di tayere b'godim mit di koshere fodim,	The precious clothes sewed with holy thread,
Mit di pasmes un mit di knopn.	With the stripes and large buttons. . . .
Lomir veynen, lomir shrayen,	Let us weep, let us cry,
Tsu dem keyser nikolayen! [24]	To Czar Nicholas!

From the very beginning of Czarist rule over the Pale sporadic attempts were made to settle Jews on land, but the progress was slow and the efforts of the government extremely erratic. Instead, the first quarter of the nineteenth century witnessed the mass expulsion of Jews from the villages in White Russia, from the western frontier towns, and from certain cities (Kiev, Sevastopol, Nikolayev). In Rumania, where the situation was especially severe, the plight of the Jewish people on the brink of complete economic ruin is described in the following song:

Shlechte yorn, bitere tsaytn,	Bad years and bitter times
Hobn mir zich yidelech do in rumania fardint.	We Jews in Rumania have lived to see.
Es falt undz tsu fun ale zaytn,	From all sides, there descend on us
Ale tog a naye vund!	Daily, fresh wounds!
Nay-geborene kaptsonim,	Newborn paupers
Zey vaksn vi groz in feld;	Grow like grass in the field,
Zey faln nebech af dem ponim,	They fall, alas, on their faces,
Fun dorsht un fun kelt. . . .	From thirst and cold. . . .
In dorf zenen mir gezesn,	We lived in the village,
Un plutsling hot men undz faryogt. . . .	When suddenly we were driven out. . . .

Fun di derfer hot men undz fartribn,
Fun di shenken mit a vildn kas. . . .

From the villages we were hounded,
From the inns, with a wild fury. . . .

Parnose vert geminert teglech
M'geyt oys far a shtikl broyt! [25]

Our livelihood shrinks daily,
We are starving for a crust of bread.

In 1807, four Jewish agricultural colonies, numbering two thousand "souls," were established in Kherson (South Russia). Although the following year the expulsion of Jews from the villages was in full swing, the number of applicants seeking to settle on the land continued to increase, as is evidenced in the eagerness expressed in the following example:

Hot ir gehert dos land chersan
Nisht vayt funem feter yishmoel,

Have you heard of the land Kherson,
Not far from Uncle Ishmael
(Turkey).

Fun foygl-milch iz dort faran—
Far yidn erets-yisroel.

They even have bird's milk there—
It's the Land of Israel for Jews.

A payem a tsig, a shof a drayer,

Goats are cheap and sheep are only
three kopeks,

A hun, a indik halb umzist.
Altsding b'zilzol, kayn zach nisht
tayer,
Un tvu-es dortn ful vi mist.

A hen, a turkey are half the cost.
Everything is reasonable, nothing is
dear,
And there are all kinds of grains,
dirt cheap.

Dos land iz gut un voyl, a vinder,

The land is good and kind and
wonderful,

Oyb lebn, brider, vilt ir fayn,
Farnemt di klimkes, vayb un   inder

If you want to live well, brothers,
Take your bundles, wife and
children,

Un lomir oyle-regl zayn! [26]

And start on foot in that direction.

In 1836 the Russian government decided to open up certain lands in the territory of Omsk, and over a thousand Jews declared their readiness to settle in the frigid Siberian steppes. But the following year, the Czar changed his mind and gave orders to intercept those who were on their way and transfer them to the Jewish colonies in Kherson. The permission granted at first was greeted with enthusiasm, as the following indicates.

Ver lebt zich azoy fray
Vi der zemledelets mit zayn plug?
Er iz zayn gezeln,
Zayn emeser drug.

Who lives so free
As the farmer with his plough?
It is his apprentice,
His true friend.

Ven di zun geyt nor oyf,	When the sun rises,
Shteyt er oyf shoyn gants fri,	He gets up bright and early,
A gezunter, a frisher,	Healthy, spry,
Opgerut fun zayn mi.	Rested after his toil.
Gebentsht iz der keyser,	Blessed be the king,
Der keyser nikolay,	King Nicholas,
Vos hot undz gegebn praves,	Who gave us privileges
Un hot undz gemacht azoy fray.[27]	And made us free.

The year 1861 saw the abolition of serfdom in Russia; 1863, the Polish insurrection. Both are reflected in children's rhymes: the first in a question-and-answer game, which reveals the sad plight of the peasantry on the eve of 1861, the second is a counting-out rhyme:

(1)

Lashinke vaysinke, avu biztu geven?	White little weasel, where have you been?
—Baym har geven.	—At the lord's.
Vos hostu fardint?	What did you earn?
—A shtikeles kez.	—A piece of cheese.
Avu hostu geleygt?	Where did you put it?
—In *popyets*.	—In a hole under the stove.
Avu iz der popets?	Where is the hole?
—Mit vaser farlofn.	—Filled with water.
Avu i' di vaser?	Where is the water?
—Oksn oysgetrunken.	—Oxen drank it.
Avu i' di oksn?	Where are the oxen?
—Dubines hobn tseharget.	—Brutally beaten with thick
Avu di dubines?	Where are the thick sticks? [sticks.
—Verem hobn tsegesn.	—Eaten up by worms.
Avu zaynen di verim?	Where are the worms?
—Hiner hobn tsepikt.	—Pecked by hens.
Avu zaynen di hiner?	Where are the hens?
—Oyfn feld avekgefloygn.	—Flew off to the field.
Avu i' di feld?	Where is the field?
—Mit krashkes farvoksn.	—Overgrown with weeds.
Avu i' di krashkes?	Where are the weeds?
—Meydlech hobn tserisn.	—Torn up by the girls.
Avu zaynen di meydlech?	Where are the girls?
—Yinglech hobn tsenumen.	—Carried off by the boys.
Avu zaynen di yinglech?	Where are the boys?
—Oyf milchome avekgelofn.	—Ran off to war.
Avu di milchome?	Where is the war?
Bizn kni in blut![28]	—Up to knees in blood!

(2)

Oy, undzere polyn, zenen antkegn yidn!	Oh, our Poles are against Jews!
Oy, undzere felder zenen fargosn mit blut.	Oh, our fields are covered with blood.
Heybt men on arumtsuyogn, heybt men on arumtsuplogn,	We begin to race about, we begin to wander about,
Dali oyf di ferd, dali tsum gever!	To horse, to arms!
Eyns-tsvey-dray, machn mir pleyte aray! [29]	One-two-three, we run off!

The general misery and oppression in the land, the tensions and the struggles for democratic rights and privileges, the brutal, exceptional laws against the Jews in every area of endeavor continued to mount and erupt in strikes, crises, and pogroms, until the turn of the century found Russia on the eve of economic collapse.

Harking back to the tragic chronicles of several centuries earlier, the pogrom songs of the nineteenth century are personal accounts of actual occurrences. The following, like the laments of the older period, relates certain circumstances of the Odessa pogrom of 1871:

Ver es hot in blat gelezn,	Whoever has read in the papers,
Vegn der barimter shtot ades.	About the famous city of Odessa.
Ach, vos far an umglik s'hot getrofn,	Oh, what a tragedy took place there,
In eyne tsvey-dray mesles.	All in a short two or three days.
Plutsling hot men oysgeshri-en:	Suddenly, someone shouted:
Ay, shlog dem yidn vi vayt ir kont!	Ay, beat the Jews with all your might!
Oy, shteyner in di fenster hobn genumen fli-en,	Oh, stones began to fly into windows,
A pogrom hot zich opgerisn in eyn moment.	A pogrom broke out in a moment.
Merder zenen in di gasn gefloygn,	Murderers flew through the streets,
Mit di hek, mit di mesers in di hent gegreyt,	With hatchets and knives in their hands,
Ay, vu nor a yidn getrofn,	Ay, wherever they came upon a Jew,
Oy, glaych im oyf an ort geteyt. [30]	They killed him on the spot, oh!

The largest pogrom prior to the Russo-Japanese War (1904) took place in Kishinev in 1903 and sent a shudder through the Jews all over the world. [31] The following excerpt from a song speaks of the looting, killing, and aimless destruction, in simple, stark terms.

In keshenev brent doch a fayer,	There is a fire in Kishinev,
Men zet nit kayn roych un kayn flam,	No smoke or flame can be seen,
Men hot geharget zeyer fil yidn,	Many Jews have been murdered,
In keshenev iz a pogrom.	In Kishinev there is a pogrom.
Moyern dray gorn tsubrochn,	Three-storied houses were demolished,
Federn z'gegangen vi shney,	Feathers fell like snow,
Zaydens un tayere sametn	Satins and expensive velvets,
Iz oychet gevezn tsvishn zey.[32]	Were also among them.

On April 24, 1905, three months after the outbreak of the Russian Revolution, the pogrom of Zhitomir took place. The brutal massacre in St. Petersburg of unarmed, peaceful Russians, headed by the priest Gapon, petitioning for bread and peace before the Winter Palace three months earlier, gave impetus to the revolutionary activities. The threat of pogroms was met by organized Jewish self-defense groups, who fought and died gallantly in the unequal struggle with the armed, Cossack horsemen. Excerpts of two songs which reveal the participation of organized workmen in the defense of Jews during the Zhitomir pogrom are the following:

(1)

Efsher vilt ir, mentshn visn,	People, perhaps you would like to know,
Vi der pogrom iz geven	How the pogrom took place.
Shabes farnacht af der polikovke,	Saturday evening on Polikovke,
Iz gefaln a chaver vi a shteyn.	A comrade fell, like a stone.
Vi mir zenen in gas aroysgegangen,	As we came out into the street,
Shrayan chuliganes: *bey zhidov!*	Rioters were yelling: kill the Jews!
Vi mir zenen tsum *ploshtshadek* tsugekumen,	As we approached the square,
Gefaln iz der student blinov.	Blinov, the student, fell dead.
Vi di kozakn zenen ongekumen,	As the Cossacks arrived,
Mit di *oruzhes* in di hent,	With their guns in their hands,
Dem ershtn vistrel hobn zey gegebn.	They shot their first round of fire
Un zhitomir af prach farbrent.[33]	And burned Zhitomir to the ground.

(2)

A shteyn klapt a tsigl, a tsigl klapt a shteyn,	A stone strikes brick and a brick strikes stone,
Un vaynshteyn der ershter, gefaln oyf podayl.	And Weinstein was the first to be killed on Podayl.

Di fentster mit di tirn hobn ongehoybn tsu klingen,	The windows and the doors began to ring,
Ale chuliganes do yogn un zingen.	All the rioters race about and sing.
Mit di royte fonen, neyn, chaverim, neyn!	With our red flags, comrades, no!
Mir torn nit shvaygn, mir muzn geyn.[34]	We must not be silent, we must go.

The Russo-Japanese War and the 1905 Revolution

The sympathy of the Jewish population was hardly with the Czarist armies and the Russian fleet in the struggle with Japan. The blood of the innocents who fell in the pogrom which swept many cities and towns cried out for revenge, and when the Czarist defeats began to mount, the Jews were convinced that an act of God was directing the hand of the Japanese victor.

Far kishinever blut batsolt yaponye gut,	Japan is settling accounts for the blood of Kishinev,
Zayn shtrof hot er endlech atsind bakumen;	The Czar has finally gotten his punishment.
Getsaygt hot im got, az ales vos er hot,	God has shown him that what he got
Iz alts shuldig di blutige pogromen.	Was because of the bloody pogroms.
Der kleyntshiger yapan, er shnaydt dem tiran,	Little Japan is cutting the tyrant down,
Der kleyner tut yetst dem groysn teytn;	The little one is now killing the big one;
Vayl du host dos folk gedrikt, umshuldige farshikt,	Because you oppressed the people, exiled innocent ones,
Rache nemen zey fun dervaytn.[35]	They are taking revenge from afar.

Another folk song, set to the somber, traditional chant of the Book of Lamentations, reveals the sardonic glee and the pent-up emotions of the Jews during this war, which was compelling many of them to serve side by side with a military which in other instances was cutting them down mercilessly.

S'helft nisht kayn tseylemen,	The sign of the cross
S'helft nisht kayn tsar,	Or the Czar won't help you,
Mit trern bavasht er zich,	The Russian fool
Der rusisher nar.	Is drenched in his own tears.

S'shtumen zayne harmatn,	His guns are silent,
S'zhavert zayn shverd,	His sword is rusting,
Zogt eycho-yishvo	Chant Lamentations
Un zitst oyf der erd.	And sit on the ground.
Katsapn zogt kines	Repent on your sins,
Oyf ayere zind,	You simple *katsaps,*
Der tsar iz oyf tsores,	The Czar is in trouble,
Es blutigt der hunt.[36]	The dog is bleeding.

The families of Jewish soldiers fighting for a government they hated sang bitterly: "How long will the war last, / How long will the blood flow? / Mothers sorrow, / Receiving no news of their children. / Orphans, widows are left behind, / Never to hear again from their men reported missing. / Their husbands were driven to their death, / And the women shall never be able to remarry. . . ."[37]

The feeling of delight that "little David" (Japan) was able to defeat the "big Russian Bear" (Goliath) was widespread, and a number of songs reflected this sentiment. In others of this period, the yearning for the end of the war was tied to the hope for an end to Russian autocracy and anti-Semitism and for the dawn of "freedom and equality of mankind." Czarist autocracy, which was oppressing all the people under its rule, was also bringing many together in the struggle against it. The following song reflects the dream of "Christians and Jews, singing a song together":

Vi baroysht iz di velt gevorn	How astonished was the world
Yaponye mit zayn krig,	With Japan's war;
Rusland hot farloyrn,	Russia was defeated,
Ge-endigt iz di krig.	The war was at an end.
Ale mir zenen tsufridn,	We are all satisfied,
S'macht nisht kayn untershid:	There is no difference between us:
Kristn tsuzamen mit yidn	Christians together with Jews,
Zingen mir yetst dos lid.	Are now singing this song.
Der sof vet zayn fun di	There will be an end to the
antisemitn,	anti-Semites,
Az rusland vet zayn fray,	When Russia will be free,
Vayl yidish blut shvaygt keynmol	Because Jewish blood never
nisht	forgets
Dem tsar nikolay.[38]	Czar Nicholas.

The spirit of the revolution was spreading like wildfire through the Russian Empire. "Through our windows in Warsaw . . . we could see

Cossacks on horseback attacking and shooting down demonstrators, leaving them wounded and dead, to be picked up later by their comrades and borne in demonstrative funeral marches. I remember the night of January 9, when we heard the news from Petersburg of the bloody occurrences before the Winter Palace, when the military shot down hundreds of unarmed peaceful demonstrators. You felt as if it were before a storm." [39]

The erratic Czar granted a constitution, guaranteeing the people broad political freedoms, and then hastily withdrew it. Once more, in the large cities, unarmed demonstrators were mowed down by armed Cossacks on horseback and rumors of pogroms in preparation filled the air. Freedom, equality, a better life became synonymous with the yearning of ever-increasing numbers of Russians, Ukrainians, Jews, and Poles for an end to the war, to tyranny, to Czarist autocracy.

Vi lang noch vet dos vildikeyt existirn mit ir sharfn trit,	How much longer will this senselessness go on with its cruel tread?
Di mentshn, m'tut zey regulirn,	The people are oppressed,
M'tsapt oys fun zey dos blut.	Their blood is drained from them.
Ven vet shoyn di frayhayt onkumen,	When will freedom come at last,
Ven vet shoyn dos vildikeyt vern ayngeshlungen,	When will this madness be swallowed up?
Demlt vet zich kontshen di milchome,	Then the war will cease,
Un di feygelech veln onheybn fray zingen. [40]	And the little birds will begin to sing freely.

The epic ballad may be rare in Yiddish folk song, but the occasional ballad on the theme of some popular folk hero or celebrity does occur. Two internationally prominent Jewish personalities, who rated being subjects of such folk ballads, were Baron de Rothschild (possibly Alphonse), of the famous dynasty of financier-philanthropists, and the French captain, Alfred Dreyfus. The fabulous wealth and influence of the Rothschilds stimulated the imagination of the people, and a popular ballad resulted, which stressed the moral of the transitoriness of wealth and the strange twist of fate. Following are three stanzas from a variant of this ballad :

Nemt zich a muser, ir groyse milyonern,	Remember this moral, you great millionaires,
Fun Rotshild dem goldenem ponem,	About Rothschild, that face of gold,
Vi azoy me ken nit mit gold shtoltsirn,	How you cannot boast with your money,

Geshtorbn iz er vi ale kaptsonim.

For he died like all paupers.

Rotshild iz in kase arayngekumen,
Un hot gevolt mit zayn gold
　　shpekulirn,
Azoy iz er teykef gefangen gevorn :
Se hot zich far im farmacht ale tirn.

Rothschild went into his money
　　vault,
He wanted to speculate with his
　　gold,
But he was immediately trapped,
When all the doors closed in upon
　　him.

Zibn mesles hot er hunger gelitn,
Un dos blut fun zayne finger
　　gezoygn.
Oy, Rotshild hot zich barimt far ale
　　keysorim,
Az er ken fun kayn hunger nit
　　shtarben.
Tsum sof zet men dem groysn
　　umglik,
Vi er ligt tsebrochn vi a sharbn.[41]

Seven days he hungered and starved,
Sucking the blood from his
　　fingers.
Oh, Rothschild was famous above
　　all rulers,
That he would never die of
　　starvation.
In the end, witness his great
　　tragedy,
As he lies there like a broken
　　skeleton.

The infamous *affaire Dreyfus,* on the other hand, deeply shocked the
Eastern European Jews, who never expected an anti-Semitic injustice
of this magnitude from the democratic French Republic. This mis-
carriage of justice and the personal tragedy of the young French Jewish
Captain was treated in the Jewish press, literature, and popular ballad.
The ballad dramatically describes the tragedy when Dreyfus is deprived
of his rank ("his golden tassels were torn off"), the viciousness of his
enemies ("they stood at a distance, gnashing their teeth"), who betrayed
not only Dreyfus "but his whole country as well," his being "shackled and
exiled like the worst bandit." Two stanzas from this ballad follow :

Klogt un veynt ir yidishe kinder,
Klogt un veynt gor on ayn tsol.
Klogt un veynt ayederer bazunder,
Far dem unshuldign man : Dreyfus.

Weep and wail, you Jewish children,
Cry and weep without an end.
Weep and wail each and everyone
For the innocent man : Dreyfus.

Alfred dreyfus, der kapitan,
Halt iber di tsores, vert gornit mid.

Alfred Dreyfus, the captain,
Bears all his sorrows and does not
　　weaken.

Er zitst oyf dem tayfl's indzl aleyn,
Un zingt zich tsu azoy ayn troyrig
　　lid.[42]

He sits on Devil's Island alone
And sings a sad song to himself.

World War I

With the outbreak of World War I in 1914, the Jewish communities in Eastern Europe were once more exposed to the tragedies of war and the excesses leveled against them as second-class citizens in the Czarist lands. Once again, the Jewish male population was called up to serve in an army and face the dangers and horrors of war in defense of a government which mistreated and persecuted them even in peacetime. The songs of this period are, in the main, somber and stark, constructed in the form and mood of dirges and laments.

In the excerpted stanzas of the following, although the singer had already served his three-year stint in the Czarist army, he is once again torn from his wife and children.

Och, toyznt nayn hundert, in dem fertsntn yor,	Oh, in the year of 1914,
Iz geven, och, ayn shlechte nabor.	There was, oh, a terrible roundup.
Me hot tsugenumen tates fun vayber un fun kinder,	Fathers were taken from their wives and their children;
Me hot undz farshikt in der shtot Lvov.	We were sent away to the city of Lwow.
Oy, af di karpate berg zaynen mir geshtanen,	Oh, in the Carpathian mountains we were stationed,
Oy, germantses hobn mir gezen fil,	Oh, many Germans did we see,
Zey hobn geton shisn mit zeyere granatn,	They shot at us with their grenades,
Un blut iz fargosn zeyer fil.[43]	And very much blood was spilled.

History has recorded the inefficiency and corruption of the Czarist military during that conflict, in which the population in the rear and the troops at the front all suffered from lack of clothing, starvation, disorganization, and exposure. The hospitals were overflowing, understaffed, ill supplied with the simplest medicaments. A tragic ballad, still retained in the memory of Yiddish-speaking Jews today, is one about a wounded soldier who releases his bride from her engagement vows because of his terrible condition. Following are two stanzas:

A brivele vel ich dir mamenyu shraybn,	Mother dear, I'm writing you a letter,
Un shraybn mamenyu, vel ich dir fun mayn gezunt.	I'm writing you, dear mother, about my health. . . .

Oy, a hant hot men mir
    aropgenumen,
Un oyf beyde oygn bin ich
    mamenyu, blind.

Oh, they've amputated one of my
    arms,
And I am blinded on both of my
    eyes.

Ich shrayb oych a brivele tsu mayn
    kale,
Un shraybn shrayb ich ir nor vegn ir
    aleyn,
Az di t'noyim zol zi tseraysn,

Un far a tsveytn tsu der chupe
    geyn."

I'm also writing a letter to my
    bride,
And to her, I'm writing only of her,

I'm asking her to tear up our
    engagement
And marry another one instead. . . .

One of the most popular soldier ballads of World War I was the song of the fallen soldier, which was based on a current Ukrainian ballad on the same theme. Below are excerpted stanzas, in which the son, even after death, thinks to spare his mother and, although the mother waits hopefully for the return of her beloved son, he never returns.

Oyf di grine felder, velder, oy vey,
Ligt mit kuglen badekt a zelner, oy
    vey.

On the green fields, in the woods, oh,
There lies a soldier covered with
    bullets, oh, woe.

Un zayn eyver iz tsurisn, oy vey,
Fun zayne vundn tut blut flisn, oy
    vey.

And his body is torn, oh,
And the blood flows from his
    wounds, oh, woe.

Kumt a foygl oyf zayn keyver, oy
    vey,
Un est zayne oygn fun zayn eyver,
    oy vey.

A bird stops upon his grave, oh,

And pecks at his eyes from his body,
    oh, woe.

Shvartser foygl, fli geshvind, oy vey,
Un zog mayn mamen ch'bin gezunt,
    oy vey.

Blackbird, fly quickly, oh,
And tell my mother I am well,
    oh woe.

Fun mayn toyt zolstu nit dertseyln,
    oy vey,
Vayl mayn mame vet zich eybig
    kveln, oy vey."

Do not tell her of my death, oh,

For she will mourn for me forever,
    oh, woe.

Notes

HISTORICAL AND TOPICAL

1. Bassin, I, pp. 31–33.
2. *Ibid.*, pp. 99–100. Transcribed by N. W. Litinsky in 1884 from the local residents in Bar, who were still singing it at the time. *Haydamakn* was a Jewish term for the Ukrainian bands of that period.
3 Weinreich, pp. 199–209. The calculated year of the coming of the Messiah by Cabalists was 1648. The day of the Nemirov massacre was the twentieth day of Sivan, which coincided with an old fast day memorializing the martyrs of the Crusades. It was appointed a day of mourning to commemorate the victims of the Cossack rebellion. Leading rabbis of the time composed a number of stirring Hebrew dirges and prayers, which were recited in the synagogue on this fateful anniversary. Stanzas 1, 3, 10, 15, 23, 31, and 44 of this lament are given here.
4. Graetz, V, pp. 141, 149.
5. Weinreich, p. 224.
6. *Ibid.*, pp. 234–252. Stanzas 2, 9, 12, 18, 34, 51, and 52 of this song are given here.
7. Bassin, I, pp. 84–86. This lament begins with: *Eycho vi zol ich onheybn tsu zingen un klogn fun dem groysn vezn, / vi tsu frankfurt am main iz ayn groyse sreyfe gevezn* . . . ("Lamentations, how shall I begin to sing and weep upon the calamity, in Frankfurt-am-Main when there was a terrible conflagration.")
8. *Ibid.*, pp. 71–72. (Author: D. Zoygersh of Kronberg and Prague.)
9. *Ibid.*, pp. 73–75. (Author: Moses Eisenshtat. A copy is to be found in the New York Theological Seminary.)
10. G. and M., No. 43.
11. Wengeroff, II, p. 156.
12. Mendele speaks of "songs of recruits who bid their loved ones good-bye as they depart for military service for many, many years. . . . Married fellows leaving their wife and children, and lads, such little ones, poor things, in their daddy's arms, in broad, long coats twice their size, saying good-bye to parents, brothers, and sisters. . . . unfortunate little souls, torn from the tree like fluttering leaves, to be carried off, far, far away, to the cold regions somewhere, among strangers and fat peasants; heaven knows where their remains will come to rest" (Mendele II, pp. 87–88).
13. Zunser describes his experiences as a victim of the snatchers, when he was a lad: "For the communal leaders of those dark days, who constantly sought to thrive on Jewish misery, this *ukase* opened a new traffic. Each Jewish commune sent out its impressors on all roads and highways; they hid in village inns and watched for prey. . . . Those who were seized were bound like sheep, brought to town and locked up in the barracks. . . . The authorities were not over-scrupulous with these unfortunates. Were they weak, sick or defective? No matter. — They were taken, dressed in military clothes, and packed off to serve the Czar. These 'bodies' were sent in place of men whose families could pay a satisfactory price. . . . They would seize young children and sell them to the community 'bosses.' . . . These were times when men

devoured men openly and with consent of the government." (Zunser—Schwarz, pp. 223–224.)

In 1868, when Zunser was thirty-two years old and his brother Akiva was still serving his twenty-five-year military term in the Czarist army, he witnessed a terrible scene while entertaining as a *badchen* at a wedding in Minsk. "At the wedding supper, when I was in the midst of my oration, snatchers and Cossacks came in and took the groom away, right before the eyes of hundreds of guests. This tragic occurrence grieved me so, that I expressed myself rather bitterly about *kahal*. Soon after, the snatchers and Cossacks came to my hotel and led me off to the barracks. . . . I wasn't detained very long but was released with a warning never to criticize *kahal* leaders again. I was silent for a long time, but in 1874, when Alexander II abolished the old system of recruitment, . . . I wrote my song 'Der izborshtshik' ('The Tax Collector'), which I sang everywhere to the delight of my audiences, who had finally been liberated from the Jewish snatchers and the *kahal* bloodsuckers" (Zunser, I, pp. 58–59).

14. G. and M., No. 44.
15. *Ibid.,* No. 50.
16. *Ibid.,* No. 51.
17. Skuditsky, 1936, pp. 241–242, No. 2.
18. Cahan, 1957, No. 473.
19. Rubin, MSS.
20. G. and M., No. 332.
21. D. and Y., pp. 312–313, No. 18.
22. Hershele, p. 101, No. 14. The poet Hershele (Danilevitsh) (1882–1941) died of starvation in the Warsaw ghetto.
23. B. and F., p. 111.
24. G. and M., No. 52.
25. D. and Y., p. 283, No. 1. ". . . The originators of the parliamentary Constitution, the landed proprietors and townspeople, were those who forced the Jews out of the cities, and drove them into land-leasing and liquor-dealing." (Dubnow, I, p. 267). "While leasing from the squire or the crown the right of distilling, the Jew farmed. . . other items of rural economy, such as the dairies, the mills, and the fishing ponds. He was . . . engaged in buying grain from the peasants and selling them . . . such indispensable articles as salt, utensils, agricultural tools, etc., imported by him from the town. He often combined . . . the occupations of liquor-dealer, shopkeeper, and produce merchant. . . . This whole economic structure, which had been built up gradually in the course of centuries, the Russian Government made its business to demolish." (Dubnow, I, p. 362).
26. Mendele, I, pp. 16–17.
27. G. and M., No. 42.
28. Cahan, 1957, No. 460.
29. *Ibid.,* No. 360.
30. Rubin, MSS.
31. The poets S. Frug and Chaim Nachman Bialik both responded to this tragic event with poems. Bialik's Hebrew "Maase nemirov" ("The Story of Nemirov"), so titled to evade the censor's wrath and later retitled "B'ir hah'riga" in Hebrew and "Sh'chite shtot" in Yiddish ("The City of Slaughter"), recalled the city of Nemirov which had yielded the largest number of victims during the Cossack massacres of 1648. Frug's "Shtromen blut un taychn trern" ("Streams of Blood and Rivers of Tears") was set to music by an anonymous composer and became popular on both sides of the Atlantic. Three stanzas, given below, cry out for aid for the stricken and maimed victims of the Kishinev pogrom:

Shtromen blut un taychn trern   Streams of blood and rivers of tears
Zidn, flisn tif un breyt. . . .   Seething, flowing deep and wide. . . .

Undzer alter groyser umglik
Hot zayn hant oyf undz farspreyt.

Our old, terrible tragedy
Has spread its hand over us.

Hert ir dort vi muters klogn,
Un fun kinder dos geshrey?
Toyte lign oyf di gasn,
Kranke faln nebn zey. . . .

Do you hear the mothers weeping,
And the cry of children?
The dead lie in the streets,
The sick fall down beside them. . . .

Brider, shvester, hot rachmones!
Groys un shreklich iz di noyt.
Git: di toyte oyf tachrichim,
Git: di lebedige broyt!

Brothers, sisters, have pity!
Great and terrible is our need.
Give for shrouds for the dead,
Give for bread for the living!

(Yaffe, pp. 27–28.)

32. Rubin, MSS.
33. D. and Y., pp. 289–291, No. 10.
34. Skuditsky, 1933, p. 71, No. 54.
35. Lehman, 1921, pp. 6–7, No. 2 (II, IV).
36. *Ibid.*, pp. 11–12, No. 4. A *katsap* was a worker from Central Russia. Among Jews the term became synonymous with crudeness and ignorance.
37. *Ibid.*, p. 4, No. 1 (I).
38. *Ibid.*, pp. 10–11, No. 3 (I, II).
39. Teitelbaum, pp. 127–133.
40. D. and Y., pp. 313–314, No. 19.
41. *Ibid.*, p. 231, No. 48.
42. Rubin, MSS. Other folk heroes treated in ballads were Hirsh Lekert and Boruch Shulman, mentioned in Chapter XI.
43. Skuditsky, 1936, p. 254, No. 14.
44. Rubin, MSS.
45. Rubin, MSS.

CHAPTER IX

Chasidic Melody and Song

AN ORIGINAL AND UNIQUE TYPE OF FOLK MUSIC WITHIN EASTERN European folk song is Chasidic melody and song, product of the Chasidic movement. Chasidism, which started first in southern Russia and Poland and then spread northward towards Lithuania, was a remarkable religious sect. Originating more than two hundred years ago, it was founded by Reb Yisroel Baal Shem-Tov (1700–1760), often referred to as the Besht— a simple Jew, not a Talmudic scholar, who was said to have been, in turn, a Hebrew teacher for young children, an assistant to a teacher, a carter, a healer, traveling about from one town to the other, preaching his ideas on humanity, Jewishness, God, and the world.[1]

Stressing human nature over human wisdom, joy rather than sadness in prayer, the Besht taught that it was not Torah learning that was the main thing but being good. The Lord does not want only our faith in him, he preached, but also that we *enjoy* this faith. He maintained that the exalted union with the Lord could best be attained not by profound learning nor pious asceticism but by joyous all-embracing ecstasy, that the plain man, imbued with naïve faith and the ability to pray fervently and wholeheartedly, was dearer and nearer to God than the learned formalist who spent his entire life in the study of the Talmud.

The tragic experiences of the Chmelnitski pogroms were still lingering in the memory of the people and the bitter disillusionment of the Sabbatai Zvi movement oppressed the heart of those who had so fervently hoped for an end to the hardships and suffering. Superstition, poverty, ignorance were rampant, and the teachings of the formal, rabbinic scholars were far removed from the mass of the simple people. Encouraging the poor, the persecuted, the suffering, Chasidism brought to the hopelessness and gloom a message of extraordinary simplicity and a ritual of intimacy and joyous brotherhood. Placing joyousness and ecstasy in prayer above scholasticism immediately raised the status of the simplest and most backward members of the oppressed Jewish community in the Pale. It was a religion and a ritual which could be grasped and performed through the senses. . . . Between the years 1782 and 1815, it reached its peak of popularity and counted its vast number of devoted adherents in all strata of the population, but especially among the simple folk.

Like their Cabalist brothers in Palestine, who had made song an important part of their movement,[2] the Chasidim held music — primarily that of the human voice — to be one of the most powerful means of attaining the blessed state of salvation through the expiation of sins, joy in prayer, and the ultimate communion with the Lord. Some Chasidic rabbis[3] even felt that tunes could be so powerful as to rid a pious Chasid of evil. The creation of melodies was consequently regarded as one of the highest virtues. Legend has it that the Besht could hear words in the notes of a tune and was able to follow the very thoughts of the singer. Another *rebe* maintained that he could hear the actual confession of the singer in his melody, though no words were uttered.

Reb Shneyer Zalmen of Liadi (1747–1813)[4] was of the opinion that melody is the outpouring of the soul and the words merely interrupted the stream of emotions. According to him, a melody with text was limited, since with the conclusion of the words, the melody was ended; whereas a tune without words could be repeated endlessly. Some *tsadikim* believed that they could reach into the heavens sooner with the power of song than with prayer. Melodies were used to purify the fallen soul, to heal the sick, and perform all manner of miracles. Some held that the sphere of music was adjacent to the sphere of penitence, and, in many cases, supernatural powers were even attributed to a tune. This approach resulted in a mass of wordless melodies, created by the Chasidic *rebeyim* and their followers.[5]

The Chasidic movement grew by leaps and bounds. The Chasidic *rebeyim* built up their dynasties and "courts" in the various parts of the Pale. Perhaps they saw themselves in the role of knights, wandering from town to town in the company of their attendants, followers, and admirers, conducting their struggles not with sword and armor but wrestling with the powers of evil for the soul of their people, saving them from Gehenna, paving the road for them to paradise and the coming of the Messiah. Every "court" developed its own style of chanting and even had its preferred mode. Every *rebe* devoted a good deal of time and thought to the creation of tunes, and, where he was not able to compose his own, he hired a "court singer," whose duty it was to study the *tsadik*'s mood and desires so that he could interpret his feelings exactly. Always appealing to the emotions, the styles of singing and the texture of the voices played an important part. In the memoirs of Chasidic followers, the specific qualities of a respective *rebe*'s voice is often recalled : "My *rebe* had a big, powerful voice, which struck fear into you. . . . Mine . . . had a small voice, but piercing . . . and every gesture was accompanied by a ball of fire. . . . When the *rebe* sang . . . everyone's thoughts concentrated on his song. . . . My *rebe* had a sweet voice, not too loud, not too soft . . . which aroused pity in your heart. . . . Our *rebe* and his son both sang . . . their eyes closed, their faces flushed, a holiness permeating their singing which made a terrific impression, stirring us fellows up."[6]

Chasidic melodies graced the public Sabbath meals, where often hundreds of Chasidim sat down at their *rebe*'s table. These songs would then be memorized by the followers, who would carry them back home, teaching them to the pious ones who had had to forego the privilege of being present on that occasion at their favorite *rebe*'s court and table. At least twice a year, on the High Holidays and at Pentecost, large pilgrimages to the "courts" were customary, for which, as a rule, special new melodies were created and sung.

Chasidic faith, ritual, spirit influenced Eastern European song, dance, and folklore. Song and dance, good fellowship and joyousness dominated the life of the Chasidic followers. In addition to the special Sabbath and festival songs and the devotional compositions for the High Holidays, tuneful melodies and dance songs were created for the public Chasidic gatherings.[7] Such music was occasionally clothed in only a few words, ecstatically uttered within the framework of the composition. From time to time, such a group song was given whole phrases and even boasted some stanzas, as the following :

Der rebele, der gabele,	The *rebe,* the elder,
Der shamesl, der bederl,	The sexton, the bathhouse attendant.
Gants kley-koydesh	All the holy townsmen
Geyt doch tantsn.	Are going to dance.
Shrayt-zhe ale hoych,	Shout then out loud
Mitn gantsn koyech,	With all your might;
Der rebele aleyn	The *rebe* himself
Geyt doch tantsn ! [8]	Is going to dance !

In time, the songs with words increased in number, although they never approached the mass of wordless tunes in circulation. There were melodies of contemplation, tunes designed to cleanse the soul of sin, wordless songs which pleaded for mercy with the Lord. Occasionally, a song of yearning, such as the following, would utilize a text of a love song, applying the tender terms to express the soul's yearning for communion with the Lord.

Volt ich hobn gilderne fliglen,	Had I golden wings,
Volt ich tsu dir fli-en.	I would fly to you.
Volt ich hobn gilderne reder,	Had I golden wheels,
Volt ich tsu dir forn.	I would drive to you.
Volt ich hobn ferd un zotl,	Had I horse and saddle,
Volt ich tsu dir geritn.	I would ride to you.
Volt ich hobn tint un feder,	Had I quill and ink,
Volt ich tsu dir geshribn.	I would write to you.
Volt ich hobn a gildernem fingerl,	Had I a golden ring,
Volt ich tsu dir gegebn.[9]	I would give it to you.

Joyous dance tunes occasionally included some text, as did, too, some drinking songs and songs to raise the spirit, such as the following, which extolled the feats of the miracle-working *tsadik*:

Der rebe, der rebe, der heyliger man,	The *rebe,* the *rebe,* the holy man,
Er iz doch a mechaye,	He is a delight,
Far im iz doch di gantse velt,	For him all the world,
Di gantse velt a fraye.	The entire world is free.
Undzer rebe, undzer sgule,	Our *rebe,* our healer,
Macht doch mofsim gor a fule,	Works many miracles,
Zayt im m'sameyach,	Make him happy,
Hulye berl, tants shmerl,	Be gay Berl, dance Shmerl,
Mit dem rebe's koyech.[10]	With the power of the *rebe*.

Primitive and secular tunes, rhythmic marches of passing military bands, songs of the non-Jewish countryside were refashioned into sacred Chasidic melodies and songs. Just as Martin Luther adapted street songs to sacred texts, begrudging the devil all the good tunes, so, too, did the Chasidic *rebe* adopt and adapt melodies from their secular environment to be placed in the service of the Lord. Legend has it that the rabbi of Koliv, Hungary, Rabbi Yitschok Isaac Toib (1750–1821), who was a shepherd in his youth and gifted musically, had paraphrased a shepherd love song into Yiddish. Both a secular and a religious version circulated among the people. "Vald, vald," the secular song, is followed by the rabbi's adaptation :

(a)

Vald, vald, vi groys biztu !	Forest, forest, how big you are !
Kale, kale, vi vayt biztu !	Bride, bride, how far you are !
Vald, vald, ver avekgenumen,	Forest, forest, disappear,
Vel ich kale, tsu dir kumen.	Then my bride, I'll come to you.

(b)

Golus, golus, vi groys biztu !	Exile, exile, how big you are !
Sh'chine, sh'chine, vi vayt biztu !	Holy Spirit, how distant you are !
Golus, golus, ver avekgenumen,	Exile, exile, disappear,
Vel ich, sh'chine, tsu dir kumen.[11]	Then, Holy Spirit, I will come to you.

Wherever Chasidic melody circulated with a text or partial text, it was usually in Yiddish or a mixture of Yiddish and Hebrew.[12] Occasionally some Russian, Ukrainian, or White Russian words were employed. Two well-known, Yiddish songs, still remembered today and ascribed to Reb Levi Yitschok of Berdichev (1740–1810), are "Du-du" ("You, You") and "A din-toyre mit got" ("A Lawsuit with God"). Since Reb Levi Yitschok was passionately committed to the role of mediator between his people and their God, many tales were current which describe his arguments with the Lord in their behalf. Such a tale surrounds the "Din-toyre" song, with which it was said he would begin his prayers during the Rosh Hashonoh (New Year) services. Following is a stanza of one version of this song, which is set in a musical recitative and pleads eloquently with the Lord to spare the people of Israel the suffering and humiliations perpetrated against them.

A gut morgn dir, reboynoy shel oylom.	Good morning to you, Lord of the universe.
Ich, levi yitschok ben sore m'barditshev,	I, Levi Yitschok, son of Sarah of Berdichev,
Bin gekumen tsu dir mit a din-toyre	Have come to you with a complaint
Fun dayn folk yisroel.	On behalf of your people of Israel.
Vos hostu tsu dayn folk yisroel?	What have you against your people of Israel?
Vos hostu zich ongezetst	Why do you pick on
Oyf dayn folk yisroel? [13]	Your people of Israel?

The song continues to entreat and to protest : "No matter what happens, no matter what occurs — it's always the people of Israel ! Sweet Father in

heaven! There are many nations in this world: Medes, Persians, Baby-
lonians. What do the Russians say?—that their Czar is Tsar. And the
Germans claim—that their king is king. And the Englishmen say—that
their ruler is monarch. But I, Levi Yitschok, son of Sarah of Berdichev
say: that the only King is He who sits on the throne of heaven! And I say
to you: I will not budge from this spot until these persecutions cease!"

Chasidim from all over the Pale, chanting to: ay-ay-ay, bay-bay-bay,
ba-ba-bam, di-di-dam, oy-doy-doy, bo-bo-bo, ya-ba-bam, tam-diri-diri,
day-di-dam-dam, and other interjections, such as "oh, sweet Father,"
"oh, dear Father," "help, the *rebe*!", created and recreated tunes and
songs they had heard at the "courts." They sang them during their
prayers,[14] at the supper table, at work, or in the company of their cronies.

Got muz men dinen,	We must serve the Lord,
Un men vet im dinen,	And we will serve Him,
Ober nit vi a goylem.	But not like a simpleton.
Adon yechidi, levo-e oylem.	The Lord is One, Ruler of the world.
Dinen muz men got,	The Lord must be served,
Got muz men dinen,	God must be served,
Derfar vos her hot undz oysgeveylt tsum dinen.[15]	Because He has chosen us to serve Him.

Some devotional Chasidic songs, couched half in Hebrew and half in
Yiddish, employed Hebrew prayer texts as their basis and the simple
Yiddish vernacular to interpret the Hebrew text—an old practice em-
ployed in the cheder.

Adir hu bo-elyonim,	You are mighty on high,
Boruch hu batachtoynim,	You are blessed down below,
Bo-elyonim batachtonim,	On high and down on earth,
Kulom moydim uma-aminim.	Everyone praises and serves Him.
Az ha-adonay echod ushmoy echod.	For the Lord is One and his Name is One.
A shtarker biztu fun oybn,	You are powerful on high,
An oysderveylter biztu fun untn.	You are the only One below.
Un fun oybn un fun untn,	And on high and below,
Ale loybn, ale gloybn,	Everyone praises, everyone believes,
Az du bizt eyner, achuts dir nito keyner.[16]	That you are One and that there is no one but you.

However, with the growth and extension of Chasidism, the simple path
indicated by the saintly Besht did not long prevail, and the roads taken

by his followers and disciples took various other directions. Since the *tsadik* served as mediator between the Lord and the common folk, there prevailed the conviction that he must be God's messenger and favorite. This resulted in a cult of reverence for him which undermined still further the scholastic and ceremonial rabbinism and wrought deep changes in some of the rituals and practices of the religious life of the Jews in the Pale. The Chasidim studied differently, prayed differently, and with the passage of time, although the movement's power rested on the mass of the poor, the courts of the Chasidic *rebeyim* took on a material splendor far removed from its original simplicity. From every corner of the Pale devout followers beat a path to the blessed door of their revered *rebe,* who in turn bestowed blessings upon his "constituents," poured forth divine favors upon his disciples, healed cripples, cured the sterile.

The profitable calling of the *tsadik* became hereditary, passing from father to son to grandson. Everywhere petty dynasties sprang up, which multiplied rapidly and endeavored to wrest the supremacy from one another.[17] The original message of the Besht seemed a far cry from this material splendor. Having for a time, at least, defeated its main religious opponents, in certain areas Chasidism literally wallowed in wealth. Below is a description of the life of Reb Yisroel Rizhiner (b. 1797), founder of the Sadigura dynasty :

". . . He built a palace for himself in Rizhin, and his whole way of life was that of a magnate. His house was full of all manner of servants. He had his own band of instrumentalists and singers. His stables were full of fancy carriages and valuable horses. The style was that of a king's court. Everything was splendidly carried through, on the dot, and everything was designed to impress and call forth adulation and admiration. The Rizhin *rebe* used to go out in a magnificent carriage with silver trimmings, led by four spirited horses, surrounded by a large suite, dressed in rich and beautiful clothes. . . . He was unapproachable to the ordinary person. Simple Chasidim had the privilege of glancing at him only from a distance, through an open door, where they could observe him seated at his table in his splendid study, looking into a book, with an expensive pipe in his mouth. . . . Thousands of Chasidim from Wolin, Poland, and Galicia would come to the Rizhiner court, bringing their gifts to the *rebe*."[18]

Measuring the religious worth of a man by the extent of his Talmudic learning, rabbinism saw in the Chasidic movement a denial of the priority of scholasticism and a serious threat to its own hierarchy. Rabbinic adherents (Misnagdim) considered the Chasidic *rebe* a dangerous type of popular priest who fed on the superstition of the masses. They accused the Chasidic followers of ignorance and considered them touched with paganism. Especially did the Misnagdim attack the lavish life of the Sadigura and other such households. Even some leaders of other Chasidic groups criticized this way of life: "They know nothing of charity, they gorge themselves and grow fat; they ride around in gilded and silvered coaches and behave like lords; their women clothe themselves like non-Jews, are bold, and other Jewish, women imitate them."[19]

In the main, the *tsadikim* were moving away from their mission of faith teachers and healers and becoming more and more practitioners surrounded by a mass of hangers-on, whose blind faith they utilized and from whose gifts and handouts they were becoming wealthy. The court of the Besht's grandson, Boruch Tultshiner (1780–1810), in Medzibozh was famous for its splendor and boasted its own "court jester" — Hershl Ostropoler, the hero of many a folk anecdote!

At the close of the nineteenth century, although Chasidism had from 3 to 4 million adherents, it functioned in an atmosphere of spiritual depression, credulity, abysmal poverty, and bitter Czarist oppression. The escape into the deification of mediocre and often inferior men created a type of *tsadik* who exerted an unwholesome influence on the mass of Chasidic followers. Spiritual intoxication was often accompanied by physical intoxication. The emphasis on joyousness carried over more and more to the earthly pleasures of eating and drinking, and, since the widespread poverty restricted this escape from the gloomy reality, many songs revolved around the theme of feasting and revelry.

Az du volst geven der boyre-oylem	If you were the Creator of the universe,
Vos volstu gemacht?	What would you make?
Ch'volt gemacht,	I would make,
Ch'volt gemacht un gemacht :	I would make and make
An oyvn a groysn	A large oven
Un tsholnt vifil s'volt arayn.	And fill it with as much roast as would get into it.
Di misnagdim un hultayes	The Misnagdim and bums
Volt ich kayn tsholnt nisht gegebn,	Would get none of it.

Nor ch'sidim, vifil es volt arayn.

Refrain: Hal'vay, hal'vay, hal'vay,

Vi derlebt men dos
shoyn? [20]

Only the Chasidim, as much as they
could eat.
Oh, that it could be, if it
only could be,
If only we could live to see
it.

The fervor of prayers became an exhibition of gestures, wherein the greater intensity was interpreted as the greater devotion to one's *rebe*.

Bay dem davenen vel ich mich
shoklen,
Machn alerley havayes.
Far dem rebn mit zayne ch'sidim,
Geyt mir oys dos chayes.
Oy vey rebenyu, ich shtey un tsiter,
Un in hartsn brent a fayer.
Ich vel zayn a chosidl a heyser,
A chosid a getrayer. [21]

When I pray I shall rock back and
forth
And make all kinds of gestures.
For the *rebe* and his Chasidim
My heart just melts.
Oh, dear *rebe,* I stand and tremble,
And a fire burns in my heart.
I will be a "hot" Chasid,
A devoted Chasid.

Chasidim abandoned themselves to revelry, neglecting their business affairs. Others were in a constant pilgrimage to their favorite *rebe,* with their families in hunger and want at home. The Chasid sought the blessings of the *rebe,* his intercession on the pilgrim's behalf with the good Lord, his aid in matters of business and work. But the *rebe* could not put an end to the poverty, the persecutions, the oppressions of the Czarist Pale. Eating and drinking, singing and dancing became a sleeping draught to dull the pain of the blows leveled at the Jewish community as a whole.

Chot mi chudi, chot mi chudi,
Ale nashi batki dobri.
Chot mi chudi, chot mi bedni,
Ale nashi batki dobri. [22]

Though we are unfortunate,
All our brothers are good.
Though we are poor,
All our brothers are good.

This intoxication rendered its adherents indifferent to study and prayer, as the following little Chabad song seems to imply:

Esn est zich un trinken trinkt zich,
Der chisorn iz nor, vos es davnt zich
nit.

There is eating and there is drinking,
The only trouble is that there is no
praying.

Esn est zich un trinken trinkt zich,
Der chisorn iz nor, vos es lernt zich
nit. [23]

There is eating and there is drinking,
The only trouble is that there is no
studying.

This preoccupation with earthly pleasures in a sea of poverty and want also rendered the Chasidic followers insensible to the various social and cultural stirrings within the Pale. Already at the beginning of the nineteenth century, however, both leaders of Chasidism and rabbinism sensed the presence of an adversary—the Haskalah movement—the movement of Enlightenment. Stimulated by the general struggles in Europe for social emancipation, justice, and freedom of thought, the Haskalah struck a new chord in the heart of Eastern European Jews, who were craving for the abolition of customs and practices founded on medieval conceptions. Secular knowledge became a goal for the youth, which yearned to be free

Herzl T. Rome, 1950

(Reprinted by permission of Schocken Books Inc. from Treasury of Jewish Folksong *by Ruth Rubin. Copyright 1950 by Schocken Books Inc.)*

and chafed under the laws of an environment in which a short jacket or a trimmed beard was regarded as a token of dangerous freethinking and the reading of books in a foreign tongue or even in modern Hebrew, treating of secular subjects, brought upon the culprit untold hardships.

The Haskalah movement attempted to transmit to the Yiddish-speaking, Hebrew-reading Jews the thought and literature of the non-Jewish world through articles, essays, plays, poems, and songs. Although it did not attack religion, it did satirize the *tsadikim* for their fanatic behavior and blind attention to outlandish rituals and customs. Among the satirical Haskalah song writers who recognized the power of melody in dealing with Chasidism were the popular folk bards, Wolf Ehrenkrants-Zbarzher, Berl Broder, Michl Gordon, and Avrom Goldfaden, who proceeded to expose what they considered to be the worst evil of the Jewish environment. These satirists utilized Chasidic song patterns as they scoffed at the *tsadikim*, who feared the bright sun of secular knowledge, and at their blind followers, who extolled the powers of their miracle-working *rebeyim*. The satirical song thus became one of the most effective weapons employed by the Haskalah movement in its struggle with Chasidism. The following example, written by Wolf Zbarzher, which pokes fun at the Chasid's fear of modern science, became very popular and is still preserved in the memory of the people in a number of variants.

Kum aher, du filozof,
Mit dayn ketsishn moychl;
Kum aher tsum rebn's tish
Un lern zich dort seychl!

Come here to me, philosopher,
With your cat's brain;
Come here to the *rebe*'s table
And learn something there.

A damf-shif hostu oysgetracht
Un nemst zich mit dem iber.
Der rebe shpreyt zayn tichl oys
Un shpant dem yam ariber!

You invented the steamboat
And boast about it.
The *rebe* spreads his kerchief
And strides across the ocean!

A luft-balon hostu oysgeklert
Un meynst du bizt a chorets.
Der rebe shpot, der rebe lacht,
Er darf es oyf kapores! [24]

You invented an airship
And think you are so clever.
The *rebe* scoffs, the *rebe* laughs,
He can manage without it!

A number of satirical songs leveled at the Chasidic saints and their fanatic followers sought to expose the hoax of the miracle-working *rebeyim*. One song humorously describes the *rebe* catching fish in the desert. Another relates an incident that reveals the power of the *rebe* which endows even his Chasidim with magical powers!

Der rebe hot gevolt in shtot arayn forn,	The *rebe* wanted to go to the city,
Un kayn ferd iz nito.	And there were no horses.
Hot er gegebn a bafel tsu zayne chasidim,	So he issued an order to his Chasidim,
Zaynen gevorn ferd in eyn sho.	And in one hour there were horses.
Der rebe fort, der rebe fort,	The *rebe* rides, the *rebe* rides,
Forn di chasidim oych mit,	And the Chasidim ride along with him,
Filn zey derbay aza min tam	And the pleasure they feel at that time
Vos kayn misnagid filt avade nit.[25]	Can never be felt by any Misnagid.

Another song of this genre describes the hilarious experiences of a *rebe* and his devotees during a perilous sea voyage of "many years," which the *tsadik* made in "one day." Following is a portion of this satire, which describes some of the wondrous things that took place during the journey.

Der rebe hot gegebn mitn oyg a vunk,	The *rebe* winked his eye,
Un mit di arbl hot er gefocht,	And waved about with his sleeve,
Hot gegebn funem yam a fish a shprung	When out of the sea there jumped a fish
Un hot zich aleyn opgekocht.	And got cooked up all by itself.
Opgekocht tsapldik frish,	Cooked while it was alive and fresh,
Un fun moyl a vortsl chreyn	And from its mouth a horseradish root
Iz aroysgeshprungen tsum rebn afn tish,	Jumped up on the *rebe*'s table,
Un der rebe hot es tseribn mit di tseyn.	And the *rebe* ground the root with his teeth.
Tsi darft ir dertsu noch gresere rayes,	Now do you need any more proof,
Az der rebe iz in der zach farmisht?	That the *rebe* was mixed up in this?
Un di apikorsim, di hultayes,	But the non-believers, those bums,
Zey gleybn in dem rebn alts noch nisht.[26]	They still don't believe in the *rebe*.

Where the above is only mildly satirical, the following song about a goat which was born to the *rebe*'s right-hand man is bitterly sardonic. The solo singer tells the tale of ceremonials and rituals attending this bizarre occurrence, while the chorus punctuates it with the refrain: *tsig-*

tsigetsapl, tsigtsap, tsig-tsig-tsap! (a play on the words *tsig* and *tsap*—goat and ram). A portion of this narrative song is given below:

Hot der rebe geheysn im putsn un tsirn,	The *rebe* ordered the goat to be adorned
Un on shayles un on maynes in mikve im firn.	And without any questions taken to the ritual bath.
Dos bekl hot men ongeton gants sheyn un gants fayn,	The goat was dressed up nice and fine
Un me hot im mit groys kovid gefirt in mikve arayn.	And taken with great ceremony to the ritual bath.
Di ch'sidim farn ek, der rebe farn horn,	The Chasidim held him by the tail, the *rebe* by the horns,
Dos bekele hot gegebn a shprung un antlofn gevorn.	When suddenly the little goat jumped up and ran away.
Zaynen ale gelofn dos bekele zuchn,	Everyone ran about looking for the goat,
S'iz afile gelofn der kohen fun duchn.	Even the priest left his meditations and his prayers.

"After him ran the second-hand dealer, Dobe, and after her the *rebe*'s fat wife, followed by Chaim the cripple. And after him, ran the pious *shochet*. The *shochet* grabbed the goat by the tail and uncovered its true personality! Then everyone saw that it was an evil spirit, and the *rebe* instructed everyone to say the evening prayer. On the morrow, the *rebe* told everyone to say the *goyml* prayer, since he had saved everybody from the evil spirit. And you, non-believers, do-nothings, who will laugh and mock at all of this, you will be burned and roasted in the other world." [27]

One of the sharpest satires leveled against false piety that seeks only to be rewarded for its good deeds, that clings to fanatic observances and outworn rituals and assumes fantastic modes of dress, is Velvl Zbarzher's "Der Bankrot" ("The Bankrupt"), which was current among Ukrainian Misnagdim (opponents of Chasidism). In this song, Zbarzher meticulously describes a number of religious community leaders and their followers: the rabbi, cantor, ritual slaughterer (*shochet*), sexton, *mohel* (performer of circumcisions), the Chasid, and an average, poverty-stricken Jew, as they stand before the Almighty, each listing his good deeds on earth and demanding his "just" rewards. So exorbitant are these demands, however, that the good Lord is compelled to declare himself bankrupt! The following stanza describes the Chasid, whom Zbarzher singles out for his most pointed caricature:

Betracht nor di kleyder durch un durch	Examine the clothes very carefully
Vos es trogt ot di heylige tsure;	Worn by this pious visage;
Oyf dem shtrayml, oyf dem verech	On the fur hat, on its tail
Ligt a matse-shmure.	Lies a holy matzo.
Oyf di shpitsn, chanuke lichtlech,	On the ends, Chanukah tapers,
A mezuze oyf der noz,	A talisman on his nose,
Arbe-koyses fun di flechtlech,	Four goblets of wine from the tassels,
Un di peyes noch der mos.	And his sideburns the proper length.
Oyf dem shtern, tsvey por tfiln,	On his forehead — two pairs of phylacteries,
Un a shoyfer oyf der tsung.	And a ram's horn on his tongue.
Un in moyl, a kos a fuln,	And in his mouth, a full goblet
Fun kidesh-havdole dem heylign trunk.[28]	Of *havdala* wine, the holy drink.

The methods employed by the Chasidim in their struggle against the inroads of the Haskalah were not always aboveboard. Since no logic was necessary and the emotional impact sufficed, the use of melody, gesture, and movement of the body in prayer became devices to attract followers. On the other hand, in their vigilance to retain their proponents and track down their enemies, they jealously guarded their adherents and vented their fury against any of them who strayed, burning their secular books, defaming, and even excommunicating them.[29]

As the Chasidic movement continued to degenerate as a popular movement, the satirical taunts leveled against it by its enemies and sometimes by its former friends increased. The following stanzas reflect the bitterness of those women who had to bear the burden of providing the family with a livelihood while their husbands, the Chasidim, sought only the atmosphere of their venerated *rebe* and the company of his carousing cronies.

Oy, du vaybl, du sheyne, du fayne,	Oh, young woman, comely and fine,
Vos zenen dir farveynt di oygn dayne?	Why are your eyes red with weeping?
—Vi azoy zol ich nit veynen, in dr'erd nit arayn,	—Why shouldn't I weep, the devil take it,
Az ich hob a chosid, a flyask far a man.	When my husband is a Chasid, a slob.
Af ale yon toyvim muz er tsum rebn forn,	Every holiday, he must journey to the *rebe,*
Er hot mir farvist di teg mit di yorn.	He has made my life miserable.

Vos chapt er baym rebn? — a loksh un nit meyn,
Chapt im a shvarts yor, a loksh iz er aleyn! [30]

What does he get there? — nothing but a noodle.
The devil take him, he's a noodle himself!

Following are three teasers, decidedly pointing up the low opinion of certain Chasidim that was becoming common in the minds of certain strata of the population.

(1)

Der rebe iz gegangen tantsn,
Hot er farloyrn ingantsn.
Hobn di chasidim gefunen,
Hot er gegebn a simen
Un hot es opgenumen. [31]

The *rebe* went dancing
And lost everything.
The Chasidim found it all,
And he gave them a sign
And took it all back again.

(2)

Der rebe zitst un shvitst,
Un es rut oyf im di heylige sh'chine,
Un di chasidim zingen, tantsn, un shpringen,
Un zey hobn hano-e funem rebn's mine. [32]

The *rebe* sits and sweats,
And the Holy Spirit is upon him,
And the Chasidim sing, dance, jump,
Delighting in the *rebe*'s expression.

(3)

Der rebe iz a groyser chvat,
Ven er macht l'chayim.
Un di chasidim raysn zich
Iber di shirayim. [33]

The *rebe* is a great fellow
When he drinks a toast.
And the Chasidim fight
Over the leftovers.

Having arisen in the middle of the eighteenth century, the Chasidic movement, in a remarkably short period of time historically, achieved a popularity unequaled in Jewish history. No spiritual movement among the Jews had ever brought so much happiness and healing, so much refreshment both for the body and the soul. By the beginning of the nineteenth century, Chasidism's break with its religious opponents, the Misnagdim, was complete and the struggle with the Haskalah, in full force. The last quarter of the nineteenth century saw a diminishing of the Chasidic influence, which had become fanatic in its behavior, leaning on mysticism and miracles, in constant strife with all manner of secular learning and ideas. It soon ceased to represent the majority of the people, nor did it offer any hope for the solution of the pressing problems which were constantly besetting the life of the Jews in the Czarist Pale. Its power waned, but a cultural heritage rich in folk music and folklore remained. Its innumerable "wonder" tales represent a type of mythology that endowed its leaders with veneration and magical powers. However, the richest portion of this cultural heritage is the treasury of songs without words, portions of which are still preserved among remaining Chasidic sects and groups in our times. These remains are but an echo of a vast collection which was current and alive among the mass of Eastern European Jews less than a century ago.

Fed by the synagogal modes, the Ukrainian and Slavic folk songs of the countryside, Cossackian dances and military marches, the melodies, created and recreated by the *rebeyim,* their Chasidic musicians, and their followers, developed a unique style which varied in character and spirit at the various "courts."[34] Though religious in purport, these songs were not employed for worship proper but for inspiration and preparation of the pious for worship. Many were genuine musical compositions and served various religious purposes: to raise the spirit and gladden the heart, seek communion with the Holy Spirit, free the soul of the miseries on earth, guide the tongue in pouring out one's heart to the good Lord. These melodies also served to bind people in gay festivities at the *rebe*'s table or among their fellow Chasidim and to lead the feet in ecstatic dances.

Although Chasidic song also includes songs with words, the wordless tune was its distinctive characteristic type, the aim and structure of which has no counterpart anywhere. Marked by a particular color and force, ranging from the freest to the most marked rhythms, these tunes embrace somber and intimate as well as gay and abandoned moods. Basically a song sung by men, its unrhythmical portion is carried by a single voice, with the rhythmical parts performed in unison by the group.

Chasidic melody, the most striking feature of the Eastern European musical heritage, exerted a strong influence on nineteenth-century, Eastern European Chazannuth ("cantorial music"). It made itself felt in many categories of the secular Yiddish folk songs, especially in the songs of merriment, the dance songs, the wedding songs, and left a strong imprint on modern Israeli music.

Notes

CHASIDIC MELODY AND SONG

1. No one knows exactly where the Baal Shem-Tov was born, whether in the Ukraine or in the Carpathian mountains of Galicia. Even his various occupations have become legendary. It is possible that his occupation as a healer, whether with herbs or cabalistic prayers and magical formulas, earned for him the name of Baal Shem—Tov—Besht—Good Miracle Man. It is not even known exactly what he himself said in his preaching or what portions were carried forward by his disciples and followers. There are some who maintain that the Besht was not concerned with ending the Galuth ("exile") but was interested in bringing joy and release to his followers as long as they were compelled to live in it. Consequently, some say that he was really not concerned with hastening the coming of the Messiah but rather with freeing the soul and lightening the burdens of his Jewish people, wherever they happened to be. Sinfulness, he is said to have taught, was merely the lowest level of holiness, and no man was too lowly to be raised to ecstasy and happiness.

2. Following closely the neomystics (Cabalists) of Safed, Palestine, Eastern European Chasidism proceeded to endow its own brand of mysticism with robust earthiness. The Cabalistic movement in the East was founded by Isaac Luria (b. 1534 or 1544, d. 1572), poet and author of several songs in Aramaic, which became popular among Eastern European Chasidim, as well as the custom, stressed by him, of receiving the Sabbath with music and song.

3. A Chasidic rabbi was called a *rebe* ("teacher") or *tsadik* ("saint") in distinction from the rabbi proper, or *rov,* who discharged the rabbinical functions within a given community.

4. In the course of its development, the Chasidic movement branched out into two directions: the system of the Besht—mostly in Poland, Southern Russia, Rumania, Hungary—and the system of Chabad, founded by Reb Shneyer Zalmen of Liadi, in Lithuania and White Russia. The Chabad branch of Chasidism stressed knowledge and wisdom and also created *the melody of the six steps,* which tried to convey musically the six stages in the soul's yearning and rising to commune with the Lord. These six steps are specifically described in Hebrew by the Chabad Chasidim as: *hishtachput hanefesh*—outpouring of the soul in its effort to rise above sin; *hitorerut* —spiritual awakening; *hitpa-alut*—possessed by His thought; *dveykut*—communion with God (at this point the music is usually slow, free, unrhythmical); *hitlahavut*— ecstasy (here the music is vigorous, often syncopated); *hitpashtut hagashmiyut*—the soul casts off its garment of flesh, becomes spirit.

5. Many sayings current among the Chasidic followers and their leaders reflect the important role assigned to the "song without words": "Silence is a great virtue when compared with speech, but when compared with song, song is the greater. . . . Language is the quill of the heart. Song is the quill of the soul. . . . He who has no feeling for song, has no sense for Chasidism. . . . A Chasidic tune is of basic importance. One must sing it simply, without any cantorial trimmings. . . . When a Chasid sings, it raises him from his lowly position to a higher level. . . . Impurity knows no song, because it knows no joy and is the source of all melancholy. . .

Music has the power to elevate one to prophetic inspiration. . . . With song one can open the gates of heaven and with sorrow one can lock them all. . . . A tune can pull you out of the deepest mire. . . ." (from *Sefer Hanigunim,* which contains songs with and without texts, personal reminiscences of the life and utterances of a number of Chasidic *rebeyim,* as told by their followers).

An interesting incident is related about a Chabad *rebe* who was passing through Shklov. Having heard of the *tsadik's* great wisdom, the elders of the city came to greet him and placed their many problems before him. The *rebe* listened but said nothing. They then decided to assemble in the synagogue, invite him to preach the Torah there, so that they might, in the proper atmosphere, again seek his counsel. The *rebe* accepted their invitation, came to the synagogue, got up on the platform and said : "Rather than preach to you and discuss your problems, I will sing you a tune. . . ." A deep silence filled the synagogue; everyone was sunk in his own personal thoughts and as the *tsadik* sang his tune, each one seemed to resolve his own problems unto himself. The Shklov Chasidim named this tune "Matan torah tune"—"the Tune of the Gift of the Torah" (*Sefer Hanigunim,* pp. 34–35 and note 51 in the Hebrew pages).

6. *Sefer Hanigunim.*

7. Many *rebeyim* were composers and some of them even good musicians. The most famous among them was the old Mozhitser *rebe,* Reb Yisroel Taub, who created scores of melodies. *Rebe* Reb Osherl Rimenover, too, was a composer of Chasidic tunes, as well as *rebe* Reb Shloyme Radomsker. There were also many anonymous Chasidic composers among the mass of Chasidic followers themselves. "In the main, however, most Chasidic melodies were created by different *chazanim* ("cantors") and *gabayim* ("deacons") who served at the courts of the Chasidic *tsadikim.* . . . A certain Reb Yosele dem Rebn's, who was one of the cantors at the court of Reb Dovidl Talner, had to create a new melody every Sabbath, which was immediately caught up and spread far and wide among the thousands of Talne Chasidim. According to them, Reb Yosele composed more than five hundred tunes" (Unger, 1946, pp. 113–115).

8. Idelsohn, X, No. 225.

9. *Sefer Hanigunim,* p. 19, No. 25. This song is accredited to Reb Mendele of Horodok, a follower of the great *magid* ("mentor") of Mezritsh, who led the exodus of Chasidim to Palestine in 1777.

10. Idelsohn, X, No. 236.

11. Unger, 1946, p. 106. Although Unger credits the rabbi of Koliv with the adaptation of this song, which according to him "is sung to the present day by all the Chasidim of Ropshits and Sandz," Kipnis prefaces his version, given below, with the following comments : "The Riminov *rebe* once walked out into the fields on a Friday evening and heard a shepherd singing a song : *Ruzha, ruzha, yak ti daleka!* ("Rose, Rose, how far you are!"), whereupon he remarked that one could not fathom the mysteries concealed in the tune. On the morrow at the third Sabbath meal (*sholes-sudes*), he sang the tune to the following words :

Royz, royz, vi vayt biztu?
Vald, vald, vi groys biztu?
Volt di royz nisht azoy vayt geven,
Volt der vald nisht azoy groys geven.

Rose, rose, how far are you?
Forest, forest, how vast are you?
If the rose were not so far away,
The forest would not seem so vast.

Sh'chine, sh'chine, vi vayt biztu?
Golus, golus, vi lang biztu?
Volt di sh'chine nisht azoy vayt geven,
Volt der golus nisht azoy lang geven.
    (Kipnis, p. 140.)

Holy Spirit, how far are you?
Exile, exile, how long are you?
If the Holy Spirit were not so distant,
Then the exile would not seem so long.

12. Explaining his use of the Yiddish vernacular in his prayers, Reb Nachman Bratslaver (1772–1810), a grandson of the Baal Shem-Tov, functioning in the Ukraine, said: "Seclusion is the highest stage in which man can attain inspiration, where he can pour out his heart to his God in a free and intimate way, and in the language familiar to him, in his native tongue. In our country this is Yiddish, for Hebrew is little known to the average man, and consequently it is difficult for him to express himself in it fluently. Therefore, whenever Hebrew is used as a medium of prayer, the ears do not hear what the mouth utters" (Idelsohn, X, Intro. ix, note 4).

13. Kotylansky, p. 29. "The Berditshever . . . at first sang with a deep humility . . . like one weeping for mercy from the bottom of his heart . . . then a great joy and ecstasy almost to fainting. . . . It is impossible to describe how deeply stirred his disciples were. . . . Everyone . . . felt . . . that the tune . . . had brought them into a higher, unknown world . . ." (*Sefer Hanigunim,* p. 25 and note no. 13 in the Hebrew pages).

14. Most of the "courts" had their own synagogue and developed their own style of devotional singing, which in the main was largely inspirational and extemporaneous. Leaning so much on spontaneity of prayer and song, it was inevitable that minor changes in Jewish religious customs should occur. This aroused the anger and fury of the Misnagdim — opponents to Chasidism — who bitterly fought against the ever greater incursion of the Chasidic movement. In their respective communities, followers of the various *rebeyim* congregated in their own *shtibl* ("prayer shack") to sing and dance. However, even the various sects among the Chasidim themselves were not in harmony, and at times the struggle between them was very intense.

15. Idelsohn, p. 427, No. 19.

16. *Sefer Hanigunim,* p. 96, No. 106. The first five lines are in Hebrew; the second five in Yiddish.

17. So violent was the competition between the courts against the encroachment of one upon the territory of the other, that in the "war" between the Chasidim who were followers of the Sandz *rebe* and those who adhered to the Sadigura court, for instance, the Sandz Chasidim "burned phylacteries and amulets written by a scribe of the Sadigura courts. . . . Never would a Sandz Chasid bring a tune to his *rebe*'s court which had been sung at the court of Sadigura, and the same the other way round." (Unger, 1946, p. 112.)

18. Ginzburg, I, "Reb yisroel rizhiner un zayn zindiger zun," pp. 100–101.

19. *Ibid.,* p. 117. When the Rizhiner *rebe* moved to Sadigura, he built himself an even more splendiforous palace than the one he left behind in Rizhin. "Life in the court of Sadigura was regal, full of splendor and wealth. His six sons and three daughters together with his daughters-in-law and sons-in-law and all of their children lived together with him in the large beautiful palace and behaved like members of a royal dynasty. One festival and celebration followed another. The Sadigurer daughters and daughters-in-law had their own riding horses and expensive breeds of dogs; they dressed and fussed and adorned themselves in the latest styles, going with their attendants to Vienna and the other large cities to attend theaters and balls" (Ginzburg, I, p. 105).

20. Idelsohn, X, No. 231. This example and the one following were obviously created by opponents of Chasidism.

21. *Ibid.,* No. 233.

22. *Sefer Hanigunim,* p. 99, No. 112. Mixed Yiddish and Ukrainian.

23. *Ibid.,* p. 97, No. 109.

24. Rubin, 1950, pp. 136–137.

25. Idelsohn, X, No. 238.

26. B. and F., pp. 389–390.

27. *Ibid.,* pp. 370–371.

28. Rubin, MSS. (*See*: *Di Yidishe Bine,* pp. 485–489.)

29. Michl Gordon published his first book of poems anonymously out of fear of Chasidic persecution, prefacing his collection with the following stanza: *Mayne lider zenen oyf der velt / Aroys azoy vi kontraband. / Mayn nomen iz oyf zey nit geshtelt / Ch'ob moyre gehat farn chosid's hant* ("My poems came into the world like contraband. My name is not signed to them because I feared the Chasid's hand"). Michl Gordon was especially bitter in his attacks against Chasidism, maintaining that the "stench of the feudal way of life of the Chasidic *rebe* and his followers" was keeping his brothers in the mire of ignorance and superstition. "Not because it is in my nature to sing did I pen my songs," he wrote, "but because my heart was breaking at the sight of the shortcomings of my brothers" (Gordon, p. 36).

30. Skuditsky, 1936, p. 137, No. 6.

31. *Ibid.,* p. 143, No. 13.

32. Idelsohn, X, No. 239.

33. *Ibid.,* No. 241..

34. "We don't know for certain whether or not there is a tune which can be traced to the Besht . . . very many melodies . . . sung by the different courts. . . . First of all there are many Bratslav and Chabad tunes; then those of the *rebe* Reb Elimelech of Lizhensk, and the *rebe* of Lublin, the Kozhenits magid, the *rebe* of Kotsk and very many from the Ropshits *rebe*" (Unger, 1946, p. 111).

Unger describes four types of Chasidic songs without words, as follows:

a. The table song: a long, slow melody, sung at the *rebe*'s table, usually not by him, but by one of his Chasidim or his son. The song has several parts, with a refrain usually toward the end. Between one part and the other, it includes a *volech* ("Wallachian tune"), which rises coloratura-like, simulating a shepherd playing his flute.

b. The dance tune: always sung when Chasidim get together, it usually consists of three parts, sung repetitively.

c. The Torah melody: sung slowly, thoughtfully, with deep feeling. Chasidim sang this soul-stirring tune when they were absorbed . . . at the table, before the *rebe* would begin his Torah preaching and words of wisdom.

d. The march: usually borrowed from passing military bands and popular among Galician Chasidim and the Radomsk and Mozhitser courts in Poland (Unger 1946, p. 116).

CHAPTER X

Of Literary Origin

FOLKLORE, SPEECH, LANGUAGE, ORAL LITERATURE, AND THE PRINTED WORD have always influenced one another. Just as the formal creators drank from the wellspring of the people's creations, so likewise did the people refresh itself at the fountains of their great and popular literary and musical artists. There are those who maintain that "folklore has always been with us"; certainly it has inspired such universal literature as *Faust, Baron Munchausen, Pantagruel and Gargantua, Tyl Eulenspiegel,* and others. Conversely, learned and artistic themes have entered the mind of the common people, resulting in folk creations approaching the stature of great works of art, such as the Old Testament, the German *Nibelungen-lied,* the Russian *Bilini,* and others. Some gifted creations of individuals, such as Sophocles' tragedies, Pushkin's *Ruslan and Ludmilla,* Shakespeare's *Hamlet,* Cervantes' *Don Quixote,* Byron's *Cain,* and Peretz's *Folkstimliche Geshichtn* utilized elements of the folklore of their respective peoples. In the field of music, this interchange has always been a natural phenomenon common to all peoples.

It becomes obvious that the source of the "common" talent is not to be underestimated and that the exchange between folk sources and professional creations is not to be ignored, for both are reflections of the living world and of the talents of their creators.

Yiddish folk song, both in its earlier, archaic epoch and in modern times, has been intensively exposed to literary influences. As far back as the fourteenth century, in the ghettos of Germany along the Rhine, a literary development began, which reached its peak of expression at the beginning of the sixteenth century. This was the epoch of epic poetry sung and recited in archaic Yiddish and marked by the performances by Jewish troubadours (*Spielmänner*) of such masterpieces as the *Bovo Buch,* the *Shmuel Buch, Megiles Vints, Kenig Artish Hof,* and others. It was a

250

time when, under the influence of German literature and song and the creative efforts of Jewish writers and musicians, new types of Yiddish poetry, songs, and tales never before heard in Jewish communities came into being. Even when the art of printing had become an established practice and the *read* book displaced the orally performed reading-chanting-singing from a hand-written manuscript, the old forms still persisted for some time. Thus, under the influence of religiosity and piety, the old sacred and some historical songs remained popular throughout the seventeenth century and into the eighteenth, but the old Yiddish folk song of the German-Jewish communities had already declined by then, giving way to a new era in the Eastern European lands. There, Yiddish folk song of the modern period blossomed out and gave rise to a variety of categories, a number of which were inspired by literary men, who continued to exert a strong influence on Jewish folk creativity throughout the nineteenth century.

Concurrent with these, the *badchen* still functioned prominently in some areas of the Pale, with his repertoire of songs, although in Central Europe after the middle of the nineteenth century the professional marriage entertainer vanished as an institution. Some of the *badchonim* in Eastern Europe were poets, composers, and performers, who published their own songs and achieved a high measure of popularity. A number of them even created secular songs, in which they expressed the prevalent ideas and aspirations of their listeners.

The Haskalah Movement

A powerful factor which stimulated the development of modern Yiddish literature in Eastern Europe and brought into play a number of Yiddish folk songs of known and unknown authorship was the Haskalah —the movement of Enlightenment.[1] Beginning with Moses Mendelssohn (1729–1786)[2] in Germany, it received a strong spurt forward in Russia a century later.

During the first half of the nineteenth century, Russia was regarded as the most backward country in Europe. Hemmed in by Czarist restrictions and hampered by their own religious prohibitions, the conditions for general knowledge among the Jews were deplorable. During the thirties and forties, the Pale presented a situation where Torah and faith influenced the entire life of the Jewish population : its social relationships, family life, and education. Daily life was regarded merely as the corridor to the afterlife, and the material world and its pursuits were important only insofar as they enabled the Jew to live and serve his Lord, study the Torah, and obey its laws. The days of the week were but stepping-stones to the Sabbath, when the Jew could completely shut out the secular world and its problems and dwell only on the peace and delight in the service of the Lord.

In such an atmosphere, knowledge other than religious, Jewish knowledge was regarded as a threat and a dangerous phenomenon. The religious leaders were constantly on guard against manifestations on the part of any member of their community that would indicate an interest in any phase of secular knowledge and fought bitterly against them (in 1815, the rabbinical judges of Lemberg excommunicated the local Maskilim).

To serve the "goddess of light and learning," the first zealots of the Haskalah left family, home, and friends and faced the strange and hostile world outside of the Pale. The suffering of these intrepid young men is described in the Russian works of Manasseh Morgulis: ". . . [they] were compelled to study the European literatures and sciences in garrets, in cellars. . . . Like rebels they kept their secrets unto themselves. . . . They looked with envy upon the great intellectual progress of their Western brethren. . . . [They] observed such secrecy that even their kinsmen and those among whom they dwelt were unaware of their existence. If through the discovery of some forbidden book any of them happened to be detected, he never betrayed his friends."[3]

In 1841, the Russian government decided to found a network of Jewish schools under the supervision of the crown. For this purpose, the Riga intellectual, Dr. Max Lilienthal (1815–1882), was engaged to visit a number of Jewish communities in the Pale to determine the sentiments of the people to the project. The mass of the people was naturally suspicious of a government which all along had persecuted them and denied them the most rudimentary privileges of citizenship. Even leading Jewish merchants, community leaders, and some prominent Maskilim wondered what would happen later, when the Jewish students graduated and could not take their place in the professions they had chosen. The following two children's rhymes reflect the strong resistance of the religious population against this project, which threatened the livelihood of the *melamdim* ("parochial teachers") and pointed to assimilation!

(1)

Nit kayn shteyn, nit kayn beyn,	Not a stone, not a bone,
Ver es veys nit vos dos iz,	He who knows not what it is,
Der iz dos aleyn.	Is *it*.
Zoln mir azoy poter vern	May we be rid of
Fun Yidishn goles,	Our exile as quickly
Vi gich me vet tsetraybn	As we'll be driven
Fun di shkoles.[4]	Out of the schools.

(2)

Besser a melamid,	Better a *melamed*,
Afile a beyzn,	Though a cross one,
Eyder a student	Than a student
In tsurisene hoyzn.	In torn pants.
Besser a bahelfer	Better a *bahelfer*
Mit a tuts kleyne kinder,	With a dozen children to care for,
Eyder a dokter	Than a doctor
Mit a tsubrochenem tselinder.	With a broken top hat.
Besser a kloyznik,	Better a Talmudic student,
Afile nisht kayn guter,	Even a mean one,
Eyder an apteker	Than a pharmacist
Vos preglt fleysh oyf puter.[5]	Who fries his meat in butter.

The accession to the throne of the liberal monarch, Alexander II (1856–1881), brought a period of reforms, during which the doors of schools and universities were swung open for Jewish students and many privileges, previously denied them, were granted. Many Jews eagerly took advantage of the liberties now at their disposal, which in turn further stimulated the spread of the Haskalah movement in the Pale. The pursuit of secular knowledge attracted adherents from the lonely Talmudist to the prosperous city merchant and generated a feeling of widespread gratitude to the liberal monarch who had made general education more accessible. This sentiment is allegorically expressed in a song by the then popular *badchen* and folk bard, Elyokum Zunser (1840–1913), entitled "Di blum" ("The Flower"), in which he compared the Jewish people to a lovely flower, left to wither beside the "highway where the nations pass," and Alexander II to an angel who restored her to her rightful place. Recalling the days when she blossomed in the royal gardens attended by many servants, "the flower" bemoans her sad fate:

Dan hot men plutsling oysgerisn mir.	Then I was suddenly uprooted.
Ich valger zich bald tsvey toyznt yor.	I wander about nigh onto two thousand years.

Vu ich bin geven	Wherever I have been
Hob ich retsiches gezen,	Cruel injustices have I seen,
Gerisn mir glid far glid;	I was torn limb from limb,
Gebrent un geshnitn	Burned and quartered,
Un noch mer tsores gelitn	And many more agonies have I suffered
Nor vayl ich bin a yid! [6]	Only because I am a Jew!

The "angel" then appears, also remembers the glory of Jerusalem and Zion when the "flower" was attained by "priests, Levites, and generals," and places it "together with all the other blossoms," whereupon it bursts forth in all its loveliness. "Tell me who you are and of your greatness," the "flower" asks the "angel," and he replies: "My name is Alexander, Czar of Russia."

Although the Haskalah regarded the Hebrew tongue as the precious possession from a glorious past, it utilized the Yiddish vernacular to reach an ever greater number with its ideas, propaganda, and instruction. Satire became one of the movement's main literary weapons, and the Chasidic movement, with its holy men and their courts and gullible followers, became its arch foe. The struggle between the two was sharp and bitter. The Haskalah poked fun at the long coats and fur hats of the Chasidim, and the Chasidic followers ridiculed the short coats of the "daytshn" ("Germans"), thus identifying the discarding of the wearing of long coats by the Mendelssohn adherents with their godlessness in shaving their beards and general departure from other Jewish ritualistic customs. Although the Haskalah seldom fundamentally opposed religiosity in the true sense, it was bitterly hostile to the outlandish modes of dress and mannerisms, the superstitious beliefs and ignorance of the millions of Jews in the Pale. Its adherents decried false piety and hypocrisy and the insensitive treatment of the mass at the hands often of their own religious and communal leaders.

Nineteenth-Century Bards and Poets

One of the first popular poets, as well as the most original and talented folk singer of the 1850's and 1860's, was Velvl Zbarzher (Ehrenkranz, c. 1826–1883). As a youth he became influenced by the Haskalah winds "blowing in from nearby cities of Brod and Tarnopol," main centers of the Galician Haskalah movement at that time. Having once strayed from "the paths of righteousness," Zbarzher left home and went to Rumania, where he stayed for twenty-five years. There, he became the most productive poet and folk singer of his generation, achieving a popularity in Moldavia and Bessarabia which equaled if not exceeded that of Zunser in the north.

In 1858, Zbarzher was already a full-fledged wandering minstrel, who, apart from the general run of *badchonim*, composed his lyrics and tunes on lyrical and philosophical, as well as topical and political themes. Although primitive in form, his songs on love, wine, and light abandon were a new phenomenon in Haskalah literature and the first of their kind in Yiddish literature, and his satirical songs aimed at the superstitions, ignorance, and outlandish practices of the Chasidic sects and their blind followers.[7] At first performing in private homes, he later appeared at inns and wine cellars, surrounded by ardent, young Maskilim and the common folk.

Zbarzher's songs are distinguished by their biting satire and humor; at the same time, they are filled with love and compassion for his suffering people. "No one has exercised a greater influence on the succeeding generation of bards than the Galician Wolf Ehrenkranz . . . who . . . delighted small audiences in Southern Russia with his large repertoire."[8] He employed every variety of folk song known to Yiddish literature at the time, handling his lyrics so skilfully that often the Chasidim themselves were not aware that the barbs were meant for them. Singing his songs in Hebrew and Yiddish, he gained prestige both from "respectable" Maskil youth and the common folk, swelling the numbers of his listeners to include many who were religious and still close to Chasidism.

A deeply satirical poem which was set to music by an anonymous composer, is Zbarzher's "Moshiach's tsaytn" ("The Time of the Messiah"), in which the ludicrous vision of a paradise on earth, overflowing with good things to eat and drink and other secular enjoyments, is humorously drawn. Such visions were often conjured up by Chasidim, promising devout followers fabulous rewards when the Messiah comes. Originally published anonymously in the sixties, the song circulated in several variants, of which two stanzas and a refrain of one are given below:

Es kon doch kayn keyser gornit farmogn	No monarch can ever possess
Dem sheynem, dem tayern vogn,	The beautiful, expensive coach

Vos der rebe vet bakumen,
Az moshiach vet kumen.
Der boyd fun taleysim

Un nit fun kayn leder,
Fun atsey-shitim veln zayn di reder,

Di aksn, di fleker, fun atsey-goyfer,

Un a baytsh fun tsitses
Vet zayn ongeknipt in a shoyfer.
Men vet oysklaybn a beheyme,
A koshere, a frume,
Nit kayn ferd, nor a poro adomo.
Oy tate ziser, a shmayser vet zayn

A soyfer oder a bal-koyre,
Un der rebe vet zogn toyre!

Refrain: Oy mir ch'sidim, mir zenen
gehoybn,
Mir veln tomid got loybn.

Az di resho-im veln dos
tsuzen,
Vet zey an ochtik geshen!
Oy, vi derlebt men shoyn
dos?
Traydiray diraydiraydi
taydiridirom,
Az moshiach vet kumen!

Ir zolt zen di sheyne un tayere
kloyz,
Vos vert gebovet baym rebn in hoyz,

Vos der rebe vet bakumen,
Az moshiach vet kumen.
Nit gebovet fun kayn shteyner,
Un nit fun kayn tsigl,
Nor fun zise macholim,
Fun tsimes un kugl,
Spirtes vet brenen der ner-tomid,

Which the *rebe* will get
When the Messiah will come.
The chassis will be covered with
prayer shawls
And not with leather,
The wheels will be made of acacia
wood,
The axles and posts of resinous
lumber,
And a whip of holy fringes
Will be tied to a ram's horn.
A kosher-pure beast
Will be chosen to pull it,
Not a horse, but a young heifer.
Oh, sweet Father, the coachman will
be
A scribe or reader of the holy script,
And the *rebe* will preach the Torah!

Oh, we Chasidim, we are
exalted,
We will always praise the
Lord.
And when the sinners will
see all this,
They will quake!
Oh, may we live to see it,

Traydiray, etc.

When the Messiah will
come!

Wait till you see the beautiful,
expensive chapel
That is being built in the *rebe*'s
house,
Which the *rebe* will get,
When the Messiah will come.
Not built of stone
And not of brick
But of sweetmeats,
Dainty stews, and puddings;
Brandies will feed the eternal light,

Un fun eyerkichlech vet zayn gemacht der omid.	And the rostrum will be made of egg cakes.
Mit gezaltsene fish veln zayn di brikn gebrakirt,	The ground will be tiled with salted fish,
Mit drelyes fun fish di vent oysgeshmitt.	And the walls will be smeared with fish sauce
Oy tate ziser,	Oh, sweet Father,
Vayn un bronfn vet zich gisn in ale ekn,	Wine and brandy will pour from all sides,
Un mir ch'sidim	And we, Chasidim,
Veln drelyes lekn ! [9]	Will lick the fish sauce from the walls !

More intricate and caustic is his satire "Der bankrot" ("The Bankrupt"), in which Zbarzher decries false piety which seeks to be rewarded for its good deeds and the blind adherence to dated rituals divested of human meaning. Set to music by an anonymous composer, this song circulated in several variants among the people and a stanza of one such variant is given in Chapter IX on "Chasidic Melody and Song."[10]

More widespread than the above was Zbarzher's "Der filozof," illustrated in the chapter on "Chasidic Melody and Song," which ridicules the Chasidic "saints" and their followers, who believed in the supernatural and shunned the miracles of modern scientific discoveries.

In the broad sense, Zbarzher and those who sang his songs accomplished more for secularization than the official Haskalah leadership. His songs were adopted by many marriage entertainers and Purim players and were sung all over Galicia, Southern Russia, Rumania, and later also in Northern Russia, Poland, Constantinople, and even Vienna, where Zbarzher, the wandering troubadour himself, appeared and was heard.

So popular were his songs that he was persecuted bitterly by the Chasidic movement and even by assimilated Jewish intellectuals who regarded the use of Yiddish as a barrier to the more speedy acceptance of Russian, German, and Polish. But the common folk, the students, artisans, and petty tradesmen, filled the coffee houses and wine cellars where Velvl Zbarzher appeared, to listen to him.

Functioning at about the same time was Berl Broder (c. 1815–1886)[11] and his *Broder Zinger* ("Singers of Brod"). Distinct from the cantorial profession, different from the traditional marriage entertainers, the singers of Brod were viewed as "a new kind of entertainment," when they first appeared in Galicia, Russia, and Rumania, with their own songs and "primitive performances." Led by their founder, Berl Broder (Margulies), who composed the songs himself for his troupe, the Brod Singers also used pantomime and character portrayal in their performances, which made their songs even more popular.

Although Brod was the Haskalah center of Galicia at that time, Berl Broder did not deal with the struggle between Chasidism and the Haskalah movement. His chief emphasis seems to have been his concern for the lowliest, the poorest, and most discontented, who were compelled to toil at the least compensated occupations and were the butt of the well to do in the average Jewish town of the Pale. These songs, which were his most popular numbers, usually began sympathetically with : "I, poor shepherd . . . I, crippled beadle . . . I, desolate coachman . . . I, humble matchmaker, I, miserable water-carrier," etc. Following are the first stanzas of two such songs which were current among the people :

(1)

Oy, ich der vister balegole,	I, desolate coachman,
Mayn horeven iz on an ek. . . .	There's no end to my toil. . . .
Ich shpil mir oys di beste rolye,	I play my best role to the end,
Der vint blozt avek.[12]	And am blown away by the wind.

(2)

Ich, nebich, oremer shoymer,	I, poor watchman,
Farvoglt iz fun mir di nacht,	I am alone in the dismal night,
Der shlof brecht mir in mayne beyner,	I am weary with sleep in every limb,
Tsi den fun ayzn bin ich gemacht?[13]	Am I then made of iron?

Broder wrote his ballads and songs on current events, often in a style reminiscent of the topical ballads of the eighteenth century. While never perhaps achieving the poetic and melodic quality nor the widespread popularity of Zbarzher's songs, Broder's performances and that of his troupe brought professional folk singing to the people, enriched the repertoire of the itinerant *badchen,* and gave to large numbers of Jews a foretaste of the coming Yiddish theater, later to be established by Abraham Goldfaden.

The most characteristic of the Haskalah poets who used his poetry and songs for the express purpose of advancing Haskalah ideas was the Lithuanian, Michl Gordon (1823–1890). Although his Yiddish poetry was at first primitive and limited in scope, it later achieved artistic quality, became popular, and a number of his poems were set to music by anonymous tunesmiths. His popularity was so great that he was considered by some to be "a giant among the popular folk poets of his day," although his militancy and the Chasidic hostility against him at first compelled him to publish his poems anonymously.

His most popular sung poems were the humorous, satirical ones, in which he tirelessly pointed up the meaningless ritualistic practices of the fanatic Chasidim. In his "Di bord" ("The Beard"), current up to the present day in a number of variants, a religious woman laments her husband's beard, which he has so shamelessly shaved off. Two stanzas and the refrain are given below :

Vos hot dir di bord geton fara ro-e?
Tsi hot zi dir gekost a kopike hoytso-e?
Tsi hot zi bay dir gebetn esn?
Tsi hot zi zich gemisht in dayne interesn?

Did then the beard do you any harm?
Did it then cost you a single penny?
Did it then ask you to be fed?
Did it then interfere in your affairs?

Refrain: Oy gevald, oy gevald,
Di bord iz nishto!

Oh help, oh help,
The beard is gone!

Zog mir, du gazlen, avu iz der ort?

Avu hostu geleygt di hor fun der bord?
In orn-hakoydesh vel ich im trogn,
Dort vel ich veynen un klogn,
Got zay mir moychl, vel ich zogn.[14]

Tell me, you murderer, where is the place?
Where did you put the hair from your face?
To the holy ark I will take it,
There I will weep and cry,
Lord, forgive me, I will say.

In his "Di mashke" ("Whiskey"), which enjoyed equal popularity with his "Di Bord," Michl Gordon poked fun at the undue use of liquor for the many family and religious gatherings which marked the pathway of Jewish life. Three stanzas of this song are given below :

Beshas der shadchen iz gekumen tsu mayn zeydn,
Dem tatn mit der mame a shidech reydn,
Hot men geret un geret umzist,
Biz dos glezl mashke hot zich arayngemisht.

When the matchmaker came to grandfather
To arrange the marriage of my father to my mother,
They talked and talked aimlessly,
Until the glass of whiskey interfered.

Tsulib der mashke iz der shidech
    geshlosn,
Der tate iz gevorn der mames chosn

The whiskey helped to consummate
    the match,
And father became mother's fiancé.

M'hot take bald di chasene gemacht
Un getrunken mashke a gantse
    nacht;
Mit groyse glezer hobn getrunken
    ale,
L'kovid dem chosn un l'kovid der
    kale.
Durch mashke hot der tate di mame
    genumen,
Durch mashke bin ich oyf der velt
    gekumen.

The wedding took place real soon,
And they drank whiskey all night
    long;
With large glasses, everybody drank,

Toasting the groom and to the
    bride.
Thanks to whiskey, father married
    mother,
Thanks to whiskey, I came into
    the world.

Mayn bisele yorn, ven ich vel
    oyslebn,
Vil ich men zol mir in keyver
    mitgebn :
A fesele mashke no-ent bay der vant,

A groyse gloz in der rechter hant;
Tsu t'chiyes-hameysim bin ich vider
    do . . .
Un trink bald mashke in der ershter
    sho.[15]

When I shall have lived my life
    through,
I want to take with me to the
    grave :
A little barrel of whiskey, lying close
    to the wall,
With a big glass in my right hand;
When the dead will rise, I'll be right
    there . . .
To drink whiskey, in the first hour of
    resurrection.

In a poem published in 1869 during Alexander II's reign, in the spirit of Haskalah endeavors, Michl Gordon called upon his people to rise and take advantage of the privileges now open to them : "The sun has long since risen, shining upon the world. It has put all people on their feet; only you still lie there, bowed down, eyes shut tight, sleeping till the midday hour."[16] Soon after its publication, Abraham Goldfaden paraphrased the first few stanzas and set a melody to it, utilizing the same title ("Shtey oyf mayn folk" — "Arise, My People"), which sorely displeased the original author. Michl Gordon's poems and songs passed from hand to hand in manuscript before they were published, attesting to their great popularity and timeliness.

Another Haskalah poet, whose thoughts and sentiments inspired Yiddish poets after him, was J. L. Gordon (1830–1892), leading Maskil and outstanding Hebrew poet of his time. Although for a number of years he treated the literary use of Yiddish with contempt, he managed to achieve eminence as a poet in that tongue. His Yiddish lyrics enjoyed considerable popularity in his day. J. L. Gordon was the first Haskalah poet to delineate sharply between the rich and the poor, championing the exploited members of the Jewish community. Yet he remained true to Jewish religion, regarding it as the only permanence for the Jews as a people through the centuries. His poems may not have been absorbed into current folk song to the same degree as those of his contemporaries, yet his "Der muter's obshid" ("The Mother's Parting"), describing the sad departure of a mother's son going into Czarist military service in 1845 for twenty-five years (!) was sung to the tune of the Russian lullaby, "Spi mladenets," one of the tunes to which Sholem Aleichem's famous cradle song was sung a generation later."

Inspired by J. L. Gordon, David Apotheker (1855–1911), in 1881, published a collection of Hebrew and Yiddish texts "to counteract Gold-faden's popular songs," which he considered to be "without purpose or meaning," whereas *he* "had always been concerned with the improvement of the lot of his brethren, to lift them out of their fanaticism and liberate them through knowledge and understanding." Following are excerpted stanzas from a folk song version based on one of the poems in this compilation ("Hanevel" — "The Lyre"), titled "Der foter mit dem zun" ("Father and Son"), in which the father, an orthodox religious man and rich merchant, is debating with his son, who is obviously a Maskil with Socialist ideas.

Dayn foter's reyd, her tsu mayn kind,	Listen, my child, to your father's words,
Ich meyn doch gants gevis dayn glik.	Surely I have your happiness at heart.
Du host doch shoyn azoyfil zind	You have already sinned so much
Af yedn shrit un oygnblik.	At every step that you have taken.
Tu shoyn tshuve un ver shoyn frum,	Repent and become pious,
Fast, zog t'hilim, vi mir gefelt,	Fast, say the Psalms, to please me,
Vet dayn neshome kumen reyn far im,	Then your soul will come pure before Him,
Far got in himl, oyf yener velt.	Before God in Heaven in the other world.
Liber foter, ich farshtey nit dayn zin,	Father dear, I don't understand you
Tsu der tshuve vos host mich tsugeret.	When you advise me to repent.

Farvos zol ich shoyn tshuve tun	Why should I then repent
Ven ich fil in zich noch gor kayn chet.	When I feel that I have not sinned at all.
Noch veynig gelebt unter der zun,	I've lived so little yet under the sun,
Noch nit geroybt yenem's gelt,	Have not stolen anyone's money,
Heystu mir shoyn tshuve ton,	Yet you tell me to repent
Un shadchenst mir shoyn yene velt.	And speak to me of the other world.
Vos redstu mayn liber zun,	What are you saying, my dear son,
Du host chato-im oyf yedn shrit.	You have sinned at every step.
Nechtn bam bet hostu a gey geton	Yesterday you walked many steps from the bed
On negl-vasser azoyfil trit.	Without first washing your hands.
Bam omid hostu zich nit gebukt,	At the prayers you did not bow,
In mitn k'toyres hostu oysgeret,	During the incense you broke the silence,
Kohanim duchenen hostu gekukt,	When the priests prayed you peeked,
Tu shoyn tshuve oyf yedn chet.	Repent then for all your sins.
Emes, foter, ich hob geton azoy,	True, father, I have done all this,
Ober ver cholile laydt derfun?	But who, pray, suffers therefrom?
Vi fun dir nechtn der goy	But you yesterday from the peasant
Vos du host zayn gelt a chapt geton?	Took the money so greedily.
Er hot nebech farkoyft zayn ku,	He, poor soul, sold his cow
Tsu tsoln shtayer derfun,	To raise money for his taxes;
Yetst zayn shtibl nemt men tsu,	Now they're taking his hut away,
Iz nisht glaycher du zolst beser tshuve ton? [18]	So shouldn't you better repent yourself?

   In a class by himself and the most prolific of all was Elyokum Zunser, the bard of Vilna and a contemporary of Mendele Moycher Sforim. Zunser wrote about six hundred songs, both in Eastern Europe and America, on practically every current topic during his long and productive life. Stirred by the Haskalah ideas, his compassion and love for his people impelled him to seek the raising of their cultural level. A workingman at first, he became a full-time *badchen* in 1861, but he was determined to be a different kind of marriage entertainer. Obviously influenced by the success of Zbarzher, Broder, and Michl Gordon, whose songs were acclaimed as much for their tunes as their texts, Zunser conceived of making the *badchen* a "singer of songs" rather than a merry clown. He decided to raise the level of the marriage entertainer to the dignity of a singer about his people, their life and struggles. Even as a lad, when he became the victim of his town "snatchers" who were impressing

Szymon Kobylinski

minors into the Czarist army, he wrote his first song in the barracks, where he expressed not only his own sorrows but also those of all the young boys there with him.[19]

Zunser's songs were so vivid that when his listeners heard his "Geshtanen tsum mishpet un aroys shuldig" ("Tried and Convicted"), in which he describes the brutal kidnapping of young children for the military, many became so angry at the town elders that they were ready to "tear them to pieces." And when they heard his "Beser nemen eyder gebn" ("Better to take than to give"), in which he relates how his employer had "sold" him to the Community Council for twenty-five rubles to be sent into the army to fill the town quota, his audience became so incensed "that they were ready to proceed at once to the village and wreak dire vengeance on the employer."[20]

Zunser attributed his immediate success in Lithuania to the fact that the songs of Zbarzher, Broder, and Michl Gordon had not yet penetrated those areas and to the fact that he was the only one to compose tunes together with their texts. Be that as it may, Zunser's gift to identify with the collective sentiment of his people resulted in his popularity everywhere. He was called to entertain at weddings throughout the land, and he sang before all gatherings, commenting on every issue that affected the Jewish community in the Pale.

When he was still a child-recruit in the barracks, he wrote his *Di Yeshu-e* (Salvation). Following the Polish insurrection of 1864, his *Der Rubl* (The Ruble), written in 1858, became popular. In 1861, when they began to build the railroad from St. Petersburg to Warsaw through Vilna, he wrote *Di Ayznban* (The Train) and in 1870 he wrote another song similarly titled. Of the two, he usually sang the second composition. A whole generation was growing up on his *Der Zeyger* (The Clock), *Der Parom* (The Ferry), *Der Zumer un der Vinter* (Summer and Winter) and scores of others.[21]

Zunser drew his tunes mainly from the *chazanim* ("cantors") in the Vilna synagogues, his taste improving with the years and his songs becoming more melodious as his skill increased. A teacher and mentor of his people, he ridiculed the fanaticism of the ignorant mass but did not hold with the assimilationists who underestimated the true worth of the Jewish heritage. Every occurrence found an echo in his songs as he scourged the hypocrites, the usurers, and false pietists who perpetrated vicious injustices upon the innocent, ignorant, impoverished mass of the people.

The pogroms of the 1880's came like a thunderbolt from the blue upon the Russian Jewish community, bewildering the assimilated, cultured Jews and throwing them into utter confusion. Like many Maskilim of that period, Zunser turned towards Zionism as the solution of the Jewish problem, writing a number of Zionist songs, among them the well-known "Shivas tsion" ("Return to Zion") and "Di soche" ("The Plow"), which are both still remembered today. In 1899, Zunser went to America, where he continued until the day of his death to respond creatively with songs about his environment in the New World. The last bard of note, always motivated by the deepest concern and love for his people, he was rewarded in turn with their affection and veneration for more than half a century, all over the world wherever Yiddish was spoken.

The disillusionment wrought among the Jews by the tragic occurrences of the 1880's resulted in the crystallization of several ideological trends. The greatest number sought the practical road of migration to America; others saw in a return to Zion and Zionism the way out of Jewish misery. Still others believed that Socialist thought and organization would solve the Jewish question in Czarist Russia, within the solution of the general problem.

Among Haskalah literary men who were using poetry and song, the two trends, Zionism and Socialism, became ever more discernible. Like J. L. Gordon and Mendele Moycher Sforim, Yitschok Yoel Linetsky (1839–1915) dramatized not only the Chasidic shortcomings but also the behavior of certain leading assimilationist Maskilim, "aristocrats . . . politicians," who were guilty of injustices towards their people. Author of the brilliant satire on Chasidism, "Dos poylishe yingl" ("The Polish Lad"), first published in the 1870's, he was soon hailed as an outstanding figure in Yiddish literature. In a poem which was set to music anonymously and was current among the people, he stressed the tricks of fate which made one man poor and the other rich and the futility of putting one's faith in material wealth. Following are excerpts from a folklore version, based on this sung poem:

A redele iz di gore velt,	The whole world is but a little wheel,
Gekatshet iz di tsayt.	Spun around by time.
Glik un umglik, kovid un gelt,	Happiness and sorrow, honor and wealth,
Katshen zich nor bay der zayt.	Merely roll along by its side.

Eyner lebt op azoy orim zayn velt,	One lives his entire life in poverty,
Der anderer lebt azoy breyt.	The other lives in great wealth.
In eyn oygnblik vert dos farkert,	In the twinkling of an eye it all turns about,
Dos redele hot zich ibergedreyt.	With the spinning of the little wheel.
Shtoltsir nit bruder, mit der guter tsayt,	Brother, don't boast when you're well off,
Bay der shlechter fal nit arop.	In failure, do not lose heart.
Glik fun umglik iz gornit vayt,	Joy is not too far removed from distress,
Mitn redele bayt zich dos op.	For both can be changed by the little wheel.
Tu nor a kuk oyf yederer zach,	Look at everything around you,
Un nem a primer fun zey.	And learn a lesson thereby.
Vestu derkenen fun orim biz raych,	Then you will realize that rich and poor,
S'iz nor gevendt inem drey.[22]	Depend only on the turn of the wheel.

Some years earlier, the Haskalah writer, Hirsh Reitman (1808–1866), had written a lengthy poem entitled "Der kitl" (a white linen robe worn on solemn occasions; also a shroud), which became so popular that portions of it circulated in manuscript before it was published in 1863, and many knew sections of it by heart. Setting his poem in the environment of the workshop with the head seamstress and her workhands, all working in sewing the *kitl*, Reitman joyfully greets the liberal reign of Alexander II and proceeds to recall the dire years of oppression in former times. The introductory lines of this poem seem very similar to the motif and setting of I. L. Peretz's "Bay dem fremdn chupe kleyd" ("Sewing a stranger's wedding gown"), of a generation later, portions of which were set to music and widely sung, as for example, "Di dray neytorins" ("The Three Seamstresses"). Eighteen lines of Reitman's poem follow:

Der shvebish ligt shoyn oysgeshpreyt,	The linen is already spread,
Altsding iz shoyn ongegreyt,	And everything is now prepared.
Nu, herts aych oyf arumtsudreyen,	Well, stop your wandering about,
Nu, lomir zich nemen dem kitl neyen.	And let us start sewing the *kitl*.
Er muz doch haynt noch fartig zayn,	It has to be finished this very day,
Nu, kukts, kinder, in toch arayn,	Come now, children, pay attention to the main thing;

Oy, arbetn muz men, der shveys zol rinen,	Oh, one must work so that the sweat pours down
Dos shtikl broyt nor tsu gevinen,	To earn one's daily bread;
Tsu machn a glik nor fun der meloche,	To succeed from your work alone,
Muz got boruch-hu ersht gebn di broche.	You must also have the Lord's blessing.
Nor shnayder-yungen, shuster-yungen,	Only tailor and cobbler fellows
Zey megn bay der arbet zingen,	May sing while they work;
Men zingt kol-nidre un adon oylom,	They sing *Kol Nidre* and *Adon Oylom*
Abi nisht zitsn vi a goylom.	To keep from sitting like a blockhead.
Di hent zoln epes mit cheyshek ton,	So that the hands may work with a will,
Tor oych dos moyl derbay nit ru-en,	The mouth, too, must not stand still;
Un az men zingt derbay a lidl,	So, when we therefore sing a song,
Geyt gor di arbet vi a fidl.[23]	The work goes merrily along.

Following the 1880's, as the literary accomplishments in Yiddish prose and poetry achieved classical eminence, the folk songs, too, reflected this development. The poems of a number of poets were set to tunes, anonymous and composed, and became the possession of the people—for example, Sholem Berenstein's (d. 1880) "Dos vigele" ("The Cradle"), which incorporated stanzas from the traditional "Unter yankele's vigele" and became as universal as the folk song, and his "Sholem aleichem malochim fayne" ("Peace unto you, lovely angels"), which enjoyed the popularity of anonymous folk song.[24] Another poet, B. Benedikt Schafir (c. 1858–1915), one of the last to imitate the art of the *badchen*, achieved considerable popularity with his "Droysn blozt a vint a kalter" ("Outdoors a cold wind blows"). Less than a generation later, another Shafir (1876–1922) entered the popular category with his "Oyfn boydim shloft der dach" ("The roof sleeps over the attic"), which was set to music by the prominent author-dramatist, Peretz Hirschbein, and is still remembered at the present day.[25]

Brought into play as a programmatic aid of the Haskalah movement during the 1830's and 1840's, a number of anonymous folk songs, poetry in folk style, and professional poetry drew sustenance from the literary men of the Enlightenment movement. A generation later, *literary* Yiddish poetry in Russia had practically "no literary traditions to fall back upon, except the folk song of the preceding generation."[26]

American Labor Poets

During the 1880's and 1890's, an interesting influence was being exerted on Eastern European Yiddish poetry and folk song by certain American-Jewish poets, writing in Yiddish: Morris Winchevsky, Morris Rosenfeld, David Edelshtat, I. Bovshover, and their contemporaries residing in the United States. Dozens of their poems were set to music by anonymous composers on both sides of the Atlantic and sung by both Jewish communities.[27]

Winchevsky's "Hert ir kinder vi es rirt zich" ("Children, do you hear the stirring?"); and "In england is do a shtot lester" ("There's a city called Leicester in England"); Rosenfeld's "Mayn yingele" ("My Little Boy"), "Mayn ru-e plats" ("My resting place"); Edelshtat's "Mayn tsavo-e" ("My Testament"), "Mir vern gehast un getribn" ("We are hated and driven") were all popular among workingmen and women, who were struggling for better conditions, a shorter workday, and in the Eastern European lands, for the end of autocracy and oppression. Portions of Edelshtat's "Der arbeter" ("The Workingman") were absorbed into Yiddish folk song in Eastern Europe, of which the following is an example:

Shnel dreyen zich di reder, es klapn
    di mashinen,
Di fabrik fun der bonifratn gas;
Der kop vert fartumlt, di oygn vern
    finster,
Finster fun arbet un fun shveys.

Fast turn the wheels, the machines
    clatter,
In the factory on Bonifratn street;
Your head swims, your eyes grow
    dim,
Darkened by toil and sweat.

Her shoyn uf, du arbeter, trern tsu
    fargisn,
Du machst doch af der arbet a flek.
Bald vet araynkumen der mayster
    der merder,
Traybt er dich fun der arbet avek.

Worker, stop shedding your
    tears,
You are staining your work.
Soon the overseer, that murderer,
    will come in
And chase us all out of here.

Do kumt arayn der mayster, azoy vi
    a vilde chaye,
Un yogt tsu der sh'chite di shof.

The overseer comes in like a wild
    animal,
Driving the sheep to slaughter.

—Vi lang vet ir dervaytern, ir
   arbeter ayere brider,

Shteyt uf un macht fun dem mayster
   a sof.[28]

—Workingmen, how long will you
   remain isolated from your
   brothers,

Arise and put an end to the overseer.

European literary influences also left their mark on certain Yiddish
folk songs, especially on a number which were current among organized
workingmen and women towards the last quarter of the nineteenth century. A motif which was evident in a number of workers' songs employed
the method of listing the wealth created by the toiling population and
pointing out that the fruits thereof were not garnered by them but by
those who exploited them. This theme, which was introduced into European literature by Percy Bysshe Shelley in his poem "Ode to the Men of
England," in 1819, appeared later in a poem by the German poet, Georg
Herwegh, a *Bundeslied* which he wrote for the General Federation of
German Workingmen in 1863. In 1891, Chaim Zhitlowsky, philosopher-
economist, based his Yiddish translation on Herwegh's poem, titling it
"Un du akerst, un du zeyst" ("You plow and you sow"). Zhitlowsky's text
was soon set to an anonymous tune and three stanzas of the folk version,
still known to Yiddish-speaking Jews everywhere, are given below.

Un du akerst, un du zeyst,
Un du fiterst un du neyst,
Un du hamerst un du shpinst,
Zog mayn folk vos du fardinst?

Vebst dayn vebshtul tog un nacht,

Grobst undz ayzn fun der shacht,
Brengst di shefa undz arayn,
Ful mit t'vue un mit vayn.

Nor vu iz dayn tish gegreyt?
Nor vu iz dayn yontev kleyd?
Nor vu iz dayn sharfe shverd?
Velches glik iz dir bashert? [29]

You plow and you sow,
You tend the flock and you sew.
You hammer and you spin,
Tell me my people, what is your
   gain?

You weave at the loom night and
   day,
You dig in the mine for ore,
You fill the horn of plenty
Full of wheat and wine.

But where is your table spread?
And where is your festive dress?
Tell me, where is your sharp sword?
And what joy is yours to share?

A poem of literary origin, which enjoyed a popularity surpassing many
a folk song, was Sholem Aleichem's lullaby about the mass migrations of

Jews from Eastern Europe to America in the 1880's and 1890's. Current in a number of textual and musical variants, it also served to inspire other cradle songs in Eastern Europe and other Yiddish-speaking communities. Two others who influenced Yiddish folk song during the last decades of the nineteenth century were Abraham Goldfaden (1840–1908), founder of the modern Yiddish theater, and M. M. Warshawsky (1840–1907), popular folk songster and tunesmith.

Goldfaden, like a number of his Haskalah contemporaries, concerned himself with the problems and tribulations of his people. "My heart was filled with pain . . . to see my people in such a low state of spiritual development. . . . I realized that it was utterly ignorant of the holy spark of its nationality, which I had thus far tried to infuse in its hearts by my songs. . . . They needed to understand their own life. . . . Historic pieces should be given that they learn their history."[30] A prolific song writer, whose poems and songs in folk style published in Europe and America would fill several volumes, Goldfaden was often criticized by his professional colleagues for the quality of his creations. Guided by his own convictions, however, he proceeded to create allegorical and historical songs in a style which had been dormant for over a century. Once, while listening to some "popular singer-jesters" performing in a wine cellar, it occurred to him that he could combine his songs by "the connecting links of prose into a tale that would make a theatrical piece." In 1876, Goldfaden launched his first theatrical enterprise, using for his first actors primitive singers, like the Brod Singers, whom he had heard perform in the wine cellars and inns. Goldfaden freely used Yiddish folk song for his stage presentations, which, in turn, made his songs exceedingly popular among the people. Such songs as "Rozhinkes mit mandlen" ("Raisins and Almonds") from his operetta *Shulamith*, based on folk motifs, still enjoys popularity to the present day. A stanza and the refrain, known to almost every Yiddish-speaking Jew anywhere, is the following :

In dem beys hamikdosh, in a vinkl-cheyder,
Zitst di almone, bas tsion aleyn.

Ir ben-yochidl yidele, vigt zi k'seyder,
Un zingt im tsum shlofn a lidele sheyn :

In the holy temple, in a corner of a chamber,
Sits the Daughter of Zion, widowed and alone,

Rocking her only son, Yidele, to sleep,
She sings him a pretty lullaby :

Refrain: Unter yidele's vigele,
Shteyt a klorvays tsigele,

Dos tsigele iz geforn
handlen,
Dos vet zayn dayn baruf,
Rozhinkes mit mandlen,
Shlof-zhe yidele, shlof.[31]

Under Yidele's little cradle,
Stands a pure white little
kid,
The little kid went trading,

This will be your calling,
Raisins and almonds,
Sleep then, Yidele, sleep.

Another song by Goldfaden which had very wide popular appeal was his "Der yiches-briv" ("The Pedigree"), an allegorical poem which stresses the greatness of the Jewish faith. Excerpts and the refrain are given below:

Der oybershter iz der mechutn,
Di toyre iz di kale,
Moyshe rabeynu
Iz der shadchn geven. . . .
Der orimer yisrolik
Iz der chosn der sheyner,
Oyf dem heylign barg sinai
Iz di t'noyim geven.

The Almighty is the in-law,
The Torah is the bride,
Moses our teacher
Was the matchmaker.
Poor little Israel
Is the handsome groom,
On holy Mt. Sinai
The engagement took place.

Refrain: Es flien yidelech, zingen
lidelech,
Yederer shrayt bazunder:
Chosn's tsad, kale's tsad:
mazltov!

Jews are rushing about,
singing songs,
Each one shouts:
To the groom's family, to
the bride's family:
good luck!

Dek oyf dayn dektuch,
Du tayere kale,
Bavayz undz dayn ponim,
Mir viln dich zen.
Zet nor ir yidn,
Un kukt tsu, ir ale:
Dos iz di emune,
Di kale geven![32]

Raise your veil,
Dear bride,
Let us see your face,
Show it to us.
Look, Jews,
Look all of you:
Our faith
Was the bride!

Till the 1880's, Goldfaden's musical plays and songs were inspired by the ideas of the Enlightenment movement, as his "Shtey oyf mayn folk" ("Arise, My People"), which he patterned after Michl Gordon's poem by the same name. In it, he passionately tried to awaken his people from their age-old slumber: "I hear . . . other nations stirring . . . with new

inventions, . . . new laws, . . . cables reach into every corner of the
earth; . . . locomotives whistle, bidding them awake and greet the day!"
But when the people slept on, hugging its dream and refusing to rise,
Goldfaden exclaimed bitterly: "My people is satisfied with a crumb
from heaven, water from a stone, the ritual length of a prayer shawl,
the prescribed contents of the ritual bath, lighted tapers, superstitions,
omens, and the cleansing of a pot that has been defiled!"[33]

The pogroms of the eighties shook Goldfaden to the core. A
song from his musical play, *Dr. Almasada,* which became very popular
and served as a pattern for subsequent Yiddish songs, contained the following:

Faryomert, farklogt, fun zayn heym faryogt,	In tears, in anguish, driven from his home
Far zayne groyse zind.	For his great sins,
Azoy umetum blondzhet arum	So wanders about everywhere
Fun got dos farsholtene kind.	The child, cursed by the Lord.
Az er zol oyf kayn ort, nit lang blaybn dort,	Never to remain long in one place,
Nor geyn un nit vern mid,	But to wander tirelessly,
Dertsu hot im zayn tate elokim,	For this, the Almighty God, his father,
Geshtemplt mit dem nomen yid.	Has branded him with the name, Jew.
Zayn kop ontsushparn bet er zich ayn,	He pleads to rest his head somewhere,
Chotsh veyn, chotsh shray, oy vey!	And though he cries and shouts, oh woe!
Neyn, entfert men im, men lozt nit arayn,	The answer is no, you cannot come in,
A yid biztu, gey vayter, gey![34]	You are a Jew and must go on, go!

Though not by a professional poet, composer, or performer, Mark
Warshawsky's songs came to be sung along with the oldest Yiddish folk
songs in Eastern Europe and wherever Yiddish-speaking Jews resided.
He authored some fifty texts and tunes. More than twenty became household songs in many Jewish homes in the Pale before they were published
and it became officially known that Warshawsky was their creator.

Mark Warshawsky's songs mirror his unbounding love for his oppressed, poverty-stricken people under Czarism of the 1880's and 1890's.
Simple, direct, musically familiar to the folk ear, retaining the folk idiom,

his songs deal with the period of disillusionment and suffering wrought by the pogroms, the migrations to America, the yearning for Zion, the daily concerns of the average Jew in the Pale. In his "Dem milner's trern" ("The Miller's Tears"), he describes the eviction of the Jews from the villages; in "Dos lid fun dem broyt" ("The Song of Bread"), he describes the joys of agricultural labor in the new colonies in Palestine; in "Der zeyde mit der bobe" ("Grandfather and Grandmother"), he describes a charming couple, ripe in years and a long happy life, surrounded by their many grandchildren; in his wedding songs "Hecher, besser" ("Louder, better") and "Di mechutonim geyen, kinder" ("The in-laws are coming, children"), he paints a vivid picture of a Jewish wedding. Whether personal or collective, Warshawsky's songs, even when they treat bitter sorrows, contain a natural optimism and joyousness. Thus, in his "A yidish lid fun rumanien" ("A Jewish Song from Rumania"), he exclaims: "When they drain my blood from me and torture me slowly, I laugh at my enemies and dance about gaily!"[35]

The success of Warshawsky's songs were immediate, especially after they were published in 1899 with an introduction by Sholem Aleichem, when both became associated as traveling performers, with Sholem Aleichem reading his stories and Warshawsky singing his songs before Jewish audiences. The most popular of all of Warshawsky's songs, regarded by most people as a "true" folk song, is "Der alef-beyz" ("The ABC"), or, as it is commonly known, "Oyfn pripetshok" ("On the Hearth"), of which the first two stanzas and the refrain are given below:

Oyfn pripetshok brent a fayerl,
Un in shtub iz heys,
Un der rebe lernt kleyne kinderlech,

Dem aleph-beyz.

Refrain: Zet-zhe kinderelech,
gedenkt-zhe tayere,
Vos ir lernt do :
Zogt-zhe noch amol, un
take noch amol,
Komets-aleph : O!

Lernt kinder, mit groys cheyshek,
Azoy zog ich aych on;
Ver s'vet gicher fun aych kenen ivre,
Der bakumt a fon.[36]

On the hearth a little fire is burning,
And it is hot in the house,
And the *rebe*'s teaching the little
children,
The ABC.

See now children,
remember dear ones,
What you're learning here :
Repeat it over and over
again,
"A" with a *kamets* is "O"!

Study, children, with great interest,
That is what I tell you;
He who'll know his lessons first,
Will get a banner for a prize.

As Zunser was the last outstanding *badchen* and the bridge between the marriage entertainer and the professional folk singer, so was Warshawsky the last folk bard of the nineteenth century, bridging the gap between the songs in folk style and the Yiddish art songs of the twentieth century.

The last decades of the nineteenth century witnessed Yiddish folk song falling ever more under the influence of professional poets representing a variety of ideological currents and different professional levels. Lyrical themes increased, and a great number of poems by leading literary men were set to music by anonymous, as well as recognized composers, and accepted into the family of popular song.

This literary influence on Yiddish folk song was maintained in Eastern Europe, through World War I, into the Soviet period, and through World War II. In the United States, where many Yiddish poets, composers, theatrical men and women of Eastern European origin came to live from the 1880's on, the old Yiddish folk songs receded and the literary influence became predominant. In time, Yiddish art song in America took the place of the Yiddish folk song from the "old home" and became, along with the popular and theatrical songs created in America, the "household" songs of the American Yiddish-speaking Jews.[37]

In Palestine, too, and in Israel after 1948, the literary influence in poetry and music was uppermost. As for Yiddish folk song of Eastern European origin in Israel, many songs were absorbed through Hebrew translation and have subsequently practically disappeared completely from the oral scene.

Notes

OF LITERARY ORIGIN

1. The Haskalah movement of Enlightenment sought to bring secular knowledge to the Jewish community in the Pale, to revive the Hebrew tongue for modern use, and to bring a critical approach to the study of the Talmud. From Germany it spread to areas in Austria, Galicia, Russia, and later Poland. In each country it adopted different paths. Whereas in Germany it took the form of assimilationism, in southern Russia it propagated productivity through handicrafts and agriculture to replace trading and unproductive occupations. In the north, in Lithuania, it sought a more intensive educational system to include the secular sciences, languages, and a deeper appreciation of Talmudic learning. The Haskalah never really attacked the fundamental beliefs of Jewish religion, struggling instead against fanaticism, false piety on the part of many Chasidic *rebeyim* and other religious leaders, mediocre and meaningless rituals, and outlandish practices.

2. An important figure in modern Jewish history, Moses Mendelssohn, grandfather of the famous composer, was called by the Germans "the Plato of German philosophy." Steeped in Jewish Talmudic learning before he became a famous German philosopher, he knew the dramatist and philosopher G. E. Lessing and is said to have inspired his treatment of the central figure in his play *Nathan der Weise.* The Haskalah movement is regarded as having begun with Mendelssohn, and his translation of the Bible and the Psalms into German incurred violent protests from Jewish religious sources. Some have maintained that what Wycliffe's translation of the Bible did for England and Luther's for Germany, Mendelssohn's did for German and Russian Jewry—but in reverse: serving for many a cloistered Eastern European Talmudic student as the gateway to German literature and Western secular knowledge.

3. Raisin, pp. 187–188. Maimon, who left his Polish home and family for the science centers of the West, achieved eminence in German philosophy in this tortuous way.

4. G. and M., No. 54.

5. *Hundert Naye*, p. 46. (*melamed* : parochial teacher in first grades; *bahelfer* : the *melamed*'s assistant.)

6. Zunser, II, p. 229.

7. Ditties, current among religious youth, bitterly attacked the followers of the German Mendelssohn, calling them *daytshn* — "Germans," singling out for ridicule their departure from traditional modes of dress and ways of life. Such an example is the following:

Geyt er di hoyzn iber di komashn,
Frest vi a goy umgevashn.

Refrain: Orntlech un fayn, fayn, fayn,
fayn,
A daytsh, a daytsh muz men
zayn.

He wears his trousers over his boots,
And eats like a non-Jew, without washing his hands.

Respectable and fine, fine, fine,
fine,
A *daytsh*, a *daytsh*, he must be.

Geyt er in gas un ganvet a bulke, He walks in the street and steals a bun,
Un um shabes reychert er di lulke. And on the Sabbath he smokes his pipe.
(Skuditsky, 1936, p. 333.)

8. Wiener, p. 77.
9. Rubin, MSS. Published in Lemberg in 1869, 1873, 1878 and in Vienna in 1865, Zbarzher's songs appeared with Hebrew and Yiddish texts.
10. *See: Di Yidishe Bine,* pp. 485–489.
11. Berl Broder's songs were never published during his lifetime, a collection appearing after his death, in Lemberg in 1876 and in Warsaw in 1882.
12. Skuditsky, 1936, p. 102, No. 3.
13. *Ibid.,* pp. 103–104, No. 4.
14. Rubin, MSS.
15. Kipnis, pp. 59–62. Example given here is based on stanzas 3, 4, and 15 of M. Gordon's original poem, which consisted of eighteen stanzas.
16. Gordon, pp. 29–36. Original poem consisted of thirty-one stanzas.
17. *See* J. L. Gordon, pp. 35–40. His poem "Tsvey chasidim," pp. 68–70, was sung to a Russian tune.
18. Rubin, MSS. *See* Apotheker, *Hanevel,* pp. 53–61. Original poem consisted of twelve stanzas. In 1888, Apotheker came to the United States, where he worked as a journalist.
19. *See* Zunser, III, p. 28.
20. *Ibid.,* p. 30.
21. *See* Zunser, III, p. 30; I, pp. 62, 138, 142, 31, 92, 50 respectively.
22. Rubin, MSS. *See* Linetsky, pp. 23–26.
23. Reitman. The first part of this poem was published in Vienna. The second was destroyed in the Brod conflagration of 1867. A copy of this poem is to be found in the library of the Yiddish Scientific Institute in New York City.
24. Berenstein was a contemporary of Michl Gordon and very popular in southern Russia. Unlike Michl Gordon with his bitter attitude toward Chasidic leaders, Berenstein sought to console his suffering brethren and made his sympathy for them the central theme of his poetry.
25. *See* Reizin.
26. Wiener, p. 108.
27. *See* Chapter XIII, "To America," for more on the American-Jewish labor poets.
28. D. and Y., pp. 345–346, No. 14. Bonifratn street is in Warsaw.
29. Rubin, 1950, p. 100. A refrain of anonymous origin was subsequently added to these stanzas, as follows:

Kling, klang, kling, klang, Kling, klang, kling, klang,
Klapt der hamer mit zayn gezang, The hammer rings out its song,
Kling, klang, kling, klang, Kling, klang, kling, klang,
Tsurayst di keytn fun shklafn-tsvang. Break the chains of slavery.

30. Idelsohn, pp. 448–449.
31. Rubin, MSS.
32. Kisselgof, p. 16, No. 34.
33. Sheet music, Hebrew Publishing Co., Chicago, 1897; New York, 1898.
34. *Ibid.*
35. Warshawsky, p. 7.
36. *Ibid.,* p. 1.
37. Many poems by I. L. Peretz were set to music by professional as well as anonymous musicians: "Shteynerne palatsn" ("Stone Palaces"); his children's songs, "Di dray neytorins" ("The Three Seamstresses"), "Di tsvey brider" ("The Two Brothers")—a portion of his long dramatic poem "Baym fremden chupe kleyd" ("Sewing the Stranger's Wedding Gown"), etc. S. Frug's (1860–1916) "Zamd un shtern"

("Sand and Stars"), "Der becher" ("The Goblet"), "Di troyke" ("The Troyka"), and others were sung to anonymously composed tunes. A. Litwin (S. Hurwitsh) (1862–1943) contributed his cradle song, "Zhamele," and "Di neyterkes" ("The Seamstresses") to the folk repertoire. H. D. Nomberg's (1874–1927) lullaby "S'loyfn, s'yogn shvartse volkn" ("Dark Clouds Are Racing"), set to an anonymous melody, was very popular among workingmen and women. The prolific Avrom Reisin had more than fifty of his poems set to music both in Eastern Europe and the United States. His "Hulyet, hulyet beyze vintn" ("Be Merry, Angry Winds"), "O, hemerl, hemerl, klap" ("Oh, Rap, Rap, Little Hammer"), and many others enjoyed a popularity on both sides of the Atlantic that many a "true" folk song would have envied.

CHAPTER XI

Poverty, Toil, and Struggle

THE BEGINNING OF THE NINETEENTH CENTURY WAS MARKED BY A PERIOD
of famine in the countryside, mass expulsions from the villages,[1] heavy
taxation. The endless decrees prohibiting Jews from owning land, exclud-
ing them from basic industries and craft guilds, resulted in a crowding
into the cities[2] and an abnormal concentration in the light-industry
occupations. The character of the Jewish parochial-education system
further tore Jews away from nature and confined many to crafts related
to their religious requirements and pursuits.

The restrictions and oppressions of the Czarist regime reduced large
masses of the Jewish population in the congested towns and cities to the
lowliest of trades, to the keeping of tiny shops and stalls, while a large
section constantly shifted and drifted, traded and bartered, compelled
to seek their livelihood at anything that would keep body and soul
together. Contrary to the conventional accusation that the Jews were a
people of petty traders, there were all kinds of laborers among the Jews,
who ". . . rendered all manner of service to their gentile neighbors, from
a cobbler's and blacksmith's to producing the most exquisite *objets d'art*
and gold and silver engraving. They were equally well represented among
the clerks and bookkeepers, and the bricklayers and stonecutters. They
took up with the most laborious employments, if only they furnished
them with an honest even though scanty livelihood."[3] Yet, although the
Jewish handicraftsmen formed the main base of service in the cities and
towns and villages, the great mass of the Jewish population was often as
poor and even poorer than the Russian peasantry.

The absorption of the Polish provinces into the Russian Empire at
the end of the eighteenth century found the Jewish people in the Czarist
Pale of Settlement in an almost medieval condition, where for generations

278

the few well to do and the network of clerical groups and their educational establishments had ruled the community ideologically and socially.

Poverty was rampant. The never-ending struggle with hunger, the constant search for a livelihood, together with the natural yearning for a better, more human life in this world brought a number of poverty songs into circulation. These dealt with economic problems on the simplest level, often on the most personal terms. Some were grim and despondent, others were tinged with satire. Still others questioned the justice in this world which doomed so many righteous, God-fearing people to a life of constant hardship and suffering.

The well-known ditty "Bulbes" ("Spuds"), which decried the monotony of a potato diet seven days in the week, is borne out by Mendele Moycher Sforim's satirical description of a scene in a workshop, when the master's wife, the seamstress, places a huge bowl of steaming, hot potatoes boiled in their jackets, on the table—the noonday dish for the workmen and apprentices: ". . . it's well worth the price of a ticket to see how skillfully the potatoes are peeled, tossed into the mouth and swallowed. Masterfully! Such craftsmen at potato eating as our tailor boys are hard to find in the world. They have become proficient in it through the years and have developed a great dexterity at it, because potatoes are their food, if you please, daily."[4] Following is a stanza of this little song:

Zuntig bulbe, montig bulbe,
Dinstig un mitvoch—bulbe,
Donershtig un fraytig—bulbe,
Shabes in a novine a bulbe kigele!

Zuntig—vayter bulbe.[5]

Sunday spuds, Monday spuds,
Tuesday and Wednesday—spuds,
Thursday and Friday—spuds,
On the Sabbath, a special treat—a potato pudding!
Sunday—spuds again.

Another song of this type is "Dire-gelt" ("Rent Money"), which bemoans the excessive rents for quarters that are often unfit to live in.

Farvos zol ich tsoln dire-gelt,
Az di kich iz tsubrochn?
Farvos zol ich gebn dire-gelt
Az ich hob nisht oyf vos tsu kochn?

Refrain: Dire-gelt un oy-oy-oy!
Dire-gelt un bozhemoy!

Why should I pay rent money
When the stove is broken?
Why should I give rent money
When I haven't anything to cook on?

Rent money and oh-oh-oh!
Rent money and oh, my God!

| Dire-gelt un gradovoy! | Rent money, watch out for the cop! |
| Dire-gelt muz men tsoln.[6] | Rent money one must pay. |

All strata of the population, with the exception of a very thin layer of wealthy merchants and top clerical leaders, felt the weight of the widespread economic degradation. Children romping in the streets skipped and played games in rhymes reflecting the environment into which they had been born.

Oy vey muter,	Oh, oh, mother,
Di kats lekt di puter,	The cat's licking the butter,
Di hiner leygn di eyer,	The hens are laying eggs,
Di kale geyt in shleyer,	The bride wears the veil,
Der chosn geyt in talis,	The groom wears the prayer shawl,
Bam kabtsn iz der dalis,	The poor man has his poverty,
Di kinder zoygn di finger,	The children suck their fingers,
Di vayber shtarbn far hunger.[7]	The women die of hunger.

A petty trader in potatoes sang a song to himself at the close of the holidays, as he contemplated the hopelessness of the economic struggle which awaited him on the morrow. Still under the influence of the holiday spirit and its songs, in this case Pentecost, he sings of the secular world in a melody from the religious chants:

Af bri—	*Af bri—*
Af morgn noch yontoyvim glaych in der fri	On the morrow after the holidays, early in the morning
Afn mark muz men loyfn,	I must run to the marketplace
Bulbes muz men koyfn—	And buy potatoes—
Un kayn gelt iz alts nito!	And there is no money!

Utas—	*Utas—*
In shtub iz kalt vi afn gas,	It's as cold in the house as on the street,
Di shoybn iz oysgebrochn,	The windowpanes are broken,
Un s'iz nito vos tsu kochn—	And there's nothing to cook—
Un kayn gelt iz alts nito![8]	And still, there is no money!

There wasn't a craft or a home or a family that escaped the devastating hand of poverty. Poverty figured in almost every situation from the cradle to the grave. Among the workingmen, whether plying the needle or working with the awl, whether in intimate or general terms, or somber, traditional or gay melodies, the economic pressures came to light in their songs. A cobbler sang : *Keyner layt nisht, keyner git kayn orves, / Ich bin a shuster, gey ich take borves* ("No one lends me money, no one gives me credit, I am a cobbler and go barefoot"). A tinsmith sang : *Ich zits un klap bay yenem fremde decher, / Ba mir in shtub, rint fun ale lecher* ("I sit mending the roofs of strangers, but my house leaks from all sides").[9] A tailor sang : *Zitst a shnayder, neyt un neyt, / Hot kadoches nit kayn broyt. / Zitst a shnayder, halt a nodl, / Un fardint kayn groshn godl* ("A tailor sits and sews and sews and has the misery, but no bread. A tailor sits and plies his needle and doesn't earn a single *groshn*").[10]

The complaints of the poor were heard everywhere, in every craft and occupation. At the butcher's stall the women cried out at the high price of meat, in the synagogue the lowly objected to the position of honor given to the wealthy of the community. Says Mendele Moycher Sforim :

The Community Council *(kohol)* terrorized the craftsmen, kept them from complaining to the community elders in matters that dealt with the day-to-day problems. A craftsman was not allowed to wear a satin frock on the Sabbath nor the circular fur-trimmed hat *(shtrayml)*. In the prayer house or house of study his place was on the furthest bench. . . . He didn't dare show himself at meetings where these 'fine folk' assembled. . . . His opinion was never sought. For impudence or some infraction he was thoroughly admonished, even thrashed, . . . taken seriously to task in the Community Council House. His children were kidnapped, given into military service, sacrificed in the place of Talmudic students who were the 'respectable' children.[11]

The sharp tilt between the few rich and the many poor resulted in songs which pointed up the contrast between them. A number of these used the traditional acrostic form and the alphabet sequence to satirize the life of the rich as it compared with the miserable existence of the numberless poor. The following employs comparisons of food and was sung to the traditional chant of *akdomes* :

Aleph—ayngemachts est der nogid,	A—The rich man eats fruit preserves,
Beyz—beyndelech hrizet der oriman.	B—The poor man gnaws bones.
Giml—gendzelech est der nogid,	G—The rich man eats geese,
Daled—dalis hot der oriman.	D—The poor man has poverty.
Zayen—zeml mit puter est der nogid,	Z—The rich man eats buttered buns,
Ches—chalasn hot der oriman.	Ch—The poor man has sicknesses.
Mem—mashke trinkt der nogid,	M—The rich man drinks whiskey,
Nun—nichter iz der oriman.	N—The poor man is sober.

The above song extends the contrasts also to clothes and other pleasures of the rich and poor.

Kof—kaloshn trogt der nogid,	K—The rich man wears rubbers,
Lamed—laptyes trogt der oriman.	L—The poor man wears straw sandals.
Samech—Sametene kleyder trogt der nogid,	S—The rich man wears satin clothes,
Ayin—Opgerisn geyt der oriman.	E—The poor man is in tatters.
Shin—Shereshevski's papirosn roychert der nogid,	Sh—The rich man smokes Shereshevski's cigarettes,
Tof—Titun pipket der oriman.[12]	T—The poor man puffs at inferior tobacco.

The poverty songs varied in their degrees of intensity. There were some which attributed their hard life to bad luck: *Oy, mazl, oy mazl, / Vu biztu fun mir antrinen? / Ich tu dich zuchn in ale vinkelech / Un kon dich nit gefinen* ("Oh, luck, oh, luck, where have you disappeared? I seek you in every corner, and cannot find you").[13] Others took their misery with a grain of salt and a humorous lilt: *Oy dalesl, nu-nu-nu, / In ale vinkelech bistu do. / Volt ich dir geholfn, / Hob ich nit funvanen. / Bet ich dich, dalesl, / Farnem zich fundanen!* ("Oh, little poverty, well, well, well—in every corner, there you are. I would help you but haven't the wherewithal. So I beg of you, little poverty, get out of here!").[14]

Each craft adapted or created its melodies to the beat of its particular occupation. For example, the tailors and cobblers sang their songs to the precise rhythmic movements of their respective crafts. The lonely coachman set his lyrics to the tread of the horse jogging easily along the road: *Az kayn hey hob ich nit, / Un kayn hober koyf ich nit, / Az der ferd vil nit geyn, / Zetz ich zich un veyn un veyn* ("Since I have no hay and do not buy any oats, the horse refuses to go, so I sit me down and cry and cry).[15]

The economic stresses borne by the working women who maintained their males in the house of study became especially intense before the Sabbath or a holiday, when additional expenses had to be met. An example of such a predicament is the following duet in which a woman informs her husband of the approaching Passover festival and the need to procure beets for the traditional *borscht* ("beet soup") and other articles. His replies were characteristic for the type of perennial student-

Louis Losowick, 1936

Warsaw Market

husband, whose mind was forever preoccupied with his studies and who expected the good Lord to take care of his family for him.

Oy mayn man, vos vet zayn m'koyech burikes?	Oh, husband, what about beets?
—Her mayn vayb, biz peysech iz noch dray vochn,	—Listen wife, it's still three weeks to Passover,
Burikes veln mir layen baym shochn,	We can borrow some from the neighbor.
Un kayn gelt iz alts nito.	And still there is no money.

The poor woman then asks her husband: What about matso meal? And he suggests that she take their zinc platters which are stored in the cellar and trade them in at the miller's. When she asks him about new shoes for the holiday, he sadly notes that his own are full of patches and "there is no money at all. . . ."[16]

Poverty interfered in the relationship between people. It prevented lovers from mating, it broke up marriages, tore brother from brother, as in the following lament:

Reboynoy-shel-oylom, vos hostu fun mir gevelt?	Lord of the universe, what did you want from me?
Vos hostu bashafn a kabtsn oyf der velt?	Why did you create the poor man in the world?
Oyf azelchene tsores, oyf azelchene noyt,	To suffer so, to be in such need,
Mir volt shoyn geven liber der toyt.	Death would be more pleasant for me.
Vos hostu dem nogid alts gegebn,	Why did you give the rich man everything,
K'dey er zol hobn afn gantsn lebn,	Enough for his entire life,
Un mir hostu gezhalevet dayne rachmones,	And from me you withheld your compassion,
Az ich mit mayn lebn, shtey mir in sakones?	So that my life would always be in danger?
. . . Fun eygene familie bin ich gevorn farshemt,	I have been shamed before my own family,
Fun eygenem bruder bin ich gevorn farfremt,	From my own brother, I have been estranged,
Er tut fun mir farmaydn ale zayne vegn,	He avoids me constantly,
Er hot zich fargesn az mir zenen unter eyn hartsn gelegn.[17]	And has forgotten that one mother bore us both.

In a moment of despair, perhaps someone would take his pack on his back and leave the town and all its miseries and problems, its conflicts with the elders and the cruelty of the insensitive rich!

Vos mer kabtsn, mer hulyake,	The poorer the man, the gayer he is,
Un vos her ich zey!	What do I care about them!
Vos mer nogid, mer sabaka,	The richer the man, the more dog is he,
Un vos darf ich zey!	What do I need them for!
Un dem pekl oyfn flekl,	I put my bundle on the stick,
Un vos her ich zey!	No more will I listen to them!
Un dem pekl oyfn pleytse,	I put my bundle on my back,
Un vos darf ich zey! [18]	What do I need them for!

During the 1860's and 1870's, the feudal system in Russia was crumbling, bringing in its wake the industrialization of large masses of Jews on the one hand and the ruination of the Jewish middle class on the other. Misery and want drove people from one town and city to another, ever in search of the elusive livelihood, while the Czarist government, through one economic decree after another, further restricted the Jewish population in the Pale. No longer able to support her males at their Talmudic studies, the average mother was compelled to send her children into apprenticeship to learn a craft. Such a step was often regarded as a tragedy, for the most despised members of the society of that day were the workingmen.

Here, too, Mendele illuminates this attitude in his autobiographical work, cited previously:

As the Jews were mistreated by the other nations, so were Jewish workingmen maltreated by their own community . . . kicked around, terribly humiliated. To admit having a worker in the family, a tailor, a cobbler, for instance, was disgraceful. Often it interfered with the consummation of a wedding match. To attain social recognition in a marriage, one sought out the rabbis, the scholars, the ritual slaughterers of *kosher* cattle, the cantors, even the poor men supported by the synagogue, and stuck into the background the worker, if he happened to be a member of the family, even denying his very existence. . . . An innkeeper, a land surveyor, a small businessman, a money lender, that now was more acceptable. In fact, these were considered fine in-laws, important leaders in the town, exerting a strong influence in the bath house, begging your pardon, in the synagogue, and the Town Council.[19]

Small wonder then that mothers wept bitterly when they were compelled to send their children into apprenticeship, often far away from home, for the destiny of workingmen in the early workshops was, at best, a station in life held in contempt by the respectable strata of the Jewish population in the Pale.

The Workshops

Living under one roof with the master workman and his wife, who acted as the overseer, the apprentices bewailed their fate in songs which described their hard life, the long hours of toil, the cruelties and humiliations which they suffered at the hands of their employers. Although these children had known hunger and want before, they longed for home. They understood the sad circumstances which had forced their parents to deprive them of a protected life in the House of Study, and were now exposing them to the dismal existence in the world of toiling adults. Exploited by the master workman who made them tend his children, take out the garbage, and perform other menial tasks, the apprentices were even beaten and starved before they were finally permitted to "master their craft." Entering the world of labor often at the tender age of nine or ten, these children, aged before their time, sang songs of helplessness, loneliness, and the hard life of the adult working world around them.

Oy bam shnayder, oy bam shnayder,	Oh at the tailor's, at the tailor's,
Iz doch zeyer bitter,	Bitter it is indeed,
Dem dritn tog a shtikl broyt oyfesn,	A crust of bread once in three days;
Abi ba dir, mayn libe mitter.[20]	But to be with you, beloved mother.

During the 1880's, when women entered industry, mainly in the needle trades, young apprentice girls added their songs on the subject :

Eyder ich leyg mich shlofn,	No sooner in my bed,
Darf ich shoyn oyfshteyn,	Then I must rise again,
Mit mayne kranke beyner	To drag my weary bones
Tsu der arbet geyn.	To work again.
Refrain: Tsu got vel ich veynen,	To God I will weep,
Mit a groys geveyn !	With a loud cry !
Tsu vos ich bin geboyrn	Why was I born
A neytorin tsu zayn !	A seamstress, why?

Ich layd shtendig hunger,
Ich hob nisht vos tsu esn.
Vil ich gelt betn,
Heyst men mir fargesn! [21]

I'm always hungry,
I've nothing to eat.
When I ask for my pay,
I'm told to forget it!

The exploitation of apprentice boys and girls and workmen in the primitive workshops of the 1880's and early 1890's was dreadful. Generally, they received no remuneration at all except for meager bed and board during the first two years of apprenticeship. In the Jewish workshops, the conception of a definite workday simply did not exist; one worked as long as "it was necessary," and during the seasons or prior to the holidays work would go on right through the night. There was generally no established attitude towards the workers and apprentices on the part of their employers and consequently no norms of hours or pay. The pressure of the rising factory system made itself felt upon the workshops, which were struggling for their existence. Consequently, these early work songs were in the main fatalistic in tone, pessimistic in mood. Simple, direct, melancholy, they yearned for a "lucky break" but saw no way out of the difficulties. In the following example, a bakery worker regrets that his father had "condemned" him to his craft:

Mayn foter hot mich geton tsu a
    bal-meloche gebn.
Er hot mich, nebich, geshochtn oyf
    mayn gants lebn.

My father apprenticed me to a
    master craftsman.
Oh, dear, he slaughtered me for the
    rest of my life.

Oy, ich nebich, zindiger beker,
Mayn lebn iz bay mir gornisht tayer,
Vayl min erev v'ad boyker,
Bren ich mich bay dem fayer.

Oh, a poor, sinful baker am I,
My life isn't worth anything,
Because from evening to morning
I roast before the fire.

A gantse nacht tu ich mich, nebich,
Brenen, brotn; brenen, brotn;
Inderfri kumt arop di bekerin

All night long, I, poor thing,
Burn and roast; roast and burn;
In the morning the baker's wife
    comes down

Shrayt zi: di zeml mitn broyt zenen
    nisht gerotn! [22]

And shouts: the rolls and bread were
    not baked right!

Here and there a feeling of bitterness and resentment is heard in a song, as in the following, which describes the "affluence" of the master workman and his bejeweled wife:

Der beker mit der bekern, zey kumen in der bekeray,	The baker and his wife, they come to the bakery,
Loyt zeyer raychtum un loyt zeyer shteyger :	Dressed according to their wealth and position :
Zi geyt ongeton a por briliantene oyringen,	She wears a pair of diamond earrings,
Un er in a goldenem zeyger.[23]	And he—a gold watch and chain.

Only rarely does a note of protest flash through, as in the following :

Oy, mayne gute-brider,	Oh, my good brothers,
Vos iz dos far a velt,	What kind of a world is this?
Mir arbetn, mir arbetn,	We work, and we work,
Mir hobn nisht kayn gelt.[24]	And we haven't any money.

In the main, however, the young lads caught in the web of the rising factory system bewailed their fate that doomed them to a life of hard work, no education, and constant want.

S'iz faranen kinder oych in mayne yorn,	There are children of my age
Doch kliger zaynen zey nisht fun mir,	Who are no wiser than I.
In raychtum, in luksus zaynen zey geboyrn,	Yet they were born into wealth and luxury,
Mit visnshaft gor on a shir.	With a great deal of education.
. . . Ober ich orem kind,	But I, poor child,
Farblibn bin ich blind,	Remained ignorant,
On visnshaft, on ale gefiln,	Without knowledge and refinements.
Vayl do in fabrik,	Because here in the factory
Oy do iz mayn glik,	I must seek my happiness
Dem hunger muz ich shtiln.[25]	And appease my hunger.

To relieve the gloom, the depressed mood was occasionally broken by a bit of horseplay. "Suddenly . . . the presser . . . starts singing a march in his high falsetto, tapping out the rhythm with his pressing iron. The workers and apprentices around the table work rapidly with the needle in time to the music, assisting him . . . each in his own way . . . rhythmically, gaily. . . . Soon, another . . . imitates in a melancholy voice the *badchen* as he sings in rhyme to the bride before the ceremony. Some of the fellows imitate the bandsmen as they play a sad little tune, while the others pretend to mourn and cry like the women. . . . Suddenly the catcalls become gay again, and the gang, as they sit at their work, end up with a . . . wedding dance to the bride !"[26]

It was moments like these that gave birth to the two-lined, saucy rhymes in the manner of the Ukrainian *chastushki,* such as the example below, which poked fun at the overseer-wife of the master workman. Such songs also served to speed the work, especially during the long hours late into the night and sometimes throughout the night, when energy flagged and spirits ran low.

Di baleboste geyt arayn,
Refrain: Hop, dunay, dunay!
　　(after each line)
Chevre, chevre, shtil zol zayn.
Refrain: Hop, dunay, dunay!

The boss's wife comes in,
　　Hop, dunay, dunay!

Fellows, fellows, let's be still.
　　Hop, dunay, dunay!

Di baleboste shteyt un kukt,

Chevre, chevre, arbet gut.

The boss's wife stands there watching,
Fellows, fellows, let's work well!

Di baleboste shteyt in kich,
Chevre, chevre, varft mit shtech.

The boss's wife is in the kitchen,
Fellows, fellows, throw those stitches.

Di baleboste shteyt in zal,

S'vert in ir tsezetst di gal.

The boss's wife is in the reception room,
Her gall is bursting.

Di baleboste shteyt af der tir,

Chevre, chevre, a make ir.

The boss's wife stands in the doorway,
Fellows, fellows, may she croak!

Di baleboste geyt aroys,
Chevre, chevre, lacht zi oys.[27]

The boss's wife goes out,
Fellows, fellows, let's laugh at her.

Prior to the holidays, the speed-up was especially intense as all the crafts were called upon to manufacture the additional articles of food and clothing necessary for the approaching festival. Working through the night was not considered unusual on those occasions. The following excerpts describe conditions in a bakery "right after Purim" — some six weeks before Passover — when the supply of matsos was being prepared.

Vi es kumt di tsayt noch Purim,
Greyt men zich tsu di matses glaych.

M'yogt zich avektsuleygn di kreftn,

Nor dem beker tsu machn raych.
. . . Vi m'kontshet nor di arbet,

No sooner is Purim past,
Than the preparations for the matso baking gets under way.
Everybody rushes to work with all his might,
Just to make the baker rich.
. . . When we finish our work,

Zayger tsene shpet baynacht,	At ten o'clock late at night,
Yeder ligt shoyn oyf zayn keyver;	Each one lies down on his "grave"
Unter tsvey tits shtroy mit a zak.	On a sack meagerly filled with straw.
. . . Fun dem krechtsn helft nisht keyner,	. . . No one comforts you when you groan,
Bay di matses tog un nacht. . . .	Baking the matso day and night. . . .

Refrain:	Shneler leygt aroyf dem valek,		Quickly, lay the rolling pin on,
	Oyf di matses velgert gut,		On the matso, roll it well,
	Di beste zach iz bay di pratse,		The best thing during the toil,
	Tsu zingen an arbetslid.[28]		Is to sing a workman's song.

Many love songs and ballads were created by women as they sewed the garments for the rich. Some worked with the needle, others at the Singer sewing machines and primitive stocking machines. Following the 1880's, when women entered industry in increased numbers, these working girls poured out their heart in plaintive songs which described their hard, colorless, often celibate lives. No rosy future awaited them, and they saw for themselves only a long life of sewing and stitching, stitching and sewing, unloved, alone, until the "grey hair sprouted." Only a prince charming in a dream could take them out of their misery.

Tog azoy vi nacht, un nacht azoy vi tog,	Day and night and night and day,
Un neyen un neyen un neyen!	And stitching, stitching, stitching!
Helf mir shoyn gotenyu, mayn sheyner zol shoyn kumen,	Help me, dear God, may my handsome one come along,
Un fun der arbet zol ich avekgeyn.[29]	And take me away from this toil.

The Factory

The second half of the nineteenth century saw the development of capitalism in Russia. With the rapid growth of industry in such large Jewish centers as Lodz, Warsaw, Bialystok, Vilna, Pinsk, and Odessa, new songs were created by the former workshop hands, now turned factory workers. These circulated side by side with the former workshop songs, many now taking on a more pronounced tinge of bitterness.

Un vi bitter iz dem orimen arbeter,

Tsu zayn glaychn nit gefinen.
Im iz tsen mol erger
Vi far a yovn tsu dinen.

Az me dint zich oys dem keyser,
Kumt men frish un gezunt.
Ba di baleboste vert men
oysgemutshet,
Me hot a verde vi der hunt.[30]

What a bitter thing it is to be a
workingman,
There is nothing to equal it.
It's ten times harder
Than to serve in the army.

When you have served the Czar,
You come home hale and hearty.
In the hands of the boss's wife you
are worn out,
And are treated like a dog.

As they described the horrible working conditions which prevailed, some of the songs took on a tone of protest and even a call to workingmen to rally in their own interests.

Tog un nacht geshpant in pratse,
Esn trukn broyt.
Kinder naket, hustn, veynen,
Oy, du shvere noyt!

Dachkes, payn, dos gantse lebn,
Shtarbn on a tsayt:
Oy vi lang vet ir es duldn,
Orime arbaytslayt![31]

Day and night, harnessed to toil,
Eating a dry crust of bread.
Children naked, coughing, weeping,
Oh, the dreadful poverty!

Want, misery, all your life,
Dying prematurely:
Oh, how long will you be patient,
Poor workingmen!

Workers, who now were compelled to seek their livelihood in the factories, at first saw in *it* the arch enemy, while others discerned in the factory owners the rogues who were getting rich on their "sweat and blood."

Zaritski hot tsen kinder,
Tsen kinder,
Un mir darfn horeven
Af yedern bazunder.

Refrain: Oy, vey, vind,
Dos beste kind,
Az s'kumt nor in fabrik
arayn,
Iz's erger vi a hunt.[32]

Zaritsky has ten children,
Ten children,
And we have to toil
For each and everyone of them.

Oh, woe, woe,
The best child
Once he enters the factory,

He's worse off than a dog.

In Western Europe the first half of the nineteenth century witnessed a stirring of many streams of thought. New ideas and movements in the

sphere of philosophy, economics, sociology, and politics were fermenting
and erupting in political and economic movements and struggles. In some
countries, existing governments were challenged and even overturned.
In the Slavic lands, however, it was not until the 1880's and
1890's that sharp clashes took place between the workingmen and the
factory owners. When they did occur, however, they were greater in
intensity than in the Western countries, due to the general atmosphere of
repression which the Czarist government maintained. Up to that time,
the small towns and villages of the Pale slumbered dreamily in feudal
oblivion. The most passionate conflicts still revolved around the battles
between Chasidism and rabbinism, while the working population passively
nurtured their resentment against their employers, poverty, ignorance,
and the brutal rule of the Czarist regime.

The Enlightenment movement (Haskalah), in its drive for secular
knowledge and worldly ways of life, had uprooted the strata of Jewish
intellectuals—the students and the petty traders—and created a genre of
Haskalah authors who utilized satire and folklore song for their programmatic purposes. Influenced by Western thought and literature, they
transferred some of these ideas and themes into their writing, which in
one form or another, became part of the oral literature of the people.
This spiritual emancipation dovetailed with the political awakening of
large sections of Jewish workingmen and women in the Pale, and both
found ways and means to express themselves despite the atmosphere of
repression which prevailed.[33]

The 1880's saw the first organizations of workers' circles and trade
unions in Vilna. The beginning of the nineties witnessed local and general
strikes in that city, the agitation for the ten-hour day, May 1st demonstrations,[34] citywide gatherings, and, in 1897, the organization of the
Bund.[35] The songs of this period took a sharp turn away from the old
patterns, styles, rhythms, themes and vernacular, although here and there
they echoed the old laments, cries, and songs which appealed to the Lord
in their stress.

Shteynerne hertser hobn di balebatim,	The employers have hearts of stone,
Zey gleybn nit dem arbeter fundanen ahin.	They don't trust the worker at all.
Ven der oremer arbeter trinkt oys abisele yash,	When the poor workingman drinks a little whiskey,

Ruft men im a shiker oyfn mitn gas.

They call him a drunkard on the street.

Proste bronfn iz nit kayn vayn,
A gilderner becher iz nit kayn kos,
Un an oremer arbeter iz nit kayn balebos.
Reboynoy-shel-oylom, farvos? [36]

Plain whiskey is not like wine,
A golden goblet is not a cup,
And a poor workingman is not a boss.
Creator of the world, why?

In an atmosphere of total political and economic repression, the Jewish factory worker, like the Russian, sang about the same current problems.

Men lozt undz nisht tsuzamen reydn,
Men lozt undz nisht tsuzamen shteyn.
Men lozt undz nisht tsuzamen shtraykn,
Men lozt undz nisht tsuzamen geyn. [37]

We're not allowed to talk together,
We're not allowed to congregate.
We're not allowed to strike together,
We're not allowed to walk together.

The more aware the modern worker became of his strength in numbers and organization, the more boldly did he attempt to realize his dreams for a better life. The songs of this period often sacrificed the poetic and musical to the thematic and topical, introducing the march rhythm and a new vernacular. There were songs of hopelessness and misery, during periods of unemployment, such as the following:

Mir zemir doch geboyrene kabtsonim;
Mir vaksn azoy vi groz oyfn feld;
Mir faln nebich oyfn ponim,
Ver fun hunger, ver fun kelt.

We are poor men born into poverty;
We grow like the grass in the field;
We fall, alas, on our faces,
Some from hunger and some from cold.

M'traybt undz arbetorer fun di fabrikn,
M'traybt undz mit a vildn has;
S'kumt undz oys tsu geyn trenken,

Entver shtarbn in mitn gas. [38]

They drive us from the factories,
They drive us with a fierce hatred;
We've no choice but to drown ourselves
Or to die in the middle of the street.

There were others, which agitated for the ten-hour day:

Nemt zich tsunoyf, oy, shvester un brider,
Vel ich aych gebn tsu farshteyn:

Gather round me, sisters and brothers,
And I'll explain something to you:

Az mir arbetn fun acht biz tsen,
Horeven mir gor umzist.
Un az mir arbetn fun acht biz zeks,
Vel ich aych gebn tsu farshteyn.[39]

When we work from eight to ten,
We toil for nothing.
But when we work from eight to six,
I will explain this to you.

Still others sang in the previous pattern of contrasting the rich and the poor, extending their comparisons to the modern situation, dramatizing the deep gulf which now existed between the few wealthy and the very many workingmen.

Seder un tsvetn un vayngertner,
Dos flantst alts oys der arbetsman.
Un gib a kuk ver est di fruchter,
Alts nit er, nor der raycher man.

Orchards and flowers and vineyards,
All are planted by the workingman.
But see who gets the fruits thereof,
Not he, but the rich man.

Salonen, palatsn un hayzer,
Dos arbet alts oys der arbetsman.
Gib a kuk ver es voynt derinen,
Alts nit er, nor der raycher man.

Salons, palaces, and houses,
All are made by the workingman.
But see who lives in them,
Still not he, but the rich man.

Ale s'choyres vos fun der gantser velt,
Dos arbet alts oys der arbetsman.
Un gib a kuk ver es nemt tsu di
    gelter,
Alts nit er, nor de raycher man.[40]

All the goods of the whole world
Are created by the workingman.
But see who takes the monies for
    them,
Still not he, but the rich man.

The patriarchal relationship between employer and worker had disappeared within the framework of the factory system, and there were songs now which stressed the class divisions which had become more pronounced. Where a factory girl fell in love with the employer's son, she was brought up short by the sharp difference in their respective positions in a society that had become more complex.

Du machst doch nor dem shpas
Fun dem orim arbetsklas,
Kayn arbetsmeydl hot bay dir kayn
    vert.
Ach, ver s'hot nor gelt,
Iz a kluger oyf der velt,
Un ver kon zich glaychn tsu dir?[41]

You are only making fun
Of the poor working class,
A working girl means nothing to
    you.
Ah, he who has the money
Is the smart one in this world,
So who can compare with you?

The dangers inherent in pursuing the ideals of freedom and brotherhood and actively opposing the tyranny of the Czarist autocracy led to tragic breaks between friends, families, lovers. Mothers feared for their children, as youth struck out for itself in its struggle to create a better world.

Ach, neyn, muter, torst dayn kind nisht shtern,	Oh no, mother, you must not interfere with your child,
Lomich geyn avu ich vil;	Let me go wherever I will;
Genug tiranen tu-en mir vern,	Enough tyrants oppose me,
Genug farshklaft iz mayn gefil.[42]	My feelings have been enslaved long enough.

There were songs which summoned the people to meetings and kept time with marching feet during demonstrations. Others served to express thoughts and opinions on current topics of the day, as they affected the collective group as well as the individual workingman and woman. The following excerpt from a lullaby, which was current in a number of variants at the time, describes a workingman dying of consumption. He sings to his infant son of his wasted life, instructs his child in the brutal facts which have ended his life prematurely, and pleads with him to cherish his father's ideals when he grows into manhood.

Ven ch'ob gelitn hunger, kelt,	When I suffered hunger and cold,
Hobn dan di milyonen geshtoygn,	Then the millions accumulated,
Ven orimkeyt hot gehersht in mayn getselt,	When poverty ruled my home,
Hobn dan di kapitalistn mayn blut gezoygn.	The capitalists sucked my blood.
Di hoyche palatsn mit di farputste salonen,	The tall palaces and fancy salons,
Zenen geven gefarbt mit mayn blut oyf royt,	Were painted red with my gore;
Darum, mayn kind, zolstu dich dermonen,	Therefore, my child, always remember,
Tsu nemen rache far mayn fritsaytign toyt.[43]	To avenge my untimely death.

In an atmosphere of repression, police terror, and brutality, the simplest economic demands flared up into political strikes, where the cry for "shorter hours, higher pay" was often linked with the demands for freedom of speech, assembly, organization, and the slogans "down with the autocracy, down with the Czar!" Workers were compelled to meet and deliberate in secret, and there were songs which described such clandestine gatherings. The first excerpt below is from a hymn sung at a secret meeting in the woods; the second, which sounds like a news item, speaks of a similar gathering, raided by the police.

(1)

Vos shloft ir, ir shlefer in finsterer nacht?	Sleepers, why do you slumber in the dark of the night?
Vos shloft ir, ir shlefer, zo lang?	Why do you sleep so long?
Tut nor a kuk tsum himl aroyf,	Look up at the sky above,
Vi sheyn iz di zone in ir oyfgang.	And see the beauty of the rising sun.
Genug shoyn tsu haltn di lodn farmacht,	Enough keeping the shutters closed,
Vos shloft ir, ir shlefer in finsterer nacht?	Sleepers, why do you slumber in the dark of the night?
Genug shoyn tsu shlofn, ir shvester un brider,	Cease your slumbering, sisters and brothers,
Vacht oyf! Fareynigt aych!	Awake! Unite!
Gicher, gicher, on a geruder,	Quickly, quickly, without any noise,
Zet az ale zoln zayn glaych.[44]	See to it that all men are equal.

(2)

Unter der sofievke hert zich a gerider,	Behind Sofievka Park, there is a commotion,
Es hobn zich sobirayet shvester un brider,	Brothers and sisters have gathered at a meeting,
Es hobn zich sobirayet a groyse kampanye,	A big crowd is gathered there,
Af der fraye un af sobranye.[45]	For freedom and the right to assemble.

The economic crisis of the 1880's, the pogroms, the effects of the abolition of serfdom in Russia on the peasants and the middle class — all resulted in a great ferment during the final decades of the nineteenth century. These occurrences, expressed in all manner of opinions, theories, platforms, and programs, took place simultaneously with the growth of the trade-union movement, economic and political strikes, the formation of Jewish workers' self-defense groups to protect the Jewish communities from the Czarist-led pogroms — all of which found an echo in Yiddish folk songs of that period. The struggle songs of this period discarded the vernacular and rhythms of the earlier work songs. Melodies, hastily adopted and adapted to fit texts of current topical songs, though they still included fragments of traditional and synagogal chants and the tunes of older Yiddish folk songs, now combined more elements from Russian,

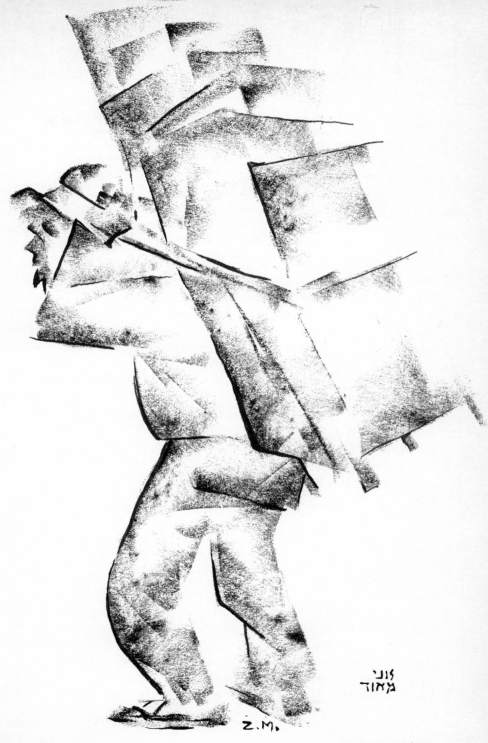

אונ
מאוד

Z. M.

Zuni Maud, 1930

Polish, and Ukrainian popular songs. They often spoke in topical terms of lofty ideals, as in the following :

Arbetn tsuzamen ale glaych
Mit a mos un mit a tsol,
Az eyner fun dem tsveytn zol nisht
 vern raych,
Fun tsufil arbetn un mit amol.

To work together equally
Within reason and within norms,
So that one does not enrich himself
 at the expense of the other,
From too much work all at once.

Far ale shklafn befrayt di velt,
Un fun nationen iz kayn
 untershid;
. . . Zolst nisht zayn untertenig dos
 giftige gelt. . . .[46]

To free all the slaves in the world,
And to do away with the differences
 between nations;
. . . Do not serve venomous
 lucre. . . .

Or they spoke in terse accents of a current strike in "Halpern's factory in Pinsk," or "Popov's shop in Odessa," or "Berke Brener's shoe factory in Warsaw." The song about the strike in the shoe factory gives the workers' demands, which were pasted up on the factory wall — ". . . two kopeks raise on every pair of shoes or we strike" — describes the employer's refusal to grant the raise and his calling in of the police, and even reproduces the shouting of the employer as the police rounded up the strikers : "clear out the rebels, quickly !"[47]

Another strike song uses the conversation pattern between two strike-bound employers, "Rabinovitsh and Lipson." Mr. Rabinovitsh felt that perhaps the workers' demands ought to be met, provided they promised "never to strike again," whereas Mr. Lipson, on the other hand, was adamantly of the opinion that :

Oy, ales vos zey fodern, vel ich zey
 nit gebn,
Dos veln zey ba mir nit oysfirn.
Ich vel mayn fabrik kayn zagranitse
 aroysfirn,
Un zey vet men do ale arestirn.[48]

Oh, I will not grant them any of
 their demands,
This, they will never get from me.
I will take my factory abroad,

And here, I'll have them all arrested.

The agitational literature distributed by the various political parties and groups (Social Democrats, Socialist Revolutionaries, Zionists, Anarchists) circulated in the Jewish Pale together with the political songs created by the people. Didactic folk songs dealing with political matters were common. As the dying father in the previously quoted lullaby sought to instruct his child in the essence of the class struggle, so did these agitational folk songs seek to teach the adults certain principles.

Der proletariat,	The proletarian
Hot kayn broyt tsu der zat,	Hasn't enough bread to eat,
Er hoybt on tsu filn, tsu visn :	He begins to feel, to know,
Mit zayn bitern shveys,	That with the bitter sweat of his brow
Macht er di velt raych un groys	He makes the world powerful and rich
Un aleyn hot er nisht tsu genisn.	But he gets nothing out of it.
Der burzhui,	The bourgeois
Zitst zich breyt bay dem tish,	Sits grandly at the table
Un trinkt zich a gut glezl vayn,	And drinks a good glass of wine,
Ober fun dem arbeter's orimkeyt,	But at the worker's misery,
Tut er shpetn un lachn,	He laughs and scoffs,
Un aleyn iz er grob vi a shvayn.[49]	While he is as fat as a swine.

The battle between political parties and their respective programs cropped up in ditties and teasers. Social Democrats taunted those who belonged to Zionist groups : *Shvester un brider, a ru-ech in ayer tatn! / Farvos zent ir nisht—kayn sotsial-demokratn* ("Sisters and brothers, the devil take your father, why aren't you Social Democrats?").[50]

Utilizing the tune of an older anti-Chasidic song ("Kum aher du filozof"), a topical song scoffed at the "brothers and sisters" both in the Zionist organizations as well as in the Bund.

Ir narishe tsionistn,	You foolish Zionists,
Mit ayer ketsenem moyechl,	With your cat's brain,
Kumt aroys tsu dem arbaytsman,	Come on out to the workingman,
Un lernt aych bay im seychi.	And learn some common sense from him.
Ir kluge bundistn,	You smart Bundists,
Oyf ale birzhes tut ir loyfn.	You run to all the exchanges.
Ven es bevayzt zich nor a kozakl,	No sooner does a little Cossack appear,
Hoybt ir bald on tsu antloyfn.[51]	Then you begin to run.

The last decade of the nineteenth century took a sad toll from the Jewish population in the Pale.

"The growth of the proletariat within the Pale of Settlement, both in business and in the trades, assumed appalling proportions. The observers of economic life in the Pale . . . called attention to the frightful increase of pauperism in that region. . . . The crop failures of 1899 and 1900 in the south of Russia resulted in a terrible famine among the impecunious Jewish masses. Whereas the peasants who suffered from the same calamity received financial assistance from the Government, the Jews had to resort to self-help. . . . At the end of the nineteenth century the ruling spheres of the Russian empire proved more anti-Semitic than at the beginning of the same century." [52]

The close of the century is marked by an intensification of the struggle of the working-class movement, wherein the economic and political demands are most often joined together, and the agitational propaganda now accuses both the wealthy and the autocracy at once.

Di rayche haltn oyf dem rusishn tsar;	The rich prop up the Russian Czar;
Zey shtitsn im, zey lozn im nisht faln.	They support him, they don't let him fall.
Zey gibn im oyf turmes, zey gibn im oyf keytn,	They provide him with money for prisons and chains,
Zey gibn im oyf ferd, zey gibn im oyf shtaln. [53]	They provide him with money for horses and stables.

Clashes with the police and the military during strikes as well as May-day demonstrations and protest marches increased. Homes and secret gatherings were continuously raided, while arrests mounted, and many were exiled to Siberia.

In dem vaytn land sibir,	In the far-off land Siberia,
Vu der himl z'tomid fun di chmares shvarts,	Where the sky is always dark with clouds,
Dort aleyn bin ich geven farshikt	I was exiled there, for shouting
Far eynem vort, far der fray.	The one word—freedom.
Mit der nagayke hot men mich geshlogn,	With the knout they beat me,
Az ich zol mer nit zogn :	To make me stop saying :
Dazdravstvuyet svoboda!	Greetings to freedom!
In dr'erd mit nikolay! [54]	Down with Nicholas!

In the main, the political movements and their songs were prominent in the cities and larger towns, but their echo was heard on occasion in some of the more isolated little towns and villages of the Pale. The following describes an incident in the little town of Lentshin (Poland), when a Polish landowner brought down a crew of workers from the big city to renovate his manor and refurbish the church and the holy pictures.

They spoke in the broad Warsaw dialect, . . . one of them played an accordion. . . . "Look, they are Jews!" We could hardly believe it. As skillfully as they worked, so did they sing. A world of song was in their mouths. . . . Parents spanked boys and girls who hung around watching them; locked them in the house, threatened them with purgatory for approaching the turncoats. Nothing helped. . . . One day . . . the police inspector of Sochatshov arrived with a whole company of armed policemen . . . followed by the peasant elders . . . with thick clubs in their hands . . . and quickly surrounded landlord Khristowsky's courtyard. The police made a big hullabaloo and threw themselves on the strangers, . . . tied the hands of each of them. . . . The strangers walked erect. "They will rot in chains. They spoke against the Czar," Jews whispered. "Serves them right, those antireligious bums," said the pious ones.[55]

The religious Jews were bitterly opposed to the organized workingmen, who in turn did not hesitate to attack the religious leaders of the Pale. Even this tilt was reflected in teasers and taunts, especially when a strike was in progress, as in the following, sung by the pious ones:

Her nor itshe-ber, kum nor do aher,
Ch'vel dir epes zogn, vestu hano-e hobn:
M'hot shoyn oysgeharget ale straykers,
M'hot shoyn far di straykers nisht kayn moyre.
M'ken shoyn geyn lernen fray di toyre.

Refrain: Sisu v'simchu b'simchas toyre,
M'hot shoyn far di straykers nisht kayn moyre.[56]

Listen Itshe-ber, come on over here,
And I'll tell you something to please you:
The strikers have all been killed,

No one fears the strikers anymore.

We can all go back to our Torah learning.

Let us rejoice in the joy of the Torah,
No one fears the strikers anymore.

To which, the strikers replied in kind:

Her nor itshe-mayer, kum nor du aher,
Ch'vel dir epes zogn, vestu dir s'ponim klogn:

Listen Itshe-mayer, come on over here,
And I'll tell you something to make your face weep:

M'hot shoyn oysgeharget ale gerer ch'sidim, / The Chasidim of Ger have all been killed,
M'hot zich shoyn genumen tsu di varshever negidim.[57] / And they've already started on the rich men of Warsaw.

Although the Anarchists were not popular in the Pale, popular ballads were created about the sacrificial acts of Hirsh Lekert and Boruch Shulman.

On May 1, 1902, Jewish workingmen in Vilna arranged for a May-day demonstration. Apprehended by the governor, Von Wahl, they were ordered by him to be flogged in public. Hirsh Lekert, the poor shoemaker, was so humiliated by this barbaric act, that he attempted to shoot the governor as the latter was leaving the theater after an evening perform-ance on May 5. Von Wahl's life remained unscathed, but Lekert was hanged on May 29, and his passionate desire to wipe out the humiliation suffered by his co-workers moved workingmen to create songs about his heroism. The ballads relate the circumstances of the assassination, often concluding with Lekert's last words as he awaited the hangman :

Oy, mir tut men shoyn hengen, / Oh, I am now about to be hung
Un ich ken shoyn gornisht tun— / And can do nothing more about it—
Betn bet ich aych, mayne libe brider, / I beg of you, my beloved brothers,
Ir zolt zich rechenen mit dem tiranen natsion. / Take vengeance of the tyrant nation.

Oy, di shtrik vos men tut mir farvarfn, / Oh, the rope that is put around my neck,
Shrekn, shrek ich zich nisht far ir— / Does not frighten me—
Betn, bet ich aych, mayne libe brider, / I beg of you, my beloved brothers,
A lid zolt ir zingen fun mir.[58] / To sing a song about me.

Four years later in Warsaw, also on May 1, Boruch Shulman assassi-nated the hated assistant Police Commissioner Constantinov, at eight o'clock in the evening on the "corner of Marshalkovske and St'k'rizhske." It is told that Shulman was met by his friend David Apt, before the act, and as soon as it was over Shulman jumped on a passing streetcar. The feeling was that Shulman could have gotten away, but that looking back he saw Apt being apprehended by the police. Shulman jumped off the streetcar, "shot three soldiers," and both he and Apt were then killed in the fray. Most of the ballads about Boruch Shulman describe his heroic disregard for his own life in attempting to save his friend and mourn the passing of his "young brave life."

Veynt nisht shvester, veynt nisht brider,	Weep not sisters, weep not brothers,
Troyert nisht muter noch ayer kind,	Mourn not, mother, for your child,
Az es falt, falt der bester,	It's always the finest that falls in battle,
Der vos hot nor getray gedint.	The ones who have served devotedly.
Sheyne blumen, tu-en bli-en,	Lovely flowers are blooming
Bay Boruch's keyver oyf der velt.	On Boruch's grave in this world.
Dos gantse folk vet kumen kni-en,	The whole people will come to kneel,
Far Boruch Shulman dem bavustn held.[59]	For Boruch Shulman, the famous hero.

Of historical significance are the political songs which were current during the Russo-Japanese war, mainly in the cities and large towns, and which tied in with the songs of the Russian Revolution of 1905.[60] It was not unexpected that the sympathies of the impoverished, oppressed Jewish population were not with the Czarist armies in their war with Japan. The blood of the pogroms in Bialystok, Kishinev, and other cities was still fresh and, seeing in these the finger of God and his punishment for the Russian excesses against the Jews, several songs exulted in the defeats of the Russian navy at Port Arthur.

The songs created during the 1905 Revolution reflected a keen grasp of the heightening tensions of the times and were often more pointed than the professional Yiddish poetry of that period. The stirring political upheavals moved even religious Jews to exclaim: *Zogt mir raboysay, vos iz dos fara yoysher? / Az mir hobn a got, to vos darfn mir a keyser* ("Tell me, people, what kind of justice is this? When we have a God, why do we need a Czar?")[61]

Political songs and ballads of this period often combined the singer's sentiments about the Russo-Japanese War and the ferment to depose the Czar, as in the following, which was current at the outbreak of the revolution:

A shvartser volkn oyf dem himl	A dark cloud in the sky
Hot zich iber rusland farshpreyt,	Has spread all over Russia,
S'iz a geshrey, a getiml,	There's shouting and a noise,
As rusland muz vern bafrayt.	That Russia must be set free.

Es roysht un es kocht in ale gasn,	All the streets are seething,
In di luftn tut zich hern a geshrey	There's a great cry in the air
Fun toyznter arbeter-masn;	Of thousands of working masses;
Nider mit dem tsar nikolay!	Down with Czar Nicholas!

*   *   *

Du host m'klompershtn gegebn a konstitutsie,	You pretended to give us a constitution,
Genumen hostu zi bald tsurik,	But took it right back again,
Du host gemeynt tsu shteln di revolutsie,	You thought you'd stop the revolution,
Mir konen shoyn dayn chazershe politik.	We understand your swinish politics.

*   *   *

Der shtrayk fun di ayznbanen,	The strike of the railroads,
Der bunt fun di matrosn oyf dem flot,	The uprising of the sailors in the fleet,
Di chochme fun yaponye's soldatn	The wisdom of Japan's soldiers
Machn dich tsu shand un tsu shpot.[62]	Mock and put you to shame.

Current also at the same time was a long satirical cradle song, written by Sholem Aleichem, patterned after his earlier lullaby of 1892. In it, Czar Nicholas is rocking his infant crown prince to sleep:

Sleep peacefully, my lovely son and heir, and you will grow up to have sacksful of money, cities, and villages. You will be wiser than I, a king among kings . . . with a land called Siberia. You will have inns and prisons and numberless churches, . . . gendarmes, Cossacks, and guards at your door — the kind that can scourge and beat without tiring. Don't be afraid of Japan. He thinks I am a fool. But Russia still lives, and a Czar is still needed. Let the Bundists prattle that they think something will be done. We'll shoot all the Socialists and torture them as much as possible. Promise the people a constitution and quietly throw them a bone and then give them a fig. . . . What if tears and blood flow out there, so long as you're all right? Let the press bark and howl, let the journalists and poets sing prettily. Even if bombs explode out there, that's not news. They will all be caught in the end, lashed and strung up, one by one. There are clubs, knouts, police, and spies everywhere.[63]

Inspired by hymns which called for the "freeing of poor slaves all over the world, from suffering, hunger, and cold," looking hopefully to the "red flag" to lead them forward, workingmen and women marched together, fought together, and died together on the barricades of the 1905 Revolution, singing :

Forverts, brider, in di reyen,
Shnel, der fon iz shoyn greyt.
Kumt zich drayster tsu bafrayen,
In dem kamf fun lebn un toyt.

Forward, brothers, in the ranks,
Quickly, the banner is ready.
Come bravely to free yourselves,
In the battle for life and death.

Ale (shneler, shneler) tsu di barikadn,
Brider, (shneler) mit gever aroys !

Everyone, quickly, to the barricades,
Brothers, quickly, come out with arms !

Nisht geshtanen, (fareynigt aych) kameradn,
Der zig iz zeyer groys.[64]

Don't stand there, unite, comrades,

The victory is very great.

The bitter, unequal struggle against the autocracy, the gendarmery, and the military, the network of *agents provocateurs* and spies increased the determination of many and degenerated the conscience of others. Such spies were usually demoralized (*lumpn*) workers who fell victim to the tempting offers to work for the police. Against these, the organized workers warned : *Oy, di lumpn / zey zenen shpionen / provokaters zenen zey. / Zey geyen oyf birzhes / un hern moves / un geyen dertseyln politsey* ("Oh, the *lumpn*, they are spies, they are *agents provocateurs*. They go to the exchanges and hear the news and then report back to the police").[65]

The 1905 Revolution was crushed. Songs of imprisonment, exile to Siberia, raids and executions, current also before, now increased in number. These described the anguish, suffering, and hardships of the primitive jails, which meted out the most cruel treatment to the political prisoners. Brave voices rang out occasionally from behind the prison bars, but these were soon silenced in the pall of reaction that followed.

Mir zitsn un shmachtn
Far hunger un kelt—
Ales far frayhayt,
Far lebn oyf der velt.
Mir vern gepaynikt,
Gemutshet mit noyt,
Mir kemfn far frayhayt,
Mit lebn un toyt.

We sit in jail fainting
With hunger and cold—
All for freedom,
For life in this world.
We are tortured,
Punished and deprived,
We're fighting for freedom,
With life and with death.

Undz shrekt nisht kayn hunger,	We fear not hunger,
Kayn turmes, kayn kelt,	Prisons, the cold,
Mir muzn bafrayen	We must liberate
Dos lebn oyf der velt,	Life in the world.
Mir muzn bakemfn	We must defeat
Di tsarishe macht,	The Czarist might,
Mir muzn fartraybn	We must banish
Di fintstere nacht.[66]	The dark night.

   The topical songs of this end-of-the-century period enjoyed the widest dissemination among the people. They are of cultural-historical significance; and two generations, raised in their spiritual atmosphere, were inspired by the determination and courage of workingmen and women who fought and died for their ideals.

Notes

POVERTY, TOIL, AND STRUGGLE

1. In 1808, 60,000 families were brutally expelled from the villages.
2. Of the one million Jews in the Pale in 1804, 400,000 resided in the cities.
3. Raisin, p. 163.
4. Mendele, II, p. 87.
5. Rubin, 1950, pp. 79–80.
6. *Ibid.,* p. 83.
7. Skuditsky, 1936, p. 283, No. 15.
8. D. and Y., p. 322, No. 2. (*Af bri*: traditional prayer song of the last day of Pentecost. *Utas*: part of the same prayer song.)
9. B. and F., p. 15.
10. G. and M., No. 320. (*groshn*: half a *kopek,* equivalent to a cent.)
11. Mendele, II, pp. 85–86.
12. B. and F., p. 382–383. Shereshevsky was the owner of a cigarette factory in Grodno.
13. Skuditsky, 1936, p. 105, No. 6.
14. *Ibid.,* p. 106, No. 7.
15. D. and Y., p. 328, No. 15.
16. *Ibid.,* p. 326, No. 10.
17. G. and M., No. 307.
18. Rubin, MSS.
19. Mendele, II, pp. 84–85.
20. Beregovski, p. 181, No. 4.
21. Rubin, 1950, p. 93.
22. Lehman, 1921, pp. 128–129, No. 66.
23. Rubin, 1950, p. 88.
24. D. and Y., p. 349, No. 20.
25. *Ibid.,* p. 335–336, No. 2.
26. Mendele, II, pp. 86–87.
27. B. and F., p. 32.
28. Lehman, 1921, p. 130, No. 67.
29. Rubin, 1950, p. 96.
30. G. and M., No. 319.
31. Glatstein, p. 75.
32. B. and F., p. 60. Zaritsky's cigarette factory was in Cherkassy, Kiev region.
33. "In the modern period . . . in the struggles between parents and children, when sections of the young generation turned away from Torah learning and religious traditions, we find their former reverence for the Torah transferred to the secular Haskalah. . . . Instead of the rabbi and the *tsadik,* the student, the doctor, the professor, the writer became important. . . . Side by side there still prevailed the hatred and contempt for the physical power of the rulers and the rich. The only difference was that now there shone brightly the new consciousness of human dignity and

justice . . . where it became worthwhile to defend these with weapons in hand, if need be. Instead of the old lament and prayer, the folk song of modern times demands stern measures for insults and humiliations" (Ansky, pp. 62–63).

34. May 1 demonstrations in Eastern and Western Europe were observed in 1886 after the Haymarket Massacre in Chicago.

35. The Bund (Jewish Socialist Workers Party) was organized in Vilna in 1897 and engaged in organizing and educating Jewish intellectuals and workingmen through its newspapers, leaflets, and pamphlets. Exerting a strong influence in the Pale, it also employed songs, the most important of which was "Di shvue" ("The Vow"), which appeared in 1896/7 and was attributed to Sh. Anski, and then became the rallying hymn of the *Poale zion* ("Workers of Zion"). Anski's "In gezaltsenem yam" ("In the Salty Sea") was also very popular among Jewish workingmen and women of the Bund. There were other Socialist groups among the Jews besides the Bund.

36. Cahan, 1957, No. 487.

37. Lehman, 1921, p. 69, No. 31.

38. *Ibid.*, p. 122, No. 62.

39. Beregovski, p. 197, No. 41.

40. Lehman, 1921, pp. 104–105, No. 55. The listing of wealth created by working men and pointing out that its pleasures were appropriated by the exploiters of labor was prominent in socialist literature in Europe at the beginning of the nineteenth century. Shelley treated it in his poem, "Ode to the Men of England," written in 1819. Much later in Germany in 1863, Georg Herwegh dealt with it in his "Bundeslied," written for the General Federation of German Workingmen. In 1891, Chaim Zhitlowsky published his Yiddish adaptation, "Un du akerst, un du zeyst" ("And you plow and you sow"), based on the Herwegh poem, which became popular among Jewish workingmen and women in Eastern Europe, and is still remembered by Yiddish-speaking Jews today.

41. *Ibid.*, p. 109, No. 56a (III).

42. *Ibid.*, pp. 49–50, No. 22.

43. *Ibid.*, pp. 112–113, No. 58 (III).

44. Rubin, MSS.

45. Beregovski, p. 197, No. 40.

46. Lehman, 1921, p. 114, No. 58 (VII). Michl Gordon's popular song, "Mayn tsavoe" ("My Testament"), was sung to the same tune as this song, which in turn is based on the melody of the Russian romance, "Moy Kostyor v'Tuman Svetit."

47. *Ibid.*, pp. 32–34, No. 16.

48. Beregovski, p. 190, No. 29.

49. Lehman, 1921, pp. 46–47, Nos. 21 (I), 21 (II). The second stanza given here, is an adaptation from a stanza of D. Edelshtat's "Der arbeter" ("The Worker").

50. *Ibid.*, p. 73, No. 35. In Palestine, during the first decade of the twentieth century, the *Poale Zion* workers in the agricultural colonies (*kibutsim*) sang this song with a Jewish-Arabic refrain of: *ya-cha-lili.*

51. *Ibid.*, p. 70, No. 32.

52. Dubnow, III, pp. 23–24.

53. Lehman, 1921, pp. 30–31, No. 13.

54. D. and Y., pp. 382–383, No. 14. The eighth line of the song is in Russian.

55. Singer, pp. 229–231.

56. Lehman, 1921, pp. 73–74, No. 36. This song was sung in Poland during Simchas Torah in a number of variants, to a Chasidic tune.

57. *Ibid.*, p. 77, No. 37. Singer also describes an incident in which a group of young carpenters were brought down to his little town by the local Jewish lumber merchants to make shingles. "These twoscore shingle workers attracted the local young tailors and cobblers who stopped praying, began to shave their beards, put on paper collars, . . . short jackets. . . . As if that wasn't enough, the shingle workers

would get together on the Sabbath, drink beer, and sing naughty songs. Among these . . . there was one which made fun of the Chasidim and their *Simches toyre,* because they had caused strikers to be arrested. I still remember one stanza: *Sisu v'simchu b'simches toyre, m'hot shoyn far di straykers nit kayn moyre."* (Singer, pp. 242–243.)

58. Lehman, 1921, pp. 52–54, No. 23.

59. *Ibid.,* pp. 63–64, No. 25. "I was destined . . . to be near an occurrence which shook all of Warsaw, and especially the Jewish quarter, when Boruch Shulman assassinated the hated enemy of the Jews, Constantinov, with a bomb. . . . It was a sunny, bright afternoon. . . . Suddenly the entire area was torn wide open by a dreadful explosion. The windows of the houses burst and shattered with a terrible crash, and, at the same moment, the electrifying words through the charged air rang out: Constantinov is killed! It is difficult to imagine what this meant to us at that time. Constantinov was the most hated Czarist hangman of Warsaw and especially of the Jews. . . . Boruch Shulman's funeral took place secretly, but his grave on the Genshe cemetery became a place where youth would come with song and flowers. The name of this humble fellow . . . became a symbol of sacrifice and fearless courage in Poland. . . . Anonymous songs were written about him, like *Boruch Shulman iz oyf der gas aroysgegangen, gegangen iz er mit a bombe in der hant* . . . ("Boruch Shulman went out into the street, he went out with a bomb in his hands") (Teitelbaum, pp. 135–139).

60. The occasional faint echo of these events in the more remote Jewish villages of the Pale is described by Singer: "Soon . . . the war between the Russians and the Japanese began. Who the Japanese were and where they were, no one knew. At the fairs all manner of rumors floated about, about rebellions, revolutions, and conspiracies. Once . . . a Russian . . . villager, who was working in a Warsaw factory, began to sing a ditty, ridiculing the Czar. He also made fun of the Russian soldiers and praised the Japanese. . . . Later . . . we learned . . . about a pogrom in Bialystok. Where it was, we did not know, but we thought Lithuanian Jews lived there" (Singer, pp. 233–235. Bialystok is about 400 miles from Warsaw!).

61. Lehman, 1921, p. 21, No. 9.

62. *Ibid.,* pp. 12–13, Nos. 5 (I, II, III). The constitution was granted by the Czar on October 17, 1905. A current ditty satirized this act: *Er hot gegebn a manifest: di toyte—frayhayt, di lebedige—arrest* ("He issued a manifesto: freedom for the dead and imprisonment for the living").

63. Sholem Aleichem, II, Moscow, pp. 280–282. Sholem Aleichem wrote a number of short stories dealing with current and political affairs: "Der feter pinye un di mume reyzl" ("Uncle Pinye and Aunt Reyzl") ridiculed the unequal struggle between Russia and Japan in the Russo-Japanese War; "Dos nay-geboyrene" poked fun at the Czar's "constitution." Touring many cities and towns before the 1905 Revolution, Sholem Aleichem was appalled at the poverty and degradation rampant in the Pale. Several variants of his "Sholf aleksey" ("Sleep, Alexei"), part of which is quoted here in translation, were current among the people. *See:* Lehman, 1921, pp. 17–19, No. 7.

64. Lehman, 1921, p. 45, No. 20, January 9, 1905, is regarded as the beginning of the first Russian Revolution, when some 140,000 men, women, and children, led by the priest, Gapon, marched unarmed, singing and pleading with the Czar for bread. They were shot down by the military in cold blood, and that evening barricades began to go up in the suburbs and the red flag of revolt was raised. This particular song is patterned after Morris Winchevsky's poem "Hert ir kinder vi es rirt zich?" ("Children, do you hear the stirring?"). A number of these struggle and protest songs were influenced by the labor poetry of the American-Jewish poets Winchevsky, Edelshtat, Rosenfeld, Bovshover, and others. *See* Chapter XIII, "To America."

65. Idelsohn, IX, No. 250.

66. B. and F., pp. 86–87.

CHAPTER XII

Out of the Shadows

THE SIMPLE, PLACID, STAGNANT LIFE OF THE SMALL JEWISH TOWNS AT the turn of the nineteenth century, far from the large centers in the Pale, was removed from the rapid tempo which prevailed for the Jewish populations in the congested cities. Limited though life in the small towns and villages was, it was ordered and controlled by the town councils, the orthodox elders, the occasional well-to-do merchant. In the cities, however, this structure was considerably weakened, the supervision of stern parents deteriorated, and young people were growing up exposed to the "alien" influences of the non-Jewish world, with which they now lived in close proximity.

Although the Jews in the cities lived in their own quarters, observing the mores and customs centuries old, the surrounding Slavic world made ever deeper inroads. Though Jews lived, conducted their business, bore children, arranged marriages, educated their young, and died — all within the laws which had bound them for generations — the economic, political, and cultural life of the Slavic land in which they had their roots became engraved on their existence, was reflected in their language, lore, and song, and became, consciously or unconsciously, part of their pattern of life as well.

The patriarchal structure of the family was deeply affected by these impacts and the rhythms of big-city life. Parents struggled to control their children, who, during the first half of the nineteenth century, were attracted to the Haskalah movement and, during the second half, were drawn to the Socialist movement. After the pogroms of the 1880's, many embraced Zionism as the solution to the Jewish problem, while others struck out across the seas to put down new roots in the democratic lands of the Western Hemisphere. There was a constant pull, a constant tug of war between parents and youth yearning to be free and build for itself on new foundations, all of which was greatly intensified in the large industrial city which hammered and battered at the old ways of life, attracting and repelling, rejecting and fascinating, creating and destroying.

The compelling characteristics of the Jewish quarters in these large, Eastern European cities of the Czarist Pale during the nineteenth century were congestion and poverty. Their courtyards, marketplaces, streets, and alleys were full of the sounds and smells, light and shadow of the various social strata of the Jewish population rubbing shoulders together: the prosperous Chasidic *rebeyim* in their satin coats, circular hats, white socks, and slippers; the emancipated free-thinking Maskilim, clean shaven, in top hat and short jackets; the Misnagdim with their "half-way" measures in short-long coats, trimmed beards, cloth caps, and canes. The marketplaces were full of fishmongers and butcher stalls, millers and furniture menders, servant girls and women shoppers, porters and stall-keepers, women vendors with baskets and sacks, and children running hither and thither in this swarming beehive. Haggling went on at the stalls and booths, at the baskets and portable tables displaying fruit, vegetables, berries, baked wares, hardware, earthenware, woodenware, dry goods, barrels of herring, jars of pickles, women's aprons, men's shirts and caps, children's underwear and pants.

Women with wide aprons and men with leather pockets handled silver and copper coins, traded, weighed, measured . . . from early morning till late in the evening, summer and winter, in good weather or bad. . . . In the sun . . . the open sacks of flour, yellow millet, brown buckwheat, and kidney beans gazed up at the blue sky above; the boxes of red apples, yellow currants, green gooseberries; the tubs of live fish.[1]

And from the symphony of bargaining and haggling, shouting and chanting of wares, separate voices could be heard energetically calling out their particular merchandise: a watermelon vendor—"A big hunk for two kopeks! Food and drink for only two kopeks!"; a chickpea salesman—"Hot peas, hot peas and beans!"; a baked-goods woman— "Fresh bagels, crisp and fresh!"; a cooked-food woman vendor—"Hot derma, nice and fat!"; boys selling lemonade—"Limonada! Komu nada!" ("Lemonade! Whoever wants it!").[2]

But there were those for whom this world of hustle and bustle, work and toil, trading and desperate struggle for a meager livelihood had no appeal. They hated the miserable life they saw, had contempt for the calloused hands and sweaty brow, the aching bones at the end of a hard day's work. Instead, they dreamed of a quick turnover, a lucky turn of the wheel of fortune that would make them rich, foot-loose, and fancy free. Such were the ones who strayed into the shadows and bypaths of the life of the gaming table, the saloons, the hangouts of thieves and prostitutes, and all the other "professions" of this world beneath the world of everyday existence.

Gaming and Gambling

The gaming table, both an international and national phenomenon, was adopted by the Jewish communities and adapted to their own needs. Gambling, its games and special vernacular, became part of the Jewish cultural baggage in Western and Eastern Europe. The German saying, *Wer Unglück hat im Spiel, hat Glück in der Liebe,* found its counterpart in the Yiddish *Az men hot glik in libe, hot men nisht kayn glik in kortn* ("Lucky in love, unlucky in cards"). The pictures of kings, princes, and queens on playing cards were replaced by the Jewish game of *kvitlech,* which eliminated these "alien" images. The English teetotum became the *dreydl,* and the rules of "put and take" — *nem* and *shtel.* Entire gaming practices, dice throwing, card games, etc., were absorbed into the leisure pastimes of the Jewish communities from their respective surrounding environments.

Gambling was a scourge against which Jewish community leaders and mentors fought through the centuries. Manuscripts dating from the thirteenth century attest to the struggle against this passion, and it must have been especially pronounced during the years following the Crusades and the Black Death. The religious fervor had evaporated by then, and the romanticism of the knights and their love cult had petered out. In Germany it was a period when knowledge and education was at its lowest level, when the bells of the clowns derided the muttering of the mystics, and satire, carnivals, primitive plays, and uninhibited dancing gripped the populace. The struggle against these excesses — dancing to exhaustion, reckless gambling, sex orgies — never ceased, no matter where and when Jews lived, through their didactic and moralistic literature, written by their mentors, teachers, lawgivers, poets, and singers.

The older Yiddish epoch undoubtedly had its Yiddish gaming songs, although few of these are extant. What there is, stems in the main from

Germany, with a number of Hebrew songs dealing with the struggle against the gambling vice originating in Italy—the two lands where gaming was widespread at that time.

Entire gambling songs in Yiddish are practically nonexistent. However, one of the oldest, dating from the fifteenth century, is a satirical description of dice throwers—a form of gaming which was apparently raging then. It seems that the author himself must have been ruined by a gang of cheats, judging from his vivid description of the evil passion of the gamblers, glued to the ivory cubes, as their number combinations spelled loss or gain for the player on the chance throw. The author bitterly accuses the swindlers who manipulate with loaded dice "which have eyes, but are blind; . . . their creators must become blind together with them and all those who submit to them." Following is an excerpt of this poem of thirty stanzas:

Morgent un' ovent, unabgelan,	Morning and night without pause,
Kayn ander kurtsvayl zi nit hon	They know of no other pastime
Ven dos zi di tsayt iber zitsn.	With which to occupy their time.
Hungerig un dorshtig un farshmacht	Hungry and thirsty and weak
Bay de teg un di nacht,	By day and by night,
Shpiln zi ven zi derhitsn	They play excitedly,
Zi shvern, graynen un baysn.	They swear, grit and gnash their teeth.
Zi visn fun kayns guten tsu zogn,	They know of nothing good to say,
Gots dinst zi zich litsl flaysn.[3]	And care little about God's ways.

Another Yiddish song against gambling, preserved in its entirety from this older period, was originally in Hebrew. Two of the Yiddish translations, as well as the Hebrew original, were sung to the tune of the *slicha* (penitential prayer) "Ani hu hasho-el," which attests to its great popularity. In this song, the author stresses the struggle of man against the passion of gambling, which rests within himself, since with his own hands he gambles away all he owns, is compelled to "wander from city to city, having no home of his own," thinking not of his responsibilities to God and man, neglecting and destroying himself and his own family. A stanza from the third Yiddish translation, published in Amsterdam in 1698, contains the following lines:

Ver zich in shpiln begibt,	He who submits to gambling,
Der lebt aylendig un betribt.	Lives in pain and sorrow.
Zayn end iz och farflucht,	His end is cursed too,
Zayn umglik hot er zelbst gezucht.[4]	For he has brought this misery upon himself.

Revealing the seriousness of the situation wherein Jews succumbed to
the temptations of the non-Jewish environment, is a warning contained
in the fifteenth-century work *Sefer chasidim koton,* in which directives
are given to Jewish communities everywhere to guard against all manner
of excesses that might begin innocently in the visiting carnivals and their
performances. Following are excerpted lines from this work :

Hit zich vayt du konst,	Guard yourself as much as possible
Nit lustig zayn oyf der velt	Against merrymaking in this world
Nit tsu der tsayt,	At the wrong time,
Saydn chanuke un purim	Except Chanukah and Purim,
Zolstu freyen zich fun gots vegn. . . .	When you may rejoice for the Lord's sake. . . .
Treft zich in shtot ba dir	Should there be in your city
Goyishe shpiln,	Non-Jewish carnivals or tourneys,
Iz hit zich zolst zey nit tsuzen.	Be careful not to witness them.
Dos eygene oych	Do likewise
Zeyere tents oder andere simches.	When they are dancing or making merry in other ways.
Demlt vestu zoyche zayn tsu zen	Then you will be rewarded
Di simche fun levyosn mitn shor habor.	With the festivity of the leviathan and the legendary ox.
Un herstu di shtim	And should you hear the voice
Fun dem hamoyn goyim,	Of the non-Jewish throngs,
Fayern un fleyt shpiln	Feasting and playing the flute
Un freyen zich,	And enjoying themselves,
Zolstu ziftsn	Then shall you sigh
Oyfn churbn yerusholayim,	Upon the destruction of Jerusalem
Un zolst got betn	And plead with the Lord
S'zol vider oyfgericht vern.[5]	To reconstruct it again.

These warnings, taken up by traveling mentors, often took the forms of
sung or chanted poems, as might have been the case with Elchonon
Kirch-han's "Eyn sheyn hisor'res lid" ("A Beautiful Song of Awakening"), where he warns against the evil of drinking with non-Jews, flirting
with women, trimming one's beard and earlocks, and gambling to excess,
because "all evil stems from card playing."[6] Kirch-han lived in Germany
during the last half of the seventeenth century and the first quarter of
the eighteenth century, but a poem, published in 1602, containing the
following stanza, attests to the struggle which was similarly being waged
against the vice of gambling a century earlier :

Ay mentsh, ay mentsh, vos hostu fir,	O man, o man, what do you gain thereby,
Du loyfst un renst, vos zol es dir?	You race and chase, but what does it bring you?
Ven du shoyn verst der aler shtarkst held,	And when you've already become the strongest hero
Un hest al dos gelt,	And possess all the money,
Noch muztu geyn oyf yener velt.[7]	You still have to go to the other world.

Not all the sentiments, however, were hostile towards the pastime of gaming, which did, in spite of all the efforts of the moralists, become part of the fabric of Jewish life. Thus a Yiddish gaming song of the beginning of the eighteenth century only mildly admonished its audience on the pitfalls of gambling, not condemning the practice but rather describing in a vivid, even humorous manner the various games which were popular at the time and the different characters of the players at the green table. This song, entitled "Eyn sheyn nay kuries shpil-lid" ("A Lovely New Curious Gaming Song"), regards gambling as a relaxing, enjoyable experience and the gaming table as a place where friends can meet and be sociable. The author points out the pitfalls but also advises his readers, including women, how to play, what moves to make, not to hesitate too long at the betting, even admonishing the watchers (*kibitsers*) to be silent, no matter what happens, even if the game ends in a bitter quarrel and an actual brawl. He warns the women to be on guard against the casual acquaintanceships that might be formed in this atmosphere, but good-naturedly advises them to play *this* game carefully as well. One of the few poems extant that seems sympathetic to gamblers, although indicating the dangers of its passion and recklessness, the corruption of the cheats and swindlers, presents, nevertheless, a vivid description of the types of people attracted to this pastime and the kinds of games played some two hundred years ago.[8]

The nineteenth century, too, had its gaming and gambling songs, both descriptive and didactic, sympathetic and hostile. The folk singers and *badchonim* derided the sad waste of time that might have begun innocently at a chance game of cards and later resulted in a deterioration of the human character, the loss of prestige and economic security, and even the breakup of the family and the home. However, though the bulk of Yiddish folk song of the nineteenth century is rich in most other categories and mirrors a wealth of cultural history, folk psychology, ethnography, and general history, it seems oddly lacking in gambling and gaming songs. Whatever is available is fragmentary, although card playing was already part of the tradition, not only during Chanukah, but as a generally accepted pastime for all strata of the people during their leisure hours.

As a normal relaxation, the playing of a casual game of cards seems to have coincided with a leisurely stroll in one of the public gardens in the big city, where young people met, promenaded, romanced. The promenade became suggestive of "playing cards," "playing at love," "taking a drink." It was the place where the blue sky, the green grass, the fresh air, and the shaded walks afforded the Jewish youth the freedom and delights denied them in the stern, orthodox home of the poverty-ridden, congested Jewish quarters. So intertwined did the "walk in the garden" become with "playing at love" and the chance game of cards, that a number of love songs, describing an unfulfilled romance, contain the following expression: *Ich hob farshpilt mayne yunge yorn azoy vi a kartovnik in kortn* ("I have gambled away my youth like a gambler at cards").

Religious leaders blamed a good deal of these practices upon certain leaders of the Haskalah movement, who encouraged assimilationist ways. Many felt that with the adoption of "non-Jewish" modes of dress and manners, and the increasing preoccupation with secular instead of religious knowledge, many young adherents of the Haskalah movement, also emulated the "alien" passions of gambling and flirting with members of the opposite sex. This age-old struggle was still evident during the middle of the nineteenth century, when not only the "straying" youth but also other strata of the population — working folk, domestics, apprentices, even traveling merchants away from home — whiled away their leisure hours at card playing, drinking and eating at wayside roadhouses and inns.

During the 1860's, the card game of "preferance" became popular in the Jewish community in the Pale, and Isaac Meyer Dik, pre-Mendele literary figure, wrote in an article about that "cursed preferance" and "everyone tries to show off his cleverness at the game and where, at one time, a good Talmudic scholar was sought as a desirable son-in-law, now a good 'preferance' player was preferred, and those who did not know the game were simply regarded as ignoramuses!"[9]

In the seventies, the card game *stukelke* became "the thing" among secularized Jews, which led one of Sholem Aleichem's star characters, Menachen Mendl, to comment about it in describing big-city ways in one

A Jewish card-player of the 18th century

of his letters to his wife, Sheyne-Sheyndl, as follows: "They have only
one fault here. . . . They like to play cards. No sooner does night fall,
then they begin their 'work,' sitting till dawn, shouting 'pass'! The rich
play a game called 'preferance,' and the poor play *stukelke* and *oke* or a
simple *tertl-mertl*."[10]

The leading *badchonim* and folk bards Michl Gordon, Elyokum
Zunser, and Abraham Goldfaden each attacked the wastefulness of the
gaming table and the pitfalls awaiting those who permitted themselves
to be carried away by its passion and fascination. The Haskalah writer,
Y. Y. Linetsky (1839–1915), in his satirical sung poem, "Der kortnshpil"
("The Game of Cards"), weaves his warnings and philosophical observations on the subject into its twelve stanzas, from which the following is
excerpted:

Di gute mide mit der shlechter,	The good deed and the bad
Geyen tsuzamen oyf der velt geport.	Go together in this world.
Punkt vi ba a muter — tsvey techter,	Like two daughters of one mother,
Azoy iz der dreydl mit dem kort.	So is the *dreydl* and the card.
Fun *nes godol hoyo shom,*	*Nes godol hoyo shom,*
Vert a tsig un volf un kroyz,	Turns into a goat and wolf and curlicue,
Un fun a tsig un volf, a terkisher dam,	And the goat and wolf become a game of chess,
Un fun a dam, oyf malke, melech, toyz.[11]	And the game of chess — a queen, a king, and ace.

Although the above indicates the occasional excesses at the gaming
table, the nineteenth-century Yiddish folk songs of the underworld expose
a whole section of the Jewish population in the Eastern European communities that, having once stumbled over the first degradations of
gambling or other vices, slipped further downward into the pit of the
criminal world.

The following describes the downward road of a gambler who started
with an innocent game of cards, lost his possessions, and then became
a thief.

Azoy vi ch'ob nor ongehoybn	No sooner did I begin
Kortelech tsu shpiln,	To play cards,
Refrain: Feygele, ketzele mayn.	Birdie, kitten mine.
Hob ich mir shoyn gemuzt	Then I had to become
A ganevl vern. . . .	A thief. . . .
Refrain	

Azoy vi ch'ob nor aroysgetsoygn,
Oy, dos ershte tsveytele . . .
Hob ich mir shoyn farshpilt
Dem zeyger mit dem keytele. . . .

No sooner did I draw,
Oh, the first little deuce . . .
Then I lost
My watch and chain. . . .

Azoy vi ch'ob nor aroysgetsoygn,
Oy, dos sheyne dritele . . .
Hob ich mir shoyn farshpilt
Dos sheyne barankove hitele. . . .

No sooner did I draw,
Oh, that pretty little three . . .
Then I lost
My pretty little fur hat. . . .

Azoy vi ch'ob nor aroysgetsoygn,
Oy dos sheyne fertele . . .
Hob ich mir shoyn farshpilt
Dos zaydene gartele. . . .[12]

No sooner did I draw,
Oh, that pretty little four . . .
Then I lost
My little silk belt.

The Underworld

The two large cities of Warsaw and Odessa actually "boasted" of a strong Jewish underworld which lived by its own laws, and the songs in this category are varied and vivid, revealing the sentiments of the criminal world in the Pale. In many ways, these songs are similar to those of the non-Jewish world on themes which dealt with the life and pursuits of housebreakers, pickpockets, hijackers, counterfeiters, extortionists, gangsters, pimps, and even murderers. These are genuine folk songs, products of anonymous singers, actual persons who daily evaded the police, faced the hostility of the respectable community, quarreled and brawled among themselves, experienced the dangers and pleasures of their "chosen professions." Children born into this environment became hardened criminals. Others, who had slipped into it, at times cherished fond memories of a once secure home, loving parents, and a life regulated by the spiritual atmosphere of the Jewish Sabbath, the festivals and holidays, the year-round customs and traditional ways of Jewish life. The following singer regrets the day in which economic reverses started him on his life of crime:

Geven a mentsh mit laytn tsuglaych,
Gehat a froy un kinderlech tsvey;
Tsi iz den geven der grester g'vir kegn mir raych,
Ven ich bin gezesn zich geshpilt mit zey?

I once was a respectable man,
Had a wife and two children;
Was then the wealthiest man richer than I,
When I sat playing with them?

Biz a finsterer tsorn iz oyf mir
gekumen,
Dos glikliche lebn hot zich
obgeshtelt—
Mayn parnose hot men mir
tsugenumen,
Ich hob nish' ferdint kayn groshn
gelt.

In farshidene chevres mitgeshlept,

Oyf banditishe onfaln mich
mitgenumen,
Mentshn baroybn iz gevorn mayn
gesheft,
Biz ich bin oyf katorge gekumen.[13]

Until a dark fury came over me,

And put an end to my happy life—

I lost my job,

And I wasn't earning a penny.

I was dragged around by different
gangs,
Taken along on bandit holdups,

Robbing people became my business,

Until I was convicted to hard labor.

Another criminal, a convicted counterfeiter, recalls his childhood and
resorts to a bit of philosophical contemplation :

Ich bin gezesn bay der g'more
ibergeboygn
Un fun kayn tfise nisht gevust;
Un mit eynmol ge-efnt di oygn,

Di g'more varfn hob ich shoyn
gemuzt.

Genumen tsu machn di linke groshn,
Ongehoybn tsu lebn a glikliche velt,
Fun mentshlichkeyt hot zich ales
ferloshn,
Ich hob nor gezucht vi tsu machn
gelt.

Ober nish' ales kon lang gedorn,
Tsu yeder zach muz kumen an ek,
In a sheyne nacht iz dos mashindl
farshit gevorn—
Un mich hot men gefirt in keytn
avek.[14]

I was sitting, bent over my Talmudic
studies,
Knowing nothing about prison life;
When suddenly, my eyes opened
wide,
And I had to quit my studying.

I began to make counterfeit money
And to lead a happy-go-lucky life,
Everything decent in me was
extinguished,
All I wanted was only to make
money.

But nothing can last long,
And everything must have an end,
One beautiful night, someone
fingered my little machine—
And I was led away in chains.

The Jewish underworld in the large cities boasted its own leaders and
henchmen, made its own laws, and enforced them mercilessly. On the
one hand, there was a fanatic devotion to each other as they faced the

hostile, respectable world about them, whose laws they were flagrantly defying. On the other, they were the victims of their own cruelties by which one "fingered" another, "squealed" to the police, "sold out" the confidences of a mate, stole another's sweetheart, brutalized the "loose" women in their employ, brawled violently to the death. Their world included the raucous atmosphere of the beer hall, the wild, lascivious dancing of their own dance halls, the "pleasure" of gluttony when they had the money to spend, the recklessness, humor, "needling" of one another, sadness of unfulfilled love, and the moments of deep despair and hopelessness when they were caught, and jailed.[15]

Their "professions" were varied, with some of them highly specialized : there were those that "covered" travelers' luggage in transit on trains; others who hijacked boxes and crates of merchandise from moving vehicles; those who broke into unlocked houses, which called for the speediest kind of operation; and those who entered second-story homes and were adept at jumping from upper-story windows if necessary. There were pickpockets who worked in a team, with one distracting the selected victim while the other "did the job." There were safecrackers and "diamond"-window cutters, who covered jewelry establishments. The following describes, with tongue in cheek, some of the above trades :

Ch'bin a yingele fayn geboyrn,
Ch'tu oys ale lachn,
Vayl ch'ob far keynem kayn moyre,
Ch'ken doch ale fachn.

I am a lad, respectably born,
I laugh at everyone,
Because I fear nobody
And am master of all trades.

Vinter, ven di nacht iz groys,
Un der tog a kleyner, zeyer,
Zuch ich mir a *masematn* oys,
Un ch'ver a *chelbene*-geyer.

In winter when the nights are long
And the day is very short,
I seek out my objective,
And cover the various shops.

Zumer, ven di nacht iz kleyn,
Der tog abisl greser,
Gey ich mir ongeton sheyn,
Ch'zog az a *taltl* iz beser.

Summer, when the nights are short,
And the day a little longer,
I am dressed so fine
And prefer housebreaking.

Ch'ob a shutef, nisht kayn *yold*,
S'klingt mit im azoy vi mit a glok;
S'iz ba mir a shlechte tsayt,
Shik ich im af *potok*.[16]

I have a partner, he's no fool,
He rings like a bell;
And when the times are bad for me,
I send him on a hijacking job.

Obviously the above singer became a crook out of choice, and he even "crows about it." The following example carries the process of selection still further, with the thief indicating his own preferences as against those of his brothers.

Ich bin salve der *blater,*	I am Salve, the thief,
Fir brider zenen mir;	Four brothers are we;
Eyner a hungeriker, eyner a zater,	One is hungry, the other well fed,
Ober blate zemir ale fir.	But thieves all four are we.
Eyner iz a *marvicher,*	One is a pickpocket,
Der tsveyter—an *alfons,* a sheyner yung;	The second—a pimp, a handsome fellow;
Eyner a *pototshnik,* a pekl-zucher,	One is a hijacker on the lookout for packages,
Un ich aleyn gey *afn-shpring.*	And I am a house thief.
A marvicher tsu zayn	To be a pickpocket
Iz gornisht gut :	Is not good at all :
Barn masematn af di gas	While you're working in the street
Vert men *farshit.*	Someone fingers you.
An alfons iz gemeyn,	A pimp is common,
Vi m'denkt :	As all agree :
Fun dem eygenem vayb	From his own wife,
Bakumt men di krenk.	He gets the disease.
A pototshnik iz zeyer biter :	To be a hijacker is bitter :
M'ken zich opraysn di lung,	You can rupture your lung,
A pekl tsu fardinen iz shver,	It's hard to earn something with the packages,
Dos beste iz tsu geyn afn-shpring."	The best thing is to be a house thief.

The following example pictures a humorous scene in which an older criminal "breaks in" a new "recruit," "shows him the ropes" of the "profession," and defines certain terms of their vernacular in the trade :

Her nor, du parshiver yat,	Listen now, you scurvy kid,
Zogt tsu mir mayn rebe ashteyger,	My *rebe* said to me, for instance,
Az ich vel tsu dir zogn : a *zner,*	When I say to you : a *zner,*
Zolstu visn : dos iz a zeyger.	Then you'll know : it is a watch.
Az ich vel zogn : *belekech* dem *yold,*	When I say : *belekech* the *yold,*
Darfstu farshteyn minastame,	You must understand of course,
Az ich hob gevolt	That I wanted
Zolst tsunemen baym *frayer* di neshome.	You to take the money from the dupe.

Az ich zog tsu dir : du zolst *kratn,*	When I will say to you : you should *kratn,*
Meyn ich : kuk mit di *blate* oygn;	I mean : keep your thievish eyes open;
Ich zog : *marvicher* dos *masematn,*	I'll say : *marvicher* the *masematn,*
Meyn ich : der baytl zol vern aroysgetsoygn.	Then I mean : the purse shall be removed.
Az ich zog a *hachtling,* meyn ich a meser,	When I say a *hachtling,* I mean a knife,
Du zolst nisht *shachern,* iz : nisht reydn.	You shall not *shachern* is : don't talk.
A *blater,* a *norke,* a *lekech,* a ganev,	A thief, a thief, a thief, a thief,
Darf konen mit a *hachtling* a keshene oyfshnaydn.[18]	Must know how to cut open a pocket with a knife.

Deftness, speed, a skill bordering on the sleight of hand was demanded of a professional criminal, who was exposed to sudden detection and apprehension. "To be a thief, you have to be quick as a wink, and then everything goes off all right," one song says bluntly and adds : "If the cop spots you and tries to blow his whistle, just show him some money and buy him off."[19] The following illustrates the work of a thief who broke into a jewelry establishment and was caught in the act.

Oy, ofetsirlech zenen mir beyde gegangen,	Oh, we were both walking respectably,
Ofetsirlech, shpet baynacht,	Respectably, late at night,
Mit a dimet dos gloz ge-efnt,	With a diamond cutter I opened the glass window
Tsu der arbet bin ich gegangen glaych.	And went right to work.
Oy, fun dem fentster glaych tsu der shafe,	Oh, from the window right to the closet,
Mit a shtam-ayzke dem shlos gehakt,	With a crowbar I knocked off the lock,
Un af mayn mazl hot zich der yold oyfgechapt,	When to my misfortune the fool watchman awoke,
Un ba mayn arbet hot men mich gechapt.	And I was caught in the act.
Fun der arbet glaych in dem mokem,	From there right to the jail,
Mit a mente, geshlosn di hent;	With handcuffs locking my hands;
Ich hob farshpilt aza zise frayhayt,	I have lost such a sweet freedom

Mit an umglik bin ich farbrent.[20]	And am burned up by my misfortune.

The songs that describe the hard life of the criminal applied only to the common thieves whose gains were small and whose risks were constant. The following is a sad commentary on the dangerous, miserable existence of the "small operator":

Baklerts nor dem ganev af di velt;	Think about the thief in the world :
Umgliklech iz er alemol.	He is always unfortunate.
Zayt im nisht mekane, ven er hot a sach gelt,	Don't envy him when he has lots of money,
Vayl tsores laydt er gor on a tsol.	Because he suffers a great deal.
M'yogt im, m'plogt im, m'harget un m'shlogt im,	He's hunted, terrorized, beaten, and knocked about,
Ba keynem hot er kayn vert.	He means nothing to anyone at all.
Shtelt zich for zayn lage, ven m'yogt im iz far im a frage—	Imagine his plight : when he's being chased he doesn't know where to turn—
Vi zayn harts klapt in im.[21]	His heart beats in him so !

The life of a criminal was hard, dangerous, insecure. The whole world seemed to be against him : the police, the community, at times his own cronies, and his sweetheart. Occasionally, an anonymous singer expressed his regret that he had not chosen a more reliable trade or craft : "I envy the workingman, even though he barely earns enough for his daily bread, / At least he lives as well as he can and is not tormented in jail."[22] Some songs express the sadness and helplessness of young people who left a poverty-stricken home and hard-working parents, only to be exposed to even more difficult conditions of insecurity and the persecution of the gendarmery. It is the rare song that speaks of theft and criminality as an uncontrollable vice :

Di g'neyve hot zich gemacht in mayn harts ayn kvatir,	Stealing has made its home in my heart,
Zi lo't mir dem kop nisht oyfheybn.	It doesn't let me alone for a moment.
Zi redt mir on az zi iz beshafn fer mir,	It tells me that it was made just for me,
Az zi kon on mir kayn minut nisht lebn.[23]	That it can't live without me for a moment.

More often than not, however, the criminal assumed a gay, dashing, debonair, arrogant, daring, and cruel manner during his moments of freedom, and a depressed, somber, pensive, helpless, and desperate mood when confined in prison. When he was "on the loose," plying his trade recklessly and arrogantly in the very thick of the congested Jewish streets of Warsaw, one singer lilted:

Gey ich mir in gas arayn,	I go out into the street,
Efn ich mir a tir,	I open a door,
Derze ich a futer,	I spot a fur coat,
Farbet ich es tsu mir.[24]	I invite it to go with me.

The following conversation song bellowed out in an Odessa hangout by members of a gang, over a bottle of whiskey, describes the night life of a "member of the profession":

Ay, t'avu biztu geven? Ay, t'avu biztu geven?	Oh, where have you been? Oh, where have you been?
T'avu hostu a gantse nacht gekrayet?	Where did you crow all night?
—Oyf der Moldavanke, mit a sharlatanke,	—On the Moldavanke, with a girlie,
Dort hob ich mayn h'roshi patirayet.	That's where I lost my money.
Ay, t'avu biztu geven? Ay, t'avu biztu geven?	Oh, where have you been? Oh, where have you been?
T'avu hostu di nacht, oy, propadayet?	Where did you spend the whole night?
—Ich bin geven bay eyner, bay Rochele der sheyner,	—I was with that one—Rochele, the pretty one,
Mit vodke mayne tsores propivayet.[25]	Drowning my sorrows in vodka.

The gay and reckless life, strong drink and women, fancy clothes and the swaggering strut appealed to the newcomers: "With the gang, in restaurants . . . where we eat the best food; and wherever there's a little job to do, I know of it and do the best of business."[26] A humorous song, which was current in many variants throughout the Pale, is the following song of a thief boasting about his "profession," which he "inherited" from his "respectable" family:

Ch'ob far keynem	I fear no one,
Kayn moyre, kayn bushe,	Nor am I ashamed,
Vayl mayn profesye	Because my profession
Kumt mir b'yerushe.	Was handed down to me.
Refrain: Orntlech un fayn,	Decent and fine,
Fayn, fayn, fayn,	Fine, fine, fine,

A ganev, a ganev Zol men zayn!	A thief, a thief Is good to be!

Ver hot nisht gehert
Fun mayn mame Zlatke,
Ale tog flegt zi
In an andere yatke—
Refrain: Nisht tsu ganvenen,
     Nor nemen, nor nemen.
	Who has not heard
	Of my mother Zlatke,
	Who, every day, would
	From another meat stall,
	    Not steal,
	    But take, only take.

Fun mayn tatn
Hot di gantse shtot gehert;
Yitschokl pobitnik,
Vos zucht nor ferd,
Refrain: Nisht tsu ganvenen,
     Nor nemen, nor nemen.
	About my father,
	The whole city knew;
	Yitschok Pobitnik,
	Who seeks only horses,
	    Not to steal,
	    But to take, only take.

Un mayn shvester
Iz oych gut bakent—
Yente di kurtse
Mit di lange hant—
Refrain: Zi halt nisht fun
      ganvenen,
     Nor nemen, nor nemen.
	And my sister too,
	Is well known—
	Yente, the shorty,
	With the long hand—
	      Who doesn't believe in
	       stealing,
	     But only in taking, in
	       taking.

Far mayn toyt
Vel ich mayne kinder
Iberlozn di tsavoe,
Yedern bazunder,
Refrain: Zey zoln nisht ganvenen,
     Nor nemen, nor nemen.[27]
	Before I die,
	I will leave to my children,
	This testament,
	To each and everyone of them:
	    Not to steal,
	    But only to take, only to
	     take.

When the gang got together in their hangout, restaurant, or dance hall, they might have roared out the following:

Solo: Mir zenen di brider Lepke
    finger,
Chorus: Oy vey, lepke finger!
Solo: Az eynem iz shver in keshene,
    machn mir im gringer.
Chorus: Oy, vey, machn mir im
    gringer!
Solo: Un az es macht eyner, vos iz a
    shverer *frayer,*
	We are the brothers, Sticky
	    Fingers,
	Oh, oh, Sticky Fingers!
	If your pocket is heavy, we make it
	    lighter.
	Oh, oh, we make it lighter!
	
	And when we strike a difficult
	    fellow,

Chorus: Oy vey, a shverer *frayer,*   Oh, oh, a difficult fellow,
Solo: Tsehakt men im dem kop,   We crack his head open and he pays
    betsolt er tayerer,   dearly,
Chorus: Oy vey, betsolt er tayerer.[28]   Oh, oh, he pays dearly.

But the day of reckoning was bound to come sooner or later and, for some, more than once. To be caught and jailed was a miserable experience for the culprit, who, on the one hand, lost face before his pals and, on the other, was pushed around, mistreated, fed slops in a dark cell, and forced into the rigors of hard labor and the confinement behind high stone walls, barred windows. In prison, a criminal who often "fingered the other guy," now moralizes soberly about his own fate :

Vos toyg mir mayn lebn? — fregt, zich eyner,	What use is my life — one asks himself,
Tsu vos mutshe ich zich?	Why do I torture myself?
Az oyf di nares valgern zich mayne beyner,	My bones lie about in the dugout,
Un az ich kum loyz, — farshit ich zich gich? !	And when I go free, I'm quickly caught again? !
Ober nisht eybig beshtat men nor yenem,	But not always does the other guy get nabbed,
Amol kumt oyf dir oych a sof.	Sometimes you get yours too.
Men hot mich gepakt, in tfise getun aynklemen;	I was caught and clapped into jail,
Yetst lig ich oyf der nare un glots mit di oygn aroyf.[29]	Now I lie on my bunk, staring up at the ceiling.

Another recalls the good old times with the gang when he was free but realizes, now that he is in jail, that perhaps the life of a thief was not meant for him.

Amol iz bay blate geven, az es iz eynem an umglik geshen,	Once, among thieves, when trouble struck one of us,
Flegt men loyfn far im in fayer;	They'd sacrifice for you to the utmost;
Ober haynt, az eyner vert farshit, kilt zich der tsveyter zayn blit.	But now, if you're caught, the others don't give a hang,
Un er vil nit gebn afile kayn drayer.	Refusing to help you even with a three-kopek piece.
Ober ich kon shoyn nit oys-haltn, mayn moyech vert mir tsushpoltn	But I can't stand it anymore, my head is splitting

Fun klern bay tog un bay nacht.

From thinking about it day and night.

Ich vel shoyn nit—ich shver—kumen do aher,

I swear, I won't come here anymore.

Vayl di g'neyve is shoyn nit far mir gemacht.[30]

Because stealing is not for me.

The songs of jailed criminals usually describe the prison atmosphere in somber terms, like the following excerpts from a longer ballad about a fellow in solitary:

Di kleyne fentster un di ayzerne kratn,
Vos m'zet zey oys dem land,
Arum bavacht fil soldatn,
Zey farhitn dem arestant.

The small windows and the iron bars,
Which you see throughout the land
Guarded by many soldiers
Watching the prisoner.

Di hoyche tfise un di breyte vent,
Di keytn klingen af fis un af hent.

The high jail and the thick walls,
The clanging chains on hands and feet.

Mentshn zitsn tog un nacht,
Tirn un shleser iz fest farmacht.

People sit day and night,
Doors and locks fastened tight.

Dos enge shtibl iz fest farshlosn,
Dort zitst a mentsh, eyner aleyn.
Taychn trern iz dort ongegosn,
Er zucht a mitl mit a geveyn.[31]

The narrow cell is firmly locked,
A man sits there all alone.
Rivers of tears are pouring there,
He seeks a way out as he weeps.

Hardened criminals were sent to Siberia under military convoy, and they knew that many would never return from that long, cold stretch. The following employs phrases which recall the songs of political prisoners exiled to Siberia, indicating the occasional contact that criminals had with revolutionaries there.

Ach, ir keytn, hert of tsu klingen
Un blaybt a vayle shteyn,
Ich vel mir mayn harts opzingen
Un dan vel ich vayter geyn.

Ah, you chains, stop your clanging,
And remain still for awhile.
I will sing my heart out
And then march on.

Mit di hoyle shverden
Firt ir dem katorzhnik, dem arestant,
Dem kop gegolt, a gele late,

With drawn swords
You lead the arrested convict,
His head shaven, with a yellow badge,

Geshlosn fis tsu fis, hant tsu hant.

His hands and feet in chains.

Ach, du frayhayt, zise frayhayt,
Ch'ob nisht gevust vi dich tsu shetsn
    dan,
Fun dir, frayhayt, ken yeder genisn,
Nor nisht der katorzhan.

Ah, freedom, you sweet freedom,
I didn't know how to cherish you
    then,
Everyone can enjoy you, freedom,
But not the convicted one.

Farn katorzhan hot men
Di tatshke mit a lopete getun
    ongreytn;
Ch'vel kopen, shlepen
Un tsum takt veln klingen mayne
    keytn.[32]

For the convict they
Prepared the shovel and wheel-
    barrow;
I will drag and pull
To the rhythm of my clanging
    chains.

Bound hand and foot, ground down by the powers he had recklessly defied, the fear of God often struck the heart of the jailed criminal:

Ich shver dir got, ich shver,
Ganvenen gey ich nit mer,
Nor helf mir ich zol oyf der fray
    aroys,
Den vestu shoyn zen,
Arbaytn vel ich geyn,
To, helf mir got, ich zol geyn loyz.[33]

I swear to you God, I swear,
I'll not steal anymore.
Only help me go free,

Then you will see,
I'll go to work,
Only help me, God, to go free.

Such sentiments gave rise to songs which recalled nostalgically the days of sweet childhood when good devoted parents who loved and cared for him sent him to cheder. Such songs are full of regret at having left the good life behind and followed the life of a criminal and a jailbird. Only God could help the criminal now. Some singers are moved to rise and pray, as the following, who got a four-year jail sentence:

Azoy vi s'iz gekumen mitvoch
    inderfri,
Ich shtel mich davenen mit a
    yomerlech geveyn!
Liber got in himl, hob af mir
    rachmones,
Helf mir, ch'zol fun mayn umglik
    loyz geyn.

When Wednesday morning came
    around,
I got up and prayed with a
    heart-rending cry!
Dear God in Heaven, have pity on
    me,
Help me to get out of my troubles.

Mame-lebn-kroyn, du zolst mayn
    ponim onkukn,
Du volst doch mich nisht geven
    derkent;

Mother, dearest dear, if you but saw
    my face,
You wouldn't recognize me;

Ch'bin doch haynt tsuglaychn azoy
vi tsu a toytn,
In kamer eyner aleyn mit di fir
vent.[34]

I am like a dead man now,

Alone in a cell surrounded by four
walls.

The monotony of prison life was such a contrast to the former life "free as a bird" that this poetic comparison often appeared in the songs of prisoners:

Vi a foygl volt ich gefloygn
Fun di tfise, di fintstere vent;
Vi a vorem volt ich gekrochn,
Gegrobn di erd mit mayne hent.

I would fly, like a bird,
From the jail, the dark walls;
Like a worm I would crawl,
Digging the earth with my hands.

Ach liber gotenyu!
Vi sheyn un vi lichtig du host di
velt gemacht,
Far ale mentshn iz zi lichtik,
Farn arestant iz zi fintster vi di
nacht.[35]

Oh, dear God!
How bright and beautiful you have
made the world.
For all others it is bright,
For the prisoner it is dark as night.

But no sooner did the jailbird go free than all was forgotten, and the old life resumed its fast pace, often with a greater intensity, to make up for the time "lost in the pen." Prison songs took on a different tone and even the good Lord, who had helped him go free, was treated with disrespect and indifference. The following, current in a number of variants both among Odessa and Warsaw gangs, was sung raucously in the city jails to taunt the keepers or at gang gatherings.

Ch'bin geven af di fray, hob ich
geganvet ferd.
Haynt zits ich in kriminal un lig
mitn kop in dr'erd.

When I was free, I stole horses,

Now I'm in jail with my head in the
ground.

Reboynoy-shel-oylem, nem mich
aroys fun tfise:
Ch'vel shoyn nisht geyn ganvenen,
nor mit di gantse chevrise.

Creator of the world, take me out of
prison:
And I won't steal again, only with
the whole gang.

Reboynoy-shel-oylem, ch'vel shvern
ba dayne fiselech,
Az du vest mich aroysrateven, vel
ich tsupasn shliselech.

Creator of the world, I swear by
your little feet,
If you'll get me out of here, I'll
make little passkeys.

Ch'bin geven af di fray, hob ich getun tantsn,
Haynt zits ich in kriminal, esn mich di vantsn.[36]

When I was free, I used to dance,
Now I sit in jail and the bedbugs eat me.

The songs of the Jewish underworld were often patterned after older Yiddish folk songs: soldier songs, children's songs, and love songs. Here and there, we encounter a phrase of a popular song by the bards Zunser and Goldfaden. The love songs, though they reflected the amoral life of the underworld and are couched in its vernacular, still incorporate many aspects—a certain naïveté, certain phrases, moods—of the love songs current among the "normal" population.

Farlibt, farlibt hob ich mich in eynem,
Zayn kop iz geven mit parfumen oysgeshmirt;
Zayne shvartse eygelech, mit zayne zise reydelech,
Zey hobn mich fun veg aropgefirt. Oy-vey!

I fell in love with a certain fellow,
His hair was smeared with perfume;
His little black eyes and his sweet talk,
Led me off the straight and narrow. Oh woe!

Tsorelech, oy, tsorelech hob ich mir genumen,
Ch'ob zey nisht getun badarfn;
A shteyn af mayn hartsn vel ich mir onhengen,
Tif in vaser vel ich mich varfn. Oy-vey![37]

Troubles, troubles, I took upon myself,
I surely didn't need them.
I'll tie a stone around my neck,
And jump into the deep water and drown. Oh woe!

Young girls who permitted themselves to be led astray by the perfumed and pomaded dandies, the debonair smarties of the underworld, were usually aware of the risks they were taking. True, such girls later "cursed the day that they were born" and warned all other innocent maidens to beware of the life of a "moll."

Mekane bin ich dos *vitishe* meydele,
Vos zi veyst fun kayn ganef nisht;
S'iz ontsuzogn a velt mit sheyne meydelech:
Gevald! a ganef iz nisht git.

I envy the average girl,
Who knows nothing of a thief;
I say this to a whole world of pretty girls;
Help! A thief is no good.

A ganef iz a takef, a ganef iz a make,
A ganef nemt aroys fun ponim di
    kolirn;
Velches sheyne meydele zi bakent
    zich mit a ganef,
Iz doch a broch tsu ire yorn.[38]

A thief is a terror, a thief is a curse,
A thief drains the color from your
    cheeks;
When a pretty girl meets a thief,

It's woe unto her life.

But girls did get caught and did fall in love with "their thief" and bore the hardships and trials of the dangerous, uncertain life. Some went to prison for their lovers, while others jilted them for a more successful "operator." Still others were in turn jilted by them. Occasionally, a love song, even in the harsh circumstances of the underworld, breathes the tenderest sentiments and is couched in terms of deep poetic meaning, as the following, excerpted from a longer ballad of a criminal who was arrested on his very wedding day:

A tayern shpigl hob ich oyf mayn
    hartsn getrogn,
Yetvider iz mir mekane geven;
Itst iz mir gevorn mayn shpigl
    tseshlogn,
Ver ken noch aza shodn oys-shteyn?

I wore a precious mirror on my
    heart,
Everyone did envy me;
Now my mirror has been broken,

Who can bear such a loss?

Oy, fintster un biter iz mir mayn velt,
S'iz oyf mir aroys got's tsorn;
Ch'ob oysgeshvumen dem gantsn
    yam,
Nor baym breg bin ich der trunken
    gevorn.[39]

Oh, dark and bitter is my world,
God's fury descended on me;
I swam the entire sea,

But at the shore I drowned.

Criminals in prison, separated from their sweethearts, were restless and concerned about them as well as suspicious of their "pals," who lay in wait for "easy prey."

Ch'volt geven a fishele in vaser,
Volt ich doch tsu dir ahingeshvumen.
Ober haynt, az ich zits
In der voyene turme farmacht mit
    di kratn,
Gevalt! vi arumert
Ken ich shoyn tsu dir kumen?

Were I a little fish in the water,
I'd swim to you out there.
But now that I sit
In the military jail behind bars,

Heavens!
How can I get to you?

Ch'volt afile a ferd-un-vogn gevezn,	Were I even a horse and wagon,
Volt ich doch tsu dir ahingeforn.	I'd ride out there to you.
Ober haynt, az ich zits	But now that I sit
In arsenal farmacht hinter di kratn,	In prison behind bars,
Gevalt! ich badoyer dayne yunge yorn.[40]	Heavens! How I pity your young life.

A saucy song current in many variants throughout the Pale and known to many Yiddish-speaking Jews up to the present day deals with a light-hearted quarrel between a thief and his "moll." She is angry with him, and he seems to think that her anger is based on false pride.

Vos geystu arum azoy farsmutshet,	Why are you so moody,
Vos geystu aropgelozt di noz?	Why is your nose so long?
Efsher vilstu visn ver s'iz dayn mishpoche,	Perhaps you'd like to know your pedigree,
Ken ich dir zogn ver un vos.	Then, I'll tell you right now.
Dayn tate iz a smarevoznik,	Your father oils the wheels of locomotives,
Dayn mame ganvet fish in mark,	Your mother steals fish in the marketplace,
Dayn bruder iz a groyser yoyne,	Your brother is a good-for-nothing fool,
Un dayn shvester iz in boyne. . . .[41]	And your sister is in Buenos Aires. . . .

A curious song is a lullaby sung by the wife of a criminal as she sits worrying about her husband, who has apparently failed to send word back to her from a "job" he has done the night before. She realizes that something must have gone wrong and that he must have been caught and sent to jail. As she rocks her baby to sleep, she makes plans for his escape.

Ich kon nisht shlofn, got zol mich nit shtrofn,	I can't sleep, may God not punish me,
Nor ich lig un kler;	But I lie there thinking;
Bay tog un bay nacht, nor ich tracht:	Day and night, I keep on thinking:
Vu nemt men mayn man aher.	How can I bring my husband back here.
Ich bin gefaln oyf a plan, un gey tsu moyshe shlisar aran,	I thought of a plan to go to Moses the locksmith
A zegele beshtel ich mir bald.	And order a little saw immediately.

Ich machl es git, in a broyt nem ich
    es mit,
Un zog em : "er zol nit zan kan
    yold." [42]

I camouflage it well and put it inside
    of a loaf of bread,
And say to him : "Don't be a fool."

In vain did mothers of wayward girls warn them against the pitfalls that waited for them on the "other side of the fence." Pathetic often was the plight of the girls when, after having defied their parents, they later cried out in misery as they sank into the pit of prostitution or fell into the web of the pimp. The following describes such a downward process :

Geven bin ich sheyn, erlich un reyn,
Fun kayn tsores hob ich keynmol
    gevust,
Biz es iz gekumen mayn merder
    tsugeyn
Un mayn unshuld hot er oysgenutst.

I was pretty, honest, and pure
And never knew of any trouble

Until my gangster came along

And used my innocence.

Ich hob im gelibt mit mayn gantses
    lebn,
Ich hob gemeynt az vos er zogt — dos
    iz var.
Biz ich hob zich tsu im ibergegebn,
Yetst bin ich geblibn tsu nar.

I loved him with all my life,

I thought that everything he said
    to me — was true,
Until I gave myself to him,
And now I'm left the fool.

Er hot mich geshlogn un tsu shand
    mich getsvingen,
Mit mayn kerper handlen zol ich;
In keltn, in regns hob ich dos lidl
    gezingen :
Kumt mit mir, oder : nemt mich mit
    zich. [43]

He beat me and forced me into
    shame,
To sell my body;
In rain, in cold, I sang this song :

Come with me, or take me with you.

From here it was but a step to the white slavery trade, which was especially marked during the period of World War I. Many were sold into prostitution and sent to distant Argentina (Buenos Aires), Brazil, and Harbin, in Manchuria.

Di hayntige voyle yingelech,
Vos zey hobn far dem keyser nisht
    kayn moyre,
Zey hobn zich ongenumen a naye
    parnose,
Tsu handlen mit lebedige s'choyre.

The smart little fellows these days,
Who do not fear the Czar,

Have hooked on to a new livelihood,

Trading with live merchandise.

Azoy vi ich lig oyf dem geleger, oyf dem geleger,

As I lie on my bed, on my bed,

Fun trern iz dos kishn nas;

My pillow wet with tears,

"Shtey of meydele, shtey of gute shvester,

"Get up little girl, get up dear sister,

Du bizt shoyn in bines-ayres farpast."

You've already been sold to Buenos Aires."

Oy, bines-ayres, oy, bines-ayres,

Oh, Buenos Aires, Oh, Buenos Aires,

Bines-ayres iz a shver shtikl broyt;

Buenos Aires is a difficult way to earn your bread;

Velches meydele zi kumt kayn bines-ayres,

The maiden that comes to Buenos Aires

Bakumt zi ach, yungerheyt dem toyt.[44]

Is doomed to die young.

By then it was too late to retreat or retrieve. Regret turned to bitter gall. "You took me away from my mother's house and promised me precious things. But instead, you brought me to Buenos Aires and made a loose woman out of me." "At your mother's house you slept in a dirty bed and ran around with just anyone. You had to wash filthy clothes, while here you sleep in fancy chambers, wear diamond rings and eat chocolates." "Ah me," sighs the doomed girl, "I'd rather sleep in a dirty bed, run around with ordinary fellows, and wash filthy clothes than be cursed forever in Buenos Aires."[45]

A most interesting facet evident in the collective character of the Jewish underworld was their sensitivity to their Jewishness, which they were ready to defend at the slightest provocation.[46] A song which reflects this aspect is a ballad about a thief, who seemed always to be trailing bad luck. As a child he was abandoned by his mother; on his first "job" he was caught and sent to jail in Pskov in northern Russia. There, he was given the choice of either accepting Christianity or exile to Siberia. He refused and was clapped into solitary. Following are several stanzas from this ballad :

Azoyvi ch'bin kayn Pskov arayngekumen,

When I got to Pskov,

Gekrign petsh hob ich bald dem ershtn tog,

I was beaten up the very first day.

M'hot mich geheysn toyfn af di katoylishe religie,

They told me to convert to the Catholic religion,

S'iz tsu mir a broch un oy, a klog.

Woe is me, woe is me.

Vi ch'ob nor dos, oy vey, derhert,	As soon as I heard this, oh, woe,
Iz mir gevorn heys un kalt;	I felt hot and cold :
Vi ken ich nemen aza sheyne religie	How can I take such a beautiful religion
Un ibergebn ir tsum galech in di hant !	And hand it over to the priest !
Azoyvi der natshalnik iz mitn galech arayngekumen,	When the chief came in with the priest,
Mit gute reyd hobn zey geredt tsu mir :	They began to talk sweet talk to me:
"Az du vest onemen undzer religie,	"If you'll accept our faith,
Vet men dich nisht shikn kayn Sibir."	You won't be sent to Siberia."
"Oy, gospodin, ir megt mir gleybn,	"Oh, Sir, you may believe me,
Az tun vel ich, oy, dos nisht :	This I will not do, oh no :
Eyder ich zol ibergeyn af a tsveyte religie,	Rather than accept another faith,
Iz kranter tsu shtarbn azoy vi a yid." [47]	I'd rather die as a Jew !"

This attachment to one's own people and traditions later led to some interesting incidents during the first Russian Revolution of 1905, when, during the wave of pogroms against the Jews, an occasional gang of underworld characters would volunteer its services to defend Jews against the organized attack of the Czarist police and military. At other times, however, as happened in Warsaw prior to the 1905 period, the organized Jewish political movement regarded the Jewish underworld as an ugly phenomenon and a bitter enemy, since it was known that the police employed Jewish criminals as spies against the Jewish revolutionary movement.

The songs of the underworld reflect the darkest corners of the Jewish streets in the large cities of the Pale, the congested quarters, narrow alleys, crowded thoroughfares filled with hustling, jostling, hawking, shouting, panhandling—a huge moving prism constantly revolving, now turning one side to the sun, now turning away from it. There, a beggar strolling by, playing his fiddle, his sightless eyes turned up towards the sky, is singing and pleading :

Oy, hert zich ayn mayne libe mentshn,	Oh, listen to me, dear people,
Oy, hert zich aynet vos ich vel aych fregn do :	Oh, listen to what I ask of you here :

Ay, vi kumt es aza veytik,   Ah, how can such a deep pain,
In a kleynem, kleynem fidl?   Be contained in such a little, little
                   fiddle?

Oy, hert zich aynet ale libe mentshn,   Oh, listen to me, all you dear people,
Hert zich aynet vos ich vel aych   Oh, listen to my question once
    fregn noch amol :   again :
Ay, vi kumt es aza shtarker veytik,   Ah, how can such a dreadful pain,
In aza kleynem, kleynem fidl?   Be found in such a tiny, tiny fiddle?
— Shenkt a nedove ! [48]   — Give me an alms !

Here a hawker, earning his living the hard way, would express his anger
with those idle ones who refuse to work even as he was forced to do !

Geyt a sharlatan afn gas,   A charlatan walks the streets
Lernen ken er gornit.   And is ignorant and uninformed.
Geyt arum pust un pas,   He walks about in idleness
Tut vos men tor nit.   And does what is forbidden.   [do,
Krank biztu tsu horeven,   You're not sick to work hard, as I
Azoy vi ich mitn bitern shveys,   With the sweat of my brow,
Geyn un shrayen : heyse bebelech,   Hawking and shouting : hot beans,
Bebelech, vaybelech, koyft ! [49]   Beans, little women, buy some !

Temptation, corruption, evil, and crime, individual conflicts, the collective misery of widespread poverty, the restrictions leveled against the Jewish community created a complex subject within the category of Yiddish folk songs of the underworld. The bravado spirit, the dash and derring-do is intermingled with the desperation and misery of the hunted and tormented. Boastfulness and courage are coupled with helplessness and tragedy. Mischievousness, humor, cockiness, tenderness in love, nostalgia for one's childhood and parents, fear of the Lord, devotion to one's "pals" — all make up the multicolored threads of this group of songs. These were heard in the shady hangouts, the favorite restaurants, dance halls (*knaypies*) and saloons, the houses of prostitution, and the abodes of the many types and characters inhabiting this world beneath the "normal" world, which in turn adopted some of the songs of this nether world and even delighted in their particular flavor and charm.

Notes

OUT OF THE SHADOWS

1. Teitelbaum, pp. 13, 103.
2. *Ibid.*, p. 104.
3. Rivkind, p. 165. This old Yiddish poem, written by Shmuel Hurglen, is given by Rivkind, together with comments, explanations, etc., in his work, pp. 155–177.
4. *Ibid.*, p. 184. Rivkind gives four Yiddish translations of this sung poem: pp. 178–186.
5. Güdemann—Shtif, pp. 141, 145.
6. Kirch-han, Song No. 13, p. 24. The song, referred to as "a song to be sung daily, so that in serving the Lord, he will provide you with everything," includes a philosophical message and moralizing about the principles and ethics on life generally and for the Jew in particular.
7. Erik, p. 305. Written by Jacob Teplits of Prague.
8. Rivkind, pp. 25–29.
9. *Ibid.*, p. 77.
10. Sholem Aleichem, N.Y., p. 71.
11. Idelsohn, IX, No. 49. The *dreydl*—teetotum—bears four Hebrew letters: *N, G, H, Sh (nun, giml, heh, shin)*. These represent four Hebrew words: *nes* ("miracle"), *godol* ("great"), *hoyo* ("happened"), *shom* ("there"). In the secularized gambling game of *dreydl*, however, the four letters represent four Yiddish words: *nem* ("take"), *gut* ("good"), *halb* ("half"), *shtel* ("put"). The *tsig un volf* ("goat and wolf") referred to in this song relate to animal figures which were substituted by the Jews for human images in the card games. This Jewish card game was "handmade" and was called *kvitlech. Terkisher dam* refers to the game of chess. *See* Linetsky. Based on his poem, "Der kortn shpil," pp. 30–35.
12. Lehman, 1928, pp. 169–170, No. XXVI.
13. Graubard, p. 36, No. CIII.
14. *Ibid.*, p. 34, No. LXXXIX.
15. Teitelbaum's mother, who was running a respectable restaurant in one of the Warsaw courtyards, was suddenly exposed to a gang of underworld characters, who had decided to make her restaurant their hangout. Teitelbaum, then a Talmudic student of fourteen, gives us a vivid description of three of these characters. ". . . I was . . . fascinated by the new guests, with their strange behaviour, loud talk, wild wrangling. Mysterious little flames shone in their thievish eyes. Their expressions seemed peculiar, their faces were arrogant, and their laughter raucous. It was fascinating to see their exaggerated devotion to one another on the one hand and their mean needling and envy on the other. Among them were some important characters, big operators, daring knifers, dangerous safecrackers. There were also the lesser ones —little chiselers, ordinary thieves, pickpockets, and such, who, before everybody's eyes, stole boxes and crates of merchandise from passing wagons. . . . There was something so colorful, so professional about them . . . with their little moustaches, long sideburns, and caps with narrow bands and patent-leather peaks pushed back on their heads. And, as in all professions, there were the 'stars' among them. . . . I recall one . . . the famous Shimele Blachazh, who was the terror and the admiration

of the Jewish quarter in Warsaw—of medium height, in his twenties, well-built, in a very short jacket, his trousers stuck into his patent-leather top boots and the well-known cap with its shiny peak. His hands were like quicksilver—always grabbing at something and squeezing it—someone's hand, neck, lapel, a bottle on the table, the back of a chair, thereby biting passionately into his lower lip. He was always ready to tear something, throw something, rip something apart so that the sparks would fly! The most remarkable thing about him were his eyes— cocky, jolly, laughing, saying: I won't hurt you, I just want you to be afraid of me! And folks *were* afraid of him, and how! And not only ordinary people . . . his own pals feared him. . . . The most insignificant incident could turn him into the bitterest enemy, and then it was the easiest thing for him to open his opponent's belly and let him lie there in the street with his innards spilling out. Shimele was a daredevil and could fight alone against twenty, and when he didn't have a knife in his hand, he'd use a hunk of broken bottle, a leg of an overturned table. Once, I saw him engaged in a bitter fight, and, at a difficult moment, he dashed into an ironmonger's shop, grabbed a ten-pound iron weight, and returned to the street to fight off a gang of non-Jews who had insulted him. Shimele wasn't afraid of the devil himself, except only—his tiny mother, the hard-working, weather-beaten Malkele, who kept a little stall in the nearby market place. . . . When he heard her voice, he'd tremble like a little frightened boy. Then, he'd either run out the back door or hide somewhere. . . . But Shimele was not the leader. The leader was Veve—quiet, gentle, restrained, with a pale, handsome face. I can't remember ever having heard him utter a single word. . . . He only came on important occasions, and even then he sat or stood, hands in his pockets in his neat suit, watching and listening with his wise, kindly eyes. Nobody knew much about Veve, and what was known was not talked about. The little that leaked out was that he was the son of a wealthy, aristocratic Jewish family, that he'd left home and a huge inheritance and had joined the underworld where, because of his tact, wisdom, and iron will, he became the leader and organizer. Veve's word, his look, was law. . . . I would stand in the shadow of the doorway leading to the dining room, watching with admiration and bated breath Veve's pale, aristocratic face, his warm, penetrating eyes, his delicate hands which handled the spoon and fork so differently, his graceful form which called forth so much obedience and respect. . . . Veve never came alone. In addition to his bodyguard, he was always accompanied by his closest aide and advisor, R'foel the Dayin (the 'Advisor'), as he was called respectfully. R'foel was the guardian of the morals and the lawgiver of the gang. His was the final decision in all controversies, and he decided what could and could not be done. And woe to him, big or little, who failed to obey the instructions and orders handed down by 'Reb' R'foel. R'foel was a huge, husky man in his sixties, with a handsome, round, greyish-black beard and bulging pockets under his stern grey eyes. He wore a short, heavy jacket, a small cloth cap, his pants stuck into his top boots and was always leaning on a thick cane, which called forth respect. He talked in a deep, bass voice, his words were deliberate, measured, and thoughtful, and when he spoke, everyone, especially Veve, hung on his every word. . . . I liked Reb R'foel because on the occasions when he came into our restaurant alone, he would lovingly pinch my cheek and ask me what portion of the Gemara I was studying at the time. . . . A strange Jew was Reb R'foel . . . with his stern eyes and good-natured smile" (pp. 107–108, pp. 110–112).

16. Lehman, 1928, pp. 104–105, No. LXVI. The underworld created its own vernacular, which included, in addition to Yiddish, also Hebrew, Polish, Russian, and even some German words. The Hebrew words reflected the religious and pious background of some of the singers. In this particular example, the following were used: *masematn*—from the Hebrew—denoting "the object," literally "the gift," which in this case might be a watch, billfold, purse, etc., on which the pickpocket had fastened his attention; *chelbene-geyer*—a corruption from the Yiddish *gevelbn*—"stores" or

"shops." In this song, the thief is contemplating trying locked doors of shops at night and entering those that are easily opened or were accidentally left open by the owners; *taltl*—from the Hebrew—to "remove," to "throw," here denoting a form of housebreaking which may involve tossing stolen goods out of an upper-story window and possibly jumping out after it; *potok*—from the Russian—hijacking merchandise from moving vehicles.

17. Lehman, 1928, pp. 109–110, No. LXX. Six words of the Warsaw Jewish underworld vernacular appear in this song: *blater* ("thief"), *marvicher* ("pickpocket"), *alfons* ("pimp"), *afn-shpring* ("house thief who can jump from an upper-story window"), *farshit* ("fingered," "caught"), *pototshnik* ("hijacker").

18. Graubard, p. 21, No. IX.
19. Lehman, 1928, pp. 101–102, No. LXIV.
20. *Ibid.*, p. 111, No. LXXII.
21. *Ibid.*, pp. 91–92, No. LV.
22. *Ibid.*, pp. 46–47, No. XXIII.
23. Graubard, p. 22, No. XI.
24. Lehman, 1928, p. 122, No. LXXXII.
25. Rubin, MSS. The Moldavanke was an Odessa suburb where criminals congregated. Three Russian words are used in this song: *patirayet, propadayet, propivayet.*
26. Graubard, p. 22, No. XII.
27. Lehman, 1928, pp. 120–122, No. LXXXI.
28. Graubard, p. 22, No. XIII.
29. *Ibid.*, p. 32, No. LXXII.
30. *Ibid.*, p. 32, No. LXIX.
31. Lehman, 1928, pp. 28–30, No. XI.
32. *Ibid.*, pp. 106–107, No. LXVIII.
33. Graubard, p. 30, No. LVII.
34. Lehman, 1928, pp. 52–53, No. XXVI.
35. *Ibid.*, p. 37, No. XVI.
36. *Ibid.*, pp. 117–118, No. LXXIX.
37. *Ibid.*, pp. 147–148, No. IX. In the love songs of the underworld, it is interesting to note that the terms *kale* and *chosn* ("bride and groom") are used, where in the current love songs the terms *lyubtshe* or *lyube* ("sweetheart") are usually employed. In the "normal" Jewish environment, the use of *kale* or *chosn* denoted that a formal match was under way. It is therefore curious that the lovers of the underworld should cling to terms of an environment which they had left and the mores of which they were constantly breaking.
38. *Ibid.*, pp. 181–182, No. XXXIV.
39. Cahan, 1957, No. 151.
40. Lehman, 1928, pp. 143–144, No. VII.
41. *Ibid.*, pp. 179–180, No. XXXIII.
42. Graubard, p. 33, No. LXXV.
43. *Ibid.*, p. 38, No. CXI.
44. Rubin, MSS.
45. *Ibid.*
46. Teitelbaum describes an incident on a Sunday, when some of his mother's Christian customers, returning from Church, got mixed up with several of the underworld characters in the restaurant. One of the church-going members was a bit tipsy and had made a snide remark about Jews. "In one moment, our big dining room became a swirling whirlpool, with everything and everybody flying in all directions—bottles, plates, chairs, tables. Heads were split open and people either jumped on or were thrown out of the windows" (p. 113). Elsewhere in the same work, Teitelbaum describes an episode which deepens the dimension of this side of the characters of

the Warsaw Jewish underworld. The festival of Purim was approaching and the young Teitelbaum, who was known to excel in reading the Torah aloud in its proper *nusach* ("cantillation") was approached cautiously by a couple of these characters in his mother's restaurant. They wanted him to come and read the Story of Esther before a group of their own people. . . . Teitelbaum accepted the invitation and . . . "at the appointed hour, on Purim eve, two of the gang waited for me, as I followed them at a distance in the twilight, with beating heart. If I'm not mistaken, they led me somewhere on Krochmalne Street, through a gate and then up dimlit stairs, into a bright, fancy house. A large number of people were already waiting there, watching out anxiously for me. I was too excited and confused to notice what they looked like. . . . I only felt their eager, grateful eyes caressing the little fellow in his long Chasidic coat and earlocks which stuck out from his Jewish cap. In the middle of the room stood a table covered with a white cloth and on it they had prepared a folded parchment scroll for me. Candles were burning. It took a little while before I was able to control my beating heart. Several men gently patted me on the back, on my head, calming me, until I finally was able to stand up and read. . . . I knew the Story of Esther by heart, and it was not difficult for me to read out of this scroll. Somehow, I felt . . . that I was doing a good thing, and my voice rose freely in this strange, fancy room, among the odd listeners who surrounded me with a deep piety. And when the chant passed from the happy portions to the somber ones, . . . you could almost feel the heartbeats of the women, who huddled there in their colorful shawls . . . and the men, seriously listening in their caps with the patent-leather peaks. They seemed to live through every moment in the tale, which they did not even understand, and they rattled their noisemakers with all their might, every time 'Haman, the enemy of the Jews,' was mentioned, in this way expressing their own sympathies for the Jewish sorrows of long ago. And when I finished reading, I saw all around me tearful, damp eyes of gratitude and contentment. . . . The two who had brought me there then quietly put the few coins in my hand and with respect and warmth led me back over the dimlit stairs and out into the night . . . till we got to Tvarda Street, whence I could find the way to my own courtyard myself" (pp. 115–116). A "Jewish" cap, in contrast to the patent-leather peaked one, had a small peak made of the same cloth as the cap itself.

47. Lehman, 1928, pp. 34–36, No. XV.
48. Rubin, MSS.
49. Idelsohn, IX, No. 699.

CHAPTER XIII

To America

IMMIGRATION TO AMERICA FROM CZARIST RUSSIA BEGAN IN 1869 WITH some 4,000 Jews annually. This was the third wave of Jewish immigration to America and, almost from the beginning, emigration from the Old World came to be identified with a deep yearning for America—land of freedom, equality, security, and opportunity.[1]

With the accession to the throne of Alexander III, the reforms instituted by Alexander II were nullified. The eighties witnessed a wave of pogroms which brought the deepest tragedies, impoverishment, and destruction to the Jewish community, creating one of the broadest movements of emigration of Jews away from Russia, with more than a quarter million men, women, and children leaving the Pale during the years 1881 and 1893 alone. Protest meetings in Western Europe and some of the large Eastern cities of the United States against the violence perpetrated against the Russian Jews did not basically improve the situation and emigration continued to move in a steady stream right up to and following World War I.

At first only those who could manage the trip financially went. A husband left his wife and child, a young man—his aging parents. Each, in the true sense of the pioneer, turned his face toward the New World in the hope of putting down new roots, of taking advantage of the opportunity to work, and then sending for his loved ones. Families were pulled asunder, some temporarily, others permanently. Old folks pined away for their children, lovers yearned for one another, wives longed for their men, who sometimes never returned. This was a period of *agune* songs, songs of the deserted wife, and the stanzas below describe the plight of the wife of a man who had gone off to America and who had apparently forgotten to send for her.

342

Oy, ongeshpart on elnboygn,
Zitst zich a froy, shpet baynacht,
Taychn trern rinen fun ire oygn,
Zi zitst doch k'seyder un tracht.

Oh, leaning on her elbow,
A woman sits late into the night,
Rivers of tears flow from her eyes,
She sits there thinking, thinking.

Mayn man iz geforn glikn zuchn,

In columbuses land.
Hal'vey volt er mir chotsh a get
    geven shikn,
Ich zol nit zayn in aza bitern shtand.

My husband has gone to seek his
    fortune
In Columbus's land.
Oh, if he had only granted me a
    divorce first,
I wouldn't be so miserable now.

Oy mentshn, mentshn, ir fort doch
    avek,
Ir fort mit shifn un mit a ban.
Fregt dortn vos er hot mir gelozt a
    viste agune,
Oyb ir zet ergets mayn man.[2]

Oh, people, people, you are
    leaving,
You are going on boats and on trains.
Ask him why he deserted me,

Should you meet my husband there.

America became the dream of millions of Eastern European Jews:
in America, one could work at anything; in America, one could worship
as one pleased; in America, the social strata were not sharply defined; in
America, young people could marry without interference of parents and
true love could be more than a dream. Such were the sentiments which
surged through the masses as they streamed from the east to the west,
across the Atlantic Ocean.

In the following song, a young man bids his sweetheart good-bye. His
parents have been interfering in their love, and he assures her that once
in America, although far from their families, they would have no such
problems to contend with, and good friends and the Lord would bless
them. Two excerpted stanzas follow:

Zolst nisht zorgn, mayn tayer-lebn,
Az du vest mayne eltern nisht gefeln,
Kayn amerike veln mir avekforn,
Un dortn a chupe shteln.

Don't worry, my own true love,
If my parents do not approve of you,
We will go off to America
And be married there.

A chupe veln mir dort shteln,
Far a minyen mentshn.
Got in himl vet zayn der eydis,

Un tsu der chupe vet er undz
    bentshn.[3]

We will stand under the canopy,
Before a *minyen* ("ten") people,
God in Heaven will witness the
    ceremony
And bless us in our marriage.

But the heart of many a young girl was troubled as, secretly bidding good-bye to her lover, she could already feel the pain of having permanently lost him to that distant unknown — America. In the following, a young seamstress, who is ready to wait "two and three and even five years" until her beloved sends for her, pleads that he write to her regularly to help her survive the long separation.

Tsvey-dray yor vel ich oyf dir vartn,
Afile finef, iz mir oych keday.
Ich vel lebn nor mit dayne brivelech,
Un mutshen vel ich mich baym
    shnayderay.

Two and three years I'll wait for you,
And even five, I'll also wait.
I shall live only with your letters,
And struggle along at my
    dressmaking.

Ich vel dich aroysbaleytn kayn
    mayne eltern
Un vel loyfn, oy, tsu dem vogzal,

I'll sneak out without my parents
    noticing
And run to see you off, oh, at the
    station,

Ich vel dich aroysbalaytn kayn
    amerike,
Un trern veln gisn vi a kval.

I will see you off as you go to
    America,
And the tears will pour like a stream
    from my eyes.

Nor betn, bet ich dich, mayn tayer
    zis-lebn,
Zolst dayn libe nit fargesn dort,

But I beg you, oh, I beg of you, my
    own true love,
That you do not forget our love over
    there,

Zolst mir bald fun dir a yedi-e gebn,

Send me a communication
    immediately,

Az hobn zol ich fun dir chotsh a
    vort.[4]

So that I get word from you soon.

America became a haven for those who sought to evade the rigorous years of military service in the Czarist army. Others looked for economic security, following the reverses at the turn of the century, the mounting crisis, the Russo-Japanese War, and the 1905 Revolution. Still others, who had already been living on the brink of economic ruin, now utterly pauperized, came to work so as not to die of starvation.

Although the American Civil War was long over and the abolition of slavery a fact, some of these historical occurrences had not been clearly assimilated by the general mass of the Jewish population in Eastern Europe. This is revealed in the following stanzas of a song in which the singer would rather be "a slave in America" than continue suffering in the Czarist Pale.

Eyn zach vel ich, got, ba dir betn,   One thing, God, I'll beg of you,
Az di zach zol mir zayn beshert,   And hope it will be granted me,
Fun rusland muz ich optretn,   That I may leave Russia
Keyn amerike vet zayn mayn pachod.   And make America my goal.

Fun keyne glikn veys ich nit,   I never had any luck,
In rusland iz mir zeyer shlecht.   I am very miserable in Russia.
Kayn amerike muz ich opforn,   I must go off to America,
Farkoyfn vel ich zich far a knecht.[5] I'll sell myself for a slave.

Another song reveals the tragic plight of impoverished Jews desperately looking to America, ready to go there on foot, and, as in the above example, "sell themselves for slaves" if need be.

Betracht nor di bitere tsayt,   Ponder on these bitter times
Ayedn in zayn profesion.   In every occupation.
Oyf yeder shrit zet men orime layt,   At every step you see paupers,
Un noch mer fun der idisher   And even more from the Jewish
    natsion.   nation.

Tsi fis kayn amerike tu-en mir laufn,   We are fleeing on foot to America
Dort a shtikl braut tsi fardinen.   To earn a crust of bread there.
Fir sklaven veln mir zich dort   We will sell ourselves for slaves,
    ferkaufn,
Abi an opru tsu gefinen.   So long as we can live in peace.

Hob rachmones groyser got,   Great God, have pity
Oyf ints atsind.   Upon us now,
Oyf ints in indzer noyt,   Upon us in our need,
Un fir ints iber dem veg geshvind.[6]   And lead us quickly across the sea.

References to the migrations of the eighties and nineties from Eastern Europe to America appear mainly in the folklore songs created in the old country. Here the first impact of the environment of the New World was overwhelming and for some even a shattering experience. Arriving from an economically backward, politically blind, autocratic land, from congested, poor quarters in small towns and villages, the new immigrants set foot in a country that had passed through a period of the most rapid economic development through ruthless methods of human exploitation. It was also a land that had pioneered in the struggle for liberty and independence, where the upheavals of eighteenth- and nineteenth-century Europe had found a sympathetic response. It was a world where into the last half of the nineteenth century were compressed the great historic upheavals of the Civil War and the abolition of slavery, the opening up of the West and the rapid expansion and concentration of industry and transportation. At the same time, this period was marked by the creation of a plutocracy brazenly flaunting its wealth, by panics and depressions, local and general strikes, side by side with the discoveries and mechanical inventions of the telephone, phonograph, the "gasoline carriage," and the airplane.

Small wonder that the new immigrants were too bewildered to create songs in those first years of putting down roots in an environment of such novel complexity. One immigrant, who had crossed the Atlantic in a cattle boat in 1892, saw the main streets of Philadelphia as

. . . a world of din . . . with a thousand sounds, . . . wide, asphalt streets, . . . large buildings and stores with shining window displays and streetcars rushing towards me and underneath me and from the side streets with a loud clanging. . . . I stared at the huge horses, as big as elephants, with legs like logs, as they dragged large wagons of merchandise over the clattering streets. I gazed at the people dressed neatly, almost in their holiday clothes, seemingly happy and eagerly hurrying toward their destination.

A week later, the same immigrant located

. . . most of my former countrymen, who were merchants and storekeepers in the old home, are now shopworkers, mostly in sweatshops. . . . Almost all of them are not happy in America. They yearn for the old home and cannot stand the hard work in the sweatshops. They all hope to save some money and open their own shop and then, perhaps, life would not be so hard and bitter.[7]

The following stanzas reflect this disillusionment in a young man who had failed to cope with the problems of the new environment:

Vos bin ich kayn amerike gelofn,	Why did I come to America,
Un vosere glikn hobn mich dort getrofn?	And what fortune did I find there?
Az elnt bin ich farblibn,	Instead, I was forlorn,
Fun foter un muter fartribn,	Separated from my father and mother,
Fun shvester un brider azoy vayt.	So far away from my sisters and brothers.

Yetst betn mich mayne eltern aheym,
Un aheym tsu kumen iz far mir nit sheyn.
Es brent in mir a fayer,
Tsu mayn liber muter getrayer.[8]

Now my parents plead with me to come home,
And I am ashamed to return.
A fire burns in my heart,
As I long for my beloved mother.

The bloodstream which bound the hearts yearning for one another across the seas was poured into letters which flowed constantly back and forth. A type of "letter song" became current at that time, several of which were as popular as folk song. One was "Tayere muter" ("Dear Mother"), by the Eastern European folk bard Mark Warshawsky, in which a son in America writes tenderly to his mother in the "old country," describing the changes that are being wrought in him and his family since he had put down roots in the New World.[9] Another, which actually became "folk song" in every Yiddish-speaking community in the world, was the prolific, popular, American-Yiddish song writer S. Shmulevitsch's ("Small") "A brivele der mamen" ("A Little Letter to Mother"). In this song, a mother pleads for letters from her only son, who has apparently forgotten his poor old parent in the scramble for material wealth in the New World. The song concludes with a description of the well-to-do son living in his "rich house in New York City, with his beautiful wife and two children," as he receives the news of his mother's death, and a refrain in which she pleads with her hard-hearted son to see to it that he not fail her this time — in saying the prayer for the dead every year, now that she is gone. However, the refrain given below, which accompanied the first stanzas, enjoyed the most popularity:

A brivele der mamen,
Zolstu nit ferzamen,
Shrayb geshvind, libes kind,
Shenk ir di nechame.
Di mame vet dayn brivele lezn,
Un zi vert genezn,
Heylst ir shmarts, ir biter harts,
Erkvivkst ir di neshome.[10]

A little letter to your mother,
Don't take too long to write it,
Write it soon, dear child,
Grant her this comfort.
Your mother will read your letter,
And she will be relieved,
You will cure her pain, her bitter heart,
And refresh her soul.

Another Yiddish song of the mass migration years of the eighties and nineties, still current today, was Sholem Aleichem's well-known lullaby, which circulated in many textual and melodic variants before it was officially published in 1892.[11]

These folk songs of popular and literary origin expressed the anxiety and loneliness, the problems and hardships of the separated families, waiting tearfully for that photograph of their "emancipated" loved ones across the sea, looking out hopefully for the precious steamship ticket, which was to reunite them with their families in the "goldene medine" ("the golden land of plenty") where chicken soup and white bread were daily fare.

The process in the American "melting pot" was intense and, under the fierce pressure of the dominant culture, the old quickly gave way to the new. Former petty merchants and storekeepers became cigar makers, shirtmakers, women's coat operators and "wrapper" (bathrobe) workers, pants makers, peddlers. The strong economic drive and the dynamic nature of the social environment tore away many cultural values, habits, manners of speech, modes of dress, work and craft patterns of centuries. The passionate desire to become Americanized weakened and severed the bonds between parents and children, parents and grandchildren.

The first decades of the mass migrations saw the emergence of a new type of Jewish workingman and woman, exploited in the sweatshops of New York, Boston, Philadelphia, and Chicago, attended by a Yiddish press, Yiddish fraternal organizations, and the first steps towards trade unionization. The carriers of the social ideas during those years were writers, journalists, organizers, a Socialist intelligentsia which devoted its energies and talents almost exclusively towards uplifting the toiling men and women of the sweatshops, the immigrant peddlers, the dislocated mass of new citizens, who had fled the ruthless Czarist regime and were now caught in the race for the dollar.

The Songs of Literary Origin on American Soil

The most prominent American-Yiddish writers at that time were Morris Winchevsky, David Edelshtat, Morris Rosenfeld, I. Bovshover, and Isaac Reingold; and some of their poetry was set to music by anonymous composers. Some of these sung poems became very widespread and were even "exported" to Eastern Europe, where a generation later they were already considered part of the folk-song tradition of the Yiddish-speaking Jews there.

By far the most versatile of the above was Winchevsky (1856–1933),[12] organizer and translator, regarded as founder of the Socialist press and literature and referred to as the "first Yiddish proletarian poet." Prior to his settling in America in 1894, he lived for fifteen years in London, England, where some of his poems, later to become popular in America and Eastern Europe, were written. Winchevsky's poetry, which was concerned mainly with social questions, came at a time when the general environment in America was perhaps not quite prepared to accept it. His poems rang out like a clarion call, as in the following two stanzas from his "Der frayhayts gayst" ("The Spirit of Freedom"), which was set to music anonymously, and sung on both sides of the Atlantic among Jewish workingmen and women.

In di gasn, tsu di masn	Into the streets, to the masses
Fun bedrikte felker-rasn	Of oppressed races of mankind
Ruft der frayhayt's gayst :	The spirit of freedom is calling :
Ich breng vafn far dem shklafn,	I bring arms for slavery,
Ich befray di arbets-shklafn	I liberate the toiling slaves
Un ich mach zey drayst.	And I make them brave.
Licht farshpreytn — recht farbreytn	To spread light — extend justice,
Kum ich un tsubrech di keytn	I come to break the shackles
Fun der tiranay;	Of tyranny;
Natsionen — fun kanonen,	Nations — from cannons,
Armeyen un fun shpionen —	Armies and spies —
Kum ich machn fray.[13]	I come to make free.

In his "Hert ir kinder" ("Children, Do You Hear?"), Winchevsky called to open battle with "capital" and foretold the workingman's realization of his power and his growing awareness. Following are two stanzas of this sung poem :

Vayl er bukt zich nit far getsn,	For he bows no more to idols
Nit far opgeter nit mer,	And no more to images,
Vilt zich mer nit lozn hetsn	Refuses to permit himself to be used
Tsu gebroychn zayn gever	To produce the weapons
Far dem nets fun zayne shinder,	For the nets of his fleecers
Kegn kamf un frayhayts-man;	Who struggle against freedom-loving men;
Oy, er kumt tsum seychl, kinder,	Oh, the workingman is coming to his senses,
Iberal der arbetsman !	Children, everywhere !

Iberal, af beyde zaytn
Fun atlantik, rirt er zich!
Er vil mer nit lozn raytn
Zayne blutzoyger af zich.
Er vil merer, vi a blinder
Ferd, nit geyn shoyn in geshpan,
Er vil fray zayn, libe kinder,
Zat zayn vil der arbetsman! [14]

Everywhere, on both sides
Of the Atlantic, he is stirring!
He refuses to let
His bloodsuckers ride him anymore.
He refuses, like a blind horse,
To trudge under the yoke anymore,
He wants to be free, dear children,
The workingman wants to be fed!

Arriving in America twelve years before Winchevsky, David Edelshtat (1866–1892), shattered by the Kiev pogrom of May 8, 1881, which he had personally witnessed, disembarked with a group of *Am Olam*[15] students. Like most of the new immigrants of those years, Edelshtat began as a sweatshop worker, but his health was frail, and he contracted tuberculosis. His poems, which dealt almost exclusively with social themes, drew on his own experiences "in the dark world of slavery," the hard struggle against it, the loneliness and suffering which characterized those early years of the mass migrations. At the same time, Edelshtat's songs yearned passionately for the good life, breathing with the impatience and exuberance of youth.

Edelshtat was the most sung labor poet, and some fourteen of his poems were set to music and became popular both here and in Eastern Europe, where several of them were absorbed into Yiddish folk song. Following are two stanzas from his "Vacht oyf" ("Awake"):

Vi lang, o vi lang vet ir blaybn noch
  shklafn
Un trogn di shendleche keyt?
Vi lang vet ir glentsnde raychtimer
  shafn
Far dem, vos baroybt ayer broyt?

How long, oh, how long will you
  slaves yet remain
And bear the shameful chain?
How long will you glorious wealth
  create
For him, who robs you of your
  bread?

Vi lang vet ir shteyn, ayer rukn
  geboygn
Derniderikt, heymloz, farshmacht?
Es togt shoyn! Vacht uf un tsu-efnt
  di oygn!
Derfilt ayer ayzerne macht! [16]

How long will you stand with your
  backs bended low
Humbled, homeless, and wan?
It dawns! Awake and open your
  eyes!
And feel your iron might!

Edelshtat's popularity was due to several reasons: the texts appeared regularly in *Di Varhayt,* the Anarchist paper where he worked following

In the sweatshop

his sweatshop period; he tried to use the folk-song patterns he heard among the workers in the shops; he spoke in terms which touched the hearts of the men and women he had toiled with. Like Winchevsky before him, his sympathies were with the brave souls pining in the Czarist prisons for their ideals, for whom he wrote his "In kamf" ("In Struggle"), which was popular then and is still alive in the memory of workingmen today. Following are two stanzas:

Mir vern gehast un getribn,	We are hated and driven,
Mir vern geplogt un farfolgt,	We are tortured and persecuted.
Un alts nor derfar, vayl mir libn	And all, because we love
Dos oreme, shmachtnde folk.	The poor, languishing people.
Nor keynmol vet undz nit dershrekn	But we shall never be frightened
Gefenkenish un tiranay.	By imprisonment and tyranny.
Mir muzn di mentsh-hayt dervekn,	We must awake humanity,
Un machn zi gliklich un fray.[17]	And make her happy and free.

Aware that his days were numbered, Edelshtat's poems were permeated with the tragedy of a life cut short by the dread disease. But his confidence in the future spoke through his poems which workingmen and women sang with tears rolling down their cheeks.

In my grave too, I shall hear my freedom song. . . . Even there, I shall shed tears for the enslaved Christian and Jew! And when I hear the clang of swords in that final struggle of blood and pain, I shall sing out to the people from my grave and inspire their hearts again.[18]

Edelshtat's "Di tsavoe" ("The Testament") soon enjoyed equal success with his "In kamf" and "his comrades promptly set a suitable melody to it, taken from a Russian revolutionary song."[19] However, his "Der arbeter" ("The Worker") was the poem most absorbed into Eastern European-Yiddish folk song, and whole stanzas from it appeared in several songs current in Eastern Europe at the turn of the century.[20]

The most lyrical of the social poets whose sung texts have lingered the longest in the memory of Yiddish-speaking Americans was Morris Rosenfeld (1862–1923), who came to New York in 1886, the year of the Chicago Haymarket Massacre. For fifteen years, he toiled and suffered from the cruel exploitation, humiliation, and dulling atmosphere of the murky sweatshops. His poems mirrored those sad experiences and were permeated with a deep love and sympathy for his people, who had fled

Czarist poverty and tyranny, only to become enslaved in the miserable clothing factories. Of all the others, he depicted most vividly the life of the Jewish-American workingmen and women during those first years of the great migrations.[21]

A poet of first rank, Rosenfeld often recited and on occasion even sang his poems before gatherings, which made his songs especially popular. Some of them became "folk songs," like his "O, ir kleyne lichtelech" ("Oh, You Little Tapers"), which spoke nostalgically of the heroic days of the Hasmoneans. As for his cradle song "Mayn yingele" ("My Little Boy"), written in 1887, its popularity equaled that of Sholem Aleichem's famous lullaby of the mass migration years. Rosenfeld in this song described a sweatshop father, driven by ceaseless toil and inhumanly long hours, who never gets to see his baby awake, neither morning nor night. Set to music by an anonymous composer, it is still current today in a number of variants, one of which contains the following stanzas:

Ich hob a kleynem yingele,	I have a little boy,
A zunele gor fayn.	A little son so fine.
Ven ich derze im, dacht zich mir:	And when I look at him I think:
Di gantse velt iz mayn.	The whole world is mine.
Nor zeltn, zeltn, ze ich im,	But seldom, seldom, do I see him,
Mayn sheynem ven er vacht.	My lovely one, awake.
Ich tref im imer shlofndig,	I always find him sleeping,
Ich ze im nor baynacht.	I see him only at night.
Di arbet traybt mich fri aroys,	My toil drives me out early,
Un lozt mich shpet tsurik.	And brings me home so late.
O, fremd iz mir mayn eygn layb,	O, strange to me is my own flesh
O, fremd mayn kind's a blik.[22]	And strange my own child's glance.

Although Rosenfeld was concerned with the Jew in every phase of his life in the New World, the social themes of the sweatshop dominated many of his poems. In his "Mayn ru-e plats" ("My Resting Place"), set to music anonymously, he reflected bitterly on the love of a worker who wastes away at the machines. In his "Kesl garden" ("Castle Garden"), which was sung to the tune of Goldfaden's "Faryomert, farklogt" ("In Sorrow, in Tears") and which recalls the style of Winchevsky, he described a scene when new immigrants were waiting to be claimed by their relatives and friends upon their arrival from the old country. Rosenfeld tries to warn these "green" arrivals of the harsh realities facing them in their new environment. His mood in this song is critical and bitter, although he attempts a hopeful attitude in the concluding lines.

Gelt fil un koyech, a gazlen, a
　　rotseyech,
Dos fodert amerike haynt.

A lot of money and power, a
　　gangster, a robber,
That's what America demands
　　today.

Yoysher un varhayt, libe un
　　klarhayt,
Leyder, dos hot men shoyn faynt.
A man fun gevisn, fun ere un
　　recht,

Justice and truth, love and
　　knowledge,
Alas, that is now hated.
A man with a conscience, honor, and
　　justice,

A mentsh mit a mentshleche herts—
Brider, dem iz in amerike
　　shlecht,
Zayn shikzal iz tsores un shmerts.
. . . Doch gibn mir tsu, as frayhayt
　　un ru,
Hobn mir do mer vi iberal.

A man with a human heart—
Brothers, for him it is bad in
　　America,
His fate is trouble and pain.
Yet we must admit, that freedom
　　and security,
We have more of here than
　　anywhere else.

Fun libe un fridn, far kristn un idn,

Tsaygt zich undz do yetst a shtral.[23]

Of love and peace for Christians
　　and Jews,
There now shines a ray here.

During the closing decades of the nineteenth century, the songs of Zunser and Goldfaden were sung in America along with the sung poems of the social poets. Always the mentor and teacher of his people, Zunser was especially productive in his new environment, where his perceptive eye and compassionate heart was deeply concerned with the miserable conditions in the sweatshops, the unproductiveness of peddling, the huge, congested cities and their inhuman pace and clamor. All of these problems Zunser treated in songs which he performed before his audiences and which, in turn, became popular among them. Below are excerpts from his "Dos goldene land" ("The Golden Land"), written in 1897, in which he described a city street, the pushcart trade, and the plight of workingmen.

In di enge gasn, vu di mase shteyt
　　gedicht,
Fil orime, finstere, der unglik ligt
　　oyfn gezicht;
Shteyen fun fri biz baynacht,

In the narrow streets, where the
　　mass stands compressed,
There are many poor and miserable,
　　unhappiness is on every face;
They stand from morning till night,

Di lipn ferbrent un fershmacht.	Their lips parched and burned.
Der iz mafkir zayn kind far a *sent,*	One sacrifices his child for a cent,
Dem varft men fun voynung far rent,	Another is thrown from his dwelling for not paying rent,
Fil grine mit shvern gemit,	Many immigrants in depressed mood,
Faln fun hunger in *strit,*	Fall from hunger on the street,
Fil dalis mit krankhayt banand,	Much poverty and sickness, too,
Alts in dem goldenem land.	Are all found in this golden land.
Dem arbeter's lebn shvimt do avek	The worker's life flows away here
In a taych fun zayn eygenem shveys;	In a river of his own sweat;
Horevet in *bizi* un hungert in *slek,*	He toils during the busy season and starves in the slack
Un iz shtendig in shrek mit zayn *pleys.*	And is always in fear of losing his job.
. . . Der proletar hot do a vert,	The proletarian has as much worth here
Punkt vi in *stritkars* di ferd,	As the horses pulling the streetcars,
Loyft, loyft, bizvanen er falt. . . .[24]	Running, running, until he falls. . . .

A poet and song writer who at first combined the characteristics of the old folk bards side by side with the tendencies of the social poets and then became a popular song writer and theatrical lyricist was Isaac Reingold (1837–1903) of Chicago. Like Rosenfeld, he performed his songs at workers' clubs in Baltimore, Philadelphia, Milwaukee, and Chicago, which popularized them and helped a number to become household songs in the nineties.

Reingold, like Rosenfeld and Edelshtat, worked in the sweatshops, where the harsh, dulling atmosphere called forth in him a series of poems of deep disillusionment with the New World. "I can't believe that the Lord intended such inequalities of rich and poor," he exclaims in one of his poems.[25] Chicago was then struggling for the eight-hour day, which culminated in the Haymarket riot of 1886. This occurrence deeply stirred Reingold, who wrote his song "Vos vet zayn der sof?" ("What Will Be The End?"), in which he called upon the "slumbering workingmen" to awake. Contrasting the productiveness of labor and its miserly returns with the wealth of its parasitic exploiters, Reingold's song was subsequently "folklorized" and sung in several variants in the large centers of compact Jewish communities both in the United States and Eastern Europe. Following are two stanzas and the refrain:

O, elnder arbetsman, shvaygzamer
    knecht,
Vos hoybt men on mit dir tsu ton?
Men roybt dir dayn frayhayt, men
    roybt dir dayn recht,
Un du nemst dayn krivde nit on!

Men lebt oyf dayn chezhbn, men ligt
    oyf dayn kark,
Un alts vos du machst un du tsaygst,
Brengt ayn milionen farmegn der
    mark,
Un du shteyst fun vaytn un
    shvaygst!

Refrain: O, troymende shlefer, ir
        halt in eyn shlof!
        O, zogt-zhe mir troymer,
        zogt, vos vet zayn der
        sof?

Du akerst di felder, du zeyst un du
    shnaydst,
Di erd shaft a raychn profit!
Doch gib a kuk elnder, ze vi du
    laydst,
Dayn feld hot far dir nit geblit!

Du shpinst oys vol—doch hostu
    kayn kleyd,
Du hungerst—chotsh du bakst dos
    broyt!
Du shafst nor fir yenem a lebn fun
    freyd,
Far zich—nor a langzamen toyt! [26]

O, lonely worker, silent slave,

What shall one do with you?
Your liberty and privileges are stolen
    from you,
And you don't stand up for your
    rights!

Others live off you, they ride on
    your neck,
And all that you make and create,
Brings fortunes in millions to the
    trade,
And you stand apart and are silent!

    O, dreaming sleepers, you
        slumber still;
    O, tell me you dreamers,
        what will the end be?

You plough the fields, you sow and
    you reap,
The earth produces a rich profit!
Yet, look at yourself, you lonely
    sufferer,
Your own field has not blossomed
    yet!

You spin the wool—yet you have no
    clothes;
You starve—though you bake the
    bread!
You create only for others a life full
    of joy;
For yourself—you prepare only a
    slow death!

The above was characteristic of Reingold's first creative period, when he dealt with the sentiments of his shopworkers and was in tune with his poetic colleagues Winchevsky, Edelshtat, and Rosenfeld. Like Rosenfeld, he also wrote lyrical and national songs and was the first of his contemporaries to move away from the Eastern European influence. The Jewish theatrical world in America was quick to recognize Reingold's facile talent as a song writer, with the result that almost overnight he became the prolific creator of theatrical songs and ditties for the American-Jewish stage. His ability to capture the spirit of the musical hits of lower Broadway and Thirty-fourth street and convert them into their corresponding terms in Jewish life resulted in a large number of Yiddish songs on every kind of topical event, set to the tunes of current American popular songs of the day. However, Reingold's theatrical and popular songs were the least inspired, although they seemed to fit the current needs of the new immigrants.[27]

The Yiddish theater played an important role in the Americanization process of the new immigrants in the large cities of New York, Boston, Philadelphia, Chicago, and the songs that emanated from it, coupled with the popular songs created for mass consumption, inexorably weaned large sections of the Jewish population away from the old, traditional, Yiddish songs from the old country. The inroads of the dominant American-English culture during this period were deep and willy-nilly, Jewish cultural patterns and habits, customs and traditions were cast off voluntarily in the scramble for identification with the new environment.

Although Jewish emigration from Europe continued to flow right up to the years of World War I, by that time the pattern of life of Eastern European Jews in America had undergone deep-rooted changes of a permanent nature. The ties with the old country had become weaker and the themes in Yiddish literature and song were dealing more often with American problems and the current scene.

Two incidents prior to World War I impressed themselves deeply on the people and were treated in popular songs: one was the Triangle Fire in New York City in 1911, and the other was the sinking of the *Titanic* in 1912.

No one, recalling the tragedy of the Triangle Fire, ever forgot its dreadful consequences; the newspapers of March 25, 1911, reported that 146 young girls, shirtwaist operators, had been burned to death at the top of a firetrap sweatshop in the ten-story Asch Building, not far from Washington Square. Nearly 100,000 east-side inhabitants followed the funeral procession, and poets, journalists, dramatists, in poems, articles, and plays expressed their horror and outrage at the criminal negligence of the employers and their deep sorrow with the tragically bereaved. Unfortunately, however, although in the memory of workingmen today there linger bits and pieces of current songs on the topic, evidence of folk songs created at the time remains at best only fragmentary.

The sinking of the *Titanic* on April 15, 1912, which took the lives of 1,513, was memorialized in Shmulevitsch's (S. "Small") popular song "Churbn titanic" ("The Titanic Disaster"). In it the song writer hails Ida Strauss, wife of the prominent east-side philanthropist, Isidor Strauss, who chose to die beside her husband, rather than save herself with the women and children on the lifeboats of the sinking liner. Below, is an excerpt from Shmulevitsch's song, followed by four lines of an anonymous topical song of the incident that was current in Eastern Europe.

(1)

Ot shteyen, mit veyen,	There stand in agony
Di toyznde in noyt.	The thousands helpless,
Un veysn az shtoysn	Knowing that death will cast them
Vet sey tsum grunt der toyt.	To the bottom of the sea.
Ot shrayt men : "geyt zey retn	There is shouting : "Rescue them,
In shiflech, froyen, shnel,	Into the boats, women, quickly !
Nit vagn zol batretn	Let no man dare to step into the boats
Kayn man gor yene shtel."	Meant for women and children."
Doch hert a froyen zele	Yet listen to one woman
Vos ken a zog ton dan :	Who dared to say just then :
"Ich gey nit fun der shtele,	"I'll not move from this spot,
Ich shtarb do mit mayn man. . . ."	I'll die here with my husband. . . ."
Zoln ern kleyn un groys,	May young and old honor
Dem nomen *ida shtroys*.[28]	The name of Ida Strauss.

(2)

Haynt, shtelt aych for, libe mentshn, di shrekliche kartine,	Now, imagine dear people, the terrible scene,
Ven dos vaser iz arayn in der mashine.	When water seeped into the engines
Un di elektritshestve iz kalye gevorn,	And the electricity was wrecked;
Az och un vey iz tsu zeyere yorn ! [29]	Oh, woe and woe unto their years !

The years following World War I and through the twenties of the twentieth century saw the development of a rich Yiddish literature in the United States. Prominent within it were Yiddish poetry and song, created by professional poets and composers who had migrated to the new land. Generally lyrical in character, these art and semiart songs included children's songs and lullabies, love songs, nature songs, national and work songs. Steeped in traditional Jewish lore and song, linked with a childhood and youth in Eastern Europe still alive in their memory, the work of these poets and composers became increasingly artistic as they mastered the modern poetic and musical media. Many wrote expressly for the Yiddish-speaking sections of the American community, and their poems and songs became the household songs in many a home, fraternal organization, club, trade union, secular summer camp and school. Concert artists performing before Yiddish-speaking audiences included many of these Yiddish art songs in their repertoire, along with "half-authored" songs, which consisted of texts by known poets, set to the music of anonymous composers.

Unusually productive in this area was Avrom Reisin (1876–1953), outstanding short-story writer and poet, who came to America in 1908. His poetic creations include at least fifty texts which were set to music in his lifetime, both by professional and anonymous composers. Several of his songs enjoyed the popularity of folk songs both here and in Eastern Europe, such as "Ma ko mashma lon?" ("What Does It Mean to Me?"), "Hulyet, hulyet, beyze vintn" ("Rage, Rage, Angry Winds"), "O hemerl, hemerl, klap" ("O Little Hammer, Rap"), "Di vant" ("The Wall"), and others.

In Reisin's "Ma ko mashma lon?", which was set to an anonymous melody based on a traditional chant, the poet describes the plight of a lonely Talmudic student, who starves in the house of study waiting for a handout, denying the desires of young life as he wilts under the rigors of his ascetic life. Following is the concluding stanza :

Ma ko mashma lon mayn lebn?	What does my life mean to me?
Vos-zhe lozt es mir tsu hern?	What is it trying to teach me?
Foyln, velkn in der yugnt,	Rotting, withering in my youth,
Far der tsayt fareltert vern.	Growing old before my time.
Esn teg un shlingen trern,	Eating a day here and a day there and choking on my tears,
Shlofn oyfn foyst dem hartn.	Sleeping on my hard fist.
Teytn do, di oylem haze,	Killing the life in the world I live,
Un oyf oylem habo vartn. . . .[30]	And waiting for the life that is to come. . . .

As Zunser in his numerous songs reflected the trials, tribulations, and dreams of his people during his lifetime a generation earlier, so did Reisin, literary man of many gifts, in his numerous stories, poems, and articles. In his "O hemerl, hemerl, klap" he draws a sympathetic picture of the poverty-stricken little cobbler. In his "Di vant" he treats symbolically the struggle of the Jewish workingmen against economic exploitation and Czarist political oppression. In his "Hulyet, beyze vintn" he allegorically compares the angry winds to the Russian autocracy, wreaking havoc on the land. Each of these songs enjoyed widespread popularity and were set to anonymous tunes. Following are two stanzas from "Hulyet" :

Hulyet, hulyet, beyze vintn,	Rage, rage, angry winds,
Fray bahersht di velt !	Rule the world at will !
Brecht di tsvaygn, varft di beymer,	Break the branches, shake the trees
Tut vos aych gefelt !	Do just as you please !
Hulyet, hulyet, beyze vintn,	Rage, rage, angry winds,
Itst iz ayer tsayt !	Now's the time for you !
Lang vet doyern der vinter,	Winter will be very long,
Zumer iz noch vayt. . . ."[31]	Summer is still far off. . . .

Up to the 1920's, the ties between the Eastern European- and American-Jewish communities were still close. Songs created in the "old country" were sung here, and songs which were popular here became part of the song treasure there. Thus, the songs created by Reisin in Eastern Europe gained a popular foothold here, just as his sung poems written here became part of the people's repertoire in Eastern Europe.

Another, who began his literary life in Eastern Europe and who lived the major part of his adult life in America as writer and folklorist, was A. Litvin (S. Hurwitsh, 1862–1943), author of "Di zoknmacherkes" ("The Stockingmakers") and the lullaby, "Zhamele." The latter, which is still sung, in several melodic variants, to an anonymous tune in our own day, speaks sardonically of poverty but tenderly of its victim, "little Ziame" ("Zhamele"). Three stanzas of this cradle song are given below in one of its current variants :

Du vest raych vern, mayn zhamele,	You'll be rich some day, my Zhamele,
Fleg mir zingen bay mayn vigele,	Thus did at my cradle croon to me,
Ale nacht amol mayn mamele,	My mother, every night, long ago,
Ich gedenk noch gut ir nigele.	I still recall her little tune so well.
Un m'kuyim iz gevorn mir,	And it all came true, at long last,
Di havtoches fun mayn mamele,	All the hopes of my mother dear,
Shver tsu krign aza groysn gvir,	You'll not find a rich man anywhere,
Aza'n oysher vi zhamele.	As wealthy as my Zhamele.

Shlofn, shloft er oyf a kerbele,	He sleeps on his little bundle of rags,
Macht hamoytse oyf a skorinke,	Breaks bread, blessing a tiny crust,
Un l'chayim fun a sherbele,	Drinks a toast from a broken shard,
Trinkt er brunim vaser klorinke.[32]	Full of clear sweet water from the well.

A popular sung poet, who came to America after witnessing the 1905 pogrom in Kremenchug, was Michl (Mitchell) Kaplan (1881–1944). He made his debut as a poet in Eastern Europe, and in the United States he wrote many poems in "folk style," expressing the sentiments of the Jewish immigrants of his generation. So vivid and true were his descriptions of the transition from the "old home" and of putting down roots in the new environment, that his poems became very popular, and a number were set to music and performed at concerts and "literary-musical" evenings. Some were even issued on gramophone recordings.

Kaplan wrote bitterly about the unrealized hopes of many who had come to America seeking security, brotherhood, and justice and found

instead a life of hardship, loneliness, and disillusionment. In one song, he draws a contrast between the hope expressed in Sholem Aleichem's famous lullaby, which speaks of the happiness that awaits everyone in America — the "white bread eaten on the weekdays," the father who immediately sends for his family, clasping them joyfully to his breast upon their arrival — with the stark reality of the dreary sweatshops, the periods of unemployment (slack), the soup kitchens, and starvation. Following are three stanzas from this song:

Ludlov strit . . . bitere, voynungen hoyche,
Finstere shtign a sach. . . .
Zunenyu, do voynt dayn tate, dayn orimer!
Opgetsert iz er un shvach.

Ludlow St . . . dreary tall dwellings,
Many dark stairways there. . . .
Dear son, here lives your poor father!
Emaciated and weak is he.

Tsdoke kich . . . tuchlekeyt . . . broyt altgebakene, . . .
Shitere, bitere yoych. . . .
Zunenyu, do est dayn tate, dayn orimer!
Klogt er zich, shpayzt zich mit roych. . . .

Charity kitchen . . . putrid . . . stale bread, . . .
Watery, bitter soup. . . .
Dear son, here your poor father eats!
Complaining, he feeds on smoke. . . .

Glust er a shifskarte koyfn oyf oystsoln,
Kloybt zich aheym shoyn fun lang. . . .
Zunenyu, slek heyst a tsayt aza bitere,
Shtert dos dayn tatn in gang.[33]

He wants to buy a steamship ticket on payments,
Planning to return home for a long time now. . . .
Dear son, "slack" is a dreadful period,
And it stands in your father's way.

Another sung poem by Kaplan describes the nostalgia for the old home, the tragedy of young lovers permanently separated by economic adversity, and the instability of those who were not able to adjust so readily to the conditions in the new home. The ballad "Baym obshid" ("At Parting"), describes two friends bidding each other good-bye. One is returning home, the other, despite the harshness of the big city, its poverty and sweatshops, remains, but sends his greetings home with his friend.

When you return safely home after your long journey, tell my folks about everything, but leave me out of it; don't tell them anything about me. . . . If my father asks about me, don't tell him how hard I work. If he wants to know how much I earn, give him the figures in rubles. . . . If my poor mother inquires about me, don't tell her everything you know. Rather tell her that I eat roasted meats and wheaten bread, and she'll be delighted with my good fortune! . . . If my dear brother asks about me, don't tell him how lonely I am. Tell him that here one can buy 'brothers' in the Verein, just by paying one's dues. . . ."

The poet lists others who were once dear to him: an old friend, his teacher, his sweetheart who waited for him so long until she married another, while all the time he was desperately trying to earn enough to bring her over. Following are two stanzas from this ballad:

Un vet oyf mir fregn a chaver an alter,	And should my old friend ask about me,
Nit zog im, mir vilt zich tsurik.	Don't tell him that I want to come home.
Dertseyl im chidushim fun sobvey, elektri,	Regale him with the marvels of the subway and electricity,
Er't meynen ich bod zich in glik.	And he'll think I'm swimming in luck.
Un vet oyf mir fregn R'foel der lerer,	And should Raphael, my teacher, inquire,
Nit zog, ch'ob farlorn mayn veg.	Don't tell him that I've lost my way.
Dertseyl im, ich shrayb in gazetn, er't meynen,	Tell him I write for the papers, and he'll think
Ich shvim azoy zicher tsum breg.[34]	That I'm solidly set on my goal.

The American contribution to Yiddish song has come to be identified, in the main, with art songs and songs in folk style. The old Yiddish folk song from Eastern Europe, which traversed the Atlantic Ocean together with the tens of thousands who came to build the largest Jewish community of modern times, did not continue to propagate itself on the new soil in the same way as it had done in the old country. Instead, like wine of centuries stored in the old vessels, it was poured into new bottles to serve the Yiddish-speaking multitudes in their new home, under new conditions.

Following the twenties, Yiddish-speaking Americans leaned more and more on Yiddish art songs and songs in folk style written by poets and composers,[35] although many still preserved the old Yiddish folk songs that had fed and inspired these professional creations. However, as the numbers speaking the Yiddish vernacular decreased, the number of "remembered" Yiddish folk songs from the old home decreased also, and substantial portions of this rich Jewish cultural heritage were forgotten.

Although practically non-existent today as a creative process, Yiddish *folk song* is still remarkably well preserved in the memory of Yiddish-speaking Americans. It is a rich source for study and investigation by scholars seeking to shed light on the life of the many-millioned, Eastern European Jewish community — the largest Jewish settlement of modern times, which is now no more. Such a study will also illuminate, no doubt, the formative years of the American-Jewish community as it was revealed in the Yiddish songs created on American soil.

Notes

TO AMERICA

1. Three streams of Jewish immigrants flowed into America. On the eve of the American Revolution, out of a total population in the Colonies of about 3 million, there were from two to three thousand Jews, of which the majority were of Sephardic descent. Following the Revolution of 1848, thousands of Jews came to America from Germany. During the 1870's, 80's, and 90's, the great mass migration from Eastern Europe took place. Today, of the 5.5 million Jews in the United States, the majority are of Eastern European origin, and in the census of 1940 some 2 million indicated Yiddish as their mother tongue.

2. Rubin, MSS. The problem of the deserted wife involves a point of Jewish law, which extends only to the husband the privilege of granting the divorce. With the husband away, unheard from, the deserted wife cannot remarry until such a time as the errant man grants her a divorce.

3. Cahan, 1957, No. 116.

4. Kremer, pp. 36–37.

5. Mlotek, pp. 186–187 (A. Litvin, MSS, YIVO, No. 904).

6. Yivo Exhibit: "Dos shtetl in mezrech eyrope 1900–1939," New York, 1958, No. 333.

7. Kobrin, pp. 36–37, p. 89.

8. Skuditsky, 1936, p. 112, No. 14.

9. *See* Warshawsky, p. 5.

10. Sheet music, Albert Teres, publisher, New York, 1921. S. Shmulevitsch (S. Small, 1868–1943) came to America in 1889 and was the author and composer of popular and theatrical songs in Europe and America. At the age of thirty he was writing texts and tunes for a number of *badchonim* in the Vilna region and composing tunes for some of Shomer's (*Shaikevitsch*) plays which appeared in Warsaw. In America, he wrote texts and tunes for more than five hundred Yiddish songs.

11. *See* Rubin, 1950, pp. 23–24.

12. As a youth in Lithuania, Winchevsky was influenced by the Haskalah movement, the popular Socialist ideas of the *narodniks* ("Populists"), collected funds for the needy in Palestine, and tried to reach Maskilim and Hebrew scholars with his ideas, in Hebrew. During his residence in London, he worked actively for the betterment of conditions of Jewish workers of the East End, and his pamphlets and articles exerted a strong influence on workingmen both there and in the United States. A master of dialect, skillful poet, man of high culture, he was conversant with the literatures of Russia, France, Germany. and England. Aside from original stories and sketches, poetry and sociological articles, he translated a number of works into Yiddish, among them Victor Hugo's *Les Misérables*.

13. I. Glatstein, pp. 100–101 (written in 1890).

14. B. and F., pp. 88–89 (written in 1886).

15. *Am Olam* ("People of the world") was an organization founded in 1881 with the purpose of organizing agricultural communes in the United States.

16. B. and F., pp. 72–73. "Of Edelshtat's fourteen sung poems, eight were written

365

during the first half of 1889: "In kamf" ("In Struggle"), "Di tsavoe" ("The Testament"), "Natur un mentsh" ("Nature and Man"), "In land fun piramidn" (In the Land of Pyramids"), "Mayn letste hofnung" ("My last Hope"), "Der shnayder" ("The Tailor"), "Der arbeter" ("The Worker"), and "Der veker" ("The Awakener"). Three of them "In kamf," "Der arbeter," and "Di tsavoe"—became Yiddish work and struggle folk songs in Russia, and revolutionary organizations there utilized them for propaganda purposes. The Czarist government consequently persecuted workers caught with Edelshtat's poetry in their possession." (Marmor, p. 50).

17. B. and F., pp. 80–81. "Edelshtat suggested to his sister that she sing *In kamf* to the tune of *Ich zits bay mayn arbet* ('I sit at my Work'), a Yiddish folk song, which soon became popular" (Marmor, p. 50).

18. *See* B. and F., pp. 84–85.

19. Marmor, p. 50.

20. *See* D. and Y., pp. 345–346, 14–15. Stanzas 1, 2, and 14 from Edelshtat's "Der arbeter" were the ones most absorbed into Yiddish folk song.

21. Rosenfeld wrote both joyous and sad poetry on lyrical, social, and national themes at a time in Jewish-American history when a new cultural epoch was coming into being. Discovered by Dr. Leo Wiener, Professor of Literature at Harvard University at that time, Rosenfeld's poetry was translated at first into English and then into a number of other European languages, which made him world renowned. Morris Rosenfeld used to appear often in concerts, reciting his poetry with a great deal of verve, and he would also sing his poems to which tunes had been written by himself or by others. "Only a few of his melodies have come down to us; others disappeared, only to re-emerge in barely recognizable form as folk songs. . . . His earliest songs were modeled on synagogue chants . . . or on the melodies he learned from his father during prayers. . . . Later, he adapted variations of Jewish folk songs and Russian melodies. . . . Some of the well-known composers who set Rosenfeld's verses to music were Platon Brounoff, H. A. Russotto, and Solomon Golub" (Goldenthal, pp. 162–163).

22. Rubin, 1950, pp. 25–26. Appeared in *Tsukunft*, New York, Jan. 1893, a monthly publication, still current today.

23. "Di yidishe bine," pp. 472–474.

24. Zunser, I, pp. 274–279. Zunser employs American expressions in this Yiddish song: *sent* ("cent"), *rent* ("rent"), *bizi* ("busy"), *slek* ("slack"), *stritkars* ("streetcars").

25. Reingold, p. 57.

26. Sheet music, New York, 1898, Hebrew Publishing Co.

27. "The catalog of his (Reingold's) adaptations is the catalog of most of the popular tunes of the eighties and nineties: 'In the Good Old Summer Time,' 'Absence Makes the Heart Grow Fonder,' 'After the Ball,' 'Break the News to Mother,' 'On a Sunday Afternoon,' to mention some of the better known" (Reingold, Intro., p. xxiii).

28. Sheet music, New York, 1912, Hebrew Publishing Co.

29. Rubin, MSS.

30. Reisin, p. 16. Reisin began publishing his poems early in the 1890's. At the turn of the century he was already regarded as the "most popular sung poet of the Jewish workingclass movement" in Eastern Europe. In America, he achieved the standing of the "most loved and popular Yiddish poet" and a number of his sung poems, both of the earlier period in the old country and those he created here, enjoyed the popularity of folk songs.

31. *Ibid.*, p. 36.

32. Rubin, MSS.

33. Kaplan, pp. 136–137. Sixty of Kaplan's Yiddish poems were translated by "L. G. and M. S." and published in New York in 1927 by the Jewish-American Literary and Dramatic Guild, entitled: *Just Folks* by Mitchell Kaplan.

34. *Ibid.*, pp. 61–62.

35. Yiddish art songs and songs in folk style in America were considerably enriched by such poets as: Yehoash, D. Einhorn, Mani Leib, Z. Weinper, H. Rosenblatt, Y. Rolnik, I. Rontsh, Z. Landau, M. L. Halperin, H. Leivick, and many others; and such composers as: H. Russotto, P. Brounoff, Solomon Golub, Leo Low, H. Lefkowitch, Michl Gelbart, Sholem Secunda, A. Ellstein, J. Schaeffer, Lazar Weiner, Max Helfman, and many more. This list is far from complete, and the whole panorama of Yiddish art songs in America calls for a thorough treatment. (*See also* Chapter X: "Of Literary Origin.")

CHAPTER XIV

To Zion

THE DISLOCATIONS RESULTING FROM THE ABOLITION OF SERFDOM IN Czarist Russia in 1861, the economic depression of the seventies followed by economic and political repressions and the pogroms of the eighties, resulted in a steady flow of great masses of Jews away from Eastern Europe. The larger stream was directed towards the United States, while smaller rivulets flowed towards Canada, South America, Australia, South Africa, and Palestine.

Several prominent Haskalah leaders began to advocate a return to the ancient homeland.

Under the shock of the first pogroms, in the autumn of 1881, Lilienblum (Moses Loeb, 1843–1910) sounded the call for a return to the ancient land of the fathers, should it take a whole century to carry it through. In 1882, Leo Pinsker (1821–1891) . . . published a brochure, in which he admonished his fellow-Jews to look for salvation in "self-emancipation," in the creation of a national retreat somewhere on the earth, preferably on the banks of the Jordan, but if necessary on those of the Mississippi.[1]

While the pamphlet was still at the printers, a group of Jewish university students in Kharkov organized a circle, called *Bilu,* with a plan to establish an agricultural colony in Palestine.[2] Peretz Smolenskin, who had consistently stressed the acquisition of a general secular knowledge and culture side by side with Jewish culture and learning, intensified his work for the development of the Hebrew language and a return to Zion.[3]

Elyokum Zunser, veteran folk bard, who wrote a number of Zion songs, described these early beginnings of the Zion migrations in his autobiographical work :

The pogroms made the Jews realize that, having been organized by the

368

Russian government itself, their blood and property meant nothing to it. . . .
A broad movement began . . . to emigrate. In this . . . there were two
trends : the practical and the idealistic. The practical people emigrated to
America, a land which received them with open arms and gave them all the
rights, together with all other Americans. . . . The idealists held that the best
home for them is the old home — Zion.[4]

When the first group of Jewish university students of the *Bilu*, from
Kharkov, passed through Minsk on their way to Palestine, they visited
Zunser. Zunser was so moved by the sacrifices of these educated young
men, coming from comfortable homes, unaccustomed to hardships, that
he wrote his "Shivas tsion" ("Return to Zion"), in Yiddish and Hebrew,
a stanza of which is given below :

Ot dize yunge mentshn,	Oh, these young people
Vet di velt zey bentshn,	Will be blessed by all the world,
Ferlozn hayzer, giter, glantz un	They leave their homes, possessions,
glik un pral;	honor, happiness, prestige;
.Mentshn geshtudirte,	Educated people,
Hoych tsivilizirte,	Highly civilized,
Viln zayn korbones far dem gantsn	Who want to sacrifice themselves
klal !	for all !
Zey hobn zich bashlosn,	They have made their mind up,
Oyf alerley fardrosn,	To face all kinds of hardships,
Nor optsuvarfn ale shteyner vos lign	And to remove the stones that bar
oyfn veg. . . .	their way. . . .
Tsu laydn shverikeytn;	To suffer all reverses;
Vi in Ezra's tsaytn,	Like in the time of Ezra,
Un zeyer nomen blaybt vi Ezra's biz	Their name, like Ezra's, will remain
di letste teg ! [5]	for evermore !

These first pioneers of Jewish Eastern European migrations to Palestine in the eighties "found a barren land, a veritable desert, where yellow
fever raged throughout the year, where . . . fresh water had to be collected
from the clay ditches after a rainfall, . . . where they were attacked by
wild Bedouins and Arabs with whom they fought desperately."[6]

When the first organized group of the *Chov'vey Tsion* ("Lovers of
Zion")[7] from Minsk founded the colony of *Chadera,* Zunser wrote his
"Di soche" ("The Plow"), a song which became popular in all Yiddish-
speaking communities and is still remembered to the present day. Following is a stanza of this song :

In soche,	In the plow
Ligt di mazl broche,	Lies good fortune,
Der varer glik fun lebn,	The true joy of life,
Kayn zach mir nit felt.	And I lack nothing more.
Es kumt der frimorgn,	When morning dawns,
Ich darf nit layen, borgn,	I need not borrow,
Der moyech darf nit zorgn,	My mind is free of worries
Oyf tog hoytso-es gelt,	For the day's necessities,
Es iz ongegreyt oyf vinter,	I have laid in a good supply
A zasik a gezunter,	For the winter,
Ich zey, ich shnayd gants munter,	I sow and reap merrily,
Fray in gotes velt.[8]	Free in God's world.

Gatherings and conferences were held in different parts of the Pale. A variety of plans and measures to colonize Palestine with Jewish farmers and laborers were everywhere discussed.[9] Although during the nineties, Yiddish and Hebrew Zion songs had already become part of the song repertoire of the people as a whole, not until Dr. Theodor Herzl came out with his *Der Judenstaat* ("The Jewish State") in 1896 was political Zionism officially launched. The Zion songs were created anonymously as well as by literary men and Zionist activists and reflected various sentiments and different approaches toward the realization of an old dream.

A predominant theme at first was the effort to recall the glorious days of old, when Israel was a kingdom and had its own rulers, its own warriors. The Czarist pogroms revived the memory of the fall of the ancient kingdom and the exile into Babylonia, and Psalm 137 became the basis for several songs, which were current among the people, such as the following:

Dort in bovl lebn ire taychn,	There in Babylonia, beside her rivers,
Zitst der alter yisroel farveynt.	Sits old Israel in tears.
Tsu zayn groysn umglik iz nito kayn glaychn,	There is no tragedy as great as his,
Dos harts in im iz gor farshteynt.	His heart is numb within him.
Men hot im fun zayn land aroysgetribn,	He was driven from his own land
Ahin kayn bovl im in plen gebracht,	And brought as a prisoner to Babylonia,
Dos land oyf ash farbrent, oyf shtoyb tseribn,	His land was burned to ashes, ground into the dust,
Ales, ales umgebracht.[10]	Everything, everything was destroyed.

Another song, popular in the United States at the time, utilized the same Psalm to list the trials and tribulations endured by the Jews during their long exile. Reingold in Chicago described the Babylonian victors taunting their Jewish captives in his poem set to a current, popular, American tune. Two stanzas follow:

Dort hobn bafoyln di groyzame faynd,
Undz machndig hilfloz un mid,
Mir zoln zey zingen vi damols zo haynt,
Fun tsion dos heylige lid.
Vi kent ir ferlangen fun undz aza zach?
Mir shtarbn shoyn liber fun shverd!
Eyder dermonen tsion's heylige shprach,
Oyf fremde, nit eygene erd! [11]

There, the cruel foe ordered us,

In our utter helplessness,
To sing as we did long ago

The holy songs of Zion.
How can you ask such a thing of us?

We'd rather die by the sword!
Rather than utter Zion's holy tongue
On strange land, not our own!

The first founding conference to unite all Zionist groups was held in Basle in 1897. Seven years earlier, a poem entitled "Dort vu di tseder" ("There, There the Cedars") saw its first musical performance in Yiddish in Lemberg and later became the most popular Yiddish Zionist hymn to grace the Basle gathering. Two stanzas are given below:

Dort, vu di tseder hoych di volkn kist,
Dort, vu di shnele yarden's-vele flist,

Dort, vu di ashe mayner eltern rut,

Dort, vu gegosn hot makabeyer-blut;

Yenes sheynes land, baym bloyen vasserzand,
Dort iz mayn libes foterland!

Un ven es iz mir fun shikzal doch bashert,
Tsu shtarbn fri oyf fremde lenders erd,
Dan leygt mir shnel in keyver's kalte vent,

There, where the tall cedars kiss the clouds,
There, where the waves of the Jordan swiftly flow,
There, where the ashes of my fathers rest,
There, where the blood of Maccabees was spilled;
That lovely land beside the strand so blue,
There is my beloved fatherland!

And if my fate has so decreed for me,
That I must die in a stranger's land,
Then place me quickly in the cold, cold grave,

Mit mayn ponim tsu tsion's hingevendt;	And turn my face towards Zion's ground;
Un shit oyf mayn gezicht tsion's vayse zand,	And sprinkle on it Zion's white sand,
Dan troym ich fun mayn foterland! [12]	And I shall dream of my own fatherland!

The above, which had originally been written by Isaac Feld in German, circulated among the people in a number of textual and melodic variants, and like Zunser's "Di soche," served a practical purpose for those who on the eve of the twentieth century had decided to revive and nurture once again the age-old yearning for Zion.

The deep desire to return to Zion, expressed in Jewish literature, lore, song, and prayer through the centuries, had become part of the traditional fabric of Judaism in all lands. "What the Jews lacked in political hopes they partly made up by their love for an idealized Zion. This love for Zion was created anew by the medieval poets of the synagogue; and in many a gloomy hour Israel found solace in the hope that once more the law would go forth from Zion." [13]

Following the tenth century, the table songs on Friday evenings or Sabbath mornings in Jewish households often included this theme. [14] Remembering Zion was a national and traditional duty, permeating many a prayer in the Middle Ages. It influenced many a Jewish custom [15] and recurred in a number of Judah Halevi's wedding odes. In some of Halevi's sea poems, it is the central motif, revolving around his decision to leave Spain, his loved ones, and a life of security, prestige, and honor to seek the distant shores of Zion. In fear and trembling for the strange unknown but driven by his passionate yearning, he crossed many seas, trod through wastes, faced the perils of mountain lions and leopards, so that once and for all he might cease to walk with head bowed to the ground in a stranger's land and could again hold the festal dance in the midst of his beloved Jerusalem. [16]

The modern Zionists naturally found in Halevi's poems an echo to their own aspirations, and Chaim Nachman Bialik (1873–1934), outstanding figure in contemporary Hebrew letters, whose poetry was one of the spiritual factors that shaped the Zionist movement, translated several of Halevi's Zion sea poems into Yiddish. Music was set to these texts, and the songs achieved a widespread usage. The following stanzas are from one of the most popular of these sea songs:

Ch'ob fargesn ale libste,   I've forgotten all my loved ones,
Ch'ob farlozt mayn eygn hoyz,   I have left my house and home.
Ch'ob dem yam zich opgegebn,   I have gone to sail the seas,
Trog mich yam, tsum muter's shoys!   Bear me, sea, to my mother's hearth!

Refrain: Un du maariv-vint   And you, West Wind, true
     getrayer,   and trusty,
     Trayb mayn shif tsu yenem   Drive my ship to that
     breg,   distant shore,
     Vos mayn harts mit   Where my heart with the
     odler-fligl,   wings of an eagle
     Zucht shoyn lang tsu im a   Has been seeking a path
     veg.   since days of yore.

Breng mich nor ahin b'sholem,   Only bring me there in safety,
Nochdem fli zich dir tsurik.   Then you can fly right back again.
Grisn zolstu ale libste,   Bring my greetings to my loved ones,
Dertseyl zey dortn fun mayn glik.[17]   Tell them of my new-found joy.

The idyllic dream of ancient Zion, the mourning at the loss of the old crown, was interpreted by a number of poets and bards toward the close of the century. Shmuel Frug (1860–1916) wept bitterly at the tragic sufferings of his people during the pogroms of the eighties and nineties. Several of his poems were set to anonymous melodies and sung everywhere, as for instance his "Zamd un shtern" ("Sand and Stars"), in which he recalls the vow made by the Lord to Abraham (Genesis 13:16; 15:5). Frug's sung poem was a bitter cry from the heart when he pointed out to the Lord that only half of his vow had been fulfilled!

Yo gotenyu, emes, vi zamd un vi   Yes, dear God, it is true that like
     shteyner,   sand and like stones,
Tsushpreyt un tsuvorfn oyf shand un   We've been scattered, dispersed,
     oyf shpot. . . .   mocked, and shamed. . . .
Nu, ober di shtern, di lichtige, di   But where are the stars, those bright,
     klore—   brilliant lights—
Di shtern di shtern vu zenen zey   The stars, the stars oh, where are
     got?[18]   they, God?

Drawing upon the mood of the Book of Lamentations, Frug, Zunser, and Goldfaden wept over the suffering of their people under Czarist brutalities and created the figure of the widow of Zion, mourning the loss of her child, Israel.[19] The "letter device" used in a number of songs created in America was used also here, in the form of correspondence between the lonely mother of Zion in Palestine, who was waiting anxiously for some word from her wandering children of Israel.[20] Nostalgic descriptions of the ancient homeland, where "the roses bloom in the vale of Sharon and Mt. Carmel exudes the loveliest scents," where the lambs frolic over the gentle hillsides and the graves of the fathers wait for the return of the exiles, filled the poetry both of the anonymous poets and the literary men. Passing from the nostalgic to the purposeful, Zionist poets on the one hand recalled the loss of the old kingdom, her treasures looted, her glory departed, her leaders slain and exiled, humiliated, persecuted, and on the other attempted to stir the people into returning to the ancient homeland again to rebuild and restore "her glory."

In this wise, did Goldfaden's song "Hashiveynu nazad" ("Let Us Return") direct his brethren to return to Zion, as he described them, uprooted, standing on the road, undecided as to which way to turn:

Dort oyf dem shlyach,	There on the road,
Elnd, on a dach,	Abandoned without a roof,
Shefelech a sach,	Many little sheep
Farblondzhete shteyn.	Stand, forlorn.
Geretet fun toyt,	Saved from death,
In shreklicher noyt,	In terrible need,
Tsurisn di hoyt,	Their skin torn
Fun velf's sharfe tseyn.	By wolves' sharp teeth.
Dos zaynen mayne brider	These are my brothers,
Fun gants faynem shtand,	Of fine origin,
Begazlt, fertribn	Robbed, driven out
Fun zeyer foterland;	Of their fatherland.
Zey zuchn a heym,	They seek a home,
A ru-ig shtikl ort,	A peaceful place,
Genug shoyn tsu zayn navenad;	Enough of this wandering;
Vos shteyt ir un tracht?	Why do you stand there pondering?
Ayer heym iz gor dort,	Your home is there,
Kayn tsion! hashiveynu nazad! [21]	In Zion! Let us go back!

Idyllic phantasies, nostalgic memories, bitter laments—these motifs were soon replaced by others which rang out with joyousness and determination about agricultural pursuits and hard productive labor that was to turn Palestine from a barren waste into a blooming garden once more. The first attempts at a wholesale immigration into destitute Palestine having failed after the first *Bilu* efforts, these were followed by a more realistic approach to establish a foothold with the few who came, small though their numbers were.

The turn of the century had already witnessed a partial realization of the fond hopes of enterprising Zionists and pioneers in the establishment of a number of agricultural settlements in Palestine. Zunser spoke

Herzl T. Rome, 1950

Roadbuilder

prophetically of Zionism as "a river which begins from a little stream as thin as a thread, becoming ever wider and deeper . . . until it becomes large enough for the biggest ocean liner to sail on it."[22] Mark Warshawsky's "Leshono habo b'yerusholayim" ("The Coming Year in Jerusalem") gained the widest popularity, describing the joy of living in peace and productive labor on one's own land, where "no more Jewish blood will flow. . . . When a stranger will come to our land, we will extend to him our friendly hand; for only he knows of another's pain who has suffered misery himself."[23]

Similarly, did Warshawsky's "Dos lid fun dem broyt" ("The Song of the Bread"), which he "dedicated to the Jewish colonists to sing in the field after their work," become a "folk song" of the people. Following are three stanzas:

Groyser got! mir zingen lider—
Undzer hilf bizt du aleyn!

Great Lord! We sing our songs—
You alone are our salvation!

Nemt tsenoyf di snopes, brider,
Biz di zun vet untergeyn.

Loz di zun undz bri-en, brotn,
Zi hot undz geshaynt tsum glik :
Zet, dos broyt iz undz gerotn.
Kinder, keynmol nit tsurik !

Lozn undzere kinder visn
Fun a lebn oyf der velt,
Az dos broyt, un yeder bisn,
Iz fun undzer eygn feld ! [24]

Brothers, gather up the sheaves
Before the sun sets.

Let the sun burn and scorch us,
It has shone upon our joy :
See, the bread that we are reaping.
Children, we will never go back !

Let our future generations
Know the good life in this world,
That the bread and every mouthful
Has been reaped from our own field !

In the United States at that time, Morris Rosenfeld responded to the movement towards Zion. In his Chanukah poem, "O, ir kleyne lichtelech" ("Oh, You Little Tapers"), which was set to music anonymously and has become Yiddish folk song everywhere, he wistfully recalled the "glorious days of old" when the Jewish nation was victorious under the Hasmoneans.[25] In his "Der yidisher may" ("The Jewish May"), he described the sweetness of spring, which brings renewed life to all the world except to the weary, plodding Jew, who can only dream of a bygone age. Attempting to rekindle in the heart of the suffering Jew a new image of himself with confidence in a bright future, Rosenfeld stirred his listeners in this sung poem, which achieved popularity and from which the following stanzas are excerpted :

Zingen vestu hirtn-lider,
Pashendig dort dayne shof.
Lebn vestu, lebn vider,
Lebn eybig, on a sof.

Keyner vet dich mer nisht traybn,
Mit zilzulim on a tsol;
In der heym vestu farblaybn
Shtil un ru-ig, vi amol.

Tret fanander nor di stezhke,
Fun dayn altn foterland,
S'glit noch dort a holeveshke,
Bay der ayngefalener vant ! [26]

You will sing shepherd songs
As you tend your sheep.
You will live once again,
You will live forever.

No one will hound you anymore
With insults endlessly,
In your own home you will remain
Quiet and peaceful as of yore.

Trod again then, on the path
Of your old fatherland,
An ember still glows there
Beside the crumbling wall !

In Chicago, the facile song writer Isaac Reingold similarly responded to the first Zionist World Congress in Basle in 1897 with his song "Ich bin a yid" ("I Am a Jew"), containing the following lines :

O tsion ! Varf arop dayn troyer,
Zol dayn vey fershtumen;
Bald kumen freydn in dayn moyer,

Dayne libe kumen!
Meg der gang zayn doplt shverlech
Meg der veg zayn vi geferlech,
Meg a velt mit gegner brumen.
Zey kumen doch! Zey kumen! [27]

O Zion! Cast off your sorrow,
May your anguish cease;
Soon happiness will enter your
   fortress,
Your loved ones are returning!
May the route be doubly hard,
May the road be full of dangers,
May a world of enemies roar.
They will come! They come!

Among the religious Jews, Zionism never did become widespread. The major part of orthodox Jewry, together with the Chasidic rabbis and their followers, were hostile to this movement, which they regarded as a threat to the idea that the Messiah would be the one to lead the Jews back to the land of their fathers. Wherever a Chasidic follower or other orthodox Jew was attracted to Zionism, however, his aspirations differed from the general secular trends of the movement. The belief in the Messiah was too deep among the orthodoxy for them to accept the notion that mere humans would be leading the Jewish exiles back to the ancient homeland. Those religious Jews who, in their suffering under Czarism, looked to a return to Zion placed their faith rather in the Lord: *Ze Got, undzere trern, / undzer noyt un payn, / veynen veln mir nit ufhern / biz di g'ule vet zayn* ("Witness, Lord, our tears, our misery and pain. We will not cease our weeping until redemption will come").[28]

However, once the program of colonization and settlement in Palestine took root and Jews were actually reconstituting a home in Zion, the majority of orthodox Jewry regarded this process with alarm and bitterly opposed the enterprise.[29] Here and there, however, some orthodox Jews envisaged the new Palestine as a future home for Jews that would also include the revival of the ancient ceremonials and a strict adherence to Jewish Law. Following is a popular folk song which combined the joys of religious ceremonials and agricultural pursuits.

Oyf di hoyche berger :
Karmel, har hazeysim,
Shpatsirn kinder kleyne,
Yisroel, am k'doyshim.

Refrain: Zingt-zhe ale yidelech,
Dem nign dem nayim,
Lernt aych di lidelech
Fun yerushalayim.

On the high hills :
Mount Carmel and Mount of Olives,
Walk the little children
Of Israel, a holy people.

Sing then Jewish children,
The new tune,
Study the new songs
Of Jerusalem.

Tvu-e veln mir zeyen,	We will sow wheat
Mayser veln mir gebn,	And give tithes,
Mir veln zich ale freyen,	We will all be happy,
Yisroel, mit undzer lebn.	Israel, with our life.
Dray mol in yor	Three times a year,
Veln mir oyleregl zayn,	We will go on foot,
N'sochim veln mir brengen	We will bring sacrifices
Fun dem bestn vayn.	Of the best wine.
Demlt vet got zogn:	Then the Lord will say:
Azoy iz mir gefeln,	All this pleases me,
Dos beys-hamikdosh zolt ir	Now you may build the Holy
boyen,	Temple
Dem mizbeyech zolt ir shteln![30]	And set up the altar!

The working-class movement in Russia which spearheaded the struggle against Czarist autocracy and terror included a number of Jewish workingmen and women, who actively participated in the revolution of 1905. There were also Jewish workers, who through their own organizations, the most prominent of which was the Bund, sought to solve the Jewish problem within the framework of the general conditions in Russia.[31] Others, in the Labor-Zionist organization (*Poale Zion*), regarded a "labor Palestine" and the unity between their labor viewpoint and the establishment of a homeland in Palestine as the only answer to the problem. This conflict is revealed in the following stanzas of a song which was current among non-Zionist workers to the tune of Warshawsky's "Dos lid fun dem broyt":

Vi kent ir arbeter zayn tsefridn,	How can you workers be satisfied,
Vos mir veln hobn undzer eygn land;	With the idea of a land of our own;
Dortn veln hershn di rayche yidn,	There, the rich Jews will only rule over us,
Nor mir verker—bay zey in hant.	And we workers will be in their power.
Derum zolt ir, arbeter, oyf dem nit kukn,	Therefore, workers, don't follow this path,
Blaybt nor nit oyf an ort shteyn,	And also don't remain undecided;
Nemt aych tsuzamen ale shvester un brider	Gather together, sisters and brothers,
Un tsum kamf muzn mir geyn.[32]	We must go forward in struggle.

A folk song in which workers of both the Bund and the *Poale Zion* groups are satirized, patterns itself after Zbarzher's "Kum aher du filozof." In it, the Zionist workers are mocked for "running to all the balls" to raise funds for the purchase of land from the Turkish government, while the Bund members are ridiculed because they run from the open clashes with the Czarist military.[33] A variant of this song presents the point of view of the Socialist Jewish workers, who believed that the solution to the problem lay within the framework of the general situation in the Czarist lands.

M'hot undz gevolt farnarn kayn tsion,	They wanted to entice us to Zion,
Mir zoln zayn tsionistn.	So that we may become Zionists.
Neyn, mir veln zayn in rusland,	No, we'd rather stay in Russia,
Mir veln zayn sotsialistn.	We will be Socialists.
M'hot undz gevolt farnarn kayn tsion,	They wanted to entice us to Zion,
Mir zoln di erd grobn;	So that we may dig the earth;
Mir veln beser zayn in rusland,	We'd rather stay in Russia,
Un di frayhayt hobn.[34]	And have freedom.

But the Zionist movement was now a fact, and the second *aliyah* ("migration") was now in full swing. The songs took on new spirit and a new rhythm: *Heybt dem becher, brider, hecher, / trinkt dem gutn karmel vayn / mir veln noch in tsion zayn!* ("Raise your glass, brothers, drink up the good Carmel wine. We shall yet be in Zion").[35] Even the popular Zionist ditty given below, which speaks of the religious Jews' sad pilgrimage to the Holy Land, concludes joyously.

Oyfn veg shteyt a boym,	On the road there stands a tree,
Shteyt er ayngeboygn.	It is bending over.
Fort a yid kayn erets-yisroel,	A Jew is traveling to Israel
Mit farveynte oygn.	With weeping eyes.
Got, got, groyser got,	God, God, great God,
Lomir davenen minche.	Let us say the *minche* prayer,
Az mir veln kumen kayn erets-yisroel,	When we come to Israel,
Vet zayn a groyse simche! [36]	There will be great rejoicing!

A sung poem in march rhythm, Morris Rosenfeld's "Zelner fun tsion" ("Sentries of Zion"), decried the pilgrimages of religious Jews who looked upon Palestine only as a place to go to in their advanced years to be interred after death.

Mir viln in tsion nit shtarbn,	We don't want to die in Zion
Nor oyflebn freylech un fray.	But live again happy and free,
Yo, binden dort undzere garbn,	Yes, bind up our sheaves there,
Un fitern shof fun dos nay.	And tend to our flocks of sheep.
Mir viln dort eylbertn flantsn,	We want to plant olive trees there
Un zingen tehilim derbay,	And sing our Psalms as we work;
Mir viln noch zen dortn glantsn	We want once again to witness the glory
Dem alt-nayem, yidishn may.	Of the old-new Jewish May.
Refrain: Mit mut, mit mut geshvinder!	With courage, courage, quickly!
Avrohom's un yankev's kinder,	Children of Abraham and Jacob,
Hoybt oyf di vayse fone,	Raise the white flag,
Un trilert mit kavone:	And sing with all your heart:
Eyn got, eyn land, eyn gloybn,	One God, one land, one faith,
Iz undz bashert fun oybn.[37]	Ordained for us from above.

    Some satirical songs even introduced an element of gentle banter, as in the following, which satirized the Chasidic vision of Zion as a Garden of Eden where goats nibble at St.-John's-bread and roast ducklings fly about in the air!

Tsi veyst ir dos land vu esroygim bli-en?	Do you know of the land where the ethrogs bloom?
Vu tsign esn bokser vi groz, oy, vi groz.	Where goats feed on St.-John's-bread like grass, like grass.
Gebrotene katshkes, gendzlech fli-en,	Where roast ducks and geese fly about,
Ts'mukim vaynen tu-en flisn on a mos, on a mos.	And raisin wine flows all around, all around?
Un mit lulovim, un mit lulovim, tut men decher dekn.	And with palm branches, with palm branches the roofs are covered.
Un mandlen, un mandlen, vaksn oyf yedn shtekn.	And almonds, almonds, grow on every stick.
Refrain: Ahin, ahin, ahin, ahin, ahin,	There, oh, there, oh, there, oh, there, oh, there,

Oh, rebenyu gevald, oy gevald !
Volt ich shoyn avek, avek, avek,
Oy, chotsh afile bald, oy bald ! [38]

Oh, *rebe* dear, help, oh, help !
There is where I'd go, I'd go, I'd go,
Oh, even right away, right away !

Weary of cultivating the gardens of "strangers" whilst "their own" stood abandoned and overgrown, with jackals roaming and the raven's raucous cry, worker-Zionists appealed to workingmen and women from the workshops and factories to join them in their movement to Palestine. A song which was sung to the same melody as the revolutionary "Mir vern gehast un getribn" ("We Are Hated and Driven") contained the following stanzas :

In varshtat baym shnayder, in kuznye baym shmid,
Baym shayn fun di funken, vos fli-en,
Derhoybt zich a nayes, a freyliches lid,
A lid vegn folk, vegn tsion.

In the tailor's workshop, in the blacksmith's foundry,
By the light of the flying red sparks,
A new joyous song there is rising,
A song of the people, of Zion.

In varshtat baym shpindl, in kuznye baym shmid,
Es hert zich fun libe un trayhayt
Tsum eygenem folk, fun fargesenem glik,
A lid fun der yidisher frayhayt.

In the spinner's workshop, in the blacksmith's foundry,
We hear of true love and devotion
To one's own people and a joy long forgotten,
A song of Jewish freedom.

Es hoybt zich alts shtarker un shtarker dos lid,
Es otimt zich munter un frayer,
S'glaycht oys zich der kerper, geboygn un mid,
Es brent in di oygn a fayer. [39]

The song rises stronger and stronger,
The singer breathes freer and gay,
The back bended weary, rises upright,
The eyes have been sparked with a bright fire.

Expressing the above sentiments, the Poale-Zionist hymn "Di shvue" ("The Vow"), said to have been written by I. Pelovits, served to rally and inspire several generations of Zionists in Yiddish-speaking communities throughout the world. [40] Those were the stirring days of marching demonstrations, where each opinion had its adherents and each group its hymn.

The repressions which followed the crushing of the 1905 Russian Revolution drove additional tens of thousands of Jews away from the Czarist lands, impelling them to seek the realization of their ideals of freedom and justice elsewhere. Three stanzas of an anonymous song in the spirit of "Di shvue" that accompanied many a contingent of workmen and women to Palestine are given below:

Mir hobn genug shoyn fir fremde geshafn,	We've created enough for strangers,
Un ze-en gants gut vos es iz undzer loyn;	And see quite clearly our reward;
Mir viln nisht lenger ferblaybn kayn shklafn,	We refuse any longer to remain slaves,
Un raych machn fremde un betlen aleyn.	Making strangers rich, while we beg for alms.
Mir hobn genug shoyn geboyt piramidn	We've built enough pyramids
Far yetvedn pare in yetvedn land;	For every Pharaoh in every land;
Shoyn tsayt zich bafrayen als mentshn un yidn	The time has come to free ourselves as people and as Jews
Fun eybign goles, fun eybiger shand.	From the everlasting exile and shame.
Shoyn tsayt tsu tsubrechn fun goles di keytn,	The time has come to break the chains of exile,
Tsu shendlicher knechtshaft zol nemen an ek:	To make an end of shameless slavery:
Un shtarkn un mutign eyner dem tsveytn,	To strengthen and encourage one another,
Bizvanen mir veln er-raychn dem tsvek.[41]	Until we realize our goal.

In serious mood and in joyous spirits, the young pioneers (*chalutzim*), few though they still were, were determined to realize the dreams of which they sang so lustily. By 1907 some of the old *Chov'vey Tsion* colonies were already twenty years old, and by 1919 there were more than thirty colonies in Palestine. The Zion songs sung in Eastern Europe by the Zionist adherents discarded the old weeping tone and adopted an air of confidence. A song which was popular both in the "old home" (in the Pale) and in the "new home" (in Palestine) was patterned after an old Yiddish question-and-answer love song which circulated in both "homes" in a number of Yiddish variants, and was sung right after the Balfour Declaration. Following are three stanzas:

Zog mir mayn shvester,
Ich vel dir fregn a por verter:
Vos vestu ton in palestina?
—Ich vel akern un zeyen,
Un zich mit mayne brider freyen,
Abi nor in palestina.

Tell me, my sister,
I want to ask you a question:
What will you do in Palestine?
—I'll plow and I'll sow
And be happy with my brothers;
Oh, to be in Palestine.

Zog mir mayn shvester,
Ich vel dir fregn a por verter:
In vos vestu geyn in palestina?
—Ich vel geyn in a layvnt kleydl,
Un vel zich rufn yidish meydl,
Abi nor in palestina.

Tell me my sister,
I want to ask you a question:
What will you wear in Palestine?
—I'll wear a linen dress
And call myself Jewish lass;
Oh, to be in Palestine.

Zog mir mayn shvester,
Ich vel dir fregn a por verter:
Vos vestu esn in palestina?
—Ich vel esn broyt oyf trukn,
Zich nisht darfn tsu keynem bukn,
Abi nor in palestina.[42]

Tell me my sister,
I want to ask you a question:
What will you eat in Palestine?
—I'll eat dry bread
And not have to bow to anyone;
Oh, to be in Palestine.

In Palestine

To Palestine the new settlers from Eastern Europe brought their songs —Yiddish and Hebrew, as well as various Slavic ones. In the beginning, this baggage of melodies and texts served as a basis for new texts, tunes, and rhythms that reflected the motifs and moods of the first Yiddish and Hebrew folk songs in Palestine. After the 1920's, however, the Hebrew songs became practically the only current, secular, song vehicle for the majority of the settlers of Eastern European origin in Palestine. The period of Yiddish folk-song creation there, consequently, was of brief duration, lasting only through the second and third migrations—through World War I and the twenties.

Those were the days when a tent was a home, the barracks—a palace, when bread and olives were a meal, and a cotton shirt and pair of khaki shorts, an outfit.

We sang in the city, in the workshops, in the workers' organizations, in the street, in the agricultural settlements *(kibutsim)*, . . . with the road-building gangs during mealtimes, at meetings, celebrations, conferences, in the evening after a hard day's work. We sang with enthusiasm, with all our heart and soul, till way into the night. . . . Children from religious homes . . . sang tunes from prayers and religious songs. . . . We also sang songs by composers and poets of our generation. But the new times demanded something different . . . to fit the new atmosphere of rebuilding the land. . . . We began to create, . . . using old tunes from all the lands we came from, . . . applying them to new texts which fitted, as we thought, the spirit of the time. . . . Many variants sprang up, . . . a song born only yesterday in isolated M'nachemya in lower Galilee was already being sung a few days later in Ramat Gan.[43]

Among the hundreds of Hebrew folk songs created in Palestine at that time, the small number of Yiddish folk songs served as the bridge between the old life, its old rhythms and crafts, and the new life with its new tempos and occupations. Former tailors, cobblers, students, seamstresses became sheepherders, road builders, drainers of swamps, construction workers, farmers, vineyard tenders. The transition took its toll. The rigorous life, the malaria, and the heat thinned out the ranks and confronted the initial enthusiasm with stark reality.

Mir hobn a land palestina,
Un mir fardinen a bishlik a tog.
Anshtot broyt esn mir china,
Un charara iz der bester kompot.[44]

We have a land called Palestine,
We earn twenty-five kopeks a day.
Instead of bread we eat quinine,
And *charara* is the finest compote.

Another one-stanza ditty utilized the old, Eastern European poverty song "Bulbes" and described the backbreaking toil of road-building:

Zuntig, montig, hakt men shteyner,
Dinstig, mitvoch, brechn di beyner.

Sunday, Monday, we break rock,
Tuesday, Wednesday, our bones ache.

Donershtig, fraytig, grobt men griber,
Kumt der shabes, ligt men in fiber.[45]

Thursday, Friday, we dig ditches,
Comes the Sabbath, we lie in bed with fever.

The Yiddish folk songs of those transition years in Palestine at first mirrored the hardships, disappointments, and disillusionment of those who came unprepared for the rigors of pioneering in a land which differed so drastically climactically, geographically, economically from the one they had left behind. A song which utilizes the refrain of *vayl mir zenen nit gevoynt tsu laydn* ("because we are not accustomed to suffer") reveals the sentiments of new settlers who were ill disposed to the difficulties and hardships of the resettlement program and contains the following lines:

Mir zenen zich chalutsimlech mit aynfershtand,	We are pioneers and all agree,
Moychl, moychl, usishkinen dos land.	We don't want any part of Ussishkin's land.
Az mir zenen gekumen in erets-yisroel, iz geven recht,	When we came to Israel, it was all right,
Un az men hot undz arayngefirt in karantin, iz undz gevorn shlecht.[46]	But when they took us into quarantine, it was bad for us.

A song of a construction worker in the city recalls wistfully the "years when my father opposed my going to Palestine, . . . but I did not listen to him and fled, and now I'm like a little bird in flight, caught in a net. . . . Not only do I eat stones and drink sweat, sleep on the hard block and drag bricks up and down all day but also have to rustle up the funds for the construction projects as well! And what reply do I get to my appeals? *Masari mafish!* — there is no money!"[47]

During the transition period, when former light-industry workers or students unaccustomed to manual labor were being transformed into manual laborers and agricultural workers, the Yiddish folk songs became the receptacles for complaints, gripes, and narrations of misery endured. Following are excerpts of a song which described the hardships in establishing the agricultural settlements.

Bin ich mir a choluts,	I'm a pioneer
Fun goles ongekumen,	Coming from exile,
Ch'ob denikinen gehert	I've heard Denikin
Un petluren brumen.	And Petlura roaring.
Vos mir idealn,	Who speaks of ideals?
Ver mir palestine?	Or of Palestine?
Ich hob glikn gezucht,	I sought security
A make hob ich gefine.	And found bad luck.
Ch'arbet vi a ferd	I work like a horse
On a haynt un on a morgn,	Endlessly

Oysgeyn far a piaster,   And haven't a piaster
S'vet dir keyner borgn.   And no one to borrow from.

Un du blaybst a poyel dort   You remain a worker here
In dayn gantsn lebn,   For the rest of your life,
Un du kukst yenem in hant,   And you look for a handout
M'zol dir epes gebn.   From others.

Shtarke vintn gor a shrek   Strong terrible winds
Fayfn in di oyern,   Whistle in your ears,
Un baytog verstu farbrent   By day you are scorched
Un baynacht derfroyrn.   And at night, frozen stiff.

Dekes, shlangen, akrovim   Creatures, snakes, scorpions
Mikol haminim,   Of all kinds,
Zumer zoygn dich fley,   Summer the fleas feed on you,
Vinter fresn kinim.   And winter — the lice.

S'feln oych araber nit   There is no dearth, too,
Vilde vi di tiger,   Of Arabs, like wild tigers,
Feter lebn, zay mir gezunt,   Uncle, fare you well,
Ch'bin shoyn nit kayn higer.[48]   I'm getting out of here.

The above song reveals a type of settler in Palestine who was not an idealistic Zionist but who came there out of need. Indeed, the Palestinian Jewish community was taking on the contours of a community which included all manner of people and ideas. The political differences within the Zionist movement in Eastern Europe were transferred to Palestine, and the struggles between the different sects, secular as well as religious, continued also in the new-ancient homeland. The secular settlers regarded the religious pioneers as an unproductive drag on the development of the community, whereas the pious pioneers felt that the others were desecrating the ancient soil of their fathers. Utilizing an old device employed by the Maskilim when they ridiculed the Chasidic *rebeyim* and their followers, the following song satirized the religious settlers who, in the midst of intense construction and reclamation of the land, concentrated most of their energies on rituals and ceremonials.

Bin ich mir a shlomi emuna,   I am at peace with my faith,
    bimbam, bimbamba,   bimbam, bimbamba,
For ich mir kayn palestina,   And I am going to Palestine,
    bimbambam.   bimbambam.

In der kolonye petach-tikve,
    bimbam, . . .
Veln mir boyen a koshere mikve,
    bimbam. . . .

In the colony Petach Tikva,
    bimbam, . . .
We will build a ritual bath,
    bimbam. . . .

Un oyfn barg har-hazeysim,
    bimbam, . . .
Veln mir boyen a fabrik fun
    taleysim, bimbam. . . .

And on the Mount of Olives,
    bimbam, . . .
We will set up a factory of
    prayer-shawls, bimbam. . . .

Ale chalutsim veln derbay shteyn,
    bimbam, . . .
Un fun kine vet zey di neshome
    oysgeyn, bimbambam.[49]

All the secular pioneers will stand
    looking on, bimbam, . . .
And from envy, their soul will
    depart, bimbam.

In the cities, pious workers refused to join the labor unions (*histadruth*), although they participated in many building projects together with other workers. A song which satirized the fear of the pious workers to expose themselves to secular practices in the labor unions contains the following stanzas:

Ch'vil nit geyn in histadrut,
Zey geyen dort on hitlen,
Arbetn veln mir
In taleysim un in kitlen.

I don't want to go to the *histadruth,*
They don't wear any hats there;
We will work in our own way
In prayer shawls and long coats.

Ich vil nit men zol zingen dort
Yeder mol hatikve.
Anshtot dem zol men geyn
Zich toyvl zayn in mikve.

I don't want them there to sing
The Hatikvah all the time.
Instead of that they should be going
To cleanse themselves in the ritual
    bath.

Tsu vos mir a kibutsl,

What do I want with an agricultural
    colony?

Tsu vos mir a kvutse?

What do I want with a farmer's
    settlement?

Ich zog mir a kapitl tilim,
Bin ich mir m'rutse.[50]

I chant my chapter of Psalms,
And I am satisfied.

The mood of pessimism and helplessness was passing, and Yiddish folk songs of good cheer were current in the cities and towns, colonies and settlements, factories and construction projects. The following reveals a singer who soberly views the prevailing difficulties yet concludes with the determination to face and conquer the hardships, come what may.

Yidn viln erets-yisroel, s'iz doch zeyer land.	Jews want Israel; well, it is their land.
Kumen balebatim, sh'cheynim raysn alts fun hant.	Bosses come from neighboring lands and grab everything from you.
Kumt men boyen zich a heym do, feln koyches fil.	We come to build our home here, much energy is needed.
Nemt men zich far altsding boygn, laydn in der shtil.	We adjust to everything, suffering in silence.
Tsvishn shteyner, berg un toln mintert men dos land,	Midst the rocks, hills, and vales we revive the earth,
Un dem elnt mitn hunger farshrayt men mit gezang.	And our loneliness and hunger we shout down with song.
Un di mide fis geyen tantsn biz tsum faln bald,	Our weary feet go dancing till we nearly drop,
Dreyen zich ale in a hora, eynik, hant in hant.[51]	Turning in a hora dance, together hand in hand.

Various aspirations in government, economic measures to be taken, methods of education to be introduced, dealing with the various patterns of culture, occupied the leaders and followers of the new Palestinian Jewish community. A humorous song current in the twenties recalled the years immediately following World War I, the exploits of the Jewish Legion, the misplaced hopes in the British, and regarded humorously the desires and dreams which at that time seemed a mere figment of the imagination, even to those directly involved. This song, with each line sung by a solo singer and replied to by the group with the nonsense term of *yokum bembe*, revolved around three facets of the Palestinian settlement at that time: certain institutions (Workers' Bank, University), leading personalities (Weizmann, Jabotinsky, Ben-Zvi, Ben-Gurion), different types of Jews (Yemenites, Sephardim, Georgians). Sung in Palestine a quarter of a century ago, in the light of subsequent historical realities this mixed-language song, employing the rhythm and pattern of an old, Yiddish, workers' dance song of Eastern Europe, contains the charming naïveté of the anonymous folk song endowed with the flash of prophetic foresight.

A yidishe meluche, yokum bembe,	A Jewish state, yokum bembe,
Palestine a medine, yokum bembe,	Palestine a government, yokum bembe,

Herzl T. Rome, 1950

Hora

Veytsman a minister, yokum bembe,
Zhabotinsky a general, yokum
    bembe,
Bentsvi a kolonel, yokum bembe,
Bengurion a proletie, yokum
    bembe,
Bank hapoalim a koznotseystvo,
    yokum bembe,
Oyfn har-hatsufim a univerzitet,
    yokum bembe.

Refrain: Razom, razom chorosho,

    Un vu iz dos geven?—
        Bachtsi halaylo!

A yidishe shif, yokum bembe,
A teymaner matroz, yokum bembe,

Weizmann a minister, yokum bembe,
Jabotinsky a general, yokum
    bembe,
Ben-Zvi a colonel, yokum bembe,
Ben-Gurion a proletarian, yokum
    bembe,
The Workers' Bank a Treasury,
    yokum bembe,
On Mt. Scopus a university, yokum
    bembe.

    Right away, right away, all
        right,
    And when did it all
        happen?—in the
        middle of the night!

A Jewish ship, yokum bembe,
A Yemenite sailor, yokum bembe,

A georgi kapitan, yokum bembe,   A Georgian captain, yokum bembe,
A sfardi lotsman, yokum bembe,   A Sephardic seaman, yokum bembe,
Un yafe a port, yokum bembe.[52]   And Jaffa a port, yokum bembe.

Yiddish folk songs continued to be heard in Palestine through the thirties, although by then their use had considerably decreased and their popularity diminished. During the twenties, thirties, and even early forties, a number of song compilations appeared, containing Yiddish folk songs in Hebrew translation. But by then Hebrew folk and composed songs had already become the main song expression of the majority of the Jews who had settled in Palestine. One of the last Yiddish folk songs to achieve wide popularity in Palestine was the following humorous question-and-answer song, which was still current in the thirties. Set to the tune of an old anti-Chasidic text titled "Az der rebe est" ("When the *Rebe* eats"), it included the following stanzas:

Avu biztu geven, avu biztu geven,   Where were you, where were you,
        tochter mayne getraye?   my devoted daughter?
—Geven in a kvutsa, gevorn a   —In a settlement I became a
chalutsa,   pioneer,
        mame s'iz gevezn a   mother it was wonderful!
        mechaye!

Un vos hostu gegesn, un vos hostu   And what did you eat, what did you
gegesn,   eat,
        tochter mayne getraye?   my devoted daughter?
—Gegesn hob ich kashe, gekocht hot   —I ate buckwheat groats cooked by
es Mashe,   Mashe,
        mame s'iz gevezn a   mother it was wonderful!
        mechaye!

Un vos hostu geton, un vos hostu   And what did you do, what did you
geton,   do,
        tochter mayne getraye?   my devoted daughter?
—Getasket hob ich shteyner,   —I lugged rocks and broke my
tsetrasket mayne beyner,   bones,
        mame s'iz gevezn a   mother it was wonderful!
        mechaye!

Un vu biztu geshlofn, un vu biztu   And where did you sleep, and where
geshlofn,   did you sleep,
        tochter mayne getraye?   my devoted daughter?
—Oyf a boydim hey, hey, mit   —In a loft of hay, hay, with

chalutsim tsvey, tsvey,
       mame s'iz gevezn a
       mechaye!

two fellow pioneers,
       mother it was wonderful!

Vos vet zayn der sof un vos vet zayn der sof,
       tochter mayne getraye?
—Ch'vel shraybn a sertifikat, m'et geyn tsu an advokat,
       mame s'vet zayn a
       mechaye.[53]

Where will it all end, where will it all end,
       my devoted daughter?
—We'll draw up a certificate and go to the notary,
       mother it will be
       wonderful!

The horrors of German Nazism and World War II set into motion additional thousands of Jewish immigrants to Palestine from Western, Central, and Eastern Europe, bringing a number of old and new Yiddish songs into the land. Some of these dealt with the dread period of the German occupation, during which, for many, the old dream of Zion became passionately identified with survival itself. One ditty from the early days of the German occupation reveals the naïve hope that the troubles will soon be over:

Klert nisht yidn, nor zayt tsufridn,
Fun ale tsores vet nemen an ek;

Az got vet gebn, mir veln derlebn,

Veln ale yidn kayn erets yisroel
    avek.[54]

Don't worry Jews, just be satisfied,
For all our troubles are bound to
    end;

With the will of God, we will
    survive,

And all Jews will go to the Land of
    Israel.

But the mounting atrocities soon resulted in other songs, one of which cried out from the death camps in a desperate hope for a return to Zion:

Ich hoyb oyf di hent un ich shver:
Kayn aushwits gey ich nisht mer!
Di taychn fun blut, in velche es
    zinken mayne trit,
Hobn mir gegebn tsu farshteyn;
Di blut di royte, di milyonen toyte
Shrayen: aheym! aheym![55]

I raise my hands and vow:
Never again to go to Auschwitz!
The rivers of blood in which my
    steps sink
Have made me understand;
The red gore, the millions of dead
Cry out: home! home!

Even before the war was over, units of the Palmach, the striking arm of the Palestine Jewish Army—Haganah, were feverishly engaged in underground work rescuing the remnants of their people from the German grip. A ditty reflecting the devious ways of the paths leading out of the Nazi hell contained the following:

Erets—	Israel—
Ven nisht der yam	But for the sea
Volt ich shoyn lang geven bay dir,	I would have been with you long before this,
Nor ich hof in gichn	But I hope in the near future
Vel ich tsu dir derkrichn	I'll be crawling to you
Oyf groyse shifn tsi oyf kleyne oych. . . .[56]	On big ships or even on small. . . .

When the war was finally at an end, the numbers of Jewish immigrants to Palestine increased considerably. Many who had survived through evacuation into the U.S.S.R., upon their return home, found their communities sadly "cleansed" of Jews. With loved ones gone and the memories of their violent demise still hovering in the air, the streams of refugees to Palestine swelled in numbers. A song sung by a group waiting to go to Palestine in 1946, on the eve of the struggle for independence, contained the following stanzas:

Fun getos osventshim, ponar un maydanek,	From ghettos Oswiencim, Ponar, and Maidanek,
Fun frontn un velder, fun hits un fun kelt.	From battlefield, forest, fire and frost.
Es halt zich der biks noch bay undz afn aksl,	We still bear the rifle upon our shoulder,
Es shturimt dos harts noch, es zidt un es kvelt.	Our hearts still are churning with sorrow and pain.
Refrain: Mir veln, mir veln tsebrechn di tsoymen,	We will, oh, we will break asunder the barriers,
Mir shteln, mir shteln dos lebn in kon.	We're ready once more to pay with our lives.
Chalutsim, chalutsim tseshparn di roymen,	Chalutzim, oh, pioneers, let's push back the horizon,
Un hoybn dem kamf ersht noch on.	Beginning our battle once more and anew.
Chotsh eybik tsu lebn mir zaynen geborn,	Though destined to live on, forever, forever,
Doch shteyen mir alts noch baym t'homign rand,	We stand on the rim of the yawning abyss.

Hobn chalutsim tsu k'doyshim geshvorn,
Tsu kemfn far frayhayt fun folk un zayn land.

Shalom ale yidn in lender in vayte,
Shalom tsu aych yidn, in noyt un in payn,
Aych ruft der chaluts in dem land vos bafrayt vert,
To lomir tsu im oyle zayn, oyle zayn.[57]

Chalutzim have sworn to their holy martyred
To fight for their freedom, their people, their land.

Greetings to Jews in distant lands,

Greetings to all in their sorrow and pain,
The chalutz calls to you from the land soon to be freed,
Come, let us go there, come, let us go.

But the Yiddish songs did not long survive in the new environment, where they had already, in a large measure, been absorbed into Hebrew translations or forgotten by the established Jewish community in Palestine. Living Yiddish folk song was actually over by the end of the twenties, and, although briefly refreshed during the thirties and forties, was creatively over before the formation of the State of Israel in 1948. The influx of additional tens of thousands of Jews from all parts of the world created an Israeli community with the majority of Jews of Near Eastern and Oriental origin. These conditions for an amalgamation of Eastern and Western Jewish cultures in a tightly knit geographical area has created a dramatic process which merits close observation and study.

Notes

TO ZION

1. M. and M., p. 697.
2. BILU represents the initial letters of the Hebrew motto of the society "*Beys Yaankev, L'chu V'nelcho*" — "O, House of Jacob, Come ye and let us go" (Isaiah 2:5). ". . . Several hundred Jews in various parts of Russia joined the Bilu society. Of these only a few dozen pioneers left for Palestine—between June and July of 1882" (Dubnow, II, pp. 321–322).
3. Smolenskin categorically rejected Michl Gordon's credo "to be a Jew at home and a man abroad," together with the fanaticism of orthodox Jewry. At the same time, he decried the indifference on the part of certain Maskilim of his day towards Jewishness. He saw in Jewish distinctiveness and the renationalization in a land of their own the only salvation for them. Thus, he was a forerunner in the movement of political Zionism a decade before Leo Pinsker and Dr. Theodor Herzl.
4. *See* Zunser, III, pp. 61–62.
5. Zunser, II, p. 250.
6. *See* Zunser, III, p. 73. "A few hundred adherents were won in Russia, but only forty arrived in Jaffa. Half were given employment in the 'Alliance' colony Mikveh Israel, and half were settled in the recently founded colony Rishon le-Zion, . . . The young pioneers could not accustom themselves to the climate and the hardships of tilling the long-neglected soil; the majority departed, making room for less educated but more hardy colonists" (M. and M., p. 697).
7. Beginning with the 1880's, a national movement, which called itself *Chov'vey Tsion* ("Lovers of Zion"), was launched in Russia and later spread to Germany, Austria, Rumania, France, England, and the United States. Predating the later Zionist movement to colonize Palestine, it aided agricultural workers in Palestine to establish themselves on the outskirts of large settlements, providing them with a cottage and small plot of land, so that they could supplement their earnings from seasonal labor in the settlements.
8. Zunser, II, p. 258. Zunser wrote this song in Yiddish and Hebrew. Later, it was translated into Russian and German and served as a stimulant and organizer of sentiment in favor of the colonization movement of Palestine among the Jews.
9. "They'd come from all the streets and crowd around the *shtibl* ('shack') where the young speaker was preaching. Most of these were young Chasidic fellows, who had sneaked away at great risk from their fathers as they were praying together in their own prayer houses. . . . They had raced over here with beating heart so that they could listen to the flaming call to return to the old-new land, and to a free, independent life. The fathers would later punish such lads severely, even smack them about, disturbing the peace of the Sabbath. But this did not prevent them from coming with bated breath to squeeze into the overcrowded shack to satiate themselves with the inspiring speeches" (Teitelbaum, p. 143).
10. Idelsohn, IX, No. 322.
11. Reingold, p. 66. Music by Herman Fidler.

12. *Kvutsat Shirim,* pp. 218–219. "It was during the last days of January, 1890, when I arrived in Lemberg . . . where I first met the Lemberger Zionists, who then called themselves *Chov'vey Tsion* . . . mostly young fellows. . . . The strongest impression on me was made by Isaac Feld . . . who was already then a doctor of jurisprudence. . . . He showed me his poem 'Dort vu di tseder' ('There, Where the Cedars'), which he had been reciting at several gatherings. . . . It was two years earlier . . . that . . . he had written it. Later he published it, . . . then . . . a certain cantor called Mots, from Breslau . . . composed a suitable melody for it. . . . On Sabbath, February 1, 1890, the hymn was sung for the first time at a gathering of the Zion Verein in Lemberg. Seven years later, the Zionist students in Basle opened their panel at the Zionist Congress with this song and Dr. Max Nordau applauded it enthusiastically" (Bader).

13. Abrahams, p. 22.

14. "Build, O rebuild Thou, Thy temple, / Fill again Zion, Thy city. / Clad with delight will we go there, / Other and new songs to sing there" (*Ibid.,* p. 134).

15. The marriage custom of breaking a glass is supposed to have been introduced by the rabbis to curb the gay mood surrounding the marriage procedures and to stimulate the thinking of more serious thoughts and the "never-to-be forgotten memory of the mourning for Zion" (*See* Abrahams, p. 187). During the seventeenth century, the wearing of black was attributed to the mourning for Zion. This custom was known also earlier. "In the mourning for Jerusalem, Jews were allowed by the Talmud to wear black shoes" (*See* Abrahams, note 4, p. 293).

16. *See* Halevi, pp. 2–39.

17. Rubin, MSS. (Sung to the melody by Z. Shneyer.)

18. *Tsion's Harfe,* pp. 33–34.

19. Frug's poem, "Tsion" ("Zion"), describes the "daughter of Zion as a widow sitting sadly at the roadside, appealing to the passing travellers: 'O tell me, have you seen my child, my lost orphan anywhere?' To which they reply: 'No, old woman, no' " (*See Tsion's Harfe,* pp. 21–23).

Zunser in his "Shivas tsion" ("Return to Zion") also pictures Zion as a widow left alone, her children scattered far and wide, and as her children—Israel—begin to return, the "widow" happily sets the table for them, saying: "Rest, my children, my darling guests; no longer will you suffer, eating at a stranger's table; once again, you will know what it is to be fed by your own mother" (*See* Zunser, II, pp. 248–250).

20. Zunser's "A briv fun der muter tsion" ("A Letter From Mother Zion"), written in 1892, decries the indifference of the American Jews to the idea of Zionism (Zunser, II, p. 262). Goldfaden's "A grus der muter tsion" ("Greetings To Mother Zion"), describes the nostalgic longing of a child for its mother, a sentiment well known to Eastern European Jews during the mass migrations to America which began with the 1880's (*Tsion's Harfe,* pp. 124–126).

21. *Kvutsat Shirim,* pp. 197–198. The title combines the Hebrew word *hashiveynu* ("let us return") and the Russian word *nazad* ("back").

22. Zunser, III, p. 62.

23. Warshawsky, pp. 48–49.

24. *Ibid.,* pp. 23–24. The above two songs, as well as several others by Warshawsky, were very popular in Zionist circles at that time. "There wasn't an evening," writes Sholem Aleichem in his introduction to this collection of Warshawsky's songs "nor a single Zionist gathering, where we weren't dragged from the Kreshtshatik to Podol and from Podol to Kreshtshatik. I had to read something aloud and Warshawsky had to sing" (Warshawsky, Intro., xi, 2nd ed.). Kreshtshatik was in the center of the city and Podol, a Jewish quarter, in Kiev.

25. *Tsion's Harfe,* pp. 145–149.

26. *Ibid.,* pp. 47–54.

27. Reingold, p. 63.

28. Idelsohn, IX, No. 219.

29. A quote from Singer's work illuminates this aspect:

. . . The door opened, and Treytl, the dry-goods merchant, a tall, thin man, . . . came in. . . . He was aglow with joy and said aloud: "Mazltov! Rabbi!"

"What's the *mazltov* ('congratulations') for, Treytl?" my father asked.

"Dr. Hertsl croaked!" he said, thereby uttering an obscene word to rhyme with *hertsl*. My father grimaced with distaste at the ugly word and asked: "Who is this Dr. Hertsl?"

"A turncoat who wanted to lead all the Jews to *shmad* ('conversion')," Reb Tretyl explained.

"Blessed be the Lord," said my father.

. . . I ran quickly to the town's rich man, Reb Joshua, to tell his grandson (who was my friend) . . . the news about the doctor, the turncoat, who had wanted to convert all the Jews. The lad . . . cursed Reb Treytl. . . . "Herzl wanted to lead all the Jews to the land of Israel. Come here, let me show you his picture," he said (Singer, pp. 227–228).

30. *Tsion's Harfe*, pp. 45–46. Mt. Carmel is in Haifa; the Mount of Olives, in Jerusalem. "It is difficult and perhaps impossible to determine the beginning of a historical process. Was it the act of Rabbi Hayim Abulafia from Ismir in settling in Tiberias in 1742, or was it the immigration of Hassidim, disciples of the Baal Shem Tov in 1777, or was it the immigration of the disciples of the Vilna Gaon in 1805? Was it the first agricultural enterprise of Moses Montefiore in 1856, or the foundation of Mikveh Israel by the Alliance Israélite in France in 1869? But I think that no doubt a special place is occupied by the founders of Petach Tikva in 1878 . . . established in our generation by the pioneer from Jerusalem Yoel Moshe Solomon and the Hungarian pioneers, Stamfer, Rab and Goodman. After them came the founding of Rishon LeTsion, Zichron Yaakov and Rosh Pina, by pioneers from Russia and Rumania in 1882" (Prime Minister David Ben-Gurion in his address before the 25th World Zionist Congress in Jerusalem, December 28, 1960. *New York Times*, January 8, 1961).

31. The Bund had its own program on the Jewish question: it was opposed to assimilation and stood for Jewish autonomy in its language and culture. Although anticlerical, it did not propagandize against religion; it was anti-Zionist, maintaining that the Jewish question could best be treated in each country where Jews resided and that a national homeland in Zion could not solve the individual problems of Jewish communities in other parts of the world.

32. Lehman, 1921, p. 69, No. 31.

33. *See* Footnotes 50 and 51 in Chapter XI: "Poverty, Toil and Struggle."

34. Lehman, 1921, p. 71, No. 32a.

35. *See*: *Kvutsat Shirim*, pp. 182–184. Author: Michl Aronson.

36. *Makkabi*, p. 74–75.

37. Sheet music, New York, 1918, Jewish Morning Journal, pub.

38. Rubin, MSS. *Esrog*: citrus fruit used for ceremonial purposes on the feast of Tabernacles.

Although the Chasidic movement on the whole was opposed to Zionism, there were exceptions where the occasional *rebe* and his followers supported it. This particular song may be a variant of another which begins: *Tsi kenstu dos land vu moshiach tsidkoni / Vet kumen raytndig oyfn vaysn ferd, oyfn vaysn ferd?* ("Do you know of the land where our Saint, the Messiah, will come riding on his white horse, his white horse" (Kotylansky, MSS).

Both songs are curiously similar to Goethe's poem, which begins: *Kennst du das Land wo die Citronen blüh'n / Im dunkeln Laub di Goldorangen glüh'n*, etc.

39. *Tsion's Harfe*, pp. 120–123. (Author: L. Yaffe.)

40. Four stanzas of "Di shvue" follow:

(1)	We raise our hands towards the east and
Mir hoybn di hent gegn mizrech un shvern,	we vow,
Bay tsion, ir fon, bay ir heyliger erd,	By Zion, her banner, her holy soil,
Bay alts vos mir shvern dos folk heys tsu	By all that we cherish, honor, and love,
Bay undzere heldn's tsubrochene shverd.	By the shattered swords of our heroes.
(2)	
Bay undzer geshichte vos iz ongeshribn,	By our history which has been written
Mit undzere trern, mit undzere blut,	With our tears, with our blood,
Bay alts vos mir shvern dos folk heys tsu libn	We vow by all this, to love our people dearly
Un kemfn fir im mit energie mit mut.	And fight for it with energy and courage.
(3)	
Mir shvern im libe, mir shvern im trayhayt,	We vow to love her, we vow to be true,
Tsurik dos gever nit tsu leygn fun hant,	We vow not to lay our arms down,
Bizvanen mir veln erkemfn in frayhayt,	Until we have won in freedom at last,
A ru-iges lebn oyf eygenem land.	A peaceful life on our own land.
(4)	
Mir shvern tsuraysn di keytn oyf shtiker,	We vow to break asunder the chains,
Fun zayne gebundene vundige hent;	That bind her wounded hands;
Aruntertsuvarfn dem yoch fun di driker,	To throw off the bondage of those who oppress her,
Farlozn dem goles, di finstere vent.	To leave the dark walls of exile.

(*Kvutsat Shirim,* p. 241.)

41. *Kvutsat Shirim,* pp. 245–246.

42. Rubin, MSS. During the thirty years of the mandate (1919–1948), more than 450,000 Jews settled in Palestine: Less than 90 per cent came from Europe, some 10 per cent from Asia and Africa, and less than 2 per cent from America and Australia. In the seventy years from Petach Tikvah to the establishment of the State, 290 agricultural settlements were established.

43. Tsidkoni, pp. 182–183.

44. Lehman, 1921, p. 174. (*charara*: a skin rash.)

45. Tsidkoni, MSS.

46. *Ibid.,* M. M. Ussishkin (1863–1941), Russian-born Zionist leader since the early days of *Chov'vey Tsion* in 1883, settled in Palestine after 1919. Under his leadership, *Emek Yisrael, Mifrats Haifa,* and others were purchased.

47. Tsidkoni, p. 183.

48. *Ibid.,* p. 184. This song reveals the singer to have fled the violent upheavals in Russia following the 1917 Revolution. A. I. Denikin, Russian general, initiated a campaign against the new Russian government in the north Caucasus in 1918. In 1919, Petlura became hetman of the United Russian and Ruthenian republics, which together with Denikin's forces aimed at the new Russian government. "Under the eyes of the Petlura government, no less than 30,000 Jews were murdered in 372 cities and small towns. . . . Graver still were the atrocities perpetrated by Denikin's *white* volunteer troops; the soldiers were openly incited to exterminate the Jews. . . . The Jews had their self-defense organizations, but they were powerless against the fury of the soldiery" (M. and M., p. 733).

49. Tsidkoni, MSS.

50. Tsidkoni, pp. 185–186. Tune and text of the *Hatikvah* hymn were authored by N. H. Imber (1856–1909) in Palestine in 1884.

51. *Ibid.,* pp. 184–185.

52. Tsidkoni, MSS. In the early days of Jewish settlement in Palestine, the Sephardic element was the dominant one. The first Jewish settlers from Yemen came to Palestine in the eighties of the nineteenth century, "almost immediately after the arrival of the first Hovevei Zion and Bilu immigrants from Russia. . . . Throughout

the mandatory regime they increased in numbers. . . . The first Georgian Jewish settlers arrived in Palestine in the sixties of the last century, and thus preceded the organized movement of the Hovevei Zion" (Ben-Zvi, pp. 30–31, p. 64). Of the million immigrants who came in during the life of the state, 47 per cent came from Europe, some 51 per cent from Asia and Africa and 1½ per cent from America.

53. Rubin, MSS. This song reflects the communal life in the early agricultural settlements and the "flexibility" of the marriage practices, where a form of "companionate" marriage existed, prior to the filling out of the application and notarizing of the marriage certificate.

54. Prager, pp. 37–38.

55. *Ibid.*, p. 231.

56. *Ibid.*, Intro., p. 39.

57. Rubin, MSS. Written in Lodz by S. Kacerginski, the tune was composed by the Vilna chalutz ("Zionist pioneer") David Botvinik. Both had fought together with the partisans.

CHAPTER XV

Soviet Yiddish Folk Song

THREE AND A HALF MILLION JEWS WERE IN RUSSIA AT THE OUTBREAK OF the 1917 Revolution. The upheavals of this historical event seemed, for a decade at least, to silence the creative process of Yiddish folk song among the Jews of the former Czarist Pale of Settlement. By the time the Russian Civil War was over, however, a number of Yiddish folk songs, both anonymous and of literary origin, had sprung up, while many of the old nineteenth-century songs had entirely disappeared.

The economic, social, and political changes instituted by the new regime wrought penetrating changes in the life of the Soviet Jews. A number of traditional institutions (cheder, Yeshiva, House of Study, ritual bathhouse), which had served the Jewish communities in Eastern Europe for generations, were drastically reduced and subsequently almost completely discontinued. On the one hand, crafts and occupations, professions and careers formerly denied to Jews in the Pale were now open to them. On the other, many former pursuits, such as private business enterprises, trading, merchandising, as well as the clerical professions of *rebe, shadchen, badchen,* etc., were sharply affected or diverted into other channels. These changes naturally resulted in the disappearance of many old customs and habits, the falling off of portions of the Yiddish vernacular, folk sayings, folklore, folk tales, and whole categories of folk song.

A song of this transition period of the 1920's that reveals the distress and confusion of the singer, who is witnessing these transformations taking place before his bewildered eyes, is the following:

A gut morgn aych reb nisl,	Good morning to you, *reb* Nisl,
Ch'kum zich durchredn abisl.	I've come to chat with you a bit.
Tsu dertseyln aych mayn biter harts,	To tell you of my bitter heart,
Aroptsutraybn dem veytig un dem shmarts.	To dispel my sorrow and my pain.

Tsores on an ek,	Troubles without end,
Fun yedn kleynem shnek,	From every little nobody,
Ch'freg bay got un bay laytn,	I ask of God and the respectable folk :
Vos tut men in azoyne tsaytn?	What does one do in times like these?
Az heyvn farkoyft der koperativ,	Yeast is sold by the Cooperative,
Taleysim farkoft men in archiv.	Prayer shawls are bought in the Archive.
Mitn cheder un mit der yeshive,	For the cheder and the yeshiva,
Men meg shoyn noch zey zitsn shive.	We might as well sit down in mourning.
Kinder hern nit di tates,	Children don't obey their fathers,
Komsomoltses, pionern, oktyabrates,	They join the Komsomols, Pioneers, and Octobrists,
Ch'freg bay got un bay laytn :	I ask of God and the respectable folk :
Vos tut men in azoyne tsaytn?[1]	What does one do in times like these?

No longer confined to the Pale, many young people hastened to take advantage of the new possibilities now open to them in the rest of the country. In the process, they quickly shed many old ways of life, which for centuries had been inextricably bound up with traditional religious orientation and practices. Although many religious chants, Chasidic melodies, and old folk-song tunes were freely utilized in the new songs, the texts now treated new motifs, new forms of conflict, new hopes and aspirations under the Soviet rule. This process was taking place, however, not in a peaceful atmosphere over a long period of time but compressed within a few decades in an environment of violent upheaval, armed struggle, starvation and death, impelled by a powerful current of organization and self-sacrifice. The ideals which had been nurtured by those Jewish men and women who had sought the solution of their problems within the framework of the general situation in the Slavic lands were now, it seemed, joined with the aspirations of others similarly inclined, in the lands formerly ruled by the Czar.

A folk song of the twenties, which utilized the first two lines of a Yiddish folk song of literary origin of a generation earlier, reveals the segment of Soviet Jewish youth that saw itself in the role of "guardians of freedom" razing to the ground the little old, "moldy" towns of the former Pale.

Oyfn boydim hengt der dach,
Tsugedekt mit shindelech.
Shteyen yatn oyf der vach,
Frayhayt's traye kinderlech.

Over the attic hangs the roof,
Covered with little shingles.
Fellows stand on guard,
Freedom's devoted children.

Alte shtetl rut zich oys,
Foylinke parshoyndelech.
Yugnt geyt in gas aroys—
Oysglaychn di beyndelech.

Little old town is slumbering,
Lazy little people.
Youth walks out into the streets
To stretch its limbs a bit.

Shimlt himl, alter s'chach,
Altinke getseltelech.
Yugnt tsindn vet dem dach—

Brenen veln veltelech.[2]

Moldy sky, wilted grassy roof,
Little old shelters.
Youth will put the torch to the
roof—
And the little old worlds will burn.

The Civil War

No sooner was the new regime set up in 1917 than Russia was invaded
by the armies of England, France, Germany, United States, Czecho-
slovakia, Japan. She simultaneously conducted a war with Poland and
during 1918–1919 was involved in a Civil War with its internal enemies:
the "white" Russians, marshaled by Generals Denikin, Kolchak, Yuden-
ich, who in their campaigns brutally murdered Jews in White Russia
and the Ukraine.[3] The land was convulsed with fighting, with battlefields
shifting back and forth, and the "red" and "white" armies advancing
and retreating across the homes and fields of the civilian populations lying
in their path.

Many young Jewish men, now equal citizens before the Soviet law,
eagerly joined passing regiments ofthe Red Army and partisan brigades
in a wave of patriotic enthusiasm.

Tsu nikolken mit geveyn,

Kloles inem rentsl.
In der roytinker armey,

Geyt men mit a tentsl.

To Nicholas' army we went with
tears
And curses in our knapsack.
Into the ranks of the Red Army,
Army,
We go with a dance.

Soyne totshet undzer aks,
Vil mit blay undz shpayzn;
Vu der shvartser fefer vakst,
Darf men im bavayzn.[4]

Enemy is threatening our power,
And wants to feed us lead;
Where the black pepper grows,
We'll send him instead.

At the front, Jewish men fought bravely. A ballad of the Civil War tells the story of Liova, the machine gunner, who was surrounded and killed by the "whites" as he vowed to drive the invaders from the land.

Oy, vi Liove iz af di frontn gekumen,
Dray mesles iz er nit geshlofn,
Di burzhutshikes hot er geshlogn,
Un a koyl hot in harts im getrofn.

Oh, when Liova came to the front,
For three days he did not sleep,
He fought the bourgeois army,
When a bullet found his heart.

Oy, vi di koyl hot in lioven getrofn,
A geshrey geton hot er fun vaytn:
—Ich bashver aych, chaverim getraye,
Ir zolt af mayn post mich farbaytn.

Oh, when the bullet struck Liova,
He shouted from afar:
—I plead with you, devoted comrades,
That you replace me at my post.

Oy, veyn nit, muter, veyn nit, libe,

Oy, taybelech, ir zolt nit vorken,
Un az ir vet di shvartse b'sure derhern,
Zolt ir nit klogn un nit ochken.[5]

Oh, weep not mother, weep not, dear one,
Oh, little doves, do not coo,
When you'll receive the dreadful news,
Don't you weep, and don't you groan.

In the rear, Jewish craftsmen were sewing and remodeling old clothes for the soldiers at the front. A popular work song contained the following stanzas:

Klapt, klapt, hemerlach,
Klapt gich, vi mashinen.
Macht ful di kamerlach,
Vi binshtokn di binen.

Rap, rap, little hammers,
Rap as quickly as machines.
Fill all the little cubicles,
Like beehives are filled by the bees.

Far di chaverim af di frontn,
Vos merer kleyder un shich.
Vos shneler zoln arbetn di remontn,
Fun alte naye nitseven mir iber gich.

For the comrades at the fronts,
Ever more clothes and shoes.
Faster, faster we must make
Old clothes into new.

Undzere royt-armeyer, partizaner, heldishe yatn,
Veln farnichtn undzere sonim bizn sof,
Undzere biksn, pulemyotn un harmatn,
Veln di bandes oys-shnaydn vi a tsherede shof.[6]

Our Red Army, partisans, brave fellows,
Will destroy our enemies completely;
Our rifles, machine-guns and cannon,
Will cut their gangs up like a flock of sheep.

The land was laid waste, and the economy collapsed in ruins. Human suffering was tragic, and no matter how patriotic one tried to be, a mother's grief upon seeing her son depart for the front could not be assuaged.

Az mayn kind iz avek mit di polkn,

Hot kayn muzike nit geton shpiln,
A mame's vey, oy, ver kon visn,
A mame's harts, oy, ver kon filn.

Un az di royte kavalerie geyt,
Un budyony iz fun fornt,
Darf men dem kop nit bahaltn,
Darf men nit zayn gor batsornt.[7]

And when my child went off with the regiment,
No music did play then,
Oh, who can know a mother's pain,
Oh, who can feel a mother's heart.

And when the Red Cavalry passes,
And Budënny is at its head,
One need not hide one's face,
One need not be troubled.

Changing Mores

When the Civil War was over and recruitment normalized, military service lost much of the terrors of the past. In the countryside, new recruits would be escorted to the railroad depot by a procession of agricultural workers in holiday attire, with flowers, accordion, song and speeches. A song which describes such a procession borders on a love song, as the singer focuses on his sweetheart, Mirele, who is the one to say a few words to the departing men. Following are two stanzas of this song:

Baleytn, baleytn, zaynen mir gegangen,
Yunge prizivnikes in armey, in armey.
Vi a royter epl iz di zun gehangen,

Un geshpritst mit funken hot der shney, hot der shney.

Mirele baleyt undz mit verter a mechaye,
Vi a shnirl perl ire tseyn, ire tseyn.

Zay-zhe mir gezunt, mayn mirele, mayn traye,
Tsum chaver voroshilov darf ich geyn.[8]

Together we all went to escort them,

The new recruits for the army, the army.

Like a red apple, the sun hung in the sky,

And sparks of light reflected from the snow.

Mirele spoke to us in words so charming,

Like a string of pearls were her teeth,

Fare thee well my Mirele, my own true love,

For to Comrade Voroshilov I must go.

An interesting group within the category of Soviet Yiddish soldier songs is the song of the border guard as he patrols the silent landscapes, far from home. In one song, a soldier bids a little bird fly east "from Lake Chasan" —in the Far East—to his tiny village "whence a letter takes so long to come." He dwells tenderly on his parents' concern for him:

Ch'veys az mayne eltern, yesurim hobn zey,	I know that my parents are worrying about me,
Ful di hertser zeyere mit laydn un mit vey.	And their hearts are full of sorrow and pain.
Ch'veys az mayne eltern shlofn nit banacht:	I know that my parents are thinking sleeplessly:
Ver veys tsi undzer zunenyu z'aroys gezunt fun shlacht.[9]	Who knows if our dear son survived the battle.

Another song in this group describes a skirmish with the Japanese before the flare-up of large-scale warfare in 1928.

Vayser shney un kalte vaytn,	White snow and cold expanse,
Luft iz ful mit frost.	The air is full of frost.
Tsvey armeyer royte raytn	Two Red Army men are riding
Tsu dem grenets-post.	To their sentry post.
Sopkes shteyen vi di shlyomen,	Hillocks crouching there like snails,
Af der vayser flach.	On the white, flat plain.
Plutsling yogn on yaponer	Suddenly the Japanese
Fun der shvartser nacht.	Come racing through the night.
Tropns blut vi funken fayer	Drops of blood like sparks of fire
Afn shney tsushpreyt,	Are spread upon the snow,
S'lign draytsn samurayen,	Thirteen Samurai are lying—
Ale saynen toyt.[10]	And all of them are dead.

The profound changes which made it possible for Jews of the former Pale to become tractor and combine operators, agronomists and aviators, scientists and military leaders, resulted in songs set to new moods and rhythms. There were songs which hailed the broader economic horizons as they mused upon the transformations that had been effected within the span of one generation. Such is the following lullaby, which recalls the "recent past" when the land was convulsed with the frightening yells of Petlura's marauding gangs and the murderous attacks upon defenseless Jews.

Ay-lye-lyu mayn tayerer,
Ver-zhe shoyn anshlofn,
Vet di mame dir dertseyln,
Vos hot mit ir getrofn.

Hushaby my dear little son,
Go to sleep now,
And mother will tell you
What happened to her.

Vi fun fuftsn bin ich eyne,
Bin ich eyns geblibn,
Gekoylet zibn hot petlura,
Orel—di tsveyte zibn.

Of fifteen only I survived,
Only I remained,
Petlura slaughtered seven of us,
At Orel, seven more were slain.

Vi s'hobn zich bahaltn
Dayn bobe mitn zeydn,
Vi in keler dort ba undz
Geshosn hot men beydn.[11]

How your granny tried to hide
And with her, your grandfather,
How in our cellar both were shot,
Both were shot together.

There were songs cast in the mold of the Ukrainian *chastushki*, created spontaneously, usually treating topical matters. Often to the accompaniment of an accordion, they soon became a vehicle for drinking and dancing songs, like the following:

Af di fonen, af di fonen,
Zaynen royte farbn.
Itst iz zeyer gut tsu lebn,
S'vilt zich gornit shtarbn.

On the banners, on the flags,
There are red colors.
It's so good to be alive now,
No one wants to die.

S'iz mayn bruder a student,
A shnayder iz mayn tate.
Mir lebn zeyer voyl un gut,
Oysgekleydte, zate.

My brother is a student,
My father is a tailor.
We live very well and fine,
Well clothed and well fed.

Mach ich mir a fetn tsimes
Fun di zise mern.
S'zaynen ale mayne kinder
Lerers, inzhenern.[12]

I make a juicy pudding
Of sweet carrots.
All my children have become
Teachers and engineers.

For some the new life meant "no longer living in a rotting hut," eating "blintses and pancakes with lots of butter and cheese," "a white cloth and wheat bread on the table," "using a knife and fork." For others, it meant building a large family, without worrying about a job and with the help of the government's bonuses. Still others identified it with the House of Culture, the clubhouse, the radio, the theater, "reading a newspaper and a book." In the following stanzas, a formerly religious woman decries her former piety, as she welcomes the secular benefits now at her disposal.

Oy, bin ich amol geven, oy, a frume
    yidene,
Yedn peysech tep gebrent,
Ale shabes licht gebentsht,
Ot a nar a yidene!

Male vos amol geven, oy, a nar a
    yidene,
Itster halt ich nit fun got
Un fun zayn bitern kompot.
Ich bin a tsefridene.

Ich bin shoyn gevorn itst nit kayn
    nar a yidene,
Ale nacht ich gey in klub—
Leyen tsaytungen, a buch,
Ich bin a tsefridene.[13]

Oh, I once was a pious woman,

Every Passover I fired my pots,
Every Sabbath I blessed the candles,
Ah, what a foolish woman!

What matters it now, what I was
    once,
Now, I don't think much of God
And of his bitter compote.
I am now contented.

I am no longer a foolish woman,

Every evening I go to the club—
I read a newspaper and a book,
And I am contented.

The element of political propaganda was strong in a great number of these songs, many of which hailed Stalin as the "wisest, kindest" man, "who protects us from our enemies . . . like a tender father his own sons and daughters." Others attacked Trotzky, sang about the "coming elections," mentioned the "Stakhanov" effort in stepping up the productive capacity. The falling away of old traditional patterns is reflected, too, in a number of songs which scoff at the old institutions of matchmaking, dowry, *kest,* social position which rested on the choice of in-laws who were pious and learned in the Torah. The following question-and-answer song, patterned on a nineteenth-century folk song still current in several variants in other Yiddish-speaking communities, reveals the parents' concern with the son's "impractical" approach in the selection of a mate.

Vos zitstu azoy batsornt, zunenu?

—Ich hob lib a sheyn meydele,
    mamenu.
Ver-zhe iz dos meydele, zunenu?
—A yunge komsomoletshke,
    mamenu.
Tsi hot zi epes nadn, zunenu?
—Tsvey goldene hent, mamenu.
Tsi hot zi epes tsirung, zunenu?
—A *kim* afn bluzkele, mamenu.

Why do you sit so troubled, dear
    son?
—I'm in love with a pretty little
    girl, mother dear.
Who is this little girl, dear son?
—A young Komsomolka, mother
    dear.
Has she any dowry, dear son?
—Two creative hands, mother dear.
Has she any jewels, dear son?
—A KIM pin on her blouse, mother
    dear.

Ver vet dich unter der chupe firn, zunenu?	Who will lead you to the canopy, dear son?
—Der gantser komsomol, mamenu.	—The whole Komsomol, mother dear.
Oy, ver vet dich bentshn, zunenu?	Oh, who will bless you, dear son?
—Oy, Stalin mit kalininen, mamenu.[14]	—Oh, Stalin and Kalinin, mother dear.

Some mothers aspired to sons who would be aviators, flying "high into the sky towards the sun," and maidens sought mates who incorporated some of the virtues and accomplishments mentioned in the following excerpted lines of a ditty:

Ich vil az mayn gelibter	I want my sweetheart to be able
Zol kenen tantsn, shvimen,	To dance and to swim,
Zayn zol er a royt-armeyer	I want him to be a Red-Army man
Ba voroshilov klimen.	Under the command of Klim Voroshilov.
Ich darf nit kayn zilber,	I need have no silver,
Ich darf nit kayn gold,	I need have no gold,
Mayn gelibter iz a stachanovets,	My sweetheart is a Stakhanovite,
Un er hot mich holt.[15]	And he loves me.

The drive to convert speedily a predominantly agricultural land into an industrial one is reflected in a number of songs which draw the contrast between the former "smoking kerosene lamps" and the "bright shining electricity," between the horse and buggy and the new automobiles. A song which speaks of an old craft, now mechanized, reveals the new rhythms and the increased tempos. Patterned after a nineteenth-century folk song, it still retains the refrain of the older song:

Mashines klapn, royshn klingen,	Machines clatter, roar, and ring,
A nay lidl vel ich zingen.	A new song to you I'll sing.
Refrain: Mit a nodl, on a nodl,	With a needle or without,
Ney ich mir b'koved godl.	I do my sewing with great pride.
A lidl zingt der nayer neyer,	A song now sings the new tailor,
A shnaydersh lidl fun konveyer.	A tailor song about the conveyer.
Neyt-zhe vayber, neyt geshmak,	Sew then, women, sew with spirit,
A pidzhak noch a pidzhak.[16]	Jackets, jackets, more and more.

The contempt for manual labor which had prevailed in the Jewish
community in the Pale was turned into "dignity and respect for the
laboring man." A former workman under the Czarist regime, deeply
moved by this transformation in his favor, begins a ballad in this way:

Ch'bin shoyn fun finf un fuftsik yor a yid,	I am a Jew fifty-five years of age,
Ober shtark, ober mechtik iz mayn lid,	But sturdy and powerful is my song;
Fun di hamers, velche royshik klingen,	From the hammers which loudly ring,
Ch'ob zich oysgelernt hilchik zingen.	I have learned out loud to sing.
Af der elter mit lider ch'bin gevorn raych,	Though I am old, I'm rich in song,
Vil ich onheybn zingen zey far aych.	Let me sing them now for you,
Mir iz shver in hartsn zey farshtikn,	It's hard for me to keep them in my heart,
Tsu di libe brider ch'vil zey shikn.	I want to send them out to my dear brothers.
Ich bin a proster arbeter fun zavod,	I am a simple worker in the factory,
In vaysrusland in babroysk, der shtot.[17]	In White Russia, in the city of Bobruisk.

The Collective Farm

The Jewish collective farms, set up and aided by the Soviet government in the Ukraine and Crimea, created an entirely new atmosphere
and a new category of Yiddish folk song. The age-old craving for the
land and a life upon it seemed satisfied at last, and a number of songs
chronicled this dramatic event, as they recalled the life under the Czar.

Bazunders, mir yidn,	Especially we Jews,
Megn avade zayn tsufridn.	May well be satisfied.
Far nikolayen hot der yid	During the reign of Nicholas, the Jew
In ergets nit gehat kayn ort.	Had no place he could call his own.
Un nit getort oysreydn kayn hoych vort.	He wasn't allowed to speak up for himself.
Itst ligt nikolay	Now, Nicholas and his gang
Mit zayn bande in der erd,	Lie in the ground,

Un undz hot men gegebn	And we have been given
Trakters mit ferd,	Tractors and horses,
Mir zoln gut ba-arbetn di erd.[18]	So that we may cultivate the land.

The drama of the sudden change from second-class citizens in congested towns and villages to farmers cultivating wide expanses of unfenced "collectives" is briefly revealed in the following topical rhymes, which describe the confusion and bewilderment of new arrivals in the countryside amid the changing times and the breakdown of the old mores.

Ver hot ven gezen	Have you ever seen
Pereselentses af tatshankes?	New settlers traveling on carts?
Zey forn zalbetsent	Riding ten at a time
Mit klumeklech, mit bankes.	With their bags and bundles.

Vaysinke brindze,	White cheese
Eygene tshabanes,	And our own sheep.
S'megn gleklech klingen	Bells may ring out
Fun sivash bizdanen.	From here to Siwash.

Chazerim vi di leybn,	Pigs like lions
Shpatsirn iber gas.	Walk along the street.
Alte tates loyfn,	Old fathers rush about,
Kinder, zayt nit blas.	Kids, don't be scared.

Vayber af tribunes	Women on platforms,
Reydn hoych un fray.	Speaking loud and free.
Haynt iz men gekumen	Today we've come to greet
Bagrisn ershtn may.	The First of May.

Tates in brigades	Fathers in brigades
Kosyen hoyche zangen.	Harvest the tall grain.
Me veyst nit mer fun shabes	We know not of the Sabbath
Un fun shoyfer klangen.[19]	Nor the blowing of the ram's horn.

A farm song which utilized the pattern of a former drinking song entitled "Yoshke, yoshke, shpan dem loshik" (Yoshke, Yoshke, harness the horse") now described Yoshke as a fleet rider with a horse with "wings of an eagle," who "races over the free earth," driving the "enemies from the fields, like frightened hares." However, the old refrain of *der rebe hot geheysn freylech zayn, trinken bronfn nit kayn vayn* ("the *rebe* told us to be gay, to drink whisky and not wine") was changed to *lomir ale freylech zayn, vayl mir veysn nit fun kayn payn* ("let us all be gay, for we know not of any sorrow").[20]

A Crimean farm song which became popular in the United States, Canada, and Palestine contained the following stanzas:

Az men fort kayn sevastopol,
Iz nit vayt fun simferopol,
Dortn iz a stantsie faran.
Ver darf zuchn naye glikn?
S'iz a stantsie an antikl.
In dzhankoye, dzhan, dzhan, dzhan.

When you go to Sevastopol,
Not too far from Simferopol,
There's a little depot there.
Why seek your luck elsewhere?
It's a special kind of depot.
In Zhankoye, zhan, zhan, zhan.

Refrain: Hey, dzhan, hey dzhankoye,
Hey dzhanvili, hey
dzhankoye,
Hey dzhankoye, dzhan,
dzhan, dzhan.

Hey, zhan, hey Zhankoye,
Hey, zhanvili, hey Zhankoye,

Hey Zhankoye, zhan, zhan, zhan.

Enfert yidn af mayn kashe,
Vu'z mayn bruder, vu'z abrashe?
S'geyt ba im der trakter vi a ban.
Di mume leye ba der kosilke,
Beyle ba der molotilke,
In dzhankoye, dzhan, dzhan, dzhan.

Jews, answer my question,
Where's my brother Abrasha?
He who rides his tractor like a train.
Aunt Leah is at the mower,
Bella is working the thresher,
In Zhankoye, zhan, zhan, zhan.

Ver zogt as yidn konen nor handlen,

Esn fete yoych mit mandlen,
Nor nit zayn kayn arbetsman?
Dos konen zogn nor di sonim—
Yidn, shpayt zey on in ponim,
Tut a kuk af dzhan, dzhan, dzhan.[21]

Who says that Jews can only be
traders
And eat fat soup with soup nuts
But cannot be workingmen?
Only our enemies can say that—
Jews, let's spit right in their faces,
Simply look at zhan, zhan, zhan.

Drinking and Dance Songs

A special category of collective farm songs were the drinking and dance songs, which marked every small or big occasion on the "road to collectivization." These described, most often in topical style, the fulfillment of the Five-Year Plans and other projected tasks. One such song tells the story of a "comrade who came down from the city and organized us into a collective farm" and then proceeds to drink a toast to "the new life . . . the fertile fields, . . . the new houses . . . the devoted children . . . old and young and everyone . . . but first of all to comrade Stalin."[22] Another, current during the Soviet twentieth-anniversary celebrations (1937), which is strongly reminiscent of the old style of the professional marriage entertainer (*badchen*), builds its rhymes in the traditional pattern, as the singer both greets and instructs the assembled guests. The singer salutes the government, thanks the leaders for having made "life on the farm secure," lists the various projects that have been successfully completed, and instructs everyone to decorate their houses, don holiday attire, march in the parade, go to the theater, and make merry at banquets with song and dance ". . . to spite our enemies, who despise workingmen. . . . But we have shown them that we know how to spill our blood for freedom. . . . Therefore, we drink a toast to everyone . . . and eat good blintses. . . . May we live till next year and not a single one of us be missing!" [23]

A drinking song which reveals the sharp struggle between the individual farmer and the collective farm ownership pokes fun at the *kulak* (independent farmer) who is "red in the face," because "we completed our harvesting on time . . . the flour has been milled and put up in sacks for the winter . . . ay-ay-ay, the fat *kulak* sits in his house, angry, because we keep adding another bull and another barn to our holdings, and a new roof to our clubhouse." [24]

Biro-Bidjan

In 1934, between the Biro and Bidjan rivers in the Soviet Far East, the Jewish autonomous region was established. At that time, the U.S.S.R. was calling young people to become pioneers and help develop the virgin lands. The rich natural resources of Biro-Bidjan attracted a number of young Jewish men and women, and some tens of thousand of settlers did go out there to build a Jewish community.

A ballad which tells a story of two such young people is one in which the singer recalls his childhood, when as a lad in a small town in the Pale, he worked for a rope twiner, "flirted with curly-headed Ethel and took her walking to the water-mill." After the revolution, when the government appealed to young people to become pioneers in the undeveloped regions, Ethel went off to Lake Baikal and became a teacher there, while he joined the army and, in two years, became an officer. One day, a letter arrived from Ethel, asking him to join her in Biro-Bidjan and there become a combine operator, and now he sits musing in the train, as it traverses the Soviet land from west to the Far East.

Herzl T. Rome, 1950

Itst fort a banele, a banele, a banele,	And now a little train is going, going,
Un s'raysn zich uf di semaforn.	And semaphores spring smartly up.
Vos brengen vet biro-bidjanele?	What will Biro-Bidjan bring me?
Geblibn zeks mesles tsu forn.[25]	I've six days traveling to do.

The severity of the Siberian climate, the hardships in cultivating the virgin earth, and the rigors of the new environment deterred and disillusioned many, while others dug in to build the new Jewish community. A song which describes the Jewish settlement some years later, when it already stood on more solid ground, includes the following stanzas:

Itst zits ich mir lebn taych biro,	I now sit beside the Biro river,
Di fish shvimen hin un tsurik,	Fish are swimming to and fro,
Un arum shpreyt zich a vald, a taige,	All around there's forest and taiga,
Far mir iz do dos beste glik.	For me this is the happiest place.
Velder mit nis un taychn mit fish	Forests with nuts and rivers with fish
Gefint ir in biro-bidjan,	You find in Biro-Bidjan,
Koyln un koks, a vilder oks	Coal and coke and a wild ox,
Un dertsu a vilder kaban.	And even a wild boar.
Biro-bidzhaner kolchozn hobn hipsh farzeyt,	Biro-Bidjan collective farms have sowed a good deal,

Ba undz iz alts gerotn—
Soye un veyts af di felder zich
    shpreyt,
Di shpaychlers zaynen ful
    ongeshotn.

And everything has taken well—
Soya and wheat are waving in the
    fields,
Our silos are full of grain.

Git nor a kuk, a shnayder fabrik,
Me neyt alts, ney un ney,

Look at our tailor factory,
Where everything is sewed and
    sewed,

Mashines naye, dos lebn iz a
    mechaye,
Es lebt zich gut un fray.

New machines, life is good,

We live well and free.

Varf nor a blik—a benkl fabrik,
Mir hobn af vos tsu zitsn.
Me macht dort bufetn, hiltserne
    betn,
Gezunterheyt tsu farnitsn.[26]

Cast your eye on the chair factory,
We now have something to sit on.
Making wooden chests and beds,

To be used in good health.

Songs of Literary Origin

From the early twenties, Yiddish song compilations were published that included the sung poems of Morris Rosenfeld, S. Frug, Avrom Reisin, I. L. Perets, M. Broderson, I. Katsenelson, and others. Later publications contained poems authored by the Soviet Jewish poets I. Bakst, I. Charik, David Hofshtein, Perets Markish, Itsik Fefer, I. Dobrushin, S. Halkin, A. Kushnirov, Osher Shvartsman, Moyshe Kulbak, L. Kvitko, Ezra Fininberg, and others, set to music by such Jewish composers as M. Gnessin, A. Veprik, M. Milner, A. Krein, S. Polonski, R. Boyarskaya, and others.

By the thirties, many categories of the "old," nineteenth-century Yiddish folk song—poverty and struggle songs, soldier songs, cheder and children's songs, love songs and ballads, Chasidic songs, marriage songs, topical and historical songs, songs of customs and beliefs, and many more relating to the life in the Czarist Pale—had practically disappeared from the current scene. Here and there a song from the old treasure was absorbed into current Soviet-Yiddish folk song, which now encompassed many fewer categories and which, prior to World War II, was in the main already the product of poets and composers.

Occasionally an anonymous song, such as the "Ballad of Kirov's Death," became popular, when in 1934 Sergei Kirov, government head of the Leningrad region, was assassinated. The feeling of isolation and hostility from the outside world, coupled with this act by an "insider," created an atmosphere of gloom, which found its expression in the following stanzas :

Mir zaynen aroysgegangen gantsfri af di gasn
Un getrofn shvartse fonen af di toyern,
Mir hobn zich dervust fun der vister yedi-e,
Az undzer land hot a firer ongevoyrn.

We came out early on the streets
And found black flags on all the gates,
We learned of the dreadful news,
That our land had lost a leader.

Farsholtn zol er zayn, der merder, der blutiker,
Farnichtet zol er zayn, der homen !
Mir shteyen af di gasn redlechvays,
Un ba yedern in hartsn kirov's nomen.[27]

Cursed be the bloody murderer,
Destroyed may he be, the Haman !
We stand on the streets in groups,
And in every heart—Kirov's name.

By then many an art song had achieved similar wide circulation, like the lullaby authored by Itsik Fefer, set to a melody by R. Boyarskaya, which described the natural beauty of Biro-Bidjan and recalled the difficult years which preceded its establishment and development.

Shlof mayn kind, farmach di oygn,
Tunkler vern berg.
S'iz an odler durchgefloygn,
Zayn zolstu vi er.

Sleep, my child, close your eyes,
The mountains are darkening now.
An eagle has just flown by,
May you be like him.

Un vi er zolstu zich hoybn,
Zayn mit volkns glaych.
Durch di ovnt-dike shoybn
Kukt der biro taych.

And like the eagle may you rise,
Level with the clouds.
Through the evening windowpane
The Biro river shines.

S'fleg dayn tate oyf di vegn
Shlepn dem geveyn.
Af amurer sheyne vegn,
Boyen mir a heym.

Your father once upon these roads
Dragged his cries along.
On the lovely Amur roads
We now build a home.

Un far der heym veln mir zich shlogn,
Bisn letstn blut.

And for this home we shall fight
To the last drop of blood.

S'hoybt di erd shoyn on tsu togn, Earth is just about to dawn,
Shlof mayn kind barut.[28]   Sleep, my child, in peace.

World War II

When the German *Wehrmacht* struck the Soviet borders in June, 1941, the country was staggered by the surprise attack. As the Germans poured into White Russia, Ukraine, Lithuania, the first and terrible victims were the Jews. The Soviet government immediately instituted a mass evacuation of Jewish men, women, and children, who moved in endless trains towards the interior, dazed and bewildered, many of whom had witnessed their homes destroyed, their loved ones maimed and murdered.

Der eshelon iz greyt,	The echelon is ready,
Mir ayln bald avek,	We're hurrying away,
O, gicher, gicher, gicher	O, quickly, quickly let us
Antloyfn fun der shrek.	Flee from all this fright.
Der gazlen sharft zich shoyn	The murderer is already sharpening
Af undz do zayne tseyn,	His teeth for us,
Er kukt fun lang shoyn	For some time now he's been
Af undz alemen aroys.	Preparing this for us.
Ade, mayn shtetele,	Good-bye my little town,
Mayn sedl un mayn hoyz.	My orchard and my house.
Dos gantse hob-un-guts	All that I possess,
Gelozt af gots barot,	I've left in God's hands.
S'iz keyner nit farblibn,	No one now remains,
Se fort di gantse shtot.	The entire city is leaving.

Refrain: Di reder klapn beyz,	The wheels clatter angrily,
In moyech dreyt,	The mind spins round,
Mir loyfn rateven	We're fleeing to save
Zich funem toyt.[29]	Ourselves from death.

The U.S.S.R. became an armed camp. Reservists were hastily called up, volunteers joined the partisan brigades, the civilian population dug in to meet the invading German armies.

Ir hot gevolt mayn tayer land batsvingen,	You wanted to enslave our dear land,
Ir hot gevolt mir zoln shklafn zayn,	You wanted to make slaves of all of us,
Ober aych vet dos keynmol nit gelingen,	But you will never succeed in this,

Es ligt, es vart der royter partizan.	Because the red partisan lies in wait for you.

Ich gey nit kemfn, vayl me tut mir rufn,	I go to fight, not because they called me,
Bay mir iz kayn moyre nit faran.	But because I have no fear at all.
Ich gey in shlacht un mutig vil ich kemfn,	I go to battle bravely and bravely will I fight,
Vayl ich bin der royter partizan.[30]	For I am the red partisan.

But the courage and determination of the Jewish fighters did not prevent the tragic toll as a result of the German atrocities. A ballad, sung by a refugee on a train bound for Tashkent in October, 1941, tells the story of the quiet, gentle Avrom-Dovid, who lived in the Ukraine with his wife, Brayne, and their five children "happily and respected by all. Suddenly, Hitler came and ordered him to build a wooden hut beneath the ground — a living grave — and forced the family to bury itself alive." Following are the concluding lines of this ballad :

On a nomen, on a tsam,	No marker, no name,
Nit kayn shum levaye,	No kind of funeral,
Nemt-zhe brider zich arop	Brothers, bear this
Fun derfun a raye.	Well in mind.
Ven me geyt dos ort farbay,	When you pass this spot,
Lozt a kol zich hern :	A voice is heard :
"Nekome nemt ! nekome nemt !	"Take revenge ! Take revenge !
Ir zolt zich do farshvern.	You must swear it here.
Undzer tsorn, undzer vey,	Our anger, our pain,
Zolt ir forgedenken,	You must never forget,
Un dem hitsl dem fashist,	Never to withhold the punishment
Di beyze shtrof nit shenken."[31]	From the *hitsl,* the fascist."

The collective farms in the Ukraine and Crimea were destroyed by the Germans and a song about hand-to-hand fighting in the south contained the following stanzas :

Fun der hayntiker milchome	About this war
Vel ich lider zingen,	I'm going to sing for you
Az se zol di gantse velt	Ringing songs
Mit di lider klingen,	That all the world may hear,
Vi s'iz forgekumen dort	How Yoshke,

Mit Yoshke dem adeser,	Who came from Odessa,
Az er hot geshlogn zich	Fought hand-to-hand
Mitn daytsh af meser.	With bayonet against the Germans.

Far di zoyg-kinder, vos ir	For the suckling babes
Hot lebedik bagrobn,	Which you buried alive,
Vet ir, treyfe hitsles, ayer	You rotten *hitsls*
Oyskumenish hobn.	Will yet pay for this.
Vayl ir hot di sheyne shtet	Because you laid
Vist gemacht un chorev,	The lovely cities waste,
Farn lebn ayern	I shall not guarantee
Bin ich zich nit orev.[32]	For your lives.

Ditties to bolster the courage of the fighters, at the front, in the rear, were created spontaneously and sung everywhere, like the following:

Yidn, rusn, ukrainer,	Jews, Russians, Ukrainians,
Poyln, totern, gruziner,	Poles, Tartars, Georgians,
Nemt farkatshet beyde hent,	Roll up both your sleeves,
Shlogt dem daytsh vi vayt ir kent.	Hit the Germans with all you've got.

Alte layt un yunge kinder,	Old men and young children,
Kegn katsev, kegn shinder,	Against the butcher and the skinner,
Kegn hitlern dem hunt—	Against Hitler that dog—
Shanevet nit dos gezunt.	Do not spare your health.

Meymest im af ale vegn,	Hit him hard on all the roads,
Er zol ufshteyn nit dervegn,	So that he can't rise again,
Lozt nit kumen im tsum shtand,	Don't let him regain his balance,
Traybt dem soyne funem land![33]	Drive the enemy from the land!

Laments, dirges, topical ballads were created by the people, in which they described the terrible tortures inflicted upon them by the German invaders. One such song chronicles the German attack on June 21, 1941, "at five o'clock in the morning," and before the sun rose "infants were slaughtered before their mothers' eyes," people were driven from their homes and buried alive, and Jewish maidens brought to shame.[34]

This tragic period was marked by a new though brief burst of anonymous song creativity among the people, and the following lament, reminiscent of the seventeenth- and eighteenth-century martyrologies when the Ukrainian Haydamak hordes overran Jewish communities with fire and sword, is an eye-witness account of a young woman who was "married on Tuesday and on the following Sabbath, early in the morning, the *hitsls* were leading us to our death and the river ran red with our blood." Here are two stanzas of this topical ballad :

Me hot nit geshoynt nit kayn alt, nit kayn yung,	They spared no one, old nor young,
Bam foter aroysgerisn hot men di tsung,	They tore out my father's tongue,
Di muter derdushet in hoyf afn mist	They smothered my mother in a pile of garbage
Un opgehakt dort ba di shvester di brist.	And chopped off my sisters' breasts.
Mayn man hot men shpiln genoyt af der fleyt,	They forced my husband to play on the flute,
Me hot im bagrobn, oy, lebedikerheyt,	And then he was buried, oh, alive.
Der malech-hamoves hot chuyzek gemacht,	The Angel of Death did mock at us,
A mise-meshune hot er undz gebracht.[35]	Bringing a horrible death to us.

Songs and ballads of fallen heroes, of maidens longing for lovers gone to war, of devastated homes and farms, marching songs and stirring hymns were created by the people in this period. So strong was the yearning for the folk for a return to normalcy and peace, that a song which already anticipated the tasks of rebuilding at the war's end contained the following stanzas :

Un az se vet zich di milchome kontshen,	And when the war ends,
Un yederer vet kumen af zayn ort,	And everyone returns to his home,
Mit di fraynt un alte gute-brider,	With friends and good brothers
Veln mir banays tsunoyfkumen zich dort.	We will get together there.
Di hoyle shteyner veln mir a kush ton,	We will kiss the bare stones,
Un ontrogn tsigl un di leym,	And bring on bricks and clay,
Af tsepukenish dem beyzn soyne,	And to spite our cruel enemies,
Veln mir zich ufboyen di heym.[36]	We will rebuild our home.

And when the victory had been won and the war was over at last,

there were songs of joy and songs which exulted in the triumph of the
Red Army over Hitler :

Bafrayt hot undz di royte armey	The Red Army liberated us
Fun di finstere necht.	From the dark nights.
Funem gantsn vind-un-vey,	From all the horror and woe.
Mir zenen mer kayn knecht.[37]	We are slaves no longer.

By then, the whole staggering picture of the German annihilation of
6.5 million Jews had come to light. Those who survived to return to
their former homes found synagogues razed, cemeteries desecrated, homes
destroyed, farms uprooted—with the memories of loved ones maimed
and murdered and buried alive, of nightmarish degradations and
atrocities hovering over all. A rare curse song, demanding the Biblical
"eye for an eye" punishment for the German crimes, contains the
following stanzas :

A klole fun der toych'che shray ich aroys,	A curse from the depths I am shouting,
Af hitler dem blut-tsaper gis ich zi oys.	On Hitler the bloodsucker, I pour out my curse.
Azoyvi du host undz dos lebn getoyt,	Just as you deprived us of life,
Azoy zol men pitslechvayz shnaydn dayn hoyt.	So may your skin be stripped bit by bit.
Un geyn in der fremd zolt ir zuchn a dach,	And may you be homeless, no roof over your head,
Un keyner zol gornit farshteyn ayer shprach.	With no one to understand your speech.
Vayl ir hot af undzern churbn gekvelt,	Because you exulted over our ruin,
Arumshlepn zolt ir zich iber der velt.	May you wander bereft over the world.
Un vu ir vet geyn, zol aych nochgeyn der toyt,	And wherever you go, may death follow you,
Un oysgeyn zolt ir ergets hinter a ployt.	May you perish alone behind a fence.
Dayn folk zol gepruvt zayn tsu filn dem tam,	May your people be made to feel what its like,
Vi kinder tsu shmirn di lipn mit sam.[38]	To have their children murdered by smearing poison on their lips.

Soviet-Yiddish folk song spans a brief creative period of one generation, marked by revolution, Civil War, and invasion. The slogan "national in form and Socialist in content," because of the particular circumstances and specific history of the Jews in Eastern Europe, came to mean for Soviet Jews, perhaps sooner than for other ethnic groups in the U.S.S.R., a rapid shedding of many traditional forms, which was apparently neither retarded nor stayed even after the establishment of Biro-Bidjan. Yet despite these conditions, Yiddish folk song in the Soviet Union was created and circulated during several decades. The songs heard during World War II are especially distinguished for their mood of determination and heroism in the struggle against German Nazism.

Together with the Soviet-Yiddish art song, Soviet-Yiddish folk song exerted a strong influence on the songs created by the Jews in the ghettos and concentration camps in the other countries under the German occupation. It may be that these Soviet-Yiddish folk songs of World War II mark the close of Yiddish folk song in the U.S.S.R. As for Soviet-Yiddish art song, with the tragic destruction of Yiddish cultural institutions and of many prominent Jewish men of letters during the dire years of 1948–1953, this phase of Yiddish song may also have been brought to an abrupt end.

Notes

CHAPTER FIFTEEN

1. Rubin, MSS The *Komsomol* is the Communist Youth Organization. The *Pioneers* and *Oktyabers* were similar organizations geared to school and preschool children respectively.

2. Rubin, MSS.

3. *See* Footnote 48 in Chapter XIV, "To Zion."

4. B. and F., pp. 472–473.

5. D. and Y., pp. 416–417, No. 3.

6. *Ibid.,* p. 415, No. 1.

7. Serebriani, p. 152. Marshal Semyon Budënny was then commander of the Soviet cavalry.

8. B. and F., pp. 470–471. Marshal Klimenti Voroshilov (b. 1881) was Chief of the Red Army at that time.

9. *Yidishe Sovetishe,* pp. 25–26.

10. D. and Y., p. 422, No. 10.

11. B. and F., pp. 466–467.

12. *Yidishe Sovetishe,* pp. 33–34.

13. D. and Y., pp. 462–463, No. 6.

14. *Ibid.,* pp. 461–462, No. 4. *KIM*—K.I.M.—represents the three Russian letters of the organization: International Communist Youth. M. I. Kalinin (1875–1946), of peasant origin, was president of the supreme council of the U.S.S.R. from 1938 to 1946.

15. *Ibid.,* pp. 449–50, No. 8. Alexei Stakhanov in the Don Basin in 1935 instituted a method of mining more coal at accelerated tempos. This method was emulated in all endeavors, and the term *stakhanovite* was absorbed into the vernacular.

16. *Ibid.,* pp. 464, No. 9.

17. *Ibid.,* p. 408, No. 25.

18. *Ibid.,* p. 437, No. 22.

19. *Ibid.,* 426, No. 4

20. D. and Y., pp. 431–432, No. 14.

21. B. and F., pp. 452–453.

22. *Ibid.,* pp. 439–440.

23. D. and Y., pp. 438–439, No. 23.

24. *Ibid.,* p. 427, No. 7.

25. D. and Y., pp. 465–466, No. 1.

26. *Ibid.,* pp. 466–468, No. 2.

27. B. and F., pp. 444–445.

28. Rubin, MSS.

29. Kupershmid, pp. 28–29.

30. Gontar.

31. Kupershmid, pp. 26–27. *Hitsl*: dog-killer, scoundrel. During the German invasion, this term became synonymous with Hitler and any German soldier.

32. *Ibid.*, p. 14.
33. *Ibid.*, p. 31.
34. *Ibid.*, pp. 25–26.
35. *Ibid.*, p. 24.
36. *Ibid.*, pp. 30–31.
37. Gontar.
38. Kupershmid, pp. 23–24.

CHAPTER XVI

The Struggle to Survive

THE YIDDISH FOLK SONGS OF WORLD WAR II WERE CREATED OUT OF suffering and deprivation, degradation and terror, struggle, heroism, and death. Texts and tunes by known and unknown authors described the day-by-day destruction of vast Jewish multitudes at the hands of a tyranny unequaled in world history. Reminiscent of the seventeenth-century chronicles of martyrdom, these songs memorialized and condemned the Nazi-German power and its personnel, which for six years engaged in sadistic expropriation of Jewish possessions, uprooted and shifted human beings from place to place, exploited and drove them until they fell in their tracks, and then physically destroyed them when they were still alive. This macabre program of a military might organized in a brutal war against an unarmed civilian population of millions is revealed in hundreds of songs written by men, women, and children, old and young, in a desperate struggle to survive.

It is generally conceded that whoever has not himself experienced the German occupation can never really grasp the complex evil process that turned countries into prison camps and human slaughterhouses and made the earth and every step upon it a yawning grave. And yet, even survivors on the very day of their liberation could not themselves believe that what their eyes had witnessed had actually occurred.[1] Disbelief, bewilderment, shock are evident in many songs current soon after the German occupation of Poland in 1939, coupled with the sincere faith that this nightmare would soon be dispelled and everything would return once again to normal. But when the consequences of German rule became evident and it was realized that no quarter could be expected from its evil men, the songs not only chronicled the tragedy but also served to rally and organize the people for survival and struggle against the tyrants. The song, the satirical rhyme, the witty saying, the humorous anecdote became extremely important and even necessary to the Jews in the German ghettos of the twentieth century. They were news bearers, morale builders, heart warmers, helping hands, as well as organizers and fighters for life and freedom.

Many categories are represented in the songs of World War II : [2] lullabies, work songs, satirical songs and ballads, prayer songs, songs of pain and anguish, shame and humiliation, songs of ghetto life, concentration camp and death camp songs, songs of courage and heroism, bitter hatred for the enemy, songs of faith and hope, struggle and joy in victory. Almost entirely absent are the songs of normal times : love and marriage, children, joy in work and study, humor and merriment. The occasional drinking and dance song has the macabre quality of the seventeenth-century dance of death; the rare love song pines away beneath the gray ghetto walls, yearning for the sight of a green blade of grass and a bit of blue sky. Created by the whole people, both by the educated and untutored, the songs contain elements of fine poetry side by side with primitive folkloric rhymes. Through all the songs, however, there flows the singleminded will to live, to survive, to preserve wherever and as long as possible every vestige of dignity, self-respect, the traditions and customs cherished for centuries, the precious habits of learning and teaching, the creative urge to write, sing, and even put on plays and concerts ! [3]

The Ghetto Songs

Most of the songs were created in the ghettos set up by the Germans in 1940 in Warsaw, Kovno, Vilna, Lodz, Bialystok, Riga, Cracow, and other centers. The songs described the crowded quarters, the food scarcities, the backbreaking toil, the irritations, abnormalities, humiliations, degradations heaped upon Jews from all over Europe, who had been driven into the ghettos together. The ghetto songs reveal the capacity for suffering and the elemental will to survive — the natural urge to create, to sing and even laugh. The ghetto had its street singers, its coffee and tea houses. It had its beggars, albeit all they pleaded for were "little old crusts, little old crumbs of bread." A poor fellow, wandering about the streets of the Warsaw ghetto, was dubbed *mandri variat* ("crazy wise man") because he would suddenly appear on the street half-naked, muttering and singing. He sang a ditty which soon became widespread :

Halt zich yingl, halt zich fest,	Hold on, fellow, hang on tight,
Di nekome vet kumen mit di ershte frost.[4]	Revenge will come with first frosts.

The same fellow would go about humming another rhyme, which similarly soon became popular: *Me hot zey in dr'erd, me vet zey iberlebn, me vet noch derlebn* ("To hell with them, we will survive them, we will yet survive").[5] Laughter became a necessity and a channel for the hatred of the enemy; it became the catalyst for expressions of anger and bitterness when the means of struggle were still not clearly defined.

Yo, yo, bay undz muz yeder freylech zayn;	Yes, yes, among us everyone must be gay;
Farges fun morgn, du muzt nit zorgn,	Forget the morrow, you must not sorrow,
Ven dos harts lacht, lachn mir,	When the heart laughs, we laugh,
Un ven dos harts veynt, lachn mir,	When the heart weeps, we laugh,
Bay undz muz yeder freylech. zayn. . . .[6]	Among us, everyone must be gay. . . .

With a song, Jews passed the dread hours concealed in a hideout behind a wall, beneath a floor, in the forest in improvised, camouflaged caves and ditches. With a tune, religious Jews martyred themselves, going to their death, singing of their undying faith in the Lord and the Messiah.[7] A ballad current among religious Jews in the Kovno ghetto speaks bravely of a future when Jews will be free and their death avenged.

In slobodker yeshive, in geto fun lite,	In the Slobodka Talmudic Academy, in the Lithuanian ghetto,
Zitst dort an alter shames aleyn.	There sits an old deacon alone.
Er zitst un zogt zayn letstn vide	He sits there saying his last prayers
Un shraybt zayn tsavoe far der briderlecher heym.	Writing his testament for the fraternal home.
Refrain: Az ir vet bafrayt vern yidelech,	When you will be liberated, dear Jews,
Zolt ir dertseyln di kinderlech,	Tell your dear children
Fun undzer payn un gehenim,	Of our pain and hell,
Fun undzer laydn un mord.	Of our suffering and death.

Vayzt di kvorim, di nemen,

Dort baym nayntn fort.

S'vet ober kumen a tsayt un di zun
vet oyfshaynen,
Un bafrayen di yidn fun geto un
noyt,
Dan ba-ern veln mir di kvorim
Vu s'zaynen gefaln yidn mit a
freydikn toyt.[8]

Show them the graves and the
inscriptions,
There, near the Ninth Fort.

But the time will come and the sun
will shine again
And liberate the Jews from the
ghetto and pain,
Then we will honor the graves
Where Jews went happily to their
death.

Those who went "happily" to their death did so with the deep faith
that in dying *al kidesh hashem* ("for the Holy Name") they were giving
their lives to save all the others. Surely the good God would be softened
by their sacrifice and spare the innocent millions? In the following, we
hear the cry of those faithful who, even as they breathed their last for
their "tortured sisters and brothers," wanted so desperately to live!

Ich vil azoy lebn;
Ich kon noch nisht shtarbn.
Men zol mir oyf oygn
Nisht leygn kayn sharbn.
Ich vil noch derlebn
Di glikliche tsayt
Tsu ze-en di brider
Fun laydn bafrayt.
Di tsayt iz nisht vayt,
Dos muz bald geshen,
Ich ober muz faln
Al kidesh hashem.
Ich loz mayn tsavoe
In klingende lider
Far mayne gematerte
Shvester un brider.[9]

I want so to live;
I cannot die yet
And have them put
Shards on my eyes.
I want to live
Until that happy time
To see my brothers
Freed from their misery.
The time is not far off,
It must happen soon,
But I must sacrifice myself
For the Holy Name.
I leave my last testament
In ringing songs
For my tortured
Sisters and brothers.

The struggle to remain alive was waged in a daily battle against
whips, clubs, and guns: beatings, looting, arson, shooting.

Ach gevald, vi halt ich oys!
Vi groys der tsar, di shand vi groys!

Vu zol ich nemen a rizn-harts

Oh, help, how can I bear it!
How great is my anguish, how
terrible the degradation!
Where shall I find the heart of a
giant

| Durchtsumachn aza groysn shmarts?[10] | To bear the terrible pain? |

Recalling the terrible days of the "snatchers" in Czarist Russia of more than a century earlier, German storm troopers roved the ghetto streets in man hunts to swell the forced-labor camps.

In der fri der zeyger klapt zeks,	In the morning at six o'clock,
Oyf ale gasn gefinen zich S.S.	The streets are full of S.S. men.
Zey yogn un traybn di groyse masn,	They chase and drive great masses,
Dos yidishe blut gist zich in di gasn.	Jewish blood is flowing in the streets.

Azoy vi es zenem gekumen di S.S. ofitsirn,	As soon as the S.S. officers came,
Hot men ongehoybn dem transport tsu firn,	They began to transport the Jews,
Kranke hobn zey oyfn ort dershosn—	The sick they shot right on the spot—
Dos yidishe blut hot zich oyf dem veg gegosn.[11]	Jewish blood flowed the whole way.

During the day, the narrow ghetto streets swarmed and hummed with activities that bore a semblance of normalcy. Trading went on and the following describes sardonically the pathetic quality of the "merchandise" sold by women and children—the men having been hauled off to the concentration camps.

Shmoktshes, banankes, veytsene kuchelech,	Doodads, bananas, wheaten cookies,
Geviklt in grine, royte papirelech,	Wrapped in green and red bits of paper,
Farkoyfn in geto iber ale gasn	Are sold on all the ghetto streets
Mames un kinder fun di orime klasn.	By mothers and children of the poor classes.

Di kvalitet fun di shmoktshes, farshteyt ir doch avade,	The quality of the doodads, you can well imagine,
Hot dem zelbn tam vos di geto-lemonade,	They taste just like the ghetto lemonade,
Un ver s'hot eynmol farzucht di produktsie fun bir,	And whoever has once tasted the beer,
Der hot gehat mitn boych klogenishn on a shir.[12]	Has had no end of trouble with his stomach.

Deprived of normal occupations, "new" ones were created in the ghetto, where the utmost resourcefulness and ingenuity were motivated by the desperate will to live. Women and children, the old and sick, and all those unfit to perform the backbreaking toil in the forced-labor camps and projects of the invaders traded with anything and everything to keep from starving to death. Others resorted to smuggling food and other objects past the German and Jewish police guards at the ghetto gates. Recalling an earlier, Yiddish drinking song, a "smuggler" describes his distasteful occupation, brought on by the abnormal circumstances:

Gey ich mir mit giche trit, giche trit,	I walk along with quick, quick steps,
Un a fule torbe shlep ich mit.	Carrying a full sack with me.
Un di fis fun midkayt boygn zich	And my legs buckle with weariness
Un dos vaser rint fun di, fun di shich.	And water oozes from my, from my shoes.
A torbe bulbes nit geklert, nit geklert,	I have a sack of spuds, and never you mind,
Un a funtl groypn iz oych vos vert,	And a pound of groats is worth something too,
Broyt a halbn labn hoych un dik,	A half a loaf of bread, big and thick,
Fleysh a fertl zaytl—an antik.	A quarter side of meat—a precious find.
Mir zenen ale shnorers gevorn haynt,	We've all become panhandlers today,
Vayl mir zaynen yidn un men hot undz faynt.	Because we are Jews and we're hated.
Fun eybik on zich tsit shoyn ot dos lid,	This tune has been heard since ancient times,
Ach vi shver un biter s'iz tsu zayn a yid![13]	Oh, how hard and bitter it is to be a Jew!

Crowding many families into one dwelling created abnormal congestion and irritations. A song that satirized the situation describes a hilarious incident in which a young man came home late at night. When he finally stumbled into his "crowded" bed, the female in it cried out aloud. He soothed and pacified her gently until she fell asleep again, but what was his horror to discover in the morning, that his female was an old crone! The refrain follows:

Ich bin nit shuldik, s'iz bay undz
    enge dires,
Ich bin nit shuldik, s'iz fintster
    umetum,
Ich bin nit shuldik, ir veyst aleyn
    farvos.
Vayl in der fintster ze ich koym
    mayn eygn noz.[14]

I'm not to blame, we live in
    crowded houses,
I'm not to blame, its pitch-dark
    everywhere,
I'm not to blame, you know the
    reason why.
Because I cannot even see my own
    nose in the dark.

The songs of M. Gebirtig, the most popular folk bard in Europe between the two world wars, were very popular in the ghettos from the very first days of the German occupation. Gebirtig endeavored to instill in his suffering, bewildered people a feeling of contempt for the brutal conquerors. In his song "Minutn fun b'tochn" ("Moments of Confidence"), written on October 2, 1940, he bids people be merry, for he hopes it won't be long before the war is ended and with it, the rule of the Germans. "Jews, be gay, don't walk about in sadness, but be patient and have faith. . . . Don't relinquish for a moment your weapon of laughter and gaiety, for it keeps you united." Following are the concluding lines of this song:

Hulyet! tantst talyonim,
Laydn ken a yid,
S'vet di shverste arbet
Undz keynmol machn mid.
Kern? Zol zayn kern!
Kolzman ir vet zayn
Iz umzist dos kern,
S'vet do nisht vern reyn. . . .
Vashn? Zol zayn vashn!
Kayin's royter flek
Hevel's blut fun hartsn
Dos vasht zich nisht avek.
Traybt undz fun di dires!
Shnaydt undz op di berd!
Yidn! Zol zayn freylech! . . .
Mir hobn zey in dr'erd![15]

Revel! Dance you hangmen,
A Jew knows how to suffer,
The most difficult work
Will never make us tired.
Sweep? Let there be sweeping!
So long as you're around
Sweeping is quite useless,
It never can be clean. . . .
Wash? Let there be washing!
Cain's red stain,
Abel's heart's blood
Cannot be washed away.
Drive us from our dwellings!
Cut off our beards!
Jews! Let's be gay. . . .
To hell with them!

As the Nazi atrocities continued to mount, Gebirtig's tone became more fearful, and in May, 1942, he wrote a song which describes "the wild foe marching swiftly forward . . . wherever he comes, life ceases . . . he advances in blood and degradation, swallowing up one country after

the other." Gebirtig hoped desperately that "from too much gorging . . .
the invader's end would result. Amen, . . ." but he never lived to see it,
although he had prophetically sensed the course of events as early as
1938, following the pogroms in Pshitik and Minsk-Mazovetsk, when
Belzhits and Treblinka were still ordinary towns and not infamous death
camps. It was then that he had written his "Es brent" ("It Is Burning"),
which became one of the most popular songs in the ghettos and concentration camps and was subsequently known to Yiddish-speaking Jews
everywhere. Following are three stanzas and two refrains from this song :

S'brent briderlech s'brent!
Oy, undzer orem shtetl nebech
  brent!
Beyze vintn mit yerugzn
Raysn, brechn un tseblozn
Shtarker noch di vilde flamen,
Alts arum shoyn brent!

It's burning, brothers, it's burning!
Oh, our poor little town is aflame!

Angry winds full of fury,
Tear and break and blow asunder
Stronger still the wild flames,
Everything is burning!

Refrain: Un ir shteyt un kukt azoy
      zich
      Mit farleygte hent,
      Un ir shteyt un kukt azoy
      zich,
      Undzer shtetl brent. . . .

And you stand there looking on

With folded arms,
And you stand there looking on

While our town goes up in flames....

S'brent! briderlech s'brent!
Oy, es ken cholile kumen der
  moment,
Undzer shtot mit undz tsuzamen
Zol oyf ash avek in flamen,
Blaybn zol—vi noch a shlacht.
Nor puste, shvartse vent!

It's burning, brothers, it's burning!
Oh, the moment can alas, come,

When our city with us in it
Can go up in flames,
Leaving it, like after a battle,
With empty, charred walls!

S'brent, briderlech, s'brent!
Di hilf iz nor in aych aleyn gevendt.
Oyb dos shtetl iz aych tayer,
Nemt di keylim lesht dos fayer.
Lesht mit ayer eygn blut.
Bavayzt az ir dos kent.

It's burning, brothers, it's burning!
Help depends only on you.
If the town is dear to you,
Take the vessels and quench the fire.
Quench it with your own blood.
Show that you can do it.

Refrain: Shteyt nit brider, ot azoy
      zich
      Mit farleygte hend.

Do not stand there looking on

With folded arms.

Shteyt nit brider, lesht dos fayer
Undzer shtetl brent![18]

Don't stand there brothers, quench the fire,
Our little town's aflame!

Concentration-Camp Songs

Europe was transformed into a vast concentration camp in which the Jews were the first and most terrible victims. Ghetto life became the threshold to the slave camp and the yawning death pits. From early dawn, the tramping feet of the forced labor brigades could be heard marching on the cobbled ghetto streets, past the guarded gates to endless hours of backbreaking toil and starvation rations, designed to work the remaining able-bodied Jews to death.

Zuntog un Montog—ligt men in di griber,
Dinstog un Mitvoch—hot men fiber.

Sunday and Monday—we lie in the ditches,
Tuesday and Wednesday—we have the fever.

Donershtog un Fraytog—hakt men shteyner,
Shabes hot men tsubrochene beyner.

Thursday and Friday—we break stones,
On the Sabbath, we have aching bones.

Shlofn shlofn men in di palatkes,
Nishto kayn hoyzn, nishto kayn gatkes,
Nshto kayn shich, nishto kayn shtivl,
Nishto kayn groshn tsu shraybn a brivl.[17]

We sleep in tents,
We have no pants nor underwear,
We have no shoes, we have no boots,
We haven't a penny to send a letter.

To cling to the last shreds of dignity and manliness became almost a heroic act in itself. Following is a song written by the old Rabbi Emanuel Hirshberg of the Lodz ghetto, which describes the Nazi use of elderly men in the place of horses.

Fintster, nas un vintn kalte
Shlepn vegn noch der tsol,
Mener shver, shoyn shvache, alte
O, vu nemt men kraft? O vu?

Dark, wet, and cold winds
We pull our quota of wagons,
Tired men, weak and old,
O, where can we find strength? O where?

Bruder! shlep un shtup dem vogn
Gants geduldik! Chotsh s'iz shver.
Gornisht kuk im oyf dem mogn,
Oysgehungert un gants ler.

Brother! Pull and push the wagon
Patiently! Though it be hard.
Pay no attention to your stomach,
Which is empty and starved.

Geyt geshpant un shlept dem vogn,	Walk in harness and pull the wagon,
Krechtst nisht, shrayt nisht, zingt a lid.	Don't moan or cry but sing a song.
Veyst, az sof kol sof vet togn,	Know, that in the end the dawn will come,
Gliklich vet noch zayn der yid.[18]	And the Jew will yet be happy again.

Every day became a battle for survival, and the weapons included all manner of ingenious devices to trick the hangmen of their prey. Songs were one of the important weapons, often flaunted courageously in the face of the invaders, like the two-lined rhymes given below which were sung in the Warsaw ghetto. Patterned on the Slavic *chastushki,* each pair of lines had a lilting Chasidic refrain : *biribi, bambambam.*

Vos darfn mir veynen, vos darfn mir klogn,	Why should we weep, why should we mourn,
Mir veln noch frankn a kadish noch zogn.	We'll live to say the prayer of the dead for Frank.
Lomir zayn freylech un zogn zich vitsn,	Let us be gay and tell jokes,
Mir veln noch hitlern shive noch zitsn.	We'll yet live to see Hitler dead.
Lomir zich treystn, di tsores fargesn,	Let us comfort one another and forget our troubles,
Es veln di verim noch hitlern fresn.	The worms will yet gnaw at Hitler.
Di sonim, vos firn undz dort kayn treblinke,	The enemies who lead us there to Treblinka
Zey veln noch vern in der erd ayngezinken.	Will yet be sinking into the earth.
Mir veln tsuzamen noch orem bay orem,	Together we will yet, arm in arm,
Imirtseshem tantsn oyf daytshishe kvorim.[19]	With the help of God, dance on the graves of the Germans.

As early as November 28, 1939, the above-mentioned Frank, governor of German-occupied Poland and hangman of the Polish Jews, ordered the organization of Jewish Committees (*Judenrat*), so that they might carry out the German orders both in the cities and areas around them. These committees, which worked together with the German occupation forces and the local subjugated inhabitants (Poles, Lithuanians, White Russians, Ukrainians, etc.), were naturally hated by the Jewish population, which made up many songs of derision about them.

The Nazi military machine had an insatiable and never-ending need of labor to dig peat, do lumbering, mend and lay railroad track, work in the factories. They conscripted men to build barracks, prisons, concentration camps, annihilation centers. The *Judenrat,* fulfilling the German orders, kept a close check on all available workhands in the ghetto, often utilizing their position as "governors of the ghetto" to make things easier for themselves. A sarcastic song which describes the functions of the Jewish Committee job holders, their methods of "cutting corners," their constant check on the population, and their arbitrary descisions in conscripting people for work in the Nazi establishments and projects contains the following stanzas:

Der komitet—dos iz der yidisher
    eltster-rat,
Velcher bayst gut tsu un iz alemol
    zat.
Er muz doch hobn koyech tsu regirn
    mit aza medine,
Az es zol nit hershn bay yidn kayn
    kine un sine.

The committee—that is the Jewish
    body of elders,
Which eats well and is always
    satisfied.
It needs to have strength, you know,
    to rule over this kingdom,
So that there be no envy and hatred
    among the Jews.

Zitst der komendant in fayne
    apartamentn,
Aynge-ordnt mit tishn, shtuln un
    andere medikamentn,
Mit byuros, sekretarn, farshidene
    agentn,
K'dey vos beser bahandlen di yidishe
    klientn.

The Komandant sits in a fine apart-
    ment suite of offices,
Furnished with tables, chairs, and
    other trimmings,
With departments, secretaries, and
    all kinds of agents,
The better to serve the Jewish
    clients.

Es iz shver ibertsutseyln di tsol amtn
    un be-amte,
Vos zaynen mitn komitet bloyz
    kroyvim un farvandte,
Un lebn oyfn chezhbn fun prostn
    oylem,
Vos horevet far zey punkt vi a
    goylem.

It's hard to count the offices and
    job holders,
Who are friends and relatives of the
    committee,
Who live at the expense of the
    common folk
Which works for them like a fool.

Er trogt di last un trogt far zey di peklech,	The people bears the load and carries the bundles,
Er arbet far zey un chapt klep tog-teglech	It works for them and gets beaten daily
Un vi der goylem hot eynmol protestirn prubirt	And no sooner does the fool only once try to protest
Hot men im tsumorgns di karte skasirt.[20]	Than on the morrow, his work card is taken from him.

Another song in this category pokes fun at the Jewish policeman at the ghetto gates, who often "split the take" with the non-Jewish guards and those smuggling food and other objects into the ghetto. Patterned after an older, Yiddish riddle song, the following poses some pointed questions to the Jewish police officials and their hangers-on : "Which one can give us a work card so that we might stay alive a little longer, and how much does it cost to be assigned to a good work brigade? Who sits in jail and who in office? What happens to the food taken away from us at the gates? Who must rise at dawn to work? Who has the misery and who the vitamins? Why do they eat white bread, hot rolls, and cakes, spend their time pleasantly with music, cards, expensive wines, and pastries? Do *they* work at the aerodrome with pickaxe, crowbar, and shovel? Which one of them reports us for making up songs about him?" The first stanza and refrain of this song follow :

Zog mir O zog mir, du geto-yidl,	Tell me, O tell me, Jew of the ghetto,
Ver shpilt in geto di ershte fidl?	Who plays in the ghetto first violin?
Un ver fun di yales, mer oder veynik,	And which of the *yales,* more or less,
Git aroys bafeln punkt vi a kenig.	Issues orders just like a king.
Refrain: Tumbalay, tumbalay, shpil geto-yidl,	Tumbalay, tumbalay, play ghetto-Jew,
Shpil fun di yidishe yales a lidl,	Play me a song of the Jewish *yales,*
Vegn di shefn un inspektorn,	About the chiefs and inspectors,
Vos zenen in geto mentshn gevorn.[21]	Who became important people in the ghetto.

Some of these derision songs mention actual names of leaders of the *Judenrat,* like Luria, examining magistrate before the war, who was known for his honesty and intelligence. In the Kovno ghetto, he was appointed chief of the Jewish workers building the aerodrome and because Luria was convinced that if the Jews proved their usefulness to the Germans their lives would be spared, he held the workers under him with an iron hand. Following is an excerpt of this song about him.

Iz in geto do faran
Eyner gor a groyser man,
Velcher iz gevorn a tiran.
Yedn morgn inderfri,
Traybt er mentshn vi di fi
Un er meynt, az eybik blaybn vet er hi.
Shrayt un shilt, shtendig vild,
Vi a vilde chaye oyf di mentshn bilt.[22]

In the ghetto there is one
Who is a very important man,
But who has become a tyrant.
Every morning early,
He drives people like cattle
Thinking, that he will live forever.

He yells and curses, is always wild,
And barks at the people like a mad beast.

The stronger ones survived a little longer, and the "luckier" ones often witnessed their loved ones, friends, and neighbors — the weak and sick, the aged and those too young to work, the ones the Germans considered "useless" — being transported to their death.

Es geyen kolones, es geyen korbones,

Finster, choyshech iz di nacht.
Der frost shnaydt vi mit a meser,
Der vint treyslt ale shleser,
Zey geyen fun shikere bavacht.

Ir geyt farbay, mir ze-en aych
Keynmol mer nit vider,
Ir geyt avek in ayer vaytn, letstn veg.
Mir blaybn do, ayere merder tsu badinen,
Mit arbet, shveys—zeyer mitleyd tsu gevinen.[23]

Columns are passing, victims are passing,
The night is gloomy and dark.
The frost cuts like a knife,
The wind rattles all the chains,
They pass, guarded by drunkards.

You pass us and we see you
For the last time,
You are going away on your long, last road.
We remain here, to serve your murderers,
With work and sweat—to win their sympathy.

Some songs deal with the feeling of guilt in remaining alive while others have gone to their death, when an accidental order at the *Umschlagsplatz* sent one to the "right," to live a little longer, and the other to the "left," to the concentration camp and annihilation center. A victim who died in Treblinka, the death camp, which from July, 1942, to September, 1943, put 800,000 Jews to death in the gas chambers, apparently briefly survived his wife and child, when he wrote this song.

Ch'shem zich farn himl,	I am ashamed before the sky,
Ch'shem zich far der erd,	I am ashamed before the earth,
Tsi bin ich den vayter	Am I then worthy
Tsu lebn vert?	To go on living?
Ch'shem zich far di beymer,	I am ashamed before the trees,
Baym bergl vos shteyen—	That stand on the hill—
Di vos hobn gehert	For they heard
Dayne letste geshreyen.	Your last cries.
Ich ze dich in roych,	I see you in smoke,
Ich ze dich in flamen,	I see you in flames,
Ich ze dos kind zich tuln	I see the child cuddling close
Tsu dir—zayn mamen.[24]	To you—his mother.

The Plight of the Children

Of all the people caught in the Nazi web, innocent Jewish children were exposed to the worst suffering. The first impact of the German occupation was felt by the mother and child. Very young children were considered unfit to labor for the Germans. Consequently, bearing children in the ghetto was forbidden. Such children, when they were born, were dubbed "hares," since they had "stolen into the ghetto unseen" and were registered as having come into the world "before the war." Mothers rocked their infants to sleep in fear, lest the sentries patrolling the ghetto streets hear the child's whimpering.

Her mayn kind vi vintn brumen	Listen, my child, to the howling winds,
Mach di oygn tsu.	Close your eyes and sleep.
Dayn tatn hot men tsugenumen,	Your father was taken away,
Ch'veys aleyn nit vu.	I know not where he is.
Ich aleyn mit dir geblibn,	Only we were left behind,
Vey un vind iz mir.	Woe, oh, woe is me.
Geven zaynen mir nefashes zibn,	Once our family was seven,
Itst nor ich mit dir.	Now it's only you and me.
Her mayn kind, men tor nit veynen,	Listen, my child, you mustn't cry,
Der postn geyt do um.	The sentry walks without.

Shisn ken er, ven er't meynen
Az men geyt arum.[25]

He can shoot us if he thinks
Someone is walking about.

Another lullaby revealing the bitter hatred for the conqueror who destroys innocent little children in his march towards aggrandizement calls prophetically to the baby who will one day be a man, to settle accounts with the invader when the time comes.

Shlof mayn zun mayn kleyner,
Mach di eygelech tsu,
Du veyst nit fun kayn zinden,
Vos di sonim shraybn dir tsu.
  Lyulyulyu.

Sleep, my little son,
Close your little eyes,
You know not of the sins
Attributed to you by the enemy.
  Hushabye.

Dayn zind iz gor a groyse—
Du host gebracht tsum krig.
Du lozt nit tsu di arier
Dergreychn zeyer zig. Lyulyulyu.

They say your crime is great—
For you have brought the war.
You prevent the Aryans
From achieving their victory.
  Hushabye.

Avekgeyn veln yorn,
Vest vern shtark un groys.
Nekome zolstu nemen
Far undzer blut un shveys.
  Lyulyulyu.[26]

Many years will pass,
And you'll grow big and strong.
Then you must take revenge
For our blood and sweat.
  Hushabye.

Each *Aussiedlung* resulted in more parents torn from their children, rendering many insane and the rest numb with the shock. In the death camp of Birkenau, a parent yearned for his lost little girl :

Lokomotiv, du shvartser, bizt zich geforn,
Host kayn birkenau mich bald avekgefirt.
Lokomotiv, du shvarster, nem mich shoyn tsurik.
Ich vil zen vider mayn meydele.

Black locomotive, you rode and rode,
Till you brought me to Birkenau.
Black locomotive, oh, take me back
I want to see my little girl again.

Oych vifil mol bin ich azoy geforn,

Fil mol bin ich shvach un krank gevorn,
Vey iz mir, ... ch'bin in daytshland doch noch a shklaf,
Un ich benk aheym, tsu mayn fayn meydele.[27]

So many times have I traveled this way,
So many times have I become weak and sick,
Woe is me, . . . I'm but a slave in Germany.
And I long for home and my lovely little girl.

In the streets of Vilna, following a similar tragedy, many children were wandering the streets, torn from their parents and lost. Following is a lullaby written by a young teacher for such a little, lost child.

Dremlen feygl oyf di tsvaygn,
Shlof, mayn tayer kind,
Bay dayn vigl oyf dayn nare
Zitst a fremde un zingt.
    Lyulyu, lyulyu, lyu.

Birdies slumber on the branches,
Sleep, my precious child,
At your cradle in the dugout
Sits a stranger crooning : hushabye.

S'iz dayn vigl vu geshtanen
Oysgeflochtn fun glik,
Un dayn mame, oy dayn mame
Kumt shoyn keynmol nit tsurik.
    Lyulyu, lyulyu, lyu.

Your cradle once did stand
Woven out of happiness,
And your mother, oh, your mother
Never will return. Hushabye.

Ch'ob gezen dayn tatn loyfn
Unter hogl fun shteyn,
Iber felder iz gefloygn
Zayn faryosemter geveyn.
    Lyulyu, lyulyu, lyu.[28]

I saw your father running
Under a hail of stones,
And across the fields there echoed
His mournful cry. Hushabye.

Left to their own devices, many children fled from place to place, hid out in caves and ditches, subsisted on herbs and scraps, gathered kindling wood to sell, begged and stole for a meager crust of bread.[29] Some managed to survive, deprived and unkempt, old before their time, bowed down often by memories of parents and loved ones done to death before their eyes. A ballad about such orphans contains the following stanzas :

Er hot oych gehat amol a tatn,
Er hot oych gehat a mamenyu,
Beyde zaynen in Shargorod
    geshtorbn,
Beyde lign ot-o-do.

He had a father once,
He had a mother once, too,
Both died in Shargorod,

Both lie there.

Er hot oych gehat an eygn betl,
Er hot oych gehat a heym,
Haynt gants aleyn ligt er un veynt
Oyf a kaltn pol fun leym.

He once had his own little bed,
He once had a home, too,
Now he lies crying alone
On the cold, clay floor.

Yogt der vint mit vayse shneyen,
Oyf dem frost yesoymim shteyen,
Vider frost un vider kelt,
Un a viste, beyze velt.[30]

The wind drives the white snows,
On the bare frost stand the orphans.
Frost again and cold again,
And a barren, angry world.

Describing the forced march from Bukovina to Trans-Dniestria, a young girl recorded the following: "We marched 30 kilometers a day. Little children and old people dropped dead. The guards beat us with iron knouts. We arrived at Kozlov Field. Several days we lay under the rain, then they drove us on to Mohilev. We fell on the grass. The Germans stepped over us, like rotten potatoes. During the night, we were awakened with yells . . . and led to the bridge over the Dniester. The Germans drove us forward and the Rumanians wouldn't let us cross. Finally, we were allowed to cross. For months we were driven from city to city and each time a number of us were counted out and shot. On the way, thousands perished. Only a few survived."[31]

A song which seems to deal with the above experiences is the following, which ends bravely on a note of hope:

S'loyfn, s'yogn di mashinen	Fast fly the wheels of the train
Un es fayft der tsug;	And the engine whistle blows,
Mir faryogte zitsn drinen,	We, who are exiled, sit therein,
M'shikt undz tsu dem bug.	Being taken where the Bug River flows.
Dortn vu der breyter dniester	There where the wide River Dniester
Shikt a grus mir tsu,	Sends us a greeting from the graves,
Fun mayn mamen, fun mayn shvester	From our mother, from our sister
Vu zey zenen shoyn do.	Lying beneath the cold waves.
Fun der heym hot men undz fartribn	They drove us from our home
In a fremdn land;	Into a strange land;
Gornisht iz undz mer farblibn,	We've nothing left to call our own,
Un mir zenen farbant.	Lost and homeless are we.
Dortn hobn undz bagegnt	There in that strange land
Hunger, kelt un noyt;	We found hunger, cold, and want;
In der vister ukraine	In the desolate Ukraine
Dort regirt der toyt.	Death is the ruler.
Lang der shturem vet nisht doyern,	But the storm will not last long,
Endikn vet zich der krig;	And the war will end;
Vider vet di zun undz shaynen	Once again the sun will shine
Un far undz, der zig![32]	And victory will be ours!

Children, doomed to the concentration camps, pined away like little birds caught in a barbed-wire cage. A parent from Siroko, watching his two little girls shrink from starvation, tried desperately to distract them with ditties and games, as he sang :

Mogn, mogn, nudye nit !	Stomach, stomach, don't bother me !
Hob ich den un gib dir nit?	Have I then something which I
	don't share with you?
Tsi hostu den fargesn,	Have you then forgotten,
Az ch'ob ersht nechtn gegesn?	That I ate only yesterday?
Mogn, mogn,	Stomach, stomach,
Her mich oyf tsu nogn.[33]	Stop bothering me.

A Libau lad in the Kaiserwald concentration camp wrote a ballad in marching rhythm, which was popular in a number of camps and sung on the interminable marches from one place to another :

Mir zingen a lidl fun hayntiger tsayt	We sing a song of modern times
Fun yidishe tsores, fun yidishe layd,	Of Jewish troubles and Jewish suffering,
Un chotsh mir zenen yinglech kleyn	And though we are still very young lads
Mir veysn dem hunger, mir konen dem payn.	We know of hunger, we know of pain.
In a finstere, tunkele, harbstige nacht,	In a dark, horrible, autumn night,
Hot men undz fun libau kayn rige gebracht.	We were brought from Libau to Riga.
Yom-kiper baynacht, ven men zogt dem al chet,	Yom-Kippur night, when the prayers of forgiveness are said,
Hot men undz fun libau gebracht in katset.	We were brought from Libau to the concentration camp.
Men hot undz tseshplitert, men hot undz tseribn,	We were splintered and pulverized,
Mir zenen fun libau gants veynig geblibn.	Few of us survived.
Oyf arbet farshikt undz, in derfer, in shtet,	We were sent to labor in villages, in cities,
Azoy iz dos lidl fun undzer katset.[34]	And that is the song of our concentration camp.

Another song, created by a twelve-year-old girl, cries out against the horrible suffering imposed on innocent children and their parents in the concentration camps and reveals the faith of the singer in the Lord's promise that Israel will live!

Eyns, tsvey, dray,	One, two, three,
Der tog vil nit farbay,	The days seem to drag by,
Shlepn tsigl, breter, shteyner,	Lugging bricks and boards and stones,
Un fun toyte mentshn beyner,	And of dead corpses, the bones,
Got! vi tut dos vey!	God! How painful it is!
Eyns, tsvey, dray,	One, two, three,
Her tsu mayn geshrey!	Listen to my cry!
Fun umbakante masn-kvorim	Of unmarked mass graves
Kleyne kinder fun chadorim	Of children from the Hebrew schools
Kayn mames do mit zey.	Without their mothers here.
Eyns, tsvey, dray,	One, two, three,
Gloybn mir getray,	We faithfully believe,
Vartn mir un hofn	As we wait and hope
Vi du host undz farshprochn,	As you have promised us:
Am yisroel chay![35]	That Israel lives!

The children sang of the horrors around them; they also sang of revenge, as in the following, which calls for a reckoning, when the time comes, with the brutal tyrants. (Like a number of others, this song is patterned after Goldfaden's "Rozhinkes mit mandlen.")

Un az du vest elter vern yidele,	And when you grow older, my little one,
Zolstu zich dermonen inem lidele:	May you remember this song:
Fun toyznter yidn nor eyner geblibn,	How from thousands, but one Jew remained,
Oy, daytshn shlechte, merder umgerechte,	Oh, evil Germans, unjust murderers,
Dayn tatn gekoylet, dayn mamen gegesn....	Who slaughtered your father destroyed your mother....
Oy, zolst es forgedenken, zolst es forgedenken,	Oh, remember it, do not forget it,
Keynmol nit fargesn![36]	You must never forget it!

The systematic destruction of life on every level convinced many that they could expect no quarter on any terms from the German invaders. People hid out behind walls, under floors, under the ground, in cellars, even in sewers, hoping thus to survive the periodic searches, the man hunts, the transports to the concentration and death camps. Those fortunate enough to escape from the ghetto hid out in the countryside, in camouflaged, improvised shelters in the forests, whence a number subsequently joined the partisans. Following are excerpts of a hide-out song:

Ich zits in krayuvke un ich tracht zich:
I sit in the *krayuvke* and think to myself:

Ich bin shoyn mid az dos oyg farmacht zich,
I'm so tired, my eyes close wiith weariness,

Ich bin geblibn aleyn, ich bagis zich mit geveyn—
I was left alone, I weep bitterly—

Tsi veln mir fun danen aroysgeyn?
Will we ever get out of here?

Refrain: Shpilt, shpilt, strunes fun payn,
Play, play, strings of pain,

Shpilt-zhe mir a yidishn nign.
Play me a Jewish tune.

Shpilt, shpilt, strunes fun payn,
Play, play, strings of pain,

Tsi veln mir derlebn dem fridn?
Will we live to see peace again?

Far dem krig hobn mir gelebt in fridn,
Before the war we lived in peace

Iz gekumen hitler un oysgemordet ale yidn.
Then Hitler came and murdered all the Jews.

Gevezn zaynen mir ru-ik, mit ale felker glaych,
We lived in peace among all the nations,

In vos bashtayt undzer zind, freg ich bay aych?[37]
Wherein have we sinned, I ask you?

A hide-out song which utilized an old Polish wedding tune satirizes a German ordinance forbidding ghetto Jews to wear fur pieces or fur coats. This was happily interpreted by the ghetto dwellers as a sign of the increasing hardships endured by the German armies in their winter fighting in Russia. The Jewish policemen and German guards at the gates would rip off fur collars and take away fur pieces and coats from Jews passing in and out of the ghetto. The song also mentions "red and yellow passes" which permitted certain men and women to work outside the ghetto. Such workers were allowed to "attach to themselves" several members of their family, and many single people would attach "a husband, wife, or child" to themselves, thus prolonging their lives as well. The song mentions Zlate, the real wife of the singer, concealed in the hide-out, and speaks of the starvation rations of bread and firewood doled out to the ghetto-dwellers by the *Judenrat*. The song follows:

Hot zich mir di shich tserisn,
Vey tsu mayne yorn,
Di kragns hot men undz opgerisn—
Ver ich doch farfrorn.

My shoes wore out,
Oh, woe to my years,
They tore off our collars,
And I am freezing.

Refrain: Tants, tants, tants
Abisele mit mir,
Oy, ir groyse frestelech,
Ir kumt doch fun Sibir.

Dance, dance, dance
A little bit with me,
Oh, you little frosts,
You come from Siberia.

Gele shaynen, roze shaynen,
Alerley kolirn.
Ven vel ich mayn vaybl zlate
Tsu zich aheym shoyn firn?

Yellow passes, pink passes,
All kinds of colors.
When will I take my wife Zlate
Home again?

Refrain: Tants, tants, tants
Abisele mit mir,
Hotsu a geln shayn,
Hob ich chasene mit dir.

Dance, dance, dance
A little bit with me,
If you have a yellow pass,
I will marry you.

Broyt oyfn sentimeter,
Holts oyfn deko.
Hot undz farzorgt der yidenrat,
Der yidnrat fun geto.[38]

Bread by the centimeter,
Wood by the dekameter,
Thus we are well supplied
By the *Judenrat* in the ghetto.

A hide-out song sung by Polish Jews in the Voronets woods in 1943 makes some pointed comments in its refrain on the great accomplishments of the twentieth century:

In tsvantsigstn yorhundert di
tsivilizatsie iz groys,
Di technik dergreycht hot ir tsil:

In the twentieth century civilization
is great,
Technical progress has achieved its
goal:

A roshe hitler gekumen iz tsu der
macht—
Er tut mit di yidn vos er vil.

A tyrant Hitler came to power

And does with the Jews as he
pleases.

Farbrenen in treblinke di yidn mit
gaz—
Dos ruft men on rasn-has.[39]

He burns the Jews in Treblinka with
gas—
And that is called race hatred.

Under the pretense of transferring Jews to other camps to work, the transports to the gas chambers and ovens continued inexorably. Only when the few escapees returned to warn of the true destination of these "shipments" was the stark reality exposed in all its dread horror. A ballad which was sung in the Warsaw ghetto and in almost all the other ghettos of the German occupation, as far as Rumania, described the transports to the death center, Treblinka. Following are excerpts from one variant:

In a kleyn shtetl gants fri fartog

In a little town early one morning

Mentshn tserudert, a geveyn un a klog.

Frightened people, weeping and wailing,

M'loyft vi meshuge halb naket un bloyz,

Running about like mad, half naked and undressed,

M'hert a geshrey : "yidn fun shtub aroys !"

A cry is heard : "Jews, get out of the house !"

Zhandarmen, politsey, ukrainer fil,

Gendarmes, police, many Ukrainians,

Tsu dermordn di yidn, dos iz zeyer tsil !

To kill the Jews, that is their aim !

M'shist un men shlogt, a moyre, a shrek,

They shoot, they beat, it's terrible, horrible,

Men traybt di yidn tsum ban avek.

They drive the Jews to the trains.

Bashraybn kon es nit kayn feder,

No pen can ever describe

Vi es dreyen zich di reder,

How the wheels go round and round.

Men firt di yidn oyf kidesh-hashem,

As the Jews are being martyred,

Kayn treblinke, kayn treblinke.

Going, going to Treblinka.

Undzere brider fun yener zayt yam,

Our brothers across the ocean,

Zey konen nisht filn undzer bitern tam

Cannot feel our bitter pain.

Zey konen nit filn undzer bitere noyt

They cannot feel our bitter anguish

Az oyf undz vart yede minut der toyt.

As death lurks over us every moment.

Di milchome vet nemen amol an ek.

The war will end some day.

Di velt vet derfarn undzer umderherte shrek.

The world will realize the unheard-of horror.

Ongefilt mit veytik iz dos yidishe harts :

Our Jewish heart is filled with pain :

Ver vet konen heyln undzer shmarts?

Who will be able to heal our hurt?

Taychn trern veln rinen,

Rivers of tears will flow,

Ven men vet amol gefinen

When they will find some day

Dem grestn keyver fun der velt

The biggest grave in the world

In treblinke, in treblinke.[40]

In Treblinka, in Treblinka.

Resistance

In April, 1943, the Gestapo gathered the last four thousand Jews of the Vilna province from the towns Sventsian, Oshmene, Tal, Vidz, and others and, under the pretext of transferring the Jews to the Kovno ghetto, shipped them in trains to Ponar, 10 kilometers away. There, the Jews were shot down in cold blood. Realizing the deception, the doomed, unarmed Jews threw themselves upon the German guards with iron bars, sticks, and even sunk their teeth into the throats of the murderers, killing several. About thirty Jews escaped, and the following ballad describes the transport and the skirmish with the guards.

Aroys iz in vilne a nayer bafel
Tsu brengen di yidn fun shtetlech,

Gebracht hot men ale fun yunge biz alt,
Afile oych kranke oyf betlech.

Tsunoyfgeshpart hot men dem lager,
Men hot zey genumen sortirn :
Oshmener yidn in vilne tsu blaybn

Un soler in kovne tsu firn.

Aroysgefirt hot men fun lager—
Yunge un frishe korbones,
Arayngeshpart hot men zey alemen glaych
In di zelbe farmachte vagones.

Der tsug iz zich langzam geforn,
Gefayft un gegebn sirenes.
Stantsie ponar : der tsug shtelt zich op.
Men tshepet dort op di vagones.

Zey hobn derzen, az men hot zey farfirt,
Men firt tsu der shreklecher sh'chite,

Zey hobn tsebrochn di tir fun vagon
Genumen aleyn machn pleyte.

In Vilna a new order was issued
To round up the Jews from the small towns,
Old and young were brought,

Even sick ones on cots.

The camp was crowded together
And then the sorting began :
Jews from Oshmene were to remain in Vilna,
And the Jews from Sole were to be taken to Kovno.

They led them out of the camp—
Fresh, young sacrifices,
They crammed them all together

Into the same sealed cars.

The train moved slowly along,
With its sirens whistling.
Ponar Station : the train stops.

The cars are detached.

Everybody realized that they had been tricked
And are being led to the terrible slaughter,
They smashed the doors open
And tried to escape somehow.

Zey hobn gevorfn zich af der gestapo

Un zey di kleyder tserisn,
Geblibn zaynen lign lebn di yidn
Etleche daytshn tsebisn.

S'hobn di getos fun der provints
Gegebn fir toyznt korbones,
Un opgefirt hot men di zachn fun zey
Tsurik in di zelbe vagones.[41]

They threw themselves upon the Gestapo
And tore their clothes.
Beside the Jews there remained lying
Several Germans, bitten to death.

The ghettos of the province
Gave up four thousand martyrs,
And their clothes were brought back

In the same freight cars.

The survivors in the camps and ghettos realized that they were faced with certain death. Dreams of freedom, the passionate desire to break out from the barbed-wire encirclements, past the walls, the brutality, the suffering, filled the hearts and minds of all. The helplessness, the demoralization and physical degradation were turning to desperate struggles. Simultaneously the hopes of the ghetto and camp inmates were being raised by rumors of the advancing Red forces from the East and the actions of deploying partisans in the surrounding areas. In the ghettos, underground partisan committees worked tirelessly to raise the fallen spirits, bolster the hopes of the survivors, and organize them for struggle. The number of satirical songs increased, along with songs expressing hatred, desire for revenge, hope in victory and determination to fight to the death for it.

A song sung in the Dinaverk concentration camp begins with pain and tears and concludes with a call for revenge:

In blut fargosene
Fun lebn yung farloshene,
Zey rufn fun der erd.
O, bruder, heyb di shverd
Un nem nekome far yederns neshome
Vos hot zayn lebn dem soyne opgegebn.[42]

Covered with blood,
Young lives snuffed out
Cry out from the earth.
O, brother, raise your sword
And take revenge for each soul

That gave its life to the enemy.

The number of marching songs increased. One which speaks of purposeful hatred, the will to live and the desire for revenge contains this stanza:

Herzl T. Rome, 1950

At the Wall

(Reprinted by permission of Schocken Books Inc. from **Treasury of Jewish Folksong** *by Ruth Rubin. Copyright 1950 by Schocken Books Inc.)*

Nor eyn gedank—er tsit mich shtark
   tsum lebn,
Er tret nisht op fun mir oyf eyn
   minut :
Ch'volt veln a nekome chotsh
   derlebn
Un zen vi blut vert opgetsolt tsurik
   mit blut.[43]

Only one thought—I want so much
   to live,
It doesn't leave me for a moment :

I want to live to take revenge

And see blood paying back for
   every life that bled.

A marching song which marked every public gathering of the Youth
Club in the Vilna ghetto contains a refrain calling ghetto dwellers to
join the young generation in its march to freedom :

Yung iz yeder, yeder, yeder ver es
   vil nor,
Yorn hobn kayn batayt,
Alte kenen, kenen, kenen oych zayn
   kinder
Fun a naye fraye tsayt.[44]

Young is everyone who wants
   to be,
Age has no meaning at all,
The old can also be the
   children
Of a new free generation.

Another song, obviously inspired by the German composer, Hans Eisler,
attempts to instruct the marchers in the difference between aimless marching and that which has a purpose. "We've been driven off the sidewalks
into the roads, beaten with the iron knout, . . . led like sheep to the
slaughter. . . . Our step rings helplessly, when we know not the reasons
why. . . ."

Nor, bruder, an anderer ritm
Vet bald tsu dayn oyer dergeyn,
Un di, vos far shrek
Geven ersht farshtekt,
Shpanen mit undz nit aleyn.

But, brother, another rhythm
Will soon reach your ear,
And those who were hidden
In fear only yesterday,
Now march right along with us, not
   alone.

Tsu eyns, tsvey dray,
Tsu eyns, tsvey, dray,
Di geslech, dem toyer farlozt !

And one, two, three,
And one, two, three,
Leave the lanes and the gates
   behind !

S'hot der trot aza klang
Gor anander gezang,
Ven du geyst un du veyst shoyn
   farvos.[45]

For your step now resounds
With a new kind of sound,
When you march and know the
   reason why.

The Soviet advance was coming closer. Already in March, 1942, the
Soviet aircraft bombed Vilna, hitting several military targets and

factories. "Some bombs fell near the ghetto, on Lida lane, where some Lithuanian military were stationed. But in the ghetto, not a splinter fell. Both the Jewish and the non-Jewish population were certain that the Soviet flyers had avoided hitting the ghetto. The mood in the ghetto was terrific." A song, containing the following stanza and refrain, was written about this incident.

Refrain: Bombes, bombes, libe, traye,   Bombs, bombs, beloved and true,
    Shoyn gevart, az yede minut,   We've waited eagerly for you
    Zolt ir kumen un varfn mit fayer,   To come and spout with flame,
    Un oyb iber undz—iz doch oychet gut.   Even over us—that too would be good.

Es nogt der gedank, di neshome,   Our mind and soul are tortured,
Tsi veln mir mentshn noch zayn?   Will we then be human again?
Dos harts gart azoy noch nekome   Our heart longs so for revenge
Far undzere tsores un payn.[46]   For our sorrows and our pain.

In the Kovno ghetto, a singer cheered his brethren with a song which already imagined on the horizon the banners of the approaching cavalry of the liberating armies.

Refrain: Nor nit veyn, yid, es kumen besere tsaytn,   Don't weep, Jew, better times are coming,
    Ich ze shoyn dos lid fun der vayt,   I now hear the song from the distance,
    Soldatn oyf ferd dort es raytn,   Soldiers on horseback are riding,
    Di fone, di fone zi veyt.   With banners, with banners waving.

Undz shrekt kayne klep, kayne tsoymen,   We fear not the blows nor the bonds,
Mir veysn, di tsukunft iz hel,   We know that the future is bright,
Di sonim, zey megn haynt shoymen,   The enemies now may be fuming,
Di frayhayt, zi vart oyfn shvel.[47]   But freedom for us now is nigh.

The air was full of news of the advancing Allied armies, and Yiddish folk songs of defiance and hope increased. Even as the remaining Jews in the Vilna ghetto were being shipped to concentration camps in Esthonia in September, 1943, the actors in the Jewish theater were performing in a musical production containing songs which stirred their listeners profoundly. Anticipating the liquidation of the Vilna ghetto, a musical entitled "Halt zich moyshe," ("Hang On, Moyshe") written in August, 1943, contained the following stanzas and finale:

(1)

Pak zich ayn, pak zich ayn,	Pack up, pack up,
S'vet fun dem gornit zayn,	But nothing will come of it.
Dos mol zaynen mir noch hige,	Now we are still here,
Morgn forn mir in Rige,	Though tomorrow we go to Riga,
Pak zich ayn, pak zich ayn.	Pack up, pack up.

Pak zich ayn, pak zich ayn,	Pack up, pack up,
S'vet der sof beser zayn,	The end will be much better,
Dos mol vet zey nit gelingen,	For this time they'll not succeed,
Mir'n zey dos lidl zingen:	And to them we'll sing instead:
Pakt zich ayn, pakt zich ayn![48]	Pack up, pack up!

(2)

Es shlogt di sho, mir zaynen do,	The hour has struck and we're still here,
Mir kukn in der vaytn.	We look into the distance.
S'vert der himl vider blo,	The sky is getting blue again,
S'kumen naye tsaytn.	New times are coming.
Un chotsh dervayl iz finster-shtok,	And although its pitch-dark now,
Vartn mir geduldik,	We wait patiently,
Es kumt der tog, es shlogt di sho—	The day is coming, the hour has struck—
Dan falt der, ver s'iz shuldik.[49]	And the guilty one will die.

The Partisan Songs

The partisan organizations exerted a powerful influence among the people caught in the German occupation army's net. Their work included all manner of actions, from the simplest to the most drastic. Their courage and heroism filtered past the ghetto gates, beckoned to the dwellers to flee the ghetto and join their brigade. They secretly instructed ghetto dwellers in diversionist acts and generally generated a feeling of hope and determination. Songs were one of their weapons, and a moving ballad, which combines the love of a man for a maid with an incident in which two partisans blew up a German military transport on the outskirts of Vila in 1942, is the following:

Shtil, di nacht iz oysgeshternt,
Un der frost—er hot gebrent;
Tsi gedenkstu vi ich hob dich gelernt
Haltn a shpayer in di hent.

The starry night is silent,
And the frost is sharp and crisp;
Do you remember when I taught you
To hold a pistol in your hand.

A moyd, a peltsl un a beret,
Un halt in hant fest a nagan,
A moyd mit a sametenem ponim
Hit op dem soynes karavan.

A girl, a short coat and a beret,
Holding a pistol firmly in her hand,
A girl with a face as soft as velvet
Guards the enemy's caravan.

Getsilt, geshosn un getrofn
Hot ir kleyninker pistoyl,
An oto a fulinkn mit vofn
Farhaltn hot zi mit eyn koyl.

She aimed, fired and found her mark
With her little pistol,
A truck full of ammunition
She stopped with one shot.

Fartog fun vald aroysgekrochn,
Mit shney-girlandn oyf di hor,

At dawn, creeping out of the woods
With snow garlands clinging to her hair,

Gemutikt fun kleyninkn n'tsochn

She was encouraged with her tiny victory

Far undzer nayem, frayen dor.[50]

For our new, free generation.

In White Russia, in the woods near Narotsh, Jewish partisans of the Voroshilov brigade were singing a song which included the following stanzas :

Veynik zaynen mir in tsol,
Drayste vi milionen,
Raysn mir oyf barg un tol,
Brikn, eshalonen,
Der fashist fartsitert vert,
Veyst nit vu fun vanen—
Shturmen vi fun unter erd—

We are very few in number,
But our courage is of millions,
On hill and dale we dynamite
The bridges and the transports,
The fascist trembles knowing not,
From where and whence it comes—
We storm them from the underground—

Yidn—partizaner.

Jewish partisans.

S'vort nekome hot a zin,
Ven mit blut farshraybst im,
Far dem heylign bagin
Firn mir di shtraytn.
Neyn, mir veln keynmol zayn
Letste mohikaner,
S'brengt der nacht—di zunenshayn,
Der yid—der partizaner.[51]

The word "revenge" makes sense
When it is written in blood,
For the holy dawn
We carry on our battles.
No, we will never be
The last Mohicans,
We bring the sunshine to the night—
We Jewish partisans.

Another song instructs partisan recruits in the disciplines of battle against German Nazism — enemy of all peoples.

Oyb s'iz nishto zat uptsu-esn,	If we haven't enough to eat,
Un oyb di glider tsitern fun kelt—	And our body trembles with the cold—
Zolt ir kinder keynmol nit fargesn	Children, always bear in mind
Az mit aych laydt di gantse velt.	That with you all the world is suffering.
Refrain: Mit feste trit marshirt in di kolones,	With firm steps let us march . together,
Shtol di nervn un dos harts a shteyn;	Let's steel our nerves and turn our hearts to stone;
Mir hobn iberlebt a sach sakones,	We have survived so many dangers,
Nor undzer folk vet keynmol untergeyn.[52]	But our people never will perish.

The heroism of the Jewish partisans was evident not only in the organized military skirmishes with the enemy. It acted as a catalyst in the ghetto, daily combating the relentless, deadening rule of the German tyrants. A ballad which memorializes Itsik Vitnberg, head of the secret partisan organization in the Vilna ghetto, set to the tune of a Russian partisan song of the Civil War of the twenties, is the following:

S'ligt ergets fartayet der faynt vi a chaye,	The enemy hearkens: a beast in the darkness;
Der mauzer er vacht in mayn hant,	The Mauser—it wakes in my hand—
Nor plutsim gestapo, es firt a geshmidtn	But wait! My heart's drumming: two sentries are coming
Durch finsternish dem komandant.	And with them our first in command.
Di nacht hot mit blitsn dem geto tserisn,	The ghetto is sundered by lightning and thunder;
"Gefar"—shrayt a toyer, a vant.	"Beware!" shrieks a tower in fright.
Chaverim getraye fun keytn bafrayen,	Brave comrades have freed our commander and leader
Farshvindn mit dem komandant.	And flee with him into the night.
Di nacht iz farfloygn, der toyt far di oygn,	But night soon is over—and death lies uncovered;
Dos geto es fibert in brand.	The flames of the city leap high.

geto, es drot di gestapo:	Aroused is the ghetto—the storm troopers threaten :
.eꜰ dem komandant !”	“Give up your leader, or die !”
ɔt dan Itsik—un durch a ɪz—	The battle ground quivers as Itsik delivers
Ich vɪ .it ir zolt tsulib mir Darfn dos lebn dem soyne opgebn? . . .”	The answer—while guns hold their breath : “Shall others be given, to pay for my living ?”
Tsum toyt geyt shtolts der komandir.[53]	And proudly he goes to his death.

But of all the songs of all the ghettos, the one which spread like wildfire, almost from the moment that it left the poet's pen, was the marching song by Hirsh Glik : “Zog nit keynmol az du geyst dem letstn veg” (“Never Say that You Are Trodding the Final Path”).[54] Set to a tune by the Soviet composers, the brothers Pokras, it became the official hymn of all the Eastern European partisan brigades and was subsequently translated into Hebrew, Polish, Russian, Spanish, Rumanian, Dutch, and English. With almost magical speed it was caught up by all the concentration camps and by the time the war was over, it was being sung by Yiddish-speaking Jews the world over and by a score of other peoples as well.

Composed in Vilna, it is most often related to the Warsaw ghetto uprising, which began in the morning hours of April 19, 1943. With the speed of lightning the news of the uprising spread to all the ghettos and camps. The poet-partisan, S. Kacerginski, recalls those days and the birth of the song :

Hello, hello, the survivors in the Warsaw ghetto have begun an armed resistance against the murderers of the Jewish people. The ghetto is aflame!” [flashed over the secret radio waves of the partisan organizations.] . . . Two short lines conveyed the flaming news. . . . We knew of no other particulars yet . . . but we suddenly saw clearly the flames of the Warsaw ghetto and the Jews fighting with arms for their dignity and self-respect. Restless days. Sleepless nights. We armed ourselves. The news of the uprising lifted our spirits and made us proud . . . and although we were in agony at their unequal struggle . . . we felt relieved . . . our hearts became winged. . . .

On the first of May, we arranged an evening on the theme : “Spring in Yiddish Literature” . . . Every speaker and every poem which was read aloud was permeated with the spirit of the fighting Warsaw ghetto. . . . Hirshke

[Glik] came up quietly beside me. "Well, what's new with you, Hirshl?"—"I wrote a new poem. Want to hear it?"—"Just like that? Well, read it!"—"Not now, tomorrow I'll bring it to you. It's a poem to be sung."

On the morrow, Hirshke came to my room bright and early. "Now listen carefully," he pleaded, "I'll sing it for you right away." He began to sing it softly, but full of excitement. His eyes glowed with little sparks... *Kumen vet noch undzer oysgebenkte sho*—The hour for which we yearned will come anew—... Where did he get his faith? His voice became firmer. He tapped out the rhythm with his foot, as if he were marching ... *Dos hot a folk tsevishn falndike vent, dos lid gezungen mit naganes in di hent* —A people midst the crashing fires of hell sang this song with guns in hands until it fell.... May, June, July, August ... we lived with the spirit of April and the Warsaw ghetto uprising. The partisan staff in the Vilna ghetto decided that the song should become the hymn of its fighters. But the people did not wait for this decision, and the song had already spread to the ghettos, the concentration and labor camps, and into the woods to other partisan brigades.[55]

Zog nit keynmol az du geyst dem
  letstn veg,
Chotsh himlen blayene farshteln
  bloye teg;
Kumen vet noch undzer oysgebenkte
  sho,
S'vet a poyk ton undzer trot—mir
  zaynen do!

Never say that you have reached the
  very end,
Though leaden skies a bitter future
  may portend;
And the hour for which we've
  yearned will yet arrive,
And our marching step will thunder:
  we survive!

Fun grinem palmenland biz vaysn
  land fun shney,
Mir kumen on mit undzer payn, mit
  undzer vey,
Un vu gefaln s'iz a shprits fun
  undzer blut,
Shprotsn vet dort undzer gvure
  undzer mut.

From green palm trees to the land
  of distant snow,
We are here with our sorrow, our
  woe,
And wherever our blood was shed
  in pain,
Our fighting spirits now will
  resurrect again.

S'vet di morgn-zun bagildn undz
  dem haynt,
Un der nechtn vet farshvindn mitn
  faynt,
Nor oyb farzamen vet di zun un der
  kayor—
Vi a parol zol geyn dos lid fun dor
  tsu dor.

The golden rays of morning sun will
  dry our tears,
Dispelling bitter agony of
  yesteryears,
But if the sun and dawn with us
  will be delayed,
Then let this song ring out to you
  the call, instead.

Dos lid geshribn iz mit blut un nit mit blay,	Not lead, but blood inscribed this mighty song we sing,
S'iz nit kayn lidl fun a foygl oyf der fray,	It's not a caroling of birds upon the wing
Dos hot a folk ts'vishn falndike vent	But a people midst the crashing fires of hell,
Dos lid gezungen mit naganes in di hent.[56]	Sang this song with guns in hands, until it fell.

The Warsaw ghetto inspired other ghettos to struggle, although none of them achieved its heroic stature and endurance. The feeling of imminent liberation was filtering through to the concentration and labor camps. Everyone felt that victory was around the corner, and, suddenly, it was here and the last survivors were being led out and away from their living graves.

A song, written on the day of liberation by a poet who was herself a partisan and one of the liberators of her city of birth, contains the following stanzas:

Ich gey itst azoy fray in gas,	I walk the streets in freedom now,
Un ch'gleyb zich nit, az ich bin fray,	And can't believe that I am free,
Dos alte libe heymshtot mayns	The old beloved city of mine,
Kumt oys mir itst i lib, i nay.	Now seems so new and dear to me.
Un ot a gut bakanter hoyf,	I see a well-known courtyard,
Vu tayer iz mir yeder shteyn—	Where dear to me is every stone—
Nor vu zaynen di libste, vu,	But where are all the loved ones,
Az ich shtey do gor aleyn?	When I am standing here alone?
Nekome nemen far mayn heym,	To take revenge for homes destroyed,
Nekome nemen farn blut.	For blood so innocently spilled,
Di biks vet mayn bahelfer zayn,	My gun will walk close by my side,
Mit ir in veg tsu geyn iz gut.[57]	To help me in this reckoning.

Veynt, veynt, yidishe fidlen, iber di felder di poylishe ("Weep, weep, Jewish fiddles, over the Polish fields") sang the Jewish street singers when Germany marched into Poland in September, 1939. On June 22, 1941, the German *Wehrmacht* struck the Russian borders and spilled over into White Russia, Ukraine, Bukovina, Moldavia. More than a third of the Jewish population of the world was murdered by the Germans. On May 15, 1945, the war was officially over in Europe. Peace had at last returned and people wept with joy and with sorrow. The war was over, but the dead would never come back to life again and the maimed and tortured never be healed.

The bulk of the Yiddish folk songs of this period were created in Yiddish, although a number were current also in Hebrew, Russian, Polish, French, Rumanian, Hungarian, and even German. These songs, which did not follow the normal course of popularization, becoming folk song almost overnight, utilized old familiar folk songs, traditional melodies, as well as tunes from current Soviet songs and dances, setting many a tragic text hastily to a gay tune out of necessity, or the other way round. Although music for many texts was created by a number of professional composers, most of these compositions perished together with their creators.

Taken as a whole, Yiddish folk song of World War II and the German occupation comprises a remarkable documentary chronicle and testament of the creative ability of a people who demonstrated their capacity for suffering, their endurance, their ingenuity and resourcefulness under the most inhuman conditions. The songs reveal the burning will to live as human beings in dignity and self-respect and the determination and ability to organize and fight unto death for that life—in freedom.

Notes

THE STRUGGLE TO SURVIVE

1. Over 6.5 million Jews, including 1 million children, were done to death under the German occupation. "Now when I look back, I often think: what happened here to us? How could we have lived thus, and died thus?" (Kacerginski, Intro., xv.)

2. Although hundreds of songs were created during this period, only several collections were actually published. Of these, the most important one was compiled by the Vilna poet-partisan, S. Kacerginski (1908–1954), with 250 texts and 100 tunes from thirty ghettos, camps, and forests. Kacerginski's compilation includes a collection of songs gathered by Zami Feder, entitled *Katsetlider* ("Concentration-Camp Songs"), published in Bergen Belsen in 1946, several songs collected by the American-Yiddish poet H. Leivick (1888–1962) during his visit to the D.P. camps in Germany in 1946 and a notebook of songs by Lusik Gerber, who perished in Dachau.

3. Ordering the Jews in the ghetto to put on theatrical performances, the Gestapo then utilized this medium to spy upon the Jews. The result was a series of musicals and songs couched in "hidden" terms, perfectly understood by the Jewish audience. The Jewish theatre in the ghetto became the institution where creative writers, musicians, and actors combined to help the people forget, for a few hours, the dreadful life they had to endure, where the performers expressed the sentiments of the collective grief-stricken heart and also stirred the people to courage and action.

4. Unger, *The Day*. The fellow's name was Rubinstein and in this ditty he was referring to the Soviet offensive.

5. Kacerginski, p. 118. Sung by the same Rubinstein of Warsaw to a Zemiroth tune.

6. Unger, *The Day*.

7. Polish religious Jews in Warsaw, Lublin, Lodz, Bialystok, first victims of the German *Blitzkrieg,* sang a Hebrew song which subsequently became popular among all Jews of Eastern European origin. It was the Hebrew song "Ani ma-amin" ("I Believe"):

Ani ma-amin, b'emuna shleyma b'viat moshiach.
V'af al pi sheyitmameyha,
Im kol ze, ani ma-amin,
Im kol ze, achake lo b'chol yom sh'yevo.
(Zemer Am, p. 3)

I believe, I am at peace in my faith that the Messiah will come.
And should his coming be delayed,
Yet will I believe,
And look forward every day to his coming.

8. Kacerginski, p. 306. Slobodka was a suburb of Kovno. Near Kovno there were a group of numbered prisons or forts. Near the seventh and ninth forts, the Germans and Lithuanians shot most of the Jews of Kovno, and Jews from Western Europe were also executed there. Axelrod, author of the text, who obviously patterned his song after Goldfaden's "Rozhinkes mit mandlen," had fled the Warsaw ghetto and perished in a hide-out when the Germans set fire to the Kovno ghetto. The concept

expressed in this song of going "happily" to one's death, is in harmony with the Jewish tradition of dying for one's faith. Death was never considered desirable as an end in itself. On the contrary, Jewish life throughout the ages regarded life as a precious and sacred trust, to be preserved. But when one's belief in the Lord and His teachings were threatened, Jews in their long history have been known to muster up their last ounce of energy and courage, under the most cruel tortures, even as they were burned to death, breathing their last joyously "al kidesh hashem," in the name of the holy God.

9. Feder, p. 1. Text: Y. Rabi novitsh.
10. Kacerginski, p. 38 Author: Diskant, a Hebrew teacher in the Kovno ghetto.
11. Prager, p. 52. The diary of a twelve-year-old lad in the Kielc region, Poland, contains the following entries: "May 9, 1942: They say there will be a raid today, because 120 more men are needed for the work camp. Every man hid, and the streets are very quiet. As I stood in the doorway, I saw three automobiles coming, and I immediately recognized them to be the same ones which had come on Wednesday. There was a panic and everybody fled to the woods, and the police began to catch people. My aunt came and said they were catching young ones like me too. I became confused and realized that I must hide somewhere. . . . May 10, 1942: The Jewish police received an order for fifty more men. Soon, they began to hunt. I didn't go anywhere but stayed in the house. Thank God, they didn't come in." (Rabinovitsh, p. 95.)
12. Kacerginski, p. 134.
13. *Ibid.*, pp. 139–140. Text: C. Cheytin. Tune: E. Teitelbaum, Vilna composer evacuated into the U.S.S.R. Thanks to the painstaking record of poets and composers kept by Kacerginski, many creators of Yiddish songs of this period were memorialized.

Starvation was one of the methods employed by the German occupation authorities to destroy the Jewish population. Smuggling food past the ghetto guards thus became a steady activity for survival. Discovery often meant imprisonment or even death. The well-known Vilna opera and radio star, Luba Levitski, met her end when she was caught smuggling some food for her ailing mother. Through her, an old Yiddish love song, "Tsvey taybelech" ("Two Little Doves") became very popular in the Vilna ghetto. (*See* Rubin, 1950, pp. 64–65.)

14. Kacerginski, p. 201. Text: A. Tsipkin, Kovno ghetto.
15. Gebirtig, p. 18. The poor carpenter, Mordche Gebirtig, was a true folk poet and tunesmith and the most popular creator of songs in folk style in Poland between the two world wars. He was shot during the German liquidation of the Cracow ghetto, on June 4, 1942, at the age of sixty-five. He wrote hundreds of songs, and a number of them were as popular as folk songs. His "Yankele," "Reyzele," "Hey, Tsigelech" ("Hey, My Little Goats"), and others are known to every Yiddish-speaking community.
16. *Ibid.*, pp. 33–34.
17. Prager, p. 147. The first four lines of this song are almost identical with one current in Palestine in the twenties. (*See* Chapter XIV, "To Zion," footnote 45.)
18. Kacerginski, p. 150.
19. *Ibid.*, p. 324.
20. *Ibid.*, pp. 181–182.
21. *Ibid.*, pp. 161–162. Text: Axelrod. In Lithuania, a German or Jewish official was called *yale*. Poor Jews often replaced wealthier ones in the labor brigades. Such replacements in Lithuania were called *malech* ("angel"). In the United States it is sometimes assumed that the popular riddle song "Tumbalalayka" is of American vintage. This Kovno ghetto song may perhaps indicate an East European source or, possibly, the utilization of the American song.
22. *Ibid.*, pp. 186–187. Text Markovsky, Kovno ghetto.
23. *Ibid.*, p. 226.

24. *Ibid.*, pp. 234–235. Said to have been written by M. Shenker, a Warsaw composer.

25. *Ibid.*, p. 122. Written in the Oshmene ghetto, a town near Vilna.

26. *Ibid.*, p. 100.

27. *Ibid.*, p. 256. Birkenau and Oswiencim were the same death camp.

28. *Ibid.*, p. 87. The young poet, Leah Rudnitsky (b. 1916), wrote this lullaby following the execution of 4,000 Jews at Ponar, on April 5, 1943, for a three-year-old child. Leah was taken to Maidanek or Treblinka, when the Vilna ghetto was liquidated.

29. In the Warsaw ghetto, children would watch passers-by, and, if they carried food, they would snatch it and, when caught, sink their teeth into it, so that the owners would hesitate to retrieve it.

30. Gontar, p. 21. Shargorod is in Poland. In 1944, a group of refugee children were rescued from the dread camps in Trans-Dniestria, near Bessarabia and Moldavia, between the Dniester and Bug rivers. Some were brought to camp *Atlit* in Palestine; others found their way to Czernowitz in the U.S.S.R. Attendants in both rescue centers recorded memoirs and songs which the children retained from the ghettos, concentration and death camps. The example cited here is from the Czernowitz source. The *Atlit* variant speaks of Lutshnits, which is near Lodz. A memoir recorded in Czernowitz from a "sixth-grade pupil, Rifke Shtanker," contains the following: "The murderers run through the streets catching Jews. They drive everyone to the trains. Children say good-bye to their parents. Voices all around are heard: 'My children are being taken to their death! My father is being led to death!' Such scenes occurred often until our whole community was *cleaned up*. Only a few, who had escaped the guards, returned. . . . They drove us to the far-off Ukraine. On the way, I lost my two sisters and mother. I had to witness, with deep suffering, how the Germans beat my mother and sister with clubs until they remained lying on the road." (Gontar).

31. Gontar.

32. *Fraye Arbeter Shtime*, Song No. 3. The similarity with H. D. Nomberg's "S'loyfn s'yogn shvartse volkns," of a half a century earlier, is unmistakable.

33. *Ibid.*, Song No. 5. Siroko is in Bessarabia.

34. Feder, p. 25. Text: Y. Rabinovitsh.

35. Feder, p. 27. Text: Esther Shtub.

36. Gontar.

37. Kacerginski, pp. 303–304. A hide-out was a *krayuvke, maline,* or *bunker,* depending on the area in which it was used. Authors: E. Magid and Gertsman, Vilna ghetto.

38. *Ibid.*, p. 205.

39. *Ibid.*, pp. 309–310. Text: E. Magid.

40. *Ibid.*, pp. 215–216.

41. *Ibid.*, pp. 32–33. The first slaughter at Ponar took place on September 6, 1941, when the Vilna ghetto was set up. "At dawn, April 5, 1943 . . . as I stood . . . not far from the ghetto gate, I saw a young fellow sneaking in, bloody, weary, disappearing quickly into a doorway. . . . When we pulled off his clothes, washed away the blood, tied up his wounded shoulder, he whispered: 'I come from Ponar!' We were petrified. 'Everyone—everyone was shot!'—The tears rolled down his face. 'Who?—the 4,000 who were being sent to Kovno?'—'Yes!'" (Kacerginski-*Tsukunft,* p. 234.)

42. Kacerginski, p. 264.

43. *Ibid.*, p. 352.

44. *Ibid.*, p. 325. Text: Kacerginski. Tune: Basye Rubin.

45. *Ibid.*, pp. 343–344. Text. L. Rosenthal, Vilna ghetto. Several Yiddish texts were set to Eisler's tunes, during this period. "I heard 'Tsu eyns tsvey dray' sung by a camp inmate before a camp audience in St. Atilien, Munich region, during my visit there. The singer stirred herself, as well as her listeners, to such a pitch . . . that

everyone responded passionately to her, with sobbing and a vow never to forget"
(Kacerginsi, Intro. by H. Leivick, xxxv).

46. *Ibid.,* p. 27. R. Buzhanski, who wrote many songs in the Vilna ghetto, based
his Yiddish song on a current Russian song entitled "Tutshi nad gorodom."

47. *Ibid.,* pp. 322–323. Text: A. Tsipkin.

48. *Ibid.,* p. 347. Text: L. Rosenthal.

49. *Ibid.,* p. 354. Text: K. Broydo. This musical production was presented by the
artists Dora Rubin, M. Shadovsky, K. Broydo, and Y. Ruthenberg. Only Dora Rubin
survived the liquidation of the Vilna ghetto.

50. *Ibid.,* p. 348. Text: Hirsh Glik. The two partisans engaged in this act were
Itsik Matskevitsch and Vitke Kempner. It is interesting to note the poet's use of
three words, *shpayer, nagan, pistoyl,* to denote the same object, an automatic pistol.
A former resident of the Vilno ghetto gave me this explanation for the poet's license:
"*Shpayer,* was current in the Vilno region; *nagan,* was the Russian word; *pistoyl*—
the German term. The use of all three within one song demonstrated the presence of
Jews from all over Europe, often herded together by the German occupationists within
one ghetto, one concentration or death camp."

51. *Ibid.,* p. 351.

52. Prager, p. 115.

53. Kacerginski, pp. 341–342. Text: Kacerginski. Tune: M. Blanter. English translation: A. Kramer. It was known that the Gestapo was pressuring the Jewish Committee for Vitenberg's apprehension. A chronicler maintains that on the night of
July 15, 1943, the Jewish Committeemen, Jacob Gens and Tsalek Tsesler, trapped
Vitenberg, shackled him, and were leading him towards the gates to be handed over
to the Gestapo. With the aid of his comrades, however, he broke away; but on the
morrow, Gens warned that if Vitenberg were not turned over at once, the ghetto
would be burned to the ground with everybody in it. Although Vitenberg knew that
the ghetto was on the eve of liquidation and was for raising the flag of struggle
against the Germans, he also knew that the ghetto population was not ready for
such a move. Not wishing to alienate the people from his point of view, he voluntarily
gave himself up, and on July 18 his body lay mutilated and dead in the corridor
of the Gestapo torture chambers, his hair burnt, his eyes gouged out and his bound
hands broken.

The following is a quote from Reyzl Korshak's book in Hebrew: *La-havut B'ofer*
("The Flame in the Dust") describing Vitenberg's escape from the Gestapo: "Suddenly, desperate cries were heard from all sides: 'Comrades, they've arrested the
commandant! Everyone to the gate, to free him!' Frightened men and women awoke
from sleep, asking: what happened? The commotion increased. Cries were heard
everywhere: we won't allow them to take our leader away! Itsik heard the cries and
realized what was happening. He broke away from his guards and began to run,
with the Gestapo behind him. But they were intercepted, knocked down and beaten
up" (Korshak).

54. Hirsh Glik was born in Vilna in 1920 and began writing poetry at the age
of fifteen. During the German occupation, he dug peat in the German labor camp
Vayse Vake, 12 kilometers from Vilna. In 1943, the Jews from this camp were transferred to the Vilna ghetto and Glik joined the partisan group there. When the news
of the Warsaw ghetto uprising reached the Vilna ghetto, Glik wrote his now famous
song, and the Partisan Command decided to make it the official hymn of the entire
underground organization. When the ghetto was liquidated, Glik, together with other
ghetto partisans, barricaded themselves in different sections of the ghetto. But he was
captured and sent to the Goldfild concentration camp. During the 1944 offensive,
when the Germans were being defeated on all fronts and were preparing to destroy
the camps nearest the fronts, Glik, with a group of his comrades, escaped. They
reached the nearby woods, but in an encounter with German troops, he fell in action.

55. Kacerginski, *Tsukunft,* pp. 235–236.

56. Kacerginski, p. 3.

57. *Ibid.,* pp. 355–356. Text: Rikle Glezer. Born in Vilna in 1923, Rikle Glezer began writing poetry in the Vilna ghetto. She joined the partisans, continued writing poetry between battles, and lived to see the day when her detachment, together with the Red Army, liberated Vilna.

CHAPTER XVII

Folksong—A Universal Language

IN SPITE OF THE SOCIAL OSTRACISM TO WHICH JEWS WERE SUBJECTED during the Middle Ages, they contributed significantly to the cultures of their dominant neighbors and were profoundly influenced by them in turn. Jewish translators in Moslem lands helped transmit Classical science and philosophy—as well as Oriental fables and tales—to medieval Europe. In Christian countries, there was a steady stream of translations from Hebrew into Spanish, French, and German—and from those languages into Hebrew. Jews were early conspicuous, too, as authors of original works in the European vernaculars.

The interchange of popular cultures among the peoples of Europe, including the Jews, was especially marked at this time. This was in part the work of migratory poets and gleemen as well as of itinerant students and teachers. Melody gave wings to folksong. Like seeds in the wind, songs were borne along by their itinerant carriers to root and grow again, often in areas far removed from their places of origin. This process of cultural interchange did not end with the Middle Ages, when Yiddish culture—like those of other nationalities—was taking shape. It has, indeed, continued to the present day.

Yiddish folksong, therefore, reveals not only some of the same themes as the folksongs of other peoples but some of the same patterns and devices as well. Number songs, cumulative songs, conversation songs, riddle songs, work songs, protest songs, cradle songs, children's songs, dancing songs, drinking songs, topical songs, war songs, hello and goodbye songs, love songs, marriage songs, laments, ballads, and humorous songs are found in many languages. Often the same song can be traced from language to language, through many variations occasioned by time and place. It is this universality of themes, patterns, and devices—only a few of which can be treated here—that makes folksong truly a universal language.

Number Songs

Many folksongs in many languages are based upon numbers. Either they begin with a string of numbers, or they fit a rhyme to a number all the way through. They may list objects or animals or activities. They may be humorous or nonsensical. Sometimes they attempt to fix in the memory solemn facts of religion.

One of the oldest Jewish folksongs, chanted in Hebrew and Aramaic toward the end of the Passover Seder, is "Echod mi yodea?" (Who Knows One?). This type of song, which uses a question-and-answer pattern and relates thirteen numbers to religious symbols, is known practically all over Europe and has been part of the Seder liturgy since the sixteenth century. It has its parallel in Latin, German, French, English, Spanish, Polish, Greek, Yiddish, American, and French-Canadian. One version is said to have been traced back to the Druids of ancient Gaul, possibly having come from the Far East.

Following are the first and last stanzas of the Hebrew chant, as enunciated by East European Jews, with the concluding verse listing the thirteen numbers and their connected religious symbols. The chant begins with "one," and after the addition of each new line all the earlier lines are repeated.

(1)
Echod mi yodea?
—Echod ani yodea.
Echod Eloheynu shebashomayim
    uvo-orets.

(1)
One: who knows?
—One I know.
One is one God who is in heaven
    and on earth.

(13)
Shloysho-oser mi yodea?
—Shloysho-oser ani yodea.
Shloysho-oser midayo,
Shneym-oser shivtayo,
Echod-oser kochvayo
Asoro dibrayo,
Tisho yarchey leydo,
Shmoyno y'mey milo,

(13)
Thirteen: who knows?
—Thirteen I know.
Thirteen attributes of God,
Twelve tribes of Israel,
Eleven stars of Joseph's dream,
Ten commandments,
Nine months of pregnancy,
Eight days of circumcision,

Shivo y'mey Shabato,	Seven days of the Sabbath count,
Shisho sidrey Mishno,	Six orders of the Mishna,
Chamisho chumshey Toyro,	Five books of the Torah,
Arba imo-oys,	Four matrons,
Shloysho ovoys,	Three patriarchs,
Shney luchoys habris,	Two tables of the covenant,
Echod Eloheyno shebashomayim uvo-orets.[1]	One is one God, who is in heaven and on earth.

An American version, which follows, was collected in 1942 from a group of people in Arkansas. The first and twelfth stanzas are given here.

(1)

Children, I'm going, I will send (sing) thee.
What shall I send thee?
Lord, I shall send thee one by one.
Well, one was the Holy Baby,
Was borne by the Virgin Mary,
Was wrapped in the hollow of a clawhorn,
Was laid in a hollow manger,
Was born, born, Lordy, born in Bethlehem.

(12)

Children, I'm going, I will send thee.
What shall I send thee?
Lord, I shall send thee twelve by twelve.
Well, twelve was the twelve disciples,
And eleven was the eleven riders,
And ten was the Ten Commandments,
And nine was the nine that dressed so fine,
And eight was the eight that stood at the gate,
And seven was the seven that came down from heaven,
And six was the six that couldn't get fixed,
And five was the Gospel writers,
And four was the four come a-knockin' at the door,
And three was the Hebrew children,
And two was the Paul and Silas,
And one was the Holy Baby,
Was borne by the Virgin Mary,
Was wrapped in the hollow of a clawhorn,
Was laid in a hollow manger,
Was born, born, Lordy, born in Bethlehem.[2]

These number songs, built originally on religious symbols, subsequently began to use secular objects in numerical sequence. This type of song was especially popular among children. A well known English example is "A Partridge in a Pear Tree," sung during the Christmas season. The first and final stanzas of its French parallel, "La Perdriole," are given below.

(1)
La premier mois d'l'année,
Que donn'rais-j'à ma mie?
—Une perdriole
Que va que vient que vole,
Une perdriole
Que vole dans la bois.

(1)
On the first month of the year,
What shall I give my love?
—A partridge
That flutters and flies,
A partridge
That flies in the woods.

(12)
Douze demoiselles, gentilles et belles,
Onze beaux garçons,
Dix boeufs au pré,
Neuf vaches à lait,
Huit moutons blancs,
Sept chiens courants,
Six lièvres aux champs,
Cinq lapins grattant la terre,
Quatre canards qui volent en l'air,
Trois ramiers au bois,
Deux tourterelles,
Une perdriole
Que va que vient que vole,
Une perdriole
Que vole dans le bois.[3]

(12)
Twelve pretty gentle maidens,
Eleven handsome lads,
Ten bulls in the meadow,
Nine milking cows,
Eight white sheep,
Seven running dogs,
Six hares in the fields,
Five rabbits scratching the earth,
Four ducks flying in the air,
Three wood pigeons,
Two turtledoves,
One partridge
That flutters and flies,
A partridge
That flies in the woods.

Cumulative Songs

As universally popular as the "Echod mi yodea?" chant is the "Chad gadyo" song, sung in Aramaic at the close of the Passover Seder. Variations of this rhyme have been traced to old French secular sources of the twelfth and thirteenth centuries, and scholars have referred to it as "the source of all similar tales" and "certainly the noblest of all stories of this type."[4] First published in Prague in 1590, it is mentioned in Cervantes' *Don Quixote*. Arnim and Brentano included it in their collection *Des Knaben Wunderhorn*. Heinrich Heine makes Jakel the Fool chant it in "The Rabbi of Bacharach," and Israel Zangwill uses it effectively in *Dreamers of the Ghetto*.

Here is the cumulative chant "Chad gadyo" (One Kid) as it appears in the Passover Haggadah. It begins:

Chad gadyo, chad gadyo!   One kid, one kid!
D'zaben abo bitrey zuzey,   Which father bought for two zuzim,
Chad gadyo, chad gadyo!   One kid, one kid!

The song then proceeds, line by line, to build a chain of actions in which the characters are: the kid, the cat, the dog, the stick, the fire, the water, the ox, the slaughterer, the Angel of Death, and the Holy One, Blessed is He. The last stanza is given below in its East European pronunciation.

Ve-oso Hakodoysh Boruch Hu,   And the Holy One, Blessed be He,
                                                                        came,
V'shochat l'malach hamoves,   And killed the Angel of Death
D'shochat l'shoychet,   That slew the slaughterer
D'shochat l'soyro,   That slaughtered the ox
D'shoso l'mayo,   That drank the water
D'chovo l'nuro,   That quenched the fire
D'soraf l'chutro,   That burned the stick
D'hiko l'kalbo,   That beat the dog
D'noshach l'shunro,   That bit the cat
D'ochlo l'gadyo,   That ate the kid
D'zaben abo bitrey zuzey,   That father bought for two zuzim,
Chad gadyo, chad gadyo![5]   One kid, one kid!

It is interesting to note that although the "Echod mi yodea?" chant is not part of the Haggadah of the Spanish, Portuguese, and Yemenite Jewish communities, the "Chad gadyo" song is.

Remarkably similar to "Chad gadyo" is an American song transcribed in New England. The first, seventh, and concluding stanzas follow here.

(1)
As I was going over London Bridge
I found a penny ha'penny, and bought me a kid.
Kid do go.
Know by the moonlight it's almost midnight,
Time kid and I were home an hour and a half ago.

(7)

Went a little further, and found rope,
Rope do hang butcher,
Butcher won't kill ox,
Ox won't drink water,
Water won't quench fire,
Fire won't burn stick,
Stick won't beat kid,
Kid won't go,
Know by the moonlight it's almost midnight,
Time kid and I were home an hour and a half ago.

(8)

Rope began to hang butcher,
Butcher began to kill ox,
Ox began to drink water,
Water began to quench fire,
Fire began to burn stick,
Stick began to beat kid,
Kid began to go.
Know by the moonlight it's almost midnight,
So kid and I got home an hour and a half ago.[6]

Many paths and bypaths were taken by this chant, which took on the coloration of each country and people who adopted it. In its simplest forms, the cumulative song is a mere enumeration from the general to the particular. This is true of the following children's song that was recorded in Georgia.

There was a tree stood in the ground,
The prettiest tree you ever did see;
The tree in the wood and the wood in the ground
And the green grass growing all round, round, round,
And the green grass growing all round.

The song then proceeds from the tree to the branch, to the bough, to the twig, to the nest, to the egg, to the bird, to the wing, to the feather, to the down, until it reaches its climax with:

The prettiest down you ever did see,
The down on the feather and the feather on the wing,
The wing on the bird and the bird in the egg,
The egg in the nest and the nest on the twig,
The twig on the bough and the bough on the branch,

The branch on the tree and the tree in the wood,
The tree in the wood and the wood in the ground,
And the green grass growing all round, round, round,
And the green grass growing all round.[7]

The first and eleventh stanzas of a parallel from Denmark reveal
a similar sequence.

(1)
Langt udi skoven laa et lille
    bjerg,
Aldrig saa jeg saa dejligt et bjerg,
Bjerget ligger langt udi skoven.

(1)
Deep in the forest stands a little
    hill,
I never saw so sweet a little hill,
Hill, standing deep in the forest.

(11)
Paa den lille pude laa en lille
    dreng,
Aldrig saa jeg saa dejlig en dreng,
Drengen paa puden,
Puden af fjeren,
Fjeren paa fuglen,
Fuglen af aegget,
Aegget i reden,
Reden paa bladet,
Bladet paa kvisten,
Kvisten paa grenen,
Grenen paa traeet,
Traeet paa bjerget,
Bjerget ligger langt udi skoven.[8]

(11)
On the little pillow lay a little
    boy,
I never saw so sweet a little boy,
Boy on the pillow,
Pillow from the feather,
Feather on the bird,
Bird from the egg,
Egg in the nest,
Nest on the leaf,
Leaf on the twig,
Twig on the branch,
Branch on the tree,
Tree on the hill,
Hill, standing deep in the forest.

Although the Danish song obviously served as a lullaby, the Yiddish parallel given below seems to have become a cumulative song
for young lovers.

(1)
Velches iz dos shenste fun der
    velt?
—A sheyner vald.
Vald fun der velt, tamtidiram,
Tamtiridiram.

(1)
What is the loveliest in the
    world?
—A beautiful forest.
Forest in the world,
Tralalala.

(9)
Velches iz shener fun dem
  bocher?
—A sheyne meydl,
Meydl fun dem bocher,
Bocher fun dem epl,
Epl fun der barne,
Barne fun dem blat,
Blat fun dem tsvayg,
Tsvayg fun dem boym,
Boym fun dem vald,
Vald fun der velt,
Tamtiridiram.[9]

(9)
What is lovelier than the young
  man?
—A beautiful young girl.
Girl than the young man,
Man than the apple,
Apple than the pear,
Pear than the leaf,
Leaf than the branch,
Branch than the tree,
Tree than the forest,
Forest in the world,
Tralalala.

Numberless cumulative patterns in endless variety are evident in the folksongs of many peoples. Below is an example popular among Spanish-speaking people, both in the Old World and the New. Here the subject matter is somewhat different, but the sequence and form are reminiscent of the older songs and tales mentioned above. The first three and final stanzas are given here.

(1)
Estaba la rana cantando debajo
  del agua;
Cuando la rana se puso a cantar.
Vino la mosca y la hizo callar.

(1)
The frog was singing under the
  water
When the spider began to sing.
The fly came and shut him up.

(2)
Callaba la mosca a la rana
Que estaba cantando debajo del
  agua;
Cuando la mosca se puso a cantar,
Vino la arana y la hizo callar.

(2)
The fly shut the frog up
Who was singing under the water.

When the fly began to sing,
The spider came and shut her up.

(3)
Callaba la araña a la mosca,
  la mosca a la rana,
Que estaba cantando debajo del
  agua;
Cuando la araña se puso a cantar,
Vino el ratón y la hizo callar.

(3)
The spider shut the fly up,
The fly shut the frog up
Who was singing under the water.

When the spider began to sing,
The mouse came and shut him up.

(12)

Callaba el hombre, al cuchillo,
  el cuchillo al toro,
  el toro al agua,
  el agua al fuego,
  el fuego al palo,
  el palo al perro,
  el perro al gato,
  el gato al ratón,
  el ratón la araña,
  la araña a la mosca,
  la mosca a la rana,
Que estaba cantando debajo el
  agua;
Cuando el hombre se puso a
  cantar,
Vino su suegra y lo hizo callar![10]

(12)

The man shut the knife up,
  The knife the bull,
  The bull the water,
  The water the fire,
  The fire the stick,
  The stick the dog,
  The dog the cat,
  The cat the mouse,
  The mouse the spider,
  The spider the fly,
  The fly the frog
Who was singing under the water.

When the man began to sing,

Came his mother-in-law and shut
him up!

Conversation Songs

A type of song shared by many peoples is the conversation song between mother and daughter on the theme of "Mother, I want to get married." In such songs the mother may offer her daughter a choice of various objects or of various kinds of husbands. In the former type, the daughter rejects all the objects in favor of a man. In the latter type, the daughter selects the kind of man she herself desires, which is often not at all what the mother had desired for her.

Below, the first and fourth stanzas of a German example are given. The conversation takes place at the spinning wheel, and the choices offered the daughter by her mother are a pair of shoes, a pair of stockings, a gown, and—a man.

(1)

Spinn, spinn, meine liebe
  Tochter,
Ich kauf dir'n Paar Schuh.
Ja, ja, liebe, liebe Mutter,
Auch Schnallen dazu!
  Ich kann ja nicht spinnen,
  Es schmerzt mich mein Finger

(1)

Spin, spin, O my dearest
  daughter,
I'll buy you some shoes.
Yes, yes, O my dearest mother,
With buckles one, two.
  I cannot spin, mother,
  My finger does hurt me,

Und tut und tut
Und tut mir so weh.

It hurts and hurts
And I cannot spin.

(4)

(4)

Spinn, spinn, meine liebe Tochter,
Ich kauf dir'nen Mann.
Ja, ja, liebe, liebe Mutter,
Dann streng ich mich an.
    Ich kann ja schon spinnen,
    Es schmerzt mich kein Finger
    Und tut und tut
    Und tut nicht mehr weh.[11]

Spin, spin, O my dearest daughter,
I'll buy you a man.
Yes, yes, O my dearest mother,
as fast as I can.
    Oh now I am spinning,
    My finger is better.
    And now, and now
    It hurts me no more.

In the East European Yiddish parallel, the mother asks her daughter: "Does my little girl wish for a dress? Then I will go to the seamstress. If it is a pair of shoes she wants, then it's to the cobbler I will go." The mother then tries a hat and a pair of earrings, suggesting in turn trips to the milliner and the goldsmith. But to each query the daughter replies: "No, mother, no. You just don't seem to understand what it is that I desire." In the final stanza, the mother at last divines her daughter's wish for a husband and hurries off to the matchmaker.

Yomi, Yomi, zing mir a lidele.
Vos dos meydele vil?
Dos meydele vil a chosndl hobn.
Darf men geyn dem shadchendl
        zogn.
    Yo, mamemshi, yo,
    Du veyst shoyn vos ich meyn,
    Du kenst mich shoyn farshteyn![12]

Yomi, Yomi, sing me a ditty.
What does my little girl wish?
The little girl wants a groom.
Then to the matchmaker I must go.

    Yes, dear mother, yes,
    You now know what I want,
    You now can understand me!

In the Italian parallel, which takes place in a vegetable garden, the daughter feigns illness, suggesting to her mother that "in the garden there is something that will heal me." The mother looks into the garden and sees tomatoes, greens—none of which seems capable of curing her daughter's illness. However, when the mother happens to notice the gardener in the garden, the cure is discovered.

Cara mamma, io sono maláta.	Dear mother, I am ill.
Ma una cosa nell'orto ci sta!	My cure in the garden you'll find.
—E, nell'orto ci sta l'ortolano.	—Well, in the garden I see the gardener.
Se tu *la* vuoi, io te la do.—	If you desire him I shall get him for you.
O mamma, si, si, si,	O mother, yes, yes, yes.
Questo va bene per farmi guari!	That is the wish of my heart.
O, quant' e cara la mamma mia,	Oh, what a dear mother you are to me
Che conosciuto la malattia.	To know the cause of my illness.
O mamma, si, si, si,	O mother, yes, yes, yes.
Questo va bene per farmi guari![13]	That is the dear wish of my heart!

The conversation in the American parallel, undoubtedly a version of the English "Whistle, Daughter, Whistle," takes place on the farm, where the mother's offers of a sheep, a cow, a goat, and a pig are all rejected by the daughter, who considers them no substitute for a man.

> Whistle, daughter, whistle, and you shall have a cow.
> I can't whistle, mother, because I don't know how.
>
> Whistle, daughter, whistle, and you shall have a goat.
> I can't whistle, mother, because it hurts my throat.
>
> Whistle, daughter, whistle, and you shall have a pig.
> I can't whistle, mother, because I am too big.
>
> Whistle, daughter, whistle, and you shall have a man.
> [Daughter whistles.] I've just found out I can![14]

Riddle Songs

Prominent in old English and Scottish ballads, the riddle song is to be found among most of the people of Europe and in the United States. In folk ballads of this type, a series of difficult questions is posed by a young man to the girl he is courting. Marriage often depends on her answers. In the Yiddish courting song below, the young woman starts the riddling contest and finally "gets her man."

[She] Nem aroys a ber fun vald	[She] Lead a bear out of the woods
Un lern im oys shraybn	And teach him how to write.
Demlt vestu, demlt vestu	Then you may, then you shall
Eybig mayner blaybn.	Forever mine remain.

[He] Ich vel aroysnemen a ber
    fun vald
Un vel im oyslernen shrabyn
Ney mir oys zibn hemder
On nodl un on zaydn.

Ich vel dir oysneyen zibn hemder
On nodl un on zaydn
Boy mir oys a leyter hoych
Tsum himl zol er shtaygn.

Ich vel dir oysboyen a leyter hoych
Tsum himl vet er shtaygn
Hob-zhe mir zibn kinder
A meydl zolstu blaybn . . .

Ich vel dir hobn zibn kinder
A meydl vel ich blaybn
Boy mir oys zibn vign
On holts un on getsaygn.

Ich vel dir oysboyen zibn vign
On holts un on getsaygn—
Bizt a kluge un ich kayn nar,
To lomir beyde blaybn![15]

[He] I will lead a bear out of the
    woods
And teach him how to write
If you will sew seven shirts for me
Without needle or silk cloth.

I will sew seven shirts for you
Without needle or silk cloth
If you build me a ladder tall
To reach into the sky.

I will build you a ladder tall
To reach into the sky
If you will bear me seven children
And a virgin yet remain . . .

I will bear you seven children
And remain a virgin
If you will make seven cribs for me
Without wood or tools.

I will make seven cribs for you
Without wood or tools—
But you are wise and I no fool,
So let us both be married!

In this English example, the two imaginative young lovers are obviously well matched in the courting game of riddles.

> Say can you make me a cambric shirt,
> Sing Ivy leaf, Sweet William and Thyme,
> Without any needle or needle work?
> And you shall be a true lover of mine.
>
> Yes, if you can wash it in yonder well,
> Sing Ivy leaf, Sweet William and Thyme,
> Where neither springs water, nor rain ever fell,
> And you shall be a true lover of mine.
>
> Say can you plow me an acre of land,
> Sing Ivy leaf, Sweet William and Thyme,
> Between the sea and the salt sea strand?
> And you shall be a true lover of mine.
>
> Yes, if you plow it with one ram's horn,
> Sing Ivy leaf, Sweet William and Thyme,
> And sow it all over with one peppercorn,
> And you shall be a true lover of mine.

Say can you reap with a sickle of leather,
Sing Ivy leaf, Sweet William and Thyme,
And tie it all up with a Tom-tit's feather?
And you shall be a true lover of mine.

Yes, if you gather it all in a sack,
Sing Ivy leaf, Sweet William and Thyme,
And carry it home on a butterfly's back,
And you shall be a true lover of mine.[16]

The Unfaithful Wife

The theme of the unfaithful wife has been popular all over Europe
and is still current in some parts of the United States. Although this
theme is not frequent in Yiddish folksong, it was known to Yiddish-
speaking Jews in Eastern Europe, and two versions were collected
by the author twenty-five years ago in New York City. The type of
song in which a husband returns home unexpectedly and discovers
his wife's unfaithfulness is usually a humorous one. This is true of
the Scottish song "Our Gude-man."

Our gude-man cam' hame at e'en
And hame cam' he.
And there he saw a saddle horse,
Whaur nae horse should be.
"Oh, how cam' this horse here,
How can this be?
How cam' this horse here
Without the leave of me?"
  —"A horse?" quo' she.
  —"Aye, a horse!" quo' he.

"Ye auld blind doited carle
Blinder mat ye be,
'Tis naething but a milk-cow
My minnie sent to me."
  —"A milk cow?" quo' he.
  —"Aye, a milk cow!" quo' she.
"Far ha'e I ridden and meikle ha'e I seen,
But a saddle on a cow's back
Saw I never nane!"

Our "gude-man" then proceeds to notice a number of other items that seem strange to him: "a pair o' jack-boots," "a sword," "a pouthered wig," "a riding-coat," all of which his wife insists are not what they seem. But the "gude-man" is never entirely persuaded, even in the final stanza.

Bed went our gude-man
And bed went he;
And there he spied a sturdy man,
Whaur nae man should be.
"How cam' this man here?
How can this be?
How cam' this man here
Without the leave of me?"
　—"A man?" quo' she.
　—"Aye, a doited man," quo' he.
"Puir blind body!
And blinder mat ye be!
It's a new milking-maid
My minnie sent to me."
　—"A maid?" quo' he.
　—"Aye, a maid," quo' she.
"Far ha'e I ridden,
And meikle ha'e I seen,
But long-bearded milking maids
Saw I never nane!"[17]

A Yiddish parallel, dating from the nineteenth century, introduces a moral dimension missing in other versions.

Gey ich mir arayn tsu mayn
　　gelibter froy,
Eyns, tsvey, dray,
In shtal shteyen ferdelech,

Eyns un tsvey un dray.
Ruf ich mich on tsu mayn
　　gelibter froy:
Vos fara ferdelech shteyen do?
Enfert zi mir: kiyelech,
Fun der bobenyu geshikt.

I come home to my loving wife,

One, two, three,
And see in the stable standing
　　horses,
One and two and three.
I say to my loving wife:

Whose horses are these?
And she answers me: Little cows,
Which granny sent to me.

Ay, kiyelech mit di lederne
zotelech,
Hey, hey, hey, dos harts tut
mir vey,
Un vilstu mich far a man,

To vozhe darfstu zey?

Gey ich mir arayn tsu mayn
gelibter froy,
Eyns, tsvey, dray,
In kich shteyen shtivelech,

Eyns un tsvey un dray.
Ruf ich mich on tsu mayn
gelibter froy:
Vos fara shtivelech shteyen do?
Enfert zi mir: shtek-shichelech
Fun der bobenyu geshikt.
Ay, shtek-shichelech mit di
zilberne shporelech,
Hey, hey, hey, dos harts tut
mir vey,
Un vilstu mich far a man,
To vozhe darfstu zey?[18]

Ah, little cows and leather
saddles on,
Woe, woe, woe, my heart hurts
me so,
And if you want me for your
spouse,
What do you need them for?

I come home to my loving wife,

One, two, three,
And see in the kitchen three pairs
of boots,
One and two and three.
I say to my loving wife:

Whose boots are they?
And she answers me: Little slippers,
Which granny sent to me.
Ah, little slippers with silver
spurs,
Woe, woe, woe, my heart hurts
me so,
If you want me for your spouse
What do you need them for?

Songs of Protest

The contrast between the life of the rich and that of the poor is an old theme of folksong. Eight hundred years ago, the French adapter of the Arthurian legends, Chrétien de Troyes, composed the lament of the "Poor Damsels," ragged and starving at their weaving:

Stitching silk, brocade, and braid,
We are soiled and scarcely clad
Because our wage is not enough,
It buys us neither meat nor stuff.
With whatever care and dread
We divide our daily bread,
It's little at morn and less at night.
With twenty pence in one week earned
We feel us into ladies turned
And yet it does not help our plight.

But those who pay this sorry wage
Grow rich upon us as we drudge.
We are driven on at their behest,
And day and night we have no rest.
If, weary, one should fall asleep,
At once they're here, with rod and whip.
We live on sorrow, live in Hell,
Poor damsels we, *Les Pauvres Pucelles.*[19]

The deplorable condition of the laboring folk during the Industrial Revolution in eighteenth- and nineteenth-century England inspired protest poems by Shelley ("Ode to the Men of England") and Hood ("Song of the Shirt") that were echoed by popular songs on the continent. In Holland, the "Lied van het Proletariat" was sung to the melody of the English song, "The British Grenadiers."

Wie delft het zware erts?
Wie brengt het uit de mijn?
Wie maakt het voedzaam brood?
De kleed'ren, zacht en fijn?
Wie brengt den rijken overvloed
Terwijl hij zelf verhongren moet?
Het is het volk dat zwoegt,
Het Proletariaat.[20]

Who digs the heavy ore?
Who heaves it from the mine?
Who makes the nourishing bread?
The clothing soft and fine?
Who gives abundance to the rich
While he is bound to starve?
It is the workingman that toils,
The Proletariat.

This was probably an adaptation of a song by Johann Most that was then current in Germany. In 1882, when Most went to the United States, he published an English translation of his song that became popular among American workingmen struggling to organize labor unions.

Who hammers brass and stone?
Who raises from the mine?
Who weaveth cloth and silk?
Who tilleth wheat and vine?
Who laboreth the rich to feed
Yet lives himself in sorest need?
It is the men of toil,
The Proletariat.[21]

The social movements of Western Europe took two generations to penetrate into the Jewish communities of Eastern Europe. Although a Yiddish version of Most's song was current in Poland before the 1905 Russian Revolution, social protest was already part of anonymous folk songs current among workingmen and women in such large Jewish industrial centers as Lodz, Warsaw, Minsk, Odessa, and Vilno. In one lullaby, a working father warns his baby about the inequalities of the world of toil. "The loveliest houses and palaces," he says, "are made by the poor man. But do you think he lives in them? Oh, no, the rich man does!" This same theme recurs in this late nineteenth-century song.

Seder un tsvitn un vayngertner	Orchards, blossoms, vineyards,
Dos flantst alts oys der arbetsman,	All are planted by the workingman,
Un git a kuk, ver est di fruchtn,	But who eats the fruits thereof?
Alts nit er, nor der raycher man.	Not he, but the rich man.
Ale s'choyres vos fun der gantser velt,	All the wares of the whole world
Dos arbet alts oys der arbetsman.	Are made by the workingman,
Un git a kuk ver es nemt di gelter,	But observe who gets the monies for them,
Alts nit er, nor der raycher man.[22]	Not he at all, but the rich man.

In France, steel workers at the open hearth sang:

(1)	(1)
Ali, alo, pour Maschero,	Ali, alo to Maschero,
Ali, ali, alo!	Ali, ali, alo!
Ils mangent la viande	They eat the meat
Et nous donnent les os,	And give us the bones,
Ali, ali, ali, alo,	Ali, ali, ali, alo,
Ali, ali, alo!	Ali, ali, alo!
(2)	(2)
. . . Ils boivent le vin	. . . They drink the wine
Et nous donnent de l'eau . . .	And give us water . . .
(3)	(3)
. . . Ils mangent le beurre	. . . They eat the butter
Et nous donnent le pot . . .[23]	And give us the empty pot . . .

The protest against inequality and exploitation was not unknown in America, the fabled land of opportunity for the masses of the European proletariat. This song reflects the sentiments of a West Virginia factory hand.

> We rise up early in the morn
> And work all day real hard.
> To buy our little meat and bread
> And sugar, tea and lard.
>
> Our children they grow up unlearned,
> No time to go to school.
> Almost before they've learned to walk
> They learn to spin or spool.
>
> The folks in town who dress so fine
> And spend their money free
> Will hardly look at a factory hand
> Who dresses like you and me.
>
> Well, let them wear their watches fine,
> Their rings and pearly strings.
> When the day of judgment comes
> We'll make them shed their pretty things.[24]

In the American South the economic struggle was heightened by racial conflict. A Negro folksong of the middle of the nineteenth century treats this theme.

> We raise de wheat, dey gib us de crust;
> We sif' de meal, dey gib us de skin;
> And dat's da way dey take us in.
> We skim de pot, dey gib us de liquor,
> And say dat's good enough for nigger.[25]

Topical Songs

Topical folksongs were inspired by events great and small, national and local. During the American Civil War, educated people composed songs expounding the political issues. The soldiers' own creations, on the other hand, were for the most part either humorous or bitter, and had little to do with duty or glory. Revealing the soldiers' resentment of the conscription laws that permitted the rich lad to avoid service by paying $300 or by providing a substitute, the following song was current at that time.

> I'm glad my dad three hundred has
> To save me from the army;
> To ma's dear aprong strings I'll hang
> And then no one can harm me.
> For I'm too sweet a little man
> For common soldier camping,
> And I should surely faint away
> To try their horrid tramping.[26]

Who can account for a Yiddish song current at almost the same time and reflecting similar circumstances in Czarist Russia? After new military service regulations went into effect in 1874, a topical song warned "rich men's sons" to stop their "frolicking," now that the new laws forbade anyone to buy his way out of the service or hire substitutes to go for him.[27]

Nineteenth-century Yiddish folksong does not include descriptions of battles or epic scenes glorifying war. In the main it deals with the deprivations of the soldiers and the miseries of families and loved ones left behind. Following is an excerpt from a Yiddish song in which two lovers bid each other adieu. He is going off to serve in the Russian army for four years, and she is fearful that when he returns he might consider her an old maid.

Ay, lomir beyde a libe shpiln,
Ay, lomir zayn fun got a por,
Oy, shvern, shver ich dir bay
    sher un ayzn,
Az vartn vel ich oyf dir tsvey-
    drey yor!

Oh, let us be as true lovers,
And let us be a pair mated by God.
I vow by my shears and my iron

To wait for you two and three
    years!

Oy tsvey-dray yor vel ich oyf
    dir vartn,
Un efsher fir iz doch oych keday.
Ay, gelt in polk arayn vel ich
    dir shikn,
Un mutshen vel ich zich bay
    shnayderay.

Yes, two-three years will I wait for
    you,
For you I'll wait even four.
I'll send you some money to the
    regiment
And work hard at my seamstressing
    trade.

Bay shnayderay vel ich zich mutshen,
Un vel zich lebn in groys noyt.
Un az du vest fun dayn sluzhbe kumen,
Zolstu nisht zogn ch'bin an alte moyd . . .

Yes, I'll work hard at my sewing,
And live in great poverty,
Hoping that when you return from the service,
You won't think me an old maid . . .

Vi nor der poyezd 't'genumen rirn
Aroysgelozt hob ich a groys geveyn!
Ay ale meydelech zey hobn chasene,
Un nor ich eyne blayb atsind aleyn. . . .[28]

But when that train began to move
My heart broke out in a great cry.
All the other girls are getting married,
The only one to remain single— am I!

A likely parallel is the beautiful song sung by Washington's men during the American Revolution—"Johnny Has Gone for a Soldier." This was the American version of the Irish "Shule Aroon" (or "Siubhail a Gradh"), popular in Ireland toward the close of the seventeenth century when Irishmen were going off to fight in the armies of France. The Gaelic refrain is still sung by Irish-Americans.

> Siubhail, siubhail, siubhail a gradh,
> Ni leigheas le faghail acht leigheas en bhais.
> O d'fhag tu mise, is bocht mo chas,
> Is go dteidhidh tu a mhuirnin slan.

Here are the English verses:

> There I sat on Buttermilk Hill,
> Who could blame me, cry my fill;
> And every tear would turn a mill:
> Johnny has gone for a soldier.

> Me oh my, I loved him so,
> Broke my heart to see him go
> And only time will heal my woe:
> Johnny has gone for a soldier.

> I'll sell my flax, I'll sell my wheel,
> Buy my love a sword of steel
> So it in battle he may wield:
> Johnny has gone for a soldier.[29]

Yiddish folksong, youngest product of Jewish folk music, is unique within its own multicultural, multilingual Jewish family. As part of world folk music, it shares the universality that combines differences which separate one people from another as well as similarities which bind all peoples together.

Notes

FOLKSONG—A UNIVERSAL LANGUAGE

1. *Hagaddah shel Pesach,* pp. 59ff.
2. Recorded by John A. and Ruby T. Lomax. A version of "The Carol of the Twelve Numbers," often known as the "Dilly Song." In Archive of American Folk Song, Library of Congress, Washington, D.C.
3. Arma, p. 104, #308.
4. Newell, pp. 33–48; Bett, p. 86.
5. *Hagaddah shel Pesach,* pp. 63–64. See Bassin, I, 64 for old Yiddish parallel published in Koenigsberg in 1699.
6. Newell.
7. Bett, p. 98.
8. Karpeles, pp. 6–7. English translation by Eileen MacLeod.
9. Cahan, 1957, p. 418.
10. Paz, p. 94.
11. Karpeles, p. 99. English translation by Maud Karpeles.
12. Rubin, 1965, p. 74.
13. Botsford, II, 226–227.
14. Thorne, Margaret, p. 24.
15. Transcribed by the author in 1948 in New York City from a 67-year-old woman born in Lithuania.
16. Winn, p. 19.
17. Shay, pp. 31–35.
18. B. & F., pp. 416–418. The Yiddish text given here seems to be close to a broadside in German translation by Franz Wilhelm Meyer widely sold in many parts of Europe in 1790.
19. Feuchtwanger, p. 303.
20. A. B., p. 5. English translation by Edith Kolinski.
21. Original song in German by Johann Most (*Proletarierliederbuch,* Chemnitz, 1875) follows:

> Wer schafft das Gold zu Tage?
> Wer hammert Erz und Stein?
> Wer webet Tuch und Lein?
> Wer bauet Korn und Wein?
> Wer gibt den Reichen all ihr Brod?
> Und lebt dabei in bittrer Noth?
> Das sind die Arbeitsmänner,
> Das Proletariat.

See Platon Brounoff, ed., *Song of Freedom,* New York, 1904, for English version.

22. D & Y, pp. 387–388.
23. Arma, p. 204, #444.
24. Greenway, pp. 140–141.
25. Douglass, p. 446.
26. Ames, p. 164.
27. Skuditsky, 1936, pp. 241–242.
28. Collected by the author in Montreal in 1955 from a 60-year-old man born in the Ukraine.
29. From the collection of John Allison in the album "Songs of the American Revolution and War of 1812."

Appendix I

FIRST PRINTED COLLECTIONS OF YIDDISH SONGS

Up to the seventeenth century, we can point to three important collections of Yiddish songs. In 1517, a manuscript of forty-three Yiddish song *texts* appeared, most of them with a parallel Hebrew text, compiled by Menachem ben Naftali Oldendorf (b. 1450). Oldendorf lived in Frankfurt-am-Main, was a scribe, and possibly also one of the more serious type of sixteenth-century performers, whose repertoire consisted of songs composed by himself and his contemporaries on themes of current Jewish interest at the time. Twenty-five of these song texts are still known to be extant.

In 1595–1605, fifty-four Yiddish song *texts* appeared, compiled by Eisik Walich of Worms (d. 1632), including popular songs on *secular* themes, apparently set to current German melodies. Considered to be the oldest collection of secular Yiddish songs, it includes love and dance songs, courtship and drinking songs, humorous and topical songs. Forty-two of these are of German origin and the remaining twelve, by Jewish authors, include Purim songs, bridal songs, a riddle song, and a *danse macabre* song.

The first collection of Yiddish songs *with music* appeared in Fürth in 1727 as Part II of a larger collection of folklore, of which Part I had appeared anonymously in Frankfurt in 1707. The compiler, Elchonon Henle Kirch-han, a Western European Jew, born during the second half of the seventeenth century, might have been a wandering mentor who traveled among the Western and Eastern European Jewish communities, accumulating the tales, fables, and customs of his people. Kirch-han set his rhymes to tunes of itinerant bandsmen and titled his collection of song texts and tunes : *Simchas Hanefesh* ("Delight of the Soul"). However, once issued in 1727, it was never republished. A copy of this rare print is preserved in the Hebrew Union College Library in Cincinnati, Ohio, and a photostatic copy with a cultural-historical introduction by Dr. Jacob Shatsky, published in New York in 1926, is to be found in the New York City Public Library.

485

Appendix II

Music for Selected Songs from the Text

1. UNTER DEM KIND'S VIGELE

LULLABY

Un - ter dem kind's vi - ge - le Shteyt a klor - vays tsi - ge le. Dos tsi - ge - le z'ge - fo - rn hand - len Ro - zhin - kes mit mand - len. Ro - zhin - kes mit mand - len iz zey - er zis, Mayn kind vet zayn ge - zunt___ un frish.___

Music: Rubin, 1950, pp. 16-17.
See: Voices, p. 31, "Unter yankele's viegele."

2. AMOL IZ GEVEN A MAYSE

LULLABY

A - mol iz ge -ven a may - se, Di may - se iz gor - nit

487

frey - lech, Di may - se heybt zich o - net Mit a yi - di - shn
mey - lech. Lyu - lin - ke mayn fe - ge - le Lyu - lin - ke mayn
kind. Ch'ob on - ge - voy - rn a - za li - be, Vey iz mir un vind.

Music: Rubin, 1950, p. 20.
Text: Voices, p. 35-6.

3. SHLOF, DVOYRELE, SHLOF

LULLABY

Shlof, Dvoy - re - le, shlof. Di fey - ge - lech zing - en in vald. Zey
zing - en un shpring - en in gri - nem groz, Zey - vel - n Dvoy - re - len breng - en vos.
Vos vel - n zey breng - en? Shey - ne fay - ne ring - en. Di
ring - en vel - n zayn mit gold ba - shlo - gn, Dos vet Dvoy - re - le tro - gn.

Music: B & F, p. 306.
Text: Voices, p. 38.

4. HOB ICH A POR OKSN

CUMULATIVE SONG

Hob ich a por ok - sn, ok - sn, Vos zey bro - kn lok - shn,
lok - shn, Ay - vun - der i - ber vun - der vi di ok - sn

bro - kn lok -shn. Dos iz mir a vun -der, ___ Dos iz mir a vun - der.

Music: Rubin, 1965, p. 38.
Text: Voices, p. 60.

5. SHEYN BIN ICH, SHEYN

SKIPPING SONG

Sheyn bin ich sheyn. Sheyn iz oych mayn no - men.

Redt men mir shi -du - chim mit groy - se ra - bo - nim. Ra-

bo - ni -she toy - re iz doch zey - er groys, ___

Bin ich bay mayn ma - men a lich - ti - ge royz.

A sheyn mey-de - le bin ich, Bloy - e ze - ke -lech trog ich,

Gelt in di ta - shn, Bir in di fla - shn,

Vayn in di kri - ge - lech, Kind -er in di vi - ge - lech,

Shray -en vi di tsi - ge -lech: Meh, Meh, Meh.___

Music: Rubin, 1965, p. 66.
Text: Voices, p. 50 (Variant).

6. DU MEYDELE DU FAYNS

RIDDLE SONG

Du mey - de - le du fayns, Du mey - de - le du sheyns

Ch'vel dir e - pes fre - gn a re - te - nish a kleyns:

Vu ze - nen do benk__ on__ fish?

Vu iz__ do__ va - ser on__ fish?

Music: Cahan, 1957, No. 499, p. 415.
Text: Voices, pp. 60-1.

7. PAPIR IZ DOCH VAYS

LOVE SONG

Pa - pir iz doch vays__ un tint__ iz doch shvarts. Tsu

dir mayn zis le - bn tsit__ doch mayn harts. Ich volt

shten - dig ge - ze - sn dray teg__ noch - an - and, Tsu

ku - shn dayn sheyn po - nim un tsu halt - n dayn hant.

Muisc: Rubin, 1965, p. 58.
Text: Voices, pp. 76-7.

8. INDROYSN IZ FINSTER

SERENADE

In - droy-sn iz fin - ster, In - droy- sn iz fin -ster s'iz shpet bay -

nacht.___ Men hert kayn zhum, kayn shorch, kayn fey-ge-le fli - en oyf der gas.

Men hert kayn zhum, kayn shorch, kayn fey - ge - le fli - en oyf der gas.___

___ A - vu biz - tu ge - ven? Ch'vil mit

dir tsvey ver - ter re - - dn.   A -

vu biz - tu ge - ven? Ch'vil mit dir tsu - za - men geyn.

Music: Rubin, MSS.
Text: Voices, p.77.

9. OY, A NACHT A SHEYNE

LOVE SONG

Oy a nacht a shey - ne,___ Di nacht iz ge-ven a - zoy sheyn.___ Di nacht iz ge-ven a - zoy sheyn.___ Af a ben-ke-le ze-nen mir ge - ze - sn,___ Di le-vo-ne hot ge-nu-men a - vek-geyn.

Music: Rubin, 1965, p. 52.
Text: Voices, p. 78.

10. ALE VASERLECH FLISN AVEK

LAMENT

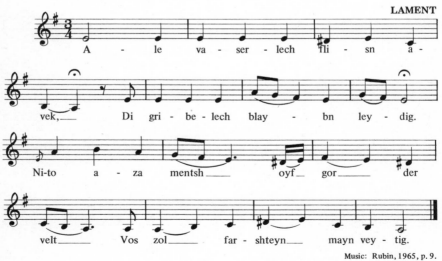

A - le va - ser - lech fli - sn a - vek,___ Di gri - be-lech blay - bn ley - dig. Ni-to a - za mentsh___ oyf___ gor___ der velt___ Vos zol___ far - shteyn___ mayn vey - tig.

Music: Rubin, 1965, p. 9.
Text: Voices, p. 82.

11. ZAYT MIR GEZUNT, CHAVERTES ALE

SONG OF THE BRIDE

Zayt mir ge - zunt, cha - ver - tes a - le,

Mayn lets - tn a - de zog___ ich aych.

Nit zayt mich me - ka - ne mi - tn no - men ka - le,

Vayl nit far ye - dn shaynt es glaych. Tsu___ der chu - pe

vert men ge - firt,___ Men vert i - ber - ge - ge - bn

tsu a tsvey - ter per - zon, Un___ da - mit___

vert men ri - zi - kirt___ Un dos le - bn shteyt_ in

kon.___ Un dos le - bn shteyt_ in kon.

Music: Rubin, MSS.
Text: Voices, p. 114.

12. DI MAME IZ GEGANGEN
IN MARK ARAYN NOCH KOYLN

LOVE DITTY

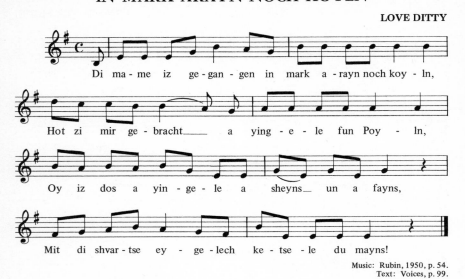

Di ma - me iz ge - gan - gen in mark a - rayn noch koy - ln,

Hot zi mir ge - bracht____ a ying - e - le fun Poy - ln,

Oy iz dos a yin - ge - le a sheyns____ un a fayns,

Mit di shvar - tse ey - ge - lech ke - tse - le du mayns!

Music: Rubin, 1950, p. 54.
Text: Voices, p. 99.

13. HOBER UN KORN

SATIRICAL MARRIAGE SONG

Ho - ber un korn,____ Ho - ber un ko - rn,

Riv - ke hot dem far - tech far - lo - rn. Yan - kl hot ge -

fu - nen,____ Yan - kl hot ge - fu - nen, Vol - tn zey zich

bey - de ge - nu - men Riv - ke zitst un

kukt _____ in shpi - gl, Un kamt zich fa - nan - der di

he - re - lech. _____ Iz tsu - ge - gan - gen

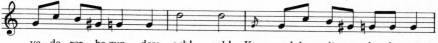

tsu _ ir _ Yan - kl un hot zi ba - sho - tn mit ke - re - lech.

Music: Fibix, p. 6.
Text: Voices, p. 109.

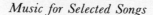

14. L'CHAYIM REBE, HOT A GUTE VOCH!

CHASSIDIC DRINKING SONG

L' - chay - im re - be, hot a gu - te voch, Shrayt

ye - de - rer ba - zun - der: och! och! Kayn mash - ke. nit ge - zha - le - vet,

lo - mir trink - en noch! Mir ho - bn oys - ge - be - tn a

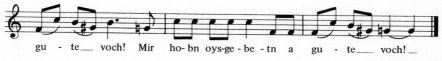

gu - te _ voch! Mir ho - bn oys - ge - be - tn a gu - te _ voch! _

Music: Rubin, MSS.
Text: Voices, p. 137.

15. VOS VET ZAYN AZ MOSHIACH VET KUMEN

SECULAR MESSIAH SONG

Vos vet zayn as Mo - shi - ach vet ku - men?

Ve - ln mir ma - chn a su - de - nyu

Vos ve - ln mir e - sn oyf der su - de - nyu?

Dem shor ha-bor mit dem lev - yo - sn. Dem shor- ha -bor mit dem lev-

yo - sn. Dem shor ha - bor mit dem lev - yo - sn

ve - ln mir e - sn, Oyf der___ su - de - nyu.

Music: Rubin, MSS.
See: Voices, pp. 140-1,
"Got aleyn mit zayn kovid
vet dort zayn."

16. GOT HOT BASHAFN HIML UN ERD

BALLAD OF ADAM AND EVE

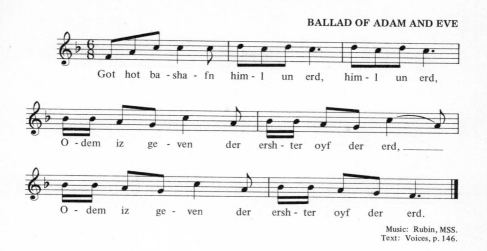

Got hot ba-sha-fn him-l un erd, him-l un erd,

O-dem iz ge-ven der ersh-ter oyf der erd, _____

O-dem iz ge-ven der ersh-ter oyf der erd.

Music: Rubin, MSS.
Text: Voices, p. 146.

17. BAY MAYN REBN IZ GEVEZN

HUMOROUS DANCING SONG

Bay mayn re-bn iz ge-ve-zn, Iz ge-ve-zn bay mayn re-bn,

Bay mayn re-bn iz ge-ve-zn a ge-ney-ve!

Zi-bn hem-der vi di be-cher, Dray mit la-tes, fir mit le-cher.

Bay mayn re-bn iz ge-ve-zn a ge-ney-ve!

Music: Rubin, 1950, pp. 130-1.
Text: Voices, p. 161.

18. EYN KOL VAYN

DRINKING SONG

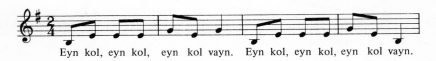

Eyn kol, eyn kol, eyn kol vayn. Eyn kol, eyn kol, eyn kol vayn.

Fine

Eyn kol, eyn kol, eyn kol vayn, Ich kon on dir nit zayn.

Eyn kol vayn, Ich kon on dir nit zayn.

D.C. al Fine

Eyn kol vayn___ Ich kon on dir nit zayn.

Music: Rubin, 1965, p. 34.
Text: Voices, p. 174.

19. S'IZ NITO KAYN NECHTN

DRINKING SONG

S'iz ni - to kayn nech - tn, S' noch ni - to der mor - gn.

S'iz nor do a pi - tse - le haynt, Shtert__ im nit__ mit zor - gn.

Tra-lay, la-lay, la-lay, lay, la-di-dam,

Tra-li-lam, tra-li-lam, tra-li-lam, tam.

Tra-lay, la-lay, la-lay, lay, la-di-dam, Tra-li-lam, tra-li-lam, tam. ___

Music: Rubin, MSS.
Text: Voices, p. 176.

20. OY, VOS CH'OB GEVOLT, HOB ICH OYSGEFIRT

DANCING SONG
(POLKA)

Oy, vos ch'ob ge-volt hob ich oys-ge-firt, ___ Zol ich a-zoy

le -bn, Ch'ob ge-volt a sheyn ying-e-le, Hot mir got ge-

ge -bn. Ch'ob ge-meynt az er iz shoyn mayn ___

Ch'ob im shoyn ba-ku-men, Iz ge-ku-men a

she-ner may-de-le Un hot im tsu-ge-nu-men.

Music: Cahan, 1957, p. 240, No. 255.
Text: Voices, p. 85.

21. GEYEN MIR SHPATSIRN

DANCING SONG
(Slow Waltz)

Gey-en mir shpa-tsi-rn in dem groy-sn vald, —

Oy - vey du — — - she le - bn,

S'iz mir zey - — - er kalt,

Oy - vey du — - she le - bn,

S'iz mir zey - - er kalt. —

Music: Rubin, MSS.
Text: Voices, p. 76.

22. VOS TOYG DI POLKE-MAZURKE

DANCING SONG
(Quick Waltz)

Vos toyg di pol-ke - ma-zur-ke, — Az

tants - n tants ich zi - nit. — Vos

toyg mir di shey-ne fi - gur-ke, — Az

ne - men nemt zi mich nit, Eyns - tsvey, Eyns - tsvey - dray!

Ay, vay iz tsu mir,____ Vay iz tsu may - ne

yor.____ A li - be hob ich ge -

firt,____ Fe - li - ke dray - fert - tl yor.____

Music: Rubin, 1965, pp. 64-5.
Text: Voices, pp. 191-2.

23. HOT ZICH MIR DI ZIP TSEZIPT

DANCING SONG

Hot zich mir di zip tse - zipt un hot zich mir tse - bro - chn.

Hot zich mir di shich tse - ri - sn Tants ich in di hoy - le zo - kn.

Tants, tants ant - ke - gn mir un ich ant - ke - gn dir,

Du vest ne - men dem ey____ dim un ich' l ne - men di shnur.

Music: Rubin, 1965, pp. 42-3.
Text: Voices, p. 193.

24. INEM TOYZNT ACHT HUNDERT NAYN-UN-NAYNTSIGSTN YOR

TOPICAL BALLAD

In-em toy-znt acht hun-dert un nayn-un nayn-tsig-stn yor,____

Hot zich ge - e - fnt a____ nay - er na - bor,

Oy vey ma-me-nyu, Fun vey-nen bin ich mat, Ich

hob nisht kayn le - go - te, ch'bin a far - ti -ger sol - dat.

Music: Rubin, MSS.
Text: Voices, pp. 213-4.

25. KAYN ESN UN KAYN TRINKEN, MAME

LOVE BALLAD

Kayn e - sn un kayn trink-en___ ma - me, nemt mich nit. Ich

bin mit may -ne hey - se tre - rn oy - vey, zat. Ich

freg un freg un key-ner__ en-fert__ nit, Farvos zol zayn__ mayn__ cho-sn a sol-dat? ____

Music: B & F, p. 111.
Text: Voices, p. 215.

26. VER ES HOT IN BLAT GELEZN

POGROM SONG
(Topical)

Ver es hot in blat ge-le-zn,
Ve-gn der ba-rim-ter shot A-des.
Ach, vos far an um-glik__ s'hot ge-tro-fn,
In ey-ne tsvey-dray mes-les.

Music: Rubin, MSS.
Text: Voices, p. 219.

27. OYF DI GRINE FELDER, VELDER, OY VEY

SONG OF THE SLAIN SOLDIER

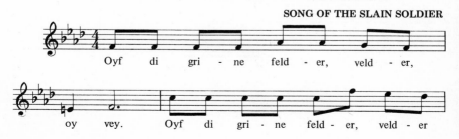

Oyf di gri-ne feld-er, veld-er,
oy vey. Oyf di gri-ne feld-er, veld-er

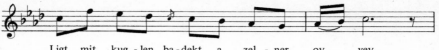

Ligt mit kug - len ba-dekt a zel - ner, oy___ vey,

Ligt mit kug - len ba-dekt a zel - ner, oy___ vey.

Music: Rubin, MSS.
Text: Voices, p. 226.

28. CHASSIDIC "NIGGUN" (Lithuania)

Ba ba ba bam yam-di-di di-di-dam, Ba ba ba bam

yam di-di di-di dam. Ba ba ba bam yam di-di di-di dam,

Ya ba ba ba bam bam bam Ya ba ba ba bam bam bam bam bam bam.

Ya ba ba ba bam bam bam bam bam, Ya ba ba bam bam bam bam bam bam,

Ya ba ba bam bam bam bam Ya ba ba bam bam bam bam bam bam bam.

D. C. al Fine

Music: Rubin, MSS.
See: Voices, pp. 230-2 for descriptive
paragraphs on Chassidic Songs
without words.

29. CHASSIDIC "NIGGUN" (Husiatin)

Briskly

Ya ba ba bam, ba ba ba ba bam, ba ba bam, Ay, ya ba

bam. Ay ba bam bam bam bam bam ba____ ba ba ba bam.

Ya ba bam bam ya ba bam ya ba bam, Ay, ya ba bam,

Ya ba ba ba ba ba ba bam, ____ ba ba ba

bam. Ya ba ya ba bam, ba ba bam, Ya ba ba bam,

Ay, ya ba ba ba ba ba bam. ____

Music: Rubin, MSS.
See: Voices, pp. 230-2 for descriptive
paragraphs on Chassidic Songs
without words.

30. CHASSIDIC "NIGGUN" (Koydenov)

Tay day day day day____ day day day day day day day day day

etc.

Music: Rubin, MSS.
See: Voices, pp. 230-2 for descriptive
paragraphs on Chassidic Songs
without words.

31. AZ DU VOLST GEVEN DER BOYRE-OYLEM

SATIRICAL CHASSIDIC SONG

Az du volst ge-ven der boy-re oy-lem Vos vol-stu_ ge-

macht? Az macht? Ch'volt ge-macht, Ch'volt ge-macht, Ch'volt ge-

macht_____ an___ oy-vn a groy-sn un

tsho-lnt vi-fil s'volt a-rayn_____ Di mis-

nag-dim un hul-tay-es volt ich kayn tsho-lnt nisht ge-ge-bn, Nor

Ch'si-dim vi-fil es volt a-rayn. Ha-l'-vay, Ha-l'-

vay, Ha-l'-vay, Vi der-lebt men dos shoyn? Ha-l'-

vay, Ha-l'-vay, Ha-l'-vay, Vi der-lebt men dos shoyn?

Music: Idelsohn, X, No. 231 (II), p. 66.
Text: Voices, pp. 237-8.

32. BAY DEM DAVENEN VEL ICH MICH SHOKLEN

SATIRICAL CHASSIDIC SONG

Bay dem da-ve-nen vel ich mich shok-len,

Ma-chn a-ler-ley ha-vay - es. Far dem re-bn mit

zay - ne cha-si-dim geyt mir oys___ dos___ cha - yes.

Oy vey_____ re-be-nyu ich shtey un tsi - ter.

Un in har-tsn brent a fay - er. Ich vel zayn a

cho-sid - l a hey-ser, a cho-sid a___ ge-tray - er.

Muisc: Idelson, X, No. 233, p. 67.
Text: Voices, p. 238.

33. KUM AHER, DU FILOZOF

SATIRICAL HASKALAH SONG

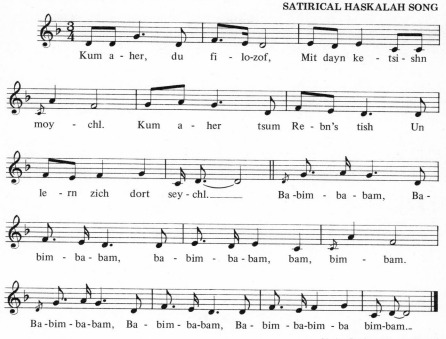

Kum a - her, du fi - lo-zof, Mit dayn ke - tsi - shn moy - chl. Kum a - her tsum Re - bn's tish Un le - rn zich dort sey - chl._____ Ba - bim - ba - bam, Ba - bim - ba-bam, ba - bim - ba-bam, bam, bim - bam. Ba - bim - ba-bam, Ba - bim - ba-bam, Ba - bim - ba-bim - ba bim-bam.__

Music: Rubin, 1950, pp. 136-7.
Text: Voices, p. 240.

34. DAYN FOTER'S REYD

HASKALAH SONG

Dayn fo - ter's reyd,_____ her tsu mayn kind,_____ Ich meyn doch gants _____ ge -

vis dayn glick. Du host doch shoyn a-

zoy - fil zind af ye - dn shrit un oy - gn

blik. Tu shoyn tshu - ve un ver shoyn frum,

Fast, zog t'hi - lim, vi mir ge - felt, Vet dayn ne - sho - me ku - men

reyn far im, Far got in hi - ml oyf ye - ner velt.

Music: Rubin, MSS.
Text: Voices, p. 261-2.

35. A REDELE IZ DI GORE VELT

MORALISTIC SONG

A re - de - le iz di go - re velt, Ge -

katsh - et iz di tsayt. Glik un um - glik,

ko - vid un gelt, Katsh - en zich nor bay der zayt.

Ey - ner lebt op a - zoy o - rim zayn velt, Der

an - de - rer lebt a - zoy breyt._____ In

eyn oy - gn - blik _____ vert dos far - dreyt, Dos

re - de - le hot zich i - ber - ge - dreyt._____

Music: Rubin, MSS.
Text: Voices, pp. 265-6.

36. OYFN PRIPETSHOK BRENT A FAYERL

Text and Tune
MARK WARSHAWSKY

Oy - fn pri - pe - tshok brent a fay - er - l, Un in shtub iz heys.

Un der re - be lern - t kley - ne kind -er - lech dem__ a - leph beyz.

dem__ a - leph beyz. Zet - zhe kind - er - lech,

Ge-denkt - zhe tay - e - re, Vos ir lern - t do,

Zogt - zhe noch - a - mol un ta - ke noch - a - mol:

ko - mets a - leph O. ko - mets a - leph O.

Music: Rubin, 1965, p. 56.
Text: Voices, p. 273.

37. SHLOF MAYN KIND, SHLOF K'SEYDER

LULLABY

Shlof mayn kind,___ shlof k'- sey - der. Zing- en vel ich
dir a lid. Az du mayn kind___ vest el - ter ye — rn,
Ves - tu vi - sn an un - ter - shid. Az un - ter - shid.

Music: Rubin, 1965, p. 67.
Text: Voices, p. 39.

38. EYDER ICH LEYG MICH SHLOFN

SEAMSTRESS' WORK SONG

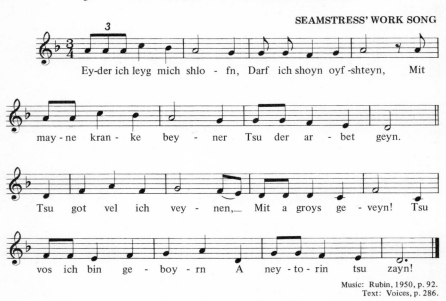

Ey-der ich leyg mich shlo - fn, Darf ich shoyn oyf -shteyn, Mit
may - ne kran - ke bey - ner Tsu der ar - bet geyn.
Tsu got vel ich vey - nen,___ Mit a groys ge - veyn! Tsu
vos ich bin ge - boy - rn A ney - to - rin tsu zayn!

Music: Rubin, 1950, p. 92.
Text: Voices, p. 286.

39. DER BEKER MIT DER BEKERN

APPRENTICE BOY'S SONG

Der__ be - ker mit der be - ker - n, zey ku - men in der be - ke - ray, Loyt zey - er raych - tum un loyt zey - er shtey - ger.__ Zi geyt on - ge - ton a por bri - lian - te - ne oy - ring - en, un__ er in a gol - de - nem zey - ger.__

Music: Rubin, 1950, p. 88.
Text: Voices, p. 288.

40. DI BALABOSTE GEYT ARAYN!

APPRENTICE BOY'S SONG

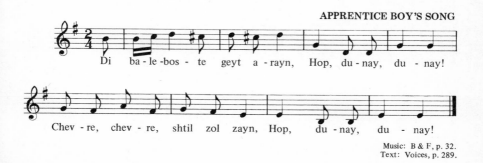

Di ba - le -bos - te geyt a -rayn, Hop, du - nay, du - nay! Chev - re, chev - re, shtil zol zayn, Hop, du - nay, du - nay!

Music: B & F, p. 32.
Text: Voices, p. 289.

41. UN DU AKERST, UN DU ZEYST

STRUGGLE SONG

Un du a - kerst, un du zeyst,___ Un du fi - terst un du neyst,

Un du ha - merst un du shpinst, Zog mayn folk vos du far - dinst?___

Refrain:

Kling klang,___ Kling klang,___ klapt der ha - mer mit

1.

zayng ge - zang!___

2.

Tse - rayst di key - tn fun shkla - fn tsvang!

Music: Rubin, 1950, p. 100.
Text: Voices, p. 269.

42. CH'OB FAR KEYNEM KAYN MOYRE, KAYN BUSHE

UNDERWORLD SONG

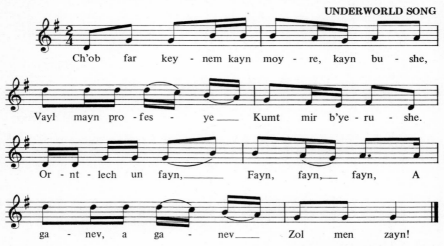

Ch'ob far key - nem kayn moy - re, kayn bu - she,

Vayl mayn pro - fes - ye ___ Kumt mir b'ye - ru - she.

Or - nt - lech un fayn,___ Fayn, fayn,___ fayn, A

ga - nev, a ga - nev___ Zol men zayn!

Music: Lehman, 1928, p. 120, No. LXXXI.
Text: Voices, pp. 325-6.

43. VOS GEYSTU ARUM AZOY FARSMUTSHET?

SONG OF THE UNDERWORLD

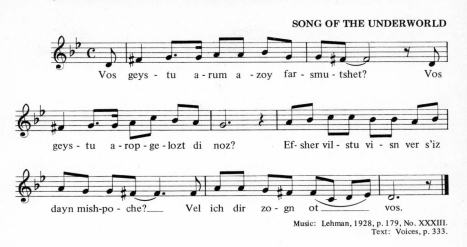

Vos geys-tu a-rum a-zoy far-smu-tshet? Vos
geys-tu a-rop-ge-lozt di noz? Ef-sher vil-stu vi-sn ver s'iz
dayn mish-po-che?___ Vel ich dir zo-gn ot___ vos.

Music: Lehman, 1928, p. 179, No. XXXIII.
Text: Voices, p. 333.

44. OY, HERT ZICH AYN, MAYNE LIBE MENTSHN

BEGGAR SONG

Oy, hert zich ayn___ may-ne li-be ment-tshn.
Oy hert zich ay-net vos ich vel aych fre-gn do:___
Ay,___ vi kumt es a-za___
vey-tig___ in___ a___ kley-nem,___ kley-nem fi-dl?

Music: Rubin, MSS.
Text: Voices, pp. 336-7.

45. ICH HOB A KLEYNEM YINGELE

LULLABY

Ich hob a kley - nem yin - ge - le, A zu - ne - le gor
fayn. Ven ich der - ze im dacht zich mir: Di
gant - se velt iz mayn. Nor zelt - n, zelt - n
ze ich im, Mayn shey - nem ven er vacht. Ich
tref im im - er shlofn - dig,___ Ich ze im nor bay - nacht.

Music: Rubin, 1950, p. 25.
Text: Voices, p. 353.

46. SHLOF MAYN KIND

LULLABY

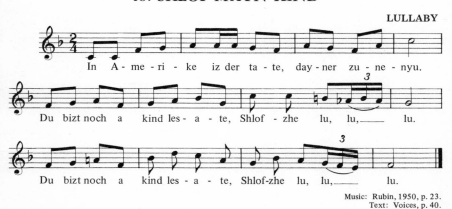

In A - me - ri - ke iz der ta - te, day - ner zu - ne - nyu.
Du bizt noch a kind les - a - te, Shlof - zhe lu, lu,___ lu.
Du bizt noch a kind les - a - te, Shlof-zhe lu, lu,___ lu.

Music: Rubin, 1950, p. 23.
Text: Voices, p. 40.

47. ZOG MIR MAYN SHVESTER

CHALUTS SONG

Zog mir mayn shves - ter, Ich vel dir fre - gn a por

ver - ter. Vos ves - tu ton in Pa - les - ti -

na? Vos ves - tu ton in Pa - les - ti - na?

Ich vel a - ker - n un zey - en Un zich mit may - ne

bri - der frey - en, A - bi nor in Pa - les - ti -

na, A - bi nor in Pa - les - ti - na!

Music: Rubin, MSS.
Text: Voices, p. 383.

48. AVU BIZTU GEVEN?

SETTLEMENT HUMOROUS SONG

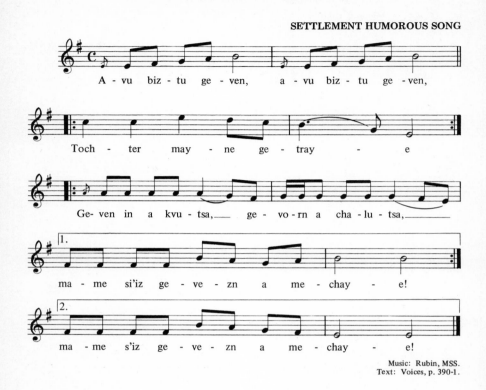

A - vu biz - tu ge - ven, a - vu biz - tu ge - ven,

Toch - ter may - ne ge - tray - e

Ge - ven in a kvu - tsa,___ ge - vo - rn a cha - lu - tsa,___

1. ma - me si'iz ge - ve - zn a me - chay - e!

2. ma - me s'iz ge - ve - zn a me - chay - e!

Music: Rubin, MSS.
Text: Voices, p. 390-1.

49. AZ MEN FORT KAYN SEVASTOPOL

COLLECTIVE FARM SONG

Az man fort kayn Se - vas - to - pol, Iz nit vayt fum Sim - fer - o - pol,

Dor - tn iz a stan - tsi - e - fa - ran. Ver darf zu - chn

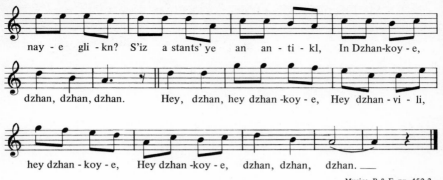

nay - e gli - kn? S'iz a stants' ye an an - ti - kl, In Dzhan-koy - e,

dzhan, dzhan, dzhan. Hey, dzhan, hey dzhan - koy - e, Hey dzhan - vi - li,

hey dzhan - koy - e, Hey dzhan - koy - e, dzhan, dzhan, dzhan. ____

Music: B & F, pp. 452-3.
Text: Voices, p. 410.

50. AY-LYE-LYU MAYN TAYERER

LULLABY-BALLAD

Ay - lye lyu ___ mayn tay-er - er, ____ Ver - zhe

shoyn ___ an - shlo - fn, ____ Vet di ma - me

dir der - tsey - ln, vos hot mit ir ge - tro - fn.

tro - fn. Vi fun fuf - tsn bin ___ ich ey - ne, ____ Bin ich

eyns ___ ge - bli - bn. ____ Ge - koy - let zi - bn

hot pet - lu - ra, O - rel di tsvey - te zi - bn.

Muisc: B & F, pp. 466-7.
Text: Voices, p. 405.

51. DREMLEN FEYGL OYF DI TSVAYGN

WORLD WAR II LULLABY

Drem - len fey - gl oyf___ di tsvay - gn,
Shlof mayn tay - er___ kind. Bay___ dayn vi - gl
oyf a na - re, Zitst a frem - de un zingt.
Bay___ dayn vi - gl oyf a na - re,, Zitst a frem - de un
zingt. Lyu - lu, Lyu - lyu. Lyu. _____

Music: Kacerginski, p. 387.
Text: Voices, p. 438.

52. AROYS IZ IN VILNE A NAYER BAFEL

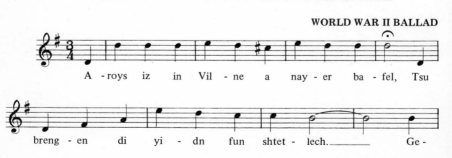

WORLD WAR II BALLAD

A - roys iz in Vil - ne a nay - er ba - fel, Tsu
breng - en di yi - dn fun shtet - lech._____ Ge-

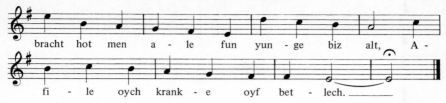

bracht hot men a - le fun yun - ge biz alt, A -

fi - le oych krank - e oyf bet - lech.

Music: Kacerginski, p. 363.
Text: Voices, p. 445-6.

53. SHTIL, DI NACHT IZ OYSGESHTERNT

WORLD WAR II BALLAD

Shtil, di nacht iz oys - ge - shternt. Un der

frost er hot ge - brent. Tsi ge - denk - stu vi ich hob dich ge - lernt.

1.
Tsu halt - n a shpay - er in di hent? Tsu ge -

2.
hent?

Music: Kacerginski, p. 428.
Text: Voices, p. 451.

54. ZOG NIT KEYNMOL

WORLD WAR II SONG

Marching rhythm

Zog nit keyn - mol az du geyst dem lets - tn

veg, Chotsh him - len blay - e - ne far - shte - ln bloy - e

teg. Ku - men vet noch und - zer oys - ge - benk - te

sho, S'vet a poyk ton und -zer trot: Mir ze - nen do!

Music: Kacerginski, p. 361.
Text: Voices, pp. 454-5.

Of the songs referred to as "Rubin, MSS.," eighteen are part of a 2,000-item field collection on tape at the Library of Congress, Washington, D.C. They represent some songs which I remember from my childhood and others which I gathered when wire and tape recorders became available to me. Following is a list of the eighteen songs and their sources:

Song No.	Source	Place	Year
8	H. Ary	Montreal	1955
11	Rachel Grover-Spivack	Montreal	1955
14	Ruth Rubin	Montreal	1920s
15	Ruth Rubin	Montreal	1920s
16	Anonymous	New York City	1950
19	Dr. Chaim Zhitlowsky	Westchester County	1937
21	Moshe Bick	Haifa, Israel	1951
24	M. Persky	Montreal	1955
26	M. Persky	Montreal	1955
27	Ch. Asher	Montreal	1955
28	F. Sultan	New York City	1948
29	J. Zipper	Montreal	1955
30	A. Yudin	New York City	1948
34	Rachel Grover-Spivack	Montreal	1955
35	I. Freed	New York City	1948
44	J. Zipper	Montreal	1955
47	Rachel Grover-Spivack	Montreal	1955
48	Ruth Rubin	Montreal	1920s

WESTERN RUSSIA
and the
JEWISH PALE
within shaded areas

Bibliography

Abbreviated Reference	*In English*

Abrahams — ABRAHAMS, ISRAEL. *Jewish Life in the Middle Ages.* Philadelphia: Jewish Publication Society, 1958.

Ames — AMES, RUSSELL. *The Story of American Folk Song.* New York: Grosset & Dunlap, 1955.

Arma — ARMA, PAUL. *Jeunesse Qui Chante.* Paris: Les Editions Ouvrieres, 1953.

Ausubel — AUSUBEL, NATHAN (ed.). *A Treasury of Jewish Folklore.* New York: Crown Publishers, 1948.

Ben-Zvi — BEN-ZVI, ITZHAK. *The Exiled and the Redeemed.* Philadelphia: Jewish Publication Society, 1957.

Bett — BETT, HENRY. *Nursery Rhymes and Tales.* London: Methuen & Co., Ltd., 1924.

Botkin — BOTKIN, B. A. (ed.). *A Treasury of American Folklore.* New York: Crown Publishers, 1944.

Botsford — BOTSFORD, FLORENCE HUDSON. *Folksongs of Many Peoples,* II. New York: Women's Press, 1922.

Cox — COX, JOHN HARRINGTON. *Folk-Songs of the South.* New York: Dover Publications, 1967.

Douglass — DOUGLASS, FREDERICK. "My Bondage and My Freedom," 1853. Quoted in *The Negro Caravan.* New York: Dryden Press, 1941.

Dubnow II, III — DUBNOW, S. M. *History of the Jews in Russia and Poland.* 3 vols. Philadelphia: Jewish Publication Society, 1916, 1918, 1920.

Feuchtwanger — FEUCHTWANGER, LION. *Raquel.* English tr. from the German by E. Kaiser and E. Wilkens, New York: J. Messner, Inc. 1954–56.

Gellert — GELLERT, LAWRENCE. *Negro Songs of Protest.* New York: 1936.

Glückel — *The Memoirs of Glückel of Hameln.* Translated by MARVIN LOWENTHAL. New York: Harper & Bros., 1932.

Goldenthal — GOLDENTHAL, LEON. *Toil and Triumph.* New York: Pageant Press, Inc., 1960.

Abbreviated Reference	*In Yiddish*

Graetz III, IV, V — GRAETZ, HEINRICH. *History of the Jews.* 6 vols. Philadelphia: Jewish Publication Society, 1949.

Greenway — GREENWAY, JOHN. *American Folk Songs of Protest.* Philadelphia: University of Pennsylvania Press, 1953.

Haggadah shel Pesach — *Haggadah shel Pesach.* REGELSON, ABRAHAM, tr. New York: Shulsinger Bros., 1951.

Hood — HOOD, THOMAS. *Poetical Works.* Boston: 1864.

Idelsohn — IDELSOHN, A. Z. *Jewish Music in Its Historical Development.* New York: Tudor Publishing Co., 1944.

Idelsohn IX, X — IDELSOHN, A. Z. *Thesaurus of Hebrew Oriental Melodies.* Collected, classified, and edited. 10 vols. Leipzig: Friedrich Hofmeister, 1932, Vol. IX: *The Folk Song of the East European Jews;* Vol. X: *Songs of the Chassidim.*

Karpeles — KARPELES, GUSTAV. *Jewish Literature and Other Essays.* Philadelphia: Jewish Publication Society, 1895.

Karpeles — KARPELES, MAUD, ed. *Folksongs of Europe.* London, England: Novello & Co. Ltd., 1956.

Landau — LANDAU, L. DR. *Teutonia.* Heft 21–24. "Hebrew-German Romances and Tales and Their Relation to the Romantic Literature of the Middle Ages." Part I. Leipzig: Arbeiten zur Germanischen Philologie, 1912.

Maimon — MAIMON, SOLOMON. *An Autobiography.* New York: Schocken Books, 1947.

M. and M. — MARGOLIS, MAX L., and ALEXANDER MARX. *A History of the Jewish People.* Philadelphia: Jewish Publication Society, 1944.

Mlotek — MLOTEK, ELEANOR G. "America in East European Yiddish Folksong." In *The Field of Yiddish.* New York: Linguistic Circle of New York, Columbia University, 1954. Pp. 179–195.

Newell — NEWELL, W. W. "The Passover Song of the Kid and an Equivalent from New England." *JAF,* XVIII, 1905.

Oesterley — OESTERLEY, W. O. E. "The Music of the Hebrews." In *Oxford History of Music,* ed. PERCY SCHOLES, Vol. VII, pp. 33–65. London: Oxford University Press, 1929.

Paz — PAZ, ELENA. *Favorite Spanish Folksongs.* New York: Oak Publications, 1967.

Raisin — RAISIN, JACOB S. *The Haskalah Movement in Russia.* Philadelphia: Jewish Publication Society, 1913.

Rappoport — RAPPOPORT, ANGELO S. *The Folklore of the Jews.* London: The Soncino Press, 1937.

Abbreviated Reference	In English

Rubin RUBIN, RUTH. *Jewish Folk Songs in Yiddish and English*. New York: Oak Publications, 1965.

Rubin, 1950 RUBIN, RUTH. *A Treasury of Jewish Folksong*. New York: Schocken Books, 1950.

Schauss SCHAUSS, HAYYIM. *The Lifetime of a Jew*. New York: Union of American Hebrew Congregations, 1950.

Shay SHAY, FRANK. *More Pious Friends and Drunken Companions*. New York: The Macaulay Co., 1928.

Shelley SHELLEY, PERCY BYSSHE. *The Poetical Works of Percy Bysshe Shelley*. The "Albion" edition. London and New York: Frederick Worne & Co., ca. 1900.

Thorne THORNE, MARGARET. *Songs from Story Parade*. Brooklyn, New York, 1945.

Werner WERNER, ERIC. "The Jewish Contribution to Music." In *The Jews, Their History, Culture and Religion*, ed. LOUIS FINKELSTEIN. Philadelphia: Jewish Publication Society, 1949. Pp. 950–984.

Wiener WIENER, LEO. *The History of Yiddish Literature in the Nineteenth Century*. New York: Charles Scribner's Sons, 1899.

Winn WINN, CYRIL, comp. *A Selection of Some Less Known Folksongs*. Vol. 2. Arr. by Cecil J. Sharp, R. Vaughan Williams, and others. London, England: Novello & Co. Ltd., 1951.

Yoffie YOFFIE, LEAH R. C. "Present Day Survivals of Ancient Jewish Customs," *Journal of American Folklore*, XXIX (July–September 1916), pp. 412–416.

Yoffie YOFFIE, LEAH R. C. "Songs of the Twelve Numbers and the Hebrew Chant of *Echod Mi Yodea*." *JAF*, LXII, 1949.

Z. and H. ZBOROWSKI, M., and E. HERZOG. *Life Is With People*. New York: International Universities Press, Inc., 1952.

Zunser-Schwarz ZUNSER, ELIAKUM. *How I Wrote My Songs*. (*Memoirs Of My People*, ed. LEO W. SCHWARZ.) New York: Farrar & Rinehart, Inc., 1943. Pp. 221–232.

Abbreviated Reference	In Yiddish

Anski ANSKI, S. (S. Z. Rappoport). *Folklor un etnografiye* (*Gezamlte shriftn*, Vol. XV). Vilna–Warsaw–New York: Ferlag Sh. Shreberk, 1925.

Apotheker APOTHEKER, DAVID. *Hanevel*. Czernowitz: 1881.

Bader BADER, GERSHON. "Der dichter fun dort vu di tseder," *Der Morgn Zhurnal*, New York (December 24, 1944).

Abbreviated Reference	*In Yiddish*
Bassin	BASSIN, M. (ed.). *Finf hundert yor idishe poezie.* 2 vols. New York: Farlag "Dos Idishe Buch," 1917.
Beregovski	BEREGOVSKI, M. *Jidiser muzik-folklor.* Moscow: Meluxiser Muzik-Farlag, 1934.
B. and F.	BEREGOVSKI, M. and I. FEFFER. *Yidishe folkslider.* Kiev: Meluche Farlag far di natsionale minderhaytn in U.S.S.R., 1938.
Cahan, 1912	CAHAN, YEHUDA LEIB. *Yidishe folkslider.* 2 vols. New York: The International Library Publishing Co., 1912.
Cahan, 1952	CAHAN, YEHUDA LEIB. *Shtudies vegn yidisher folks-shafung.* New York: Yiddish Scientific Institute (YIVO), 1952.
Cahan, 1957	CAHAN, YEHUDA LEIB. *Yidishe folkslider mit melodyes.* New York: Yiddish Scientific Institute (YIVO), 1957.
Di Yidishe Bine	*Di yidishe bine,* ed. Y. KATSENELENBOGN. New York: Farlag Katsenelenbogn, 1897.
D. and Y.	DOBRUSHIN, I., and A. YUDITSKY. *Yidishe folkslider.* Moscow: Meluche-Farlag *Der Emes,* 1940.
Erik	ERIK, MAKS. *Di geshichte fun der yidisher literatur.* Warsaw: Farlag Kultur-lige, 1928.
Feder	FEDER, ZAMI. *Katset un geto-lider.* Bergen-Belsen, 1946.
Fibix	FIBIX, SARRA. *Yidishe folkslider.* Moscow: Gosudarstvenoye Izdatelstvo Izkustvo, 1939.
Fraye Arbeter Shtime	"Kindershe lider fun yidishn milchome-churbn, tsar un ye-ush," *Fraye arbeter shtime,* New York (December 1, 1944).
Gebirtig	GEBIRTIG, MORDECAI. *S'brent.* Cracow: Voyevodishe Yidishe Historisher Komisie, 1946.
Gelbart	GELBART, MICHEL. *Fun m'shor'rim lebn.* New York: Farlag Moyshe Shmuel Shklarsky, 1942.
Ginzburg I, II	GINZBURG, SHAUL. *Historishe verk.* 2 vols. Shaul Ginzburg 70 yoriger yubiley komitet, 1937.
G. and M.	GINZBURG, S. M., and P. S. MAREK. *Yevreiskiya narodniya pesnya v'rosii.* St. Petersburg, 1901. Published by Voskhod. Voskhod.
Glatstein	GLATSTEIN, I. *Di fraye muze.* Warsaw: Ferlag *Lire,* 1918.
Gontar	GONTAR, A. "A pekl briv un geto-lider," *Einikeit,* Moscow: April, 1946, p. 21.
Gordon, J. L.	GORDON, J. L. *Sichat cholin.* Warsaw, 1885.
Gordon, M.	GORDON, MICHL. *Shirey M. Gordon yidishe lider.* Warsaw: 1889.
Graubard	GRAUBARD, P. "Gezangen fun t'hom." In *Bay undz yidn.* Warsaw: Ferlag Pinches Graubard, 1923. Pp. 19–41.

Abbreviated Reference	In Yiddish
Hershele	HERSHELE. "Funem folk's moyl." In *Bay undz yidn*. Warsaw: Ferlag Pinches Graubard, 1923. Pp. 95–110.
Hob Ich Mir	*Hob ich mir a lidele*. Warsaw: Farlag Kultur Lige, 1922.
Hundert Naye	*Hundert naye folkslider*. Warsaw: Farlag S. Goldfarb, 1925.
Kacerginski	KACERGINSKI, S. *Lider fun di getos un lagern*. New York: Tsiko Bicher Farlag, 1948.
Kacerginski-Tsukunft	KACERGINSKI, S. "Zog nisht keynmol, az du geyst dem letstn veg," *Tsukunft*, New York (April, 1949), 234–236.
Kaplan	KAPLAN, MICHL (Mitchell). *Gezamlte shriftn*. Newark, N.J.: Michl Kaplan Yugnt Kultur Grupe, 1947.
Kaufmann	KAUFMANN, FRITZ MORDECHAI. *Die Schönsten Lieder der Ostjuden*. Berlin: Jüdischer Verlag, 1920.
Kipnis	KIPNIS, M. *80 Folkslider*. Warsaw: Farlag A. Gitlin, n.d.
Kirch-han	KIRCH-HAN, E. H. *Simchas hanefesh*. Fürth, 1727. Photostatic reprint, New York Public Library, with Introduction by Dr. JACOB SHATSKY, 1926.
Kisselgof	KISSELGOF, Z. *Lider-zamlbuch*. Berlin: *Juwal* Verlagsgesellschaft für jüdische Musik, 1914.
Kobrin	KOBRIN, LEON. *Mayne fuftsig yor in amerike*. Buenos Aires: Farlag Yidbuch, 1955.
Kotylansky	KOTYLANSKY, CHAIM. *Folksgezangen*. Los Angeles: Chaim Kotylansky Book Committee and YCUF Farlag, 1944.
Kremer	KREMER, ISA. *Album of Jewish Folk-Songs*. London: Chappell & Co., Ltd., 1930.
Kupershmid	KUPERSHMID, S. *Folkslider fun der foterlendisher milchome*. Moscow: Meluche Farlag *Der Emes*, 1944.
Kvutsat Shirim	*Kvutsat shirim*. New York: History Publishing Co., 1924.
Lehman, 1921	LEHMAN, S. *Arbet un frayhayt*. Warsaw: Folklor Bibliotek, 1921.
Lehman, 1923	LEHMAN, S. "Di kinder-velt." In *Bay undz yidn*. Warsaw: Ferlag Pinches Graubard, 1923. Pp. 113–149.
Lehman, 1928	LEHMAN, S. *Ganovim-lider*. Warsaw: Farlag Pinches Graubard, 1928.
Linetsky	LINETSKY, I. J. *Der beyzer marshalik*. Part II. Warsaw: 1879.
Litvin	LITVIN, A. Manuscript collection of Yiddish folk songs. Yiddish Scientific Institute (YIVO), New York.

Abbreviated Reference	*In Yiddish*
Marmor	Marmor, Kalman. *Dovid Edelshtat.* New York: Ykuf Farlag, 1950.
Mendele I, II, VI, VII	Mendele Moycher Sforim (S. I. Abramovitsh). *Ale verk.* 8 vols. Warsaw: 1913. Vol. I: *Di alte mayse;* Vol. II: *Shloyme reb chayim's;* Vol. VI: *Dos kleyne mentshele;* Vol. VII: *Dos vintshfingerl.*
Nayntsig Geklibene	*Nayntsig geklibene yidishe folkslider.* Warsaw: Farlag M. Goldfarb, 1926.
Pines	Pines, M. *Di geshichte fun der yidisher literatur.* Vol. I. Warsaw: Farlag B. Shimen, 1911.
Prager	Prager, Moshe. *Min hametser korosi* (Yiddish and Hebrew). Jerusalem: Musad Harav Cook, 1956.
Rabinovitch	Rabinovitch, Israel. *Muzik Bay Yidn.* Montreal: Eagle Publishing Co., 1940.
Rabinovitsch	Rabinovitsch, Dovid. *Dos tog-buch.* Warsaw: Farlag Yidishbuch, 1960.
Reingold	Reingold, Yitschok. *Geklibene lider.* Chicago: L. M. Stein Publisher, 1952.
Reisin	Reisin, Avrom. *Lider tsum zingen.* New York: A. Reisn Yubl Committee, 1947.
Reitman	Reitman, Hirsh. *Der kitl.* New York: Yiddish Scientific Institute (YIVO) Library, n.d.
Reizin	Reizin, Zalmen. *Lexicon fun der yidisher literatur prese un filologie.* 4 vols. Vilna: Vilna Farlag B. Kletskin, 1928, 1929, 1930.
Rivkind	Rivkind, Isaac. *Der kamf kegn azartshpiln bay yidn.* New York: Yiddish Scientific Institute (YIVO), 1946.
Rubin, MSS	Rubin, Ruth. Private manuscript collection of Yiddish folk songs, collected by Ruth Rubin.
Serebriani	Serebriani, I. "Sovetishe yidishe folks-shafung," *Heymland,* No. 1, Meluche Ferlag Der Emes, Moscow, 1947, pp. 151–156.
Shiper	Shiper, I. *Geshichte fun yidisher teaterkunst un drame.* 2 vols. Warsaw: Farlag Kultur-lige, 1927.
Sholem Aleichem, N.Y.	Sholem Aleichem. *Oysgeveylte verk.* 6 vols. New York: Published by Tog-Morgn-Zhurnal, 1959. Vol. I: *Menachem Mendl.*
Sholem Aleichem, Moscow	Sholem Aleichem. *Ale verk.* 3 vols. Moscow: Meluche Farlag Der Emes, 1948.

Abbreviated Reference	In Yiddish
Shtern	SHTERN, YECHIEL. *Cheder un besmedresh. (Yivo Bleter*, Vols. XXXI–XXXII.) New York: Yiddish Scientific Institute (YIVO), 1948. Pp. 37–130.
Singer	SINGER, I. J. *Fun a velt vos iz nishto mer.* New York: Farlag New York, 1946.
Skuditsky, 1933	SKUDITSKY, Z. *Folklor-lider.* Edited by M. VINER, Vol. I. Moscow: Farlag Emes, 1933.
Skuditsky, 1936	SKUDITSKY, Z. *Folklor-lider.* Edited by M. VINER, Vol. II, Moscow: Farlag Emes, 1936.
Teitelbaum	TEITELBAUM, A. *Varshever Heyf.* Buenos Aires: Tsentral Farband fun Poylishe Yidn in Argentine, 1947.
Tsidkoni	TSIDKONI, YANKEV. *Yidishe folkslider fun erets yisroel. (Di goldene keyt, No. 7).* Tel-Aviv: Histadrut haklalim shel ha-ovdim ha-ivrim b'erets yisrael, 1951.
Tsidkoni, MSS	TSIDKONI, YANKEV. Unpublished private collection of Yiddish folk songs current in Palestine in the twenties. Resident of Jerusalem, Israel.
Tsion's Harfe	*Tsion's harfe.* Warsaw: Ferlag Hazomir, 1917.
Unger, 1946	UNGER, M. *Ch'sides un lebn.* New York: 1946.
Unger, *The Day*	UNGER, M. "Lider vos idn hobn geshafn in der geto," *The Day* (April 28–29, 1946).
Viner	VINER, M. *Tsu der geshichte fun der yidisher literatur in 19tn y.h.* Vol. I. New York: Ykuf Farlag, 1945.
Warshawsky	WARSHAWSKY, M. M. *Yidishe folks-lider.* Introduction by SHOLEM ALEICHEM. New York: Max N. Meisel, 1918.
Weinreich	WEINREICH, MAX. *Bilder fun der yidisher literatur geshichte.* Vilna: Farlag *Tomor* fun Yoysef Kamermacher, 1928.
Yaffe	YAFFE, L. *Lider farn folk.* Vilna: Farlag Sifrot, 1920.
Yid. sovetishe	*Yidishe sovetishe folkslider mit melodies.* Kiev: 1940.
Zunser, I, II, III	ZUNSER, ELYOKUM. *Ale verk.* 3 vols. New York: A. Katsenelenboygn, 1920.
Zunser, Songs	ZUNSER, ELIAKUM. *Selected Songs of Eliakum Zunser.* New York: The Zunser Publishing Co., 1928.

In Hebrew

Korshak	KORSHAK, REYZL. *La-havut b'ofer.* See E. Vortsl, "A nomen vos blaybt umfargeslech," *Morning Frayhayt* (August 9, 1954).
Sefer hanigunim	*Sefer Hanigunim.* Edited by Rabbi Samuel Zalmanoff. Brooklyn, N. Y.: 1949.

Abbreviated Reference	*In Hebrew*

Zemer am   *Zemer Am.* Translated into Hebrew from the Yiddish by I. ADL, J. STUTCHEWSKY, S. MELTSER, D. SHTOK. Tel-Aviv: M. Newman, 1945.

Zichron   *Zichron Yankev.* Edited by Reb Yankev Halevi Lifshitz M'Kovno.
yankev   Part I. Frankfurt-am-Main: Nota Halevi Lifshitz, 1924.

Miscellaneous

A. B.   *Twaalf Vrijheidsliederen* (uit het Engelsch e.a.). Amsterdam: H. J. Poutsma, 1899.

Halevi   HALEVI, JEHUDA. *Selected Poems.* Hebrew poems, translated into English by NINA SALAMAN. Philadelphia: Jewish Publication Society, 1946.

Güdemann   GUDEMANN, MORITZ. *Geschichte des Erziehungswesens und Kultur*
—Shtif   *der abendlandischen Juden während des Mittelalters und der neueren Zeit.* 3 vols. Vienna: Alfred Holder, 1880–88. Vol. III *(Die Juden in Deutschland im 14 und 15 Jahrhundert)* translated into Yiddish by NOCHEM SHTIF *(Yidishe kultur-geshichte in mitlalter).* Berlin: Klal Ferlag, 1922.

Makkabi   *Makkabi Liederbuch.* In Yiddish, Hebrew, and German. Berlin: Jüdischer Verlag, 1930.

Wengeroff   WENGEROFF, PAULINE. *Memoiren einer Grossmutter.* In German. 2 vols. Berlin: Verlag von M. Poppelauer, 1908, 1910.

General Index

Camp Atlit, 459 (n. 30); Yiddish folk-songs in, 383–4; Yiddish folksongs translated into Hebrew, 390

Palmach, 391

Pantagruel, 250

Paris und Viene, 22

Passover, Seder, 19, 31, 149, feast, 58–9; ceremonial, 58; story, 157 (n. 9); *Haggadah,* 129, 193; chants, 58, 463, 465, 466; conversation song, 282–84

patroness of Yiddish literature, 23, 27 (n. 21)

paytan, paytanim, 17, 25 (n. 3)

Pelovits, I., 381

Pentateuch, 125 (n. 12)

Pentecost, 21, 232, 280, 307 (n. 8)

Peretz, I. L., 250, 266, 276 (n. 37), 413

Persia, 68 (n. 33), 129

Petach Tikva, 396 (n. 30), 397 (n. 42)

Philadelphia, 345, 348, 355, 357

Pines, M., 72

Pinsk, 291, 298

Pinsker, Leo, 368, 394 (n. 3)

Poale Zion (Labor Zionism), 308 (n. 35), 308 (n. 50), 378–9, 381; hymn, 381

Podol, 395 (n. 24)

Podolia-Bessarabian border, 213

pogroms (*See* Nemirov, Odessa, Zhitomir), during the 80's in Czarist Russia, 265, 296, 310, 342, 368–9, 370, 373, 397 (n. 48)

Pokras, 453

Poland, Polish, 22–3, 26 (n. 11), 44, 99–100, 236, 257, 278, 308 (n. 56), 433, 478; Jewish settlements, 23, 26 (n. 20), 98–9, 126 (n. 5); *Haskalah* in, 275 (n. 1); Chasidism in, 216, 230, 246 (n. 4), 249 (n. 34); War with Russia, 401; Polish Insurrection, 108, 218, 264; dance calls (*See* dance chapter); German occupation of, 423–455; "Hangman of Polish Jews" (Frank), 432

Polone, 202

Polonski, S., 413

Ponar, 445, 459 (n. 28)

"Poor Damsels," 476

Popular songs, 22. (*See also* chapter on songs of literary origin, and section in chapter "To America": "Songs of Literary Origin on American soil," 348)

Port Arthur, 303

Poznan, 206

Prague, 23, 208, 465

Psalms, 144, 196 (n. 7); translated into German, 275 (n. 2); theme of Psalm 137 in Yiddish folksongs, 370–1

Pskov, 335

Purim, 19, 21, 149, 178, 257, 290, 341 (n. 46)

Pushkin, 250

Rab, 396 (n. 30)

"Rabbi of Bacharach, The." 466

Rabbi Emanuel Hirshberg, 431

Rabbi Hayim Abulafia from Ismir, 396 (n. 30)

Rabbi of Koliv, 233, 247 (n. 11)

Rabbi Yitschok Isaac Toib (*See* Rabbi of Koliv)

rabbis, 18, 20, 26 (n. 15), 68 (n. 33), 73, 98–100, 125 (n. 11), 227 (n. 3), 246 (n. 3). (*See also* Chasidic rabbis; rabbinate, 71; rabbinical schools, 99)

Rabina, 196 (n. 4)

"Rabinovitsh and Lipson," 298

Rabinovitsh, Y., 458 (n. 9), 459 (n. 34)

Ramat Gan, 384

Rappaport, Shloyme Z. (*See* Anski, S.)

Reb Elimelech of Lizhensk, 249 (n. 34)

Reb Levi Yitschok of Berdichev, 234; The Berditshever, 248 (n. 13)

Reb Mendele of Horodok, 247 (n. 9)

Reb Nachman Bratslaver, 184, 248 (n. 12)

Reb Osherl Rimenover, 247 (n. 7); Riminov *rebe,* 247 (n. 11)

Reb Shloyme Radomsker, 247 (n. 7)

Reb Shneyer Zalmen of Liadi (founder of Chabad sect of Chasidism), 184,

Song Index

First lines of songs are italicized. Excerpts of songs are in italics and quotation marks. Titles of songs are in quotation marks.